STAND WITHOUT APOLOGY

75th

ANNIVERSARY EDITION

THE HISTORY OF
Bob Jones University

DANIEL L. TURNER

BJU Press, Greenville, South Carolina 29614

Library of Congress Cataloging-in-Publication Data

Turner, Daniel L., 1950-

    Standing without apology : the history of Bob Jones University /
Daniel L. Turner—

      75th anniversary ed.

        p. cm.

    Includes bibliographical references and index.

    ISBN 1-57924-672-9—ISBN 1-57924-710-5 (softbound)

      1. Bob Jones University—History. I. Title.

LD457.T87 2001

378.757'27—dc21   2001043115

NOTE:

The fact that materials produced by other publishers may be referred to in this volume does not constitute an endorsement by Bob Jones University Press of the content or theological position of materials produced by such publishers. The position of Bob Jones University Press, and of the University itself, is well known. Any references and ancillary materials are listed as an aid to the student or the teacher and in an attempt to maintain the accepted academic standards of the publishing industry.

Standing Without Apology: The History of Bob Jones University
75th Anniversary Edition

Photo credits: From the archives of Unusual Films, back cover from the archives
  of Creative Services

Edited by Steven N. Skaggs

Cover design by TJ Getz

Interior design by Rich Cutter

© 2001 Bob Jones University Press
Greenville, South Carolina 29614

ISBN 1-57924-710-5

15   14   13   12   11   10 9 8 7 6 5 4 3 2 1

To my parents, Altyn James and Iva Mae Turner,
with deep gratitude and love

Congratulations
on becoming a member
of the
President's Club!

Bob Jones III

PETIMUS CREDIMUS

Table of Contents

PREFACE

◆

This book began originally at the University of Illinois as a doctoral dissertation on cultural history. That paper, "Fundamentalism, the Arts, and Personal Refinement: A Study of the Ideals of Bob Jones Sr. and Bob Jones Jr.," immersed me in both cultural history and American religious history, fields that were complementary to my study in educational history and music education. Through the course of that research, it became evident that the history of Bob Jones University was essentially oral and undocumented; this necessitated a redocumentation of the school's history in order to complete one chapter of the dissertation. About the same time I noted that the scholarship dealing with Fundamentalism and evangelism generally relegated BJU and the Joneses, if mentioning them at all, to footnotes. Many of these works dedicated little or no space to BJU and summarily dismissed the Joneses as embittered iconoclasts or combative dictators, thereby diminishing their impact and influence. While all three Joneses have been true individualists and the University that bears their name is definitely individualistic, the dismissals applied to them seemed more than simply uninformed; they seemed unjustified and sometimes downright vindictive.

Interest in Fundamentalism by scholars George Marsden, Martin Marty, and Ernest Sandeen, with their more balanced portrayals of the movement and the forces within it, has aided in focusing national attention on the Fundamentalist element of conservative Protestantism. Recent attention to the Joneses and the University by scholars Mark Taylor Dalhouse and Howard Edgar Moore has at the least recognized the institution as a major player within Fundamentalism.

This book is not intended to correct any past injustice and hopefully will not be received as a hagiography. It is an attempt to present a documented record of Bob Jones University within the changing political-economic contexts of this century. This is a record, not infallible, of the cultural, spiritual, and academic development of the institution. This is a record of a unique place—founded and operated without funds from government, philanthropies, or religious denominations, yet financially robust and growing; unaccredited by associations and independent, yet widely recognized for the quality of its graduates; unhesitatingly adhering to its creedal foundation, yet astonishing in its breadth of inclusion; standing without apology for what it believes, what it is, and what it produces. It is one of the few schools in America with an official formulation of creedal truth, proper behavior, and cultural boundaries that is coherent, consistent, and cultivated among its students to produce Christians unafraid to live what they believe. Bob Jones University retains its orthodoxy by being unorthodox.

What the institution produces is a direct result of the quality of people which make up its faculty and staff. They are men and women of greatness, with open spirits and large souls; they are leaders and servants; they are gifted, creative, and productive; they are highly educated and trained professionals who are passionate in their pursuit of academic excellence and God's truth. They are not always right, but in their hearts they wish to be. What the institution is, it is because they believe and live as they do.

Some readers, I am certain, would wish to know about skeletons in the institutional closet. The closet is clean. It is kept so by the administration's vigilance, "the washing of the water of the Word," and the fire that keeps the chapel platform hot. There have been a few "nuts" in the place, but they were shaken from the institutional tree. There have been characters and individualists; there still are. It is not a perfect place, but it strives to be. It is unusual in nearly every aspect.

This book is organized in four major sections: short biographies of Bob Jones Sr., Bob Jones Jr., Bob Jones III, and important campus personalities; the founding of the College in Florida through its departure in 1933; the Cleveland, Tennessee, years; and the growth and development of Bob Jones University in Greenville, South Carolina. Within these four sections, the material is presented chronologically with occasional excursions into contextual information or topical discussions of culture, New Evangelicalism, or other issues. The focus of the book is not issue oriented. Only those issues that directly affected Bob Jones University have been dealt with. Thus, some readers may look in vain for certain cultural events; these events are omitted not because they lack importance in themselves, but because they have limited relevance to the institution.

Standing Without Apology is a record of what God can do with men who have the courage to "do right." May that courage continue. *Soli Deo gloria.*

ACKNOWLEDGMENTS

◆

The research and writing of this book has, at times, been almost a team effort, with the author drawing on the strengths, talents, insights, and perceptions of many colleagues and friends. To the following go many thanks for their help.

Finding documents and data was often a daunting task. Several BJU staff members, however, were extremely helpful and gracious in the search. Although the President of the University had extended me great freedom in my research, Mrs. Iris Jackson, the former University office manager, acted as my clearinghouse for letters and file documents. Her nearly total recall of persons, correspondence, and events made it possible to find documents in the University's General Files; Mrs. Gail Dunbar, file supervisor, was patient and efficient in locating reams of material; and Shelagh Johnson of the Records Office located numerical data important to the book. Dr. Bert Wilhoit and Mrs. Marion Spence were of great help in finding information located in the University Archives. Mr. Dayton Walker, Greenville city councilman, provided assistance in obtaining copies of the minutes of the Wilson zoning hearing of 1960. Mr. E. Roy Stone Jr. and Miss Martha Stone of Stone Realty graciously provided documents dealing with Bob Jones University's move to Greenville in 1947.

Dr. Katherine Stenholm was extremely helpful and extended me the use of her late husband's personal diaries, dating from 1934 through 1976. The diaries recorded in detail many of the events that affected the Bob Jones College and University community over the years. Gilbert Stenholm's record was invaluable in providing context, often allowing me to put dates to events only distantly remembered by others.

Many people submitted to hours of interviews or acted as a sounding board for ideas, which often kept me from wasting time in my search for information. Among those most helpful were Dr. Dwight Gustafson, dean of the School of Fine Arts, who showed great patience with my seemingly endless questions; Mr. Roy Barton, chief financial officer, who made himself available for interviews and discussions that helped clarify the Bob Jones University tax case; and Dr. Philip Smith, provost, for his interest and encouragement of this project.

I also wish to acknowledge several students for allowing me the use of their research and writings about Bob Jones University: Bob Jones IV, for his work on the National Association of Evangelicals and BJU; Rebecca Tabler, for her materials relevant to *Bob Jones University v. United States of America;* and Bryan Suhr, for his work on the Supreme Court and nonpublic schools. Dr. Jack Matzko also opened to me a wealth of student research completed for the Bob Jones University History Seminars.

STANDING WITHOUT APOLOGY

Drs. Jack Matzko and Carl Abrams spent long hours reading the manuscript and gave encouragement and suggestions that brought more focus and refinement to it. Dr. Mark Sidwell, production coordinator at Bob Jones University Press, was a willing listener, helped keep the book balanced, and provided material about the Neo-Puritanism movement that began in the late 1950s.

I wish to thank Dr. Bob Jones III, President of Bob Jones University, for his support, encouragement, and deep interest in this project. His insistence on balance and accuracy made the writing both challenging and rewarding. The Chancellor, Dr. Bob Jones, was gracious enough to read and comment on the manuscript and provided insights into many of the events that have been woven together to form the University's tapestry.

Jamie and Jess, my wife and son, listened patiently to long dinner-time discourses about this material and advised me on key points. The key question, asked by Jess, was, "Dad, Mom's book only took her a year to write. Why is yours taking so long?"

To all of these, I am most grateful.

ABBREVIATIONS

Bob Jones University
stands without apology
for the "old-time religion" and
the absolute authority
of the Bible.

CHAPTER 1

Bob Jones: The Man

Robert Reynolds Jones was born on October 30, 1883, on a farm near Skipperville, in Dale County, Alabama.[1] Bobby, as he was called, was the eleventh child of the twelve children born to Georgia Creel and William Alexander Jones. Robert Reynolds Jones was named after Robert Reynolds, a Confederate army buddy of his father's from the Civil War. When Bobby was three months old, the family moved to a farm at Brannon Stand near the southeastern Alabama town of Dothan.

In Alex Jones's veins flowed the blood of a fighter inherited from his rugged, two-fisted Welsh-Irish pioneer stock. He was a tempestuous man who fought for the Confederacy with Company H of the Alabama Thirty-seventh

Bob Jones Sr. (ca. 1884)

Regiment during the Civil War. Alex often regaled the family with stories of the war and spoke tenderly of the men with whom he fought at the Battle of Chickamauga, where he was wounded in the right knee.[2] His buddy, Robert Reynolds, cared for the wound, but Alex's knee remained lame in spite of the kindness of his friend and was a testimony to the ferocity of the battle.

Old soldiers in the South, especially those of the Confederacy, were treated with great honor, and the "Lost Cause" was held high in quiet devotion. The Jones family, in fact, often joked that their father's old knee wound was more important to him than they were.[3] During his evangelistic days, Dr. Jones Sr. often reflected on the irony of old Yankee veterans sitting in his meetings—a son of the Confederacy, at whose father they had been shooting.

To the family, Alex Jones always stressed the honor of battle. He believed in meeting life head-on and "finishing the job." Dr. Jones Sr. recalled that

> a few days before my grandfather died, there was a husky young fellow who came by the house and was very discourteous in what he said to my grandfather. My father, who was about seventeen years of age, came in and some of the family told him what this fellow said to my grandfather.

My father said, "I'm going to go over and whip him. . . ." A few days later my grandfather died, and [my father's family] moved away.

When my father was twenty years of age, he kept thinking about this young upstart who was impudent to his father. So he got on a horse and rode back up to that [lumber] community and hunted this man up. My father weighed about 135 pounds. The other man weighed about 180. My father walked up to the man and said, "You were the fellow who was impudent to my father just before he died, and I have come here to whip you." And this man said, "If you do, you will be the only man who ever did." They fought for two hours and my father finally got the best of the man, . . . and the man finally said, "Take him off!" The two men got up, shook hands; he got on his horse and rode back home [with the job finished].[4]

From family stories like these Bobby not only learned about human frailty, but he also learned to fight for principle, honor, and integrity. Interestingly, during his evangelistic meetings Bob Jones had the opportunity to bring to the love of Christ many of those who had opposed his father's views and many who had fought on the other side from his father in the War Between the States.

William Alexander and Georgia Creel Jones

As passionate about life as Alex Jones was, his wife, Georgia Creel, was the opposite. She was quiet, patient, tender, and loving, and greatly admired by those who knew her. She was a woman of integrity who had a keen sense of spiritual discernment that she passed on to her son. A woman of great industry, she lived each day to its fullest.[5]

Life was hard for Alex Jones, a peanut and vegetable farmer in the cotton belt of Alabama. The Civil War and Reconstruction had destroyed agricultural markets, and generations of abuse had ruined the farmland. It took years to bring the land back to productivity, but apparently Alex Jones was successful. He "never attended an agricultural school in his life, but he knew how to tickle the ground and make it smile with harvest. He could produce yam potatoes as big as you ever saw, and ears of corn that made the neighbors almost worship at the granary shrine," his son commented.[6]

The South at this time was essentially a two-crop society. Cotton was indisputably king and his knave was tobacco. As late as 1938 the situation remained essentially the same. A report of the New Deal National Emergency Council stated that "the farming South depends on cotton and tobacco for two-thirds of its cash income. More than half its farmers depend on cotton alone. They are one-crop farmers, subject year after year to risks which would appall the average business man. All their eggs are in one basket which can be upset, and often is, by the weather, the boll weevil, or the cotton market."[7]

When Bobby was born in 1883, cotton prices averaged 9.5 cents per pound. By 1894-96, however, cotton prices had fallen to 5.8 cents.[8] In some states, cotton prices fell to a record low of 3.4 cents per pound. "Times were hard," young Bobby remembered. "People were hungry. There was no money to buy clothes. . . . We ate cornbread and molasses. We lived through the hard time. We may have been a little undernourished, but we built some character."[9]

All the Jones children, including Bobby, had to pull their weight on the farm by plowing, planting, weeding, tilling, and caring for animals. By the time he was nine years old, Bobby was an experienced plow hand who could plow straight and reportedly spent a portion of his days sermonizing to his father's mules.[10]

Alex Jones was sympathetic to Populism, both agricultural and political, and as an officer in the local Farmers' Alliance, attempted to rally area farmers in support of both the agricultural initiatives of the Alliance and their progressive political reforms.[11] The Southern Farmers' Alliance had been formed in Texas as a cooperative venture of small ranchers to protect themselves against land syndicates and cattle barons. By the 1880s, after some initial successes, the Alliance diversified its interests into agriculture in general and sent teams of organizers with evangelistic zeal throughout the cotton South. The message to the southern farmer was simple: diversify your crops, use scientific methods, organize cooperatives, and expand your markets.[12] Alliance supporters believed this to be the only solution to southern agricultural poverty. Bobby often accompanied his father to Alliance meetings and other political gatherings where progressive ideals were debated, and Bobby developed a lasting interest in politics.[13] In fact, his first recorded public speech was made from a dry-goods box in front of the Nix Drugstore in Dothan, Alabama, where in 1895, as a twelve-year-old, he exhibited unusual ability as a public speaker and quick thinker in a twenty-minute defense of the Populist Party.[14]

Alex Jones was the first farmer in south Alabama to diversify his small farm away from cotton into growing vegetable crops.[15] He became known as "Peanut Jones" for his dedication to the cause of peanuts, and he worked hard to develop a small vegetable business.

Young Bobby would sometimes accompany his father on the vegetable rounds and at times would be called on to handle the route himself. Before dawn in the summer, when Bobby was ten or eleven years old, his father would send him to Dothan with a wagonload of vegetables. Bobby recalled being afraid of the dark, and seeing "the pine trees dancing out by the side of the road, but I had to be in town by daylight. . . . I drove around in town, rang doorbells, and sold vegetables. I would take an armful of turnips, greens, collards, cabbage, field peas, . . . butter, and eggs and milk and sell them. I would take in all the money I could and then drive home about the middle of the day."[16]

Doubtless, these experiences were influential in shaping his character, and many of these experiences later found their way into his sermons in the form of anecdotes and illustrations.[17]

> One day my father said that if I would get a certain amount of money and would bring it to him I could have anything that was left over. Well, I gave the customers good measure that day, but I didn't heap up the measure. I was honest all right, but I didn't give them anything they weren't entitled to! I made one quarter for myself. I know that amount of money doesn't look like anything to you, but that was money when I was a boy. You could almost rear a family on that amount! . . . On my way home I took that quarter out and looked at it, and flipped it up, and caught it. I had earned it! . . . But along the way, while admiring it, I dropped it. It fell through a crack in the wagon into the sand. I stayed there until sundown sifting the sand but never did find it! I drive that road sometimes now with a pain in my heart. I learned that day a lesson. Things don't always turn out as you think they will turn out.[18]

The Jones family was devoutly Christian, closely knit, and sentimental. Every Sunday after church, the family would spend part of the afternoon at the Clark Cemetery where two of the Jones daughters were buried. Bob Jones carried this family sentiment with him through life and often visited his boyhood home to renew old friendships and visit the graves of his family. He said, "I have been to that cemetery many times and I have sat by [my mother's] grave until the twilight faded and I have listened to a funeral dirge played by the wind in the pine trees near-by."[19]

Alex Jones was an "immersed" Methodist, and Georgia Creel Jones was a Primitive Baptist. Since there was no Baptist church in the area, the entire family attended the Methodist church near their home. In 1894 an elderly preacher held meetings at the church and spoke about the poor crippled man who was brought to the house of a Pharisee and could not get in. The preacher told about the men climbing up to the roof of the house to let the afflicted man down into the presence of Christ, how the Great Physician told him to take up his bed and walk, and how the man was healed and went home rejoicing that he had found Christ. If the crippled man could get to Jesus, young Bobby knew that he could find Him too.[20] As an eleven-year-old boy Bob Jones answered that altar call and made a public profession of his faith in the Lord Jesus Christ as personal Savior. Later that same night, he felt called of God for His service.[21]

4

Though Bobby was converted in a Methodist meeting, his mother persuaded Alex to allow Bobby and several of the other Jones children to be baptized by immersion in the creek that ran near the Methodist church.[22]

Shortly after his conversion, Bobby came under the influence of one great truth: "I had to live somewhere forever. . . . I've got to live. I've got to live until God dies. I've got to live until angels sing a funeral dirge over His grave."[23]

This thought fired Bobby's purpose as a young boy. He soon abandoned preaching to mules as he plowed and began preaching to people. Extant records from the Beulah Church, which the Jones family attended, indicate that in 1894 or 1895 Bobby took part in a Children's Day service and "really preached a sermon."[24] His speaking was so powerful that by twelve years of age he was made Sunday school superintendent over men "old enough to be his grandfather." In 1895, as a twelve-year-old, Bobby held his first revival meeting at his home church in Brannon Stand and saw sixty conversions during only one week of meetings.[25] That same year he built a brush arbor and held meetings that resulted in the founding of a church he later pastored. He said, "The first two or three years I walked . . . and begged for any kind of place to preach. In one community I built a brush arbor and conducted a revival meeting for a week. We organized a church with fifty-four members. I did not receive one cent for my services, but I had good food, a place to sleep, peace of conscience, and the sweet assurance that I was doing God's will."[26]

Before the age of fifteen he was licensed to preach by the Methodist Episcopal Church, South, the dominant middle-class church of the era, and at age sixteen Bobby was called to pastor the Headland Circuit, a circuit of five churches. During his two-year ministry on the Headland Circuit, over four hundred made professions of faith in Jesus Christ and joined the churches.[27] As a teenager, Bobby was preaching throughout southeast Alabama and was widely known as the "boy preacher, Bob Jones."

"I realize," Dr. Jones said later, "that I must have been rather dumb. In my early ministry it never seemed anything out of the ordinary that the public was following me and that the businessmen in the community would come to listen to a little country boy preach. The wonder is that the devil did not trap me. He tried to do it. I was pulled here and there and from house to house. People flocked to hear me preach. The buildings could not hold

Bob Jones Sr., age fifteen
(ca. 1898)

the crowds; people even stood outside and stuck their heads in the windows to listen. It is a wonder it did not spoil me."[28]

Bobby's early education was obtained in two schools, both of which operated only a few months a year. The Jones children, Dr. Bob remembered, started attending school around seven years of age and "just learned as fast as we could."[29] Though lacking a formal education, Alex Jones loved to read aloud to the family from the Bible, religious literature, newspapers, and the classics. When a particularly striking passage caught his attention, Alex Jones would copy it, have Bobby memorize it, and call upon him to "say your speech" for the family or the many guests who were regularly invited to dinner.[30] "I do not know any child more timid and self-conscious than I was," Dr. Jones later recalled. "I did whatever my father said to do, but when he told me to 'say the speech,' I suffered agony that nobody could possibly know."[31] Included in his memorization were large portions of Scripture, prose, and poetry. He continued to memorize pieces of this type throughout his life, but one particular poem, "Building the Bridge for Him," by W. A. Dromgoole, became a favorite which he often quoted in chapel talks.[32]

Bobby's ability to "say his speech" ultimately brought him the opportunity for further education. During the summer of 1896, while selling religious books and setting up Sunday schools, Dr. Charles Jefferson Hammitt[33] stopped at the Jones farm and was invited to stay for a meal. Following supper, Alex Jones called on Bobby to "say your speech." Hammitt listened to the recitations and realized that the boy had much potential. He questioned the Joneses about Bobby's education, and when he thought of the limited opportunities available in the Brannon Stand area, Hammitt offered to board Bobby with his family in Kinsey, Alabama, fourteen miles away, so that the boy could attend Mallalieu Seminary.

Mallalieu, a Methodist secondary school of which Hammitt was the principal, was the religious, cultural, and educational center of the Dothan area and one of only two secondary schools in southeastern Alabama.[34] Endowed by northern Methodists, the school had opened in 1882. Tuition was free, but each student paid an "incidental fee" of one dollar per term. The courses offered, many of which Bobby probably took, included the "three R's" as well as physiology, Latin, Greek, algebra, rhetoric, Roman history, New Testament history, geology, music and art courses, and a course in home economics.[35]

Prior to his conversion, Dr. Hammitt had studied for a career on the stage. He was widely known as dignified and disciplined and as a godly, highly educated man—the most educated man in all south Alabama.[36] From him, Bobby came to appreciate the importance of education for those called of God to His service, as well as the importance of the personal polish that helps one radiate the gospel.

In late summer of 1896, Bob Jones became a student at Mallalieu Seminary where he stayed through 1900 when he completed his high school studies.[37] During these years, Mallalieu enrolled between 150 and 180 students, depending on the price of cotton.[38] Even though tuition was free, Bobby had to work to earn money for his books and his board with the Hammitts. Alex Jones helped with his son's expenses by delivering produce, sweet potatoes, and cornmeal to the seminary.[39]

For his board Bob recalled doing chores for Mrs. Hammitt, waiting tables for the family, and drawing "water out of a well sixty feet deep to water an old cow that never had enough water in her life. You couldn't fill her up! I was ordered around by kids in the home. And I never wasted a cent of money. I had none to waste."[40] The Hammitt children in turn remembered that young Bobby was so poor that his pants had "patches on patches."[41]

Shortly after he left home to study, Georgia Creel Jones, the fourteen-year-old boy's mother, died. Bobby had been close to her, and her death gave him a renewed determination to "do right" and to succeed.[42] He often related the story of his last visit home before her death and remembered the words of his mother as he left to return to Mallalieu: "You are going away, Son. Be a good boy." Two weeks later he was brought home to stand by her deathbed. When she realized he was there, her first question to him was, "Have you been a good boy, Son?" She looked up at him and said, "Son, you have always been a good boy. I want you to trust God and follow Him and let Him make something of you. I am going away. I want you to be a good boy and meet me in heaven."

After the funeral, as he returned to school, he realized that "this time, there was no mother to go with me to the gate and kiss me goodbye and say, 'Be a good boy.' But I had the sweetest kiss I ever had. Mother threw me a kiss from Heaven. I seemed to hear a sweeter voice than I had ever heard. I heard it with the ears of my soul. It was Mother's voice mingled with the music that angels make on harps of gold saying, 'You are going away now, Son. Be a good boy.' "[43]

Three years later, in 1899, Alex Jones died, leaving Bobby on his own.[44]

Following the completion of his secondary schooling at age sixteen, Bob Jones enrolled at Southern University, a Methodist school in Greensboro, Alabama.[45] While at Southern, he was a member of the Alpha Tau Omega fraternity, pastored several Methodist churches in circuit, and held as many evangelistic meetings as would fit into his schedule.[46] With his sharp mind, he was known at the college as a gifted debater, and he had an interest in dramatics and speech.[47] Dr. Jones recalled that Southern had a "very practical, cultured approach . . . with high standards of refinement and decency."[48] While there, he studied Greek, Latin, mathematics, and science but "did not set the woods on fire academically."[49]

A salary of twenty-five dollars a month paid by his circuit of churches, offerings from evangelistic meetings, and loans from friends paid his expenses for the three years he spent at Southern, from 1901 to 1904.[50] "Many times," he said, "I became discouraged and blue, but not once did

Jesus fail me. I borrowed what money I could not earn by preaching around the country or by doing extra jobs to meet the bills as they came due." These experiences undoubtedly made him determined to "make stepping stones, not stumbling stones" out of his difficulties.[51]

Even though he began preaching before he was fourteen years of age, it was not until his college days that it became a full-time calling. By 1903 he was scheduled for revival campaigns throughout the states of Alabama and Louisiana. Typically, these meetings would be sponsored by one church, be held in the summer, and last fourteen to twenty-eight days or possibly longer. Invitations to preach revival meetings became increasingly frequent, so that by the time he reached his senior year in college, Bob was constantly kept busy preaching or preparing to preach. He did not complete his college program at Southern.[52]

While a student at Southern University, Bob met Bernice Sheffield and fell in love. They married on October 24, 1905.[53] Bernice briefly traveled with Bob in his evangelistic ministry. Ailing, she was diagnosed as having tuberculosis, and for her health they went to Colorado Springs, Colorado, hoping for rest and a cure. While the young couple was there, her condition began to deteriorate, and they decided to return to Alabama. As they traveled, she weakened and contracted pneumonia. She died within days of arriving in Birmingham, on September 7, 1906, after less than eleven months of marriage.[54] Shortly after this, Bob himself was diagnosed with "tuberculosis of the throat." He returned to the West for a year to recover.

Sometime between the years 1906 and 1909, Bob Jones Sr. may have served one year under James M. Gray of Moody Bible Institute as a regional evangelist. During this time Bob Jones began developing citywide, cooperative campaigns along the same lines as the previous generation of evangelists—namely, Finney, Moody, and Sunday. During this era a revival meeting was an event of considerable interest in the cities and towns of the nation. In many instances the entire population of a town as well as many folks from surrounding areas would come to meetings simply to observe the happenings.[55] With the advent of citywide campaigns, all orthodox churches in a locality were invited to participate in the sponsorship of a meeting. Some meetings lasted as long as twelve weeks with many thousands in attendance.[56] It was not uncommon for three thousand to five thousand adults to be at an evening service. For meetings of this size, huge wooden "tabernacles" were constructed or industrial warehouses were rented and remodeled to hold the crowds. "They never had a tabernacle that accommodated the crowds," Mrs. Jones Sr. recalled. "They always overflowed."[57] Often, the adulation of the crowds would turn the head of an evangelist, and after a short period of time, no more would be heard of him. Such was not the case with Bob Jones.[58]

In 1907, Bob Jones held a meeting in Uniontown, Alabama, and while there met a gracious and cultured young woman who was singing in the choir. Following a year's courtship, Mary Gaston Stollenwerck and the twenty-four-year-old evangelist were married on June 17, 1908. The newly married couple established their home in Montgomery, Alabama, and on October 19, 1911, the evangelist's only child, Robert Reynolds Jones Jr., was born in Montgomery.

The Stollenwerck family, though not considered wealthy, was one of the cultured, socially prominent plantation families of Alabama.[59] Mary Gaston's mother, Estelle Siddons Stollenwerck, was a refined woman of the Old South. She was a small and delicate woman of charm, intellect, and education who had been converted

Bob and his new bride, Mary Gaston Stollenwerck Jones (1908)

at age fourteen.[60] She loved books and art, and she spoke fluent French. Bob became quite close to her and called her "Mother." She regularly accompanied the family on his evangelistic campaigns.[61]

Dr. Jones Sr.'s first encounter with the ecclesiastical machinery of the Methodist Church came when he was fourteen years old. A "highbrow" bishop refused to approve the ordination of young Bob on the grounds that he was only a boy, untrained and untested in theological matters. An old preacher at the ordination council reportedly suggested that the bishop preach a sermon followed by one by Bob Jones. The people present could then vote on the ordination based on who preached the better sermon. Knowing young Bob's skill as an orator, the bishop declined the invitation, and Bob Jones was ordained by unanimous consent.[62]

Some years later, the denominational leadership passed an ordinance that stated that no Methodist preacher could hold a religious meeting in any circuit without the local pastor's permission. This was seen by many of the evangelists of the era as an attempt to build a denominational machine and to silence the voices of religious nonconformity represented by evangelists such as Bob Jones, Sam Jones, and others.[63] While many Methodist preachers and evangelists knuckled under to the demands of the denomination, Bob refused, continuing to build a reputation as a preacher of character who could not be stopped by the demands of petty bishops.[64]

In the second decade of the twentieth century, Bob Jones made his first forays into the North under the auspices of the Baptists and Presbyterians. His meetings produced dramatic results with large numbers of conversions

Mr. and Mrs. Bob Jones Sr. leaving for their wedding trip, June 17, 1908. The couple is seated in the fourth row from the front.

and hundreds seeking Protestant church membership. Recapping a six-week campaign in 1917, the *Zanesville (Ohio) Times-Recorder* reported that the Bob Jones campaign ran for eight weeks, during which time the evangelist preached 102 times. The actual head count for the entire campaign totaled more than 266,000 people, with seventeen churches cooperating in the meeting. There were 3,284 converts and the "free-will offering to Mr. Jones was $6,000."[65]

Each campaign had several themes which Dr. Jones hit as he preached. He lambasted the sins of men. In special services for women he denounced the sins of women.[66] His message, though having a social significance that in many respects paralleled the message of the Progressives of his day,[67] was primarily spiritual. He fought social ills vigorously, preaching against the sins of the gambling interests and the fledgling Hollywood movie industry,[68] crooked politicians, and the election of tainted public officials.[69] Corruption in the church, the school, and the home were standard themes of each campaign. Vice, police corruption, unfair wages for labor—all had a place in his preaching. He was an "ardent admirer" and public supporter of William Jennings Bryan,[70] campaigned throughout the South against Al Smith in the election of 1928,[71] fought for Prohibition,[72] supported the progressive reforms of Alabama Governor Bibb Graves,[73] and was known by men of influence in politics, religion, education, and journalism during his lifetime.

In every town in which a campaign was held, he railed against the liquor trade, and the trade was always affected and, sometimes, even closed down.[74] In Hartford City, Indiana, for example, it was reported that within two months of the Bob Jones revival, sixteen saloons were put out of business and the city voted dry for the first time since 1842.[75] Following six weeks of meetings in Quincy, Illinois, where one of his most dramatic campaigns was held, the saloons were closed, and many thousands in the town were converted to Christianity and joined Protestant churches.

The successes of his revivals were not without incident. On numerous occasions threats were made on Bob Jones's life.[76] On at least three occasions actual attempts were made on his life: twice during Prohibition days in Montgomery, Alabama, and once in Quincy, Illinois, in 1916. In Quincy, a predominantly Catholic, rough-and-tumble river town, a conspiracy was hatched by the owners of the local saloons to murder him in the pulpit as he preached. A mob of ruffians was raised to carry out the plan, but the plot was uncovered and revealed to Dr. Jones before the service began. While admitting he was frightened, he would not turn away from a fight. Years later, recalling that night, Dr. Jones said he

> talked to that crowd—toyed with them like a cat toys with a rat for about fifteen or twenty minutes. They [the mob] were good-hearted fellows; they had been stirred up by dirty saloon keepers, crooked politicians. And after a while, I leaned over the pulpit and said, "Now they tell you I'm here to fight the Roman Catholic Church. I've got all I can do to fool with these backslidden Protestants.
>
> "Suppose you fellows down here today were formed to come here tonight and kill me. Suppose there should be such a condition here. And suppose you had it all fixed up that at a certain time, [at] a certain signal, somebody would rush up here, the lights would be cut off, and you'd kill me. I think you've got too much sense to do it, because you would not get another drop of liquor in this town. . . . [The townspeople] would put those saloons out and you would not get any more liquor."
>
> God helped me and the power of God came down. When I gave the invitation, every member of the mob came forward and wept their way into the arms of God.[77]

Bob Jones never backed down from a fight. The news writers of 1911 passed to Bob Jones the "mantle" of Evangelist Sam Jones.[78] By the 1920s the name "Bob Jones" was a household word not just in the South, but in many parts of the country.[79] One description, penned in the 1920s, says, "Bob Jones is a crusader, not a crank. He accepts all science that is science; but he refuses to believe or teach what is yet nebulous, negative of revelation, and not fully proven. His religion is foundation-solid and fool-proof. Hence the magnetism of his leadership and the popularity of his protagonism."[80] By 1925, his name was nearly as widely recognized as Billy Sunday's.

Before his thirtieth birthday in 1913, he had preached in twenty-five states. By 1923 he estimated that he had preached 12,000 sermons to audiences totaling fifteen million people.[81] Between the years 1908 and 1930, he conducted more than eighty revival campaigns in the major cities of the United States and Canada, including New York City; Chicago; Atlanta; Jacksonville, Florida; Philadelphia; Pittsburgh; Los Angeles; Portland, Oregon; El Paso, Texas; and Montgomery, Alabama. He also held campaigns in smaller cities such as Owensboro, Kentucky; Columbia, South Carolina; Binghamton, New York; Quincy, Illinois; and Zanesville, Ohio. The *Montgomery (Ala.) Advertiser,* in 1953, called the Bob Jones revival of 1921 "the religious event of the century" in that city.

For his faithful service as an evangelist, Bob Jones was awarded an honorary doctor of divinity degree from Muskingum College, New Concord, Ohio, in 1921. He was thirty-eight years of age.[82]

The Ku Klux Klan supported Bob Jones Sr.,[83] as it did most conservative Protestant ministers and evangelists of both the North and the South.[84] There is evidence to suggest that he sympathized with the Klan's professed position for religious orthodoxy, Prohibition, and the elimination of the teaching of evolution.[85] However, he spoke out strongly against "lawlessness" and "lynching."[86]

Bob Jones Sr. was not frightened by progress. He studied the technological advances in communications and culture in general to determine their usefulness and effectiveness for evangelism. During his early campaigns he often gave radio interviews, and during at least one campaign the evening message was broadcast nightly for an entire six weeks. In the late 1920s he recorded radio messages for a small network that included stations in Dothan and Montgomery, Alabama; Pittsburgh; and New York City.[87]

Film, as a tool in mass evangelism, also fascinated Dr. Jones. In 1925 he financed, wrote, and produced a dramatized sermon film that was shot on location in Philadelphia while the Joneses were taking a six-week vacation between evangelistic campaigns. The film, entitled *The Unbeatable Game,* starred Bob Jones Sr. and members of his evangelistic organization, as well as actors and actresses from the Philadelphia area.[88] The film's portrayal of certain sins against which he preached was too graphic for the State Censorship Board, and they "slashed the film into an unrecognizable mess."[89]

In 1927 Bob Jones Sr. traveled the Chautauqua Circuit, famous for bringing noted speakers and musicians to small communities, where he lectured on general social issues in a dramatic address entitled "The Perils of America."[90]

Print media were also important. During the early days of Bob Jones College, mass mailings were sent out containing information about the school. In 1928 the *Bob Jones Magazine* was introduced to inform the public of Bob Jones Sr.'s ideas of "religious, political, and social life."[91] The magazine, which was published until January 1931, included such articles as

"Intelligence and Orthodoxy,"[92] "Pontius Pilate: A Religious Drama,"[93] "The Atonement,"[94] "Music at the Bob Jones College,"[95] and "Why I Am Not an Evolutionist,"[96] as well as political commentary.

At the height of his evangelistic career, with hundreds of thousands of people thronging to his meetings and with his name a household word in many areas of the country, he became determined that his "dream" to establish a school based on the "old reliable 'faith of our fathers' . . . shall come true."[97]

In 1927, Bob Jones College opened its doors, and the evangelist was now also an educator. The question is, why?

CHAPTER 2

◆

Why Start a College?

Did the South need another college? It had a long tradition in higher education extending back to William and Mary, established in 1693, and including the first state-supported universities—Georgia in 1785 and North Carolina in 1795. Before the Civil War, more than half of the colleges in the country were located in the South.[1] With the Civil War most southern colleges ceased operation for lack of students or because of the Yankees' torch. Following the war, the schools slowly reopened, but problems finding qualified students among the applicants plagued the colleges.[2] The loss of thousands of the South's finest young men in battle, the war's interruption of education on all levels, and the slow postwar reopening of secondary schools caused a scarcity of students ready for college-level study—a fact emphasized by one critic in 1884 who wrote, "We have too many so-called colleges and universities, and too few preparatory schools. There has been no great advance, if any, in college work in the South since the war, and in preparation for college there has been a positive decline in most of the States."[3] The Civil War scattered, maimed, or killed the teaching faculties and reduced the southern college and university to a ruin that took nearly sixty years to rebuild.[4]

By 1900, 216 institutions of higher learning were operating in the South. Of these, only 56 were independent of some form of denominational or sectarian control, and many were in some way state supported. Between 1900 and 1920 many new schools opened to meet the educational needs of black Americans, women, and the growing Protestant denominations.[5] A "New South" was on the horizon, prosperity had come, and education was viewed as the key to the door of the future.

Between 1870 and 1930 the emphasis of undergraduate higher education shifted from a classically oriented curriculum to one that stressed the scientific method.[6] To many educators, "science" meant one thing: evolution and the application of the evolutionary hypothesis to their field of study. Evolutionary scientific methods based on the research model of Hegel and others also brought a freethinking, critical examination of knowledge.[7] The new views of social psychology, based as they were on the behaviorism of J. B. Watson and E. L. Thorndike and the psychological explanations of man proposed by Freud, brought other issues into the arena as well.

In 1916, James H. Leuba, professor of psychology at Bryn Mawr College in Pennsylvania, published a landmark study entitled *The Belief in God and Immortality*.[8] His work focused on the beliefs of undergraduate students and science professors in American colleges and had a profound impact on political and religious leaders. It was freely quoted by Fundamentalist leaders, including William Jennings Bryan and John Roach Straton, both of whom were friends of Bob Jones Sr., as incontrovertible evidence that Christian orthodoxy was under attack by American higher education. The challenge hurled at orthodoxy came primarily because of the intellectual embrace of evolutionary science, Spencerian social Darwinism, social psychology, and higher criticism. Repeated incidents convinced Fundamentalist leaders such as Bryan, Straton, Reuben A. Torrey, William Bell Riley, and Bob Jones Sr. that "the teaching of evolution as a fact instead of a theory caused the students to lose faith in the Bible, first in the story of creation, and later in other doctrines which underlie the Christian religion."[9]

The Belief in God confirmed that more than 50 percent of the science professors in American colleges and universities embraced Darwinian evolution as fact and had "discarded belief in a personal God and in personal immortality."[10] Based on the evolutionary hypothesis, professors rejected the supernatural; cast doubt on the Mosaic account of man's creation found in Genesis and on the inspiration of the Bible and its authority; and publicly expressed doubt about the virgin birth and the bodily resurrection of Christ.[11]

It came as no surprise to conservative religious leaders that Leuba reported that 45 percent of American college graduates had discarded their faith in God and the doctrines of the Bible because of the influence of unbelieving professors.[12] What did shock Fundamentalist leaders, however, were the results of a 1919 survey of religious colleges that indicated that three-fourths of these schools taught evolution as scientific fact instead of theory and that most of the science professors were evolutionists of some type.[13]

Fundamentalist writings of the period contain numerous accounts of young people returning home from college only to renounce their belief in biblical stories and doctrines.[14] Amazingly, the major liberal theologians of the day, while scoffing at such stories as spurious, capricious, or a scare tactic, recorded personal experiences that corroborated the Fundamentalists' claims.[15] Even secular novelists picked up the theme and wrote of the bitter inner struggles when a young man in college faced the choice between modern science and old-time faith.

James Lane Allen, a pulp novelist of the era, wrote of a young, backward ministerial student who came in contact with science and theological higher criticism for the first time. The final words of Allen's main character seem to be characteristic of the Modernist and the scientist of the era: " 'Science! Science!' the boy shouted. 'There is the fresh path for the faith of the race! For the race henceforth must get its idea of God, and build its religion to him, from its knowledge of the laws of his universe.' "[16] Thus, orthodox, conservative scholars, pastors, and evangelists, including Bob Jones Sr., saw the new faith in science in general and the teaching of evolution in particular as dangers to the faith of the young.

A second threat, found firmly established in American seminaries and colleges by the 1920s and fed by the faith in science and evolution, was the abandonment of the doctrines of the Christian religion by educators and theologians.[17] Following World War I, the "New Era" emphasis on scientific inquiry brought amazing technological innovations, and the scientific method brought both religious and political changes that disturbed conservative leaders. The impact of the New Era was nowhere more evident than in religious life.

Using "scientific" higher criticism to "de-mythologize" the Bible, college professors began to attack the authorship of the Pentateuch, the books of Daniel, Job, Psalms, Isaiah, and others. They attacked the writings of the apostles Paul and John, the Gospels, the record of Christ, and His historicity and miracles. Every tenet of Christianity was attacked by science and the new criticism.[18] As a result, a new "social gospel" was developed and was widely adopted. Church attendance ballooned, but missionary efforts declined dramatically and coincided with an increased interest in humanitarianism, humanism, scientism, and behaviorism.[19] Because of these new influences and the seeming dissolution of American society, many churchmen demanded a religious revival.[20] The upheaval in society that followed World War I was, to many minds, the result of the denial of biblical truth. With this view Bob Jones Sr. agreed.[21]

The America in which Bob Jones Sr. moved and to which he preached through 1920 could rightly be described as Protestant, orthodox, and evangelical.[22] In addition, the South in which he had grown up was not overtly sectarian or denominational, although it was dominated by Protestantism. There was a freely shared faith that stressed basic beliefs over sectarian interpretations of Scripture. These believers of differing denominational stripes supported each others' revivals, reforms, Bible conferences, and schools.[23] Thus, with a freely shared faith, the South exhibited a more homogeneous quality than other sections of the country.[24] The promise of widespread support was therefore not lost on Bob Jones.

Because of the Civil War and Reconstruction, southerners had developed a resistance to change and progressive thought—especially that which was imported from the North. The southern churches to which Bob Jones Sr. ministered between 1903 and 1917 held to more conservative positions theologically, embraced new ideas more slowly, and thus gave little attention to the ideas of the higher critics within the northern seminaries or the social gospel of Baptist theologian Walter Rauschenbusch.[25] The dynamic tensions within the northern churches between conservatism and Modernism wrought heated discourse on the true meaning of the gospel.[26] John Roach Straton, the Fundamentalist pastor of Calvary Baptist Church in New York City, wrote of the dire need for social awareness and social service but also declared that "we cannot substitute social service for personal salvation. The true aim of social service is to open the way for spiritual service. Mere

Bob Jones Sr. (1912)

reform, apart from Christ, cannot permanently heal the sores of our society."[27] To many, the social gospel had become the equivalent of the gospel itself and "seemed to undercut the relevance of the message of eternal salvation through trust in Christ's atoning work."[28] By the 1920s social awareness was rising within the southern church, and, like its counterpart in the North, this social concern was equated with religious experience and conversion. For the southern church, a time of decision as to which ideas to embrace and in what direction to head was near.[29]

Even as the northern denominations and seminaries gradually moved away from their historic doctrinal positions, their southern counterparts remained largely orthodox. One explanation for this may be found in southern reactionism. Another may be found in the fact that late in the nineteenth century, doctrinal skirmishes occurred in the South that kept the religious liberals at bay. A series of uproars and heresy trials in southern church-related colleges between the 1870s and 1920s helped to restrain the rising tide of the new theology for a time.[30] Such trials occurred in Methodist,[31] Baptist,[32] and Presbyterian[33] colleges and universities. State universities were not untouched by these ideological conflicts; one trial led to the resignation of the president of the University of North Carolina.[34]

For the Fundamentalist, Modernism was an attack on the person, veracity, and work of God. To many Fundamentalists, Modernism was not Christian at all; it was pantheism.[35] (For more on the Fundamentalist-Modernist controversy, see Appendix A.) The powers of Fundamentalist oratory and persuasion were the means to attack the thought of those who would dare to attempt to bring down the throne of God. To the Modernist, Fundamentalism was a dangerous, reactionary reaffirmation of the tired dogmas of the past. The powers of education and the media were to be used to attack those who attempted to deny science and progress their rightful place. The Fundamentalists became masters of discourse, logic, and debate; the Modernists became masters of the classroom, the cause of humanity, and the media.

Against the rising tide of educational scientism and new theology stood a rapidly eroding wall of politicians, ministers, and denominationally controlled Christian colleges. While Fundamentalists opposed the teaching of behaviorism, evolution,[36] and higher criticism in state educational institutions, they reacted violently to the teaching of these same things in Christian schools or schools supported primarily by church funds.[37] Evangelist Billy Sunday expressed this reaction bluntly in Elmira, New York, in 1924: "If anyone wants to teach that God-forsaken, hell-born, bastard theory of evolution, then let him go out and let him be supported by men who believe that blasted theory and not expect the Christian people of this country to pay for the teaching of a rotten, stinking professor who gets up there and teaches our children to forsake God and makes our schools a clearing-house for their God-forsaken dirty politics."[38]

In a stinging criticism, Fundamentalist Presbyterian J. Gresham Machen wrote that modern education was a "soul killing system" of schools that teach "their materialism, their discouragement of any sustained intellectual effort, their encouragement of the dangerous pseudo-scientific fads of experimental psychology" and scientism.[39]

William Jennings Bryan

Bob Jones Sr. recalled a conversation with the great Christian statesman William Jennings Bryan at Winona Lake, Indiana, in 1924. During a preaching service at the Bible conference center, Bryan leaned over and said, "If schools and colleges do not quit teaching evolution as a fact, we are going to become a nation of atheists."[40] Fundamentalists agreed with this frightening assessment. The logical end of the teaching of evolution, most Fundamentalists preached, was the disavowal of belief in the cardinal doctrines of the Bible and the embracing of a philosophy of relativism or pragmatism on the part of the student.

Bob Jones Sr. was aware of and concerned about the teaching of evolution in public schools and colleges.[41] In his powerful and popular Chautauqua lecture, "The Perils of America," he said, "The educational institutions in America are sleeping over atheistic volcanos. . . . Is this Old Book, written with the finger of inspiration . . . to flee the stage because Mr. Darwin guessed about how everything was made?"[42] To the Fundamentalist, the answer was a resounding "No!"

Though the teaching of evolution was a major issue to Bob Jones Sr., more important to him was the actual condition of belief and behavior of college-age students that was commonly reported to him by parents around the country.[43] Mrs. Jones recalled that even as early as 1916 or 1917 the spiritual conditions among college students had made an impact on her husband's mind. One day while traveling in Florida, the evangelist and his wife were talking about the future of young Bob Jr. Mrs. Jones recalled that she turned to her evangelist husband and asked,

"Where will we send Bob to college?"

He replied, "Honey, I don't know. There are many fine schools and some good Christian schools in the United States, but I don't know of any one that exactly suits me in educating my boy."

Like all mothers and fathers, we thought we had a prodigy. And we wanted the best for him in an educational way, but we were determined not to expose him to teachers who did not know and believe the Bible.[44]

Mrs. Jones also recalled her husband saying,

"I'm going to see that someone organizes or founds a Christian school—a real Christian school."

So, with that in mind and with prayer behind it, of course, he began to talk to people that he thought could do it. They all agreed with him and admitted there was such a need for it, but they didn't have time or they didn't know how to go about it. And, of course, anything like that has to have a financial foundation and so many different things. And Dr. Bob was so busy with his evangelistic work he didn't know when *he* could do it. . . . But the need became greater and greater, because everybody that would come to him would say, "We would love to have a place to educate our [children], Dr. Jones. Can you recommend a place?"

Later on, he would have so many young people come to him and tell him stories, tragic stories, about losing their faith.[45]

Bob Jones was often met by disturbing reports from parents and students alike of the ideas propounded in colleges and universities in the country. The product of this education he called "shipwrecks."[46] "In my evangelistic contacts," he recalled, "I had found hundreds of young people who had been brought up in Christian homes and who went to college and university. Then these young people came back home to their parents with shattered faith and sometimes with wrecked morals."[47] He was often confronted by heartbroken parents with stories of their child's moral decay, dis-hallowed spiritual life, or suicide.

Following one meeting, a local pastor related to Dr. Jones the story of one of his faithful members. The man and his wife had reared a daughter who, by all appearances, was a Christian. After graduation from high school, the girl went to college for further study and returned having lost her faith in the Bible and in Christ as God's Son. "She laughed at the old-time religion," they said. Her parents were heartbroken and tried to speak with her about her beliefs and the condition of her faith. "One day, she rushed upstairs, stood in front of a mirror, took a gun, and blew out her brains."[48] This, and other stories like it, deeply affected the evangelist.

In an editorial entitled "Worse Than a Common Thief," he protested vigorously against the "atheists and infidels" in church schools who were stealing the faith of the young while in the employ of church-sponsored schools. In his words, "Bootleggers and harlots will stand a better chance in the day of judgment than the teachers in colleges called Christian which damn boys and girls from Christian homes."[49]

Bob Jones Sr., seeing increasing moral decay in the educational, political, and religious institutions of the country[50] and viewing the teaching of evolution[51] and behaviorist psychology[52] with alarm, "felt there ought to be an institution that stood for the old-time religion, emphasized evangelism, had high academic standards—where students could go and not have evolution rammed down their throats."[53] He wrote, "I am tired of leading boys and girls to Jesus Christ and then seeing these boys and girls attend institutions which shake their faith in the deity of the Christ whom they trust and in the Word of God which they have been taught to believe."[54]

These long-standing concerns played on the mind of Bob Jones Sr. The idea of a Christian college that could "pass muster" gradually formed in his mind—a college that would be a "continuous Chautauqua, with the greatest Christian scholars and teachers in the world there";[55] one in which every class "is opened in prayer, where boys and girls learn to pray . . . [where] every session opens with a revival."[56] This was to be a college in which "the faith of a boy or girl is worth more than an education."[57]

The stage was now set.

CHAPTER 3

◆

The Founding of Bob Jones College

By 1925 Bob Jones Sr. was one of the most sought-after evangelists and public speakers in America, booked for campaigns at least four years in advance and traveling on the Chautauqua lecture circuit.[1] At this time, his income from the campaigns was the largest of any evangelist in America except Billy Sunday.[2] Before the Great Depression it was not unusual for love offerings to total $1,000 to $1,500 per week above expenses. In the 1920s Bob Jones Sr. may have enjoyed an income of $50,000 to $75,000 a year.[3] By all standards he was a successful man, and he could have become a rich man. Yet from the time he first mentioned a school to his wife in 1916 or 1917, the thought weighed on him. He began to look for someone to start a school in the South that would stay true to the fundamentals and have broad appeal, but "he could not find anyone. Finally he could not stand it any longer."[4]

In early April 1925, while traveling to south Florida for a rest from evangelistic meetings, Dr. and Mrs. Jones were talking about the condition of the country and the need for a school. Around lunch time, they stopped to buy sandwiches at a roadside restaurant or drugstore in Kissimmee, Florida. To eat their lunches, they pulled in at a roadside rest area by the banks of the Coco River. Mrs. Jones remembered that while sitting under some shade trees,

> just as a clap of thunder out of a clear sky, he said, "Mary Gaston, I'm going to found a school." I knew with him, to think was to act. . . . I replied with amazement, "Robert, are you crazy? Honey, you don't know anything about a school. You're not an educator, you can't found a school."

> "I know I can't, but God can!"

> [Bob] just wheeled that car around and went straight back. I said, "Where are we going?"

> He said, "Let's go to Panama City, to see R. L. McKenzie. He is a wonderful friend, and I've got to have somebody help me find a location—that will be the first thing."

> I said, "Why do you want to build [a school] in Florida instead of Alabama, our home state?"

> "Well," he said, "It's just over the line from the part of Alabama where I was reared. I know the country there and the needs, and I believe that would be the best place. From the sounds of it, I believe Florida will have an appeal for northern people. Most of my meetings in recent years have

been in the North and I just believe many people would love to send their children to Florida for the winters."

When we got to Panama City, we got in the hotel and he contacted Mr. McKenzie—called him on the phone. They met at the hotel and stayed up nearly all night in discussions. The next day they met with bankers and other men, including the lawyer, Mr. Sapp, and by the next afternoon, all was decided. We left for Montgomery late that afternoon and arrived home about 2:00 A.M.[5]

A Board of Trustees was formed, the school was incorporated as a "corporation not-for-profit," and the school charter was approved by the circuit court in Panama City on April 14, 1925.[6] The first board included Governor Bibb Graves of Alabama, Georgia congressman William D. Upshaw, real-estate broker R. L. McKenzie, lawyer and judge J. M. Sapp, banker Raymond Crane, Mrs. Bob Jones Sr., and Bob Jones Sr.[7] The board also recommended that the college be named "Bob Jones College," over the strenuous objections of Dr. Jones. They felt that because of his widely known name, established reputation, and intimate connection with the founding of the college, any other name would be inappropriate.[8]

Dr. Jones pledged to the Board of Trustees to personally underwrite at least twenty thousand dollars yearly to pay teacher salaries and other expenses. He also refused to take a salary from the college, preferring instead to live off a portion of his campaign offerings and to give the rest to the school treasury.[9] He was opposed to soliciting funds for construction, so a "cold-blooded business" plan, based on real estate sales, was devised to raise money for the school while providing an investment for all donors.[10]

A great land boom had started in 1920 in Miami and gradually moved north until 1925 when it struck the Panhandle. Land speculators made enormous sums of money in short periods of time, and stories abounded of men who purchased "forty acres for $45.27" and later sold them for $40,000 or more.[11] Wealthy northerners snapped up huge tracts of land; holdings between 75,000 and 225,000 acres were typical, and in one instance, the Hoover family of Chicago held over one million acres. Typically, the land was sold to a speculator, who cut roads and resold it to syndicates or investors at higher prices. They in turn built more roads, divided the acreage into estates or lots, and sold it for handsome profits to "settlers" who either held the land for resale or subdivided the lots and created more investors and settlers.[12]

The boom that swept through the Panama City area made it a scene of "prosperity and optimism" with homes "being built everywhere." From appearances, Panama City, though at the end of the boom, was one of the liveliest places in all Florida.[13] By 1926 it had two new luxury hotels and a major golf course designed to attract the tourist trade. A railroad link had been developed to Dothan, Alabama, and prime land was still plentiful and relatively inexpensive.

After looking over several sites in the Panama City area, Bob Jones decided on what was then known as Long Point on St. Andrews Bay. The point was part of a 2,500-acre plot owned by the New York–based land development and real estate firm Minor C. Keith Corporation, which was developing properties in north Florida.[14] In January 1926, after a highly successful evangelistic campaign in Birmingham, Dr. Jones and Minor C. Keith met to discuss locating the college on Long Point. At that time Keith Properties, under the local supervision of Berry Collins, was completing the Panama City–St. Andrews Bay Country Club Development and dividing the land on Long Point into residential lots. In order to sell the 2,500 acres of land on the point, a deal was struck changing the name of Long Point to College Point and forming the College Point Development Company. The agreement was that Dr. Jones would lend his name and influence to Minor C. Keith's Development Company for the promotion of land sales, beginning in February 1926. In exchange, the college was given a 470-acre tract on which to build the campus, the college treasury was to receive 25 percent of the proceeds from the sale of 300 prime acres, and Dr. and Mrs. Jones were given the lot of their choice on which to construct a home.[15]

Mrs. Jones suggested that the family simply build a garage with an apartment over it until the school got off the ground. The evangelist would have none of this suggestion and refused to consider it, saying, "That's the last thing I want to do. There have been so many fly-by-night things opened up" that made promises to people and never followed through. Building his home by the bay, he thought, lent the new Bob Jones College a sense of permanence and purpose.[16]

In the spring of 1926, the Development Company launched a sales campaign with the slogan "Give Till It Hurts," while the slogan "Public Duty to Give" was trumpeted by local newspapers advertising College Point.[17] True to the norm, roads were cut, sidewalks were promised, and electric power poles were positioned. The lots ranged in price from one to two thousand dollars each, depending on size and location.[18]

During the first six months of the year, Dr. Jones scheduled a large number of short meetings throughout Alabama, Georgia, and north Florida, sometimes as many as three or four a day in different towns, to sell the land development idea. He argued that those who bought lots would "do four things: make a safe investment, line your pockets with profits, boost your community, and endow a college."[19]

He was able to sell many lots based solely on his reputation while at the same time receiving many small cash donations toward building the school.[20] It had been the practice of the Bob Jones Evangelistic Association to file the names and addresses of supporters and converts from many of the campaigns. Many of these individuals were contacted about the development and the college.[21] Others were recruited to become sales representatives for the College Point Development Company by reporting that "one man made

College Point, Florida, July 5, 1926

$630 yesterday in commissions," promising that "the best buying season is just ahead of us," and inviting them to meetings with Dr. Jones and a Development Company representative.[22] According to publicity reports, more than 350 lots had been sold by late June 1926.

A grand finale to the publicity campaign occurred on July 5, 1926, when a great land sale was to take place on College Point. A motorcade of 175 automobiles, accompanied by R. W. Sorrentino's Band, wound through Panama City from the Bob Jones Tabernacle out to Bay County.[23] After a tour of home sites and the proposed college campus, the crowd of fifteen hundred gathered under a huge tent for speeches by Bob Jones and local dignitaries. A box lunch was served to all by the Protestant churches of Panama City, and the afternoon was spent in swimming races, canoe-tipping contests, sack races, and a watermelon-eating contest. The day's events were to be capped off by a pie-eating contest. The contest had to be called off, however, when the makeshift tables on which the chocolate pies were sitting collapsed![24] Many tracts of land were sold by August, providing enough funds to begin construction of the college.

Support for the new college was widespread. Journalist Sam Small, a brilliant reporter for the *Atlanta Constitution* and an associate of Joel Chandler Harris, published his support of the college. Small wrote, "Cultured and financially competent men and women in many states are giving encouragement to the Bob Jones college enterprise knowing its genesis and that it is not a 'boom bubble,' a speculative promotion, or a get-rich-quick scheme of any sort. Those who know Dr. Jones know all that with absolute confidence."[25]

Within three months of the July extravaganza, however, real estate values in Florida plummeted and the land boom collapsed. One Panama City citizen recalled, "My dad was in the real estate business, and I saw one piece of property change hands three times in one day, and it went from $300,000 to $1,000,000—in one day. [The boom] just couldn't last. Whoever owned [the property] last was stuck. Everybody was land poor."[26]

A general economic depression soon followed in Florida; most of the mortgages on College Point lots had to be foreclosed by the Keith Corporation, and land sales were halted. Following the completion of the Panama City–St. Andrews Bay Country Club Development, the Keith Corporation pulled out of Florida, leaving the college to pave the roads, lay the sidewalks, run electric lines, and spend thousands of dollars on work that Keith had agreed to do. To complete the construction and furnish the buildings, hire and maintain a faculty and staff, and cover other expenses, more funds were needed. The college board voted to issue at least $500,000 in College Development Bonds, which, they wrote, constituted "a safe and worthy

Groundbreaking ceremony, College Point, Florida, December 1, 1926; *left to right:* J. M. Sapp, R. L. McKenzie, Bibb Graves, Bob Jones Sr., Willis Haymaker, Mrs. Jones Sr., Mr. Boone

investment."[27] In lieu of fulfilling their agreements, the Keith interests swapped $500,000 in mortgages—some good, some foreclosed, and some unsold properties—to the school in exchange for college bonds "with the understanding that if the mortgages were not collected, that [the college would] never pay the bonds. Those mortgages went on record with a group of three bankers who said they were worth 100 cents on the dollar."[28]

To reassure investors, Dr. Jones took out a life insurance policy of $500,000 to guarantee the value of the bonds and to guarantee the existence of the school in the event of his death. He never felt comfortable about soliciting funds outright for donations to the college. "Now remember," he wrote to supporters, "we are not asking you to make a gift to our college. We want you to purchase a bond, and have an interest in this proposition. I will give you my word of honor that the bonds are good. You can write any bank in this town and they will vouch for what I am telling you."[29]

The groundbreaking ceremony for Bob Jones College took place on December 1, 1926. With more than seven hundred invited guests in attendance, Governor-elect Bibb Graves of Alabama attacked "God-less education as a curse" and eloquently prophesied that thousands would be drawn to the college from all parts of the nation, "magnetized by the power of Jesus Christ."[30]

Artist's conception of Bob Jones College, College Point, Florida; dated March 16, 1927

Construction on "the city rising from the primeval forest" began in early spring of 1927 "with the chug of gasoline engines, the scratch from cross-cut saws, the click of sharp axes cutting through live timber, the smoky sweet aroma of pine woods burning under an open sky and the calls of scores of men at work."[31]

The new campus, as conceived by the architects, was to be the hub of a surrounding city. An artist's conception of the college showed seventeen buildings located within a mile-long circular drive. Spokelike roads led to a central administration building with an impressive bell tower. Two girls' dorms were planned on one side of the campus; on the other side were two boys' dorms. Also shown were a formal flower garden, a dining hall, two classroom buildings, a chapel, a library, an art building, a science building, a gymnasium, a heating plant, and a huge stadium. The projected cost to complete the campus was $5 million.

The surrounding town was to be centered on the campus bell tower, and the city was to be reserved for orthodox Protestants who could live the tenets of Christianity without interference from "worldly" interests.[32] One promotional booklet read, "The . . . evangelist saw the spires of a great, Christian college, founded on the Rock of Ages, and dedicated to the eternal perpetuity of religious orthodoxy. 'Round about it, his eyes could see a model city—a city of homes, and schools and churches—a city permeated with the spirit of a religious renaissance—a city at whose gateway was flung down the gauntlet to modernism."[33]

Bob Jones Sr. had maintained a nonsectarian approach throughout his evangelistic career and was determined that the college should not overemphasize any scriptural interpretation that would be divisive. Rather, he hoped to unify orthodox believers around the fundamental precepts of God's Word. Although Dr. Jones was a Methodist by upbringing, the college was founded as a "nondenominational, interdenominational" institution that could be supported by all Protestant denominations who subscribed to the fundamental truths of the Scripture as stated in the college creed. He took pains to insure that different denominations were represented on the faculty and declared that the "denominational integrity of every student" would remain unchallenged. One thought, writ large in the mind of Dr. Jones, was the "possibility of denominational cooperation without organic church union. We must not," he said, "have church union, but we must have . . . cooperation."[34]

While Dr. Jones Sr. left the organizing of the college's academics to others, he took the writing of the college creed on himself. He discovered writing the creed to be more difficult than he had imagined. He called on many of his friends for help but simply could not "fix it just right." Finally, during a visit to the college site by Atlanta journalist and good friend Sam Small, the evangelist related the problem of the creed to him. Without hesitation, Small "reached in his pocket and took out an envelope and took a pencil. He wrote the second paragraph of this college charter with a pencil on the back of an envelope. We put it in our college charter without changing a comma, a period, or even having to dot an 'i' or cross a 't.' . . . It was the most perfect little gem you ever heard of or ever saw. . . . It's a marvelous statement."[35]

The back of that envelope read,

> The general nature and object of the corporation shall be to conduct an institution of learning for the general education of youth in the essentials of culture and in the arts and sciences; giving special emphasis to the Christian religion and the ethics revealed in the Holy Scriptures; combatting all atheistic, agnostic, pagan, and so-called scientific adulterations of the gospel; unqualifiedly affirming and teaching the inspiration of the Bible (both the Old and the New Testaments); the creation of man by the direct act of God; the incarnation and virgin birth of our Lord and Saviour, Jesus Christ; His identification as the Son of God; His vicarious atonement

for the sins of mankind by the shedding of His blood on the cross; the resurrection of His body from the tomb; His power to save men from sin; the new birth through the regeneration by the Holy Spirit; and the gift of eternal life by the grace of God. This charter shall never be amended, altered or changed, as to the provisions hereinbefore set forth.[36]

Thus, the charter revealed the uniqueness of the college.[37] Bob Jones College was to be independent from any denominational controls, educationally conservative, theologically orthodox, and was to emphasize cultural education.[38]

Fundamentalist Christians were considered by many, especially in the Northeast, to be superstitious, ignorant, crude, and backward. This idea seems to have sprung from the popular writings of H. L. Mencken prior to and during the Scopes trial of 1925. Mencken had become something of a spokesman for the liberal secular press during this era, and repeatedly his writings and those of others published under his direction in the *American Mercury* reflected poorly on the South in general and on Fundamentalists in particular. Invariably, the portrait, painted in broad strokes, was one that was anticulture, antiarts, and antiprogress: "Dispatch from the up and coming Arkansas town of Stuttgart in the *Little Rock Gazette:* 'The Rev. Dr. M. M. Culpepper, pastor of the Grand Avenue Methodist Church, in discussing National Music Week at the request of the local Musical Club, scored the members for devoting their time to the study of grand opera, which, he said, "no one can understand, and if they did, it would do them no good!" ' "[39]

Dr. Jones was determined to have a college that defied the caricature of these satirical writers. He said, "This college was founded [to] neutralize in this country the idea that if you are conservative and believe the Bible, that you are sort of a fanatic, or you're lopsided or something. Some people—worldly, highbrowed, snooty people—think that if you're a Christian, that you are queer. . . . So we wanted to build a college that would neutralize in the minds of the public the idea that culture does not go hand in hand with the old-time, conservative, Christian approach, and so we started off on that basis."[40]

Other orthodox Christian colleges did exist in 1927, but they either were operated by denominations, stressed narrow theological distinctions, or emphasized scholarly pursuit above godliness. The founding of Bob Jones College was not without opposition from some within these colleges. J. Oliver Buswell, who had just been appointed president of Wheaton College in Illinois, took Dr. Jones Sr. publicly to task for starting a school.[41] He "objected to [the] founding of Bob Jones College, since Wheaton was a biblical institution and doing everything that needed to be done."[42] Buswell wrote, "One [orthodox school] is enough. We ought to stay by that."[43]

The college's independence from any sectarian or denominational financial support or control was problematic to some denominational leaders. Dr. Jones tried to reassure pastors in Florida and adjoining states that Bob

Jones College would not be in conflict with any other school which stood for the fundamentals of the Christian faith. "THE SCHOOLS OF ALL KINDS ARE OVERFLOWING SO THERE IS PLENTY OF ROOM FOR US. . . . We are close to you; we are neighbors; WE CAN WORK TOGETHER LIKE BRETHREN."[44]

Nevertheless, pastors and denominational leaders often discouraged prospective students from attending Bob Jones College because "the college was not Methodist" or because it was "unaccredited and the college work would have to be validated" by the denominational leadership or because the college was too "strict."[45]

On the other hand, many Christian leaders did support the college and were eager to serve on its board or speak in the daily chapel services and at the annual Bible Conference, which began the first year.[46] Leaders who took an active interest in the founding of the college included Dr. Henry Clay Morrison,[47] Evangelist Billy Sunday,[48] Dr. Harry Ironside,[49] Dr. William Bell Riley,[50] Dr. Leander Whitcomb Munhall,[51] Dr. William E. Biederwolf,[52] Dr. Paul Radar,[53] and Dr. John Roach Straton.[54] Bob Jones Sr., convinced that Fundamentalism could cut across denominational or sectarian lines, brought men of different denominational backgrounds to the college as speakers. Some

Billy Sunday, Nell Sunday, Bob Jones Sr. (1932)

years later he commented, "I think all of these [Protestant] denominations have been called into existence to underscore something that should be underscored, but all of them are built upon the same essential foundations of the Christian faith. And I made up my mind that a school could be built that would appeal to all the evangelical Christian groups if you would stick to the fundamentals. . . . I don't want to divide God's people; I want to unite them on the essential fundamentals of the faith."[55]

Bob Jones College advertisements promising a thoroughly Christian education began to run in newspapers in August of 1926: "Do you want your son or daughter educated in a Christian school which believes in the Bible from cover to cover, in a school which emphasizes the necessity of the new birth and holds uncompromisingly to the 'old time religion'? If you do, send your son or daughter to Bob Jones College." The college advertised that it would accommodate two hundred students, offer studies in education, English, history, mathematics, music, science, foreign language, Bible, and religious education beginning in the fall of 1927.[56] The Founder promised that "fathers and mothers who place their sons and daughters in our institution can go to sleep at night with no haunting fear that some skeptical teacher will steal the faith of their precious children."[57] Recruiting students became another full-time passion of Dr. Jones, even as preaching, selling lots, and raising money for construction had become passions.

Harry Ironside with Bob Jones Sr.

Amazingly, the buildings were finished on schedule in spite of the normal Florida summer rains and some small problems with supplies. The eighty-five students signed up for the first year were consumed with excitement about becoming "pioneers for the Lord."[58]

CHAPTER 4

◆

Bob Jones College:
College Point, Florida

The Bob Jones College buildings were completed on schedule and the College opened with gala ceremony on September 14, 1927. Present at the opening were such luminaries as Governor and Mrs. Bibb Graves of Alabama and Congressman William D. Upshaw of Georgia. Representatives of the departments of education of Florida and Alabama attended, as did the presidents of colleges, local judges, elected officials, and ministers from Florida, Alabama, and Georgia.[1]

Speeches were made by various dignitaries; a prayer of dedication was offered; the crowd of two hundred joined in singing "Faith of Our Fathers" and then watched silently as the newly hired faculty filed past a lectern and signed the College creed.

A banquet for the guests had been planned, but it was a near disaster. The Dining Hall director, hired by Dr. Jones without consulting his wife, was incompetent and "couldn't do a thing. She did not know how to take hold, and she knew nothing about planning portions or purchasing food!" Mrs. Jones had to plan the meal, oversee the cooking, bake the desserts, brew the tea, and even crush the ice.[2] Because of the feverish preparations for the banquet, no meal had been planned for the students or the faculty members and their families. Just before the banquet was to begin, Mrs. Jones realized the error, and she and a friend's cook baked cookies and made sandwiches and handed lunches out the kitchen window to the students and staff while the banquet was going on in the dining room. One week later, a second banquet was held specially for the students and the faculty. Mrs. Jones, however, never entirely overcame her embarrassment at this early blunder.

Set on 470 acres of pine woods, titi, and wiregrass that bordered the St. Andrews Bay, the campus on opening day consisted of six Spanish-style stucco buildings: Jennie Brandenberg Hall, a dormitory for 125 girls; Bama Hall and Southern Hall,

Bob Jones College on opening day, September 14, 1927

dormitories for 200 boys and faculty apartments; a separate faculty apartment hall; an administration and classroom building; and a dining hall.[3] Other buildings included the President's home, which was nestled on the bay nearly a mile from the campus; bathhouses; and servants' quarters. The College also had a twenty-acre truck farm that produced many of the vegetables used at the College, a canning plant, and a dairy barn. Buildings built a few years later included the Dixon-McKenzie Auditorium, designed to seat one thousand, and a campus store containing the post office and club room.[4]

Bob Jones Sr. recognized that he did not possess the educational background that one should have to found a college. "I have the training and know what I want to do," he said; "with the help of God, I will borrow the brains that I need to establish the right kind of academic standards."[5]

Dr. Jones used the term "borrow brains" to communicate the idea that he sought the advice of experts in education, finance, and religion when confronted by problems. He said, "I always go to somebody that knows when I want information,"[6] because "we are out selling an educational gospel to the public."[7] In the initial stages of the College, he sought to hire people who could develop and administrate academic and social programs that paralleled his own thought. Also, during this era in America, the role of the expert was extolled, and those with expertise were held in high esteem. To generate public acceptance of the College's programs, it was necessary for the public to perceive expert opinion as backing those programs.

A bit of "borrowed brains" came from Dr. Henry Clay Morrison, the great Methodist preacher. In the first year of the College, he gave Dr. Jones two pieces of sound advice. He said that "one of the hard things in the educational business is [that] your graduates develop other loyalties. Students who seem very loyal in college, sometimes when they get out and get involved in other things, will not always be loyal to what they have learned. You've got to figure there is going to be some loss."[8] Morrison also advised Dr. Jones to maintain the spiritual life of the school by keeping the "chapel platform hot." Dr. Jones decided to institute daily chapel services that included "red hot" preaching instead of adopting the sentimental, devotional chapel services then in vogue at other southern schools.[9]

Chapel in these early days was never overly formal. One day Dr. Bob Sr. asked the audience to sing "O God, Our Help in Ages Past." The singing was very poor, so he stopped the piano and organ and said, "Wait a minute! None of you seem to know this. I want every one of you—faculty and student body—to memorize this, and the day after tomorrow, we'll sing it again. I want everybody to know it."[10]

In another chapel service during the first week of school, the evangelist told the students that they all had to perform something in chapel on a given day—read a poem, give a speech, sing a song, play an instrument—just anything they could do. After each student finished, he critiqued the performance.[11] Dr. Jones also used the chapel platform to hammer home his ideas of culture for the students and the school by preaching, "A Christian will always be a lady or a gentleman."[12]

From the school's founding, Dr. Jones intended that it have the highest academic standards and the finest faculty possible.[13] To accomplish this goal, he hired two men who had backgrounds in school administration: J. Floyd Collins, who became the principal of Bob Jones Academy, a coed high school with a military division for boys; and W. E. Patterson, who became the first dean of the College. The high school program as developed by Collins was approved by the Florida Department of Education, and by the end of the first year, credits earned from the College were recognized by the University of Florida.[14] The Founder's initial goal was to start a junior-college program to provide solid

J. Floyd Collins, first principal of Bob Jones Academy

religious training with two years of college work and thus "ground [students] in the faith." He then proposed to channel the students to other colleges or universities for completion of their degree programs.[15] Two-year courses leading to associate degrees were offered in a number of fields, including premedical studies, precommercial studies, business administration, and home economics.[16] In 1929 he expanded his vision into a four-year program, but the school's academic majors were limited to religion, music, and speech—the disciplines most necessary to Christian evangelization or the

W. E. Patterson, first dean of Bob Jones College

pastoral ministry.[17] A "teachers' curriculum leading to Normal diploma" was added in 1932-33, and the Theological Seminary opened that same year and offered the M.A. degree in religious education.[18]

From the beginning, Dr. Jones was opposed to holding membership in any regional accreditation organization, but he wanted the College to meet or exceed all the academic requirements set forth by the associations. Early salaries and degree requirements approximated those of other Florida colleges and universities, and the standards and programs of the University of Florida were held as the academic model for Bob Jones College.[19]

Nevertheless, extant records indicate that academic standardization and curriculum construction were problematic in the early years of the College. Discussions of academic standardization occurred regularly in meetings of the faculty, and minutes of these meetings indicate that such normal curricular matters as the scheduling of exams and the planning of the next semester's courses were often left until the last minute even though course offerings were published in the *Bob Jones College Catalogue and Announcements.*[20] In one instance, W. E. Patterson requested the instructors to be "thinking about the courses to be offered for the second term" and announced that an examination schedule was impossible to construct, "the exact dates to be left to the individual teachers."[21]

Although academic requirements were short on planning in the initial stages—years later Dr. Jones Sr. readily admitted that "we didn't know what we were doing then"[22]—students from the Florida era all agreed that the work was challenging and of high enough quality to allow them to gain entrance into the graduate schools of their choice.[23]

Dr. Jones applied consistent pressure on the dean and faculty to develop and maintain "high academic standards." He had announced his intentions that no diploma would be issued "that is not standard from the standpoint of culture and science," and about this point he was adamant. One explanation for his interest in academics was his desire to challenge the prevailing notion propagated by cynics like H. L. Mencken and others that Fundamentalists were ignorant rubes.

For instance, an article by Dean Patterson in the *Bob Jones Magazine* stated that while the median entrance scores of the Alpha Test of intelligence for college freshmen at "several colleges of high standing" was 150, the median score for Bob Jones College freshmen was 158.55. If the IQ of students entering BJC was higher than that of students in secular colleges, the dean argued, then orthodox belief was not necessarily a hallmark of intellectual ignorance.[24]

Bob Jones Sr. was determined to have a school in which both academics and a fervor for evangelism could flourish. In his mind, academics, scholarship, and the fine arts ought to be joined with Fundamentalist Christian belief. To Dr. Jones, a saving Christian experience was foundational to true intellectual development and "the greatest mental stimulation" one can have "is fellowship with God. The greatest thing on earth is to think God's thoughts after Him," he said. "It is the greatest thing for your own intellectual development."[25]

He stated that Christianity was the school's primary emphasis, and it was never to be subjugated to the rationalism of intellectuality. He meant business when he said that real education was knowing God first. He wrote, "No shoddy work is tolerated. . . . We believe the spiritual is more important than education."[26] As important as education is, "there are some things that education alone cannot do. Nothing but God in the soul through the miracle of regeneration can save the individual and make the type of character that will save our civilization."[27]

In 1933, in the midst of financial turmoil, when it would have been easy to lower standards to attract students and financial supporters, he preached: "High educational standards we are going to have! But the big thing is [still] the blood of Christ, the prayer room, and the mourner's bench."[28] One student remembered Dr. Jones saying many times, "I'll do away with history, English, or science before I'll let anything be put ahead of my Lord."[29]

The school motto, which was first published in the course catalog of 1933-34, summarized the educational philosophy of Bob Jones Sr. and has appeared annually in the catalog ever since. It reads, "No college shall exceed us in the thoroughness of our scholastic training; and, God helping us, we endeavor to excel all other colleges in the thoroughness of our Christian training."[30]

Bob Jones also promised his constituency in an editorial in the *Bob Jones Magazine* that no teacher in the College would "steal the faith" of the students.[31] Other Fundamentalist leaders considered the College to be a spiritually safe atmosphere for the education of their young people and were supportive of it.[32]

Another element of Bob Jones Sr.'s educational philosophy was that education should be affordable, and he therefore sought to keep expenses at the College as low as possible.[33] In 1928 tuition and fees per semester were $62.50. Room and board was set at $25.00 per month. Expenses for music and dramatic arts instruction were $54.00 for nine months of private instruction and $10.00 for nine months of class instruction.[34] By 1933 tuition had risen to $110.00 per semester and room and board to $30.00 per month, but lessons in music and speech were offered at no extra charge.[35]

On September 14, 1927, the College opened with eighty-five students, and the Academy opened with forty-seven students. By the end of the second semester, the school may have matriculated as many as 135 students on both levels.[36] Recruiting students the first year was a challenge, and Dr. Jones Sr. recalled that "we got them where we could get them—we didn't check them very carefully."[37] Some parents took advantage of the College and tried to use it as a means to reform their children. This caused Dr. Jones to write in the *Bob Jones Magazine*,

> While we are only in our second year as a college, we have learned two very interesting things. First: The best boys and girls gravitate to us. They are happy in the atmosphere of the college. We have a number of students now who will stand out in coming years as great leaders. Second: Some parents who have children they cannot control think that if they send them to us that we shall be able, by some magical process, to transform them into wonderful boys and girls. To be frank, this is our greatest problem.

> We do not want boys and girls who are the unruly type. We are not a Reformatory; we are a Christian college. If a bad boy comes to us and we

don't convert him, the folks at home think we have failed. If we do convert him . . . when he goes back home—changed—every mother in his community who has a boy of this type will want to get her boy in our school. . . . This year, we have had to expel some boys and girls, because it was not fair to our "fine and noble" boys and girls to keep them.

We are limiting our attendance next year to 300 and we want the best boys and girls. We are going to investigate all applicants as carefully as possible.[38]

The first school year opened with a revival meeting, as have all succeeding school years. At the 1927 opening, forty of the eighty-five students came to the mourner's bench either to "get right" or to be converted. Of these eighty-five first-semester students, seventeen were expelled—"shipped" in BJC jargon—for violations of campus rules.[39]

In the second year the College matriculated nearly two hundred students but shipped a larger number than the previous year.[40] Because of the large student turnover, admissions requirements were tightened during the second year of the school. The expulsions also caused a bit of a furor in Panama City. The reason for the uproar appears to have been the penalty "meted out to some of the students who were expelled from the school for the violation

Students and faculty of Bob Jones College; College Point, Florida, September 14, 1928

not only of the known rules, but of the known spirit of the Bob Jones College." Eighty-four students wrote and signed a resolution that declared their loyalty to the principles of Bob Jones College and pledged "to refuse, in the future, to patronize business leaders in Panama City, or elsewhere, who make it their business to reflect upon the good name and Christian Spirit of the Bob Jones College."[41]

Students were attracted to the College for various reasons. For some, it represented a "safe haven" where an education could be gained without having one's faith and morals destroyed. For others, the emphasis on music and speech was highly attractive; and for still others, Bob Jones Sr.'s influence and reputation sold the College to them.[42] Some of these Florida students later became influential in the development of the College. Among those from the Florida years who had an impact are Bob Jones Jr., Fannie May Holmes Jones, Monroe Parker, James D. Edwards, and R. K. Johnson.[43]

From the beginning, the College had rules by which the students were expected to live both on the campus and away from it. Most of these rules and policies were simply "made up" by Dr. Jones Sr. or were decided in faculty meetings as a practical need arose. Some were determined on the basis of written student petitions to the faculty. Others were dictated by what Dr. Jones Sr. and the faculty viewed as the "right thing to do" based on Scripture.[44] "We have discipline," Dr. Jones wrote. "We live by rule. . . . If they don't live up to the rules of the game, we have prayer with them and give them a chance. Then if they do not live up to the rules, we send them home."[45] The aim of the College was to challenge the students to live by the "highest principles"—Bible principles.

During the first year of the school, discipline problems were handled publicly from the chapel platform, in front of the entire student body. On one occasion a student, for being habitually late to the required breakfast meal, was "required to make a two-minute speech in the dining hall every day for a week on 'The Importance of Being at Breakfast on Time.'"[46] Dr. Jones later said, "If a boy was shipped from the school, we told them [the student body] all about it. . . . We were trying to help the fellow that wasn't shipped by showing him the danger."[47]

Beginning with the second semester of the first year, students requiring discipline appeared before the entire faculty, and discipline penalties were meted out by the faculty.[48] On March 8, 1931, the President's son, Bob Jones Jr., along with eighteen other students, was brought before the faculty for "kissing." Bob Jones Jr. later recalled that he kissed his girlfriend on the cheek and got caught by the chaperone. To keep the chaperone from reporting him, he kissed her as well! All nineteen students, including Bob Jr., were given "four weeks campus during which time no letters or notes were to be exchanged, no social priviliges [sic] granted, no speaking [to each other] except 'good morning.' They must act above suspicion."[49]

Faculty Meeting Minutes are replete with such statements as,

The faculty met April 15 and discussed the cases of Sammy Jackson, Frank Smith, "Cat Head" O'Gwynne, . . . who had been guilty of drinking. It was decided that they would [not] be expelled but put off by themselves to be observed and if Dr. Jones saw fit they would be reinstated at the end of the year and allowed to take their exams.[50]

Chisholm Welch was put on probation, he is not to attend the Bryan [Literary Society] banquet, and is to be automatically expelled if he violates another rule of the college.[51]

Wayne Williams was expelled because of continual violation of rules, the last being that of going to Panama City at night to see a girl without permission and returning to the dormitory after doors were locked.[52]

Sometime later, probably around 1932, a panel of both students and faculty was organized to dispense justice, although Dr. Jones would still occasionally deal with discipline issues publicly in chapel.

Bob Jones Sr. was determined to keep the College from coming under the domination of any influence that would cause it to have to "hedge" on a principle. Money was one such influence. Athletics was another. During the first years, the College participated in intercollegiate sports, although all the games were held at home.[53] Football, basketball, baseball, track, and tennis teams were developed for the men, and intercollegiate basketball for the women. The College teams—in fact all the students—came to be known by the derogatory name "Swamp Angels" because of the prevalence of marshy land in the Florida Panhandle and the high standards of Christian behavior expected of the students. All of the athletic teams posted outstanding records—the basketball team was undefeated in 1931, and the football team lost only one game in four years.[54] The Swampers played hard to win but also tried just as hard to be a good testimony. One opponent said, "Those were the best men I ever saw. They would knock us down and then help us up and say, 'God bless you, buddy.' We would take God's name in vain, and they would say, 'We will pray for you, friend.' "[55]

Problems accompanied the sports program, and the Faculty Meeting Minutes record numerous decisions made about football, game times, and academics. It was decided that all athletes "must pass in all subjects"[56] and that football players in particular had to maintain a B average.[57] Apparently one year's team had trouble measuring up to the standard,

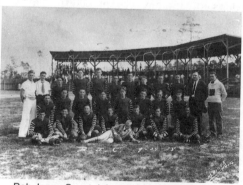

Bob Jones Sr., at right, with the Swamp Angels football team, September 29, 1928

because a student petition in 1930 asked that the players "be given another six weeks to make their grades."[58] In 1931 the coach questioned the participation standard of "B average with no failures" and proposed that the general average should be C with a passing grade in twelve out of fifteen credits.[59] Games sometimes interfered with class meeting times, much to the displeasure of the faculty.[60] Apparently these and other decisions taxed the faculty and the President.

The school found that the better their team, the more the wrong kind of student was drawn to the institution because of his desire to participate. Many of these students, it was found, worshiped physical prowess and had little or no interest in spiritual things.[61] Fans also bet on games, and fans of visiting teams left beer and whiskey bottles and other trash strewn about the campus. In time, Dr. Jones felt that football was "not conducive to the spiritual welfare of the students." Mrs. Jones remembered after one game the team

> came back with all their honor and glory. Dr. Bob got up in chapel and announced, "I'm sorry boys and girls, we're not going to have any more football." Well—you've just never heard! You would have thought the earth had come to an end!
>
> "Why!? Why!?" they all said.
>
> "Well," he said, "We love it too much. I love it too much. We can't do our work and run around the country here playing football. That is not what God called this school down here to do!"[62]

The College abandoned intercollegiate sports in 1933. After a discussion of the problems in faculty meeting, a vote was taken, and all but three voted against having intercollegiate athletics of any kind.[63] Dr. Jones admitted that this was a "severe test, but we did what was right."[64] In the place of interscholastic sports, an intramural sports program was developed between the existing student organizations—called "literary societies"—in order to allow broader participation among the students.[65] The four original literary societies were Chi Delta Theta and William Jennings Bryan for men and Sigma Lambda Delta and Sigma Kappa Rho for women. Debate was one important aspect of student life that was offered through the literary societies and for which the students were very enthusiastic.[66]

There was also an array of student clubs available to provide other opportunities for fun, leadership, and service: the Masque, for those interested in public speaking and drama; the Methodist student organization, Epworth League; the Presbyterian student organization, Christian Endeavor; the Baptist Young People's Training Union; the J Club of sports lettermen; the Life Service Band for Christian workers; and the Pioneer Club, which had five stated purposes—to pray for the College each day, to be present at the yearly banquet, to assist in any way possible in College activities, "to ask for the resignation of any atheistic or modernistic teacher who does not believe in the doctrines set forth in our Creed," and to close the school if it ever "gives way to modernism."[67]

Student life was busy, orderly, and disciplined, but not dreary. Trips to nearby St. Andrews Bay for swimming, diving, sailing, fishing, and other water sports were common recreation, as were trips into Panama City and Lynn Haven. Monroe Parker, who later became director of Religious Activities, remembered that the 1929-30 school year was "a busy time for me. I was president of the student body, was active in the Chi Delta Theta Literary Society . . . and was fullback on the football team; I boxed and ran cross-country and took a heavy academic schedule. . . . I was in several plays . . . and would go out and preach somewhere every week."[68]

At the end of the "flapper era," popular music, particularly jazz, became an issue of concern. Dr. Jones Sr. recounted one incident as follows:

> One day, I decided to help [the students] to have a little club room where they could go and drink a little soda water. We fixed up a real cute place and put a Victrola in it. We had some real nice records in it. Some were hymns and some were classical music. It was so nice, and I was so proud of it. One day I was going across the campus and heard them playing, "Hallelujah! I'm a Bum." I went in and said, "Give me that record." I went to the [chapel service] and broke it on my knee and stepped on it and preached on the irreverent spirit of our day. "Hallelujah! Thine the Glory, Revive Us Again"—"Hallelujah! I'm a Bum." That's the Slimy Serpent tramping on human character.[69]

The faculty also passed resolutions on November 16, 1931, and November 23, 1931, opposing the playing of jazz over the club room radio. Discipline penalties were also placed on the misuse of the club room.[70]

Dress standards were another early problem, as indicated by Dr. Jones when he said,

> I remember in the early days of Bob Jones College, just after the first terrible world war, in the little dispensation of time called the "flapper age," the dresses got awfully short; they kept cutting a little more off the bottom and a little more off the top, and I got nervous. Well, we're not in the institutional business for money, so when it was necessary to make a rule to be decent, we made a rule to be decent. If we can't run a decent college, we just won't run a college. . . . So I said, "Now girls, I don't want to have to tell you how long your dresses should be. And I'm not going to have somebody coming around here with a tape measure, unless I have to, and say you must stop one inch below the knee, or one inch above the knee; but you've got to let those dresses down."

> Most of the girls . . . like they have always done, respected the standards.[71]

Mrs. Jones Sr. remembered this era by commenting, "One little girl was called in about her dress and I watched her. Before she went in the door, she stopped and pulled the skirt down a bit to cover her knees. A few moments later, when she came out, she gave that skirt a tug and walked off with it up above her knees."[72]

A faculty of at least nine greeted the first students who arrived in the fall of 1927. Of these, all had master's degrees and four held doctorates.[73] It is unclear exactly how these teachers were recruited. Many had been previously acquainted with Bob Jones Sr. because of his evangelistic work and came to him seeking employment when the school's opening was announced. Others may have been recommended by Christian leaders or school presidents.[74] Several were older teachers from Alabama public schools who were retired from teaching and agreed to join the faculty of the new college.[75]

W. E. Patterson, formerly a professor of education at the University of Alabama and the first dean of the College, helped Dr. Jones recruit faculty.[76] Although the applicants were investigated as thoroughly as possible during the short period between the groundbreaking and the opening, some teachers did not fit in with the religious or academic direction of the school and therefore did not stay long.[77]

Bob Jones Sr. himself did all hiring and firing of faculty and more or less ran the day-to-day affairs of the institution, including the financial aspects of the school, during the first two or three years of operation. He also maintained a full schedule of evangelistic meetings.[78] Dr. Jones was a demanding administrator and in 1929 found it necessary to fire a staff member, the bookkeeper, for not being "financially straight."[79] A few months after the firing, the Faculty Meeting Minutes record some developing faculty unrest about the school's financial health. Unknown to the faculty and in spite of the rumors generated by the former employee, Dr. Jones was carrying the financial burden of the school himself and giving most of the offerings from his evangelistic meetings to the College. He informed the faculty that "out of 52 weeks' work last year, he kept out for his own expenses and obligations, the money collected in 8 weeks. The offerings for 44 weeks went to the school."[80]

In Dr. Jones's absence from the school, Dean Patterson made operational decisions, but Faculty Meeting Minutes for the years 1928-33 indicate that action on important decisions was often deferred until Dr. Jones was on campus.

Dr. Jones was quick to credit early College faculty members for their contributions to the College's cultural and academic growth. Especially prominent were J. Floyd Collins and Eunice Hutto.[81] August Greisel became academic dean in 1932 when W. E. Patterson left the College to become the president of a state vocational school in Birmingham, Alabama.[82] Though Patterson seems to have been a fairly good leader, the College's schedules and internal organization did not develop until Eunice Hutto replaced Greisel and became dean in 1933.[83] She was an organized, efficient woman who demanded that the College's course work be raised to a higher level. Miss Hutto also did much to standardize the College's academic program. Dr. Collins, in addition to being principal, served as a disciplinarian for the Academy boys when necessary.[84] Faculty Meeting Minutes indicate that young men were occasionally remanded to Collins for infractions of rules. On November 19, 1929, for example, the cases of a few students for "impudence and disrespect for teachers" was left to "Collins's discretion as to the use of a rod or a belt."[85]

Eunice Hutto, dean of Bob Jones College

Dr. Jones stressed personal refinement as one element of the Christian life and articulated that one goal of the College was to make ladies and gentlemen out of the students. The students had regular lectures in etiquette presented by Mrs. Jones Sr.[86] and were required to attend formal banquets, parties, and outings, all of which were chaperoned. In addition, one student recalled that "dates were *required* for college functions," and if a student failed to get a date, "the staff arranged one for him." Dr. Jones often preached on personal refinement in chapel and said, "Here at Bob Jones, we believe in educating the whole person. It is just as important for a man to know how to get in and out of a lady's parlor as it is for him to have book learning."[87] "A Christian," he said, "will always be a lady or a gentleman."[88] In later years he added, "If you are not a gentleman at heart, there is something wrong with your religion."[89]

The four literary societies at Bob Jones College provided many opportunities for leadership, sports and recreation, and debates. Society outings, however, were the social event of each year and "competed with each other" to try to plan "the most popular function of the year."[90] Each society had one day in which its members would sponsor a banquet, take a boat excursion, or enjoy some other special outing. Mrs. Jones Sr. recalled that one society traveled into Panama City to one of the large new hotels and decorated the lobby with ribbons and banners in the society colors—even the gelatin at the meal was in the society colors. "Of course, so many of our students came from rural communities," she said, "so that was very beautiful to them. To even come into a hotel with elevators and all that" was very special. "They would have their dates, and all would walk around on the mezzanine until the dining room doors were thrown open for them to come in."[91]

Other student organizations sponsored parties, and the College administration also organized many teas, banquets, and social events for the students. To break the ice at the beginning of each school year, the school sponsored a get-acquainted party for the students and staff. Each student was to stand, introduce himself, tell where he was from, and give one reason he had come to Bob Jones College. One country girl from Alabama stood, gave the information requested, and then reportedly said, "I came to be went with, but I ain't yet."[92]

Dr. Jones Sr. believed that part of the process of refinement was exposure to the fine arts of music, speech, and drama. This belief gave rise to a weekly recital-like program—later known as Vespers—which sought to synthesize the Christian message with the musical and dramatic arts.[93] Initially known as "Twilight Musicales," the programs were produced under the direction of the Music and Dramatic Arts Departments and were held weekly on Sunday afternoons. The first one was held on October 9, 1927.[94] These Sunday afternoon programs, combined with the meetings of the Epworth League, Christian Endeavor, and Baptist Young People's Training Union, substituted for Sunday evening church services since transportation into Panama City was limited and rather difficult. The rare student who did have transportation often took a load of students and attended evening services in town in addition to the required Vespers.[95]

The College music faculty developed a choir and an orchestra and encouraged the first year's students to bring instruments and music to college.[96] The "orchestra" picture in an early course catalog shows students playing a violin, clarinet, saxophone, banjo, drum set, piano, trumpet, and cornet. With a group of this instrumentation, finding appropriate music was difficult, especially in the Swing Era. The Faculty Meeting Minutes for 1932 report that the orchestra, which had been playing for Saturday morning student body meetings, had been observed playing inappropriate music, and the faculty therefore recommended that it be discontinued.[97] The music faculty, though, successfully organized vocal ensembles and a college choral club, which toured more than fifty schools during 1927-28.[98] A recital series of faculty and student music programs also began in 1930.[99]

Though not a trained musician, and certainly no singer, Dr. Jones had a great desire to sing and could recognize good singing.[100] In 1931, the quality of the singing in school services must have concerned him because he requested that the faculty and students meet once a week with the voice teacher to study "sight singing."[101]

Bob Jones College "orchestra," College Point, Florida (ca. 1927)

In support of the College's cultural emphasis, townspeople from Lynn Haven and Panama City attended many of the concerts, plays, and programs at the College.[102] The College also attracted students from around the country whose interests lay in the fine arts, and in 1929, as a way to attract even more students, Dr. Jones announced that music, speech, and art would be offered at no additional charge above tuition. This policy both attracted a somewhat more serious type of student than those who may have been attracted by athletics and also provided a springboard for the examination of culture in the light of Christian ethics and beliefs.[103]

By 1928-29, the faculty had grown to at least fifteen, and by 1929-30 there were twenty-two faculty members—twelve men and ten women—all with master's degrees or more.[104] By school year 1932-33, the faculty had grown to twenty-seven.[105]

Other problems developed in late 1929 that directly challenged the attitude, faith, and fidelity to principle of Dr. Jones Sr. Dr. W. J. Hall, assistant editor of the *Bob Jones Magazine* and professor of history and religious education, was dismissed before the end of the school year for "modern-ism."[106] Dr. Jones Sr. wrote that Hall "broke down with his subtle propaganda, the morale of the student body. . . . He almost wrecked the institution the second year."[107]

Hall's dismissal followed his continued promotion of Harry Emerson Fosdick in the classroom as a "great Christian man."[108] After the first occurrence of Hall's support of Fosdick, Dr. Jones personally reminded Hall of his agreement with the College to uphold its doctrinal standards, and Hall agreed to do so.[109]

Shortly thereafter, Hall again praised Fosdick in the classroom and publicly criticized the College in Lynn Haven and Panama City. Dr. Jones recalled, "I went to him two or three times, and the last [time], I said, 'Now listen! You're going. I promised the parents of these children and I told the folks that put their money in Bob Jones College that we are going to keep it orthodox. We are not going to surrender. So just pack your clothes and get off this campus."[110]

Hall was dismissed but his influence on the history of the school was far from ended.

CHAPTER 5

◆

Bob Jones College:
Depression and Collapse

Financial calamity struck the entire country on Black Thursday in October 1929, two years after the opening of the College. "Everyone was wiped out and completely broke," Dr. Jones Sr. said later. "I got scared and it gave me a complex that has followed me to this day."[1]

But the financial bubble in Florida had actually burst in 1926. Unable to sell lots, the Keith Corporation abandoned its Florida projects in December 1926, gave the College $500,000 worth of mortgages, and purchased $80,000 of Bob Jones College Development Bonds with the understanding that the bonds would not be called due if the mortgages were uncollected.[2] As the national depression deepened, most of the property owners forfeited, and by 1930 the cash amount due the College from the mortgages exceeded $200,000.[3] By the end of 1932, this amount had swelled to $352,000.[4] One source of operational income for the College was completely gone.

The depression years were difficult for both the College and the students. Very few students paid in full; most paid through work; some paid in commodities useful to the College. One student paid his entire year's school bill with collard greens, which became a daily item on the menu that year. The students joked that "BJC stood for Big Juicy Collards."[5] Monroe "Monk" Parker, a student at this time, remembered accidentally poking a hole in the sole of his worn-out shoes, sitting on his bed, and "weeping like a child" because he did not have money for new soles.[6]

As Christmas 1931 approached, the student body of Bob Jones College passed the following resolutions at a chapel service:

> Make no gifts to loved ones and friends except those of necessity.

> Recommend money used to buy presents be used as a gift to the Lord, to help students in dire financial situations return next term.

> To have a special Christmas tree in the chapel for the whole community the night of December 21, on which money gifts with letters of praise and thanksgiving for the blessings of God could be hung.

> Ask loved ones for no gifts but money for the student help fund.[7]

During the depression years, Dr. Jones Sr. worked continuously to raise money for the College. He gave the school's treasury virtually every cent raised in his evangelistic campaigns. He cashed in his $500,000 life insurance policy with New York Life for its cash value of $20,000 and sold the land on which his boyhood home sat in order to pay the debts of the College.

He sometimes spoke three or four times a day to raise money for the beleaguered school. In addition, he continued his evangelistic meetings full-time and arranged speaking tours in high schools during the day, speaking at as many as four schools a day on behalf of the College.

Sensing the danger of the situation, Dr. Jones Sr. wrote all bondholders in November 1929, asking them to return their bonds to the College for a refund of their investment if they felt they could do so.[8] On January 1, 1930, he discussed the financial condition of the school with the faculty, requested them to look for "paying students," and for the first time asked "those faculty who could, [to] wait for their January checks." In February of 1931, the First National Bank of Panama City closed its doors, causing more loss and hardship for the College.[9] By March 1932 the financial condition of the College had deteriorated to the point that "Dr. Jones gave a short talk on the financial condition of the school in which he suggested that the faculty members voluntarily take a 10 percent cut in salary. . . . He stated that in any event, if the money is available, full salaries will be paid."[10]

Shortly after this March faculty meeting, the entire salary scale of the College had to be restructured. Salaries thereafter were based not on academic degree, rank, years of service, or tenure, but on need. In April 1932 there were not enough funds available to print the College annual or to pay the royalties on a play performed on the campus. To raise money, the College drama department performed three one-act plays in Lynn Haven, for which they charged admission.[11]

On May 28, 1932, Dr. Jones Sr. spoke to the faculty about the financial condition of the College and explained that the salary structure of the school would have to change so that the College could survive. For the College to hang on, "the first money received from all sources" would be applied to immediate expenses such as lights, fuel, food, and so on. The "next money" would be applied toward reducing "certain embarrassing debts"—the bonded indebtedness. The remainder would be "distributed on a pro rata basis among the faculty and employees of the institution."[12] He said simply, "We are broke, and we can't continue to pay the large salaries that we've been paying. We will give you a place to live and something to eat for all members of the family, plus a little cash."[13]

Professor Mountain of the music faculty stood and said, "Let me see if I understand you correctly, Dr. Bob. Did you say that you would give us a place to live, plus the food we eat, plus some cash? I have never been any better off than that. I will take it."[14]

The new salary plan was passed by the faculty without opposition.[15] The faculty also voted unanimously to accept a 10 percent reduction in salary. "The faculty were as well off with us as they were with anybody else," Bob Jones Jr. commented. "It was like a family. You just pull in your belt and go ahead and do the best you can."[16] Bob Jones College continued to operate on a shoestring and to pay its bonded indebtedness long after the state of Florida and Bay County in which it was located had defaulted on theirs.

In 1932 W. J. Hall stepped forward to join forces with the Keith Corporation to threaten the existence of the school. After his firing, Hall had taken advantage of his influence with a small but outspoken group of Lynn Haven and Panama City church people who held Bob Jones College Development Bonds. The group refused to return their bonds for a refund, and when the College finally reneged on its interest payments in late 1932, Hall's group and the Keith Corporation gained control of a majority of the bonded indebtedness of Bob Jones College.[17] In spite of Dr. Jones's protestations to the contrary and because no written record could be found of the Keith agreement not to call the bonds, Keith and Hall's group filed suit for payment, and the court served papers to foreclose on the mortgages of the College.

Bob Jones College, which in the beginning had depended on land sale royalties, then on mortgage payments and the sale of Bob Jones College Development Bonds, and finally on donations, now faced ruin. Dr. Jones Sr. called together the Executive Committee, which consisted of McKenzie, Graves, and Mrs. Jones; and the committee recommended that, given the circumstances, the board turn the property over to the bondholders. He later said, "We were out of house and home. We had nothing."[18]

The official record reads,

TO THE MEMBERS OF THE BOARD OF TRUSTEES OF THE BOB JONES COLLEGE I respectfully submit this report:

First. For the last three years we have run the college on a cash basis and have reduced the floating indebtedness approximately ten thousand dollars. Even now, in spite of the nationwide depression, we are paying our current expenses.

Second. An investigation will show that we have kept the college buildings in good repair . . . up-to-date and in good condition. The grounds, as you will note, are well kept and beautiful.

Third. We have spent on buildings, equipment, and improvements since we started six years ago about $485,000.

Fourth. We have owing the college (and most of it is long past due) approximately $352,000. Most of the indebtedness is secured by mortgages on real estate, but due to the depression the real estate has at this time practically no value. Most of the people who owe us are "broke." A few years ago many of them were well-to-do. Most of the people who owe us are our friends and are loyal to the testimony of the college. They would pay if they could, but they can't. I do not consider these debts worth one cent on the dollar.

Fifth. The college owes in bonded indebtedness about $350,000. While the bonds are secured by a mortgage on the land owned by the college and on the college buildings and equipment, it was our purpose, as you know, to retire these bonds with the collection of these mortgages, and from the sale of other real estate which the college owns and which good business men considered valuable. Of course, every one knows that these bonds could not be retired from the income of the college. A Christian college cannot even make enough money to pay running expenses, but must be supported in its running overhead by income from outside sources. As you know, I have brought into our college treasury thousands of dollars every year since we started. In order to keep the record straight, I should like to remind you that we sold the real estate in our college subdivision after the Florida boom was over. . . . Our financial trouble is not the result of the Florida boom.

Sixth. While we were able to pay, even under the stress of these days, our current expenses, we are not able to pay interest on our bonded indebtedness. We did, however, pay the interest on our bonds after many municipalities and institutions stopped paying their interest on bonds.

Some of our bondholders have grown restless. . . . The trustees for these bondholders feel that it is their duty under the terms of the bond (and I think they are right in their interpretation) to foreclose the mortgage. They have begun proceedings and the papers have been served on me as president of the college.

Under the present financial conditions, we all know that the property can bring only a very small amount. . . .

Please note carefully this serious problem which we will face even if we should be able to buy in the property. Our attorney advises that under the terms of the bond the court, when the property is sold, will give a deficiency judgment against the college corporation. . . . This will make it impossible for the college to operate successfully.

Seventh. I do not need to remind you that we are in no way responsible for the inability of the college to pay its bonded indebtedness. . . . The Bob Jones College has back of it no convention, no conference, no state, no church. Single-handed and alone, supported by the grace of God and the unselfish co-operation of this Board and the prayers and help of our friends, we have demonstrated that even in this time of distress we can run the college on a cash basis. . . . If times were normal we would have no serious financial problems. . . .

I call special attention to the fact that the Bob Jones College is a corporation *not for profit*. I am the founder and the president, and the college is named for me, but it *does not belong to me*.

Six years ago last December we broke ground for our first building. At that time I was personally in comfortable circumstances financially. On this altar of Christian service I have given all my worldly possessions and six years of the hardest work I have ever done in all these strenuous years of my busy life. . . .

If you ladies and gentlemen cannot find a plan by which we may continue to operate here at College Point, we will go elsewhere. I have already been approached with a view of moving the college to another place where there are well-equipped buildings. I do not think this is desirable, and would only be willing to move as a last resort. If by moving the school we could pay one hundred cents on the dollar to our bondholders, I would feel it our duty to move. But I cannot see how anybody could be profited by moving the institution to some other community.[19]

The national financial crisis caused many colleges and schools to release a number of their teachers, some schools simply closed never to reopen, and many other colleges, religious organizations, and businesses sought protection from creditors and investors in bankruptcy court.[20] When it became obvious that all options had been exhausted, that the school could not meet the bondholders' demands, that a plan for rescuing the school financially could not be developed, nor that a buyer of like ideals could be found, the Board of Trustees recommended, on January 9, 1933, that bankruptcy proceedings be initiated.[21] Ironically, a year earlier as the financial crisis was unfolding, Dr. Jones, in revival meetings in Dothan, Alabama, had said, "Instead of trusting God, we trusted the dollar and now we've got it in the neck."[22]

Sermons, chapel talks, and letters of Bob Jones Sr. from the era show the depth of emotion that pervaded the discussions pertaining to bankruptcy and to relocating the College. Transcripts of these messages record Dr. Jones Sr.'s voice breaking with emotion as he spoke of the College and God's hand in its affairs.

On January 26, 1933, the receivership agreement was finalized in district court, and Dr. Jones returned to College Point after having signed the College assets over to the court and being appointed receiver for the liquidation. He had exhausted all of his energies and the school was broke. "I have done the best I could. I have given all I have of strength and nervous energy," he wrote. "I have sacrificed my own small personal fortune."[23] On January 29, with renewed confidence, he said in a Sunday sermon, "I have never been so confirmed in my faith as I have been the last thirty days. Our hope is in prayer; ours is not in a bank account. It isn't resources we want—we want the stamp of His approval. . . . God has directed everything in this college. We have one asset and just one, and that is the approval of God. . . . God isn't broke."[24]

This experience made an indelible impression on him, steeled his resolve, toughened his financial procedures, and reinforced within him the belief that the College would succeed and grow only in proportion to his faith. Years later, in recalling these days, he said, "I shall never forget when . . . in the depression, I knew how badly we needed money, and one day it dawned on me that I didn't need anything but God Almighty. That's the day that Bob Jones College picked up."[25]

Even prior to 1933, Dr. Jones Sr., Bob Jones Jr., and several members of the board had discussed the possibility of moving the school to a more accessible region of the country.[26] The Panama City–Lynn Haven area, though holding promise, was still somewhat isolated, with only one narrow-gauge railroad connecting the area to the North. On Christmas Day, 1932, Bob Jones Jr., while driving between Knoxville and Chattanooga, Tennessee, passed a boarded-up college in Cleveland, Tennessee. Upon inquiry, he learned that it was the Centenary College, owned by the Holston Methodist Conference, and that it had been closed for seven years. The fact that the school was thirty miles from Chattanooga and less than a two-hour drive from both Knoxville and Atlanta made the property attractive. Bob Jones Jr. apprised his father of the deserted school, and after a phone call to the Cleveland Chamber of Commerce by Dr. Jones Sr., the wheels that ultimately took Bob Jones College to Tennessee were set in motion.

Word spread quickly that the College was considering a move. On April 1, 1933, the *Lynn Haven Free Press* reported that "it was unthinkable among residents that Bob Jones College would be moved to another location."[27] Delegations from communities throughout the Southeast extended invitations to Bob Jones Sr. and the College board with promises of monetary support, land, or buildings if the College would relocate in their community.[28] The board narrowed the choices to two communities: Anniston, Alabama, and Cleveland, Tennessee, and voted on April 1 to accept the invitation of Cleveland, Tennessee.[29]

The objectives of Hall and his group of bondholders, which included former board member Jennie Brandenberg, are unclear. It is doubtful, however, that their intentions were totally financial. It is clear that the College intended to pay the bonded indebtedness as it could. It is also clear that the Keith Corporation, by reneging on its early agreements and abandoning the College project, forcing the school to pay for construction and improvements for which Keith was under contract, created some of the financial burden with which the school wrestled. The Keith interests may also have been eager to acquire the property in its improved state.

Arguing that "under the circumstances, [Bob Jones College was not] morally obligated to the Keith Corporation," Dr. Jones stated to the dissidents' lawyer that "all the [bond] money put up by your client, was used in putting in sidewalks and other improvements which the Keith Corporation was under contract to do themselves"; and "they well knew that they were under contract . . . and that they were relieved from this contract and were saved from spending thousands of dollars." He closed by writing, "I hope these bondholders will find a way to do something with the property so they can realize something on their investment. I have done the best I could."[30]

The legal action and the resulting liquidation of the assets of the school, though providing some small remuneration, forced the College to relocate. The Lynn Haven community was devastated, and a group of investors from

Panama City, led by R. L. McKenzie, organized to try to raise the money necessary to rescue the College and keep it in the area. It was to no avail—Hall, the Keith interests, and the disaffected bondholders foreclosed. On May 1, 1933, even before the school year ended, the College's assets and property, at one time valued at more than $500,000, were sold to Dr. R. H. Bartee of Lynn Haven for $3,100. Bartee, hoping to make some quick money, agreed to transfer the property to the majority of the bondholders within thirty days if they could raise $3,500. In the event that they declined or failed to raise the money, he stipulated that the land was to be offered to the city of Lynn Haven for the same amount. Neither the bondholders nor the city was able to raise that amount, and the land was eventually sold for taxes to H. C. Lister of Wewahitchka, Florida, a turpentine company owner. Lister systematically liquidated the buildings and equipment, tore down some of the buildings, and sold off the land. At the liquidation auction, the turpentine producer received a total of $7,800.[31] Furnishings were auctioned to local residents and businessmen and the monies raised were used to pay off any school debts still outstanding.[32] Even the Joneses' own home, built for $18,000, was sold to a banker for $6,000.[33]

Later, Dr. Jones Sr. viewed Hall as "the man that brought the wrath of man to praise [God]. If we had not fired that preacher from Bob Jones College in Florida, we would have been in Florida now, located out there [in the woods] where we were. That man's hatred and animosity and influence were the horses that God hitched to the chariot that pulled the school through the gate into the field of success."[34]

May 31, 1933, marked the final Commencement Day of Bob Jones College in Florida.[35] Mrs. Jones Sr. remembered that the day was one of sadness for having to leave that beautiful bay area, yet one of excitement for the challenges ahead. As soon as the "Amen" was pronounced, she and Bob Jr. climbed into a car that had been brought to the back door of the auditorium and left immediately for Cleveland, Tennessee, to begin the work of preparing the new campus.[36]

The College was destitute. Had it not been for two contributions, the school would have been unable to transport its equipment and books to the new location. Moving expenses were partially covered by faculty member Grace W. Haight, who donated three thousand dollars toward the move, and Board of Trustees member Raymond T. Crane of New York, who donated another three thousand dollars.[37] The six thousand dollars from the sale of the Joneses' home helped to pay for the College's moving expenses as well. Because of the limited funds, the faculty was asked to select for moving only those items of equipment that were most essential to the continuation of the College. The Florida plant, therefore, was left intact, nearly completely furnished.[38] College Point and the Bob Jones College campus gradually fell into disrepair as the area reverted to turpentining. Occasionally Lynn Haven groups rented the old college auditorium for special events, but by 1946 the campus was only a crumbling ruins.

A concrete and bronze marker now stands at the site of Bob Jones College on Harvard Boulevard, Lynn Haven, Florida. The marker reads, "I have set before thee an open door and no man can shut it for thou hast . . . kept My word and hast not denied My name" (Rev. 3:8).

CHAPTER 6

◆

Bob Jones College: Cleveland, Tennessee

Cleveland, Tennessee, was a picturesque industrial town of ten thousand people, nestled in the Tennessee hills between Chattanooga and Knoxville. In the early 1930s it boasted a few well-to-do families and only one large industry—the Hardwick Stove Company. In Bob Jones College, the town fathers saw an opportunity to bring economic growth, to attract new residents, and to revitalize the community with increased educational and cultural opportunities. Excitement in Cleveland ran high, and the local newspapers exulted, "Bob Jones College, Located in Florida, Will Be Moved Here"[1] and "Bob Jones Is Given Hearty Welcome Here."[2]

Financial arrangements for purchasing the Centenary College property were completed in late April 1933.[3] Because of the depression, Centenary College had closed in 1929, and the Holston Methodist Conference, which operated the school, owed $66,000 on the property to Cleveland business-man George Hardwick. The Methodists had been unable to pay any interest on the debt for several years, and Hardwick was unwilling to sue for payment or foreclose on the property. When his own financial difficulties arose and his need for income from the property became urgent, Hardwick offered the college buildings and property to Bob Jones Sr. for half of the outstanding debt—$33,000—payable by 1936. The Holston Methodist Conference, however, had to agree to pay the remaining $33,000. When and if both the College and the Holston Conference paid their share of the note, the deed for the property would be transferred to Bob Jones College. In addition, Hardwick offered the College a five-thousand-dollar donation at such time as both the College and the conference paid their entire debts. The conference, which stood to gain a 50 percent reduction in its debt obligation, agreed to the terms. Some members of the Holston committee believed that Bob Jones College would eventually fail and that they would be able to reclaim the buildings in good repair and at a price significantly below the indebtedness.[4]

When Dr. Jones Sr. first visited Cleveland, shortly after Christmas in 1932, his personality "electrified" the members of the chamber of commerce. Jones and Bibb Graves, who accompanied him, talked business to the chamber of commerce, "not as a minister unskilled in the ways of the commercial world, but as a business man."[5] As a sign of good faith, and as a result of the evangelist's persuasiveness, the Cleveland Chamber of Commerce raised $7,500 cash in one day and promised to provide a total of $10,000 plus the necessary manpower for the repair and refurbishing of the

Centenary College property. Cleveland ultimately donated $25,000 for building repairs and improvements.[6]

Centenary College, located in the heart of Cleveland, consisted of "five permanent buildings, constructed of red brick and stone, connected as to be under one roof."[7] It was essentially one large three-story building—Old Main—with several smaller outbuildings. Old Main was T-shaped with circular stairways leading up from the main lobby to

Boys' dormitory room, Bob Jones College, Cleveland, Tennessee

the second floor. The classrooms, auditorium, administrative suite, library, dining room, and a swimming pool took up the ground floor; and dormitory suites, designed for two students each, were on the second floor. Initially the boys' rooms were located on one end of the second floor and were separated from the girls' end by a partition. The outbuildings consisted of a fallen-down garage, an old heating plant with a "dirty old smokestack sticking up," a kitchen, and other unsightly shacks; these made up the "eyesore" that was the Centenary property. Dr. Jones Sr. later said, "We took that property [and] cleaned it off. . . . We doubled the value of every piece of property on this side of the street. . . . [Now] you can't buy property near this college."[8]

On June 1, 1933, immediately following the Bob Jones College Commencement exercises in Florida, Mrs. Jones Sr., Bob Jones Jr., and the College business manager, Don Cochran, left for Tennessee to oversee the mammoth task of remodeling.[9] College staff and Cleveland citizens worked diligently to prepare the campus for its September opening. They hauled mounds of rubbish from broken-down structures and had to replace nearly every pane of glass in Old Main because the windows had been broken out by vandals in years past.[10] Because of the depression, everyone was begging for work; even "first-class carpenters were getting twenty-five cents an hour and that was big money," a staff member recalled. That same staff member worked at the College "for fifteen dollars a week plus [board] for my family, and that summer was one of the happiest I have ever known. . . . I saved one dollar a week for thirteen weeks and offered the money to Dr. Bob to help get the school opened; but he would not take the money. . . . Dr. Bob had the energy of several men; and yet he was so human, always joking with the help."[11] The work proceeded smoothly, with few problems, and the campus was cleaned, painted, wallpapered, mowed, trimmed, and hedged, and ready for use on schedule.

More than seven hundred people filled the BJC auditorium for the opening meeting on September 6, 1933. Cleveland had not "manifested such interest in an event" for many years, and the two-hour program featured speeches by the mayor of Cleveland, eight other local leaders, and the Founder.[12]

To conclude the meeting, Dr. Jones Sr. familiarized the crowd with the principles upon which the school was founded and ended by saying, "Education with God left out will ruin our civilization; education with God left out is worse than no education. The aim of Bob Jones College is to combine learning with the principles of Christ."[13] Later that week he announced that enrollment had increased 50 percent over the previous year in Florida and that already the new campus was crowded. "Room will be made for all who come," he said, "even if members of the faculty have to be crowded out into private homes, or nearby residences have to be engaged to house the overflow."[14]

When school opened that September, the students were welcomed warmly, and the faculty felt relieved to have their teaching positions.[15] Some students, especially those from large cities, were not very impressed with Cleveland. One described it as "an old-time town; a little town with a small town mentality. Culture was far, far beyond it. [The townspeople] did not understand anything of an intellectual or spiritual nature. . . . They had 'spit-and-whittle' clubs, where the old fellows would sit on the courthouse lawn whittling away with their knives and spitting tobacco. The snake-handling preachers from the Church of God would run up and down with their snakes."[16]

The influx of several hundred new residents simply overwhelmed the merchants. Shortages were common and student frustration at shopping in Cleveland caused one to say, "The stores were so small that you had to walk in slowly or you'd hit the back wall!"[17] After getting settled in the new surroundings, however, the student body was "wild about the school."[18]

Bob Jones College not only had a new home, it also had a new administrator. In 1931, following his graduation from Bob Jones College in Florida at the age of twenty-one, Bob Jones Jr. had been appointed to the faculty as an instructor in history.[19] The next school year he was elected to

Boys' dormitory room in Cleveland, Tennessee

the Board of Trustees and appointed to the office of vice president, with the title of Acting President in the absence of his father.[20] In 1934 Bob Jones Jr. was installed as acting college president and handled the day-to-day affairs of the College while his father was on a four-month European preaching tour that took him to Ireland, Poland, and Russia. Dr. Jones later wrote that "my son ran the college successfully in my absence, and it is a great joy to know that we have an organization which can function without my being here."[21] Also in 1934, business manager Don Cochran left Cleveland to become a traveling representative of the College and Robert Kirthwood Johnson, though still a senior in college, began managing the school's business affairs. He was appointed business manager in 1936 and became a member of the Executive Committee of the Board of Trustees.[22]

Dr. Jones Sr.'s interest in the College never waned. He remained thoroughly involved in the school and made it clear in chapel talks to the students that his role was to "keep it right." To a certain degree he saw himself as a caretaker and a promoter, keeping the College close to the Fundamentalist philosophy on which it was founded.[23] The Florida collapse and resulting bankruptcy continued to play on Bob Jones Sr.'s mind so much so that when he was on campus, he would daily check incoming contributions and track enrollment for the next year. "Every day he wanted to know where we stood business-wise," said a staff member. "He kept his finger on that. But he would not take a postage stamp out of the office. He was absolutely ethical. Every penny had to be accounted for."[24]

Part of Dr. Jones Sr.'s philosophy—"Work as if it all depends on you, trust God as if it all depends on Him"—was evident in the development of the College in Cleveland. Dr. Jones characterized himself by saying,

> I am an asset to this college in three particulars. First, I have had years of evangelistic experience, and I know how to keep the religious stimulation. Second, I have the enthusiasm. Third, I am an expert propagandist. All three things in which I excel I can carry on with my evangelistic work. . . . I can "blow into" the college about one week in three and set it on fire, "pep it up," generate enthusiasm, keep things on a high pitch, and then go out into the world and preach the Gospel and contact the people over the radio and come back home and set the college on fire again. Bear in mind, all the time I am out, I am selling the school, putting out propaganda, lining up students, and making financial contacts.[25]

As one writer expressed it, "his personality was, from the first, [the school's] chief asset."[26]

Financially, the school started to rebound. By 1936 the College had paid its half of the $66,000 note. Still floundering from the depression, the Holston Methodist Conference, after much pressure, some "arm-twisting," and personal fund-raising efforts by Bob Jones Sr., raised the money for its share of the debt as well. The deed was transferred, and Bob Jones College owned its new plant outright.[27] Dr. Jones also collected on George Hardwick's promise of five thousand dollars.

With a gradually improving financial condition and the addition of Bob Jones Jr. to the administration, it was possible for Dr. Jones Sr. to devote more of his time to evangelism. His preaching had the dual effect of bringing to the College both more students and increased financial support from Fundamentalists around the nation.

Dr. Jones Sr.'s primary motivation in life was to reach people with the gospel of Christ. In this, he was indefatigable. Founding a school was only one means of reaching people—building Christian leaders to go into the world to win others. He had interests in many other areas, yet the goal of these interests was to reach people with the gospel. In the 1920s he had witnessed the rise of moving pictures, realized the potency of a Christian theme on film, and attempted to produce what may have been the first Christian moving picture.

He had perhaps been the first evangelist to make live remote radio broadcasts from a revival crusade.[28] He developed a radio broadcast called the "Bob Jones College Hour"while the school was in Florida, which was carried by five stations in major metropolitan areas. From 1928 to 1933 he published the *Bob Jones Magazine,* a periodical containing religious and political commentary.

In Cleveland, the College broadcasted a daily program through a radio network centered in Chattanooga, with stations from New York to Los Angeles. Dr. Jones also began writing a syndicated newspaper column, "Comments on Here and Hereafter," which was carried by a large number of papers. In 1933 Dr. Jones opened the Bob Jones Gospel Centers in several southern cities. These centers offered daily Bible studies, nightly preaching services, businessmen's meetings, and youth activities and were opened under the auspices of the newly formed Gospel Fellowship Association,[29] a fellowship founded by Bob Jones to encourage evangelism. The centers were staffed by Bob Jones College preacher boys.[30]

Dr. Jones felt a burden to reach the thousands of college and high-school age young people with the gospel and therefore founded the Young People's Fellowship Clubs in 1932 in Florida. Many Bob Jones College preacher boys got their start in preaching, evangelism, and youth ministry during school by leading a club in the areas surrounding Cleveland or in the summer by starting clubs in their hometowns. Often a Bob Jones Gospel Center would sponsor four or five Young People's Fellowship Clubs in surrounding communities, and in this way hundreds were touched by the gospel. Another important part of this ministry was the *Fellowship News,* which was the official newsletter for the Gospel Centers, the Fellowship Clubs, and the Gospel Fellowship Association. Grace Haight, a veteran missionary who joined the College faculty in Florida to teach missions, edited the *News.*[31]

Though initially spacious, facilities in Cleveland soon became overcrowded. Enrollment at the College increased more rapidly than existing facilities could be expanded or new ones built. Much of the new construction was made possible because of the generosity of John Sephus Mack, president of the G. C. Murphy Stores, U.S.A.[32] Mack first met Bob Jones Sr. in Pennsylvania when he served on the organizing committee for a 1927 Jones revival campaign in McKeesport, near Pittsburgh. In 1936 Dr. Jones Sr. was again in the Pittsburgh area conducting fifteen days of revival meetings, and their acquaintance was renewed. Initially, Mack and his wife offered to donate $45,000 to the construction program if the College could match the gift.[33] Dr. Jones Sr. contacted the Board of Trustees, the faculty, and students and raised the needed funds in a matter of weeks. After this, Mack became increasingly interested in the College, but before putting large amounts of money into the school, he wanted assurances that it was a lasting venture and that Dr. Jones could both be on the road preaching and manage the school at the same time. In a lengthy letter, Dr. Jones answered Mack's concerns and as a result, Mack and his wife became extremely generous in their giving to the school.[34] Margaret Mack was added to the Board of Trustees in 1936, and by the late 1930s J. S. Mack had gone so far as to tell Dr. Jones to "construct your buildings and send me the bill."[35] After a visit to the campus in the spring of 1939, Mack sent eight hundred shares of G. C. Murphy stock to the College and thereafter sent generous monthly checks. Shortly after this visit, J. S. Mack fell ill. He died on September 27, 1940, leaving a small legacy to the College.

In the thirteen-year span that the College was in Cleveland, one new building a year was built on the campus, not to mention the purchase and remodeling of many houses, and major maintenance. Some of this new construction was done while paying off the early long-term debt of $33,000. Beginning in the summer of 1933, the College built a classroom building. In 1935 a large-scale building program was announced, and construction began on a new gymnasium, an auditorium, and a dormitory for two hundred men. The following year the first major campus additions were completed—Margaret Mack Auditorium and a gymnasium.

By 1937 the student body had grown to the point that men were being housed in auditorium dressing rooms and in the gymnasium. On the advice of J. S. Mack, the College began purchasing every property adjacent to the campus as it became available.[36] These were transformed into student residence halls, faculty apartments, or instructional facilities and were given interesting names—Harmony House, Honeymoon Hall, Melody Hall, Bachelor Hall, and the Stable, to name a few.[37] J. S. Mack promised to put up 50 percent of the money needed for the acquisition of these properties.[38]

Beginning in 1939 and continuing for the next decade, tensions in Europe, war, and the production of war materiel for U.S. armed forces made construction virtually impossible. When a building was needed on the Bob Jones College campus, however, God brought the construction about. Dr. Jones Sr. preached, "We need three hundred thousand dollars for building right now—really we could use a million. That's not what we need. All we need in Bob Jones College is to keep this college in the center of the will of God, that's all. . . . If you do that, every time you need a building, you'll get it. Every time you need a book, you'll get it. Every time you need a teacher, God will send one. Every time you need a piano, you'll get one second-handed maybe. All we need is there."[39]

One goal of the Founder and a keystone in his educational philosophy was that student tuition and fees should be reasonable—even cheap. He remembered his own struggle to get an education and was sympathetic to students trying to get a college education during the depression.[40]

In order to allow needy students to come to college, Dr. Jones personally arranged jobs for students with area businessmen.[41] During 1934, Dr. Jones contacted Berea College in Berea, Kentucky, noted for its student work program, requesting suggestions for items that could be manufactured by students and sold to provide work and income. He also made inquiries in Cleveland about setting up a clothing factory on the campus that would employ women students. Although the expense was prohibitive and the factory was never started, he went so far as to select a factory site in Cleveland, contact cloth mills about supplying material, and approach the Singer Sewing Machine Company about purchasing equipment.[42] These inquiries were instrumental in Dr. Jones's decision to start a campus work scholarship program, funded by the Student Loan Endowment Fund, whereby students could work for the College to receive financial credit toward their bills.[43]

He was determined to keep a BJC education affordable. In 1933-34 tuition per semester was $87.50 with room and board listed at $25.00 a month, for a total of $400.00 a year.[44] Expenses remained at this level through 1936-37 when a student activity fee of $5.00 was added to cover the expenses of the yearbook (*The Vintage*), society athletic events, and Artist Series programs.[45] Tuition and room and board were raised approximately every five years through 1946-47, at which time tuition was $125.00 per semester with room and board listed at $150.00 per semester, or $550.00 a year. School year 1946-47 saw the addition of a matriculation fee of $25.00, which replaced the student activity fee.[46] Lessons in music and speech were available at no extra cost to the students, which tended to attract talented students.

The lessons learned in Florida were indelibly stamped on Dr. Jones Sr.'s mind. He conceded that the Florida experience made him very cautious—even a bit paranoid—in financial matters. In order to get the Cleveland campus in shape, it had been necessary to borrow money, and repaying these loans while keeping the current expenses covered was a huge strain. Between 1933 and 1937 the College spent over two hundred thousand dollars for construction and necessary improvements. To survive, everything had to be done on a strict budget and the College's financial organization, as developed by Dr. Jones Sr. and R. K. Johnson, was extremely conservative. In a letter to J. S. Mack, Dr. Jones wrote, "We are asking the Lord to supply our needs, and this He is going to do. . . . My burden for nine years, both in Florida and Tennessee, has been the struggle of digging up money. The worst days are over. I am not going to involve this school in debt, and we are going to operate on a cash basis, God helping us."[47]

After J. S. Mack examined the College's financial records in 1939, he invited business manager, R. K. Johnson—"Lefty," as he was called—to the home office of the G. C. Murphy Company to receive training from Murphy Company accountants. When Johnson returned to Cleveland, he brought with him a new system of bookkeeping that was used at least until the early 1970s. College finances were restructured so that all operating overhead, including operational expenses, maintenance, and faculty salaries were covered by student tuition and fees.[48] This financial arrangement kept the College from relying on outside sources of income to meet the daily expenses of the school. Campus construction and special projects were financed by donations and fund-raising drives.

Mack also gave Johnson other practical advice about the College. Drawing an analogy between works of art and the grounds, Mack said, "I look at landscaping as the frame of a picture. I have seen good pictures badly marred and their beauty obscured by the cheap, unsightly frame." To correct the Cleveland frame, J. S. Mack sent his landscape engineer to work out a master plan for beautifying and improving the campus.[49]

Bob Jones College in Cleveland, Tennessee, opened on schedule in 1933 with about two hundred students—fifty more than the previous year.[50] Growth continued through the war years. Between 1941 and 1945, enrollment increased 141 percent.[51] By September 1945 the combined enrollment of the College, the graduate school, and the Academy reached the limit the Cleveland campus could accommodate: 1,264 students.[52] An influx of returning war veterans swelled the College student body to nearly 1,500 in January 1946.[53] An immediate problem with student housing was resolved when the College purchased and relocated from Oak Ridge, Tennessee, fifty trailers owned by the United States government. The trailers, which housed single men students and some married couples, were placed on a lot owned by the College and on part of the athletic field.[54] With additional housing available, a total of 1,861 students were enrolled in September of 1946.[55] Problems with instructional facilities were not so easily resolved. Class sizes had to be doubled and multiple sections of courses were added.

The faculty also grew in proportion to the student body. The last year in Florida, the faculty had numbered twenty-seven. For school year 1933-34 in Tennessee, the faculty numbered twenty-six and remained at that level through 1935-36. In 1936-37, the faculty grew to thirty; in 1937-38, the faculty numbered thirty-six; and by 1946-47, the faculty had grown to sixty-six.[56]

The faculty had some remarkable people. Former missionary Grace Haight had joined the faculty in Florida; now she continued to teach missions courses and edit the *Fellowship News*. Linguist and religion professor Charles Brokenshire came to Bob Jones College in January 1943, preceded by a week-long mail delivery of his books.[57] He became dean of the School of Religion and established the Princeton tradition of orthodox Christian

Grace Haight (ca. 1935)

scholarship in which he had been trained by Robert Dick Wilson, Benjamin Warfield, and J. Gresham Machen.

Sometime prior to 1936, Dr. Jones Sr. received a bit of advice from J. S. Mack that became a part of the hiring and personnel philosophy of the College. On building an organization Mack wrote that "education is a slow process. The easy thing to do is to hire and fire folks. But that doesn't tend to develop an organization. To build an organization, you hire and train folks and the longer they are in their job—if they are good—the better they become at their work."[58] Dr. Jones Sr. later told of a faculty interview he conducted with a young teacher of impressive credentials, which perfectly illustrated Mack's point. Dr. Jones recalled, "I was greatly impressed by her. I told her to come to the college for an interview with her expenses paid. . . . Well, I made the prettiest speech you ever heard. 'We have the Lord here at BJC,' I said, 'and we believe the Bible from cover to cover.' I made it plain. My heart was burning with great zeal and fervor. I talked to her for thirty minutes and when I finished my nice speech she said to me, 'How much do you pay?' And I said, 'Not one cent, sister.' I wouldn't have her here. She had a hireling heart. She had the spirit of a hireling."[59]

Taking Mack's advice and adapting it to the personnel policies of the College, Dr. Jones Sr. and Dr. Jones Jr. began looking increasingly to graduates to provide instructors and staff members.[60] They felt that their former students would be more likely to agree with the school's theological position and have a keener sense of purpose and a stronger sense of loyalty to the College and the cause of Christ. Thereafter, an increasing number of Bob Jones College graduates joined the faculty, many of whom became gifted teachers in their respective fields. These included such well-known campus teachers as James D. and Elizabeth Edwards, in history and speech; Gilbert and Katherine Stenholm, in religion and speech; Monroe and Harriette Parker in religion and music; Karl Keefer in music; Marshall and Anna Loyd Neal in Bible and speech; Ted and Alice Mercer in English; and many others.

Further, Dr. Jones felt if a job in the organization needed to be done for which no one was specifically trained, he could look within the organization to find a skilled person to be transferred into the area of need. Bob Jones Jr., commenting on this aspect of the personnel philosophy of the school, wrote, "We have selected . . . likely graduates and given them what instruction we could for other jobs for which we thought they had hidden capabilities. More often than not they have become proficient, capable, and in some cases, amazingly secure—indeed, expert."[61] The growing College needed faculty members of flexibility who were willing to wear "many hats" and operate in several fields comfortably.[62]

While the Founder and the Acting President considered Fundamentalist Christianity, the discipline, and the culture of the College its most important assets, they also valued the academic standing and preparation of the faculty. To further expand the education of the teachers, the school strongly encouraged faculty members to get additional education, and in some instances faculty were sent away to continue their educations. Even in these early years the College may have paid a portion of the expenses for pursuing an advanced degree.[63] Eventually, the school established a loan fund for faculty education to enable the teachers to pursue advanced work.[64] Such advanced study served to provide credibility to the College's programs.[65] In addition, Dr. Jones Sr. also believed that the acceptance of BJC graduates into graduate schools was proof of the College's high academic standards.

There was, of course, faculty turnover during the years 1933-47. Some of this turnover may be attributed to faculty retirement and World War II. There were no faculty dismissals of a theological nature, such as occurred between 1927 and 1933. Other problems, concerning salary, interdepartmental conflicts,[66] and loyalty to administrative policies, did develop among faculty and led to several dismissals.[67] One faculty member had to be dismissed because she organized prayer meetings for the sole purpose of praying against Shakespearean plays at the College.[68] Another faculty member was dismissed because his wife was a malcontent and a gossip.[69] And another was dismissed for refusing to enforce campus social regulations, for unprofessional behavior in the classroom, and for behaving in a way generally incompatible with the standards of the school.[70]

The issues of loyalty and trust were to become issues of major importance for retaining faculty members and administrators.[71] Dr. Jones Sr. boiled the school's philosophy down to the concise statement "We are not going to pay anybody to 'cuss' us. We can get 'cussin' ' free from the outside." He said in a chapel talk, "We have never been a divided college. . . . We are of one mind in this school. We have not always had smooth sailing, but we have thrown the Jonahs overboard. If we get a Jonah on the ship, and the ship doesn't take him, we let the fish eat him! We throw him overboard. . . . 'United we stand, divided we fall.' That is the reason that in this school we have no 'griping.' Gripers are not welcome here. If you are a dirty griper, you are not one of us. . . . God helping us, we are going to keep Bob Jones College a kingdom that isn't divided and a house that stands together."[72]

To keep the house united, to preserve the spirit, and to be consistent with the hiring philosophy proposed by J. S. Mack, Bob Jones College hired graduates in growing numbers. In 1933-34, three of twenty-six faculty members were BJC graduates; by 1938-39, twelve of thirty-six were graduates; and by 1946-47, thirty-two of sixty-six were graduates of the College. These graduates felt a special kinship with Dr. Jones Sr. They loved him, respected his spiritual insight, admired his single-mindedness, and trusted his judgment even while recognizing his human weaknesses and rugged individualism. "You should put your ear to the keyhole when the faculty meets sometime," he told a chapel audience in 1935. "We have one to offset the other. . . . We check each other. I might turn this school into a camp meeting, but Miss Hutto [dean of the College] says, 'No, this is a college.' So she keeps me reminded that this is a college and I keep her reminded that we have to keep our religion. . . . Two or three of the faculty pull this way, and two or three pull the other way, and we pull against each other and stay in the middle of the road."[73]

Even though the faculty signed statements of agreement with the creed and philosophy of the College, and a growing number of BJC graduates were on the faculty, problems and differences developed. Since the school provided housing for the faculty, there were some complaints about living conditions, heat, space and furnishings, salaries, or departmental responsibilities.[74] By and large, these issues were settled amicably to everyone's satisfaction after being brought to the attention of Dr. Jones Sr. or Dr. Jones Jr. There was a concerted effort on the part of the administrators to be evenhanded and fair in dealing with the living conditions of the teachers, especially in the midst of the depression.

Since the days of the collapse in Florida, salaries had been figured on the basis of family need and the institution's ability to pay. Because this was still a time of depression and money was scarce, all salary negotiations were confidential, personal, and based on good faith. Dr. Jones Sr. "asked each teacher to make out a list of his needs and in the event we could not supply his needs then we would not want the teacher to come. All who came with us to Cleveland came on that understanding."[75] In 1933, to provide a savings opportunity for faculty and also to help the school, "Dr. Jones stated that the college would be glad to give a note, signed jointly by the college and Dr. Jones personally, payable September 15, [1934], bearing 8 per cent interest, to any or all faculty members for any sum of money due them as part of their monthly salary which they would permit the college to hold out of the salary due."[76] To further help the faculty, the College developed a group life insurance program in which all staff members under age fifty-five were covered for one thousand dollars. This coverage was doubled in 1945.[77]

The agreement for one faculty family, the husband holding a Ph.D., was a suite of rooms, meals, plus a $100 cash salary each month for twelve months. A bonus was also promised at the end of nine months if "the college income justifies it."[78] In 1940, a single man with a bachelor's degree, in his first year of teaching, received $40 a month, a room, and meals. The next year, following his marriage and a master's degree, he received $125, an apartment, and meals.[79] A single woman with several years' teaching experience, who was about to complete a Ph.D., was paid $75 a month;[80] while another woman who had been with the college for eight years was paid $65 each month for twelve months.[81] A different faculty family, a husband and wife who also were caring for an aged parent, was paid a salary of $175 a month for twelve months and given their meals. However, they were asked to rent or purchase a home in the Cleveland community.[82] All salaries continued to be handled on an individual basis, confidentially and personally.

The end-of-the-year bonus was much anticipated and greatly appreciated by the faculty, giving them a sense of reward and appreciation.[83] Bonuses were even paid to faculty who left the College at the end of a year.[84] Bonuses for summer work were also given throughout the Cleveland years.[85]

The reason for the school's existence was bound up in the creed, which was affirmed in each chapel service. Emphasis on the Bible and its truth was no less strong in Cleveland than it had been in Florida. Chapel was held four days a week. Each Wednesday, the freshman through senior classes had class meetings and each Saturday, society meeting. Each class meeting and society meeting was closed with a chaplain's message, so the gospel was preached every weekday to the student body. Sunday services consisted of Sunday school, with the student body divided into classes by denominations, a formal morning worship service in the Margaret Mack Auditorium, Vespers in the afternoon, and denominational youth meetings in the late afternoon. On Sunday evenings the students would often attend church in Cleveland or drive to Chattanooga for a service. Most of the student body were also active in evangelization activities, many of which were held on Sundays. By 1943 the College had twenty-five different Protestant denominations represented among the student body, including Presbyterians, Methodists, Episcopalians, Lutherans, and Baptists.[86] It was during these years in Cleveland that Dr. Jones Sr. coined some of his chapel sayings, which he thereafter used regularly when preaching to the students.

Because of the common belief that religious schools did not maintain high academic standards, Dean Eunice Hutto often challenged the faculty to keep academic pressure on the students, to demand a high level of work, and to avoid giving grades that were too high.[87] In at least one case, Dr. Jones Jr. instructed the teachers to

Society spirit in Cleveland

"assign more work; let the students do more work and check more thoroughly on assignments."[88]

During the Cleveland years the degree offerings were greatly expanded. The College continued to emphasize the fields of religion, speech, and music but added minors in English, history, mathematics, and foreign languages. In 1933 the school opened its Business Col-

Study time in Cleveland, Tennessee

lege as a one-year program for secretarial and bookkeeping training.[89] The bachelor of science degree in elementary education was added in 1941 and degrees in commerce and home economics in 1942.[90] The Theological Seminary first offered the master of arts degree in religion in 1942,[91] and the Ph.D. in religion was added in 1943.[92]

In Cleveland the College's teacher training program, established in Florida, was delayed pending approval by the Tennessee State Board of Education. Education courses appeared in the Bob Jones College catalogs from 1933 to 1936, and the director of the University of Tennessee College of Education believed that the teacher curriculum would easily meet state certification requirements.[93] Approvals by the Tennessee State Board of Education for the teacher training program were finally announced in 1934, and Dr. Jones Sr. felt that this again showed that "our standards are as high as those of any similar institution anywhere in the world."[94] To insure that the College maintained its academics, examination teams from the state of Tennessee regularly came to the College to evaluate the type and quality of work offered.

The Tennessee Department of Education recognized the College's degrees in 1934 as did Vanderbilt University and Peabody Teachers' College. The University of Tennessee, however, did not recognize the undergraduate degrees of Bob Jones College graduates, accepting only three years of credits from the College.[95]

Although Bob Jones College course credits were accepted by major institutions such as Princeton Theological Seminary, Union Theological Seminary, and the University of Chicago Divinity School, the administrators of other Bible colleges and seminaries tended to refuse credits earned at BJC. Correspondence gleaned from the letter files of these colleges and seminaries for the years 1933 through 1947 are noteworthy in their refusal to transfer Bob Jones College credits on the same basis as other nonaccredited schools and for the sometimes acrimonious tone with which refusal was made.[96] Refusal may have been based on reservations about the quality of the academic work of the students, disagreement with the religious position of

Bob Jones College, or on a bias against the regulations governing student behavior and academic life.[97]

Another explanation, however, may be the jealousies or feelings of competition among leaders of certain of the colleges and seminaries in question. In 1929 J. Oliver Buswell, president of Wheaton College, and other conservative religious educators had tried to persuade Bob Jones Sr. to lead a national fight against educational standardization. Dr. Jones had refused to involve himself, saying that he wanted to cooperate with public educators and not fight them, and, further, that he desired academic standardization in Bob Jones College, not accreditation.[98]

Several years later, in a reversal of their earlier position against standardization, some of these men under Buswell's leadership formed an accrediting association for religious schools, which Bob Jones Sr. and the College refused to join.[99] Extant letters indicate that though he did not criticize those who chose to join these associations, and though agreeing with the need for standardized work, Bob Jones Sr. believed that membership in any association was not in line with the beliefs of the Bob Jones College administration or board.[100] For holding this position, Bob Jones Sr. was criticized for being uncooperative, and the College was labeled anti-intellectual. On at least two occasions the College was attacked by Buswell because it remained unaffiliated with the Bible college group of which Buswell was president.[101]

The issue of academic accreditation continued to be a problem for the College. In 1949 Bob Jones Sr. wrote Oliver Buswell that "it cost us something to stay out of an association, but we stayed out. We have lived up to our convictions."[102] Bob Jones Sr. did not elaborate on the cost, but lack of accreditation must have complicated student recruitment, faculty recruitment, and academic recognition. Nevertheless, this lack did not keep the College from growing both in academic and cultural offerings and in reputation. By 1945 Bob Jones College was the largest liberal arts college in the state of Tennessee, enrolling over nine hundred students, and its future growth would be even more dramatic.[103]

As the College grew in size, regulations on student life grew as well. (See Appendix B.) Some regulations were necessary because of the crowded living conditions, while others addressed social behavior and etiquette. Still other rules dealt with spiritual standards. Students who violated the rules met a committee of faculty and students who administered demerit penalties, and students who accumulated 150 demerits in one semester were expelled. Primary among all the rules was " 'Griping' will not be tolerated." This was followed by "Hazing is positively prohibited. Penalty: Minimum 50 demerits."

Other college rules included the following:

3. The use of tobacco in any form . . . prohibited. Penalty: expulsion.

6. Students must protect and preserve all college property and any willful damage to college property will be punished with a minimum of 50 demerits. . . . Damage must be paid [for].

8. The Bob Jones College endorses high class music. Students who persist in inflicting any other type music on the institution will be dealt with by the faculty committee.

10. Gambling, drinking of alcoholic beverages, profanity, obscenity, dancing, card playing, dice throwing will not be tolerated.

11. Attendance at chapel each week day and at morning church service and Vesper service, compulsory. Penalty: 25 demerits.

30. All students will leave the dining room at the same time. The gentlemen will remain standing at each table until the ladies at the table are seated.[104]

Little Moby's Corner: soda fountain, snack shop, and bookstore (Cleveland, Tennessee)

It was not uncommon for student petitions to be brought before the faculty, either for modifications or for exceptions to rules to be granted.[105] All couples on dates had to be chaperoned or in a public area on the campus like the social parlor or snack shop. Students found together in private without chaperones were dealt with strictly, as in the case of Pat and Aubry: "Leon A. went to the laundry room to take his clothes and found Pat W. and Aubry S. there. Discipline Committee met and shipped Aubry. Pat is campused for the rest of the year and if she gets as much as 5 demerits, she is shipped."[106]

Discipline was delivered fairly and with impartiality. Family connections, wealth, or reputation did not matter. On one occasion the daughter of a New York investment banker was sent home because of breaches of campus regulations. Dr. Jones Sr. said,

> Her daddy was a pretty nice sort of fellow; he had a lot of money, too, and the school was up against it in those days—we needed money! One day, we had to expel that girl. Of course, we had a discipline committee made up of students and faculty. But folks always blamed me if somebody was expelled. I felt sad about it, to tell you the truth, because her daddy was going to give us $100,000, and I needed $100,000. We had an awful struggle in those days. So, the girl came in and asked if I would talk to the committee. I said, "I can't do it. They did right. You'll have to go home. Your father's a friend of mine, and I'm sorry . . . but I can't let friendship affect me in a matter like this. You'll have to go home. . . . You're doing

the institution harm by not upholding our standards, and you won't be the right sort of representative of this school when you go out. So, you'll have to go." You ought to have seen the letter that girl's father wrote me. . . . He set that paper on fire. He said in so many words, "I'd let everybody on that campus starve before I'd send you any money." Well, I expected that. But you have to do right.[107]

Eventually the College rules grew to handbook size, and the students were asked to sign a statement of agreement and intended compliance with the rules.[108] Dr. Jones Sr. made it clear that no teacher or student could be a troublemaker and remain in the College. Discipline was not meted out carelessly, but it was exacted expediently; each case was pondered and prayed about. Very often, students were given second and third chances to make good.[109]

The College was purposely rigorous in academics and discipline. The system of discipline—a committee of faculty and students deciding penalties or excusing demerits for the students—as well as the basic rules continued unchanged through the Cleveland years. Discipline, Dr. Jones Sr. preached, was a primary element of the Christian life and part of the cultural program of the College.[110] He stressed that the school intended to teach the students "not just to make a living, but how to live."[111]

The idea was to help the student develop self-discipline by providing external discipline and structure to the student's life.[112] "Listen, you've got

Giovanni Sperandeo (ca. 1935)

to learn discipline; that is one of the essentials of culture," Dr. Jones Sr. preached. "No man is a gentleman that is too rotten lazy to get up out of his chair when a lady comes up, unless she has a cigarette in her mouth—then keep your seat."[113]

To the faculty, Dr. Jones Sr. preached, "It takes character to fit into this institution. . . . You can't adapt yourself here unless your heart is right."[114] When he said, "We are going to keep Bob Jones College a kingdom that isn't divided and a house that stands together,"[115] he meant it. Disunity among the faculty or student body would not be tolerated. There were instances in which the unity was threatened and in which Bob Jones Jr. as an administrator was tested. Two specific cases that warrant some attention are those of Giovanni Sperandeo and Ruth Flood. The Sperandeo case was handled by Bob Jones Jr., and the Ruth Flood case was handled by the

Founder. Both illustrate the philosophy "We are not going to pay anybody to 'cuss' us."

Giovanni Sperandeo was an operatic tenor who also spoke fluent English, Spanish, German, and French, as well as his native Italian. In May 1934 he was hired and began teaching French and German and giving voice lessons[116] that September.[117] His wife was hired to teach piano and violin and to organize and conduct the orchestra. Perhaps sensing Sperandeo's temperamental nature, Dr. Jones Sr. wrote, "We would expect you to come to us with a cooperative spirit and work with us in the solution of whatever problems might develop."[118]

During the 1934-35 school year, students made periodic complaints about Sperandeo's intimidating methods and his wife's teaching and playing. He was asked to sing at a revival meeting with Mrs. Loren Jones instead of his wife accompanying him.[119] He protested singing with her and the next school year refused to sing for a College concert altogether, demanding satisfaction over his perceived slight of his wife. Because Dr. Jones Sr. was in Europe on an extended preaching tour,[120] the situation fell to Bob Jones Jr. to handle. A meeting was arranged, at which time Sperandeo flew into a rage and attacked the head of the Piano Department as "incompetent" and declared that he "would not care to go on teaching."[121] Following a heated discussion, the Acting President wrote him that "unless you could accept the ruling of the administration and the Head of the Piano Department in regard to the matter of an accompanist, we should have your resignation."[122] Not willing to take Dr. Jones Jr.'s decision as authoritative, he demanded a meeting with the President, which was soon arranged, and listed a number of grievances concerning the treatment of him and his wife as artists. Within days of this session, in late January 1936, the man was fired. He demanded his full year's salary, went to the Cleveland press to expose "the exploiting of innocent teachers [who] work for you and your son for little or nothing," demanded a hearing by the Board of Trustees (which he never got), and publicized his salary, which at the time was among the highest of all the faculty.[123]

When the conflict finally ended, Dr. Jones Sr. wrote the man that "we are Christians. We wish you well. . . . I have tried to help you in every way possible, and at the same time take care of the welfare of the College and people who are under my protection. That is my responsibility and the Lord is helping me to take care of it. He is going to keep on helping us

Ruth Flood (ca. 1935)

take care of this institution because we are
doing it for Him."[124] Sperandeo was the first
test of twenty-five-year-old Bob Jones Jr.'s
authority as Acting President.

The second case is that of Miss Ruth
Flood, one of the original faculty members of
Bob Jones College who had moved from Florida with the school. Miss Flood had been responsible in large part for the burgeoning
interest in acting and "expression," as speech
training was then called. She joined the faculty
in 1927, shortly after finishing her own undergraduate work, and completed a master's degree in speech at the University of Michigan
by 1933.[125] She had played in the first Shakespeare productions and appeared regularly on
Vespers programs. In Cleveland she was both
respected by and popular with her students.[126]
She traveled to England with Bob Jones Jr. in

Dorothy Seay (ca. 1937)

1934 or 1935 to study Shakespeare at Strat-
ford-upon-Avon and was generally thought of as a "beautiful interpreter" of
poetry and a very fine actress.[127]

Following a serious physical and emotional breakdown in the spring of
1936, she left the College for more than nine months and returned to teaching
on January 6, 1937.[128] The 1938 annual was dedicated to her, and by all
appearances she was a loyal, dynamic, productive, and well-liked member
of the faculty.

In 1936 Ruth Flood had become acquainted with Dorothy Seay and Mr.
and Mrs. Joseph Free. Dorothy Seay was hired in August 1936, as replace-
ment for Sperandeo, to teach French, Latin, and Greek, and she lectured
occasionally in sociology and psychology. She was completing a dissertation
for the Ph.D. in classical Latin from the University of Chicago and came to
teach at Bob Jones from Winthrop College in Rock Hill, South Carolina. She
came with the idea of "conforming" to the outward standards of the College.[129] Within weeks of the opening of school, Seay had become the center
of a swirl of disputes. She mimicked and mocked students both publicly and
privately; she denigrated other faculty members to her classes; in violation
of school rules she invited male students to her apartment for long "study
sessions"; and she refused to cooperate with the school in matters of student
discipline. She publicly criticized elements of student life that she found
"outlandish."[130] After only three months of employment, Dr. Jones Sr. had
held two conferences with her about her behavior and stated the conditions
of her future employment.

First: There must be absolute loyalty to the administration. If something happens in the administration which you do not like, your protest is your resignation. If you stay here you must not under any circumstances criticize the administration.

Second: You must not "hobnob" with students.

Third: You must cooperate with the policy of the administration in its method of handling the individual student and you must not employ any method contrary to the method of the administration.

Fourth: You must not criticize other departments and charge them with failure as you did. . . .

Fifth: You must not criticize, to your students in class or elsewhere, other students.

Sixth: You are not employed to philosophize about life in the classroom, nor are you employed to comment about things and people. . . .

If you return after Christmas I shall take it for granted that you thoroughly understand the situation and that you are determined to follow the suggestions I have outlined.[131]

Dorothy Seay did return after Christmas and was rehired for the next school year as well, but her attitudes appear to have remained unchanged. Although her classroom behavior was more ethical, she freely shared her criticisms with her friends Ruth Flood and Joseph Free.[132]

Dr. Jones did not know that his patience would earn him and the College a malicious article in H. L. Mencken's national magazine, the *American Mercury.*

There is a college where your boy may be put in solitary confinement for a month for smoking one cigarette, where your daughter is restricted to the campus for refusing a boy a date, where four hundred boys and girls do not dare speak to each other except when crowding into the dining room. These young people—I nearly wrote "inmates"—dare not complain when their roof leaks, because complaints are considered sinful; they wouldn't dare write home about an outbreak of ptomaine poisoning because letters are read in the office and withheld from the mail. Outlandish though this must sound, it is right here in the United States, and I am a member of its faculty. When I accepted the appointment I did not dream that my pedagogical duties would include spying on my students or that I would be plunged into an almost hysterical awareness of *Sin.* . . .

Dr. Jones keeps his evangelistic hand in, so to speak, by his sermons to the student body. The religious fervor that he works up results in mass confessions of wrongdoing, mostly imaginary, of course. . . . Blank College and its kind take students from Maine to California and turns them out sin-conscious and snoop-minded. They graduate boys and girls knowing more of philandering than philosophy, and more of evil than evolution.[133]

Dr. Jones had questioned two of the faculty about Seay but lacked satisfactory evidence to fire her. At a meeting of the student body, Dr. Jones Sr. said he felt "someone in the faculty was a hindrance,"[134] preached to them, and prayed a powerfully worded prayer that the person would be discovered.[135] After two days of investigation, a faculty meeting was held, the evidence presented, and twenty-five faculty members voted to release her. Four abstained. Dorothy Seay was fired, but her influence had been felt by Ruth Flood.

Joseph Free came from Ann Arbor, Michigan, to teach speech and work with debate. He fell in with Dorothy Seay, and he and his wife were close to her. His teaching was intellectual and credible, and he characterized his work at the College as "mutually profitable and enjoyable." He did, however, do his "best to disrupt the speech department."[136] In comments to students and faculty he characterized Dr. Jones Sr. as "conceited" and said that statements made by Dr. Jones Sr. in his "emphatic way, in faculty meeting or in chapel . . . were far too absurd for any debate teacher to accept."[137] He openly criticized the College and its rules for being "paternalistic" and squelching personal development, accused R. K. Johnson of lying and being crooked, pointed out to his classes the "fallacies of logic" contained in chapel messages, and recommended that BJC students attend other schools.[138] He also made a case for "open minded" tolerance to all ideas and taught that several chapel messages were "absolutely incompatible with certain truths that I felt it my duty to teach certain of my classes."[139] When all this came to light, Joseph Free was fired.

As a member of the speech department, he worked closely with Ruth Flood and registered his criticisms of logic and action with her. Dorothy Seay's criticisms, when coupled with the intellectual arguments of Joseph Free, changed Ruth Flood. "Floodie" herself kept silent. Dr. Jones Sr. had

conferences with her on four occasions to warn her of the Frees' potential for harm, but she seemed attracted to them. From a teacher "held in great esteem," she suddenly changed.[140] Nothing at the College now suited her. Dr. Jones wrote: "The impression in general to the students is that she is off mentally due to her depleted nervous state. I must say . . . it is probably spiritual."[141] Ruth Flood resigned on May 25, 1938.[142]

These faculty problems serve to illustrate the control that the President and Acting President held over the school, a control unlike that in secular institutions. While trying to accommodate individuals to the fullest extent possible and give them the benefit of the doubt, they

Joseph Free (ca. 1938)

held the good of the institution and the welfare of the students paramount over personal considerations. As one faculty member remarked some years later, "Remember, Dr. Bob will never consciously do anything to harm the school."[143]

Dr. Jones Sr. believed that no institution, organization, or individual could survive in which self-control and self-restraint were not the rule. He preached, "The Satanic philosophy is a philosophy of 'live as you please'; 'have what you want'; 'don't let anybody tell you what to do'; 'it's your life, you have got a right to live it.' " Both Seay and Free advocated such a philosophy. "The Christian philosophy," however, "is a philosophy of self-denial, self-control, and self-restraint." The College would not survive with any other philosophy being promoted, Dr. Jones Sr. believed, and to be a good teacher, you had to "live what you teach the best you can."[144]

Though these events did not have any lasting effect on the institution, they do show the convictions of Dr. Jones Sr. and Dr. Jones Jr., convictions that would be severely tested some years later. Dr. Jones Sr. believed he was training leadership for the spiritual future of America, and he wanted Christian leaders with sweet Christian character and refined culture. He prayed, "Lord, don't let us waver, don't ever let us waver."[145] And he never lost sight of the needs of the young students.

CHAPTER 7

◆

Combing Out the Cultural Kinks

The charter of the College clearly charged the institution with the mission to educate "youths in the essentials of culture . . . with special emphasis on the Christian religion and the ethics revealed in the Holy Scriptures."[1] The faculty and student body were often reminded of this in chapel talks and faculty meetings in which the "essentials of culture," from an enlightened Fundamentalist perspective, were emphasized by Dr. Jones Sr. and Dr. Jones Jr. "Our greatest assets," the Founder often remarked, "are our religion, our discipline, and our culture."[2]

The essentials of culture were organized in a way consistent with Fundamentalist theology and the truth of a spiritually lost and dying world. The Founder's vision for the school was to develop young people to be spiritual "salt and light" within the world.[3] He wanted a product that could withstand scrutiny and compete on an equal footing with the world's product, a product that would take Christ to every level of society—from the slum to the mansion, from the "down-and-out to the up-and-out." The school was conceived in Florida by Dr. Jones Sr. and developed and maintained in Cleveland by Dr. Jones Jr. as an institution that emphasized all the elements that go into making one cultured: a recognition and understanding of the cosmos—the world's spiritual, political, and economic systems; personal discipline and refinement; and familiarity with the great products of man in the arts. The emphasis on culture at the College, mandated in the charter, is rooted in these three areas.

To understand the cultural program of the institution is to understand much of the motivation of the Founder in establishing the school and molding its policies. To understand the College's cultural climate in Cleveland, we must look to Dr. Jones Sr. and then to the College's years in Florida.

Prior to founding the College, the great evangelist spent his time "magnifying the cardinal doctrines of sin and salvation, the Book and the Blood . . . [and] Christ on Calvary" as the only

A classic pose—Bob Jones Sr. (1940)

77

escape from defiling sin.[4] Bob Jones Sr. was first a Christian, second a Fundamentalist, and third an evangelist. He did not view himself as an educator.[5] His thoughts on culture were generally presented while preaching or in letters in response to specific questions.

Bob Jones Sr. preached on three different types of culture: the cosmos, the fine arts, and personal refinement. He generally determined which type to speak on based on the audience he was addressing. Thus, when on the Chautauqua Circuit in 1927, he lectured on general social issues.[6] In the citywide revival campaigns of 1911 through approximately 1935, he dealt with individual sin, issues of personal spirituality, and community morality.[7] While addressing students at the College, he often dealt with discipline, personal decency and refinement, and the fine arts.[8]

Dr. Jones was not an aesthete and to him life was "not divided into the secular and the sacred."[9] He viewed life as a "total world"[10] or a synthesis of all its elements—social, educational, recreational, creative, and spiritual. Developing and disciplining all of these areas was part of the responsibility of Bob Jones College.[11]

The ideas of Bob Jones Sr. were based on several basic truths. All truth is God's truth, and truth is one characteristic of God. Truth is revealed to man in God's Word, the Bible—the verbally inspired, infallible, and authoritative divine revelation to mankind.[12] Man as portrayed in Scripture is a fallen creature, totally depraved and redeemable only through the specific, atoning sacrifice of Jesus Christ on the cross.[13] Because man is depraved, his social organizations and his world system—the cosmos—are inherently antagonistic to God. There is not and cannot be a "good society" because there is none that "doeth good" in the supreme sense of the word.[14]

Society has as its primary need neither physical nor social repair. It is a society that is in need but is incapable of moral reformation. The affairs of society require divine intervention, and man requires divine restoration to his Creator.[15] The ills of society were viewed by Bob Jones Sr. as spiritual ones, rooted in individual sin and transgression against God, not in environmental, behavioral, scientific, political, or social factors as preached by American Modernists of the era.[16]

Two elements pervaded Bob Jones Sr.'s social pronouncements: patriotism and morality. These two essentials were based on the requisite of personal salvation, adherence to biblical teaching related to government, and the application of Christian standards to personal behavior. In politics he was independent—sometimes supporting Populists such as William Jennings Bryan; sometimes supporting Republicans such as Herbert Hoover; sometimes campaigning for Dixiecrats such as Strom Thurmond; and occasionally falling into line with the rest of the Democratic South—but he always applied Christian standards to the candidates and weighed their policies on the scales of principle.

Dr. Jones was no demagogue. He was strongly patriotic and denounced in the strongest terms Fascists,[17] Communists,[18] and those who would rend the fabric of American life through sexual promiscuity and perversion.[19] He did not propose the suppression of any religious, political, social, or racial groups, however, because he believed that any government that had power to suppress one faith had the power to suppress all faiths. He spoke, therefore, with restraint when dealing with Americans' basic rights to believe and to act on that belief. He was outspoken, though, in his opposition to what he considered to be false doctrines that lead people into sects and cults; these included Christian Science, Mormonism, Jehovah's Witnesses, spiritism, and Modernism, which was considered by most Fundamentalists to be a new pagan religion.[20]

Bob Jones Sr. also opposed Catholicism as a system of religious belief that was "devilish" and that enslaved those who followed it. He said, "The Devil has plenty of religious systems. He's no enemy of religion. He is the enemy of the Bible."[21] He loved the souls of Catholics, tried to win them to Jesus, and pitied those who were duped by Catholicism's mysticism and superstitions.[22] He told of trying to win a Catholic lady to Christ: "We had a hard time getting to [Jesus]. The priest was in the way. The virgin Mary had blocked traffic, and all the saints stood in the door, but I think she climbed over altars and beyond priestly robes and saints, and somehow or other, I think she got to Jesus."[23]

Dr. Jones Sr. also fought Catholicism as a political institution.[24] During the presidential election of 1928, the Catholic issue forged a political alliance between Modernists and Fundamentalists in opposition to Al Smith, the Catholic presidential candidate from New York. Modernists feared foreign immigration; Fundamentalists feared Catholicism. Both feared for the dominant place of Protestantism in American culture.[25] *Bob Jones Magazine,* which had been founded as a vehicle to spread Bob Jones Sr.'s ideas of "religious, political, and social life"[26] devoted two complete issues to the election, Catholicism, and foreign immigration, all of which were hot political issues for Protestant Americans.[27] Bob Jones Sr., however, did not encourage or support violent acts against Catholics or immigrants, as was sometimes the case with other Protestant preachers. To Dr. Jones, the law was to be obeyed and acts of hatred could not be justified in any case. Simply put, it was never right to do wrong.

In his famous Chautauqua lecture of 1927, "The Perils of America," his social thought was developed into eight broad perils to individual and civil morality.[28] Eventually, he distilled the eight into three "fundamental perils": peril to the home, peril to religion, and peril in education. He closed his lectures with a call to "Christianize the inevitables" of labor, business, and education,[29] and asked for a dedication of effort to the cause of Christian education and to the preaching of the gospel. He said, "How [do we change people]? Christian education! . . . We have not tried it. There isn't a Christian city in the United States. There are a few Christian homes. Still fewer Christian schools."[30] He then concluded his thoughts on education by presenting the philosophy and atmosphere of Bob Jones College.[31]

Like other Fundamentalists, Bob Jones Sr. defined the faults of society in spiritual terms and saw society as containing both Christian and pagan elements.[32] He believed that the resolution of social problems was found in "real Hell-fire and damnation preaching,"[33] preaching that was intended to "change people." He said, "Conditions are a result [of people], not a cause. So long as people are greedy, we'll have the results of greed. Dictatorships—unemployment—crime—war. [We must] change people."[34] He laid at the feet of Christians the responsibility for many of the social and political problems of the day. If Christians did their duty as they should, he argued, many of the day's problems would not exist. In 1948, while preaching about Christians' failures to evangelize the world, he preached, "Suppose Hitler had been converted. If Hitler and Mussolini had been [converted], the sons of America that are sleeping in the silent tombs of death on the battlefields of Europe would have been home today with Mother and Dad."[35]

Bob Jones Sr. tried to develop a college that was truly Christian and would distance the "perils" from the lives of the students. Dr. Jones Sr. told the students, "You can't reach the right object without the right nature. . . . You cannot reach a Christian goal without a Christian heart. This college cannot achieve a Christian object without having a Christian nature. This college can never receive Christian results on earth unless it is Christian itself."[36] He encouraged the students to study God's Word and "think God's thoughts."[37]

"The Christian philosophy," he often said, "is a philosophy of self-denial, self-control, and self-restraint."[38] Dr. Jones set the policies of the school in such a way that the students' lives were regulated by rules that called for "clean living" by "higher principles" than the "behavioristic" gratification of self.[39] The Christian's life, he said, to be a life of grace, should evidence control by such higher principles. A strong work ethic was therefore encouraged, and social unrest on the campus was not tolerated.[40] Sunday was reserved for worship and religious activities, not for sports or parties. The students were taught to "render to Caesar" those areas of life incumbent on citizens—military service, payment of taxes, obeying laws, voting, and other duties—without sacrificing the standards of God's Word.

Bob Jones Sr.'s idea of personal grace and refinement—the personal, social, and educational disciplines necessary to become fully integrated into society—were clearly defined. The refinement of the person made up a large portion of the ideals of Bob Jones Sr. and was often represented by him as "putting to practice the ethics revealed in the Holy Scripture."[41] Dr. Jones believed that Christianity is "the most refining influence that came to a human heart. . . . A man is inherently a gentleman who is a Christian. If you are not a gentleman at heart, there is something wrong with your religion."[42]

This emphasis had the effect of creating a need within the students for the elements of culture.[43] The issue of personal refinement and culture was "hammered in" and was linked by Dr. Jones Sr. and Dr. Jones Jr. to the disciplinary standards and social rigors of the school. In their eyes, refinement was one way of gaining acceptability in society. As one mem-

Bob Jones Sr. preaching (1940)

ber of the College faculty put it, "Dr. Bob Sr. was, in his own way, a very earthy person. But he was earthy in the sense that he was down-to-earth in order to pull you up out of it. [Speaking against] the baggy pants, dirty nose, that kind of thing, is a good illustration. Culture understood in this sense is one means of doing that—of elevating [the perception] of Fundamentalist Christianity to a higher level. . . . The culture of the institution was a great way of giving [Fundamentalism] a status in the minds of the public."[44]

Both Bob Jones Sr. and Jr. often railed on the uncouth appearance, ignorance, and loutish behavior of some Christians, constantly reinforcing the idea of "selling an educational gospel to the public."[45] The social emphasis was not on a relaxed, "sweatshirt culture," but on a more formal one of "language and refinement."[46] One major goal of the College was to make ladies and gentlemen out of the students; Bob Jones Sr. often preached, "A Christian will always be a lady or a gentleman."[47] In this connection, the students received lectures on etiquette by Mrs. Jones Sr. or by the dining hall supervisor before meals.[48] The meals were all "family style" to give students a sense of community and belonging. Family-style meals also gave students the opportunity to practice good manners and display good breeding under the supervision of the faculty, who served as hosts and hostesses at each table. Students were also required to meet certain dress standards for both morning and afternoon classes, for Sundays, and for social events.[49] They were taught to be punctual and to treat others with Christian consideration.[50] Social functions were numerous and well chaperoned, with as many as six formal banquets, one formal tea, and five dinner parties for the students. At these functions Dr. Bob's "boys and girls" were expected to behave with poise and dignity.[51]

Even in the school's first year, one major goal was to teach self-control and refinement. Dr. Jones Sr. recalled, "When we opened college the first year, I looked out across the street on the campus and saw a girl, and . . . a boy shoved her around. I went out there and said, 'Take your hands off that girl. This is no roughneck establishment. Girls are treated like ladies here.' If they are not ladies, then they go home. We teach young folks refinement, Christian refinement."[52]

Dr. Jones Sr. believed and preached that "there is nothing in this world that takes the place of Christian grace and hospitality."[53] "Politeness and courtesy" were part of that which goes to make up culture.[54]

Personal ability, as a gift from God, is to be developed, not suppressed. He preached, "If you are a good singer, sing. If you can talk, talk. Fill your own place. God has a purpose for your life."[55] Somewhat later he said, "Sing the best you can; play the best you can. Learn all the science you can; learn all the literature you can; learn all the history you can. Take all the training [you can]."[56] In 1935 he preached, "If you are taking music, God expects you to play the best you can play. You ought to be ashamed to do less than your best."[57]

Loyalty as a character trait was given much attention,[58] and personal discipline was constantly stressed.[59] Strong character and godly temperament were the hinges on which the door of evangelism swung. Dr. Jones Sr. said, "It is your business to sell Jesus Christ and Christianity to your community by your life."[60] The whole reason for education was stated succinctly when he said, "All these things we learn here like Greek and Hebrew and French and German and Spanish and all we learn about history and civilization—all of that simply is to give us a contact to preach the gospel."[61]

Personal habits were scrutinized so that offensive ones could be eliminated.[62] He preached, "You're a Christian. Keep your hands clean, comb your hair, keep your shirt clean. Your Christian influence is a great thing."[63] Bob Jones Jr. described his father's thought by saying, " 'If a man can't get out of lady's drawing room gracefully, he is not a well trained man.' He saw so many uncouth [Christian] people who looked upon any kind of . . . culture as sinful, and therefore they were misfits in society and were unable to make a good impression or reach people. He was interested in the down-and-outers always, but he thought that the up-and-outers were being neglected. . . . He felt that to reach them, a man ought to be able to discuss the arts and anything that was current at the time."[64]

To train Christians in these areas, Bob Jones Sr. believed, was partly the role of education—to add to faith, virtue; and to virtue, knowledge. He admonished the students to "get all the education, get all the [intellectual] equipment you can. Be the best human instrument possible."[65] "We want you to know literature. We want you to know some history. We want you to know music. We want you to know a little about art. We want you to know how to get in and out of a lady's parlor and be a gentleman. We want you to know how to say 'thank you.' . . . If you haven't got enough culture to say 'thank you' and to write a courteous letter, you are not educated like you ought to be educated in the essentials of culture."[66]

Bible characters provided vivid examples of personal refinement, and Dr. Jones Sr. often used their lives as examples. Job was one such example. "Job was a gentleman," he said. "He did not go across the street and spit in the face of a fellow. . . . There is nothing so dignified, so powerful, as true purity and true virtue."[67]

"Jesus was a gentleman everywhere He went," Dr. Jones said. "He was a gentleman when a wicked woman was kissing His feet and pouring out tears there. He was a gentleman when Nicodemus, a scholar, met Him at night. He was a gentleman."[68] "He knew how to take babies out of their mother's arms. He saw people going down the street, old, tired, women. He said, 'Come to Me and let Me carry your burden for you.' This is a college of Christian ladies and gentlemen. . . . When you come on the Bob Jones College Campus, you're received like a lady and like a gentleman, and if you don't like that kind of atmosphere, go back and get with the 'roughnecks.' "[69]

He often spoke of the apostle Paul, saying that "Paul had all the marks of a man of culture. He had education, travel, position, authority, and character."[70] When we think of Paul, "we don't think about his intelligence. We think of him for his missionary journeys and for what he stood. We don't discredit the books, but I don't want to make [them] an end in [themselves]."[71]

The third area of culture, the fine arts, was expounded by Bob Jones Sr. as the product of many years of intellectual struggle with the issue of the fine arts and Christianity.[72] The earliest extant pronouncement on the fine arts came in 1934. Culture in terms of the fine arts did not come to the forefront of Dr. Jones's consciousness until the College was located in Tennessee, when the facilities and the size of the student body could support a program of more than a rudimentary nature and when the music and speech faculties were established.[73]

Bob Jones was the sole controlling personality in the early days of the College and made all decisions relative to the cultural, religious, and academic life of the school. The whole cultural program, though perhaps the idea of others, shows Dr. Jones's commitment to the fine arts. Overlaying his basic presuppositions of man, God, and truth was the idea that "every good thing comes from God,"[74] because God is inherently good. God is also, by nature, creative. The gifts of God to man are creative gifts and were thoroughly good in their original state.[75] Man is created in God's image, and one way in which he reflects that image is in his ability to create, an ability that was "good" in its original state. All the fine arts come from God as a direct gift to man. Because the arts are from God, they are "good." As such, they are reflective of Him in all His attributes, among which are His creative urge, purity, holiness, love, and humor. Man's creative output in the fine arts should attempt to reflect the character of God rather than the fallen nature of man. "All good music comes from God. Every good thing comes from

God," he preached. "The Devil doesn't own anything that is good except what he took away from God and perverted. . . . The Devil comes in and steals everything. He takes all the beautiful in life and drags it down and commercializes it and steals it away from decent people."[76] He also believed that all the fine arts—architecture, music, literature, drama, painting, sculpture, and some forms of dance—had expressive import as "an effort of man to explore the unexplored depths of his soul."[77]

The Founder did not deal specifically with each of these arts. He was, however, forced to defend his position on several artistic areas to numerous critics. A 1929 article in the *Bob Jones Magazine* stated the position of the College on music when it reported, "Music is the natural expression of the soul of man. It is a revelation of his character. It is the instinctive universal expression of human experience. Music crystalizes the very thoughts and imaginations of our very self-hood. . . . Bob Jones College is a school where the heart and soul are cared for as carefully as the mind and body. We stress the finer things of life as well as the material. Our aim is to train young men and women to take the [religious] inspiration gleaned here to the people of the world."[78]

The position of the College and Bob Jones Sr. on drama was difficult for some Fundamentalists. Bob Jones College began dramatic productions in its first year and received tremendous criticism for doing so. To justify drama, Dr. Jones went back to his basic philosophy that all things that are good are from God as a gift to man to use for Him. He also used as an example the biblical story of Job, calling it the "greatest drama ever written," and made the observation that all the great preachers of history were dramatic, including the apostle Paul and Jesus Christ.[79] To answer critics of the fine arts program of the College, he often quoted James 1:16-18—"Do not err, my beloved brethren. Every good gift and every perfect gift is from above, and cometh down from the Father of lights, with whom is no variableness, neither shadow of turning. Of his own will begat he us with the word of truth, that we should be a kind of firstfruits of his creatures."

He also cited the example of the apostle Paul: "I am made all things to all men, that I might by all means save some. And this I do for the gospel's sake" (I Cor. 9:22-23). Bob Jones Sr. cited the educational background, philosophical study, intellectual insight, literary background, knowledge of Jewish and Roman law and custom, and social ease with which the apostle Paul comported himself as an example of the goal of the Christian student.[80] He preached,

> Paul said, "I am all things to all men." Paul could not have been all things to all men if he had not been an educat[ed] man. . . . Paul said he was all things to all men for the sake of the gospel. Not just because he wanted to know. It is all right to want to know, but the fellow that wants to know just because he wants to know doesn't have a Christian conception. A fellow who wants music simply because he wants music, just to

sit down and satisfy the emotional make-up in his life is not upholding a Christian life, in a sense. It is all right to enjoy it. [But] Paul said he wanted to know so that he might go out for the sake of the gospel of Christ. . . .

You ought to understand the labor movement of our day. You ought to understand the business approach of our day. You ought to know about the international problems of our day. You ought to know something about music and culture.[81]

Each cultural concept coincides roughly with the various stages in the career of Bob Jones—evangelist, Founder of a Christian college, and college President. Fundamentalist theology plus dynamic evangelism undergirded the concepts of culture found in the College. The purpose of evangelism to Bob Jones was to change man's spiritual nature, thus changing his desires and lifestyle, and thereafter changing society. Education follows evangelism, first to discipline and refine the person, then to remake society into one of spiritual vitality. Refinement should develop man's sensibilities and tastes and provide an emotional outlet and creative expression in the arts for the purpose of further evangelization in society. Dr. Jones tried to "hammer in" the value of the cultured life. Yet the message of Christ was supreme. "It takes more than culture to save a people," he said.

Jesus, who knew what was in man, recognized the hopelessness and helplessness of human nature when He told Nicodemus, a cultured, elegant gentleman, he must be born again or he could not "perceive" of the kingdom of God.

This school believes in the Liberal Arts, classic literature, classic music, believes in scientific laboratories, believes in mathematics . . . but Christianity in this college has the right of way. The Christian religion has the first place. This is one place where "the sky is the limit" for the Christian religion.[82]

Dr. Jones preached that "culture is the method by which to put over the message of Christianity."[83] And he meant to enforce it on the students because, as he put it, "Christianity is more than a creed; it is a life."[84]

CHAPTER 8

◆

Culture Comes to Cleveland

Cultural development in the fine arts was important from the beginning of the College and is demonstrated by the fact that Bob Jones Sr. limited the areas of study to three majors—music, speech, and religion—two of which were fine-arts oriented. All three areas, however, were also related to the gospel ministry and evangelism.[1]

To initiate the fine arts program during the first week of the school in Florida and to see if there was any talent among the student body, Dr. Jones required the students "to perform something—read a poem, sing, or play an instrument" in a school assembly. After each student, the Founder critiqued the performance.[2] Following this public talent audition came the first cultural undertaking—a weekly program presented on Sunday afternoons, called "Twilight Musicale" and renamed "Vespers" in its second year. The Musicale was evidently the idea of music teacher Susie Kelly Dean, who had been a piano teacher in Panama City, Florida, and was also active in Bay County cultural organizations.[3]

Twilight Musicale attempted to combine a rather vague Christian message with the musical and dramatic arts.[4] The program was intended to be cultural and inspirational and was "in composition . . . classical in nature and consisted of instrumental and vocal trios and solos interspersed with [dramatic] readings."[5] Bob Jones Jr. later said these programs were "like tea recitals . . . like they would have had in Britain at teatime in a hotel. Looking back on them, they are very funny." Dramatic readings were interspersed with semiclassical vocal and instrumental ensembles. The programs were artistically unsophisticated at first, but "most of the people who came had never seen anything at all, so they thought it was great."[6]

The Bob Jones College Glee Club Mixed Double Quartet, College Point, Florida

The first Musicale was Sunday, October 9, 1927, at 5:30 P.M., and was presented in the Dixon-McKenzie Auditorium.[7] Bob Jones Jr.'s first speaking appearance and his only appearance singing were in the Twilight Musicale presented on December 11, 1927.[8]

The musical quality of the selections was wide but tended toward the banal.[9] As the faculty matured and the students made progress and gained experience, the selections improved, although sentimentalism was still the rule of thumb. Sharing the programs were readers, vocal soloists, pianists, violinists, and the College choir. The choir was directed by Charles W. Mountain[10] and the orchestra was under Susie Kelly Dean during the first year.

By 1931 the Vespers were assigned to different members of the College speech faculty, who planned and coordinated the programs. In addition, senior-level speech students all planned and directed a Vespers as part of their requirements. Credit was also given to students participating in the productions.[11] As Vespers became larger in concept and scope, more rehearsal time was necessary to polish the

Vespers program in Florida

program. Accordingly, in 1932 the faculty voted to set aside every Wednesday evening for rehearsal.[12]

In February 1928 an original drama, *A Woman Who Dared,* based on the biblical account of Queen Esther, was presented.[13] As the first drama, this play opened the way for other original dramas and may have prepared the College family for secular drama as well. All Vespers drama was prepared under the direction of Ruth Flood, instructor in speech,[14] and dramas became a regular feature of the Vespers programs during the Florida years. The early dramatic attempts were perhaps unpolished, the scenery was juvenile in design, and the costuming was rough, but everyone was "just learning." The stage

> had a kind of a curtain [material] that cost fifteen cents a yard. It was what they called "misprint." It was material at the first of the run of printed cotton when it went through, before the ink got right. Everything was sort of a dirty color, and we made curtains out of that. You couldn't turn on the stage lights until you opened the curtain because everybody could see through the curtain. [Mrs. Dean] would put candles out along the front of the stage for atmosphere, and [if] somebody would open the door, the curtains would blow and would catch fire. We had to have one fellow sit

on the front row to smack out the fire every Sunday—that was his business. After a few weeks, there were kind of oval holes all in the curtain. . . . We didn't use those very long. But we were learning.[15]

In spite of the rehearsals, things occasionally went awry during performances. During one religious drama, as a long, solemn processional was making its way down the aisles and up the front stairs of the stage, the last man, costumed as a Roman guard with spear, sword, and armor, tripped and fell to the stage with a thud. He let loose a noticeable and notable obscenity for which he was later disciplined.[16]

Shortly after the first biblical drama was presented, secular plays of a generally lighter nature were performed independently of the Vespers productions. Among them were *The Importance of Being Earnest, The Patsy, Everyman, The Little Minister,* and *Quality Street.*[17] They were apparently entertaining enough to draw crowds from Panama City.[18]

The driving force behind drama at the College, and ultimately the force behind the formation of the Shakespeare repertory group, was Bob Jones Jr.[19] As a college student he wrote letters to Shakespearean actors and producers and asked for advice and suggestions. He explained to them that "we were trying to build a good Shakespeare repertory company, and we were starting from scratch. They were always very kind and helpful." As specific technical problems arose, he contacted companies who advertised in *Theater Arts* or other of the trade magazines for advice and information.[20] When things needed to be done to advance the Players, he was perhaps "a little sneaky about some things." On one occasion after he had joined the faculty, swords were needed for a production, but the business manager would not agree to purchase them without Dr. Jones Sr.'s approval. Money was scarce, and it was certain that the elder Jones would not agree to the expenditure. A few weeks later, on a trip through New York City, Bob Jones Jr. bought the swords he needed and simply had the business manager take a few dollars a month out of his paycheck until they were paid for, thus eliminating the need to ask his father. "I never deceived my dad," he said. "I sometimes took advantage of his absences to do things that he might have been reluctant to do had he been there. My dad was always tolerant because he liked the results; but some things I did not discuss with him before I did them."[21]

In the fall of 1929 the Classic Players, the school's dramatic production group, was formed, and their first play, *The Merchant of Venice,* was performed on June 2, 1930. *Merchant* was directed by Ruth Flood, but Bob Jones Jr., then only a college sophomore, designed and executed the sets and costumes.[22] All the roles were played by students, with eighteen-year-old Bob Jones Jr. taking the role of the aged Jewish merchant, Shylock.[23] The College's second Shakespearean production, *Othello,* was produced on June 2, 1931, with Bob Jones Jr. playing the title role.[24]

Since 1930, at least two plays have been performed annually by the Classic Players, and on at least two occasions the Classic Players took

The Merchant of Venice by William Shakespeare (Bob Jones University Classic Players, 1930); Bob Jones Jr. as Shylock is on the far right.

productions into neighboring cities.[25] Amazingly, during Commencement activities in 1932, two different plays—*The Taming of the Shrew* and *Hamlet*—were both performed the same day, and Bob Jones Jr. played the lead role in both.[26]

After the move to Tennessee, cultural draws both continued and were strengthened. The response in Tennessee was much like that in Florida. The local people were amazed at the beauty of the programs, as well the performance skills of the students.[27] In Cleveland the format of the Vespers programs remained similar to that of the early Twilight Musicales, with musical numbers—sacred, classical, and semiclassical—interspersed with dramatic readings, fully staged dramatic scenes, and recitations of poetry or Scripture. Unlike the Vespers programs in Florida, which were essentially little concerts, the programs in Tennessee gradually became centered on a particular theme—a verse or thought from Scripture, a well-known hymn, or a special event or holiday.[28] The intent was to present an inspirational-cultural program, not simply a cultural one as in Florida.[29] Yet, as the Music Department attracted students of a higher caliber and as the teachers gained greater experience, classical music became an integral part of the programs and was included nearly every Sunday.[30]

Plays and pageants also continued as part of the Cleveland Vespers programs and were popular with both the students and the townspeople. These included *The Rock,* a play about the apostle Peter,[31] and *The Star of the East,* a pageant set in Persia in the fifth century B.C.,[32] as well as standard seasonal plays at Christmas and Easter. One fully costumed pageant depicted the history of ancient Israel from Abraham through the apostle Paul.[33] Not every selection included on Vespers was of a sacred or decidedly religious nature, however. For example, Bob Jones Jr. once presented

Cardinal Wolsey's "Farewell to His Greatness," from Shakespeare's *Henry VIII* as part of the Vespers program.[34]

In Cleveland the Vespers were first performed in the College chapel and remained there until 1936 when the auditorium was built.[35] With the addition of Margaret Mack Auditorium, an enlarged stage area with increased depth made new staging and lighting options possible. Designed by Bob Jones Jr., the auditorium was described by the area press as "one of the best equipped in this region," and the stage reportedly had the most advanced lighting system then possible.[36] It had thirty curtains, six of which could be displayed on the stage at any one time, and a contour curtain designed by Bob Jones Jr.

The building also had a radio studio, dressing rooms, a scene shop, a costume room, a greenroom, and studios for the speech therapy clinic of the Speech Department.[37] Solo spotlights were available for the first time, and the increased stage depth made more spectacular productions possible.[38] With the new stage facility, the directors were encouraged to be creative and try new ideas.[39]

Margaret Mack Auditorium, Cleveland, Tennessee

The Classic Players soon developed as well, and critical acclaim followed them. By the time the College moved to Cleveland, the performances were up to excellent quality—at least "as well as anybody else was doing."[40] The first play produced in Cleveland, Tennessee, was Shakespeare's *Hamlet* on October 20, 1933, and was directed by Bob Jones Jr.[41]

Performances of the Classic Players were compared favorably in the press with those of professional touring companies[42] and with only one exception, the Cleveland and Chattanooga critics who reviewed the plays pronounced them "triumphs," "amazingly fine in acting, setting, costuming and stage management."[43] The Classic Players was hailed as unique and peerless—the only college company specializing in Shakespeare in the country.[44] The Players gained a good bit of notice for the College in the *Shakespeare Association Bulletin,* which called the group "young, enthusiastic, intelligent, and flexible . . . under the stimulating guidance of Bob Jones, Jr."[45]

In Florida, the Classic Players' repertoire included only five Shakespearean plays: *The Merchant of Venice, Hamlet, Othello, The Taming of the Shrew,* and *Macbeth.* In Cleveland, the Players performed these five plays but expanded their repertoire to include *King Lear, Henry V, The Tempest, Twelfth Night, Henry IV, Richard II, Julius Caesar, As You Like It, The Comedy of Errors, Romeo and Juliet, Much Ado About Nothing*, and *The Winter's Tale*. In all of these, with the exception of *Romeo, Julius Caesar, Twelfth Night*, and *The Winter's Tale*, Bob Jones Jr. played the male lead.

During the Cleveland years the troupe also played regularly in Chattanooga, Tennessee, and Dalton, Georgia; the group was scheduled to perform at a convention of the Southern Association of Teachers of Speech in Chattanooga when World War II intervened.[46]

The promotion of drama at Bob Jones College was, as stated earlier, problematic for many Fundamentalists. Many believed that drama eroded the spiritual sensitivity or receptivity of the American people. They felt that any activity or entertainment where wrong was "gilded over with wit, humor and beauty," which drew attention away from the "basic problem of individual sin," or which appealed to the "lower instincts of the race, rather than to its higher and nobler ideals" was immoral.[47] Christians attributed much of the "general decadence" found in American society to the theater, its supporters, the amorality of its actors and actresses, and the "theater trust."[48] Bob Jones Sr.'s friend, John Roach Straton, pastor of Calvary Baptist Church in New York City, described the theater as "sordid commercialism . . . awful iniquity" and a "violation of the highest and most sacred laws of God." He described those who made their career on the stage as "brazen licentiates . . . often the mothers of illegitimate children and scoffers at the things that are holy and pure!" and "the very embodiment of the worst destructive tendencies of our civilization."[49] Most Fundamentalist leaders feared that young people would seek a career on the stage if exposed to its glamour and fame.[50]

Accordingly, Dr. Jones Sr. was hesitant to produce Shakespeare, let alone modern drama—even the light comic plays that were performed in the first two years of the school. As an observer of American culture, he sensed the direction that modern drama would move and knew that it could become deleterious in the lives of young people.[51] Bob Jones Jr. was "always pushing for the drama," however, and persuaded his father to allow Shakespeare and the classics.[52]

The move into Shakespearean drama was a major decision for Bob Jones Sr. "We decided to major in Shakespeare and the classics for two very important reasons," Bob Jones Jr. wrote, "the first being their substance and quality and the second . . . being that we felt people could hardly legitimately criticize the presentation of great and highly moral dramas on the stage when they have been consistently studied in the classroom for several hundred years."[53] Shakespeare, he said, gives helpful insight into the thought processes and nature of man.[54] He has also stated that "Shakespeare is the most lofty of dramatists. His great characters are larger than life but drawn from a deep insight of life. He is the most moral of playwrights. His lines may be sometimes blunt and unrefined, but he is never obscene. His spiritual vision and understanding never permit him to make vice attractive. No sin goes unpunished, and vice is always the object of judgment."[55] Because of these values, Bob Jones Sr. encouraged the ministerial students and others to involve themselves in the Classic Players.

Bob Jones College went against the grain when it began the Classic Players in 1929. Although there was no outcry of indignation against the College for performing the secular dramas mentioned previously or for performing short religious plays at Vespers, when the Classic Players was formed to do Shakespeare, pious religious critics attacked the school for its worldly amusements.[56] Bob Jones Jr. wrote, "We were criticized more for presenting Shakespeare than for anything else."[57]

Another concern that Dr. Jones Sr. registered was that an overemphasis on dramatic activity, or any activity, could ultimately subvert the Christian standards on which the College was founded and change the direction he intended the College to go.[58] He came to believe, however, that in addition to the dramatic substance, literary quality, and educational value that the plays offered, drama gave young preachers the opportunity to learn a sense of dramatic timing, poetic expression, and something about "putting over the message." He felt that "our young ministerial students preach better sermons when they have been playing Shakespeare."[59] He also came to believe that the act of simply viewing Shakespeare was cultural in itself.[60]

In 1933, as another approach to culture at the College, Bob Jones Jr. organized an annual lecture series for the student body and the town of Cleveland, which continued until the College left Tennessee. Among those brought to the College were Major W. H. Drane, assistant director of the Federal Bureau of Investigation;[61] Ruth Bryan Owen, U.S. minister to Denmark and the daughter of William Jennings Bryan;[62] explorer Von Wormer Walsh;[63] Cornelius Vanderbilt Jr.;[64] and world-traveler Richard Halliburton.[65]

In 1934, in another first for the Cleveland area, the Music Department formed its first real orchestra for the College's presentation of Handel's *Messiah*.[66] After this, the orchestra rehearsed regularly and appeared on Vespers programs and in other programs and Music Department recitals.[67]

Bob Jones Jr. was responsible for developing what came to be called "Artist Series"—a concert and drama series that brought professional performers to the College and to Cleveland, Tennessee.[68] The initial budget for Artist Series at the College was fifteen hundred dollars and was supplied by student fees.[69] The first appearance by a guest performer was on February 6, 1934, when V. L. Granville, an English actor, presented a program of dramatic monologues.[70] Other early performers included the Davies Light Opera Singers[71] and Fernanda Doria, mezzo-soprano of the Chicago Civic Opera.[72]

Bob Jones Jr. selected and booked these programs but initially "borrowed the brains" of a program director involved in Chautauqua programs with the Florida Forum and Assembly at Daytona Beach.[73] The latter suggested securing artists with "a Radio following" to attract big crowds, because "people will pay money to see someone like Nelson Eddy . . . but they will not pay to hear artists who are not well-known."[74] For the first season, Bob Jones Jr. booked a piano trio, a well-known actor, a concert violinist, a group of Russian singers, and actress Cornelia Otis Skinner.[75] He also gave his one-man show, "Curtain Calls," each year from 1933 through 1945 as part of the Artist Series season. Though large state universities had concert series in the 1930s and 1940s, no other Christian college had a regular drama, lecture, or concert series at this time.[76]

Opera had been a love of Bob Jones Jr. since his boyhood, and even his evangelist father had occasionally attended operatic performances in major cities. Recognizing its benefits, he went along with his son's plan to bring opera to Tennessee. The first attempt to bring fully staged opera came in 1938 as part of the Artist Series programs, but the attempt ended in failure. Opera-on-Tour, a troupe of forty-three singers, was scheduled to appear on November 12, 1938, in a fully staged production of Gounod's *Faust*. The singers were accompanied by long-play recordings made by the London Philharmonic under Sir Thomas Beacham, but after the troupe began its tour, a strike was called by the Musicians' and Stagehandlers' Unions because of the use of prerecorded sound. The production was unable to strike and load its sets from a performance in Nashville, causing the Bob Jones College performance—"the first grand opera in this section"—to be canceled.[77] It was not until 1942 that grand opera was again attempted at the College. Only a small number of universities were producing opera in the 1940s, and no other Christian schools were presenting opera at all.[78]

Bob Jones Jr. was the moving force behind the Opera Association—a passion of his second only to his love of Shakespeare. During his national and international travels, Bob Jones Jr. took every available opportunity to attend operas and to make the acquaintance of many singers and managers.[79] To Bob Jones Jr. opera was the ultimate fusion of the arts, bringing "together all of the [arts] that represent culture in one fell swoop . . . the orchestra, the drama, the music, the vocal, the whole business."[80]

On May 8, 1942, Gounod's *Faust* was finally staged in Cleveland with a

Final bows from *Faust* by Charles Gounod (Bob Jones University Opera Association, May 1942); *left to right:* John Dudley (?), Oliver Steiner, Hilda Burke, Bob Jones Jr., Norman Condon

cast of Bob Jones College students and guest artists from the Metropolitan Opera.[81] Little is known about this first performance, except that it was conducted by Oliver Steiner, a music teacher at the College who had no previous experience in instrumental conducting, let alone opera. Among the artists that first year were two outstanding voices: soprano Hilda Burke as Marguerite and the renowned bass Norman Condon as Mephistopheles.[82] When the singers arrived from New York, one day was spent in piano rehearsal, another was spent with the orchestra and singers in a stage rehearsal, and the third was the day of the performance.[83]

The orchestra at this time was small—thirty to thirty-five pieces—and had an unbalanced instrumentation. To fill in missing voices, a Hammond novachord was used. Participants in this performance recalled that there were no breakdowns and that the performance went so well a second opera was scheduled for December of 1942.[84] This first performance reportedly made a great impression on the students, many of whom had grown up listening to Texaco's Saturday afternoon Metropolitan Opera broadcasts. Most, however, had never actually seen an opera and had mixed feelings about the experience.[85] The performance of *Faust* apparently made an impression on the Cleveland community as well.[86]

Aida by Giuseppe Verdi (Bob Jones University Opera Association, December 11, 1943)

Oliver Steiner conducted two more productions at the College: *Il Trovatore* (1942) and *Aida* (1943).[87] *Aida* was heralded as a "big hit" and a "great success,"[88] and the *Opera News* reported the Bob Jones Opera Association production by saying,

> Frederick Jagel's recent impersonation of Verdi's warlike hero at Bob Jones College, Cleveland, Tennessee, was no pinch hit. Indeed it was the climax of the season for the dozens of students who sang with him, the inspiration of the young men and women who will henceforth boast of how they shared the stage with a Metropolitan star.
>
> In May 1942, Dr. Bob Jones Jr. decided to invite a few leading artists of the Metropolitan to sing the chief roles of Gounod's "Faust" in a college production. Scenery and costumes, chorus and orchestra were all homemade. The success of "Faust" was so great that "Trovatore" was staged just a year ago, with the help of Doris Doe, John Gurney, and others.

Encouraged by the enthusiasm with which these masterpieces were received, "Aida" was chosen for the Pre-Christmas Festival this year and a distinguished group of principals invited to participate. These included two former Metropolitan Opera Auditionists of the Air. . . . A recent letter from the Cleveland, Tennessee, college states that the triumphal scene is to be repeated at Commencement, while the "Barber of Seville" is planned for March with an all-student cast.[89]

The fourth production, *Rigoletto,* was conducted by Karl Keefer, whom Bob Jones Jr. had sent to the Cincinnati Conservatory for a summer session in orchestral conducting. Jones Jr. expressly requested Keefer to attend rehearsals and performances of the famed Cincinnati Zoo Opera to learn as much as possible about opera production. While in Cincinnati, Keefer was able to observe Sir Thomas Beacham, as well as other top rank conductors, both in rehearsal and in performance. Back in Cleveland, Keefer conducted *Rigoletto* and the Verdi *Requiem* later that same year.[90]

Generally, the guest artists were contracted to sing both an oratorio and the scheduled opera. The two performances were separated by only one day, which was spent in rehearsal; often, however, the performances were actually scheduled on consecutive days.[91] Most of the guest artists were from the Metropolitan, the Chicago Civic, the San Francisco Opera, or other American or European opera companies.[92] Most were genuinely supportive of the school's attempts to stage grand opera, and the performances were considered well done from the standpoint of the student orchestra, sets, costuming, and staging. The problems that did develop were nearly always with the guest singers, although most were helpful and truly desired to see the Opera Association succeed.

Karl Keefer recalled that during his first opera conducting assignment, Robert Weede, a big star in those days, was giving him problems in rehearsal, demanding that things be done in certain ways. When Dr. Jones Sr. "got wind of what was going on," he came and sat in rehearsal to give Keefer "moral fortitude." After the rehearsal, Dr. Jones made a comment to Keefer "which was intended to say, 'Don't pay any attention to him and all his airs.' "[93]

The Opera Association revived one seldom performed opera, Verdi's *Ernani,* which they sang in English. The performance, the first in America since 1928, was met with mixed reviews.

Doris Doree . . . who has distinguished herself in recent years by her outstanding performances of seldom-done roles, added another success to her list of achievements in the part of Elvira. . . . [She] showed herself a master of her art and gave a convincing performance in this difficult part. Arthur Tree sang the tenor lead as Ernani, doing a very creditable job vocally. Unfortunately his poor acting detracted from the effectiveness of his singing. . . . Nino Ruisi, basso, was cast as Silva. It is to be regretted that Mr. Ruisi's fine vocal abilities were marred by the fact that he did not seem to know his part very well, or rather badly bungled several important cues.[94]

As with Shakespeare's plays, the opera librettos were occasionally edited not only for length but also so that the opera would not present situations antithetical to the Christian position of the school. Bob Jones Jr. selected the opera repertoire, requiring that each one teach a strong moral lesson, have beautiful music and a good story line, and provide interest to the young audience for whom the performances were intended. He commented that "what we try to do is get operas where the story is not bad, and that is very hard in opera."[95]

As previously mentioned, the College also included performances of oratorios as part of the Artist Series, beginning with the first *Messiah* performance on January 26, 1933.[96] The *Messiah* was sung almost yearly in Cleveland, beginning in 1937, with other large choral works such as the Verdi *Requiem,* the Bach *St. Matthew's Passion,* the Rossini *Stabat Mater,* and the Brahms *German Requiem* substituted occasionally.[97]

The cultural offerings of Bob Jones College were particularly striking for a mountain town in Tennessee. They clearly showcased the philosophy of Dr. Jones Sr. and one mission of the College. He said, "This institution has stood for refinement. That is one emphasis of this school—the emphasis on the fine arts mixed with everything else. Any of these things left alone would not be sufficient. The Gospel: all right. Discipline: all right. Good academic work: all right. Hard study: all right. The fine arts . . . scrambled in with everything else we have here is one of the most wonderful things that ever happened for the training of young people."[98]

The cultural program of Bob Jones College sought to combine selected artistic elements of the fine arts with personal discipline, refinement, and academics, in order to send out students who would make a spiritual impact for Christ on society.

CHAPTER 9

♦

Closing the Book on Cleveland

World War II reached Cleveland, Tennessee, on December 15, 1941, eight days after the Japanese bombed Pearl Harbor—a civil defense blackout was declared that night at 7:00 P.M. Promptly at 8:30 P.M., however, Sydney Montague of the Royal Canadian Mounted Police began a lecture at Bob Jones College as part of its Pre-Christmas Festival just as scheduled.[1]

With war came interruptions to the routines of campus life. Teachers had to substitute for other teachers who were drafted.[2] Many students were drafted or joined up to fight. In October 1943 the campus newsletter reported that 215 former students were serving in the military. By April 1944 that number had grown to over 250.[3] Chapel programs were occasionally given over to war news in order to keep the students abreast of the international situation.[4] A prayer meeting for the war effort and for the BJC students who were serving was held daily at 12:15 P.M.

The war brought hardship and challenge to the College, just as it did to the rest of the country. Everything of any worth was rationed—clothing, gasoline, tires, tools, sugar, coffee—anything and everything seemed to be obtainable only with a coupon. "Shoes are rationed!!! Coupon #17. Good for one pair until June 15," one faculty member recorded.[5] Students, faculty, and administrators wept over the Allied armies' defeats as well as over their victories. One faculty diarist recorded that the "Fifth Army is having a tough time in beach head south of Rome. Gen. Clark feels that victory toward Rome will come soon"; and that "MacArthur's Troops Landed on Leyte in the Philippine Islands. 250,000 landed on invasion." He exulted when "Gen. Patton's Third Army crossed the Rhine."[6] Finally, the frightening news came through that the "ATOMIC BOMB FALLS ON HIROSHIMA! WIPES OUT MOST OF CITY."[7] Eight days later, Japan surrendered and joined the other Axis powers in defeat. America rejoiced. The College held a day of prayer. The boys could now come home.

American colleges lost numbers of the young men to the war effort, and Bob Jones College was no exception. Campus records, however, show only nine fatalities among former students, with many more wounded in action.[8] As Christian young men, they went off to war for the cause of human freedom; yet while fighting human enemies, they also fought spiritual battles for the souls of men. Many hundreds of young men and women in the armed services were brought to Christ as a result of the Christian witness of Bob Jones College boys who had learned how "to shoot the gospel gun" at BJC.[9]

Those who died for country were memorialized and many of those who lived through the campaigns of the war returned to Cleveland to study.

Through World War II the College was able to sustain its growth in the student body, soon becoming the largest liberal arts college in Tennessee. Because of its crowded conditions, Bob Jones College was able to obtain permits, find building materials, and erect new buildings each year in spite of the war and the government's general ban on construction.[10] To do so required creative thinking and quick action, but R. K. Johnson and Dr. Jones Sr. generally got what they asked for. In one instance, they appeared before the War Production Board in Chattanooga, who referred them to the Knoxville office, who sent them to Atlanta, who suggested they go to Washington, D.C., for permission to purchase needed building materials. The permissions were obtained one week after the first meeting in Chattanooga.[11]

In one instance, because of War Production Board regulations, R. K. Johnson was unable to find timbers of the correct sizes already cut at area sawmills, and a lumber company which had the correct sizes in stock could not sell them because of the regulations. Johnson, however, was able to "borrow" the timbers, critical to the building program, and repaid the "loan" thirty days later.[12] Later in the war years, War Production Board regulations prohibited all building except with timber from one's own land. The school was able to purchase several pieces of choice timberland which thereafter provided all the board feet for building.[13]

By 1944 the College's facilities included twenty-five buildings.[14] By 1946 twenty-seven buildings were in use,[15] and the campus had a book value of $2,242,000.[16]

As Table 1 below shows, the student body continued to swell, with the College having only one "down" year in enrollment. During the war years it was not unusual for enrollment actually to increase for the second semester. In fact, in 1944, thirty students left the College after first semester but more than one hundred new students enrolled. In 1946, new students swelled the second semester enrollment by 240![17]

During the war, Christmas vacations, which in the late

Bob Jones College, Cleveland, Tennessee (1946)

1930s had run from mid-December through mid-January, were shortened to a four-day break or canceled altogether.[18] Because military personnel generally filled the trains and buses, civilian travel was extremely difficult to the point that it was nearly impossible for students to reach home during a two- or three-week break. Even with the hardships of war and world uncertainty, students came to Bob Jones College in increasing numbers, and after the war the College's growth accelerated.

Table 1

First Semester Enrollment Bob Jones College & Academy, 1933-47[19]

Year	College	Academy	Grad./Spec.	Total
1933-34	NA	NA	0	NA
1934-35	158	52	0	210
1935-36	214	56	15	270
1936-37	233	82	21	315
1937-38	335	65	0	400
1938-39	383	61	0	444
1939-40	416	76	0	492
1940-41	433	64	0	497
1941-42	455	85	0	540
1942-43	563	97	6	666
1943-44	543	249	28	820
1944-45	672	279	40	991
1945-46	915	311	38	1264
1946-47	1581	216	65	1861

Thousands of GIs returned stateside with the promise of a college education paid for by Uncle Sam through the GI Bill of Rights.[20] Known formally as the Servicemen's Readjustment Act of 1944, the GI Bill included job placement services, unemployment benefits, mortgage guarantees, and educational benefits for each veteran who applied. In education, the bill subsidized tuition, books, and fees, and provided a subsistence allowance, paid directly to the veteran.[21] The effect of the bill, originally framed to placate veterans' groups and to minimize the effects of joblessness and economic distress caused by rapid demobilization, surprised both the Veterans' Administration and the country's educators.[22]

They believed that only a small number of GIs would take advantage of the education provisions. Yet 88,000 troops entered American colleges in 1944, and by 1946 the number had swelled to 1,013,000 veterans, all enjoying the education benefits of the GI Bill. Every college was transformed in some way by the servicemen. Quonset huts and portable barracks sprouted to house the students and, in some cases, their spouses. Many colleges doubled their enrollment, college rules were rewritten to reflect the veterans' seriousness and discipline, "classes were jammed, [and] facilities were strained beyond capacity. . . . Somehow, everyone took the situation in stride."[23]

The end of the war also brought a new reality to bear on the American psyche: it was now noted that racism was deeply embedded in American life and law. This racism was not only of the de jure type lived in the South but also the de facto racism of the Northeast, Midwest, and far West. Military service, which was nearly universally segregated, and wartime indoctrination against fascist and communist ideologies brought the beginnings of "a new consciousness, a new willingness" on the part of black Americans, "to insist that [American] society make real the promises of its democratic creed."[24] Having taken root shortly before the war under the aegis of liberal church leaders such as Reinhold Niebuhr and "Christian radicals" such as Buck Kester (who promoted the idea that the South's religious conservatism was the greatest threat to social justice, and that "no alteration or amelioration of social conditions" was possible until "the basic religious pattern has been radically and fundamentally changed"), the racial equality movement was slowly growing in the South.[25] The movement's "new consciousness" eventually was embraced by southern religious liberals and later grew into the Civil Rights movement of the 1960s.

Bob Jones College was affected by the influx of veterans, the slowly changing attitudes, and the laws that controlled the southern racial ethic.[26] Requests for admission by black students were answered promptly, but in the negative.[27]

In 1943 the Bob Jones College campus facilities were full. By 1945, with an increasing number of veterans, the campus was bursting at the seams. By 1946 the size of the College brought unique problems. Rising bell was at 6:00 A.M. so that everyone could be fed at the required breakfast meal. Attendance at all meals was required, even though it took three shifts to feed everyone. Classes began at 7:00 A.M. and continued until 8:00 P.M. Chapel was required of all, and the students rotated their seating so that each one sat in the auditorium once a week. There had to be two church services and two Vespers services on Sunday, and Artist Series programs and lectures had to be held for two nights.[28] Something had to be done to house single students, newly married GIs, and faculty as well.[29] The needs were acute. Dr. Jones Sr. called the government Home Preparedness Office and asked for help in housing students.[30] Shortly thereafter, R. K. Johnson was sent to Atlanta. He recalled that

> Dr. Bob had taught me not to ask for anything to which we were not entitled; but if we were entitled to it, then I must never stop until we got what we went after. This advice has paid off well many times. The Lord prepared the way again, and we found the government men cordial and

cooperative. They told us that they had many trailers at Oak Ridge, Tennessee, that were not in use and that we could have fifty of these trailers if we would move them. The second semester was beginning in less than three weeks, and we had many new students coming with no place to put them. I thanked the men and told them I would be in Oak Ridge the next morning.

It snowed several inches during the night and everything seemed to go wrong, but the hard trip was worth the effort. The men at Oak Ridge picked out fifty of their best trailers, tagging them "Bob Jones"; and then they helped fill out the necessary papers for the release. I left Oak Ridge rejoicing, thanking the Lord, and promising the men that we would start moving the trailers the next day. Bad weather set in. . . . [We] had every trouble imaginable—they broke axles, bogged down in the mud. . . . To set the trailers on their foundations and install water, sewerage, lights, and heat, we had to crawl in mud. But God was with us and we were ready for the extra students when they arrived for the second semester.[31]

Trailer housing in Cleveland, Tennessee (1946)

The trailers were placed on a lot owned by the College and also covered half the athletic field.[32] By February 2, 1946, the trailers were in place, crews of students and faculty had made the necessary connections and adjustments to each unit, concrete sidewalks were poured, and landscaping was underway.[33]

The federal government also agreed to lease to the College seven barracks-style housing units which were available from the Army Air Corps Base at Tullahoma, Tennessee.[34] The College acquired these units, probably in late 1945, and brought them to Cleveland where they were rebuilt on land leased from the Church of God, whose national headquarters were in Cleveland. In early 1946 Bob Jones Sr. and business manager R. K. Johnson went to the housing site to check on the progress and, on a whim, decided to visit the office of Reverend John C. Jernigan, the General Overseer of the Church of God. Unknown to Dr. Jones, the leadership of the Church of God wanted to consolidate its national headquarters, its college, and its publishing house in the same city and were considering Cleveland for the location. During this informal visit Jernigan casually offered to buy the Bob Jones College campus in an offhand comment that Dr. Jones took as a joke.[35]

On February 26, 1946, an official delegation from the Church of God contacted Dr. Jones Sr., inquired about his decision regarding the sale of the campus, and officially tendered an offer of $1.5 million for the campus.[36] Now realizing that the offer to purchase the campus was a serious one, the President agreed to call a special meeting of the Board of Trustees on April 4, 1946, to consider the delegation's offer.

With 1946 came seemingly un-limited prospects for spreading the gospel. Calls for missionaries over-seas and a renewed interest in Chris-tian ministry at home accompanied the postwar explosion of college-bound young men and women. To evangelize these men and women, numerous organizations, some of which began during the war, began aggressive ministries. These in-cluded Word of Life, headed by Jack Wyrtzen; Inter-Varsity Christian Fel-lowship; the Navigators; Youth For Christ International, headed by Tor-rey Johnson; Campus Crusade for Christ led by Bill Bright; and others. Most of these groups had wide sup-port on the Bob Jones College cam-pus and many BJC graduates went

Gilbert Stenholm (ca. 1946)

into Christian service with these organizations.[37] Bob Jones Sr., Bob Jones Jr., Gilbert Stenholm (the head of Ministerial Training at BJC), and Monroe Parker traveled extensively in the postwar years speaking at youth rallies and areawide campaigns and serving on the cooperating boards of these organizations.[38] Involvement in these youth activities gave the College great visibility among American young people and attracted a large number of students to the school.[39]

Before the summer of 1946 ended, more than two thousand students, many of them veterans, had to be turned away from Bob Jones College.[40] There was simply not enough room for them. The time for decision had arrived: the school could either participate in the GI educational boom by expanding or else turn away hundreds of students, limiting its size to the existing buildings.[41]

Beginning in 1935 or 1936 the school had followed the advice of J. S. Mack and had quietly but systematically purchased houses and lots in the vicinity of the campus as they became available. By 1945 attempts by the College to purchase more land met with strong resistance and outrageous prices from the owners. The faculty were apprised of the situation and asked to pray for a solution to the problems facing the school. Dr. Jones Sr., in requesting prayer from the faculty, said, "There is only one thing that we are praying for, and that is that we will please God in what we do."[42] The school was hemmed in on all sides by houses, and expansion was impossible. Dr. Jones Sr. wrote, "We are congested beyond endurance."[43]

If the school were to remain in Cleveland, more land had to be purchased. In late February or early March, the College administration and the Cleveland Chamber of Commerce launched a campaign to persuade nearby property owners to sell their land to the school. The campaign brought to the surface long-held animosities by some owners. After what Bob Jones had done for the Centenary property and for the town, "wouldn't you think that all the neighbors around here would be for the college?" the school's banker asked.[44]

The animosities seemed to be centered on three themes: congestion and traffic caused by students and faculty; a property tax exemption enjoyed by the College; and antagonism toward the religious and discipline standards of the school.[45] Bob Jones Sr. went on the radio to defend the school and to appeal to the citizens of Cleveland for help in solving the impasse.[46]

The fact was that Bob Jones College had put Cleveland, Tennessee, on the map in American educational and religious circles, and the whole region

The Cleveland campus "congested beyond endurance"

had begun to prosper as a result of the College.[47] Nevertheless, some neighbors of the school were unwilling to sell to meet the needs of the College.

There are three explanations for this reticence to sell. For some, it was a sentimental decision to not sell the "old family home." For others, the decision would mean moving out and rebuilding, a difficult prospect when building materials were still controlled by the government and permits for new construction were still difficult to obtain. A third explanation is the residents' business sense—they simply wanted to hold out for the highest possible dollar.

Three key pieces of property were needed by BJC if the College were to continue in Cleveland. The school offered one man two thousand dollars more than his lot was worth, but he refused several offers—that is, until the school later announced its intentions to move. One vital piece of land was owned by a widow and situated across from Victory Hall, one of the men's dormitories. Three appraisers evaluated the property and the highest appraisal came in at $28,000. The widow and her sons refused to sell for anything less than $56,000. Another piece of land—eight acres—was needed for a new athletic field since the old field now had trailers on it and was needed for construction. The owner refused to negotiate, arguing that the school's leaders were "bluffing" about leaving just to get his property. Members of the chamber of commerce, the mayor, and a board member called on the man and asked him to reconsider. "All right," he replied. "If they pay me $40,000 they can have it."[48] The prices were too high for the College to pay.[49]

The Cleveland newspaper, the *Daily Banner,* proposed establishing a fund, made up of citizens' donations, to be used by the College to pay the inflated price of the needed land. The paper, defending the wounded honor of the town and the integrity of its citizenry after Dr. Bob's radio speech, published a rebuttal explaining that the College "had been hampered in its expansion program because of unanticipated advances in real estate values." The paper claimed that this was a "perfectly normal" postwar occurrence and that the prices were equivalent to those in other Tennessee cities. The city, it continued, could not be blamed for the College's "lack of foresight and planning."[50]

To Dr. Jones Jr. these arguments were "nonsense." The war had ended some months earlier and life was becoming more normal. Real estate prices were considerably higher in Cleveland, especially around the College, than in any town, North or South, that Dr. Jones Sr. had investigated.[51] (Real estate values plummeted after the College announced its decision to move, thus leaving no doubt as to the truth of the Joneses' statements.)[52] As one World War II veteran put it, "Dr. Bob is considering leaving because he has no room to expand, which shows only one thing: that Cleveland has failed to keep pace with the progress of the school. This hurts more than losing the college!"[53]

The *Chattanooga Times,* reporting the move of the College, quoted Bob Jones Sr. as saying,

> I, personally, am willing to recommend the plan which could be carried out successfully in Cleveland if the citizens of the community will give satisfactory cooperation. . . .

> Personally, we would like to carry on our work here and have a real part in the material, cultural, social and spiritual upbuilding of the city and surrounding territory, but my conscience will not permit us for lack of accommodations to turn away hundreds of young people from the best families . . . who wish to get their education in the atmosphere of Christian culture which Bob Jones College offers.[54]

In the March 26 chapel service Dr. Jones Sr. implied that "we would move from Cleveland." When Dr. Jones at a later date announced that the College was definitely leaving Cleveland, one student recalled that "he never heard a more explosive roar in his life." In the eyes of this student, wherever the school located, it had to be better than Cleveland.[55] Later that day, Dr. Jones flew to Orlando, Florida, to meet with a delegation about moving the school there. Two days later, on March 28, the President flew to Asheville, North Carolina, to meet with their delegation.[56]

On Sunday, March 31, Dr. Jones made a formal statement about the College's remaining in Cleveland. He said,

> We have studied this expansion thing, and the college has money to expand but it does not have the money to pay the prices which the property holders near the college want for their property. . . .

> We want to settle this expansion problem once and for all. We do not want to be hemmed in here when we add buildings in the future.

> If we can buy the property at reasonable prices I will recommend to the board of trustees to stay in Cleveland. . . . If we can't get co-operation in our expansion program, we will be forced to move. It's God's business and not mine.[57]

"Cleveland Has 3 Days to Save Jones College," reported the *Daily Banner.* An ultimatum had been delivered: "The college president in an 'open letter' address on [radio station] WBAC at 5:30 P.M. to Cleveland said residential neighbors of the college will be asked to quote prices on their property for consideration of the Board of Trustees. If the college finds its expansion program too costly, it will leave Cleveland, he said."[58] Many in town considered the announcement a ploy.

Sensing that the April 4 board meeting was of great importance, many members traveled considerable distances to be in attendance. One member from California wrote, "Faced by the fact of phenomenal success in its present location, the board moved slowly. I doubt if a member present wanted a change. But that board faced a great necessity."[59] The board asked Dr. Jones for his recommendation. "I don't have any recommendation to make," he responded. "It will suit me just fine if you keep [the college] just like it is. It would be easier on us. We don't think we want any bigger job than we have. . . . You do what you want to do."[60]

Several board members arrived with their minds made up and "came to the meeting to get the school moving."[61] At the four-hour session, an eightfold resolution was passed unanimously. In it, the board unitedly resolved to authorize a special committee to relocate the school to a suitable locale if land in Cleveland could not be obtained; authorized "Bob Jones College [to] expand into a Christian university"; and directed that "its name be changed to Bob Jones University." The resolution also called for the new university to be planned to accommodate "a minimum" of three thousand students and to emphasize the areas of "the fine arts, the Bible, missions, evangelism, pastoral training, history, journalism, education, Christian education, theology, international relations, the social sciences, and languages, both ancient and modern."[62]

The meeting ended in a season of tears, praise, thanksgiving, and prayer for guidance and blessing, and the board offered the Cleveland campus to the Church of God for $1.75 million, unless the College could conclude agreements for the needed properties in Cleveland.

The Church of God leadership considered their position and the College's offer. They held to their offer of $1.5 million. The Expansion Committee accepted it and the board approved. A tentative timetable was discussed and agreement was reached that Bob Jones College would begin the 1947 school year elsewhere. If unable to vacate by the agreed date, the College was to pay one thousand dollars a week to the Church of God for the use of the property until the College could move into its new plant.

The Expansion Committee had several criteria for selecting a new home for the school. First, the new location must provide the opportunity to expand so as to avoid a repetition of the Cleveland expansion problems. Second, the new home must offer "the best spiritual, cultural, and financial support" and building materials must be readily available. Third, Dr. Jones Sr. wanted to occupy the new facilities for the 1947-48 school year—seventeen months in the future.

Special prayer meetings were held asking for God's guidance, the news was carried by the national wire services, and offers to the College poured in from across the country: Chattanooga; Atlanta; Hendersonville, North Carolina; Asheville, North Carolina; Detroit; Boston; Kansas City, Missouri; Orlando; and Knoxville. Of all these offers, those from Orlando and Knoxville were most appealing.[63]

Kansas City, Detroit, and Boston each offered the school excellent opportunities for expansion and a "big city" environment that was culturally attractive. A Christian organization in New England offered to purchase twelve hundred acres of land outside Boston for the school. Kansas City, Missouri, at the encouragement of Dr. Walter Wilson, offered a city park; Detroit offered a vacant estate. The size of the offers were overwhelming, but Dr. Jones Sr. felt that each location had definite drawbacks: Kansas City and Boston both had few strong churches; therefore, ministry opportunities for students would be limited. The Northeast was also generally less conservative than the South, and Boston's location would have made transportation inconvenient for the majority of the student body. Detroit was eliminated, as were Boston and Kansas City, because Dr. Jones Sr. felt the school should remain in the South.[64]

Besides Orlando and Knoxville, serious consideration was given to Chattanooga, Atlanta, Hendersonville, and Asheville. Chattanooga offered a quick move with relatively few complications, and friends there offered to buy the land for the school's relocation. Atlanta offered a tract of land in Marietta, Georgia, and both Asheville and Hendersonville sent delegations to Cleveland to meet with the Expansion Committee. Their enthusiasm was impressive, but the committee simply did not feel that the Lord was leading to any of these locations.[65]

Orlando offered $1.15 million in financial aid plus an old air base if the school would locate there. A Florida construction company offered to purchase one million dollars of development bonds as incentive for the committee to select Florida.[66]

Knoxville offered three hundred acres of land for $100,000 which a friend of the school offered to purchase if the school would stay in Tennessee. Educators from the University of Tennessee also encouraged the College to remain in the state and were anxious to have the College close to its Knoxville campus.[67]

Each offer was accompanied by opposition from local ministers. "Everywhere we had an invitation to go," Dr. Jones reported, "there was some preacher that opposed us. The only people that opposed Bob Jones College when we were moving were preachers. The businessmen were for us. The [educators] were for us. They said, 'we know how you stand, we know what you believe and we're sympathetic.' "[68]

Within days of the board's announcement on April 4, the Expansion Committee—Dr. Jones Sr., Dr. Jones Jr., and R. K. Johnson—had eliminated the two original candidate cities. It is reported that Orlando was eliminated because the city was unable to guarantee the needed land options prior to an agreed-upon date. Orlando also was considered too far south for the school's constituency.[69] Asheville was eliminated because a group of local ministers made it clear through newspaper advertisements, sermons, and gossip that they would fight every aspect of bringing the school to the area and that the new Bob Jones University would be unwelcome in their community because of its Fundamentalist theology.[70]

After visiting sites in Florida, Georgia, North Carolina, and Tennessee, and after much prayer, the committee reached an agreement: Knoxville, Tennessee, would be the new home of Bob Jones University. Dr. Jones Sr. told the *Daily Banner,* "I am convinced that we are going to stay in eastern Tennessee; I think you can put it down unequivocally that we will move to Knoxville."[71]

Gradually, the magnitude of its loss dawned on Cleveland, and the city fathers scrambled to turn the tide. H. B. Carter, president of the Cleveland Chamber of Commerce, organized a last-ditch effort on behalf of the school and "a group [of] Cleveland business men came out forty strong to see what could be done to get B.J.C. to stay. They unanimously voted to do their best, but were not too emphatic."[72] The group raised only twelve hundred dollars. One owner of property needed by the school for expansion even contacted the school offering a lower, but still outrageous, price for his land.

Summing up the situation by comparing the city to a freight train, Cleveland Mayor Willard J. Parks said, "We regret that we are going to lose this college for it has done a great deal for our city. . . . The only friction that the institution has ever caused is the same friction which a stream-lined modern train making a hundred miles an hour produces when it passes a freight train making fifteen miles an hour."[73]

CHAPTER 10

◆

Miracles, Pressed Together

As far as Dr. Jones and the members of the Expansion Committee were concerned, Knoxville, Tennessee, would be the new home of Bob Jones University. On Thursday, April 18, 1946, Bob Jones Sr. and R. K. Johnson arrived in Knoxville to work out the final details, with "enough money in their pockets" to purchase the land. While completing the papers, the woman who owned the land stated reservations about selling, because it was "hard to give up land that has been in the family for many years." Johnson was eager to close the deal and responded impatiently, "I cannot understand this; you knew this was inevitable. I have been up here many times working out the plans." Dr. Bob interrupted him and said, "Lefty, do not coerce. If the Lord is in this, the plans can be worked out satisfactorily; if not, He must have some other plan for us."[1]

Sometime between March 26 and March 31, a junior music major from Greenville, South Carolina, ended a letter to her parents with a postscript. "By the way, the college is considering a move," Martha Stone wrote. "Maybe it could come to Greenville?"[2] That innocent postscript motivated her father, E. Roy Stone, an "aggressive" realtor in Greenville, to take action.[3]

The Stones' first acquaintance with the College extended back to the early 1940s when Clifford Lewis, a Bob Jones College graduate, had organized a Greenville chapter of the Young People's Fellowship Club, the youth organization founded by Dr. Jones in 1933. Stone and his children were so impressed with Lewis and the other Bob Jones College students who helped in the club that in 1943 Norwood Stone enrolled at Bob Jones and Martha soon followed.[4] Mr. Stone was therefore familiar with the College and its standards, and he recognized the asset the school would be to Greenville.[5] Between late March when he received Martha's letter and April 18, Stone worked diligently.

On April 4, following the meeting of the College Board of Trustees, the proposed move of Bob Jones College was carried by the national news wire services and created great interest. After reading the news report that confirmed the move of the College, Stone wrote Dr. Jones Sr. enumerating Greenville's advantages as a new location for the school. "Greenville is located in the heart of the so-called Bible Belt," Stone wrote. It "is in healthful surroundings and has excellent transportation." The city desired to become a cultural center, and the College would help achieve that goal. Not to be overlooked, he continued, was that the Greenville area, with nearly three million people within a one-hundred-mile radius, would provide numerous opportunities for Christian workers since the area was nearly "99½ percent" Protestant. "The mountains," he added, "should also be great proving grounds for young Christian workers." Denominationalism was not the controlling religious factor, and the people were not hidebound by it. Finally, Stone wrote, "You and the members of your fine faculty would have a wonderful opportunity to render a much needed service for the Lord in this vicinity."[6] Evidently, Dr. Jones did not give much thought to the letter by Stone; there is no evidence of a response. The Greenville query was cordial enough, but the Knoxville site was very attractive.

Meanwhile, Stone approached Richard Arrington, the Greenville Chamber of Commerce president and president of Union Bleachery, a leading textile firm, with the idea of attracting Bob Jones College to Greenville. Arrington called Ken Miles, the executive secretary of the chamber, and asked him to follow up on Stone's idea. After some telephone research about the students, the business ethics, and the financial condition of the College, Miles and Arrington presented the matter to the chamber of commerce board. As a result, President Arrington ordered the board to form an eight-man Liaison Committee with instructions to get the College "whatever the cost."[7]

On April 16, Miles wrote to Dr. Jones Sr., officially inviting him and the Expansion Committee to come to Greenville to view several tracts of land.[8] Sensing the imminence of the decision, the next day Miles telegraphed Cleveland, begging Dr. Jones to make no decision until visiting Greenville.[9] As it happened, Dr. Jones received neither the letter nor the telegram until later; he was already in Knoxville reviewing the terms of the Knoxville purchase. Greenville's Liaison Committee investigated several parcels of land but did not seem to move quickly enough for Stone. On the night of April 17, Stone appeared before the chamber board and convinced them, for the good of Greenville, to take action. After the meeting, Stone prayed for leading about the school. That night he awoke from his sleep about 2 A.M., and later said, "The answer came through. I decided to call."[10]

That morning, Stone located Dr. Jones and R. K. Johnson at the lawyer's office in Knoxville and talked to the evangelist by phone for thirty-five minutes, attempting to persuade him to visit Greenville and consider its proposal. Stone insisted that the signing be delayed until the Expansion Committee had the opportunity to view several tracts of land in Greenville. Finally, with some reluctance, Dr. Jones Sr. agreed. The Expansion Committee asked for and received a ninety-day option on the Knoxville land, put down some earnest money, and returned to Cleveland.

On April 22 the Greenville chamber chartered an airplane, and Richard Arrington and Ken B. Miles flew to Chattanooga to discuss the precise needs of the College and to bring the Expansion Committee to Greenville.[11] Bob Jones Jr. had been previously scheduled for a preaching tour, so he requested that his mother make the trip to Greenville in his place.

When the Joneses and Lefty Johnson arrived in Greenville, they attended a briefing that provided information about the progressive nature of the Greenville area, and Dr. Jones was favorably impressed with the city. He was impressed even more, however, by the character of the men who represented Greenville. They seemed like men who would follow through and keep their word.

As the group drove to the different sites suggested by the chamber, only one area impressed Dr. Jones. It was not an awe-inspiring vista—only muddy hills, gullies, and a corn field. As Mr. Stone told it, "I can remember so clearly when Dr. Bob walked out on this piece of land and stood by the tree out in front of the spot on which the library is built. He looked around, swung his arm, and said . . . , 'Lefty, this is it.' Then he turned to me and said, 'Mr. Stone, this is the land, isn't it?' "[12]

That night, the chamber of commerce hosted a banquet in honor of the Expansion Committee and made official their invitation to come to Greenville. The chamber offered 180 acres of land bordered by U.S. Highway 29 (then called the SuperHighway), S.C. Highway 291, Old Spartanburg Highway, and White Oak Road, which they estimated could be purchased for $175,000. Arrington warned the gathering not to "make any promises to Dr. Jones that we cannot fulfill. We do not wish to mislead them, but if they will consider coming here, then they can rest assured that we will stand by them and do everything we can to cooperate with them, and will protect them at all times."[13] This statement made a deep impression on Dr. Jones.

Knoxville had already been selected, Dr. Jones told those at the banquet, and an option on the land had been executed. Many other cities had made lucrative offers, some including land plus one million dollars and more; the least Greenville could do, he said, was to purchase the land under consideration for the school. If Greenville did that, they would give the city due consideration. In closing, he said, "We want to place our school where God would have it placed."[14] On April 25, in only three days, the committee would announce its decision, he told them.

The Greenville chamber worked feverishly for the next two days to acquire options on the land, and by the afternoon of April 24 most of the parcels of land had been secured. Miles telegraphed Cleveland with the news that the "options [are] already in hand for [a] major portion of it." He continued, "Mr. Daniels [sic] at our meeting this afternoon assures us again that buildings can be completed by August 1, 1947, provided necessary priorities are secured. In telephone conversation with Washington officials today, we are assured no difficulty will be experienced in this respect. . . . Our board unanimously extended most cordial invitation to you and your associates to cast your lot with us. We like you and we hope you like us. We are convinced that with our joint efforts you can realize for your college in Greenville all your dreams."[15]

Meanwhile, telegrams, phone calls, and letters of good wishes poured into Bob Jones College from the citizens of Greenville. Miles himself called or telegraphed at least twice a day![16] The chamber appointed four of its members to get to Cleveland as quickly as possible to keep the pressure on the school.[17] The group drove all night through torrential rain and arrived in Cleveland in the early morning hours of April 25 to meet with Dr. Jones and the Expansion Committee. The decision was to be announced at the chapel service that morning. Chapel was delayed to allow the Expansion Committee to meet with all concerned parties: the Greenville delegation assured the committee that all was settled and the land was in hand; a last-ditch effort to induce obstinate landowners in Cleveland to sell was unsuccessful; and the Reverend Mr. Jernigan of the Church of God guaranteed the purchase of the Cleveland campus.

Finally, the student body gathered at 10:30 A.M. for the official announcement. The atmosphere was charged with excitement. Bob Jones Sr. first described the situation leading up to the decision to move and commented that "thousands have been praying . . . that the fear of God might direct me and the Expansion Committee in the choice of a location."[18]

He then read two formal statements: one of acceptance to the delegation from Greenville, South Carolina, and one to the citizens of Cleveland, Tennessee.[19]

For all involved, the service was one of deep emotion; there were tears of sorrow and of rejoicing. While reading his concluding remarks, Dr. Jones Sr. was overcome by emotion, requiring his son to finish reading the statement. It said, "Bob Jones College's business is not like a commercial business. It is a corporation not-for-profit. Our service is an unselfish service. We have an obligation to God to do the best we can with the light we have. In view of everything, though we regret to leave our friends in Cleveland, we feel that we must move on into a larger opportunity of service."[20]

On May 1 Bob Jones Jr. and R. K. Johnson arrived in Greenville to address a dinner meeting of 350 citizens to explain the school's academic, cultural, and religious programs; talk about construction; and establish the necessary contacts to manage the business needs of the school. At this time, representatives of Furman University, Presbyterian College, and Clemson University all met with Bob Jones Jr. and assured him of their best wishes and support.[21] Sometime during the site search Dr. Jones Sr. had also contacted the South Carolina state superintendent of education and the president of the University of South Carolina, both of whom agreed that Bob Jones University was a welcomed addition to higher education in the state and that they would work with the school in every way possible.[22]

Nevertheless, even before construction began, opposition and problems surfaced. On May 30, John C. Jernigan, general overseer of the Church of God, telegraphed Dr. Jones Sr. with the news that the executive council of the Church of God, "because of some opposition of some of our preachers," felt it necessary to postpone the purchase of the Cleveland campus until the end of August when the agreement could be presented to the general convention. Dr. Jones immediately phoned Jernigan and expressed in no uncertain terms that he and the Church of God were obligated both ethically and legally to purchase the facilities. It was too late to turn back in Greenville. The Church of God must live up to its agreements or they would not be able to "look society in the face."[23] Jernigan eventually pulled the Church of God together, and the deal was completed.

Meanwhile in Greenville, Arrington, Miles, and the chamber had formed seven fund-raising teams to raise the $175,000 needed to purchase the University site.[24] On May 17 the chamber began a promotional campaign by newspaper and radio, and on May 21 the chamber kicked off its fund-raising with a breakfast meeting. They asked community leaders to rally behind the cause, give liberally, and bring an institution to town that will "fit in with Greenville's general scheme of life."[25] The campaign started with a bang. On the first day, thirty thousand dollars was collected for the school.[26] By June 28, all the options on the land had been exercised, and ninety thousand dollars' worth of land had been purchased. The chamber publicized their expectations that the school would yearly add more than $4 million to the Greenville economy.[27]

Greenville began to feel the economic impact of the school's move almost immediately. By June the chamber of commerce had "received inquiries from thirty-seven families in Ohio, Florida, Pennsylvania, Nebraska, New York, and Washington, D.C., that wish[ed] to purchase homes near the college."[28] The office of E. Roy Stone took numerous calls for property and housing close to the new school and even set up a referral service to handle those needing short-term housing during construction and the University's first year in Greenville.[29]

Nevertheless, "a satanic whispering campaign," as Bob Jones Sr. called it, dampened the fund-raising campaign, which eventually sputtered and stalled.[30] According to one source, the Methodist bishop of Tennessee related to the bishop of South Carolina incidents about Bob Jones College and its independent evangelistic outreaches, whereupon South Carolina Methodists became concerned that their denominational strength would be diluted by the Joneses' independent thinking. They began opposing the relocation of the school.[31]

The Southern Baptists also became concerned about their hold on the region, and the president of Furman, Dr. John Plyler, registered a complaint with E. Roy Stone about the University's moving to Greenville.[32] A letter to long-time BJC antagonist Dr. Louie Newton of the Georgia Baptist Convention indicates that Southern Baptist supporters of Furman University were also upset because the city had supported a drive for BJU when an earlier drive to benefit Furman had failed. The Furman campus at this time was located in downtown Greenville in a group of old, somewhat dilapidated buildings. The contrast between the Furman buildings and the proposed Bob Jones campus was striking, and eventually enough pressure was brought to bear on the South Carolina Baptist Convention that a new campus for Furman was built north of the Bob Jones campus and the city.

Observers commented that the area's religious leaders feared conservative Christianity because it would slow the growth of the social gospel movement that was then gaining strength in Greenville; it would hinder their humanitarian appeals; and it would make students at their colleges appear less Christian because they did not live a public Christian testimony or maintain any evangelistic zeal. The BJU students' zeal was a threat, they said, because the town was used to seeing students whose religious faith had little impact on their daily living.[33]

Dr. John McSween of Greenville's Fourth Presbyterian Church accused the school of recruiting students away from state Presbyterian colleges and publicly criticized those in Greenville who gave money to bring the school to Greenville.[34] Dr. Jones Jr. later characterized McSween's statements, and those of other religious leaders in Greenville, as "malicious and deliberate falsehood and slander [by] preachers, some of whom were warped with denominational bias and prejudices and some of whom resent the orthodox theological stand of this institution."[35] By mid-June it was nearly impossible for the chamber to raise another dime for the land.

Debate over the wisdom of bringing the University to Greenville began within the chamber itself, and its membership was polarized over the issue. Liberal religious leaders in the area convinced several members of the chamber that it was fruitless to try to raise the money through pledges because it would never be collected. They were also successful in convincing some chamber board members that Bob Jones would develop a fanatical following of religious radicals in Greenville who would ultimately hurt the social development of the area and take over the town. Since E. Roy Stone had been instrumental in initiating contact with the College, he was at the center of the debate, and for a year his office received daily calls about the College, its students, and its religion.[36]

Dr. Jones Sr. had foreseen such opposition. "The only opposition to Bob Jones College is the opposition to its religion," he had said a year earlier, "and there is a rising tide of hatred against an aggressive Christian testimony."[37]

The chamber group that supported the school ran a full-page ad in the *Greenville Piedmont* entitled "Bob Jones College As We See It" to try to counteract the rumors that had been circulating. This ad stated the virtues of Bob Jones College and the probable impact—religiously, socially, culturally, and economically—that the school would have on the Greenville community. The letter began, "The honor and integrity of the Greenville Chamber of Commerce are at stake!" and it was signed by the chamber's officers and directors.[38] The fund-raising drive stalled in June; by October 2, 1946, only $65,000 had been collected.[39] Through repeated appeals by the chamber, another $32,000 was raised before the drive finally died at a total of $97,000. The school was left with two choices—scale back construction or purchase the land itself. The school purchased the most vital land out of its own treasury, spending over $50,000 immediately.[40] Simply put, the chamber of commerce did not keep its word.[41]

As a result of the chamber's failure, the school could acquire only a portion of the land originally promised.[42] When the chamber failed to pay, the options expired and the owners began to negotiate directly with the school and to hold out for higher prices. Eventually some of the land promised to the school did come into its possession, but at a significantly higher cost. In 1961 R. K. Johnson reported that the school had already spent over $265,000 for land that was promised in the original package.[43] In 1969 he reported that the school, out of necessity, had spent a half million dollars for land that would have cost less than $78,000 in 1946![44]

The chamber in succeeding months and years continued to renege on its agreements with Bob Jones University. In the initial negotiations with the Expansion Committee, the chamber board had agreed to float development bonds to cover the cost of running sewer and water lines to the new campus. Because of the opposition toward Bob Jones that developed within the board, these bonds were never executed and, within thirty days of occupancy, the sewer and water lines had still not been installed. In order to expedite this situation, the University itself floated bonds with the Jefferson Standard Life Insurance Company of Greensboro, North Carolina, and financed both the pipe and the labor to run the lines. About 1951, after rather heated debates between the school and the chamber, the chamber and the city assumed the debt and upkeep of these lines.[45]

After 1947, when K. B. Miles's term as president of the chamber ended, the chamber board's attitude toward Bob Jones University was clearly one of disdain and embarrassment over having the school in the area. As early as June 1948, a map of Greenville issued by the chamber showed a proposed shopping area to the east of the campus area and a housing development that had been started in 1947 on land adjacent to the campus; the University, however, was omitted from the map, leaving the area blank. This happened even though construction on the University had started in 1946. An official tour book of the Greenville area published in 1953 by the chamber named twenty-seven businesses, schools, colleges, parks, and city areas by name, including Furman University and Clemson University, but did not mention Bob Jones University.

Dr. Jones Sr.'s response was heated and direct. "Something could have been put in this *official* tour bulletin," he wrote, "and would have been if someone had not wanted Bob Jones University left out. . . . Somebody . . . in this city tries to play Bob Jones University down. We are determined to place the responsibility wherever it belongs, and we are willing to face this thing at the bar of public opinion. . . . We are not going to be ignored *intentionally* or *unintentionally* when conventions are here without protest to the public."[46] On tours of the area for visiting businessmen, BJU was regularly skirted while Furman University was never missed. When Johnson contacted chamber officials about the oversight, they cited "the constraints of time schedules" as the reason.[47]

Records indicate that the chamber of commerce, after failing to raise the funds to purchase the land, then denied their responsibility to lay the sewerage and water lines and went through a long-term cycle of denial that any of these agreements were real. Moreover, they claimed that if any agreements had been made, they applied only to the specific board that had made them and not to succeeding chamber boards. After years of denying the existence of any agreements, then stating that all agreements were nonbinding, and then finally suggesting that no records about any agreements existed, the chamber, under the leadership of Dick Greer in 1981, issued a statement saying that the chamber owed a past debt to the school and settled for $50,000.[48]

Other problems occurred with the construction. Charles E. Daniel, a member of the Greenville chamber and owner of Daniel Construction Company, the largest construction firm in the Southeast, attended the first meetings pertaining to the school's coming to Greenville. Daniel had guaranteed Dr. Jones Sr. that his company could handle all aspects of construction and finish on schedule and on budget. Construction was set to begin on June 1, and a crew of five hundred men, to work ten-hour shifts five days a week, was readied for the assault; but just before construction started, problems caused a delay.

Wartime restrictions were still being enforced, and all new buildings had to be approved by the War Production Board in Washington, D.C. These approvals were difficult to obtain, and on the first attempt the school's building permits were denied because steel needed for the buildings was still being stockpiled for military use. Dr. Jones and K. B. Miles flew to Washington and spent several days working on the problem with "key men" in the government. Within a week, the proper permits were issued.[49] The official, formal groundbreaking was held on September 1, 1946.

Costs for the new campus were estimated at $3,030,000 for the first unit of construction.[50] The Cleveland campus had been sold to the Church of God for $1.5 million—a price significantly below the school's book value of $2.25 million. To finance construction in Greenville, a $1.9 million loan was secured from the Jefferson Standard Life Insurance Company.[51] Construction of the new plant took all the financial reserves of the school, but donations from Fundamentalist Christians across the country flooded in to aid construction.

Bob Jones Sr. divided the responsibilities of the effort among himself, his son, and R. K. Johnson. Dr. Jones Sr. assumed the role of fundraiser and student recruiter. Dr. Jones Jr. administrated the Cleveland College, planned the new facility with the architects, and handled Greenville community issues. Johnson was the on-site supervisor in Greenville. Dr. Jones Sr. said jokingly, "I am not going to build the college. I'm not going to have anything to do with it. . . . If it isn't right when it is all over with, then you can say, 'Bob Jr. didn't know anything about architecture.' "[52]

R. K. Johnson moved to Greenville and lived on the building site throughout the construction of the new plant and was intimately involved in all aspects of the building—from settling disputes and motivating the workers to hunting down scarce building materials. In spite of his driven determination and several bitter disputes that developed with the job supervisor and the architects, for which Johnson ultimately had to apologize, he came to be admired by all those associated with the project for his stamina, determination, management skills, and ability to motivate others. The pressures were intense, but he had the mind to work; those under him followed suit or were replaced.[53] Johnson recalled that "miracles were numerous during those construction days. . . . God opened doors that we wanted opened, and He kept closed doors that should not have been opened. To Him goes the praise for everything."[54]

Construction proceeded on schedule with few delays. The weather was normal for South Carolina—unpredictable—and during the time of construction, "we had alot of rain. But over and over again, it would rain all around the campus and the campus remain dry. Many a time, the rain stopped just across the street or in the middle of the road and did not strike the campus. This did not happen once, but many times, through the construction process," making it possible for construction to continue unhindered.[55]

Following the September groundbreaking, it took some weeks to level the hills, fill in gullies, and lay foundations. To the casual passerby, it seemed as if little was going on, since no building was visible from the road until March 1947. Even R. K. Johnson recorded some doubts about completing the plant on time.[56] By July 1947, however, the buildings were "going up fast. You enter the grounds near the Administration building. Nearby are the Art Studio, the great Dining Hall, and the Music Building. These are all being constructed of steel and

View of construction from Rodeheaver Auditorium parking lot (ca. 1948). Note Student Center and original Dining Common in the background.

reenforced concrete, faced with buff brick, and present a beautiful picture."[57] The campus was designed in what was then described as "modern functional architecture."[58]

The construction of the campus shows the administration's level of commitment to the arts. The Rodeheaver Auditorium, which also contained speech and music classrooms and faculty studios, was constructed at a cost

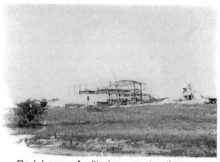

Rodeheaver Auditorium construction (1947)

exceeding $600,000, nearly 25 percent of the school's construction budget for the entire first unit.[59] The auditorium plan was conceived by Bob Jones Jr. both to provide an excellent preaching environment and to "afford the best possible facilities for dramatic productions."[60] The impressive auditorium was designed to seat three thousand, with one balcony and a proscenium stage with a forty-five-foot arch.[61]

Construction of the plant was not without its problems. One major problem was that of getting doors. No one could supply doors earlier than the spring of 1948, and school had to open by the fall of 1947. "Can you imagine this school without doors?" Johnson asked. "Curtains would have had to be stretched across the bedroom doors, and big boards would have had to serve as outside doors. We would have been willing to do even this; we had to open school." At this time, Dr. Jones Jr. was in revival meetings in Seattle, Washington, and he told some Christian businessmen about the school's need for approximately six thousand doors. The businessmen secured a sawmill and lumber, "and those doors were here months ahead of schedule—not in the spring of 1948, but in the spring of 1947. How good God is to us," Johnson commented.[62]

Shortly after construction began, the steel company informed Johnson that too much steel had been figured for the buildings and the error would cost about twenty thousand dollars. Should the work halt and "should we refigure?" they asked. Johnson knew that a delay in steel delivery might jeopardize the entire project, making an on-time opening impossible. He also knew that if the buildings were not ready on time, the University would have to rent the old campus in Cleveland from the Church of God for one thousand dollars a week. He decided to lose the twenty thousand dollars rather than put the opening of school in doubt.[63]

Because of the war, steel was scarce and expensive, and shortages occurred regularly in steel products. At one point, the builders could not find nails and the project was threatened. Johnson called the College and asked John Ludwig, the head of the Maintenance Department, to get a station wagon, find all the nails he could, and bring them directly to Greenville. Ludwig collected nails from the Cleveland area, loaded the car from floor to ceiling, and brought them to Greenville.[64]

For a time, the University's opening was also threatened by delays in approvals to run the sewer lines to the campus, but Dr. Jones Sr. and K. B. Miles were able to receive the proper state clearances within thirty minutes at a special meeting arranged in the state capital. This came after the requests had languished in a state office for several weeks.[65]

Perhaps the most serious problem was a shortage of electrical transformers. The Daniel project managers told Johnson about the shortage and declared, "You won't be able to open school. We can't get transformers. They are unobtainable." They reported that all electrical transformers were being sent to Russia on a government Lend-Lease program. Duke Power Company had had an unfilled order for these same transformers since 1945 and could not offer any help, so Johnson flew to the Westinghouse Company headquarters. The vice president to whom Johnson spoke could not offer any immediate assistance but promised to "move Heaven and earth to try to help you." Johnson wrote later,

> Back in Greenville, I called Dr. Bob and asked him to write a letter to Westinghouse. Two weeks later I was on the plane on my way back to Westinghouse. The vice-president . . . reported that they had been able to secure a few small transformers and would keep trying to locate the larger ones. . . . At that very time a big company out West turned down some large transformers. Why? God led them to do it. The transformers were headed to Greenville, and one man commented, "Whoever gets those transformers will be getting a miracle." He did not realize what a miracle it was. The result was that we had every transformer except one when school opened, and I think God tested us about that one to see what we would do. Duke Power Company kindly lent us that one until ours arrived.[66]

Miracles did not occur only with buildings, equipment, and supplies;

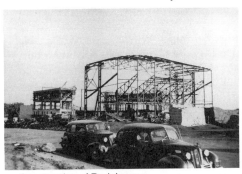

Construction of Rodeheaver Auditorium (1947)

miracles of protection happened as well. During the entire construction process, only one serious accident occurred: some trusses in the gymnasium fell, "throwing three men to the floor," yet only one man was injured.[67]

On December 5, 1946, Dr. Jones Sr. went to Atlanta to handle some pressing business.[68] After arriving, he checked into the Winecoff

Hotel and called Johnson to bring some information down from Greenville. The business was completed on December 6, and Dr. Jones decided to leave for Mobile immediately for his next meeting rather than stay the night in Atlanta. He told Johnson to take his room at the Winecoff and check on some business the next day. After arranging for a room in Mobile, Dr. Jones changed his mind and insisted that Johnson go to Cleveland, Tennessee, to get some information for the next day's meetings. Johnson wrote,

> I did not want to go to Cleveland, and I argued with Dr. Bob. I knew I could call Cleveland and get the information which I needed. But Dr. Bob was insistent.

> "Is there any reason why you cannot go to Cleveland?" he asked. I said, "No, Dr. Bob, but I have not come prepared to take that trip. I can stay here tonight, can attend to the business in Atlanta tomorrow, and can get back to Greenville, where I am needed desperately by tomorrow night." Finally, Dr. Bob agreed that if we could get an appointment with a certain business man in Atlanta the next morning, I would not go back to Cleveland. We investigated the matter and found that the man . . . had just left for Nashville, Tennessee, and would not be back for several days. I must go to Cleveland.

> I was more than a little disappointed. There were no plane or train reservations available. That meant that I must travel by bus. At 5:30 P.M., I checked Dr. Bob out of the hotel and put him in a limousine to go to the airport. Then I walked slowly up the street to the bus station. . . . I was tired, for I had been up since 3:30 that morning. Boarding the bus, I found "standing room only." In a weak moment of discouragement, I said, "Lord, I cannot understand it. I am trying to serve Thee; and yet as tired as I am, I am having to stand on this bus."

> The bus missed its connections to Cleveland and I found myself in the little town of Ocoee, ten miles out of Cleveland, in the bitter cold. I called James D. Edwards, Dean of Administration at Bob Jones College, who drove out to get me. Because of the lateness of the hour, there was little time left for sleep.

> At breakfast the next morning, Dr. Bob's secretary came to the table and anxiously inquired about Dr. Bob. I told her that he was in Mobile. She asked if I were sure he was in Mobile. I said, "Yes," and went on talking. Finally she grabbed my arm, shook me and asked, "Are you positive he left Atlanta?" I said, "Marjorie, are you crazy? Of course I'm positive. I put him in the limousine to go to the airport, and I know that he left."[69]

Gilbert Stenholm's diary reads, "One of the most terrible fires in U.S. history occurred in Atlanta when 127 people perished in the Winecoff Hotel fire which began at 3:00 a.m."[70] The fire began on the fifth floor, with the most death and destruction coming to those on the sixth floor—the floor of

Dr. Jones's room. Had either Johnson or Dr. Jones been at the Winecoff that night, his injury or death would have been a devastating blow to the school.

In spite of the problems mentioned and numerous smaller difficulties in the acquisition of equipment and building materials, the first unit of the campus was completed on schedule and on budget. The buildings of the Greenville campus, rising from the red clay and mud of South Carolina, were completed, and ready for the influx of students by October.[71]

When it came time to "possess the land," the move from Cleveland was organized with great precision. The College offices ended the workday in Cleveland on noon one day, were packed, loaded, transported that night, and were unloaded and ready for business by noon the next day. A professional moving company brought sixty-three tractor-trailer loads of material over the mountains to Greenville and amazingly suffered only one minor accident when a truck axle broke.[72]

Details of the campus construction had been closely guarded, and the students and faculty, after praying diligently for months for the work to progress rapidly, were full of excitement. Everyone looked forward to leaving the cramped conditions in Cleveland. Students would sometimes take weekend trips to Greenville to see the construction, and interest at the College was heightened as they returned with descriptions and photographs of the gigantic operation. One trip to Greenville, however, produced a tragedy.

Monroe and Harriette Parker (1945)

On December 30, 1946, Monroe Parker, the director of Religious Activities, and his wife Harriette, the head of the Music Department, began a drive to Greenville to look over the new campus and the construction. On the way, their car collided head-on with a large truck, and Harriette was killed. A young composer who had studied at the Cincinnati Conservatory, Harriette had written numerous works for Vespers and the BJC Church Choir and had composed the music for the University Hymn, to the words of Bob Jones Jr.[73] The new year began with sorrow for the College family.

Throughout 1946 and 1947 Bob Jones College in Cleveland continued in its routine with

123

seemingly no interruptions. Bob Jones Jr. carried out his duties of designing the new campus, managed the daily affairs of the College with alacrity, and kept an active preaching schedule as well. His load was lightened significantly by able men, all BJC alumni, who had become active in the administration of the school—Monroe Parker, assistant to Dr. Jones Jr. and director of religious activities; James. D. Edwards, dean of the College; Karl Keefer, registrar; and Ted Mercer, dean of men.

Not only had the school a new name—Bob Jones University—and a new home; it also had a new president, Bob Jones Jr., who was installed by the Board of Trustees on May 28, 1947.[74]

CHAPTER 11

Bob Jones Jr.

The new President of Bob Jones University had actually assumed teaching duties at the College in 1931 when he was appointed to the faculty. In 1932 Bob Jones Jr. assumed administrative duties also when he was appointed vice president of the College, with the title "Acting President" during the absences of his father.

Bob Jones Jr. was born in Montgomery, Alabama, on October 19, 1911, and as a child often traveled with his parents on his father's evangelistic campaigns. Because Mrs. Jones was kept busy during campaigns with women's meetings, prayer meetings, and social functions, a nanny was hired to travel with the Joneses.[1]

Bob showed an interest in things dramatic and when traveling with his parents would sometimes create a stage in their hotel room by hanging sheets

Bob Jones Sr., Mary Gaston Jones, and Bob Jones Jr.

for a stage curtain. He would then perform plays from his imagination with the nanny or his grandmother as his audience.[2]

When Bob was five, his grandmother, Estelle Siddons Stollenwerck, assumed some direction of his early education. She was a "scholarly" woman who "loved the beautiful in life," and she reinforced in him his parents' spiritual lessons.[3] She introduced him to the wonders of books and imparted a love for literature that he never outgrew. She taught him French when he was six years old.[4] He also memorized the entire Methodist hymnal "word for word" in order to please her.[5]

As a child of six years of age, Bob Jones Jr. came under the burden of sin about which his evangelist father preached. In Aurora, Illinois, young Bob trusted Christ as his personal Savior and became determined to serve Him.

When Bob was school age, his father would sometimes take him from school in Montgomery rather than leave him and his mother in Alabama during evangelistic meetings. On such occasions, his parents hired tutors "who struggled with [him] for a few hours each day" on his lessons.[6] By his own admission, he was a reluctant and sometimes recalcitrant student who loved literature and history but disliked mathematics and never "bothered with spelling."[7] For five years he was tutored by Gussie Woodruff, who, with her sister, operated a private academy in Montgomery, Alabama. "Miss Gussie" took him in tow with what he remembers as "firm discipline, tough tutelage, and vigilant eyes." He felt as if she had "eyes in the back of her head" and that she was always one step ahead of his mischief.[8] She believed in the "foot rule and the Golden Rule" and used both impartially. She also was proficient with Octagon soap when correcting the speech and attitude of her ward.[9]

Young Bob read voraciously. His tastes were diverse and included a large and steady diet of the Bible, Tom Swift stories, the works of Edgar Rice Burroughs, and the science fiction of Jules Verne. Before he was twelve, Bob had read a collection of fifty missionary books that his father had given him and *Foxe's Book of Martyrs,* and by age fourteen he had read all the novels of Alexandre Dumas, *The Wandering Jew* by Eugene Sue, and *Les Misérables* by Victor Hugo.

Bob Jones Jr. was a good student, though somewhat stubborn and shy. In 1923 his parents sent him to Starke's University School, better known as Starke's Military Academy, in Montgomery, Alabama, because they felt that he needed discipline, intellectual rigor, and opportunities to mix with people.[10] As a headstrong twelve-year-old, Bob disliked the eighty-member military school and resented taking orders from his peers simply because they had rank.

Professor Starke, like Bob's father, possessed a sense of humor but also had a strong sense of honor and integrity that could not tolerate deceit, pretense, or dishonesty. Much of this sense of honor rubbed off on the young Jones. Many years later Bob wrote, "Four things I despise—deceit, illogical thinking, evasive speech, and muddled writing. Pomposity and verbosity are irritating. . . . Lack of clarity and originality are unforgivable."[11] The virtues which he admired most were consistency, conviction, and courage. "Falsehood and

Bob Jones Sr. and Bob Jones Jr. in his Starke's Military Academy uniform (ca. 1927)

slander," he said, "are among the sins I most deplore."[12]

While he was a student at Starke's, Bob learned how and when to fight. Once, after Bob had run from a fight, his father told him that if he ever ran again, he would get spanked. Soon after this, Bob came home somewhat bloodied and disheveled. "Did you run away this time?" his father asked. "No," Bob said. "I just retreated, fighting as I went." After boxing lessons with Zed, the Joneses' mechanic, yardman, and cook, Bob never had to retreat again, and he learned "how to take on any customer," whether in "fisticuffs or debate, to be careful about handing out challenges," and never to let himself "be bluffed or terrorized."[13]

Starke advocated quick and logical thinking, public speaking, and debate. Each day opened with a Scripture lesson, followed by "mental arithmetic." The boys then studied the great books, physical culture, mathematics, and Latin, for which Bob was required to memorize and recite the first oration of Cicero against Cataline.[14] Jones credited Starke with sparking his interest in debate and public speaking—interests that were later refined and put to use in both the College and the ministry.[15] At the 1927 commencement exercises, Bob was a finalist for the Hill Speaker's Medal, speaking on "The Sign of the Cross."[16] Unknowingly, Starke taught young Bob an important lesson about fidelity to the Christian faith.

> I used to sit in our pew at church before I ever knew Dr. Starke and watch him. He sat in the "amen corner." . . . I used to wonder at him. He sang the hymns but whenever the Apostle's Creed was recited, he sat and said nothing. I used to think it strange that a man as intelligent as this man was supposed to be, because everybody in town knew of his brain, couldn't learn the Apostle's Creed. I used to wonder why such a brilliant man couldn't learn something that I knew at four or five years of age. After I was his student, I gathered my courage and asked him why he didn't say the Creed. . . .
>
> [Starke answered,] "That preacher is a liar. He doesn't believe the Apostle's Creed and he doesn't believe in the virgin birth of our Lord. I won't repeat the Creed with a man that doesn't believe it and I'm not going to be a party to such hypocrisy and dishonesty." That is the kind of character that man had.[17]

In 1924 as a twelve-year-old boy, Bob Jones Jr. accompanied his father to the Democratic National Convention in New York City, where he witnessed William Jennings Bryan's final speech to his party. The antagonism displayed toward Bryan made an indelible impression on the young Bob Jones. He recalled that the Tammany Hall "rabble booed [Bryan] and tried to laugh him off the platform." Bryan's dignity and sincerity were "tremendously impressive, and one sensed that here was a good man and a real statesman. . . . It was, of course, apparent that those who set themselves against him were ruffians beneath contempt."[18]

In the same year Bob accompanied his parents to Europe and the Holy Land. During this, his first trip overseas, he was fascinated with the European art treasures, and he spent many hours exploring galleries, cathedrals, and other public collections.[19]

At fourteen Bob was made a deputy chaplain at Kilby Penitentiary by his father's good friend, Bibb Graves, governor of Alabama. He taught Sunday school lessons, conducted Bible studies, and helped the chaplain with Sunday morning services. The experience showed him the worst in human character, and he learned much of value for his later preaching career. In addition, the experience brought him in contact with rough, unrefined men—a sort of people he had not previously known.[20]

When Bob was fifteen years of age, he saw the last of the great touring Shakespeare companies—Robert Mantel and his troupe.[21] Although drama fascinated him and stirred his imagination, he considered the works of Shakespeare "a terrific bore" until two or three years later. After he turned sixteen or seventeen and had begun memorizing lines from the plays, he "began to realize the greatness of the man and his works."[22] He became acquainted with the American opera scene at an early age through one of his aunts, who was a patron of the Metropolitan Opera's yearly performances in Atlanta.[23] During the family's European trips, Bob also attended opera performances with his parents.[24]

In 1927 sixteen-year-old Bob Jones Jr. transferred his high school credits from Starke's and became a member of the first graduating class of Bob Jones Academy, operated in conjunction with the newly opened Bob Jones College. The following year he entered Bob Jones College as a freshman with a major in speech and a minor in history, and continued to read widely.[25] While in college, Bob was active in debate, dramatics, and student government. Through his influence in 1929, the College formed the Classic Players, a Shakespeare repertory company, and in 1930 it staged the first Shakespearean production on the campus, *The Merchant of Venice,* in which Bob Jones Jr. played the role of Shylock.[26] The play caused a considerable stir among the students, supporters of the College, and area residents who paid attention to such things.[27]

After several years of campus Shakespearean performances, Bob Jones Jr. came to the attention of the noted actor Fritz Leiber, who invited him to join his touring Shakespeare company.[28] Bob declined the offer. Likewise, when in 1937 Warner Brothers Studios in Hollywood approached him with the offer of a screen test and a contract, he again refused, believing that the Lord had something vastly different for his life.[29]

Bob Jones Jr. graduated from Bob Jones College in 1931 and pursued a master of arts degree in history at the University of Pittsburgh, completing it in 1933.[30] As part of his master's work, he spent one quarter of study at the University of Chicago Divinity School. He also took postgraduate work in drama and theater at Northwestern University in Evanston, Illinois.[31]

After he graduated from college in 1931, he was appointed to the College faculty as an instructor in history, teaching several courses, including ancient and medieval history, Hebrew history, and somewhat later, homiletics. He also became the faculty sponsor of the Classic Players.[32] The next year he was named vice president, with the title of Acting President in the absence of his father from the campus, and began his career as college administrator, if only part-time.[33] In 1934, when Bob was only twenty-three, Asbury College in Wilmore, Kentucky, presented him an honorary doctor of letters degree for his work as a Shakespearean actor. Dr. H. C. Morrison, a close friend of Bob Jones Sr., was then president of Asbury.[34]

During the summers of 1934 and 1935, Bob Jr., along with Ruth Flood of the College faculty, spent several weeks at Stratford-upon-Avon studying with members of the Shakespeare Company of the Memorial Theatre. The "Shakespeare Fortnight Hostelry" was operated by American actress Fanny Bradshaw and was noted as a place where aspiring actors or teachers could take an intensive course of study in Shakespeare and observe the rehearsals and performances of ten plays.[35] Enrollment in the summer program was widely sought but was limited to only six participants each summer. The students took private acting lessons with actors of the Royal Shakespeare Company and studied Shakespeare's characters, period costuming, stage deportment, fencing, and eurythmics. Dr. Jones wrote,

> Most of our classes met in the conference room of the theater, a large hall behind the stage . . . beside the Avon. When the weather was nice we would take our fencing lessons and our course in stage deportment and eurythmics outdoors. The latter course, I could never take seriously, and I suspected neither did the teacher, a tiny English ballerina who seemed to have as hard a time as I did in keeping a straight face when some matronly English teacher tried to jump over a hedge gracefully. She would say to us, "Now I want you to move in character. . . . Bob, you be Hamlet. Now walk across the fields, head up, back straight, eyes forward." Off we would go trying to maintain the character while avoiding the cow droppings.[36]

In 1936 Bob Jones Jr. was introduced to the distinguished actor Otis Skinner (1858-1942), who encouraged him to make a career of theater.[37] Jones did not take Skinner's advice, but he did develop a one-man show (apparently in 1933) in which he portrayed seven or eight of Shakespeare's most dramatic and entertaining characters.[38] Known as "Curtain Calls," the show was carried by a professional agent for a short time[39] and was scheduled for four weeks of performances each year until December 1945.[40] Curtain Calls, performed in "authentic costumes and makeup, [with] special stage setting and lighting effects," and accompanied by classical music on the piano or organ, brought acclaim to Jones Jr. as a Shakespearean interpreter.[41] The Shakespeare Association of America invited him to present Curtain Calls at their 1935 annual convention,[42] and one writer called the program "an outstanding contribution to the American theatre."[43] Bob Jones Jr. was hailed by the International Lyceum Association as the "best young actor of Shakespeare in America"; and by virtue of the name association, Bob Jones College also gained a reputation in the southern public's mind.[44]

Bob Jones Jr. in various Curtain Calls roles (ca. 1936)

Wherever the show played, critical acclaim followed, and a reputation of growing importance was established for Jones Jr. as an actor and dramatist. One critic wrote, "What a joy to have a Hamlet that is young, alive, and goodlooking. Bob Jones brings to the part youth, fire, and fine acting."[45] Another critic called the program "so realistic that those of the audience could feel themselves in the atmosphere of the real situation."[46] After a performance at Denison University, the director of drama wrote that Bob Jones Jr. had "done more toward setting these students on the road to a fuller appreciation of that genius, Shakespeare, than any program in years! Already there is a demand for a return engagement."[47] One performance at Hunter College in New York City, obviously marred, was reported thus:

> Everything mechanical went wrong. Fuses blew, curtains stuck, the stage was too small; costumes donned in a frenzy in an inadequate dressing "room" that lacked everything including room, were as often as not thrust on backwards as well as frontwards. Richard III, with his deformity slung in front, instead of in back, looked more like Falstaff than his wicked self.

> Yet, I judged Bob Jones Jr. on the basis of what I saw this evil night. For nothing daunted him. He kept right on. The lights might fail, but not the show. The wig might be askew, but never the character. Tights might become loose, but never the love lines. Romeo wooed in spite of falling nether-garments; Othello killed regardless of a slipping beard. Bob Jones Jr. did not make his audience forget these things; he so held them they never suspected they existed. He made Shakespeare live.[48]

Bob Jones Jr. found four elements in Shakespeare especially attractive: "The language of the plays is beautiful—almost sensual. The rhythm of the speech is lyrical, musical, and evocative of mood. The quality of the drama is the finest." But for the characters, especially, he holds great affection.[49] "My affection for Shakespeare, especially his plays," he writes, "is second only to my love for the Bible. I have learned a great deal about human nature not only from the Word of God but also from my study of Shakespeare, whose perception and delineation of character are always psychologically accurate."[50]

As an executive of Bob Jones College, Dr. Jones Jr. served on the College board, presided at faculty meetings, organized and administered the school's academic and social programs, oversaw campus cultural events, greeted campus guests, traveled hundreds of miles in preaching engagements, and did some of the faculty hiring and firing along with his father. During his years as Acting President, several Bob Jones College graduates came on the faculty who, in the later years of the institution, played a prominent role in campus life and affairs. Among them were James D. and Elizabeth Edwards, Gilbert and Katherine Stenholm, and Hazel Claire Riley.

As Acting President of Bob Jones College, part of Dr. Jones Jr.'s responsibility was to preside over or preach at the daily chapel service when his father was away from the school. Not a trained theologian, Bob Jones Jr. began a study which led him through some of the great works of systematic theology and into the sermons of the Puritan divines as well as those of more contemporary preachers. Among the sermons which he studied were those of Alexander Maclaren and William Muncy, but he often said that his theology was learned from the great preachers who frequented the Bible conference grounds of America during the early days of his life and from those who preached on the campus of Bob Jones College at the chapel services and Bible Conferences. Many of those with whom Bob Jones Jr. became acquainted in this way represented the leaders of American Fundamentalism and various political causes in the first half of the twentieth century.[51]

By the mid-1930s Bob Jones Jr. began preaching regularly in campus chapel services and was invited to preach revivals and young people's meetings. By the late thirties he was highly sought as a preacher. In addition to his preaching, traveling, and administrating, he also managed to present lectures on Shakespeare.

By all accounts, the busy young college president, then a bachelor, was considered the catch of the campus. He was eventually caught by Fannie May Holmes, who he claims had to be "sold" on him. They were married on June 1, 1938, in Cleveland, Tennessee. The night before, Bob Jones Jr. had played Richard II, one of the longest Shakespearean roles, without "fluffing a line." At the wedding, however, he fumbled his memorized vows twice.[52]

Left to right: Joy, Bob Jr., Bob III (standing), Jon, and Fannie May Jones (early 1950s)

On August 8, 1939, Robert Reynolds Jones III was born. Bobby gained a brother, Jon Edward, on February 19, 1944, and a sister, Joy Estelle, on April 20, 1945.

Shortly after the birth of Bobby, the Jones family took a major but painful step toward its denominational independence. At a Bible conference at the Broad Street Methodist Church in Cleveland, the featured speaker, a well-known Modernist professor from Candler Seminary, debunked the Book of Revelation and subtly denied the major doctrines of the Faith. After the service ended, Bob Jones Jr. told the pastor that as a matter of conscience and principle he must withdraw his family's membership from the Methodist church. He told the pastor that "I cannot be a member of a church that will bring this kind of a man to its pulpit or sit under the ministry of a pastor who praises this kind of infidel and exposes his people to these heresies."[53]

Though not at this meeting, Dr. Jones Sr. soon followed suit and removed his membership. Shortly thereafter, Dr. Jones Sr. joined Dr. Bob Shuler's Methodist church in Los Angeles, California, and the Jones Jr. family joined a Christian and Missionary Alliance church. After the school moved to South Carolina, they joined a local independent Baptist church.[54]

From the Bible he learned the nature of man; from Shakespeare and the Kilby prison, he learned the twists of human character. From studying Shakespeare and the Bible, he developed a fluid, elevated vocabulary; and from his training for the classical stage, he developed a smooth style of presentation that brought a sense of drama to every sermon. These qualities, with the addition of his academic background, and his Fundamentalist theology, combined to form a preaching style that was unusual in its breadth, range, and eloquence.

Bob Jones Jr.'s preaching was often criticized and compared negatively to his father's forceful style. Because of great differences in language, he was considered simply too refined, too poetic, and too dramatic. Jones Jr. made no claims to being a minister or evangelist.[55] He was a teacher, administrator, and actor. He felt keenly the natural comparison made between him and his powerfully persuasive father, and he hoped to develop himself in areas in which his father had little or no expertise.[56]

Some of the school's supporters were concerned with his "pretty speeches" and "eloquent sermonettes," viewing only the presentational style of the message—little shouting, no pacing the stage, no pulpit pounding or leg kicking. They overlooked the substance of the messages, which was no different from that of his father's sermons. Bob Jones Jr. was an outspoken Fundamentalist who opposed Modernist theology just as his father did.[57]

Before World War II, Bob Jones Jr. tried to remain on the campus as much as possible, attending to the details of the administration of the College. Between the years 1935 and 1947, even though invitations to preach and hold revival campaigns poured in, he spent much of his time and energy establishing the College's fine arts program, developing the faculty, and broadening the College's cultural offerings. From his early interest in Shakespeare, his cultural interest at the College moved next to grand opera, and through his influence, the first opera performances in central Tennessee were staged in 1942. He also established a concert series which presented guest musicians from around the world.

The new Greenville campus, far more spacious than that in Cleveland, allowed Dr. Jones to pursue other of his interests as well. Following a preaching tour to Europe in 1948, he returned to the school in Greenville with the goal of building a University cinema program. As noted earlier, his father had shown interest in the Christian use of film and thus was enthusiastic about a cinema program.

Construction for a sound stage began in 1950, and the first film was released in 1951. When Dr. Jones Jr. suffered from pleurisy and was put to bed for several weeks in 1950, he wrote the novel *Wine of Morning,* which became the basis for the first feature-length religious film produced by the school.

In Greenville Bob Jones Jr.'s interest in art, painting, and sculpture also blossomed. For two summers in the late 1930s he had worked as a European tour guide for several independent tour agencies. As such he led several groups to prewar Europe to see the great museums and galleries, the operas, and the concert halls of London, Rome, Paris, and Vienna.[58] Bob Jones Jr.'s interest in art grew until, at his urging, the school's Executive Committee approved the establishment of the Gallery of Sacred Art to be paired with the Bowen Museum of Biblical Antiquities located on campus.[59]

During Dr. Jones's term as vice president and Acting President, the College experienced great growth, becoming the largest liberal arts college in Tennessee. On May 28, 1947, Bob Jones Sr. stepped down as President of the College and Bob Jones Jr. was named by the Board of Trustees as President.[60] He was responsible for planning, designing, and building the new University plant in Greenville, and under his leadership the University became widely recognized for its academic programs, spiritual fidelity, and cultural richness. After the move to Greenville, he carefully scrutinized the day-to-day affairs of the University. The school was firmly under his control, even though the Founder sometimes interjected himself in daily affairs, took executive liberties, and handled things his own way.[61]

When Dr. Jones Jr. noticed problems or lapses of vigilance in an area, he was quick to put his thoughts forward in a forthright and direct manner. On a personal level, he was generous and soft-spoken, never harsh, unkind, or obdurate. Those who received memos or letters written in moments of displeasure sometimes felt otherwise, however. As President, he was authoritative and decisive, personally considerate but guarded, and somewhat distant and aloof. Unlike his father, who exuded great personal warmth, a charismatic magnetism, and just "loved people" and loved to be in crowds, Bob Jones Jr. was simply a different man, loving instead the privacy of his office and study or the school's art collection. During his tenure as President, he built the Greenville plant and added nearly a building each year thereafter, successfully staved off an internal rebellion by dissident administrators, fought the battle against New Evangelicalism and compromise evangelism, strengthened academic programs, and instituted ideas that brought the school to a higher level of academic achievement. While trying to give all areas of the University equal administrative and financial attention, he realized that the School of Religion "was the important school," but he was always concerned that the fine arts areas "didn't get pushed aside." It was this attitude that enabled all the programs of the school to grow throughout his tenure.[62]

Bob Jones Jr. was widely traveled, and his preaching career took him to every inhabited continent of the world, many countries, and every state in the union.[63] He preached to millions of people, saw many thousands converted to Christianity, and earned the devotion of friends and acquaintances around the world. Yet neither he nor the school made allies easily within the established Greenville power base.

Because the Greenville Chamber of Commerce had failed to fulfill its promises to the school regarding land acquisition and other matters pertaining to the school's move, Dr. Jones Jr.'s attitude toward the city fathers manifested itself in noninvolvement in the community's social and political life. For many years the leaders of the city, though recognizing that they were welcome as visitors on the campus, treated the institution as if it simply did not exist. These attitudes sometimes led to clashes between the school and the Greenville political establishment and tended to isolate the school from the community.[64] Some within the community never truly accepted either the presence or the importance of the institution to the fabric of Greenville's cultural, spiritual, economic, and intellectual life. Only when the chamber of commerce finally settled its obligation with the University in the 1980s did this situation begin to change.

In addition to his role as educator, preacher, actor, art collector, and world traveler, Bob Jones Jr. authored numerous books (sermons, poetry, and two novels); a play on the life of Jon Huss; and a nationally syndicated newspaper column, "A Look at the Book," carried by more than three hundred newspapers. He represented the conservative and Fundamentalist viewpoint in anthologies of religious essays and on the NBC television series *What They Believe.*

His roles as educator, evangelist, scholar, cultural advocate, and apologist for Fundamentalism made Bob Jones Jr. a powerful influence in American Fundamentalism. Furthermore, those qualities—along with his aggressive leadership and demanding personality—likewise shaped Bob Jones University as a Fundamentalist institution. His contribution, like his father's, was immeasurable.

CHAPTER 12

◆

"The Most Wonderful Place in the World"

Though the structures of Bob Jones University were finished between mid-August and mid-September, a staggering amount of work remained to be done before the campus was habitable. All the floors of the classroom buildings, the dormitories, and the Student Center had to be hand scrubbed to remove the red stain of Carolina clay; the concrete floors then had to be sealed, waxed, and buffed. The dormitories and classroom buildings had to be cleaned, the windows washed, and the furniture installed. Students' and teachers' desks had to be moved into the classrooms from warehouses scattered throughout Greenville; books remained to be shelved in the library; offices had to be readied for use. The job list seemed endless. With the help of faculty and student workers who had arrived early, R. K. Johnson saw to it that the campus was ready for occupancy on time.[1] Surveying the campus, Dr. Jones Sr. described it as "the most wonderful place in the world."[2]

When the faculty arrived on September 27 all the projects were nearly complete. By the time the students arrived on October 1, everyone was "amazed to see such a big campus and buildings. Everything looks great!"[3]

Bob Jones University, Greenville, South Carolina (1948)

The new buildings were impressive and the campus was spacious, but it was far from attractive. "There were no trees. There was no shrub nor blade of grass when we arrived," one student recalled. A student joked that it was not necessary to post "Keep off the grass" signs; there was no grass. It was "one bleak, barren clay spectacle," another commented.[4] Everything had been cleared for construction with the exception of a lone oak tree that had somehow avoided destruction. Still "it was really quite exciting."[5]

Bob Jones University created a stir among the journalists of the area. Feature articles about the school ran in papers throughout the Southeast, including a three-part series published by the *Charlotte (N.C.) News.* Though skeptical, these writers were fascinated by the strict rules (which they termed "many unique restrictions"), the emphasis on Shakespeare and high culture, the importance of academics, and the emphasis on "old-time" Bible Christianity.[6] Most denominational schools had abandoned strict social regulations during the 1930s, allowing dancing and social drinking and eliminating such things as chaperonage. The arrival of GI Bill war veterans "forced" schools to further liberalize their discipline policies—especially their dating regulations. The differences between Bob Jones University, which held to its standards, and many other schools such as the Presbyterians' Winthrop College or the Baptists' Furman University, which did not, were now striking.

To these journalists, rigorous discipline mixed easily with conservative religion. But neither strict discipline nor religion mixed well with high culture or academics, they believed. Why would students attend a school noted for strictness and discipline? Why would a school that believed in the "old-time religion" devote effort to Shakespeare, opera, concerts, and other elements of high culture? Why would militantly conservative Christians be interested in book knowledge? One writer observed that "the Christian ideals of the school do not prevent the college from having the highest academic standards."[7] Why nearly twenty-five hundred students would travel an average of one thousand miles each to attend such an institution was a mystery.

In considering these questions, one writer said, "What brings them here is a craving for learning in an atmosphere of the old-time religion—but the people are not religious cranks. 'How could they be?' asks Bob Senior. 'You put a fanatic here and let him study science and mathematics, and he'll cool down. We aren't running a nut factory. We let the fools go before they finish.' "[8]

On October 1, 1947, Bob Jones University opened with 2,494 students.[9] Amazingly, even the new campus was not large enough. Because of space limitations, over 3,200 applicants had been turned away![10] The campus dormitories were designed to accommodate only 2,000, yet to make room for as many as possible the school moved trailers from Cleveland and added a trailer park for single men in the back campus area. In the same area, the school placed six barracks units and moved in two small, three-room houses.

Across from the campus, east of S.C. Highway 291, three private trailer parks opened for the benefit of Bob Jones students. Most of this housing was used by married students, many of whom were veterans, who were, in spite of the conditions, grateful to be in Greenville, have a roof over their heads, and be among those enrolled in school.[11] Some of the on-campus trailers and barracks later became faculty housing.[12]

The student body's diversity was unmatched by any other school in either of the Carolinas. Students came from forty states and several foreign countries. As in every year since the school's first, evangelistic meetings opened the term. Dr. Jones Sr. preached and many of the young people made decisions for Christ. The auditorium was not yet completed, so students were assigned to two different locations in the Student Center complex for the opening service—the War Memorial Chapel and the gymnasium.[13] A blown fuse in the Student Center, however, made it necessary for the first evangelistic meeting on the new campus to be held in the Dining Common.[14]

Classes began on October 6, 1947, and the new University was in full operation. The academic organization of the University was significantly different from that of Cleveland and was first announced to the faculty by the new President, Bob Jones Jr., in a faculty meeting on January 6, 1947.[15] The University was organized into six schools: the College of Arts and Sciences, the School of Fine Arts, the School of Education, the School of Aeronautics, the School of Religion, and the School of Commerce.[16] Even with the addition of the schools of Commerce, Education, and Aeronautics, Bob Jones University offered the largest number of majors in the School of Fine Arts, while the largest number of students were enrolled in the School of Religion.

The curriculum of the University, as expected, was greatly expanded from what it had been as a college. For example, the University language departments offered instruction in French, German, Spanish, Russian, Chinese, Italian, ancient Greek, Hebrew, and other languages; eleven majors in languages were available in all. More than seventy-five music courses were carried in the course bulletin, and a full range of biology, botany, chemistry, and physics courses was offered.[17] BJU expanded from twelve majors in Cleveland to offering thirty-three undergraduate majors, eleven master's degrees, and a Ph.D. in religion that first year in Greenville. Deans were appointed to manage each school of the University and to organize the academic affairs of that school.[18] Long-time associate James D. Edwards, though officially dean of students, had oversight over the faculty as well.

After a rather normal summer which had helped to expedite construction, an unusual amount of rain fell that first October and November. The campus was turned into oozing, creeping rivers of red mud and gluelike red clay that stained everything it touched: shoes, clothing, floors, and carpets. When asked to describe the new campus, the students responded, "MUD! Mud everywhere."[19] Many of the sidewalks had not yet been poured when

J. Y. Smith and Bibb Graves Halls (boys' dormitories), Mack Library at far right (ca. 1948). Note the "mud everywhere."

the rains hit, so temporary boardwalks were laid and makeshift bridges were constructed from wooden planks to span the muddy flow of unpaved sections of the streets. The landscape was almost surreal—red clay earth with yellow brick rising from it. The campus in the fall of 1947 was a barren, wet, muddy, mucky mess.

In spite of the muck, the formal dedication was held on Thanksgiving night as the crowning event of that week's festivities. The service, held in the "massive" new three-thousand-seat Rodeheaver Auditorium, opened with a one-hundred-voice choir singing the Hallelujah Chorus. The student body and visitors recited the University creed, then joined in singing the University hymn. Both Bob Jones Sr. and Jr. offered comments, as did the mayor of Greenville and other state and local officials and visiting college presidents.[20]

After the introductions of the distinguished guests, words of welcome, and comments from the dignitaries present, the President offered the dedicatory prayer, calling upon God to enlighten the minds of those who teach and study in the institution, so that "no youth here shall ever lose his faith." He prayed that the school should "never be a spot where wisdom boasts of its own power. Thine it is," the President concluded fervently. "We pray Thee that it shall ever be Thine."[21]

The Founder, in his remarks, assured the audience that "high academic standards [will] be maintained" but that "we [will] never strut our academic standards"; rather, the faculty, staff, and administration were determined to stay true to God Almighty and do what He called the school to do. "This institution," he said, "has put Jesus Christ first in everything. The school already belongs to God. The devil is a four-flusher. Everything he has is stolen. Everything belongs to God. This is simply our recognition of the fact that this school is God's."[22]

The crowd rose and joined in singing the Doxology, and William Ward Ayer, pastor of Calvary Baptist Church of New York City, offered the benediction.

In mid-December, the school began a concerted effort to beautify the barren grounds. A plant nursery in Liberty, South Carolina, was contracted to supply the campus with trees and bushes.[23] One student recalled that it was not uncommon to look outside a window during class and see a full-grown, twenty-five-foot tree pass by on the bed of a truck, on its way to be planted.[24] Within one year, the lawns were seeded and thriving and the first plantings by the soon-to-be shaded and oak-arched streets and sidewalks had been completed.

A writer had concluded that "surely the miracle of building construction at Greenville will be matched by a miracle in Christian education when Bob Jones University opens its new home."[25] This was the case. To those who came to study and to those who taught, "everything seemed just perfect."[26] Dr. Jones Sr. had always preached that Christian education could occur only as Christian teachers work with Christian students in a Christian environment of discipline, loyal dedication, and loving service. Indeed, Faculty Meeting Minutes for the early Greenville years and the recollections of those early faculty members show an amazing singularity of purpose. Personal ambitions paled, for a short time, in the light of "the Cause." Total dedication was the expectation and the norm.

At the time of the dedication, Bob Jones Sr. was sixty-four years of age and was full of vitality and exuberance for life and the gospel. He called himself "the Budget Boy" and kept close track of donations and the school's financial outlook. He was seemingly haunted by the depression-era events in Florida when the school almost closed its doors. Although he was a demanding boss, he was also a thoughtful one. After being away from the campus for an extended period, he would often return to the office, call impromptu meetings of the staff and "really go after" them to root out inefficiency. He feared wasting God's money and losing God's blessing. "Not slothful in business, fervent in spirit, serving the Lord!" he reminded the staff. After such a session he would sometimes feel bad about getting after the office staff, and the next day before they arrived for work, he would place a nickel on everyone's desk to cover the cost of a coffee break just to encourage them.[27] On the campus, the faculty children flocked to him for hugs, pats on the head, and the shiny nickels that seemed to line his pockets. All these were given with a kind word and a twinkling eye.

R. K. Johnson and Dining Common employees

141

Campus expenses were staggering, yet God provided for the needs. To save money, provisions for the dining hall were purchased and delivered on a daily basis so that little or no waste in the food would occur. The financial strain was immense and was carried by the Founder, the President, and R. K. Johnson. Payments on the loan from Jefferson Standard were accelerated, maintenance costs were large, and so were the expenses of landscaping and completing the furnishing and decoration of the new buildings. Faculty needs also increased with time—medical care, life insurance, salaries, and housing all needed attention.

The "first unit" stood as a tribute "that God did what man said couldn't be done."[28] Along the front curved drive stood an impressive array of new structures. On the east, the Administration Building, with its tower, held twenty-five offices and a fully modern switchboard. The Dining Common, at the rear of the Administration Building, was constructed in the shape of a huge square, with a copper-topped octagonal tower rotunda for a main entrance. Fifteen hundred could be seated for the family-style meals; hence, two shifts for all three meals were necessary. The Student Center was to the west of the Dining Common; it was shaped like an elongated H. It was anchored on the east by the gymnasium and on the west by the War Memorial Chapel. The second floor held the Social Parlor, a powder room, and three formal parlors. Downstairs, shops for student convenience were opened: Little Moby's (the snack shop), a formal tearoom, barber shop, campus store,

post office, *Vintage* office, and photo shop. When school opened in October the auditorium, standing at the back of a large, central common, was not yet completed. The Alumni Building, west of the Student Center, housed three floors of classrooms and a wing of faculty offices. Next in line was the impressive Mack Library, with its "closed stacks" (i.e., bookshelves accessible only to library workers), three reading rooms, and on the top floor, the Bowen Museum of Biblical Antiquities. A second group of buildings went up on the east side—two women's dormitories and Grace Haight Hall and Faculty Court for faculty and staff families. Located on the west edge were two

Bob Jones Sr. preaching in chapel (1949); Dean James D. Edwards is seated at left.

men's dorms, music practice studios, and maintenance offices.[29]

Following completion of the "first unit," dramatic growth in facilities occurred.[30] The University raised funds and made needed improvements or built buildings at the rate of nearly a building a year. In 1949 BJU built radio station WMUU (for "World's Most Unusual University") on the campus for the purpose of "providing religious, educational, and cultural broadcasts, as well as high type entertainment. No swing, no hillbilly, no jazz" was broadcast, unlike any other station in the Upstate.[31]

In 1950 an art gallery was constructed and a cinema building was built and outfitted. The next year, four army barracks were moved from Cleveland, Tennessee, and placed back campus in a quadrangle. One was outfitted for University science labs and classrooms, one became the campus hospital, one was decorated and turned into a home economics house, and one became the Academy building.[32]

In spite of growing needs and expenses, the Founder and President were determined to give back to God a portion of all that was received. In March of 1952 Dr. Jones Sr. announced that henceforth 50 percent of all funds received in offerings would be used for missionary projects around the world; the other 50 percent would be used for building and maintenance needs on the campus. That same March, the Student Loan Endowment Fund was established with a goal of one million dollars to aid students on work scholarships.[33]

With a newly established art museum, a cinema program, a radio station, concerts, lectures, and exciting special events, Bob Jones University was one of the most exhilarating places to be in South Carolina.[34] It was, as one former dean described it, a "high pressure" organization.[35] Yet BJU was the most wonderful place in the world. It was God's place.

CHAPTER 13

◆

Clouds on the Horizon

The years between 1947 and 1953 seem to the casual observer to be tranquil enough both at the University and on the national religious scene. However, upon closer examination, it is evident that the clouds of a series of storms that would reach full intensity when passing the campus were forming on the horizon. Three of those "storm clouds" were Ted Mercer, the National Association of Evangelicals and New Evangelicalism, and Billy Graham.[1] Each of these storms tended to shift the focus of the public away from the University's educational work toward the personality and beliefs of the Founder and the President and the underlying Fundamentalist philosophy of the institution. In many ways the situation involving Ted Mercer (see Chapter 14) was an outgrowth of some of the events that developed on the campus between 1947 and 1953.

The hiring philosophy of the school, first proposed by J. S. Mack in 1933 and instituted during the Cleveland years, remained unchanged. The primary goal of the Founder and the President was to build an organization that would be loyal in all particulars.[2] The majority of the faculty, therefore, had received their undergraduate education at Bob Jones College. Because of this, the internal bond of the College was strong and a strong goal orientation existed.

Administrators, secretaries, and office staff routinely worked six days a week and worked not just eight hours each day but until that day's job was finished. Sometimes office personnel worked from 8:00 A.M. to 10:00 P.M. or later to "finish the job," and they seemed to thrive on the challenges.[3] Some administrators, such as R. K. Johnson, often returned to work on Sunday afternoon after church or Vespers.

The executives set the pace and were the example for everyone else to follow. Their schedules were extraordinarily rigorous. They managed campus affairs, received official visitors, continued their preaching schedules, kept correspondence current, raised money, and recruited students. In addition to these things, Dr. Jones Sr., for example, opened all donation mail when he was on campus and often answered donation letters personally and at some length.[4]

The internal bond of the organization was harder to maintain after the College became a university. The expansion required a larger faculty with greater academic diversity in order to carry out the requisite course offerings of a university.[5] The President, therefore, aggressively sought out and recruited new faculty members. Some of these faculty were former GIs, saved during the war, who became interested in the school. Others were college teachers who contacted the school about faculty positions; occasionally, Dr. Jones Jr., during preaching trips overseas, would recruit a teacher from a European college or university.[6] Some of these teachers were "brought on board" without a thorough check of character or academic or religious backgrounds, and sometimes they simply did not fit in.[7] They were, however, required to be "born-again Christians [who] . . . could ascribe to the creed."[8]

Many of the new teachers found that the University was run differently from anything they had previously experienced in the academic world—the University "required a . . . Christian discipline and a practice of administrative authority" that was unique.[9] The sum effect of the rapid growth of the school was, therefore, a rather hodgepodge group of faculty, some with great peculiarities. Most, though, were academically sound. The University opened with seventy-nine faculty members, including forty-one who were new to the school. A large number of graduate assistants with Bob Jones bachelor's degrees were hired to teach freshman-level classes while working on advanced degrees.

Statistics from the Cleveland years show an increasing number of faculty holding bachelor's degrees from Bob Jones College. (See Table 2 below.) An examination of the University's *Catalogue* confirms that this trend continued in Greenville as well.[10] This pattern also reflects the hiring advice given by J. S. Mack many years earlier.

Table 2

Percentage of Bob Jones Undergraduate Degrees on BJU Faculty[11]

Year	Faculty	BJ Degrees	Percentage
1947-48	79	38	47
1951-52	96	55	57
1955-56	106	50	47
1959-60	139	91	65
1963-64	145	110	76
1967-68	175	117	67
1970-71	199	144	72

Life at the school was rigorous for the teachers, and the schedule was demanding. The faculty carried large teaching loads—twenty to twenty-five credit hours.[12] Living conditions were Spartan and salaries were meager. The bonus system that had been in effect in Cleveland as a way of rewarding the faculty for their work continued in Greenville, even though the University was under extreme financial pressure. The bonuses, in fact, were in the form of a written contract, paid to the teachers at the end of each semester, and bonus amounts were often the equivalent of several months' salary.[13] Wives were required to work on the campus. All faculty were required to live in University-supplied housing. The faculty, if not on an extension ministry, were required to attend Sunday church and midweek prayer meetings on the campus. All meals were taken at the Dining Common at the same time as the students' meals.[14] The faculty and students were like one large family, and thus campus life re-

In the Dining Common: Dr. Bob Jones Sr.'s 69th birthday (1952)

quired a type of "community living" that put unique pressures on all the teachers, and many of those who came from other academic settings found these arrangements difficult.[15]

Study of the faculty suggests that turnover was high—averaging 32 percent between the years 1947-48 and 1954-55, with an increase to 55 percent during 1953-54.[16] Teachers left Bob Jones University for reasons not unlike those found in other institutions: graduate assistants completed their academic work; faculty took Christian ministries in other parts of the country; some left to pursue advanced degrees; others left for health or family welfare. Others left because they were disgruntled.

It should not be assumed, therefore, that events coming in 1953 were those which caused faculty turnover. Rather, the turnover may in fact have caused the events. Things transpired during this time that had the effect of testing the faculty's loyalty, either drawing them into a tightly knit and cohesive unit or causing them to dissociate themselves from the institution. These events also aided in formalizing the administrative structure. One dean characterized things by writing,

> In my view, the high rate of faculty turnover at the university between 1950 and 1953 . . . was at least in part the result of the school's sudden growth from a college to a university. By that, I mean that the immediate acquiring of a larger number of faculty with a greater diversity of expertise was required. The school did this in two ways—by going into the ranks of its own recent graduates to secure genuinely Christian faculty members. The faculty was composed, therefore, of a large proportion of very young people, many of whom were recent graduates of the Cleveland years. However, it is interesting to note that there is a significant number of longtime faculty members like myself who received undergraduate degrees in 1952 and 1953, who then became teaching assistants as graduate

students, and now still remain on the faculty. These young teachers "weathered the storm" of 1953 better than some of their older colleagues.

Also, it appeared to me as a student that the University reached out considerably to find educators in the general academic community. Of course, these people had to ascribe to the creed of the University and had to attest to the fact that Christ was their personal Savior. In those days, the lines between Fundamental Christianity, New Evangelicalism, and what are now the liberal churches of the main-line denominations had not been drawn. Faculty members who were born-again Christians and who could ascribe to the creed could be drawn from many main-line sources. . . .

It [was] my impression as a student that some of these outside academics had come into a situation which required a type of community living, Christian discipline, and a practice of administrative authority that they would not necessarily experience in a secular academic community. As a student, I noticed that some of these academic people would stay with the school for only a year or two.[17]

This same dean recalled having three different speech teachers during his first semester of freshman speech in 1948 because two teachers simply left the school in the middle of the semester. But for most of the faculty, the University was a great place to live, work, and rear a family, even in the face of difficult circumstances.

The storm that broke in 1953 appears now, with the passage of time, to have been brewing on the school's horizon since the relocation to Greenville. It was no secret that life at the school was demanding of time, energy, talents, and personal character. One staff member during those years summed it up by saying, "Everyone either worked hard, all pulling in the same direction, or you got out."[18] The executives demanded effort, and they also demanded loyalty. Dr. Jones Sr. would often preach, "A man who isn't loyal isn't anything."

Between the years 1948 and 1954, there was increasing incidence of preaching on the subject of loyalty—specifically, loyalty to God, loyalty to His Word, loyalty to authority, loyalty to the government, and loyalty to the school.[19] In one chapel talk soon after the opening of school in Greenville, Dr. Jones Jr. preached,

I understand we have a [town student], an old student, who came here in connection with the school, who says we are too strict out here, too narrow-minded. He is critical of the school. Now, son, you can just pack up your wife and family and house, and go somewhere else. We are not interested in folks who are not interested in the program of this school. A fellow who is disloyal to this school, he has no place in the school. If we are going to have critics, we had rather have them outside.

Young people, there is nothing that can hurt this institution as long as it is "right" on the inside. "If God be for us, who can be against us?" If you are a griper in this institution, the trouble is you have got a sin buried in your heart. . . . We are going to insist upon loyalty and cooperation.

If you can't back the program of Bob Jones University . . . if you don't believe that a Christian ought to live the life of a Christian, then you are not a Christian. You don't belong to Bob Jones University. Bob Jones University is in the business of training Christian leaders.[20]

The chapel talk is remarkable for its prescience. Even more remarkable is that from the beginning of the Greenville years, these same chords were struck repeatedly in chapel. Bob Jones University, its administrators, faculty, and students were being prepared for the issues to be faced and the battles to be fought in coming years.

In Cleveland, Tennessee, Dr. Jones Sr. often expressed his admiration for the faculty and staff and for their servants' spirit and willingness to sacrifice personal ambitions for the sake of the College and the cause it represented. In a chapel talk made just before leaving Cleveland, Dr. Jones said that "we do have teachers that sacrifice. These teachers work hard. There is one thing about our teachers—there isn't a crowd of teachers anywhere on earth that work like we do. But we work for the Lord. That's the reason we do it."[21] Conditions in Cleveland were such that sacrifice was necessary. Salaries, though modest, were regular and satisfactory.

In housing, sacrifice is clearly evident. In Cleveland, two or three faculty families often lived in one large house, sometimes sharing bath and kitchen facilities. Some single teachers lived in dormitory-like apartments. Some married couples lived in rooms that also served as that couple's classroom, music studio, or office. Mr. and Mrs. Oliver Steiner of the music faculty, for example, lived in the studio space in which they both taught. The studio, with a couch and chair, and their grand piano, served as their living room with a bedroom and bath attached.[22] All faculty also took their meals in the Dining Common with the students.

As odd as these arrangements may seem today, the nation had just emerged from depression and world war. Little private construction had been allowed during the war, and with thousands of GIs returning home, government restrictions remained on almost everything. With industry continuing its war-related production, housing was stretched beyond reasonable limits all across the nation, often with the same effects as those felt on the campus. There was a spirit of personal sacrifice still evident in the country and "the Cause" was everything—whether the cause was the war effort or the cause of Christ at the College. As one observer put it, "Living was simpler and harder for everyone in those postwar years."[23]

Living on the campus was unique in that faculty life was oriented on the campus community. Salaries were based on need, not on education or position. Housing, said to be as equal as possible, was provided by the school. Meals were available for all in the Dining Common but at the same time and in the same room with the students. The campus was a somewhat cloistered community unto itself.

Dr. Jones Sr. recognized the hardship these conditions placed on the faculty. He therefore communicated his sincere desire to provide each faculty family with its own house or apartment, a desire some faculty members took as a promise to be fulfilled when they arrived in Greenville.[24] When the faculty arrived, housing was at a premium and disappointment was easy to come by.[25] Although two permanent apartment units were constructed with the original plant—the Faculty Court Apartments and the Grace Haight apartments—the units contained housing for perhaps twenty-five to thirty families. With a faculty approaching one hundred in 1952—some forty to fifty families plus numerous single teachers—it is obvious that a severe shortage of suitable housing occurred and the "promise" of a house for all was unfulfilled.

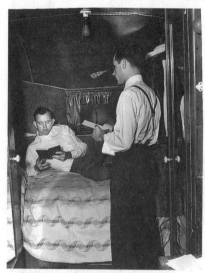

Interior of trailer housing for single staff men (ca. 1950)

Single faculty and staff women, during the first year in Greenville, were housed on the ground floor of Graves Hall, a men's dormitory, in a wing that had been partitioned off from the rest of the building. Single staff men lived in trailers, and several old-time faculty, such as Dr. Broken-shire, had small houses in the back-campus area. Married faculty with children were assigned to apartments in Faculty Court or Grace Haight Hall based on seniority, family size, or other criteria. Married faculty not in the apartments were placed in small trailers or in one of the prefab barracks units erected on the west edge of the campus.

There was, however, an undercurrent of dissatisfaction that developed because of the burdens of housing, work, or medical care.[26] In housing, for example, it was not until 1963 that the first single-family houses were actually built for faculty members.[27] The Jones home, properly constructed first, had been built in 1949, but it was built with funds donated by Mrs. Stollenwerck. Administrators, like some of the faculty, lived in the apartment buildings until homes for administrators were completed in 1954 and 1955. It took eight more years before any permanent faculty housing plans were laid.[28]

Faculty families, in large part, remained in housing that was in many ways substandard—uninsulated, some lacking bath facilities, others having no kitchens, and always extremely small. As families increased in size, the small one- and two-room apartments of the barracks units forced the faculty to become creative in managing their families. One faculty member constructed an "addition" to his tiny dwelling out of cardboard. By tacking boxes to the barracks siding and using a window as a crawl-through door, he built a cardboard bedroom for his children. Another faculty member designed and built a swing-away berth attached to the wall and ceiling of their one room. On this berth, which swung down over their bed, the parents could bed down their three children. Dr. Grace Haight simply referred to the barracks units and trailers as "The Slum."[29]

The Founder and the President both relied on R. K. Johnson to manage the housing and financial arrangements with the faculty. They assumed, because housing or financial problems only occasionally came to their attention, that the faculty were well provided for and happy. This assumption was unfounded. There was unrest because of perceived inequities in housing, salaries, staff work hours, and wives' jobs.[30] Often, faculty would approach the business manager with dire financial or personal needs. Johnson would spend time going over faculty expenses and often find solutions to the problems. Sometimes it was necessary for him to caution the complainants to examine their hearts for a spiritual problem and live by faith. For some, personal circumstances became so severe that seemingly the only solution was to seek employment elsewhere, resign, and leave, which they did with a heavy heart. Many of the details of these situations never came to the attention of the President or the Founder, though they were informed of the situations.[31] Sometimes they did intervene, as in the case of one young married faculty member[32] and one administrator.[33] Very often, though, they felt it unnecessary to pursue further matters that R. K. Johnson had settled, since they trusted his judgment.[34]

"Silver City" trailer housing in Greenville (ca. 1950)

In instances where a clear-cut decision was difficult, Johnson or other administrators took the details directly to the Founder or the President for action. In their absence, Monroe Parker, and later Ted Mercer as assistant to the President, or James D. Edwards as dean of students, weighed issues and made decisions, but they also discussed them with one of the Drs. Jones. There were seemingly very few matters of which the Founder or President was not apprised. "At that time if there was a problem, it went right to Dr. Bob Sr. . . . [The school] was run like a tight ship."[35]

The financial and housing matters were laid at the feet of the business manager, who was in the difficult position of fulfilling his mandate—keeping the school financially solvent, as secure as possible, stable, and running efficiently—while at the same time being sensitive to the increasingly urgent needs of the faculty. He wrote, "I am trying to run the business end of this school the best I know how, and Dr. Jones Sr. and Jr. are looking to me to keep everything coordinated and running smoothly and efficiently."[36] "I am discharging my responsibility as business manager of this school and doing the best I can with all the light I have."[37] This mandate he managed with great skill, turning exceedingly small income and assets into a strong, financially robust organization, even though the school reportedly "did not have two nickels to rub together."[38]

In spite of what was felt by some old-time faculty as a growing isolation from the Founder and President, there was yet a deep sense of personal loyalty to Dr. Jones Sr. and Dr. Jones Jr. and an even greater sense of loyalty to the cause which they and the school represented.[39] The Founder had a powerful personality and a warmth of spirit that motivated people to willingly set aside personal interests for the cause. In spite of the undercurrent of problems with some of the faculty, there was a sense of unity on the campus among most of the faculty and the students. This was a unity of doctrine and direction.

One of Dr. Jones Sr.'s goals in founding the school had been to create a campus environment that was centered on the fundamental doctrines of Scripture around which all conservative Christians could rally. By 1948 this dream was largely reality: the student body was drawn from twenty-five different denominations, including Assembly of God, Baptist, Brethren, Congregational, Episcopal, Evangelical Reformed, Friends, Lutheran, Mennonite, Moravian, Methodist, Nazarene, Presbyterian, and Salvation Army.[40] The faculty was equally diverse. Yet sectarian and theological division was unheard of among the faculty, staff, or students until the rise of Neo-Puritanism in the 1960s.

The storm that broke in 1953 was not one of theology, but one arising from the undercurrents described.

CHAPTER 14

◆

The Storm of '53

Theodore C. Mercer (1921-86) graduated from Bob Jones College in 1943 and completed an M.A. degree from the College in 1944. By the time the school moved to South Carolina, Ted had been appointed to the administration and had served in various capacities, including director of Religious Activities (1944-45), dean of men (1945-47), registrar (1947-53), and assistant to the President (1951-53).

As registrar, Mercer served the school commendably. He possessed a brilliant mind and was efficient, well spoken, responsive to requests, charming, and personable. Most importantly, he enjoyed the full confidence of the Founder. Following the 1951 resignation of Monroe Parker, who was entering full-time evangelism, Bob Jones Sr. appointed Mercer to the position of assistant to the President, making him the "number three man" in the organization. Mercer was specifically charged to "safeguard the institution" in the absence of the Founder and the President.[1] In the event of the death of the President, he would "take over the responsibility of the executive head" of the institution.[2]

Mercer's appointment was made over the objections of both Mrs. Jones Sr. and Bob Jones Jr.; nevertheless, the President acquiesced to his father's wishes, thinking that he was perhaps misjudging Mercer. "When Dad decided we go ahead and use him, I dismissed whatever doubts I had and went with my Dad all out," Dr. Jones Jr. wrote, "boosting Ted and backing him in every way possible."[3]

After nearly fifteen years with the institution as both students and faculty members, Ted and Alice Mercer were popular among the faculty and administration, and they were a model couple. Yet at a special meeting of the Executive Committee of the Board of Trustees, held on June 15, 1953, Ted Mercer was fired as a result of evidence presented.[4] On July 8 fourteen members of the Board of Trustees unanimously passed a resolution supporting the action taken by the Executive Committee.[5]

The firing came as a shock to everyone, although one contemporary wrote that something was "fundamentally wrong with Ted" and that Mercer had "created a problem all year."[6] Records indicate, though, that just days before the firing, Mercer still had the confidence of the Founder. For example, on May 8, 1953, Dr. Jones Sr. responded to a bank query that Mercer "has been with us for a number of years. He plans to be with us next year."[7] On June 1, Dr. Jones Jr. wrote him a note about vacation time, urging him to take a quiet, restful vacation and not stay for an extended time "in the

153

home of one of our constituency. . . . It tends to produce a sense of obligation which is apt to influence a man in his dealings."[8] On June 6, Ted Mercer spoke in summer school chapel,[9] but by June 15, he was fired.

Mercer credited a 1951 disagreement with Dr. Jones Sr. over the selection of a physician as the "beginning of the end" for him, when in reality, a visit by one student's parents brought about his downfall.[10] During an October 1952 campus visit, these parents conferred with the dean of men, the dean of women, and Mercer about their daughter and her boyfriend. They came away confused by what they heard and later wrote that they sensed "there was something wrong" and that they "felt a Satanic force" on the campus. They began to pray that God would "clean up the school."[11] After the visit, the dean of women began checking some of the particulars mentioned by the parents and talked at length with Mercer about the situation and his relationship with the students in question.

It was widely known around campus that Mercer had gathered a group of "very bright but unspiritual" young men with whom he had regular "chat sessions" and confided information that was private and confidential about faculty members, administrators, school policies, and campus financial matters.[12] A dormitory hall monitor from this time recalled that it was common knowledge among the students that Mercer had a group of student friends who were immune from campus regulations and for whom Mercer would destroy or overlook demerits.[13]

On at least one occasion Mercer took no action against a student leader, whom he liked very much, for cheating on an examination—an offense punishable by expulsion. He destroyed the cheating evidence, tried to persuade eyewitnesses to change their stories, and finally instructed them not to discuss the case with anyone. Mercer told the offender, after he privately confessed, "not to mention the incident to anyone and that we would forget it."[14] Sometime later, another of Mercer's student friends was caught by a night watchman climbing out of a window with his girlfriend at 12:25 A.M. The incident was reported to Mercer for disposition, but he took no disciplinary action against the students.[15]

Mercer offered his office to students for unchaperoned dating.[16] He purchased clothing for a group of student admirers and on at least two occasions paid a student's expenses to accompany him to conventions and share hotel accommodations.[17] He also routinely called some of these young men out of classes and rehearsals for long, private conversations, sometimes lasting up to four hours.[18]

A major public spectacle occurred after he had represented the University at a convention for college registrars. While there, the president of the student body, a close friend of Mercer's, with the help of Mercer's secretary, instigated a card and letter shower for Mercer at the Minneapolis convention. Following the convention, instead of returning to campus as expected, Mercer went to visit a male student at that student's home and stayed until

Dr. Jones Sr. contacted him by telephone and ordered him to return to Greenville immediately. Mercer returned, thinking he would be fired.[19] Nothing was said to him about this incident. At his first opportunity to speak in chapel when both the Joneses were absent, however, Mercer "strode on stage wearing a big cowboy hat, carrying all these letters and cards, much to the delight of the students." He took the entire chapel time reading student messages to himself from the chapel platform.[20] Infuriated by this exhibition of pomposity and self-indulgence, at least one administrator left the platform, and Mercer was called to defend his actions.

Three administrators—Gilbert Stenholm (director of Religious Activities), James D. Edwards (dean of students), and R. K. Johnson (business manager)—had conferences with Mercer on May 1, 1953.[21] The discussions dealt with the chapel service and their perceptions of his being "too friendly" with students. (At this time the specific cases mentioned above had not yet come to their attention.) All three administrators hoped to see a change in Mercer, but none occurred. At some point between May 26 and June 10, Edwards, Stenholm, and Johnson met with Dr. Jones Sr., informed him of their concerns, and related the details of their conference with Mercer. He subsequently met with Mercer and asked for an explanation of the chapel shenanigans and the "hobnobbing" with students.

Left to right: Bob Jones Jr., R. K. Johnson, Ted Mercer, Hazel Riley, and James Edwards (ca. 1946)

The family previously mentioned revisited the campus in late May and again met with Dean Riley. They said that they still felt uneasy about things but would not go into any details. When Riley reported this conversation to the other administrators at a June 10 meeting at which Mercer was present, Dr. Jones Jr. instructed her to request the parents to write and explain in detail what they were referring to in their conferences. "We know that our organization is not perfect," Miss Riley wrote to them, "but we are always striving to make it so. If there is something here that is wrong, we will see that it is made right."[22] A copy of this letter made its way to the University files, but the letter itself was never received by the parents.[23]

When the dean of women followed up the letter with a phone call to the parents and realized that it had never arrived, she reported this to the other

155

administrators. As a result of this and the Founder's conference with Mercer, a meeting of the Executive Committee was called on June 15, and a letter to the University President was drafted instructing him to release his assistant.[24] To fulfill the committee's instructions, the University sent a check for five hundred dollars to the Mercers as severance pay with a note stressing that there was no personal animosity held for either Ted or Alice, but that the policies of the institution had to be maintained.[25]

Suggestions that Mercer had been immoral angered those who knew him well and later increased the intensity of the attack on the University. One dean wrote, "I was not shown evidence to indicate that Dr. Mercer was inefficient, crooked, and by implication, immoral."[26]

Another aspect of the situation that has recently come to light is that Mercer, in his contacts as registrar, was perhaps seeking ways by which the school could accept accreditation. Much of his later published criticisms dealt with institutional issues that would be problematic only in gaining acceptance in an association. Among these were faculty salaries and benefits, faculty teaching loads, faculty ranking, library size, and so on. It seems probable that Mercer's vision for Bob Jones University was that it be accepted by the educational world at the expense of the spiritual.

Dr. Jones Sr. saw the school as an island of tranquility in a world crazy for hell. When the Mercer affair broke and the irrefutable evidence of failed standards was established, the tranquility of the campus was shattered and the battle was now at home, a battle that hurt Dr. Jones Sr. deeply.[27] He felt betrayed by one whom he had promoted, groomed for leadership, and treated as a son.[28] The issue, as Dr Jones Sr. saw it, was loyalty. Mercer's actions, he felt, were disloyal and a repudiation of the cause.

Ted Mercer knew why he was fired. However, he was accurate in writing later that he was not told the details that led to his firing. He wrote that "my only inkling comes as I review the conferences I had and the subjects of their displeasure with me."[29]

Four days after the firing, after both of the Joneses had left to begin evangelistic campaigns or attend meetings in different parts of the country, Mercer came to the campus, held a meeting with his office staff and secretaries, cleared a number of items from the office, and ultimately had to be escorted from the campus by security officers. Within four weeks of the firing, Ted Mercer published a twenty-page booklet detailing from his perspective the events that led to his dismissal through July 1953. Shortly after this booklet was distributed, a second booklet of twenty-four pages was published containing more substantive issues that related to salaries, faculty housing, and academic issues. The tone of this tract was belligerent and charged the sixty-nine-year-old Bob Jones Sr. with self-aggrandizement, negligence, deceit, and purposeful obstruction of the progress of the school.[30] A third statement appeared in August, defending Mercer's relationship with one pair of students.[31]

As registrar, Mercer had access to all student records, and when he left, he apparently took with him the only complete copy of student home mailing addresses that existed. He sent copies of these booklets to each student, as well as letters, some duplicated and some personal, attempting to dissuade them from returning to BJU. He sent copies of his material to all members of the Board of Trustees, asking them for an audience. Mercer also wrote the University's textbook suppliers and urged them to have no further business dealings with the school. He wrote letters to the South Carolina Department of Education, the United States Office of Education, the National Education Association, and other professional organizations urging, them to investigate Bob Jones University and sever educational ties with it.[32]

The school was forced to rebut the avalanche of Mercer material. Secretaries worked feverishly, reconstructing the stolen mailing lists and answering the questions of students, board members, and Christian leaders. All the teaching faculty were contacted by the administrators, and those who returned to school in the fall were awarded a fifty-dollar loyalty bonus.

The University did not publicize Mercer's firing in any way, beyond informing the Board of Trustees of the action of the Executive Committee. The first public report of the firing came on June 27, 1953, when three deans—Karl Keefer of the School of Fine Arts, Benedetto Ciliberto of the School of Commerce, and Laird Lewis of the School of Education—joined Ted Mercer for a press conference in Greenville. These deans, who by this time had also resigned, denied that their resignations were connected with Mercer's firing. But the press conference underscored the fact that faculty unrest was increasing and that the unrest was centered on the living conditions, salaries, and administrative structure of the school.[33] The interviews, though short on specifics, gave Mercer the opportunity to take private information to the non-Christian public for judgment—an event that caused "regret" in the heart of at least one of the resigned deans.[34]

When the *Greenville (S.C.) News* contacted the Founder in Birmingham, Alabama, he gave no specific reason for the firing but said in part, "Mr. Mercer was discharged after information was imparted to the seven members of the executive committee. . . . Every member of the executive committee voted to discharge Mercer. That is the only comment we have to make."[35] The Board of Trustees concurred with only two exceptions.[36]

By the time the news of the firing became public on June 27, most of the faculty had already heard about it, and those who were disgruntled also resigned.[37] After everything was sorted out, some fifty-three teachers left the school during the summer of 1953, but Dr. Jones later wrote that only twenty-three left because of Mercer.[38]

A group of students also withdrew from the school. Some of the dissident faculty, deans, and students created a "Joint Committee of Alumni and Former Students of Bob Jones University." They planned several meetings in major cities for the purpose of informing alumni and students of the "truth" of Mercer's firing.[39] The "committee" also authored and disseminated bitter letters of contempt toward Bob Jones Sr., many of which were sent to him anonymously.[40] Several thousand of these were mailed to faculty, students, and Christian leaders nationwide and contained numerous charges against the old warrior, Bob Jones.[41] Bob Jones Jr. recalled that for a short while, "it seemed as if the lid came off hell itself because of all the hatred" directed at the school.[42]

The board never made public the charges against Mercer. In fact, all the materials relating to this case have been sealed until now. The Founder and the President stated from the beginning, "We have no desire to reflect upon Dr. Mercer." Material sent out by the institution was, in tone and content, restrained but direct, answering Mercer's charges. The whole affair was dealt with in chapel that fall, and the theme for the year was "Morale Building."[43] The whole affair caused harm to the University's reputation for a short time. As rumors spread and became embellished, the public perception of the University became that of a troubled institution. Public confidence in the school was shaken for a time, as evidenced by correspondence received and answered by board members.[44] Mercer's letters to Christian leaders, to prospective students, to the dissident administrators, and to former students and faculty continued for nearly four years and caused some decline in enrollment. From 1953 through 1957, University enrollment gradually declined from 2,022 to 1,893; enrollment in the Graduate School fell slightly, but enrollment in the Academy increased.[45]

To many of the students who returned in September 1953 there was no discernible change in the school. "It was as if nothing had happened. None of the [resigned] faculty seemed to be missed."[46] Among the returning faculty, "there was a more intense spirit of loyalty [to the school] than before."[47] To Dr. Jones Jr. "it was like a new institution. The faculty that came through were unwavering and unmovable, and they became the nucleus" for the great advances that the school was able to make.[48] These young teachers "weathered the storm" of 1953 better than some of their older colleagues.[49]

The Storm of '53 had the effect of solidifying the previously untested administrative structure of the University and removing dissident administrators, faculty members, and students. In the final analysis it unified the remaining faculty and students and rallied them around the authoritative, Fundamentalist position of the school. Lines of responsibility were clearly delineated, and it was now obvious to all that school policy and administrative action had to be consistent. Not even the assistant to the President was exempt. These events may also have spurred the administration into a more responsive posture toward faculty concerns and needs.

With forty years' perspective, Dr. Jones Jr. saw the Storm of '53 as the hand of the Lord purifying and uniting the faculty in preparation for the battles against the New Evangelicalism and compromise evangelism that would be embodied by the Billy Graham Association.

On September 9, 1953, at the beginning of the next school year, the old evangelist, visibly weakened from the summer's struggle, preached the opening service. He discussed three "satanic attacks" the school had faced in its history: an attack on the creed by W. J. Hall in Florida; an attack on the Christian philosophy of self-control and self-restraint by Dorothy Seay and Joseph Free in Tennessee; and finally the recent attack on administrative policies by the spread of unrest. "Did you know that no Christian institution was ever destroyed by forces outside?" he preached. "They are always destroyed by forces inside. The Devil can't put enough guns on hell's battlements to blow up a Christian institution. He comes inside." Then he closed his message with a fervent prayer.

We thank Thee for handing this school down to us in spite of the world, the flesh, and the Devil. We thank Thee that we are here tonight in this wonderful place, and we dedicate it all anew to Thee, everything here. . . . Everything around here is Yours.

We are Yours. Lord God, we dedicate our own lives to Thee tonight with all we have and are. Let the power of God come upon the President of the University, upon all the staff, the deans, and all the faculty, Board of Trustees, and all these students. . . . Keep us what we ought to be.

Lord God, protect us in this day of moral looseness. Keep our lives right. Forgive us all our sins. Fill us with Thy Holy Spirit. Use us for Thy glory, for Jesus' sake. Amen.[50]

With this prayer, the future of Bob Jones University began anew.

CHAPTER 15

$\blacklozenge$

"What Difference Does It Make?"
BJU and the New Evangelicalism

From the earliest days of the school, both Bob Jones Sr. and Bob Jones Jr. had vigorously fought Modernism and had been proponents of separation—refusing organic union or cooperation with liberals or Modernists in any type of religiously oriented activity. They felt a kinship with all who supported the historic doctrines of the faith, and the University was an organization in which denominationalism was secondary to the tenets of historic faith. The unity thus promoted by the Joneses and the University was a unity of doctrine. The unity that came to be stressed in the 1950s in this country, however, was one of "mood, perspective, and experience" and not one of theology.[1] A movement toward separation developed, and since the 1950s separation has been the defining issue among conservative Christians.

Some years earlier the Founder had warned, "There are multiplied thousands of holy men in the pulpit, but don't you think that because a fellow has on a long-tailed preacher's coat [that] he's a good man. You judge him by the things he stands for."[2]

With the dissident element gone, the institution moved toward its maturity without diminishing its heritage, a heritage born out of the ideological and spiritual combat of the Fundamentalist-Modernist controversy of the 1920s. In the 1920s, the term "Fundamentalist" denoted one who held firmly to basic orthodox Christian beliefs and who fought for the "defense of the faith." By the 1930s and 1940s, the term was more commonly used as a pejorative, connoting that those who held such beliefs were unrefined, uneducated, fractious, and vituperative. Gradually, some Fundamentalists, hoping to stress the evangelistic zeal of Fundamentalism over the theological contentiousness, set aside the term and reappropriated the term "evangelical." In the late 1940s, the terms "orthodox," "evangelical," and "Fundamentalist" all held approximately the same meaning in the minds of the general public but conveyed varying degrees of erudition and pugnacity.[3]

The National Association of Evangelicals[4]

In the winter of 1940-41, Bob Jones Sr., along with 146 other orthodox Christian leaders, signed a letter urging conservative Christians to unite in forming an interdenominational body to represent evangelicals.[5] The letter specified that membership "be on a basis of the traditionally accepted evangelical position" and called for a meeting to be held in St. Louis at which the particulars of the organization would be discussed.[6] In St. Louis,

J. Elwin Wright stressed that the delegates were there "not to discuss a denominational union" but to resolve misunderstandings, and "to find common ground" on which to fight the "dictatorship of either government or ecclesiastical combinations" that restrain Christian liberty and evangelism.[7] With these aims, Bob Jones Sr. and Bob Jones Jr. agreed.

In May 1943 representatives of more than fifty denominations and numerous Christian schools and organizations gathered in Chicago and approved a constitution for the "National Association of Evangelicals for United Action" (NAE). The organization was to be a voluntary and democratic organization open to all who affirmed the doctrinal creed of the association and who were "evangelical in spirit and purpose."[8]

The doctrinal statement was strong and biblical, and it was accepted without dissent despite the numerous organizations, the many denominations represented, and the varied backgrounds of the delegates.[9]

The association agreed to focus on (1) evangelism, (2) the government and evangelicals, (3) the local and national use of radio, (4) public relations, (5) preservation of church and state, (6) Christian education, and (7) freedom for home and foreign missionary endeavor.[10] The Joneses were justifiably excited about the proposed organization because Dr. Jones Sr. was the "spiritual daddy of all" of the young evangelists; both Joneses were active in radio; and both were leaders of a growing, vibrant Christian college that was by far the largest in the country.[11] Bob Jones College became a member in the NAE's first year and actively supported the organization for the next ten years. Dr. Jones Sr. praised the spirit of unity that prevailed within the group, and he believed that "if orthodox Christians would magnify the things about which they agree as much as they emphasize the things about which they disagree, there would be more harmony among God's people."[12] The harmony he encouraged, however, was harmony of doctrine.

Both Joneses were active in the NAE and served in varying capacities. Bob Jones Sr. was named a director of the Religious Broadcasters from 1944 through 1947.[13] He was also elected to the Committee on Evangelism but was assigned a diminished role in spite of his long years of experience and thorough understanding of evangelistic methods.

Generally, Bob Jones Jr. took a more active and visible role in the organization than did his father. The younger Jones was elected to the Committee on International Relations and served at least through 1950.[14] In 1947 he was elected to the NAE's Board of Administration.[15] In 1950 Bob Jones Jr. was elected as one of two vice presidents of the NAE.[16]

Developing concurrently with the NAE was the American Council of Christian Churches (ACCC), Carl McIntire's separatist organization. The ACCC drew its membership from two small denominations—the Bible Presbyterians and the Bible Protestant churches—and a few small religious organizations. The dominant concern of the ACCC was fighting the Modernism of the Federal Council of Churches of Christ (the forerunner of the

National Council of Churches). The NAE and the ACCC shared some common goals, but the ACCC, while promoting unity among believers, showed delight at doing battle and promoted a "unity based on criticism" rather than the unity of common experience promoted by the NAE.[17] The NAE approached McIntire, hoping that common ground could be found to join together in the fight against Modernism, and invited him to present the goals and direction of the ACCC to the board of the NAE.

McIntire met the NAE board in October 1941, but they found no real basis for cooperation. Those present came to differing conclusions about the meeting. The historian of the NAE recorded that "it was the feeling of the larger group that [the ACCC] did not properly express and implement the constructive ideals which [the NAE] had in mind."[18] He continued, "A certain sector of American evangelical life had early withdrawn from the main stream of the new evangelical movement." It seemed to the NAE that the settled policy of the ACCC was never to cooperate with anything that it did not originate and to "brand as heretical that which did not conform to its *modus operandi*."[19]

Carl McIntire's recollections differ. He wrote that the NAE leadership backed away from its early support of his group after he presented a "clear-cut position . . . on separation from the Federal Council." He wrote, "The reasons they gave . . . for not coming with the American Council were: First, because the American Council planned to attack the Federal Council [of Churches of Christ] and oppose it, and because a line was drawn against it in the American Council's constitution. This they said would be unwise and we would not get anywhere. Second, the spirit of controversy that prevailed in the American Council leadership would be disastrous."[20] McIntire further expressed "that a 'mighty controversy was taking shape in Protestantism'—not a controversy between conservatives and modernists, but between separated conservatives and those who refused 'to take a stand against the Federal Council' " and to call for a repudiation of it.[21]

The dialogue ended as a dispute, and the Joneses and the University were caught in the middle. The University leadership weighed the two approaches, and though they supported the battle against the Federal Council, they sympathized more with the inclusive and constructive approach of the NAE; they therefore joined that organization. "We didn't wait to see how things were going," Dr. Jones Sr. wrote. "We didn't wait to find out whether it would hurt us with the American Council of Christian Churches or any other people. We knew the sacrifices we would have to make."[22] One immediate sacrifice was the financial support of folks in ACCC churches. Dr. Jones Sr., however, felt that the NAE "might be the last chance we would ever have in this country to do the job [of evangelism]. The NAE could have captured the imagination of all the conservatives and also the preachers and religious leaders on the borderline between conservatism and modernism and could have swept this country."[23] With its narrow platform, the ACCC could not have accomplished this goal.

In addition, Bob Jones Jr. disliked McIntire's methods and felt that the exclusion of Pentecostals from the ACCC was wrong because "they represented a strong, Bible-believing force" that would have been an asset.[24]

McIntire attacked the NAE and, by virtue of its widely publicized association, Bob Jones University. Attacks on the school by Modernists were not troubling, but attacks from separatist evangelicals "must have been particularly galling."[25] Pressure on the Joneses also began to mount inside the NAE itself. Dr. Jones Sr. was made a junior member of the Committee on Evangelism, a "snub" he tried not to take personally.[26] He expressed his opinions about the NAE's tendency to attack Romanism instead of Protestant Modernism, and there were clashes over other issues, all of which he said were "misunderstood" by other members of the committee; his opinions were clearly held suspect by the other committee members. More painful than this, however, was the rejection of the newly built BJU campus as the site for the NAE national convention.[27]

As troubling as these things were to Dr. Jones Sr., the largest problems occurred in the arena of the NAE's educational committees. In 1946 the NAE established the Commission on a Christian Philosophy of Education to develop a guiding ideology for Christian education.[28] Although this commission was to include "representatives of every sphere of evangelical educational activity," Bob Jones University was conspicuous by its absence.[29]

Dr. Jones Sr. was stunned that with "twice as many students as the largest other well-known evangelical school in America," BJU would be unrepresented when it came to writing a philosophy statement.[30] Hurt feelings were not the issue, Dr. Jones Jr. argued. "We are convinced that the convictions and attitudes of Bob Jones University will have to be represented, at least to some extent, in any report that sets forth the broad evangelical viewpoint of what constitutes a Christian philosophy of education since this institution has had a growth and an appeal unparalleled" in American educational history.[31]

A major objective of the NAE Commission on Education, from its inception in 1943, was to gain intellectual acceptability of evangelical religious beliefs by secular and Modernist scholars. The commission, therefore, encouraged Bible schools and Christian colleges to seek membership in accrediting associations.[32] The commission, while stating that the proclamation of the truth be "in the demonstration of the Spirit and of power," also supported the view that "scholarly" attacks on belief need to be met with "equal and better scholarship."[33] The position of the University on the issues of accreditation and "matching wits" was well known and may account for the reasons that BJU was not represented on the philosophy committee and that the final report did not reflect any dissenting viewpoints. When the committee's report, *Christian Education in a Democracy,* was published in

1951, it took a position of unqualified support of accreditation: "The best scholastic progress has come about through voluntary acceptance of standards formulated by accrediting agencies." It offered that institutional membership brings healthy self-examination and criticism vital to destroying the educational complacency that existed in some Christian education.[34] The report conceded that young colleges with limited resources should not expect to receive immediate accreditation, but no concession was made to established schools that rejected accreditation out of religious conviction. In fact, convictions against accreditation were met with skepticism, and NAE committee member Carl F. H. Henry wrote Dr. Jones Jr. that "all too often a negative attitude toward the accrediting agencies implies also a refusal to meet certain worthwhile academic standards."[35]

The commission report also spoke to the need for a Christian university. The opinion expressed was that "as yet American evangelicals have no university, in the strict sense of the term, that they can call their own. . . . No university maintaining all or most of the graduate departments is fully committed to a consistently biblical philosophy of education."[36] The committee, with its agenda for acceptability, had overlooked or dismissed BJU and the potential for evangelicalism and scholarship that it represented.

The University took another direct hit when Fuller Theological Seminary, established in 1947 as an outgrowth of the NAE's interest in education, questioned the University's educational standards. "Will you please send me a list of the fully accredited seminaries which have given you assurance of the acceptability of graduates of Bob Jones University?" Carl F. H. Henry wrote to Bob Jones Sr.[37] The Founder's response, in part, was one of disappointment that "an orthodox seminary [would turn] 'thumbs down' on graduates of an orthodox educational institution" whose graduates were well trained.[38] Speaking for Fuller, Henry responded, "lacking this evidence, we could only embarrass ourselves at some future date" if Fuller admissions practices were examined by an accrediting committee.[39]

The last straw in the relationship between BJU and the NAE came in the form of a list of evangelical colleges published in the official NAE periodical, *United Evangelical Action*. The list was first published in 1948 with Bob Jones University included among the schools. The same was true of the 1950 directory. The 1948 list had been compiled without the knowledge of the Joneses, however, and by 1950 Dr. Jones Sr. had given the first directory close scrutiny. Some of the schools listed, though religious or church affiliated, had well-known Modernists or liberals on their faculties. These teachers destroyed the faith of young people and sent them home as "shipwrecks," Dr. Jones said. The list, he believed, indicated tacit approval of the schools by the NAE and its constituent members. He simply could not stomach the thought of his or the University's membership fees going for the promotion of schools that would shipwreck young people. An all-inclusive list should never have been published, he argued, but a list of

NAE member institutions was acceptable and even desirable. His idea was rejected by the NAE leadership.[40] Rather than support a list that he felt would do "untold moral and spiritual harm," Bob Jones Sr. chose to resign quietly from the organization.[41]

Shortly thereafter, the University, instead of creating a public spectacle over the events, simply withdrew its membership from the NAE.[42] Bob Jones Jr. also withdrew his membership without making a public statement.[43] The leaders of the NAE begged both Joneses to reconsider and one later wrote, "I regret you and Bob Jr. are not still in NAE. Your school is built on NAE principles—not Am[erican] Council—exclusivistic—'everybody is wrong but us' position. . . . Neither of you are that type."[44]

The separation from the NAE, amicable but out of conviction, came after many years of close cooperation from the Joneses. Bob Jones Jr. wrote that "this action is not to be taken as any evidence of unfriendliness toward the National Association of Evangelicals or of any lack of desire on our part to co-operate with the NAE whenever we can conscientiously do so."[45] His father concurred when he wrote, "We do not wish to stir up strife. We are friends of the NAE. . . . We have sacrificed for the NAE. We have taken it under the chin; and . . . we have been snubbed by the NAE. But that doesn't matter."[46]

This was the first instance in which Bob Jones University and the Drs. Jones separated from brethren over an issue. It was done without rancor or publicity and was done out of firmly held conviction. The fracturing of Evangelicalism and Fundamentalism remained more or less behind the scenes, even though leaders like Harold Ockenga of the NAE (and president of Fuller Seminary) were calling for a "new evangelicalism" that would cross theological boundaries and bring about a conciliation with Modernism. The split in ideology was soon brought to the forefront of national attention with the "ecumenical evangelism" of Billy Graham—an evangelism that may be seen as the logical extension of the NAE practices of the early 1950s.

The Billy Graham Evangelistic Organization

The Billy Graham crusade in New York in 1957 marked the beginning of the public division that had been brewing in conservative Christianity for nearly a decade and continues to this day.[47] Because of their opposition to the Billy Graham organization and its "compromise with unbelievers," the Joneses and Bob Jones University have found themselves in the vortex of this controversy.[48] The University's Founder and its President became two of Fundamentalist Christianity's chief spokesmen and joined others, such as John R. Rice, Ernest Pickering, Charles Woodbridge, Bob Shuler, and Carl McIntire, in opposing the Billy Graham Evangelistic Organization's methods and the rising tide of New Evangelicalism.[49]

The relationship between Bob Jones Sr. and Billy Graham began in 1936. At the advice of evangelist and BJC graduate Jimmie Johnson and after listening to the glowing reports of his friend and BJC student, T. W. Wilson, Graham left Charlotte, North Carolina, to become a student at Bob Jones College. Graham was highly likeable and charming, handsome, and popular with his classmates. His one semester at Bob Jones College, however, was marked by poor academics and carelessness about the regulations. Rebellious, discouraged, and sick with allergies and flu, he left school for Christmas vacation and sought a doctor's advice. The Charlotte doctor advised him to consider a warmer climate, so the Graham family decided to visit the Florida Bible Institute, located outside Tampa, because of an advertisement they had seen in the *Moody Monthly*.[50]

When Graham returned to Cleveland, Tennessee, he broadcast that he and his roommate, Wendell Phillips, were leaving Bob Jones College. Dr. Jones Sr. called both young men in for "talking up" the Florida school and Phillips defied Dr. Jones to his face—something that Dr. Bob's temperament could not abide—and, among other things, told him that he was leaving. The effect was incendiary. During the session, Phillips remembered that Billy was "like a wounded dog with his tail between his legs. . . . He just sat there and bit his nails."[51]

After finishing with Phillips, Dr. Jones Sr. reportedly looked at Graham and said, "Billy, if you leave and throw your life away at a little country Bible school, the chances are you'll never be heard of. At best, all you could amount to would be a poor country Baptist preacher somewhere out in the sticks." Dr. Jones, however, recognized Graham's potential and continued, "You have a voice that pulls. Some voices repel. You have a voice that appeals. God can use that voice of yours. He can use it mightily."[52]

Graham left Bob Jones College in January 1937,[53] and he attended the Florida Bible Institute, where he completed the Christian Worker's Training Course Diploma after three and one-half years of study.[54] He eventually went to Wheaton College and completed a bachelor's degree in anthropology. He met and married Ruth Bell, the daughter of missionary doctor and surgeon L. Nelson Bell, who later became a chief apologist for his son-in-law.

Following a short pastorate at a small Illinois church, Billy Graham embarked on a career as a youth evangelist for Youth For Christ.[55] Billy's reputation as a speaker grew and he persuaded T. W. Wilson to join him for the huge, citywide youth rallies planned by YFC. The largest of these rallies was held at Soldier's Field in Chicago on Memorial Day, 1945.[56] After Graham had gained the attention of newspaper publisher William Randolph Hearst,[57] his name began to appear regularly in the American press.[58]

Billy Graham also joined the National Association of Evangelicals at about the same time as Dr. Jones Jr. and served with him on the International Committee on Evangelism.

In 1947, against his better judgment and over his initial opposition, Graham was made president of Northwestern Baptist Bible College in Minneapolis, Minnesota, the school founded by Fundamentalist leader W. B. Riley.[59] In 1948 Bob Jones College conferred an honorary doctorate on Billy Graham, and in 1949 Northwestern conferred an honorary degree on Bob Jones Jr. That same summer Billy Graham attended the organizing sessions of the World Council of Churches as an observer for Youth For Christ.[60] During a rather difficult five-year stint as the largely absentee president of Northwestern, Graham learned much about management and often asked Bob Jones Sr. for advice.[61] In 1951 Billy Graham resigned from the college and with his team of aggressive, like-minded young men, began full-time evangelism. The group included singer George Beverly Shea and Bob Jones College graduates T. W. Wilson, Cliff Barrows and his wife Billie, and former BJC student Grady Wilson.

Early in 1949 Billy Graham met Chuck Templeton, an old friend from YFC days. Some years earlier Templeton had urged Graham to do graduate work with him at Princeton Theological Seminary. During their discussions, Templeton admitted that he had lost his faith as a result of his Princeton studies and challenged Graham's beliefs in the Christian doctrines of the inspiration of Scripture, the deity of Christ, salvation, and the Genesis record. Though Graham finally confessed complete faith in Christ and simple reliance on God's Word as inspired, inerrant, and infallible, Templeton rebuked him. "Bill, you cannot refuse to think. To do that is to die intellectually. . . . Not to think is to deny God's creativity. Not to think is to sin against your Creator. You can't stop thinking. That's intellectual suicide."[62] He chided, "Your faith is too simple. You will have to get a new jargon if you want to communicate to this generation."[63]

These comments from an old friend shook Graham and may have in some ways encouraged him to be more "open-minded" and accepting of those whose belief had become Modernistic. In fact, in talking with reporters about this period in his life, Billy Graham later said he had become skeptical of the Bible—"I didn't know if any part of the Bible is true. However, I overcame my skepticism with an act of faith, and I am not now the Biblical literalist that I am widely supposed to be."[64]

A hugely successful campaign in Los Angeles in 1949 was held, during which Los Angeles radio personality and singer Stuart Hamblin and a well-known West Coast crime figure were converted. On the final day of the meeting, William Randolph Hearst, attuned to the patriotic and anti-Communist rhetoric of Graham, sent a telegram to his Los Angeles editor which read, "Puff Graham." One biographer writes, "That nova burst came just as the crusade was tapering to a monotone and desultory finish, on the final Sunday night's service. When Graham arrived at the tent, as he later recounted, 'I suddenly noticed reporters and cameramen crawling all over the place.' Not a little giddied by this abrupt inexplicable clamor [of attention],

Left to right: Cliff Barrows, Billy Graham, Bob Jones Jr., and South Carolina governor Strom Thurmond (1950). Within a few years Graham pursued a policy of ecumenical evangelism that placed him and the University in opposing camps.

he finally managed to tug aside one reporter to inquire what it all meant: he was informed it had all been set off by a memo just delivered down from Hearst—*Puff Graham.* And with no more than that, he happened. His genesis took place."[65]

The crusade suddenly took on "bigger than life" proportions and Graham decided, since the media attention seemed to warrant it, to lengthen the crusade. The meetings ultimately lasted eight weeks. Graham preached "all he knew," ran out of prepared sermons, and began losing his voice. Friends supplied him with books of sermons, and he called on others to preach. Bob Jones Jr., preaching in Ventura, California, at the time, came and took one service for him.[66]

Within days, the Los Angeles crusade was featured in *Time, Life,* and *Newsweek,* as well as in all of the press wire services. Billy Graham now had the nation's attention. The next six years were filled with campaigns in the United States and Europe with varying degrees of success but always with a maximum of publicity. During these years Billy Graham gathered a large group of advisers and established an organization that mastered the necessary organizational and management techniques needed to make meetings memorable and apparently successful.

In 1950 Billy Graham held a campaign in Columbia, South Carolina, which was supported by Bob Jones Sr., Bob Jones Jr., and University faculty, staff, and students.[67] Dr. Jones Jr. was unable to attend the Columbia meetings because of illness, but Billy invited Bob Sr. to preach one campaign message. The elder Jones declined but, when introduced at the Columbia meeting, spoke to the crowd for about ten minutes.[68] After Henry R. Luce, publisher of *Time* and *Life* magazines, attended a service and then held a lengthy conversation with the evangelist, Graham was again featured in both *Time* and *Life*, but this time not in altogether glowing terms. The writer pointed out that Graham's seven thousand Columbia decisions were slight when compared with Billy Sunday's twenty-five thousand decisions in 1923. He also reported that 80 percent of those responding to invitations were already church members.[69]

The crusade was a major event in the state. Governor Strom Thurmond invited the evangelist to address a joint session of the state's general assembly, arranged speaking engagements in public high schools and the state's colleges, and declared the closing day of the crusade to be South Carolina Revival Day.[70]

Following three weeks of preaching in the state's capital, a two-week satellite campaign of one-day meetings was arranged in the major cities of South Carolina, including one in downtown Greenville at Sirrine Stadium. Billy Graham was also invited to speak in a BJU chapel service.[71] Greenville's mayor requested that all stores close and that schools be dismissed for the afternoon rally.[72] Rain came, however, so Bob Jones Jr. offered Rodeheaver Auditorium for the meeting. On March 20, 1950, two services were held—10:00 A.M. and 3:00 P.M.—and "around 170 were dealt with and given decision cards."[73] Throughout the Columbia campaign, BJU students, faculty, and staff served nightly as counselors for those who made decisions. The three-week Columbia campaign also brought Willis Haymaker into the Graham organization, at Bob Jones Sr.'s suggestion. Haymaker had been the advance organization man for Jones Sr.'s evangelistic campaigns for nearly forty years.[74]

In the 1950s Billy Graham was never fully out of the collective national consciousness. Between Luce and Hearst media coverage, his own publicity releases, his nationwide radio broadcast, and some clumsy though effective political activism, Graham found introduction to many of the powerful political and social elite of the twentieth century.[75]

Through the 1950s Graham stayed in close contact with both Bob Jones Sr. and Bob Jones Jr. His letters indicate a close kinship of spirit and a "need for your advice and counsel . . . [because of] your long years of experience to help guide me across the many pitfalls."[76] Sometime prior to the 1950 Los Angeles crusade, Graham asked Dr. Jones to consider him "one of his boys" even though he had attended BJC for only a few months. The warmth, depth of feeling, and satisfaction that Dr. Bob Sr. received from the early ministry of Billy Graham are evident in his letters.[77] Dr. Jones Sr., however, was very direct in relating dangers he saw developing in the Graham organization. It embarrassed the elder Jones when Bob Jones College failed to appear in Billy Graham's press releases and biographical sketches, especially since he had asked Dr. Jones to consider him "one of his boys" and Dr. Jones had "boosted" Graham at every opportunity. Very often people quizzed the Joneses about Graham, asking if he had been expelled from the school or was ashamed of his record. Because of the omission in the publicity, Dr. Jones felt that some in the Graham organization simply did not want the connection made known.[78]

Billy Graham asked Dr. Jones for advice and warning when it was needed, and Dr. Jones took the request seriously. Letters indicate that as far back as 1946 advice flowed freely, as from a father to a son, from the pen of the Founder. Some was witty; all was frank. For example, in 1951 he wrote encouraging Graham to shun publicity: "In your heart you love Jesus, and you are happy to see people saved; but your love for glamour and your ambition (which is the strongest ambition I have ever known any man in evangelistic work to have) and your desire to please everybody are so dominant in your life that you are staggering from one side of the road to the other."[79] A year later Dr. Jones Sr., from his years of experience as an evangelist, wrote,

First: You have the headlines. It is going to be impossible for you to maintain the headlines very long unless you strain after effect. That will hurt the cause of evangelism. . . .

Second: I would advise you to take a few campaigns in small towns and pull your budget way down. It will do your soul good to get away from the cities and into small communities where Americans live and where there is not so much glamour. . . .

Third: Make it clear that you are not in the business to get church members, but to get church members converted.

Fourth: Now, politics has been my weakness. It is going to be a weakness with you. Watch about your association with politicians. If you are not careful, you will be used sometime when you are not conscious you are being used. . . .

Now Billy, you can't judge a man's work over a period of a few years. It takes a long time for the returns to come in. I have never tried to be a glamorous evangelist, and I have never tried to make the headlines, and I have never tried to clamor for anything that was big. . . . No man can travel with ecclesiasticism today and maintain for long, spiritual contacts. That is not the way the Spirit of God is moving. You know at the close of the age, ecclesiasticism is going into apostasy under the anti-Christ. . . . The man who pats ecclesiasticism on the back today is patting on the back the apostasy; and when he does it, he is helping build the machine that is out to crush [God's testimony].[80]

To this, Graham answered, "The modernists do not support us anywhere. We have never been sponsored by the Council of Churches. . . . We have never had a man on our committee that denied the virgin birth, the vicarious atonement, or the bodily resurrection."[81] By 1956, however, this had changed.

In 1953 Dr. Jones Sr. wrote, "I have talked about the impression being made that America is having a great revival when, as a matter of fact, we are not having a great revival, though many people are being saved. I have talked over and over again about the danger of the liberals taking over the movement, and that is what they are trying to do."[82]

Billy Graham at this point in his career was becoming very much the product of his public relations machine. Thanks to Chuck Templeton, he had also reflected on biblical Christianity and its meaning to a new generation of American Christians. He weighed the friendship of Evangelicals and Fundamentalists and made decisions on the basis of those friends' influence and national prominence. Billy Graham was also feeling pressure from Modernists and liberals because of his early Fundamentalist messages and results. He wrote, "The Devil is attacking on every side. Modernists are beginning to write letters against me. Articles are beginning to appear in certain papers attacking the thing for which I stand."[83] Having never faced opposition, Graham was greatly concerned, because his stated goal was to become all things to all men, and he did not wish to alienate any part of the Protestant audience. In 1951, still feeling some of the sting of the Modernists' criticisms of him, he wrote to Bob Jones Sr. asking for his continued prayers, friendship, and "enthusiastic support of soul winning."[84] Dr. Jones responded in a way characteristic for him: "Let me assure you that I have nothing in my heart for you except love. I have a real affection for you and always have had. Anything personal that you may have done to me affects me only as it is related to the cause of evangelism, for which I have fought, bled, and died for fifty-two years. . . . I want you to remember that the fellow who wrote you this letter loves you and wants you to be what God wants you to be."[85]

Through 1955 Billy Graham described his beliefs as Fundamentalist. However, it appears that as early as 1947, he shared reservations about Fundamentalism with other young evangelicals—especially those involved with YFC—because of the "unfortunate connotation of the word" and the "pugnacious dogmatism" and separatism of those who were Fundamentalists.[86] Billy Graham came to prefer the more intellectualized, socially responsive, noncontroversial, and nonseparatist Christianity represented by his friends Harold Ockenga, Carl Henry, and those among the National Association of Evangelicals who considered themselves the "new evangelicals."[87] Though not "ecumenical" in the early meaning of the term, one key element of New Evangelical strategy was to gain a hearing for evangelical ideas in mainline denominations, and Graham realized that one could not gain entrance to these religious leaders and their people with too shrill a voice or too direct a confrontation of their modern theology.[88] Thus, accommodation became the key to developing an audience.

The concept of ecumenism may have begun to fascinate Graham when he attended the World Council of Churches meetings as an observer in 1948, and he found his 1949 discussions with Chuck Templeton challenging.[89] Though uncomfortable with the liberal theology dominating the WCC, Billy Graham was attracted by the concept of a unified Christian community and called the 1948 sessions "one of the most thrilling experiences of my life up to that moment."[90]

The 1954 WCC meeting in Evanston, Illinois, was marked by open criticism of Billy Graham's style of evangelism, but he "thrilled at the whole process of seeing world churchmen sitting down together, praying together, discussing together." Although the WCC promoted "universalism"—the belief that, however one might conceive of salvation, all human beings will ultimately receive it—a religious vision with which Graham disagreed, he was intoxicated by his contact with the world's religious leaders.[91]

Though rejecting the World Council's views on universalism, Graham began to ponder ways of uniting the various spectrums of belief within Christianity.[92] Accommodation of beliefs soon became Billy's goal, and his position with respect to Fundamentalism and Modernism became public. In 1955 on a preaching tour of Great Britain, Graham began his practice of inclusivism—placing Modernists and liberals on his platform—when he welcomed the Archbishop of Canterbury to the platform to challenge the converts and pronounce the benediction for one service and gave public affirmation to the liberal leaders of the Church of Scotland. This alarmed some American Fundamentalists, but for the most part, they gave Billy the benefit of the doubt and adopted a watchful attitude, unaware of the change in Billy's thinking.[93] Their private caution changed to public criticism because of a crusade scheduled in New York City in 1957.

Prior to 1957 Billy Graham had refused two invitations to go to New York. The first was in 1951 when a committee of Fundamentalists invited him. Graham insisted that a number of Modernists be invited to join the executive committee, a fact that disturbed the Fundamentalist members. Jack Wyrtzen called together a group of influential Fundamentalist pastors and explained that he could not work with a mixed multitude. They agreed, drew up a statement of faith, and presented it to Graham, who approved it. The Fundamentalists requested that all members of the executive committee sign the doctrinal statement, which specified "the basic doctrinal faith upon which the Crusade will speak to the hearts and minds of our city—that this include the Bible as inspired of God and the only infallible rule of our faith and practice, the deity and virgin birth of our Lord Jesus Christ, the vicarious and substitutionary atonement wrought by Him on the Cross, His bodily resurrection from the dead and the salvation which is ours by faith in Him alone."[94]

Liberal New York pastor John S. Bonnell dissented, refused to sign the statement, and resigned from the committee, taking twenty-six others with him. When Bonnell refused to participate, Graham rejected the invitation and said that the sponsorship did not "represent the broad spectrum of belief" of the churches of New York City.[95]

By 1954 Jack Wyrtzen had organized another campaign committee that was evangelical and unified around the statement of faith. He invited Graham back to New York, and he assured Graham of great attendance and wonderful meetings. The Graham organization announced that it would consider a campaign in New York only if there was broad sponsorship, and it rejected the pleas of conservative, Bible-believing Christians to come to rekindle the fires of the old-time religion. Shortly thereafter, Graham's organization negotiated an invitation from the Protestant Council of the City of New York, a member of the liberal National Council of Churches and World Council of Churches.[96] The Protestant Council leadership was made up largely of clergy who denied the virgin birth of Christ, His deity, His bodily resurrection from the dead, His second coming, the inspiration and infallibility of Scripture, and virtually every other historic Christian doctrine for which Bob Jones Sr., his University, and other Fundamentalist leaders had fought.

Billy Graham accepted the council's invitation, and, in accordance with crusade policies, a committee partially composed of laymen was named by the Protestant Council and publicized as sponsor of the crusade. This allowed the Graham organization to claim that the crusade was not under the auspices of New York Modernists, but under an independent committee, and thus counter the claims of critics.[97] To further increase the breadth of his appeal, Graham began to accept invitations to speak at liberal seminaries in the Northeast—Union, Colgate, and other centers of American Modernism. One biographer writes,

> At Colgate Rochester Divinity School, [Graham] attempted to bridge the differences between his own theology and that of the eminent neoorthodox theologian and social critic, Reinhold Niebuhr. When [Graham] spoke of "the central need for a personal experience of Jesus Christ," he added, as if they were synonymous conceptions, "or what Niebuhr would call an encounter with the living God." A fundamentalist reporting on this event objected that "no man in his right mind would believe for a moment that what the neoorthodox Niebuhr means by 'an encounter with the living God' and what Jesus Christ defined as being 'born again' are one and the same." At New York's Union Theological Seminary, Graham had the temerity to say kind words about "known liberals," including his old friend Chuck Templeton, who was then serving as an evangelist for the National Council of Churches. His hobnobbing with Anglicans in Great Britain and with Church of Scotland pastors in Glasgow added fuel to the fire. To make matters worse, he had invited some prominent

American liberals, including New York pastor John Sutherland Bonnell, who publicly acknowledged that he did not believe in the Trinity, the Virgin Birth, the Resurrection, the inerrancy of Scripture, or heaven and hell, to sit on the platform with him during services at [Union]. When Scottish reporters tried to pin down Graham's location on the contemporary spectrum, he declared . . . "I am neither a fundamentalist nor a modernist." To make matters worse, he told another reporter, "The ecumenical movement has broadened my viewpoint and I recognize that God has his people in all churches."[98]

Billy Graham's direction was set. In spite of warnings by Bob Jones Sr., Bob Jones Jr., and others, he was intent on drawing common ground with those who disavowed the person and work of Christ, the inspiration and infallibility of His Word, and His true kingdom. He wanted their rapt and eager acceptance and chose his language in such a way as to attract the Modernist without repelling the simple evangelicals who were then pouring millions of dollars and hours of prayer into his organization.[99] He intended "to go anywhere, sponsored by anybody, to preach the Gospel of Christ if there are no strings attached to my message."[100] To many American Christians, this sounded almost Pauline, but in practice, Billy promised "many people many things" in order to win their support. For example, to a group of fifty New York Anglican and Episcopalian priests, Billy promised to "give more emphasis" in his preaching to "the sacraments of Baptism and Holy Communion."[101] In an interview with a leader of the Lutheran church, he commented that although he was not certain about infant baptism for salvation, all of his children had been baptized as infants. He said, "I do believe that something happens at the baptism of an infant, particularly if the parents are Christians. . . . I believe a miracle can happen in these children so that they are regenerated, that is made Christian, through infant baptism."[102]

The message of social reclamation seized the evangelist, and the message of personal salvation to a lost and dying world became mixed with nuclear disarmament, the elimination of poverty, crime reduction, racism, and other social issues. In a 1956 interview, Billy Graham declared his new theological heritage: "I am neither fundamentalist nor modernist." He was now the "spokesman of the convictions and ideals of the New Evangelicalism."[103]

Graham staked his flag between the National Association of Evangelicals and the Modernists of the World Council, this to the exclusion of Fundamentalists and the less accommodationist-minded of the NAE. The line was drawn. Billy Graham sought the recognition and support of the liberals, Modernists, Neo-orthodox, and eventually, Roman Catholics—all of whom "did not retain God in their knowledge"—and he was therefore disobeying God and His Word.

Bob Jones Sr. vocally opposed Billy Graham's New York crusade and the new "cooperative evangelism" or, as Fundamentalists called it, "compromise evangelism."[104] The Fundamentalists of 1956 lacked cohesion and a spokesman of the national stature of a William Jennings Bryan or a Billy Sunday, while Billy Graham was that spokesman for the New Evangelicalism. More importantly, Fundamentalists lacked an entree to the national media and the religious press. Their voices of protest were successfully muted by the NAE because *United Evangelical Action* and *Christianity Today,* edited by Carl F. H. Henry, published only favorable reviews of Graham. Protest was not silenced, however. Bob Jones Sr. placed all of his considerable influence and gave his full voice in opposition to the actions of the Billy Graham Evangelistic Association, and Evangelist John R.

Bob Jones Sr. and John R. Rice (1958)

Rice eventually took up the battle in his national religious weekly the *Sword of the Lord.*[105]

Fundamentalists were not the only ones who opposed Graham. Radical Modernists—the Unitarians and Universalists—also opposed him, but their opposition was based on their philosophical stance rejecting the deity of Jesus Christ, the Son of God.

The impact of Jones Sr. and Rice, as with the Fundamentalist leaders of the 1920s, was limited. Graham, since the Hearst and Luce fascination with him, had the support of the secular media, enjoyed its implicit credibility, and was the darling of the religious press, appearing in at least one religious publication nearly every month.

Graham's reaction to publicized criticism was swift. Lumping together the radical Modernists with Fundamentalists, and showing a disdain for historic Christian doctrine and a loathing for those he had earlier professed to love, he stated that the badge of "Christian discipleship is not orthodoxy, but love," fully forgetting Christ's injunction to His followers: "If ye love me, keep my commandments."[106] He bitterly commented that Fundamentalists "whose orthodoxy knows nothing of the spirit of God or the love for their own brethren . . . are a stench in the nostrils of God" and "prevent revival in the church." He continued that he would not stoop to answer the "petty little fights over nonessentials" brought out by his critics, thereafter stating that "I make it a policy never to answer critics."[107] The task of rebuttal was assigned to hired publicity agents, Billy Graham Evangelistic Association staff members, *Christianity Today* editor Carl Henry, team members such as

T. W. Wilson, and Billy's father-in-law, Nelson Bell, all of whom took up the attack. "Why the sudden fury?" they asked, seeking to make the breach between the old-time Fundamentalists and the Billy Graham Association appear hasty and unreasonable, the result of jealousy and a lack of piety and Christian charity.[108] The force of evangelical Christianity was on their side and souls would be won to Christ. Wasn't winning souls the function of the evangelist? Why would any good Christian brother be against winning souls?

Besides, Billy Graham asked, "What difference does it make who sponsors a meeting" if good will come from it?[109] It made all the difference to Bob Jones Sr., Bob Jones Jr., and the Fundamentalist Christians who composed Bob Jones University.

CHAPTER 16

♦

"Wounds of a Friend, Kisses of an Enemy": BJU and Cooperative Evangelism[1]

Billy Graham was both a person and the embodiment of the New Evangelical movement. As such, his allies could claim that criticism leveled at his actions as the embodiment of the New Evangelical movement was personal and therefore un-Christian. That is not to say that there were no personal attacks—there were some. But the objections that the Joneses and Bob Jones University raised were not personal. They were directed at Billy Graham as the embodiment of the movement toward cooperative evangelism.

Those who defended Graham's New York campaign characterized his critics in two ways: spiritually cold or simply jealous of Graham's popularity. Neither of these characterizations holds up under examination.

Between 1954 and 1956 some of Graham's supporters claimed that the division was caused by "technical" Fundamentalists who were strict Calvinists and therefore lacked any zeal for soulwinning. This may have been accurate for some but certainly not for Bob Jones Sr. or Bob Jones Jr.[2]

Most Graham biographers still readily and uncritically accept Graham associate T. W. Wilson's characterization of criticism of Billy Graham as stemming from jealousy.[3] After lengthy correspondence about the New York crusade, Wilson, in a peremptory and sarcastic letter to Bob Jones Sr., wrote, "What is the matter? Many times I have heard you say, 'I have preached to more people than any man in America.' Now that you can say this no longer, could it be that you have actually let the green-eyed old Monster of Jealousy creep into your heart?"[4]

The record does not corroborate the widely reported assertion of jealousy as a cause. The point of separation between the Joneses and Billy Graham was not personal animosity—they were friendly toward each other and expressed that fondness in each letter that passed between them. The separation that followed the New York crusade caused the Joneses great personal pain.

Bob Jones Sr. had taken a principled stand against Modernism. He had fired a liberal faculty member from the College in its first years; he fought against the liberal Federal Council of Churches; he rebuked Modernists during his evangelistic campaigns; and he had always fought vigorously for the fundamentals of the Faith. He simply could not support Billy Graham's crusades as long as Modernists were officially involved.[5] One writer put it succinctly: "The New York crusade did not cause the division between the old Fundamentalists and the New Evangelicals. . . . But it did provide an event around which the two groups were forced to define themselves."[6]

The division that occurred confused many in conservative circles, including many churches and individuals that supported Bob Jones University, and many "orthodox Christians refus[ed] to be caught up in the swirl."[7] The division, though, was not the sudden controversy Graham's supporters claimed. It had been brewing privately for several years. Seeing "harm to the Cause in the future" of evangelism and believing Willis Haymaker could make a difference, Dr. Jones wrote him in 1951: "I'm afraid the permanent is about to be sacrificed on the altar of the immediate" because of Graham's eagerness to please everyone.[8]

In 1956, however, Billy Graham wrote that Haymaker "says that Dr. Bob used to go and hold city-wide meetings on exactly the same basis that we go today."[9] To the degree that Haymaker was speaking of organizational details, this was true. It was not true of sponsorship.[10] Bob Jones Sr. "never knowingly held a campaign in [his] life under the sponsorship of a ministerial group where one of the men did not believe in the fundamentals" of the Faith.[11]

The issue between Bob Jones and Billy Graham was that of sponsorship, fellowship, and accommodating unbelief. Had the differences of belief been the relatively minor areas of denominational distinctives and had the pastors been uniting behind a statement of faith for the cause of Christ and the revival of the church, there would have been no issue. As it was, members of the executive committee of the New York crusade rejected outright the major doctrines of the faith, including the deity of Christ and His virgin birth, while at the same time Billy Graham was stating publicly that no Modernists had ever served on one of his committees and was defending the committees.[12] In establishing formal spiritual relations with these men and by giving them recognition as Christian brothers, friends, and advisers, Graham was accommodating error. When he called two leaders of the liberal National Council of Churches, both of whom rejected the deity of Christ, "godly men," one observer said it was "too much to swallow. They are *not* godly men."[13]

Graham believed "that the ground of our fellowship is [not] to be the inerrancy of Scripture, but rather, the ground of our fellowship is to be the deity of our Lord Jesus Christ."[14] By lowering the standard regarding inerrancy and its foundational doctrine, the inspiration of Scripture, Graham allowed himself to come under the influence of men whose views on other doctrines differed from conservative Christians' and which were blatant error. Thus, "lowered or weakened views of Biblical inspiration finally result[ed] in weakened views in other areas of theological thought."[15]

Dr. Jones Sr. often quoted II John 9-11: "Whosoever transgresseth, and abideth not in the doctrine of Christ, hath not God. He that abideth in the doctrine of Christ, he hath both the Father and the Son. If there come any unto you, and bring not this doctrine, receive him not into your house, neither bid him God speed: For he that biddeth him God speed is partaker of his evil deeds." Dr. Jones Sr. believed that to the extent that Billy Graham gave prominence to those who denied God, His Word, and His Son, he was a partaker in their evil.

Graham and Bob Jones Sr. also disagreed about the role of the evangelist in the church. To Graham, the work of the evangelist was to win souls, and winning souls was the single most important responsibility of the evangelist. Thus, anything done in the name of winning souls was justified.[16] Dr. Jones Sr. answered this argument when he wrote, "keep in mind . . . that as an evangelist it is not just your business to win souls. You are given to the saints, and it is every saint's business to win souls. Your greatest responsibility as an evangelist is to perfect the saints to do the work of the ministry."[17] To Graham he wrote, "Paul told Timothy to do the work of an evangelist—reprove, rebuke, exhort. I have never read one of your sermons where you were reproving or rebuking these false prophets who are leading people astray. It is a sin to put your converts in churches whose pastors do not believe in the deity of Christ."[18]

Dr. Jones Jr. wrote Graham, "In your effort to make friends with the modernists and the neo-orthodox folks, you have put yourself in the position where you can't even speak out against that theological system which is at enmity against the Gospel and which the Word of God so vigorously condemns." Citing the example of the apostle Paul, he continued that Graham had a responsibility to warn the converts "against modernism and the deceivers that enter in unawares." Summing it all up, Bob Jones Jr. wrote, "You have sold yourself a bill of goods, and your position, Billy, is contrary to the plain teaching of the Word of God, and anything that is contrary to the Word of God is wrong."[19]

As a dividing point between Fundamentalists and New Evangelicals, the New York crusade looms large. Two other events, however, brought the Billy Graham controversy very close to the BJU campus. The first was the wide circulation of a letter Dr. Jones Sr. had written to Graham's father-in-law, Nelson Bell. The second was a Billy Graham crusade scheduled for Greenville in 1966.

As part of the preparation for the 1957 New York crusade, Billy Graham representatives visited Christian colleges across the country to organize a prayer effort on behalf of the crusade. In November 1956 Ralph Mitchell, an executive of the Billy Graham organization, wrote Dr. Jones Jr. requesting an invitation to represent the Billy Graham Association on campus, speak in chapel about the New York crusade, and organize a prayer effort. Dr. Jones Jr. declined to issue an invitation, saying that "as much as we love Billy personally, if he came to Greenville on the same basis as he goes to these other cities, we could not cooperate or in any wise endorse a campaign." He wrote that he believed that "what Billy is doing in seeking the sponsorship of the liberals and the modernists . . . is contrary to the plain teaching of Scripture" and that such sponsorship is "unfair to the brethren who have stood for the Gospel and endured the attack of these . . . liberals and modernists. Our sincere and heartfelt conviction," he continued, is that "in the long run Billy is going to wreck evangelism and leave even orthodox churches, if they cooperate, spineless and emasculated."[20]

As the New York crusade gained national attention, Dr. Jones Sr. was besieged with letters from pastors and laymen from around the country about the crusade. His response to one such letter from L. Nelson Bell became a four-page form letter that was used to answer the thousands of requests that came to the school and in which Bob Jones Sr. stated his full position. He stressed that he took "pride in Billy Graham and his organization" and that "Billy Graham is a charming personality. There is nothing personal between us and never has been." The issue was that "Billy Graham has violated the Scriptures. . . . It is not a question of Billy Graham giving the Gospel to people. God tells us to preach the Gospel, but he also tells us some other things." Citing his long evangelistic career and his firsthand knowledge of the methods of Billy Sunday and other famous evangelists, he continued, "The Bible makes it plain that if I . . . give a man the recognition given a Christian and the man rejects the doctrine of Christ, I am a partaker of his evil deeds. I am patting an anti-Christ on the back. Billy Graham needs to stop and think. It is not right to do wrong to get a chance to do right. It is not right to violate the clear teaching of the Word of God to get a chance to preach the Gospel."[21]

The tone of Dr. Jones Sr.'s letter was constructive and based on biblical principle. Often, however, those who received the letter did not realize the years of advice and pleading that Dr. Jones Sr. had given to Graham, encouraging him to stay true to the Lord and do the true work of the evangelist: reprove, rebuke, and exhort the saints with "long-suffering and doctrine" to perfect them for the work of ministry, making them able to withstand the "cunning craftiness" of those in error.[22]

Shortly after Dr. Jones composed his letter, L. Nelson Bell wrote the Founder and charged that a group of students had been threatened with expulsion for praying for Billy Graham.[23] Dr. Jones responded that the prayers of a student, faculty member, or administrator were between him and God. Dr. Jones himself prayed for Billy every day, he said, and no students had been so threatened. An organized prayer meeting of a group of Bob Jones University students "to ask God to bless the evangelistic movement which Billy Graham is heading up in New York," however, would be inconsistent with the school's position and "we would not permit it."[24]

Bell's response came quickly. As a chief apologist for the New York campaign and angered either by the Founder's letter or the rebuff that Mitchell received for his request for formal prayer meetings, Bell obtained the consent of a disgruntled BJU student who had been employed by Billy Graham and reprinted a letter the student had written condemning the school.[25] To this, Bell appended his own thoughts, and the result was a ten-page letter in which he savaged Bob Jones Sr. and Bob Jones University but in which he failed to deal with the issue of Modernistic sponsorship.[26] He charged that the school was prohibiting free prayer and free thought. He charged that students had been expelled for praying. He claimed that the Graham campaign was using the same methods Bob Jones himself had used. Among other things, he charged the Founder with extreme jealousy, "begetting hate instead of love . . . inoculating [students] with the deadly virus of hatred, distortions, jealousies, envying, malice, false witnessing and untruthfulness," and being deficient in the fruit of the Spirit.[27] Bell mailed the letter to most members of the faculty and the student body, the University board, known supporters of the school, and thousands of pastors across the country.

John R. Rice took up the defense in the *Sword of the Lord* and rebutted Bell's scathing personal attack in an article descriptively titled "God's Blessed Man, Dr. Bob Jones—The Man Who Could Not Be Bought nor Bluffed nor Scared, Who Avoids the Counsel and Company of the Wicked, Who Delights in and Defends the Bible."[28]

Prior to 1957, this conflict had been limited and somewhat private. The Founder wrote, "I tried to handle this just as quietly as possible, but the issue kept coming up until I had to take a stand openly. I am an old man. I did not want to get into a battle but I am not going back on the Lord Jesus Christ."[29] The battles that had been waged were in private conversations and letters to Billy Graham, T. W. Wilson, and others from the Billy Graham Evangelistic Association. With the Nelson Bell letter, the battle became public, and the issue was thereafter dealt with openly and often from the chapel platform in order to give the students biblical principles to prepare them for the inevitable clash.

Bob Jones University declared itself on the side of the clear teaching of the Word of God. The Billy Graham Association, the National Association of Evangelicals, *Christianity Today,* and most other Christian colleges could not see beyond the soulwinning aspect of the Graham crusades and declared themselves to be for accommodation, unification, and ecumenical dialogue with liberalism. As an institution, Bob Jones University stood nearly alone in the conflict.

In 1956 Dr. Jones Jr. had written that if Billy "came to Greenville on the same basis as he goes to these other cities, we could not cooperate or in any wise endorse a campaign."[30] The school had opportunity to test these words when, a decade later, Billy Graham, seemingly in an attempt to force the University to acquiesce or be publicly humiliated in its hometown, arranged a ten-day crusade in Greenville. The Graham team had only three meetings scheduled that year: two in Europe—London and Berlin—and one in America—Greenville. Never, neither before nor since, has the Graham team conducted a campaign in so small a community. Some in Greenville felt that the crusade was not so much for Christ as it was against Bob Jones.[31] Thirteen months before the Greenville crusade began, Bob Jones Jr. made clear in chapel what the response of the institution would be to the Billy Graham crusade in Greenville. He preached, "If Billy Graham comes to Greenville, we will pray that the Lord will forgive the preachers in Greenville that are supposed to believe the Bible but cooperate with those who don't believe the Bible. We will pray for God's mercy, but we are not going to ask the Lord to bless what He says in His Word He forbids."[32] After laying out the history of the controversy for the students and dealing with the issue of sponsorship, Dr. Jones Jr. said,

> You cannot be a party to this kind of thing. No Bob Jones University dormitory student will be permitted to go to a single meeting of the Greenville crusade. No Bob Jones University adult student, if he is married or lives in town, may attend the crusade and remain as a student in Bob Jones University. You can go if you want to go; you are an adult. But you cannot be seen in that unscriptural mess and be identified as a Bob Jones University student.

> You cannot say I have not made our position clear well ahead of time. . . . It is not going to be until March 1966. This is thirteen months from now. . . . Young people, we must be consistent. We have taken a stand. We are going to be consistent with the public. We are going to be honest with you, and we are going to be open and honest before God.[33]

When Billy Graham arrived in Greenville for the March 1966 crusade, he issued a statement to the Greenville newspapers saying he really did not know what accounted for the split between him and Bob Jones University and did not know why the University did not support his crusade![34] Prior to the announcement of the crusade Dr. Jones Jr. had been scheduled to be out of the country, but fearful that the Graham organization might deflect or misstate the truth, he prepared a response to be released to the media if the situation warranted. After Graham falsely claimed no knowledge of a reason for the separation, the University released Dr. Jones Jr.'s statement.

> I am addressing this statement to the citizens of Greenville who are interested in the facts and to remind Dr. Graham that the objection of Bob Jones University to the Billy Graham crusade is purely on a scriptural basis. What Dr. Graham is doing is forbidden by the Bible, which we believe is the infallible and authoritative Word of God.

> The Bible commands that false teachers and men who deny the fundamentals of the faith should be accursed; that is, they shall be criticized and condemned. Billy approves them, Billy condones them, Billy recommends them. . . .

> We object to Billy and to what Billy is doing on the basis of the Word of God, which forbids it. There is nothing personal about this. It's purely a matter of obeying the Scripture. . . .

> So our objection is on the basis of his sponsorship, which is unscriptural, and on his practice of turning his converts back over to unscriptural churches and to false teachers, and recommending such men. I think that Dr. Graham is doing more harm in the cause of Jesus Christ than any living

man; that he is leading foolish and untaught Christians, simple people that do not know the Word of God, into disobedience to the Word of God. That is wrong, and it is doubly wicked in that he is doing it under the pretext of being a soul-winning ministry.[35]

The Upper Piedmont crusade in Greenville chalked up a total attendance of 278,700, with 7,311 who answered the invitations for rededication, prayer, salvation, or some other kind of help.

Graham's defenders have through the years pointed to the size of the crowds and the numbers of decisions as proof of God's blessing.[36] In response to this justification, Dr. Jones Sr. wrote,

> I do not judge an evangelist by how many people he wins to Christ. I judge an evangelist by what he does to the Body of Christ. Now, the Body of Christ, as you know, is made up of born-again Christians—not modernists—not people that repudiate the virgin birth, the blood, etc. Now, if Billy is hurting these orthodox, born-again Christians, he is prostituting his office of an evangelist because the evangelist, pastor, and teacher are given to perfect the saints for the work of the ministry. There are many soul winners who are not evangelists, and there have been some great evangelists who were not great soul winners. . . . Our position is that when a man is Scripturally wrong, even if some people are converted, there will be permanent harm done to the cause of the Lord Jesus Christ.[37]

Billy Graham's courtship of Modernist Protestants is only half of the story. The other half is Billy Graham's embrace of Catholic leaders as Christian brothers and his growing ecumenical alliance with them.[38] To historic Christian believers, the pope and Roman Catholicism have been many things: persecutor of the believers, purveyor of spiritual darkness, perpetrator of monstrous injustice, the church of the Antichrist, "the Seat of Satan," the man of sin, and the Antichrist.[39] In the 1950s it was unthinkable that an evangelist, calling himself Fundamentalist in theology and evangelical in practice, would align himself with the church of Rome. Such alignment was a repudiation of Protestant distinctives and history.

Through 1957 Graham held to the historic Protestant stance toward Catholicism. There were weaknesses in this stance, however: in 1952 Graham commented that many Pittsburgh converts had joined the Catholic Church and "he hoped to hear Bishop Fulton Sheen at one of the masses at St. Paul's Cathedral tomorrow."[40] For the 1957 New York campaign, Graham announced that his goal was to return people to their places of worship—Catholic, Protestant, Jewish[41]—and that Catholics who accept Christ will be better Catholics.[42]

In 1958 in San Francisco, in spite of vocal protests by Fundamentalists, the Graham organization's counseling and follow-up remained as it had been in New York, sending converts to both Catholic and Seventh-Day Adventist churches.[43] Representatives of the Billy Graham organization, however, in response to skeptical Evangelicals, claimed that converts were never sent back to Catholic churches but were channeled into "Bible preaching" churches.[44]

During the 1959 crusade in Sydney, Australia, the Roman Catholic hierarchy attempted to ban the crusade and forbade their parishioners to attend. A member of the Graham association flew to Australia and appealed to the bishop to lift the ban because "any Catholic who makes a decision at a Graham meeting will be referred back to his church."[45]

In 1964 Graham sought out a Catholic prelate and thanked the cardinal for his support for the crusade in Boston. Cardinal Cushing, an enemy of outspoken Protestants in the Boston area, declared, "I'm 100 per cent for Dr. Graham and . . . I would encourage all Catholic people to attend the meetings." To Graham, he said, "No Catholic can listen to you and not become a better Catholic."[46]

By late 1967 Billy Graham had accepted the official sanction of Catholic colleges by accepting honorary doctorates from Belmont Abbey in North Carolina and from Boston College. At Belmont the capitulation of Billy Graham to ecumenism was completed. He solemnly declared that the time had come for Protestants and Catholics to "meet together and greet one another as brothers."[47] In São Paulo, Brazil, Graham asked the Roman Catholic bishop to join him on the platform, and at the invitation the bishop stood beside him "and blessed the converts as they came forward."[48] In 1971 the bishop of Oakland, California, heaped lavish praise on the evangelist and joined him on the platform of the Oakland crusade.[49] A few years later, Graham spoke at the dedication of Oral Roberts University, thus aligning himself with the Charismatic movement as well.[50]

Bob Jones Sr. had warned Billy Graham in 1949 that through compromise with Modernists and liberals, the cause of Christ would be harmed, evangelism would be emasculated, and ultimately the church would be left confused and weakened. This did occur. Billy Graham and his organization have been the defining issue in Protestant Christianity for over forty years. Bob Jones Sr., Bob Jones Jr., and other Fundamentalists who opposed conciliation and accommodation with Modernists and Catholics, who opposed spiritual leaders who were disobedient to the clear teaching of God's Word, were slandered, lied about, caricatured, and dismissed as "pharisees—legalists" who forgot that "the greatest of all Christian virtues is love."[51]

"Billy Graham could have led this country back to the conservative position," Bob Jones Sr. wrote in 1957, "and could have helped the men on the borderline to stand firm."[52] Instead, as the logical extension of the mood of the National Association of Evangelicals, he broke down the walls, led to compromise, and entered into the ecumenical movement. The break with the NAE had little effect on Bob Jones University, but the school took a terrific beating during the years of the Mercer affair and the Billy Graham issue. Through it all, however, Dr. Jones Sr. and Dr. Jones Jr. remained staunch and unmoveable.

The impact of the Mercer affair was rather short-lived and had a purifying effect on the institution, preparing it for the battle with cooperative evangelism. Many of those who left because of Mercer eventually found themselves within New Evangelicalism and became advocates, if not active supporters, of Billy Graham and his ecumenical ministry by virtue of their association with evangelical causes.[53]

Those who survived the Mercer propaganda in the summer and fall of 1953 thus were somewhat prepared for the Graham propaganda of 1956-57. The attack by Mercer was pointed and personal, but primarily internal. The attacks by L. Nelson Bell, T. W. Wilson, and others representing the Graham organization were brutal and personal but national in scope and cloaked in piety. Since 1957 Bob Jones University has been recognized not only for the academic preparation of its students but as the place that "didn't like Billy Graham." The cumulative result, however, was a purifying one.

To some observers, the seemingly rigid position of Bob Jones Sr. and Bob Jones Jr. on the matter of "ecumenical evangelism" was surprising. To others, however, the Joneses' opposition was the result of applying their beliefs in a consistent way. During the time of the New York crusade and the months immediately following, the publicity that was accorded the University by the national media and the Graham organization had a negative effect on enrollment. By the school year 1957-58 enrollment stood at a ten-year low of 1893.[54] (See Table 3 below.)

Table 3

First Semester Enrollment Bob Jones College, University, & Academy, 1947-60[55]

Year	College	Academy	Grad./Spec.	Other[56]	Total
1946-47	1581	216	65	0	1862
1947-48	2209	218	67	0	2494
1948-49	2298	230	68	0	2596
1949-50	2313	215	127	0	2655
1950-51	2248	229	155	38	2670
1951-52	2141	285	139	22	2587
1952-53	2122	357	147	23	2649
1953-54	2022	289	91	12	2414
1954-55	2018	285	125	0	2428
1955-56	2030	338	129	0	2497
1956-57	1939	309	99	0	2347
1957-58	1893	345	86	7	2331
1958-59	1986	382	102	11	2481
1959-60	2175	415	84	25	2699

The Mercer affair apparently caused few board members to resign. (In fact, records of only one resignation have been found.)[57] The Billy Graham issue was somewhat different. Of a board of approximately 105 members, fifteen members resigned between 1956 and 1959. Of these, seven tendered their resignations in support of Billy Graham; these included Billy Graham Evangelistic Team members T. W. Wilson[58] and Cliff Barrows.[59] Some of those resigning from the board defended Billy Graham and his inclusivism; others had intended to quietly support both sides but ultimately resigned.[60]

Between 1957 and 1959 few faculty members resigned because of the Graham issue. The combined effects of Mercer and Graham were to cull the faculty and allow the executives the opportunity to appoint to the administration and bring to the faculty a large number who were recent BJU graduates and who were loyal to the founding precepts of the institution. These people respected the leadership of Dr. Jones Sr. and Dr. Jones Jr. and grew as scholars, teachers, intellectuals, and humble Christian servants. Among this group were Emery Bopp, Stewart Custer, Walter Fremont, Dwight Gustafson, Joe Henson, Marshall Neal, Edward Panosian, and Robert Pratt. To them goes much of the credit for the academic and cultural growth the institution experienced in its next twenty years.

CHAPTER 17

◆

"Not Letting the Devil Grind His Ax"

Even as the Graham controversy stewed nationally, campus life at Bob Jones University continued unabated. Bob Jones Sr.'s emphasis on culture was an important ingredient in the overall success of the institution and was a major element in its ability to attract students of good quality. Bob Jones Jr., with his personal interest in and aptitude for the fine arts, implemented and superintended the growth of the cultural programs. "You know," the Founder said, "we are not interested in bringing students here to this school to just get the training we have in music, in speech, in culture. We are not interested in letting the devil grind his ax on our grindstone."[1]

In Greenville the cultural program of the school contained seven elements: discipline, Vespers, Artist Series, drama, opera, cinema, and the Collection of Religious Art.[2] Of these, two were developed in Greenville—cinema and the art collection—but all seven were raised to new heights.

The school's emphasis on discipline remained unchanged from the years in Cleveland. The standards of conduct were clearly stated and consistently enforced and had a refining influence in the lives of the students. The school's emphasis on personal development and exposure to high culture was designed to cultivate well-rounded Christian young people who would effectively represent Jesus Christ and be "salt and light" in a world of spiritual decay and darkness. Besides merely having the students know something about these areas, Dr. Jones Jr. believed that the cultural opportunities would give the students a point of reference from which to build a gospel witness to the "up-and-outers." The arts should be the servant of Christ and His gospel, he said, and for the Christian the arts must reflect truth accurately, including the truth that "you reap what you sow."[3] Yet the ease with which culture could substitute for the truth was well understood by the Founder, as was the ease with which religious ritual or intellectual attainment could substitute for true spirituality.[4]

Many Greenvillians viewed the University's drama, musical offerings, and art collection as a great boost to the area's generally weak cultural life—Greenville had never hosted musicians or dramatists of such peerless caliber until BJU came. As the *Easley (S.C.) Progress* reported it, "Bob Jones has done a wonderful job in bringing big city music and drama to our area."[5] Residents also rightly believed that the University's programs would help attract industry.[6] Other Greenvillians remained disinterested or even hostile to the school because of the types of events presented or the Christian morality that governed the productions.[7]

Drama and the Classic Players

The Classic Players held a unique place in American colleges and universities as the only college-based repertory group in the nation. Though occasionally critical, the Greenville press was generally supportive of the Classic Players. Following the Classic Players' first Greenville performance—*Richard III* on January 14, 1948—one critic praised Bob Jones Jr.'s malevolence in the role and skill as an actor and went on to commend the "superb scenery, brilliant costumes, and well-handled lighting effects."[8] Another wrote that "never before [has] such . . . drama been presented" in the entire area.[9] In Greenville the Classic Players' repertoire expanded to include twenty-three Shakespearean plays, one Greek tragedy, and *Prologue: A Drama of Jon Huss* by Bob Jones Jr.

Evangelist John R. Rice defended the school's drama program against other Fundamentalists' attacks[10] and stated unequivocally that "Shakespeare is great literature" worth studying and performing.[11] Of course this attitude was not universally held by all within the Fundamentalist camp. Perhaps the most caustic attack ever leveled at the school in this regard came from James Oliver Buswell, president of Wheaton College until 1940. Buswell had kept drama studies out of Wheaton and was quick to attack theater, regardless of its form; this included the Shakespeare plays at Bob Jones College and Bob Jones University.[12] In 1949, Buswell reviewed a sermon by Bob Jones Sr. by saying,

"And He Pitched His Tent Toward Sodom." I have not found anything to criticize in [the sermon]. The following words which Abraham is imagined as speaking to Lot are excellent:

"Yes Lot, but it is a rotten place to rear children! It is all right for your cows . . . but what about your children?"

These are good words! But Dr. Jones, let me ask you a question or two. Your own educational program is reeking with theatricals and grand opera, which lead young people, as I know, and as you ought to know, into a worldly life of sin. . . . Let me ask you to read what you have written on the subject and think it over.[13]

The charge of "reeking with theatricals," a serious charge for the time, brought on a maelstrom. John R. Rice published a three-page defense of the University in the *Sword of the Lord* in which he said that he saw no "difference in learning how to speak or sing by seeing how the greatest artists do it, even though they are not Christians, and riding on a railroad run by non-Christians, when it goes where you need to go." He concluded that "Dr. Buswell's statement that the Bob Jones University educational program 'leads young people into a life of sin' is utterly untrue."[14]

With the passing of time, however, the criticism grew less intense, with an occasional parent taking a critical stance toward drama.[15] Most students and graduates shared a genuine sense of pride and anticipation about the Classic Players' performances.[16]

Vespers

The Vespers programs continued to challenge and inspire the University family in Greenville.[17] Though the programs gradually changed with the times, the goals remained for Vespers to be "dramatic in its music, in its presentation;"[18] to be an exciting program but not a preaching service;[19] and, practically speaking, to give students experience and "the opportunity to hone their craft."[20]

The weekly program also allowed the directors to experiment with new techniques, staging, lighting, and costuming.[21] The techniques introduced included such concepts as Group Interpretation or Readers' Theater,[22] dramatic monologues, and choric speaking.[23] Perhaps the most dramatic change in the program came in 1977, when as a result of pressures on the Fine Arts department and the stage facilities, Vespers was changed from a weekly to biweekly schedule. In the 1980s directors began to stress themes more directly applicable to the problems of Christian living in contemporary society.[24] They developed faster-paced programs that focused on the concern that scriptural truth forcefully and artistically confront the audience and demand action on their parts.[25]

Perhaps more than any other University innovation, Vespers has had the widest impact and has been introduced by graduates into churches and schools across the country. In this area, however, BJU, though often imitated, is never reproduced.

Opera

Like Cleveland before it, Greenville was fertile ground for the Bob Jones University Opera program. The first Greenville opera in 1948 was *Aida,* which met with rave reviews for Marjorie Lawrence and the other guest artists.[26] The program grew, but it truly began to mature after 1955 when Dwight Gustafson conducted that year's performance of *Aida.* Thereafter, he assumed artistic control of the productions and has conducted virtually every opera performed on the campus through 1996.[27] Because of Dr. Gustafson's growth in stagecraft and conducting, and the fine vocal training available from outstanding University teachers, the opera program of the University soon rivaled the quality of the best regional companies and was far superior to any other productions in South Carolina.[28]

Some of the eminent singers of the 1950s through the 1970s appeared in Bob Jones University Opera Association productions, with guest singers taking the leads and faculty and students performing all other parts.[29] The opera productions were limited primarily to the standard French and Italian repertoire, although three American operas have been staged.[30] The association successfully revived two seldom performed operas—Verdi's *Ernani* in 1945, which was repeated in Greenville in 1949 and 1966, and *La Juive* by Halevy in 1963.[31] A national music journal reported that the latter production was "one any opera house might be proud of." Though offering some criticism, the reviewer ended by saying that "it was gratifying to hear a college operatic production which could be evaluated on a professional level. Few schools can boast such a high degree of operatic proficiency."[32]

According to Bob Jones Jr., opera is important for the same reasons as drama: as a required activity to broaden the student's experience. "There is nothing wrong with good music. There is no reason why Christian people should not enjoy it," Dr. Jones Jr. wrote.[33] "Anything that depicts human nature without an overemphasis on the sensual helps to give an understanding of what man is like."[34]

Artist Series

The first Artist Series program in Greenville was Phil Spitalny and His All-Girl Orchestra, of the popular radio program *Hour of Charm*.[35] After this rather interesting series opener, notable performers were booked by Bob Jones Jr. and have included a wide array of truly great artists.[36] The twice yearly productions of the Classic Players, the opera by the Opera Association, performances of the University Oratorio Society, and the annual Commencement Concert are also included in the series.[37] From 1934 through 1971 Bob Jones Jr. was responsible for booking the artists, and since 1972 Dr. Jones III has assumed the booking responsibilities.[38]

In order to protect the school and save guest artists from embarrassment, the artists are informed in advance of the religious and moral standards of the school. Concert programs are therefore discussed in advance.[39]

The Artist Series provided exemplars of the musical and dramatic arts for the students and was often cited by Bob Jones Jr. as a means of broadening their overall education.[40] On one occasion Dr. Jones Jr. made the point forcefully by telling of a student who was expelled because "he cut the Artist Series program [and] went to town. When we called him in and asked him about it, . . . he said, 'The Lord told me to go down and do personal work.' He was a nut. He violated the rules and regulations [and then] talked pious. A guy like that

The first Greenville Artist Series program: Phil Spitalny and His All-Girl Orchestra from *The Hour of Charm* (1947)

needed a little culture. [It] wouldn't hurt him a bit to look at a pretty, big, blonde woman sing a few songs. Wouldn't have hurt him at all."[41]

From the chapel platform, the President sometimes drew lessons from the performances.[42] After the performance of contralto Claramae Turner, he told the students that "you preachers could learn something from that gal. She came out like she had a job to do and she was going to do it. . . . That woman knew how to interpret a song; she knew how to set the mood for a song. The fact that nobody was tempted to applaud [at an inappropriate moment] indicated that the woman knew how to put a message over. You can learn something from that."[43]

Even though attendance was required of all the students, the impact of the programs was significant on even the most culturally unaware. To former students, the Artist Series programs were amazing in the quality of talent they brought to the campus—often artists at the peak of their artistic powers.[44] Every alumnus, it seems, had a "most memorable" Artist Series program. These ranged from the strangeness of the performance of Benjamin Britten's *Curlew River* or the chanted, dramatized version of *The Book of Job* performed in mosaic patterned costumes, to magnificent performances by Sherrill Milnes, the American Boy Choir, and the Empire Brass Quintet, and even included the Artist Series at which Dwight Gustafson had to inform the audience that the artists, the Salzburg Mozarteum Orchestra, were backstage, dressed and ready to perform but their instruments had been mistakenly shipped to Greenville, *North* Carolina![45]

To those who criticized the school for bringing "unconverted" guest artists to the campus to perform, the President wrote, "We do not bring [the musicians] here as Christians or recognize them as such. Whether it be a singer or a symphony orchestra, we hire them to do a job" as one would hire a lawyer, doctor, carpenter, or electrician.[46]

To a pastor who questioned bringing the great singer Eileen Farrell to the campus in 1961 with the Bach Aria Group, Dr. Jones responded that "God does not give men the gift of music, or the gift of art, or the gift of language and expect them to leave the talent buried and the gift unexercised." He commented that a "negativistic attitude" that ignores or excludes things that are beautiful does not honor God. The President then wrote, "We brought her here as an artist to demonstrate her technique and her skill as an artist. Our students can benefit and learn something from a great and finely trained talent that will help them in the developing of their own gifts."[47]

As part of the educational process, former students see the benefit of required attendance at the concerts, and they recognize this as a major point of BJU's uniqueness among all other Christian colleges and universities.

Art Gallery

Bob Jones Jr. collected the pictures that now make up the Bob Jones University Collection of Religious Art. The idea for a gallery dedicated exclusively to sacred art came from art historian and collector Carl Hamilton in 1948.[48] Shortly after Hamilton made the suggestion, Dr. Jones Jr. discussed the possibility with the Executive Committee, and pointed out that "with an excellent School of Fine Arts and a strong School of Religion," it would be especially appropriate to "confine the Collection to religious art."[49]

Dr. Bob Jones Jr. in the Art Gallery (1954)

The Executive Committee agreed and established an acquisition fund of thirty thousand dollars and empowered Bob Jones Jr. to administer it and act as the first gallery director.[50] Two selection criteria were established—only works on biblical themes would be collected and only works from the thirteenth through the eighteenth centuries would be featured.[51]

During World War II major European collections were broken up and dispersed. Following the war, baroque paintings were in disfavor with museums and collectors, and the art market was flooded with seventeenth- and eighteenth-century paintings, thus holding prices down.[52] Baroque pictures were "plentiful, available, and inexpensive."[53]

Bob Jones Jr. said, "You could buy a Rembrandt for $50,000 then, and Rubens's works? They were falling from the sky like manna on the children of Israel."[54] Between January 1951 and the opening of the gallery in November, Dr. Jones was able to collect the gallery's original pictures, which included works by the great masters Botticelli, Botticini, Ghirlandaio, Tintoretto, Veronese, and Ribera.[55]

Carl Hamilton gave counsel, and art historians and scholars like Federico Zeri and Carlo Volpe offered insightful advice. Respected dealers like E. and A. Silberman in New York, Julius Weitzner in London, and M. and C. Sestieri of Rome also assisted in acquiring some of the works.[56] Pictures were also donated by individuals and corporations who had an interest in art and the University. To house the collection, a gallery of two rooms was constructed adjoining the Bowen Collection of Biblical Antiquities—a group of artifacts collected by Frank and Barbara Bowen, missionaries and archaeologists.[57] The Bob Jones University Collection of Sacred Art opened with much fanfare on Thanksgiving Day 1951 and presented twenty-five paintings. True to the wishes of the Executive Committee, all were religious themes and ranged in period between the thirteenth and the eighteenth centuries.[58] By the time the first catalog of the collection was produced in 1954, the holdings had grown to at least forty works.[59]

In 1956, when the Fine Arts Building was constructed adjoining the gallery, several new rooms were added to enlarge the display area. All of the older gallery space, including the museum, was redecorated and period furniture was then added to the collection and displayed in conjunction with the pictures.[60] Included in this new gallery space was a Tondo Room,[61] a French Gothic Room, a Northern Gothic Room, a Baroque Room, and a Renaissance Room. Also displayed for the first time were Russian icons from the collection of the last Tsarina, Alexandra Feodorovna, in the Icon Room.[62] The collection grew until the 1962 catalog of Italian, French, Spanish, Flemish, Dutch, and German paintings numbered 211 pictures, among which were two works by Rubens, two by Van Dyck, and one by Giordano.[63] Visiting art critics and historians were amazed by the collection, and one art historian commented that "although one hears a great deal about the Bob Jones University Collection, one really has no conception of the extent and the excellence of the collection until one has seen it firsthand."[64] Through gifts and acquisitions, the collection eventually grew to encompass nineteen rooms and finally outgrew the museum building entirely.

Of major importance was the 1963 acquisition of the seven-canvas series "The Progress of Revealed Religion." These works by American Benjamin West, commissioned by King George III of England, were intended for the king's proposed private chapel in Windsor Castle.[65] Because of the king's illness and eventual madness, the chapel was never built and the paintings were never hung at Windsor. They were separated and fell into private hands where they remained until 1963. Bob Jones University acquired the series for presentation in the newly remodeled War Memorial Chapel.[66]

When the University constructed its new Dining Common in 1965, the Gallery moved into the old Dining Common after several months of extensive renovation and redecoration. The new Art Gallery and Museum opened on Thanksgiving Day 1965 with a gala banquet at which local and state dignitaries, museum directors, art historians, and internationally recognized dealers were guests. In connection with the opening, a two-day symposium on "Culture and the Visual Arts" was held, featuring papers by six prominent museum directors of the leading art galleries in the United States and Canada, all of whom lavished praise on the Bob Jones Collection.[67]

The new facility contained thirty galleries, twenty-seven given to the display of the University's permanent collection of religious art, one for the display of the James Cole Collection of Ecclesiastical Textiles and Vestments, and two for special exhibitions.[68] Also included were a restoration shop, work area, reception center, and offices.[69] The gallery gained national prominence when a number of the paintings—possibly as many as twenty-one—were included in three NBC Television *Project Twenty* specials on national TV: "The Coming of Christ," "He is Risen," and "The Law and the Prophets."[70]

By 1968 the collection had grown to nearly 350 works in the permanent collection of sacred art, as well as a small collection of secular works which were hung in the Rodeheaver Auditorium, the Administration Building, the Mack Library, the Fine Arts Building, and later in the Founder's Memorial Amphitorium.[71] By 1990, the collection had over four hundred works on permanent display, was recognized as the finest collection of religious art in the Western Hemisphere, and was visited by more than twenty-two thousand people each year.[72]

Early on, critics challenged the University to justify the Collection of Sacred Art. The criticisms most often expressed were "the fantastic cost" and the "Catholic" theology portrayed.[73] Many of the paintings were actually donated to the school, and the remainder, Dr. Jones Jr. wrote, were a "better investment than real estate or stocks or bonds."[74] The collection, he said, was meant to provide aesthetic enjoyment, historical instruction, and a chance for religious reflection. "Just as there are books in our library with theological content and interpretations with which we may not agree," he wrote, "so there are in the gallery paintings by men with whose interpretations we do not agree."[75] The gallery, he wrote, "is not intended to teach theology."[76]

In recent years, numbers of national and international exhibitions have borrowed from the Bob Jones Collection, including a long-running exhibition at the famed Ringling Museum in Florida and one at the Walraf-Richartz Museum in Cologne, Germany.

Cinema

Unusual Films, the Bob Jones University Department of Cinema, was organized in 1950 as an educational department within the School of Fine Arts. It was also intended to operate as a fully functioning film production unit to make Christian films.[77] Film, as a tool in mass evangelism, had fascinated Bob Jones Sr. in the early years of his evangelistic work. As noted earlier, in March 1925 he produced a dramatized sermon film on location in Philadelphia.[78] Although no copy of this film survived, the interest of Dr. Jones Sr. in the medium apparently did, because some years later, probably 1938 or 1939, Dr. Jones Sr. appointed a staff member to try to make a film about Bob Jones College. The effort ended about two weeks later when Dr. Jones realized that filmmaking was more difficult than it appeared.[79]

Bob Jones Jr. shared his father's interest in the medium as a tool for mass evangelism. The idea of developing a film program at the University may have been discussed among the Joneses during the 1940s because

Bob Jones Jr. met with Arthur Rank of the famed Arthur Rank Film Studios of Great Britain in 1948 to gather information about filmmaking.[80] During the next two years Bob Jones Jr. began to examine critically the quality of Christian films, and he became convinced that a film production unit on the campus could be successful and could fill a great need in American evangelicalism. "Motion pictures," he believed, "can be a most effective medium for getting out the gospel. They can be used in churches and by means of television they can reach into the homes and speak for the Master."[81]

At the urging of both the Founder and the President, the University board approved the construction of a cinema studio, for which ground was broken in June 1950.[82] At the time of construction, no film staff had yet been hired, but in line with the personnel philosophy of the school—selecting individuals and letting them grow with a position—Dr. Jones Jr. selected two staff members to pioneer the studio: Katherine Corne Stenholm, director;[83] and Bob Craig, photographer.

Dr. Jones Jr. first approached Stenholm about the film studio while she was directing rehearsals for *Cyrano de Bergerac*.[84] She was completing her doctoral studies at Northwestern University but decided to abandon them in the summer of 1950 to enter film school at the University of Southern California. While there, she worked mornings on the Hollywood film lot of director Stanley Kramer and became acquainted with Kramer's production designer, Rudolph Sternod. From Sternod she learned many of the secrets of the trade, including equipment, makeup, special effects, set construction, sound recording techniques, and photography.[85] Bob Craig also entered the USC film school and became BJU's first cinematographer and worked with Unusual Films for eight years.

In September 1950, following her first summer of study, Stenholm began teaching cinema courses and started preplanning for *Macbeth,* the first production of Bob Jones University's "Unusual Films."[86] Bob Jones Jr. narrated and starred in the 105-minute color film.[87] A second project, *Light of the World,* a dramatized sermon by Bob Jones Sr., was premiered April 1, 1951.[88] *Macbeth,* though started before *Light,* was finally premiered on September 8 that same year.[89]

In July 1951 the studio produced *Pound of Flesh*, a film sermon on the theme of law and grace from Shakespeare's *Merchant of Venice*. In the middle of the sermon, Bob Jones Jr. turned from the pulpit and pushed open the large doors behind him. As Shylock, he then entered a Venetian courtroom where the scene was acted out. The film closed with Dr. Jones again in the pulpit, contrasting the sinner's appeal to law with that of the penitent throwing himself upon God's grace.

That same year, the campus film studio produced three *Hour of Decision* television programs for the Billy Graham Evangelistic Association.[90] In addition, the film *You Can't Win,* based on Bob Jones Sr.'s sermon to men (possibly very similar to the Founder's 1925 film *The Unbeatable Game*), was completed in March 1952. That same year Unusual Films received its first national award from the National Evangelical Film Foundation for the film *Vesper Melodies,* as the best musical production.[91] Amazingly, between 1950 and 1957 Katherine Stenholm and her staff produced the Billy Graham TV programs, the *Frontiers of Faith* television series with Bob Jones Jr. (sponsored by the American Council of Christian Churches and broadcast on NBC), and eight films, one of which was feature-length.[92]

The feature-length picture, *Wine of Morning,* based on Bob Jones Jr.'s novel of the same name, was premiered in 1955.[93] The film was shot entirely on the campus, had seventy-five speaking parts, and used over eight hundred students in the cast. All the leading roles were played by University faculty and students, and the music was composed by a music faculty member and performed by the University orchestra.[94] *Wine of Morning* was selected by the University Film Producers Association to represent the United States at the International Congress of Motion Picture and Television Schools in Cannes, France, and following a showing at the Congress, garnered praise from the international film community.[95] *Wine of Morning* was also awarded four "Christian Oscars" from the National Evangelical Film Foundation for Best Film, Best Actor, Best Director, and Best Producer. [96]

Other major film productions of the University's studio include the 1963 release of *Red Runs the River,* the story of Civil War generals Stonewall Jackson and Richard Stoddard Ewell;[97] and *Flame in the Wind,* a story set during the sixteenth-century Spanish Inquisition and released in 1971. *Sheffey,* the touching story of an itinerant evangelist of the late nineteenth century, was released in 1978. *Beyond the Night,* a missionary film based on events in the life of missionary surgeon John Dreisbach, was released in 1983, followed by the 1990 release of *The Printing,* a dramatic story of persecuted believers in the former Soviet Union.[98] Interspersed with these feature-length projects were a number of shorter films for commercial clients, five promotional films for the University, and a large number of student projects that regularly won national awards.[99]

In 1957 a nationwide survey of undergraduate and graduate cinema programs was published by the Journal of the Society of Motion Picture and Television Engineers. It ranked Bob Jones University

Katherine Stenholm, at right, directing *Beyond the Night* (Unusual Films, 1982)

third behind the University of California at Los Angeles and the University of Southern California.[100] In 1963 a United States Office of Education Bulletin reported national survey results which indicated that "there is probably no institution in the United States or abroad which is so well equipped [for teaching cinema] in relation to the number of students being trained."[101] BJU is still one of only a handful of American universities to offer a master's degree in cinema.

The film department of Bob Jones University was unique in Christian higher education. "There is no other school in the United States who has done what we have done in [feature-length] films," Katherine Stenholm said. "And the reason for it—background. . . . If we hadn't had costumes exactly in period, if we hadn't had art, if we hadn't had the music, if we hadn't had the emphasis on doing it right . . . [our films] would not have been possible. The whole [cultural] foundation had to be made right."[102]

The cultural program of Bob Jones University was diverse and unlike that of any other college in the world. It came of age in Greenville in the campus environment of excellence demanded by Bob Jones Jr. Imitators in other Christian colleges have tried to duplicate BJU's cultural and social opportunities, but never with complete success. Undoubtedly the most significant element of the program was the underlying goals: first, "to develop the student's knowledge and talent in the liberal arts so that he can be 'all things to all men' and, thereby, 'win some,' just as Paul used quotations from two Greek poets in order to gain the consideration of worldly philosophers. The second purpose was to develop the student's understanding, discrimination, and taste in harmony with the teaching of God's Word."[103]

Even as expenses associated with these programs have skyrocketed, Bob Jones III has remained committed to continuing the cultural emphasis.[104] As the Founder said, "We insist that every good and perfect gift comes from God and that when the devil takes music, or drama, or art, he holds stolen property."[105] Through each production Bob Jones University has sought to reclaim that which was stolen.

CHAPTER 18

♦

"Brains Are No Substitute for God!"

It took several years following the move to Greenville and the change to university status before majors and course offerings were stabilized. The new, young members of the administration and faculty who came to the school following the Mercer affair and the stand against Billy Graham injected creativity and a renewed enthusiasm that carried the institution to new heights of academic and spiritual progress. The Founder's note was sounded: Godly humility with intellectual prowess was the goal.[1] "Don't worship at the shrine of intellectuality," he preached. "Get your degree, but don't go out and strut yourself and say you don't need anything else, . . . because intellectual conceit breaks the heart of God."[2]

Progress in upgrading the academic program of the University was consistent and noteworthy. The education that the University offered in several areas began to gain national recognition. The School of Education was one such area.[3] In 1952 the Bob Jones University chapter of the Future Teachers of America was selected as that organization's National Banner Chapter.[4] The previous year, the School of Education's dean reported that on the National Teacher Examinations (NTEs), 90 percent achieved scores high enough for South Carolina "A" teaching certificates with the other 10 percent receiving scores high enough for South Carolina "B" certificates. He also reported that "the average of our graduates . . . exceeds that achieved by [those] which were chosen for sampling and the establishment of norms."[5]

Under Walter Fremont, who became dean in 1954, the NTE results became even better. In 1957 the results indicated that BJU students scored forty to fifty points above the national average.[6] By 1962 this score improved to 98 percent "A's" and 2 percent "B's," which was the highest score in South Carolina;[7] by 1963 the score was 100 percent "A's."[8] For twenty consecutive years, BJU's NTE test scores remained above the national average.[9]

Fremont also succeeded in challenging the School of Education faculty to send graduates into the developing Christian day school movement instead of the public schools. In 1960, for example, 46 graduates of the School of Education went into the Greenville area public schools and another 143 began teaching in newly organized Christian schools across the country.[10] Between 1960 and 1970 more than 1,000 BJU graduates were certified to teach and were teaching in public, private, and Christian schools in at least forty-eight states.[11]

Under Dean Laurence Lautenbach the School of Business gained a national reputation for its graduates because of their thorough understanding of the various fields of business with the added bonus of highly developed personal character.[12] Results of the American Institute of Certified Public Accountants Testing Program for 1962 reported that the lowest score a Bob Jones University accounting student received was at the national average and all others were significantly higher. Two years in a row a BJU student scored in the one hundredth percentile on this test, and all business seniors had been hired well before their graduation.[13] In 1964 the average score of BJU accounting students on the National Achievement Tests of the American Institute of Certified Public Accountants was 40 percent above the national average with three students scoring in the ninety-eighth percentile.[14] Graduates of the School of Business were widely recruited by industry and highly respected for their integrity and for the fact that "they give more than a day's work for a day's pay."[15]

The School of Religion, the largest of all BJU academic schools during the 1950s and 1960s, prepared a large number of pastors, evangelists, Bible teachers, and missionaries for Christian ministry both in the United States and abroad. In 1950 the "Preacher Boys" class had eleven hundred members;[16] in 1961 approximately eight hundred young men were counted as Preacher Boys.[17] The influence of these men is immense. In 1971 alone, the Preacher Boys held 27,600 services, dealt with more than fifty-five thousand people, and saw more than six thousand people converted.[18] As the years passed, however, and American society became increasingly materialistic and secularized, the number of Preacher Boys continued to drop, causing concern among pastors and school officials.

It is the exception to find a Christian school, college, or Bible school that does not have at least one BJU alumnus on its faculty, and many of the Christian colleges that began after 1950 were initially staffed almost entirely by Bob Jones University graduates.[19] Often the expressed desire of the founders or first presidents of these schools was to "make a little BJU" out of their institutions.[20] Hiring BJU graduates seemed to be the best way in which to do this.

In 1967 the School of Religion and the Graduate School joined forces to produce a journal of Fundamentalist Bible scholarship entitled *Biblical Viewpoint*. Published twice yearly, the journal focused on one book of the Bible per issue and was prepared by the University's religion professors and other conservative Christian scholars.[21]

The School of Fine Arts, under the leadership of Dwight Gustafson since 1954, matured greatly with faculty receiving state and national recognition and students competing and placing for top awards in state, regional, and national competitions.[22] Within the School of Fine Arts was the fledgling Cinema Department that demanded the efforts of all areas of the arts—music, scriptwriting, scenic design, acting, and costuming. As the Cinema Department became more widely known for its superior productions, the School of Fine Arts' reputation also grew.

Test results of standardized tests like the NTE, the Graduate Record Exams, and various business examinations were often cited by the University as proof of "high academic standards" and helped many graduates gain admittance into major graduate programs even though the school remained a nonaccredited institution.[23]

Because Bob Jones University was not accredited by a regional or national association, the faculty felt an increased responsibility to prepare the students to the highest possible extent in their major areas. When a BJU graduate entered a graduate school, he was there on the strength of his own personal record, not on the strength of a school's accreditation. BJU's reputation in academic circles gradually became more respected for the intellectual preparation and strong character of its graduates. By the 1960s several graduate schools actively courted University alumni, and BJU graduates were accepted into most of the major graduate programs in the country despite the school's opposition to regional accreditation.[24]

A review of the graduate schools attended by University faculty who held undergraduate degrees from BJU shows the level of acceptance which they and the University in general enjoyed. Most of the faculty, with the exception of those in religion, took advanced work at secular colleges and universities, including prestigious professional schools and research institutions.[25] The faculty's training was thorough and academically impeccable.

The record of BJU graduates from these years in pastorates, the chaplaincy, the mission field, and in youth ministries is also dramatic. Students in the University were continually challenged to be busy about the Lord's business, and during each school year literally hundreds of evangelistic outreaches were undertaken by students and faculty in the immediate Greenville area. These included children's Bible clubs, prison and jail ministries, street preaching, nursing home work, camp work, and outreaches organized by local churches. In addition, musical groups from the University as well as summer mission teams represented Christ and the school in the United States and all over the world.[26]

In 1957 the University opened the Institute of Christian Service as a Bible school training program for "individuals of mature experience or irregular academic background" who were not interested in a formal university or college degree.[27] Under the leadership of Ken Hay, the curriculum and faculty were separated from the University, and students who were deficient in certain areas of their academic background or were somewhat older in age or had been away from study for several years were encouraged to enter this program.[28] The scope of the three-year program was designed to be practical in nature but required the students to take an academic core of general subjects such as English grammar, speech, psychology, and business, as well as courses in Bible and practical Christian service.[29] The Institute opened with seven students in 1957, grew to over one hundred by 1961, and eventually grew to over two hundred in the 1970s.[30]

The fifties were the decade of the Cold War. They brought a sense of imminent danger to much of the nation. Atomic attack from the Soviet Union was perceived as a very real national threat, and the government encouraged the citizenry to take precautions to insure survival if such an attack occurred. Government agencies themselves actively prepared for such an eventuality as well. At two different times in 1961, representatives of the United States Navy and the Internal Revenue Service surveyed the Bob Jones campus for possible governmental use in the event of an atomic attack on Washington, D.C., or Atlanta. Dr. Jones Sr. took the navy request to the board, which decided that in national emergency, "the greatest service we can render our country is the training of Christian leaders for the future" rather than as billet for the military. A similar request from the IRS was also denied.[31]

In spite of growth in the student body, growing educational offerings, the cultural richness of the school, and the economic impact of the University on Greenville, a cold war of sorts developed between the school and some of Greenville's leaders, including members of the chamber of commerce. Affairs reached a climax between 1961 and 1963 when the school, the city of Greenville, and the chamber of commerce clashed in a zoning controversy over a proposed shopping center to be built adjacent to the University.[32]

The school and nearly all its neighbors opposed the zoning change from residential to commercial, feeling that the center was unneeded and would endanger the lives of the nearby residents and students as traffic increased.[33] In addition, the new Wade Hampton Shopping Center was only one block from the school, and W. Harrell Wilson's shopping center would be next door with the exits emptying directly onto the campus itself.[34] The issue became increasingly heated until the President appeared before the city council and in effect threatened to move the school if the issue could not be resolved.[35]

Wilson's zoning proposal passed two of the required three readings in city council, each with the vote of six to one. After the second reading on July 5, 1962, the school filed lawsuits against the city, the chamber of commerce, the Wilson Development Company, and the Wilson family.[36] Nevertheless, the city council approved the zoning request on the third reading.[37] W. H. Wilson had been unfriendly to the school for many years and had declared that he would never sell his land to Bob Jones, but he never broke ground for his new Carolina Shopping Center. Soon after the issue was resolved, he fell ill and was forced to sell the property to pay his expenses. The land passed through another developer's hands and eventually was purchased by Jack Shaw, a Greenville realtor and developer. Shaw ultimately offered it to Bob Jones University.[38] Ironically, by losing the suit against Wilson, the University paved the way for eventual ownership of the property and guaranteed land for its expansion in the 1980s.

The Mercer (1953) and Graham (1957) disputes took a toll on enrollment (see Table 4 below), and by 1957-58 enrollment stood at a ten-year low of 1,893, a drop of nearly one thousand students since the opening in

Greenville. Enrollment steadily improved until the year following Graham's Greenville campaign (1963-64), when enrollment again dropped somewhat. By 1967-68, however, enrollment had rebounded to 2,841 first-semester students. And by 1971 Bob Jones University was the largest Fundamentalist Christian university in the country, enrolling 3,300 undergraduate students, 163 graduate school students, and 487 high school students, for a combined total of 4,121.[39]

Table 4

First Semester Enrollment Bob Jones University & Academy, 1957-71[40]

Year	Univ.	Academy	Grad./Spec.	ICS	Total
1957-58	1893	345	86	7	2331
1958-59	1986	382	102	11	2481
1959-60	2175	415	84	25	2699
1960-61	2388	457	83	44	2972
1961-62	2405	401	64	109	2979
1962-63	2402	417	51	86	2956
1963-64	2250	389	48	97	2784
1964-65	2462	457	93	143	3155
1965-66	2508	410	116	163	3197
1966-67	2632	422	131	195	3380
1967-68	2841	370	120	170	3501
1968-69	2942	436	121	195	3694
1969-70	3091	406	156	189	3842
1970-71	3300	487	163	171	4121

Costs for tuition and room and board remained low. In 1947 tuition was listed at $125.00 per semester and room and board was $172.00 per semester, for a total of $594.00 per year. A $25.00 matriculation fee was also levied on the students.[41] By 1970 tuition had risen to $325.00 per semester and room and board was $472.50, for a total of $1,595.00 per year, plus a matriculation fee of $50.00 per semester.[42]

For those students who required financial aid to complete school, the University's Student Loan Endowment Fund gave aid to students through a work scholarship program similar to the work program developed in the 1930s in Cleveland, Tennessee.[43] Since its beginning in 1952, the fund has helped thousands of students pay for their college education while providing important services to the school.

Following the completion of the seventeen-building first unit, the University raised funds and constructed approximately one building a year. Dramatic growth occurred between the years 1947 and 1971. In 1950 the

Unusual Films studios were added to the back of Rodeheaver Auditorium. The next year the art gallery building was completed, the Bowen Museum was moved from the library to the new facility, and the Academy Quadrangle was constructed.[44] The cool comfort of air conditioning came to Rodeheaver Auditorium in 1953. In 1955 a $1.5 million expansion program was announced; this included a new girls' dorm (Georgia Creel), the Fine Arts Building (1956), a new gymnasium and swimming pool (1959), new faculty housing, and a nursery building.

Desperately crowded for science teaching space, the University dedicated the beautiful Howell Memorial Science Building in 1960, along with two new dormitories—Estelle Siddons for women and Ernest Reveal for men—and expanded the Academy. In 1965 the Administration Building was modernized and a new three-story wing was added; the 3,500-seat Dixon-McKenzie Dining Common was completed; and sixteen new faculty homes were constructed overlooking the athletic fields on the back campus. The grass common in front of Rodeheaver Auditorium was transformed into a reflecting pool with cascading fountains and sprays—all part of the new campus air conditioning system—with a bridge and a small island in the center. More faculty housing—104 apartments—was added in 1968 with the construction of Campus View Apartments; and the next year, the four-story, full-care W. J. Barge Memorial Hospital, with seventy-nine beds, two operating rooms, examining rooms, a physical therapy room, and x-ray, pharmacy, and obstetrical departments was dedicated. The University's new elementary school was built in 1970, and a new faculty wing with sixty offices and two lecture rooms was added to the Alumni Building, the main classroom building. (One English professor quipped that an aerial view of the new wing unfortunately gave the building the shape of a giant F.) Ground was also broken for the mammoth Founder's Memorial Amphitorium.

Many remodeling projects were completed during these years, including

Towers of the Founder's Memorial Amphitorium under construction (1972)

the 1960 transformation of the old Student Center gymnasium into a 700-seat Concert Center and the 1963 redecoration of the War Memorial Chapel to prepare it for displaying the huge Benjamin West masterpieces.[45] Following the construction of the Dixon-McKenzie Dining Common in 1965[46] and the conversion of the old dining hall into a new art gallery area, the former gallery was remodeled for use as speech classrooms, becoming part of an expanded Fine Arts Building.

Construction on campus buildings never began until the need was pressing. The greatest example of this was the construction of the Founder's Memorial Amphitorium. Announced in 1970 and completed in 1973, the Amphitorium—a name coined by combin-

A view from Rodeheaver Auditorium of the Amphitorium construction (1972)

ing the words *amphitheater* and *auditorium*—was constructed as an enclosed amphitheater, acoustically tuned for preaching, and was designed to seat the entire student body and faculty under one roof. By 1968 the student body had outgrown Rodeheaver Auditorium making it necessary for chapel, Sunday morning worship, and Artist Series programs to be carried by closed circuit television to the Concert Center. By 1971 the faculty had to be seated on the auditorium stage, and students filled Rodeheaver Auditorium, the Concert Center, and the War Memorial Chapel; and during Bible Conference and Commencement, the Science Lecture Hall, Alumni Lecture Halls A and B, and the Social Parlor were pressed into service as well. Students were often required to attend live concerts in formal attire in a building where the program was carried by radio or fuzzy black-and-white television. One student recalled an Artist Series featuring the Little Angels, a Korean folk music troupe, where all that was seen displayed on the Concert Center screen was an occasional head, feet moving in the background, and scarves swirling across the screen.[47] One performer, baritone Sherrill Milnes, actually left the Rodeheaver stage and went to the Concert Center to perform one number live.[48] To bring the University family back under one roof, it was imperative to construct an appropriate-sized building.[49]

The Amphitorium, which measures 290 feet by 290 feet, encloses more than an acre of land and contains almost three acres of floor space in its various levels. It contains sixteen million pounds of concrete reinforced by 400,000 tons of steel, all under a 230-foot clear span roof having an additional one million pounds of steel supported by eight towers. The building has seven thousand seats; a choir loft for three hundred; a projection booth; a sound room; dressing rooms; a stage office; a fully equipped multitrack recording studio with control room, offices, tape duplication, and storage facilities; and the Pauline Rupp Assembly Room for seminars and small campus meetings.

To support the accoustic needs of the building, over three thousand watts of audio power were available through more than eight thousand pounds of speakers and baffles. In addition, the Allen Organ Company installed what at that time was its largest and most sophisticated electronic organ.[50] Shortly after completion, the Amphitorium received the National Design Award of Merit from the Armco Steel Corporation.[51]

The University became increasingly well known not only for its outspoken, separatist, Fundamentalist theology and the academic preparation of its graduates but also for the discipline it required of its students. Discipline was a major selling point of the University, especially during the turbulent 1960s, and helped attract many students to the school. The high standards of social behavior set for students during the Florida days and carried through the Cleveland years continued in Greenville.

Student life was not "all work and no play," however. The University's student literary societies continued in Greenville and prospered with the growth of the institution. In 1948 sixteen societies existed for the students.[52] By 1954 the students had thirty-two societies from which to choose—sixteen women's societies and sixteen men's societies—and the societies were the center of athletic competition and student social life.[53] As the student body increased, some societies grew to be extremely large, thus limiting leadership opportunities within those societies. To correct this, eight new societies were created in 1969 by cutting the membership of each existing society and assigning those students to the new organizations. No society was to be larger than eighty members, and those that exceeded the limit had to be cut by ratios. The arbitrary manner in which the cuts were made created some hurt feelings among the students who were reassigned. The new societies were financially broke, having to raise nearly every cent needed for sports and cheerleading uniforms, outings, and other needs.

In 1980 growth in the student body again necessitated creating fourteen more societies, for a total of fifty-four. To minimize the types of problems created by the 1969 expansion, Bob Jones III announced that 1979-80 would open with "Pioneer Days," which offered students the chance to "be a pioneer" and "get that pioneer spirit!"[54] Jim Berg, the administrative assistant, supervised the planning and implementation of Pioneer Days and urged the students to consider volunteering to help establish a new society.[55] Buttons, posters, bulletin boards, and pep talks spread the message, and the students enthusiastically responded.

Society life has remained relatively unchanged through the history of the school. Each year the societies have fielded athletic teams, held pep rallies, sponsored banquets and outings, had prayer meetings and extension ministries, provided social opportunities, and generally have raised the spirit of the student body. The Inter-Society Council (organized in 1953 to replace the old Pan Hellenic Council, a holdover from Cleveland days) undertook campus and community projects that required large numbers of volunteers.

These projects included planning and creating Thanksgiving decorations and organizing the halftime festivities for the Turkey Bowl (the school soccer championship), planning the basketball championship festivities, and organizing other student events, such as urban cleanup days.

Worldly amusements such as theatrical movies, dancing, listening to or performing jazz or rock-and-roll music, were strictly forbidden, as were beards and styles of clothing considered immodest, revealing, or "hippie."[56] Conservative hair lengths were required for men students, and neckties were worn for morning classes and any time a young man was off campus. Sport coats or suits and ties were also required for the evening family-style meals. In short, the atmosphere was one of organized activity, and student life was such that in 1967 one national magazine named the University "the most square University in America," and ranked it the third most conservative school in the nation.[57] That same year another magazine, in a study of college culture, reported, "BOB JONES: Pot: there isn't any. You get expelled here for smoking a Kent. Liquor: soft drinks. Girl guests: prim, proper, arms-distance. Hippie hangout: none. Kicks: none. Law and Order: Dr. William Liverman, Dean of Men."[58]

Even around conservative Greenville, the deportment of Bob Jones students did not go unnoticed. A columnist for a Greenville newspaper wrote, "My theological position and my style of life is far removed from those of the people at Bob Jones University. But BJU students who come into our place of business always have nice manners and a cheerful outlook. It is refreshing to do business with them. I envy those fundamentalists a little."[59]

During the most turbulent days of the late 1960s, the administration of Bob Jones University remained firmly in control of the students and their campus activities. Student radicalism was nonexistent on the campus, and the national turmoil created by the Civil Rights and antiwar movements had little visible impact on the student body. While students in colleges across the country were protesting the Vietnam War, invading campus buildings, looting offices, and destroying property and equipment paid for with public money, Bob Jones students were being taught in the classroom and from the chapel platform how to live.

Even though Dr. Jones Jr. was "sympathetic to people in need" and felt sorry for folks who lived in areas where "there is not enough work to go around,"[60] the teaching emphasis of Bob Jones University was not on social reclamation or reconstruction, personal freedom, or civil rights, but "personal responsibility and civil obligations. In a day when rascals in clerical garb join hands with anarchists in mob violence and law breaking," Dr. Jones Jr. said, "Bob Jones University sends out men and women who stand for the fundamental principles of Constitutional Americanism." He declared that the University stood for "old-fashioned decency, honor, integrity, and truth." While he recognized that grave social conditions existed in American society, he maintained that "the preaching of the Gospel is the great need of our day" and that "the grace of God can change men's hearts. Apostate prophets have talked about changing conditions and improving the world. Conditions are changed—but for the worse," he preached. "We are not sending you out to change conditions. We are sending you out with a message that can change men."[61]

Part of that message was old-fashioned self-discipline and self-control. "All this philosophy of the day—express yourself—is contrary to God's Word," he preached. "God's Word says deny yourself. He that will be greatest among you, let him be the servant of all. If any man will come after me, let him take up a cross daily and follow me—that willingness to take up hardships and difficulties and self-discipline . . . is not letting yourself do what you want to do."[62] During the turbulent 1960s he stressed obedience by saying that "there is no man who is not subject to God's law. . . . There is no respect of persons with God; every Christian is under the same obligation. . . . Don't you get the idea that if you get prominent that you are freed from obligations to obey Scripture. God doesn't set some man above His purpose and His revealed will. Obedience is enjoined on every child of God."[63]

Dr. Jones Jr. described the school as a human place with imperfect students, imperfect executives, and an imperfect President, but said that "we try our best to keep it as perfect as we can. We do the best we can with imperfect human material, but we have hearts that are sincere before God."[64]

The 1960s were a period of at least formal transition in the executive leadership of the school. In 1964 Bob Jones Sr. retired as chairman of the Board of Trustees, Bob Jones Jr. was elected to that position, and Bob Jones III was named vice president of the University. Dr. Jones Sr. was named chairman of the Cooperating Board, a position he held for two more years. In 1966 the eighty-two-year-old evangelist, worn from a life of preaching and serving Christ, tendered his resignation to the Cooperating Board. It was accepted, and Bob Jones III was named a member of the Executive Committee.[65] The great evangelist was hospitalized for the final two years of his life.

Even in the mental confusion of grave illness, the Founder would ask his visitors if they knew Jesus and preach sermons in his sleep. No matter how muddled his thinking became, his prayers remained clear

Left to right: Bob Jones III, Bob Jones Sr., Bob Jones IV, Bob Jones Jr. (December 1966)

and powerful.[66] His death, though not unexpected, was still difficult for those who had fought the battles beside him and supported him in "the Cause."[67]

A writer in the 1920s had said, "Bob Jones is a crusader, not a crank. . . . His religion is foundation-solid and fool-proof. . . . Live or die, he is determined that 'the dream shall come true.' That sort of man can't be defeated."[68] Undefeated in life, Bob Jones Sr. died in Greenville, South Carolina, on January 16, 1968, at eighty-four years of age. Thousands came from around the world to pay their respects to the last of the old-time evangelists.[69]

The reports of his death carried such personal descriptions as the following: "When he met his Maker face-to-face on Tuesday, he stood four-square as a man of conviction—not compromise." He had been "a militant defender of fundamental Christianity" and "was never a man to avoid a battle over the gospel."[70] The Greenville paper said, "He was utterly and completely consistent . . . in his beliefs, his principles, his thoughts, his way of life, and his relations with the world. . . . He never retreated from a position and was willing to defend his opinions against all critics. His adamant outlook on life was anathema to many liberals, particularly those . . . disillusioned with historical ethics. What he leaves is a post, pleasing or displeasing, to which a philosophy can be tied firmly. His is a tough philosophy to follow."[71] As his son wrote, "Only the pages of God's Heaven can reveal the measure of his life; only a recording angel report it fully."[72]

Edward Panosian reads the eulogy Dr. Bob Jones Jr. wrote for his father (January 1968).

Noel Smith wrote that "Dr. Jones, considerate and generous and charitable as he was, never 'mellowed' to where he would tolerate the mixing of the truth of the Bible with modern infidelity. He never wavered in his loyalty to the Bible as the very Word of God. . . . He would permit the friendship of no man to neutralize his loyalty to the Bible and to the principles he held to be right."[73]

Bob Jones Jr. stated it most eloquently in a written eulogy for his father. Triumphantly, he wrote, "This should not be a day for weeping. This is a time for rejoicing. This should not be a moment for sorrow. This is an hour for gladness. A fight has been fought, a race has been won, a crown is laid up."[74] (See Appendix C for the complete tribute.)

On the little island in the middle of the fountains in front of Rodeheaver Auditorium, Bob Jones Sr.'s body was laid to rest. Inscribed on his tombstone are these words, written by his son:

> A fight well fought,
>
> A course well run,
>
> A faith well kept,
>
> A crown well won.

Three years later, in June of 1971, the seal of the office of President of Bob Jones University passed from the Founder's son to the Founder's grandson, Bob Jones III. Bob Jones Jr., who had been either Acting President or President of Bob Jones College since 1931, now took the title of Chancellor. He had been largely responsible for the growth of the institution from a small liberal arts college in Tennessee into a mature, respected Christian university, and he now felt it was time to pass the torch to the third generation.

Dr. Robert Reynolds Jones Sr.
October 30, 1883–January 16, 1968

CHAPTER 19

◆

Bob Jones III

On Commencement Day, June 2, 1971, Bob Jones Jr. placed about the neck of Bob Jones III the seal of Bob Jones University and thereby divested himself of the heavy presidential responsibility he had borne since 1947. At his installation as President of Bob Jones University, Bob Jones III laid to rest all questions that the school would begin to soften its Fundamentalist stance. "The God of my fathers is my God," Dr. Jones III said. "Should there be any possible doubt in any-

The installation of Dr. Bob Jones III as President of Bob Jones University, June 2, 1971; *left to right:* Bob Jones Jr., Bob Jones III, R. K. Johnson

one's mind that this University in the years ahead, as God tarries, will be any less militant in its defense of the Faith, any less earnest in its evangelistic fervor, any less thorough in its academic program, any less resolute in its character-building aspect, let me say with all clarity that I am resolutely and irrevocably committed to the furtherance of what God has ordained from the day of its foundation should be the ministry of Bob Jones University."[1] With these words, Bob Jones III began his tenure as President and took on himself

Left to right: Fannie May Holmes Jones, Mary Gaston Stollenwerck Jones (holding Bob Jones III), and Estelle Siddons Stollenwerck (1939)

the mantle of leadership—a mantle he had tried to escape.

Born in Cleveland, Tennessee, on August 8, 1939, Bobby showed a determined will, which caused his grandfather to write a friend that "if he gets converted early in life and gets lined up with the Lord, he will do something."[2] As the child of a well-known evangelist and university president, and living in an intellectually stimulating university environment, Bobby had rich spiritual and cultural experiences and had the opportunity to make the acquaintance of many great preachers and great artists as they visited the campus.

As a child of five, Bobby made a profession of faith in Christ as his personal Savior. He began to doubt this profession as a teenager, however. Burdened with the fear of being forever lost in hell, he came to full assurance of his salvation after a fierce inner struggle.

Bobby sometimes traveled to Europe and the Holy Land on his father's summer tours. He also attended many recitals, concerts, and opera productions, and regularly played minor Shakespearean roles in the Classic Players productions. As a fifteen year old he played the role of Dysmas in the film version of his father's novel *Wine of Morning*. In most things, he was a serious, thoughtful young man, who in many ways "was never really young" and always had "that dimension of maturity and seriousness because he knew . . . the kind of responsibility he faced."[3]

Bob Jones III has been strongly influenced by four men: his grandfather, the aggressive evangelist and Founder of the school; his father, the studious, artistic, and creative President of the school; Ernest Reveal, founder of the Evansville Rescue Mission and an enthusiastic soulwinner;[4] and Paul Vanaman, a good friend, BJU graduate, and pastor in Michigan whose ministry of encouragement often came at the needed moment during the most difficult days.[5]

In 1955 when Bobby was fifteen, he went to Indiana and worked for eight weeks in the summer camp sponsored by the Evansville Rescue Mission and the mission's founder, Dr. Ernest I. Reveal. Reveal was a member of the University board and a close friend of both Dr. Jones Sr. and Dr. Jones Jr. He had taken a keen interest in Bobby when the boy was only six years of age and prayed for him—kept him "hooked on at the Mercy Seat"—for many years.[6] His interest in Bobby never waned, and during the summer Bobby worked at Camp Reveal, the old preacher kept him busy in activities somewhat unusual for a teenager. Dr. Reveal's impact on Bobby was "enormous."[7]

The campers were the children of the down-and-outers who were housed at the rescue mission, along with large numbers of children from the "tough" areas of Evansville, a rather hard-living, hard-drinking Ohio River town. Dr. Reveal gave Bobby many opportunities to preach on the radio—every third day—preach in the camp's evangelistic meetings, give devotional talks, and counsel the young toughs at the camp. Reveal wrote Bobby's father that "he is preaching with power. . . . The Lord has given you something in that boy. He is getting good experience here and is seeing the rough side of life."[8]

During his stay at the camp, the power of prayer became evident as Bobby saw serious needs met in miraculous ways as a result of Dr. Reveal's prayers. Just talking to Dr. Reveal was a lesson in prayer. Dr. Jones III often tells that when driving in a car, one moment Dr. Reveal would be talking with him, "the next moment, he would be talking to God. It was that kind of a natural relationship."[9] One particularly memorable event occurred during the summer that Bobby was in Evansville. The area had experienced a long drought, during which the well at the camp ran "bone dry." The camp was in dire need of water in order to continue operating. Reveal called the staff together and prayed for water in the well so that the children would not have to be sent home "stinky and dirty" and thus "reflect on God's work." The next day the well had water in it, and it stayed full during the entire summer while the other wells in the area remained dry. For Bob Jones III, this was a great object lesson of God's provision.[10]

A second lesson learned from his summer at Camp Reveal was simply that humanity needs Christ. Contacts with the unkempt, unloved, and often unwanted children at Camp Reveal helped Bobby to develop the same type of love and compassion for people that his grandfather possessed.

Bobby's early education was in the public schools of Cleveland, Tennessee, and Greenville, South Carolina. He attended Bob Jones Academy during his high school years. As a student, Bob excelled. He finished high school in three years, completing the last of his Academy requirements in 1956, after entering Bob Jones University in 1955.[11] He was a member of the Bryan literary society and was active in student government and sports—especially enjoying basketball. As a teen he also developed what has become a continuing love for tennis, hunting, fishing, and all types of outdoor activities. He received his bachelor of arts degree in 1959 and immediately began work on a master of arts degree that fall. In December 1959 Bob married Beneth Peters, who was also a graduate student in speech.

Beneth grew up in Olympia, Washington, and had moved to Phoenix, Arizona, where she attended the Phoenix Christian High School for her junior and senior years. While in high school, she showed great promise in both speech and music, and two of her teachers recommended that she consider Bob Jones University for her college education. Following their advice, she applied, was accepted, came to Greenville in 1955, and majored in speech. During her sophomore year, she read for the part of Roxane in *Cyrano de Bergerac* and never dreamed she would

Beneth Peters as Roxane in *Cyrano de Bergerac* by Edmond Rostand (Bob Jones University Classic Players, May 13, 1957)

have a chance at the role. She knew that Bob Jones III was slated to play Christian, the romantic male lead, but thought little of it. Beneth received a callback for a final audition, and, unknown to her at the time, Katherine Stenholm, the director, had invited Bob to attend that reading by the four women under consideration. When the auditions ended, Stenholm turned to him and asked, "Well, which one do you want for Roxane?" Much to her delight, Beneth was selected for the part. Bob had been interested in her for some time and now had the perfect opportunity to court her, although rather publicly. When the play ended, they began to date and with the encouragement of Dr. Jones Jr. were married in December of 1959, during their first year in graduate school.[12]

Many of the school's supporters assumed that one day Bob III would simply take the helm of the school. For many years, however, he was of a different mind. He wanted to pursue a military career because he loved airplanes and flying. The military's structure also appealed to his sense of "making his own way" outside the realm of the fame of his father and grandfather. When he reached his senior year in college, however, Bob III began to feel God's direction to stay at the University to try to "help perpetuate the ideals and standards," he said, "which my grandfather had set up when he founded the school."[13] As a graduate assistant, he taught speech while working toward his M.A. and also served in the dean of men's office as a dormitory supervisor.

After their marriage, Bob and Beneth Jones attended summer classes in speech and drama at Northwestern University, and Bob later took postgraduate work at New York University. He received his first honorary degree, doctor of literature, in 1963 from Pillsbury Baptist Bible College in Owatonna, Minnesota, and has been similarly honored by San Francisco Theological Seminary and Maranatha Baptist Bible College in Watertown, Wisconsin. Meanwhile, in 1960 he was elected to the Cooperating Board and appointed Assistant to the President.[14] He was elected to the regular board in 1962,[15] and in 1964, following the resignation of Bob Jones Sr., he was appointed to the Executive Committee of the University and was asked to serve as vice president.[16]

On January 14, 1963, the young Joneses were thrilled by the birth of their first child. Complications developed, however, and within hours after the baby boy's birth, Bob III had to inform the family that "God has taken him back." The family's second child arrived on December 12, 1964, and was named Roxane for the role her mother had played at the beginning of her parents' courtship. Two years later, Robert Reynolds Jones IV was born on December 11, 1966; and a third son, Stephen, was born on December 31, 1969.[17]

The years between completing his graduate program in 1961 and assuming the reins of the school in 1971 were filled with an increasing number of administrative duties, major roles in numerous Shakespearean productions, preaching for campus services and for a growing number of engagements off-campus, plus major roles in two feature-length films: the role of General J.E.B. Stuart in the Civil War story *Red Runs the River* and the role of Fernando, a Bible smuggler during the Spanish Inquisition, in the film *Flame in the Wind.*

During this decade Bob Jones III also began to learn firsthand the challenges of operating a Fundamentalist Christian university in the midst of an increasingly unsympathetic culture. In 1966 a reporter from *Harper's* visited the campus to gather information for his article "The Buckle on the Bible Belt." After several days of casual observation and one formal interview with Dr. Jones III, the writer came away from the school bewildered by an institution out of step with 1960s cultural norms. His published story was unsympathetic, defamatory, and sarcastic; for Bob Jones III, however, it was something of an early introduction to the misunderstandings that the secularist viewpoint promoted as it looked at the institution.[18]

A second incident that showed the flawed viewpoint of the secularists and also served to elevate Dr. Jones III to the position of a spokesman for Fundamentalism occurred in 1977 when NBC, under the sponsorship of General Motors, prepared a film version of the life of Christ for presentation during the Passion Week. Directed by Franco Zeffirelli, the film, though it had artistic merits, portrayed Christ as "an ordinary man, gentle, fragile, simple"[19] and showed "the humanity of Jesus."[20] In response to the secularized and humanized *Jesus of Nazareth,* Bob Jones III began a campaign against GM by calling on "those who love and know the Lord Jesus Christ, God incarnate" to "make their protest known both verbally and by spending automobile dollars elsewhere."[21] In a matter of days, thousands of letters opposing the film poured into both GM's and NBC's headquarters. The pressure worked: General Motors withdrew its support, losing over $4.5 million, and thousands of Evangelical and Fundamentalist believers boycotted the broadcast.[22]

When Bob Jones III took the University's reins in 1971, he found the school to be in good financial condition. The Amphitorium construction was nearing completion; the student body was growing; and the faculty was strong and loyal. However, the institution and its President were facing a severe

Ted Koppel interviews Dr. Bob Jones III on *Nightline* (1982).

test of principles as both faced the wrath of the federal courts and the Internal Revenue Service and as Bob Jones III carried the weight of the fight with the government. (For more details on the BJU tax case, see Chapters 20 and 21.)

During this period, Dr. Jones III bore the hostility of the American media on such programs as the *Phil Donahue Show,* ABC's *Nightline* and *Good Morning America,* NBC's *News Magazine,* the *MacNeil-Lehrer Report* on public television, the *Freeman Report* on Cable News Network, and the *Larry King Show* on Mutual Radio.

The appearance that probably garnered the most attention and had potentially the largest single audience was the *Phil Donahue Show,* which then reached nearly forty million viewers. Taped in Chicago, the program audience included a contingent of Bob Jones University alumni who spoke with devotion and clarity about the school. By their presence, they helped to stifle the ridicule and fallacious characterizations of the school that Donahue tried unsuccessfully to make. Donahue was genuinely amazed at the school's regulations, and Dr. Jones III had to keep bringing the discussion back to the main issues. During the program, in the midst of the conversation about the religious and constitutional issues represented by the BJU case, an incredulous Donahue turned to Dr. Jones and asked him, "Does anybody get to heaven if he's not born again?"

Dr. Jones III replied, "Absolutely not. Jesus told Nicodemus, a religious man, 'You must be born again.' . . . The Lord Jesus said 'I am the way, the truth and the life. No man cometh to the Father, but by me.' " The President continued and gave a summary of the message of salvation.

Donahue responded sarcastically, "I just think that's real unfair to God to say that." Even as Dr. Jones was answering, Donahue had shaken his head, muttering, "Uh huh. Yeah, right." Eventually, Donahue changed the subject amid the somewhat derisive laughter and scattered applause of the overwhelmingly antagonistic audience.[23]

Perhaps the most hostile interview on the school's case was aired on *The Mid-Day Report* in New York City. Dr. Jones III was interviewed for half the program, and then he was confronted by a panel consisting of the director of the Urban League, a lawyer from the National Council of Christians and Jews, and the president of the Gay Atheists Society. The session was not a friendly one, and when it ended, the director of the Urban League turned to Dr. Jones III and said, "I bet all this exposure that your school is getting will bring you millions of dollars from people who agree with you." Dr. Jones recalled looking at him with "my nicest smile and [saying] in my nicest voice, 'I certainly hope so.' "[24]

As difficult and challenging as these interviews were, they always seemed to work for the good. For instance, a housewife, while working at home, stopped to listen to part of the Donahue program and was struck by Dr. Jones III's use of the phrase, "Ye must be born again." These words so plagued her that she determined to find their meaning for herself. After asking several people for help, including a nun who told her to say the rosary and do good deeds to get to heaven, she finally met a Christian who took a Bible and showed her what Scripture had to say about being born again and getting to heaven. The woman was born again as a result of Dr. Jones III's appearance on the show.[25]

The pressures of these interviews and the public scrutiny that arose from the IRS action took a physical and emotional toll on Bob Jones III. In retrospect, however, those days, as his wife observed, "may have been the most spiritually fulfilling days" ever experienced by the young President. He felt, beyond any doubt, an extra measure of God's power.[26] In addition to the pressures wrought by the court case, he had the demands of the school to bear as well: maintaining the spiritual, cultural, and academic fervor of the institution; charting a course for future growth; and keeping a positive "faith attitude" that God was in control.

Lightening the burdens were a group of loyal and gifted administrators who skillfully guided the academic affairs of the institution. James D. Edwards had been a close family friend and adviser since he joined the administration of Bob Jones College in Tennessee in 1936. As dean of administration (1953-81), he elicited great respect and brought stability, consistency, and a godly common sense deeply rooted in his association with the Founder and the Chancellor. Philip D. Smith had been trained under Dean Edwards and had shown brilliance for organization and details, first as registrar, then as provost (1981-present). Dwight Gustafson (dean of the School of Fine Arts 1954-97) had been handpicked by Bob Jones Jr. to lead the cultural life of the institution. His administrative ability, artistic sensitivity, and skills in music and speech, coupled with his spiritual fervency, made the School of Fine Arts stable. Guenter Salter, dean of the College of Arts and Science (1971-98), brought a disciplined academic outlook. Deans Marshall Neal (1965-78) and Thurman Wisdom (1978-2000) in the School of Religion combined a biblical scholar's insight with evangelistic zeal and strong organizational skills. In 2000 Dr. Wisdom retired and Dr. Royce Short was appointed to the office. That same year, Dr. Steve Hankins was appointed dean of the Bob Jones Jr. Memorial Seminary and Center for Evangelism. Richard E. Leiter (1974-85) and Bob Taylor (1985-98), deans of the School of Business, emphasized the spiritual over the material yet moved the business school forward in professional reputation. In 1998 Bob Taylor became dean of the College of Arts and Science, and Dr. Dick Stratton took the helm of the School of Business. Stratton's initial major challenge came with adding the business school's first graduate degree, the M.B.A., in 2001. Walter Fremont (1953-90) presided over the School of Education with great energy, goal orientation, and spiritual fervency until his retirement. James Deuink (1990-present) solidified the graduate school and has maintained the high standards and reputation of the School of Education. Richard Rupp (1977-91) followed Gilbert Stenholm (1964-77) as director of Ministerial

Training and aggressively helped develop the church planting ministry. Bruce McAllister (1991-present) continues in this office and leads with determination and dedication. Roy Barton (1974-present), the director of Financial Affairs and, later, chief financial officer, with his expertise in banking and investment, successfully brought the institution through its most financially troubled time, oversaw its reorganization, and increased its financial stability.

Also of importance to the ministry of Dr. Jones III and the institution was the 1977 appointment of Bob Wood as executive vice president. Wood came from a background in the transportation industry but had also founded and pastored an independent Baptist church because of his desire to be in the gospel ministry. With a fervent heart, keen intellect, and refined business instincts, he became influential in University financial matters, developed the flight and aviation programs, and reorganized the nonacademic support divisions of the school. As a preacher, when the President was away, Wood kept the chapel platform "hot." (For more on Bob Wood and several others mentioned above, see Chapter 25.)

Dr. Jones III is described by those who work most closely with him as sharing his grandfather's "personal touch" and love for people. He shares his father's appreciation of the fine arts but without his father's immersion in them. He also has his father's love for acting and the stage. Dr. Jones III has shown tenacity in the face of opposition and has a broad vision for moving the University forward to face the challenges and obstacles that today's society has erected against the gospel. At the forefront in his mind is better ministering to the needs of the students and the faculty and working for the greater cause of Fundamentalist Christianity. Like his predecessors, Bob Jones III is somewhat impatient and driven—"a true 'Type A' personality."[27] He is highly competitive by nature, and when institutional opportunities and challenges arise, he is often inclined to "go for it."[28] By all accounts, he sets the tone for the administrators with his work ethic: a workday of sixteen hours.[29] He maintains a demanding travel and speaking schedule, which takes him to all parts of the country for meetings.[30] Bob Jones III is also fascinated with organization, planning, and "tinkering and experimenting" for the betterment of the University. He enjoys the challenges of administration.[31] Unlike his father, he possesses an inquisitiveness about developing technologies and their applications for Christian ministry.[32]

Dr. Jones III shares a deep-seated desire to minister to the needs of the students and faculty and to be an encouragement to faithful pastors and missionaries throughout the world, regardless of the size of their ministries. Dr. Jones III is in great demand as a speaker and is therefore away from the campus a great deal in churches, Christian schools, conferences, and pastors' meetings. He is also noted as one of the most lucid and persuasive spokesmen for the Christian school movement in America and is often called upon to represent the interests of Christian schools in educators' and legislative

Left to right: Beneth Jones, Joshua Robinson (grandson), Bob Jones III, Bob Jones Jr. (Commencement 1991)

meetings around the country. Dr. Jones III shares his father's interest in missionary activity as well. Since taking the presidency, he has encouraged University faculty and students to form summer missions teams that have ministered all over the world, and he established two scholarship programs for foreign nationals, the WORLD Fund and the Timothy Fund, at the University. (See Chapter 24.)

Since assuming the presidency in 1971, Dr. Bob III's leadership has been instrumental in many important areas: a national television ministry; a positive relationship with the Greenville community; the Bob Jones University Press; a community educational outreach; new technology for Christian schools; forming partnerships with home school families; expanding the academic range of the University; beginning more aggressive marketing of the institution; and facing the challenges posed by the retirement of the "second generation" of faculty and planning for the needs of the "third generation."[33] In short, Bob Jones III envisions three avenues of outreach for Bob Jones University: furthering the cause of Fundamentalist Christianity in the nation and throughout the world; building bridges to the Greenville community and the state of South Carolina; and meeting the campus needs of faculty, students, and prospective students.

The growth of the school in size, from fewer than a hundred to several thousand students, amazed Bob Jones Sr. Growth of the institution continues under his grandson—albeit on somewhat different fronts of activity—because of his unique skills, interests, and personal aggressiveness. The multiplying outreaches in communication and publishing are examples of the different areas in which the University has grown under Bob Jones III. The school's tradition of academic and cultural excellence, the broad impact of new technologies, and above all, the solid foundation of the "old-time religion," for which the institution has always stood, have been combined in the University to make an impact on the world for the cause of Christ. About these issues, Dr. Jones III says simply, "This is God's school; He can do anything with it He wishes."[34]

CHAPTER 20

"It's Religion, Not Race"

The issues of race, civil rights, and the Christian's response to these have been problematic to believers of all races in both the South and the North. In the early twentieth century, the status quo was segregation of the races either by law (de jure) or by practice (de facto) in the South, North, Midwest, and Far West for African Americans, Native Americans, and Asian Americans.[5]

During the world wars, segregation of the races was the policy in the military, and this reflected the practice in American society. African American veterans who had fought and returned home from war did so with a determination to create change. Through subsequent use of the American court system, they first "won the theoretical recognition of a set of basic rights" in education: *Brown v. Board of Education* (1954).[2] They next won protected participation in all aspects of American life through the Civil Rights Act (1964), although the act was aimed specifically at the de jure segregation of the South.[3]

By the mid-1960s, with extremes of agitation from both sides, white and black, legally organized marches and demonstrations eventually led to race riots, looting, and random acts of violence in Birmingham, Atlanta, Chicago, Detroit, Boston, Los Angeles, and other American cities. It was evident that the nation was in the throes of a new revolution.

The Founder and the Chancellor, both sons of the South, had grown up under the de jure segregation that existed during their youth and adulthood. While difficult for them to imagine life different from how it had always been, both rejected the extremism and violence on both sides of the issue. They preferred to walk a narrow middle ground: arguing for equal rights and against violence, while at the same time speaking out for the state's rights to settle these issues as well as the rights of black and white churches and schools to remain as they wished to be. They believed that no one "should be discriminated against in this country under the law because of his creed, or his color, or anything else." They were disdainful of all radicalism and reacted strongly to the coercive tactics employed by both sides.[4]

Bob Jones Sr. in his radio messages and Bob Jones Jr. in his chapel talks urged those on both sides to obey the law.[5] The law is the law, they said, and disobedience is always wrong: "Remember," the Founder said, "it is never right to do wrong in order to get a chance to do right."[6] Dr. Jones Jr. repeatedly preached that "if the law requires that we have to do something, we will do it. You have to do what the law makes you do."[7] If a law is wrong, he argued, the "legitimate thing to do is to get the law changed."[8]

Over the years, the Founder had received queries from black students about attending Bob Jones College or Bob Jones University. Because of the segregation laws of Tennessee and South Carolina (as well as the rest of the South) in force until 1964, it was impossible for the school to admit any. When such requests came, the President contacted one or two orthodox schools in the North and "was able to arrange for the enrollment of a number of fine" black students who wanted "to be in a Christian institution."[9] Dr. Jones Sr. had given thought to starting a school for black students operated on the same basis as Bob Jones University, one in which "people could get their education in an atmosphere where their talents in music and speech and art and all could be preserved and handed down. We wanted to build that kind of a school," he said.[10]

BJU's administration believed that in many ways black Americans had been subjected to discrimination and had often been ill treated.[11] They also agreed that the proper course of action was to establish judicial equality for all. The Joneses, however, argued for the University's right to exist for its own purposes and to define its own governance. If you want "to have a school for bow-legged people," Dr. Jones Sr. often said, "you ought to have the right to have one."[12] Bob Jones University was not going to cave in to any external pressures.[13]

Bob Jones Jr. was critical of such leaders as Malcom X and Elijah Muhammed because they, at best, advocated a separatist black state and, at worst, wanted to overthrow the United States government. He was also highly critical of many of the leaders of the civil rights movement such as the Rev. Ralph Abernathy and Martin Luther King Jr. He opposed their religious Modernism, denounced their alleged Communist ties, and pointed out their dubious personal morality.[14] Dr. Jones believed that many Civil Rights leaders were bitter "against other classes of people."[15] "All of this strife comes not because of social conditions—it comes out of the condition of the human heart. God's Word makes that clear," he said.[16] Answering the claims of Modernist theologian Nels Ferré that the civil rights movement was an introduction into a broader spectrum of spiritual truth, Dr. Jones responded that "integration sit-ins are not a broader spectrum of Christian truth"; such actions were violations of the law and the law must be obeyed.[17]

"God is the author of peace and concord," he preached. God is not going to send somebody down to stir up civil strife and disobey the law. God commands you to be obedient to the law and to render unto Caesar the things that are Caesar's."[18]

The civil rights movement and its ramifications eventually had a direct impact on the University. In 1965 Bob Jones Jr. refused to sign documents of compliance issued to all American schools by the U.S. Department of Health, Education, and Welfare (HEW), in which schools pledged to comply with all of the then unwritten regulations that would flow out of the Civil Rights Act (1964) and its entitlements.[19]

These documents, Dr. Jones Jr. said, would "put this institution under the control of HEW" and give the federal government control "over God's institution. We are not going to do that. We are going to do what God tells us to do" and where God says to give "Caesar" authority, "we'll give it to him."[20] For the University, Caesar's authority ended at the point at which biblical injunction began.

Bob Jones University's admissions policy was one such point. In the 1960s, the University admitted only a small number of Asian students and no black students. This policy was not unique to BJU, but was nearly national in scope, as de facto segregation in the North and East and de jure segregation in the South.[21] Dr. Jones Jr. stated publicly that for him the issue was a religious conviction, one then held in evangelical circles, against interracial marriage and not an issue of race.

The President argued that the school refused to accept African American students for several reasons. First, the school was located in the South and South Carolina law would not permit integrated schools at that time. If the school were located elsewhere or if state law changed, admissions would perhaps not be an issue.

Secondly, Dr. Jones Jr. saw forced integration as a method of unifying the world for the Antichrist. Those in the movement advocated "a world for Antichrist, and today the cry is 'One world, one church, one race.' Bob Jones University . . . cannot be party to this."[22]

Thirdly, integration, he believed would lead to intermarriage, a key element of the "one-worldism" promoted by the ecumenical church and the national government. He believed that young people brought together at the age when most find "romantic attachments" would lead to marriages that were against the principles of Scripture and contrary to the rules of the school.[23]

Interestingly, the policy regarding dating was put in place in the mid-1950s because of a threatened lawsuit by a set of angry parents. A white male student was seriously dating an Oriental girl against the parents' wishes, and the young man's parents threatened to sue the school for allowing social contacts between the couple. Until this time no problems of this kind had surfaced and all students were allowed to date. The wisdom of a dating policy seemed strong as a way to head off any potential difficulties. A rule was added that reflected the then-commonly-held view of interracial dating and marriage. Thus, all students who attended the school were not allowed to date outside their race and no Scripture texts were cited as proof texts for this policy.[24]

On these grounds, the Founder and the President supported racial separation. The separation for which they argued did not come from an ideology of racial superiority or from a radical interpretation of Scripture.[25] It found its biblical roots in the attempt at unifying the world recorded in the Old Testament account of the Tower of Babel and in the apostle Paul's sermon on Mars Hill in the Book of Acts.

Paul's sermon in Acts 17:26-27 indicates that God made all men from "one blood" (literally, "one flesh") and established the boundaries of each nation's habitation so that they should "seek the Lord." Dr. Jones Sr. therefore maintained that the races were established by God as were their national boundaries. By this separation, God's purpose—that man would have cause to seek Him—would be accomplished.[26]

The fact that slavery broke down this separation, as wicked men sold others into slavery and "evil men" carried slaves from one part of the world to another, did not set aside God's plan. Slavery was not part of God's will for man. Instead, Dr. Jones Sr. said, slavery and the importation of slaves was of satanic origin and was an attempt to break down the boundaries that God designed because Satan does not want "man to find God."[27]

The Founder argued that "God gave every race something [unique]" and made each race and nation for a special purpose. God commanded the Jewish race to separate themselves "from among the nations of the earth. God chose Israel" and gave the Bible and the Messiah through Israel, whom He commanded to "live segregated lives." He continued, "God made of one blood all nations, but He also drew the boundary line between races."[28] Interracial marriage, he believed, was simply another satanic attempt to erase God's boundaries, create one world, and as such defy the plan of God.

Dr. Jones Jr. cited the account of the Tower of Babel (Gen. 11) as a biblical record of man's rebellion and pride in seeking to unify and elevate himself to the height of heaven, as well as the first biblical instance of the philosophy of "one world." The ensuing judgment of God, the confusion of languages, thus divided men into nations, causing them to scatter over the earth. Drawing on a modern analogy, it was, he said, "the first United Nations. . . . Their idea is that the sum of human good is a society where everything is leveled off to one low level of equality, where everybody is like everybody else; everybody keeps the same hours; everybody lives the same life, eats the same food, worships the same god. . . . We are all members of the same state. It is Anti-Christ's program."[29]

In the face of increasing government and social pressure, erudite and cautious critics of forced integration were silenced by the media and more radical leaders.[30] Bob Jones Jr. became increasingly resolute on the point of forced integration as a tool for social unity and government intervention into the affairs of private organizations, and ultimately, BJU became a point of difficulty for the federal government.

Following the Civil Rights Act (1964) and after Dr. Jones refused to sign the documents of compliance issued by HEW in 1965, BJU was placed on a list of noncompliant institutions and was thus brought to the attention of the Internal Revenue Service. In July 1970, an IRS form letter announced a new policy denying tax-exempt status to any private school that practiced what the agency considered to be racial discrimination.[31] In November 1970, following a ruling by the district court for the District of Columbia that barred all private schools in Mississippi from retaining or obtaining tax exemption,[32] the prohibition was expanded to include all private schools in the country, including religious schools.[33] The IRS, "after careful study, concluded that private schools with racially discriminatory admissions policies" were not legally entitled to federal tax exemption and began to survey the admissions policies of all private schools with the intent of identifying those that discriminated.[34] The survey required that supporting documents be included. It warned that all schools that "were not able to show . . . racially nondiscriminatory admissions policies"[35] to the satisfaction of the IRS or failed to publicize their policy broadly enough were threatened that their tax-exempt status would be challenged.[36] After seven months passed, the acting commissioner of the IRS wrote a congressman that Bob Jones University had not yet responded to the survey.[37] The focal point of discovery at this time was the issue of the admissions policy.[38]

The role assigned to the IRS in policing compliance with civil rights legislation and the pursuant Supreme Court decisions was unclear. Congress, in the Civil Rights Law of 1964, had not charged the IRS specifically with the enforcement of the law. The IRS commissioner, however, believed his bureau's jurisdiction to be open-ended. The IRS, when threatening to revoke tax status for failing to comply, acted without direction from Congress or the executive branch. The service was thus "on the cutting edge of developing national policy" without any previous experience in such sociological or religious issues.[39]

Late in 1971, the University filed suit to prevent the IRS from removing its tax exemption.[40] The school, under its newly installed president, Bob Jones III, argued that the IRS had overstepped its lawful authority and sought to deny the school its First Amendment rights to free exercise of religion, and the court agreed. On September 9, 1971, the U.S. District Court of South Carolina forbade the IRS from revoking the University's tax-exempt status. The next day Dr. Jones Jr., chairman of the Board of Trustees of Bob Jones University, announced that the admissions policy of the school was being changed to admit a "fine young married black" and Marine Corps veteran.[41] The Executive Committee, no longer feeling federal coercion, believed that the University could integrate in this way without capitulating to the one-world philosophy or "jeopardizing its convictions against interracial marriage."[42]

The IRS appealed the September 9 ruling, and the Fourth Circuit Court of Appeals overturned the district court's decision. Citing the Anti-Injunction Act of the Internal Revenue Code, the court "prohibited the university from obtaining judicial review by way of injunctive action before the assessment or collection of any tax."[43] This meant that the IRS could not be ordered "not to do something it had not yet done."[44] The IRS was free to revoke the school's tax exemption. The University appealed, and on January 7, 1974, *Bob Jones University v. Simon* was heard before the United States Supreme Court. The Supreme Court ruling concurred with the circuit court and the ruling stated that the IRS position represented an effort to enforce the technical requirements of the tax laws and that the IRS position had some legal basis. It did, however, raise the issue of the role of the IRS as an agent for a social agenda and stated that "taxes are intended to raise revenues, not to regulate activities."[45]

Four months later, on April 16, 1975, the IRS notified BJU of the proposed revocation of the school's tax-exempt status.

On May 29, 1975, the University Board of Trustees authorized a change in the admissions policy of the institution to conform to another Supreme Court decision that affirmed that private schools, including religious schools, must submit to government regulations and adopt open, nondiscriminatory admissions policies.[46] Bob Jones III wrote: "This institution's Bible-based convictions are against interracial dating and marriage" as "the first line of defense."[47] It was, he later wrote, "a line in the sand that was drawn" against the encroaching one-worldism of Antichrist.[48] Because "we are law-abiding citizens," he said, the admissions policy was changed to one that was "racially neutral . . . to admit students of any race to all rights, privileges, programs and activities generally accorded or made available to students at the University: and the University does not discriminate on the basis of race in the administration of its educational policies, admission policies, scholarship and loan programs, and athletic and other administered programs." The letter went on to state that the school would continue to prohibit its students from interracial dating and marriage and specified the penalties.[49]

But this change in admissions policy did not go far enough for the IRS, however, and on January 19, 1976, it notified the school that "the proposed revocation is final and your exempt status is revoked effective December 1, 1970."[50] Clearly, nondiscriminatory admissions were not the issue—the issue was the internal policies and religious beliefs of the institution, even though the school now had an open admissions policy and was fully integrated. The battle lines were drawn over the rights of a private, religious institution to have its own standards, beliefs, and policies. As Dr. Jones III put it, the battle was in resistance to the developing "one world"; the battle was not "for our rule, we are fighting for our right to it. [This] is a religious freedom issue."[51]

Per the instructions of the court, the University filed tax returns under the Federal Unemployment Tax Act for December 1, 1970, to December 31, 1975, and paid a twenty-one-dollar tax for one employee for calendar year 1975. The school then requested a refund, which was denied. The University then filed suit to recover the twenty-one dollars. The government counterclaimed for $489,675.59 plus interest and penalties for federal unemployment taxes for tax years 1971 through 1975.[52] On December 26, 1978, a federal district court ruled that the University was entitled to its tax exemption as a religious and educational institution and ordered the IRS to refund the twenty-one dollars.[53]

The Justice Department, on behalf of the IRS, appealed, and almost two years later, in a split decision, the Fourth Circuit Court of Appeals reversed the lower court's decision because of its interpretation of the wording of the IRS tax code §501(c)(3), and the meaning of the word "charitable."[54] This tax code states that tax exemption may be declared for "organizations organized and operated for religious, charitable, scientific testing for public safety, literary, or educational purposes, or for the prevention of cruelty to children or animals." The code further states that an organization may be exempt if it is "organized and operated exclusively for one or more" of the listed purposes.

The court of appeals argued that §501(c)(3) must be read against the background of charitable trust law. To be eligible for an exemption, the divided court ruled that an institution, in addition to the other conditions listed in §501(c)(3), must be "charitable" in the common law sense and thus must not be contrary to public policy.[55] They argued that tax exemption is made in recognition of a public benefit derived from the organization and that organizations that operate counter to "public policy" are therefore not providing a public benefit and are not "charitable." Such organizations therefore do not qualify for exemption.[56] On December 30, 1980, the court ordered the school to pay its tax.

The University requested a hearing before the full ten-judge panel of the district court of appeals but was denied: thus, an appeal was filed with the Supreme Court. The court agreed to hear the case in early 1982.

Following the circuit court's decision, the case gained notoriety, as did a case involving Goldsboro Christian School of Goldsboro, North Carolina.[57] Many religious groups, alarmed by the growing power of the IRS and recognizing the capricious nature of "public policy," filed *amicus curiae* briefs with the court, arguing in favor of BJU.[58] Numbers of southern congressmen and senators showed support for the University, including Mississippi's Trent Lott, North Carolina senator and Nixon nemesis, Sam Ervin, and South Carolina senator J. Strom Thurmond. Nationally syndicated conservative columnists such as Patrick Buchanan and James J. Kilpatrick attempted to balance the media's generally biased reporting of the case. After stating the IRS case, Kilpatrick wrote that "public policy of the government approves of interracial marriage; therefore, Bob Jones is not charitable and does not qualify. This is incredible. The government is contending, in effect, that the First Amendment's guarantee of freedom of religion must yield to bureaucratic determination of 'public policies.'"[59]

Amazingly, on January 8, 1982, on the eve of the hearing, the Treasury and Justice Departments of the Reagan administration approached the Court and asked that the Bob Jones case be declared moot, that it be dropped, and that previous court decisions against the school be vacated. They also announced that the IRS would revoke its antidiscrimination policy and issued a statement which said in essence "that the IRS had no business making national policy." The Justice Department continued that "granting or withholding of tax exempt status should not be determined by the whims of an administrative agency, especially not by its interpretations of what constitutes 'federal public policy.' "[60] The IRS was ordered to reinstate the tax-exempt status of more than one hundred schools whose exemptions had been denied.[61] Bob Jones III in the wake of this action, which was "unprecedented in the history of jurisprudence," responded that "no court forced the IRS to be at peace with Bob Jones University—God did."[62]

The media and civil rights groups exploded angrily. One editorial screamed, "Outrageous!" "Subsidizing Racism," claimed another. The Americans for Democratic Action called the action "obscene."[63] Benjamin Hooks of the NAACP accused President Reagan of "pandering to the worst racist attitudes in this nation"[64] and "rattled off so many epithets and insults at the president . . . a shorthand teacher couldn't have gotten them all down."[65]

Dr. Jones III was invited to write guest editorials for the *Washington Post* and other major papers[66] and television talk shows, such as the *Phil Donahue Show*, and radio's *Larry King Live* invited him to appear to defend his school, often in the face of great animosity and verbal abuse from both host and studio audience. For several weeks the school became the topic of nightly news programs. In all, Dr. Jones III's position was that the school was in God's hands, that the school desired God's will to be done, and, he stressed over and over, that the "issue is religion, not race."[67]

Because the government abandoned the case against the University, the NAACP's legal committee requested on January 11 that the Supreme Court allow it to replace the Justice Department in prosecuting the school. On April 19, the Court announced that it would not allow the NAACP to join the case, and in a step considered unprecedented by legal scholars and "extraordinary" even to the NAACP's leadership, the Supreme Court appointed a prosecutor of its own—black attorney and civil rights activist William T. Coleman. Bob Jones III commented that "this puts the court in the position of creating an issue to be litigated and insisting that an issue be heard when one of the two litigants declares 'no contest.' "[68]

Within a few days of the first Justice Department announcement, the circuit court of appeals placed a restraining order on the Reagan administration, making it impossible for the promised tax exemption to be granted.[69]

An embarrassed Reagan administration then reversed itself and asked the court to reinstate the Bob Jones case, even though the Justice Department's argument to the court would be that the IRS had no statutory authority for the action it had taken.

CHAPTER 21

◆

"The Power to Tax Is the Power to Destroy"

On October 12, 1982, the Supreme Court heard *Bob Jones University v. United States of America*. Because of what it felt were significant differences between Goldsboro's case and BJU's case, the University requested and was granted a separate hearing from Goldsboro, although the cases were argued together.[1] At the time of the oral argument, it was rumored that four of the nine justices were leaning against the University with two undecided.[2] William Ball, attorney for BJU, argued to the Court that the University, as an exclusively religious organization, qualified as a tax-exempt organization under the plain and universally understood meaning of IRS section §501(c)(3). Citing the legislative history of §501(c)(3), he showed that the court of appeals erred in holding that all tax-exempt organizations must be "charitable" as defined in *Green v. Connally*—that is, that to be charitable, an organization must comply with anything that can be called "public policy" and be in conformity with "Federal public policy." He also argued that the reasoning in *Green* was "erroneous" when that decision declared that "non taxation is tantamount to subsidy."

Ball further argued that "Bob Jones University is a pervasively religious ministry whose raison d'être is the propagation of religious faith. Its rule against interracial dating is a matter of religious belief and practice. Denial of tax exemption to a religious ministry because its established teaching and practice violates 'Federal public policy' violates rights of that ministry protected by the Free Exercise Clause of the First Amendment. The compelling constitutional interest in religious liberty may not be made to yield to an indefinitely stated 'Federal public policy' respecting race."

Ball further argued that the decision of the court of appeals violated the Establishment Clause of the First Amendment by establishing "a minimum floor of acceptable church doctrine to which every church doctrine of every religion must subscribe or else suffer taxation." Thus, religions embracing the government's doctrines are "favored," creating "excessive entanglements of government with religious bodies."

"The power to tax is the power to destroy," Ball argued. "Liberty and property are taken without due process of law by force of the [appeals court's] decision . . . which would destroy the entire religious enterprise known as Bob Jones University solely because it follows a religiously dictated policy respecting dating by its students."[3]

William Bradford Reynolds represented the Justice Department and argued that the Reagan administration was "unflaggingly committed to eradicating all forms of racial discrimination" but that "these cases do not call into question that issue. We found no indication that [Congress] intended to grant broad authority to the IRS."[4]

William T. Coleman, who had been appointed by the Supreme Court to present the case after the Reagan administration withdrew, argued that

1. The IRS ruling against exemption was a natural result of antidiscrimination laws dating back to the Civil War.

2. Congress intended to grant tax benefits in a common law sense, meaning that BJU must conform to government public policy.

3. Congress had repeatedly refused to revise the IRS regulation in question although it had made other alterations. Thus the rule was being enforced as Congress intended.

4. Not allowing the tax exemption did not prohibit BJU's right to hold or teach its religious practices.

5. Bob Jones University would not qualify for tax-exempt status even if discrimination were not a factor. The University could not be considered a purely religious school because it offered a curriculum consisting of more than religion courses.[5]

During the ninety-minute session, both Coleman and Ball were interrupted with questions by Justices Byron White and Sandra Day O'Connor, and at one

Bob Jones III, William Ball, and Bob Jones Jr. speak to reporters outside the Supreme Court building after the Court heard *Bob Jones University v. United States of America,* October 12, 1982.

point, after some verbal sparring with White, Coleman simply retreated from his argument and said, "Let me try again."[6] When questioned by O'Connor about the nature and meaning of "public policy," Coleman expressed his opinion that there was no firm "public policy" regarding sex discrimination or other types of discrimination and argued that a decision in this case would not ripple into other areas of social interaction.

On May 24, 1983, Bob Jones III took the platform for the daily morning chapel service, announced his Scripture text from Isaiah 59 ("And judgment is turned away backward, and justice standeth afar off: for truth is fallen in the street, and equity cannot enter"[verse 14]), and said, "Young people, we serve a sovereign God who does as seems good unto Him, and it seemed good unto God for Bob Jones University to lose its tax case this morning." He went on to say that for the thirteen years of the dispute, "we have asked God to do His will. We have said again and again that the will of God is all we wanted, and we meant that with all of our heart." The court's 8-1 vote came as a surprise to everyone, and Dr. Jones III told the chapel audience that "whichever way it went," he had expected the vote to be close.

He went on to explain some of the possible future implications of the decision, and stated, "We have incurred the wrath of the state, but we will not give way to the dictates of the state where they contravene the dictates of the Word of God as we understand them." He closed the service by saying, "Let us exalt His name together. Let us trust His provision. He is going to provide. . . . Do not worry one bit about the future of this school. Do not worry about the finances. That is in God's hand. God is working His perfect will."[7] The chapel service closed with the student body and faculty singing "Praise God from Whom All Blessings Flow."

The United States Supreme Court had affirmed the findings of the court of appeals. Chief Justice Warren Burger wrote the majority opinion and was joined by justices Brennan, White, Marshall, Blackmun, Stevens, and O'Connor; and was joined in part by Justice Powell. Justice Rehnquist dissented. The majority opinion was that

1. The IRS ruling properly interpreted §501(c)(3) as prohibiting tax-exempt status for private schools having a racially discriminatory policy, since racial discrimination is against public policy and such institutions cannot be viewed as conferring a public benefit.

2. The IRS did not exceed its authority when announcing its interpretations, since the IRS has broad authority to interpret the tax laws. Institutions at odds with public policy could not be seen as charitable within the meaning of tax code sections under dispute.

3. The IRS's interpretation did not violate the free exercise clause of the First Amendment as applied to schools discriminating on the basis of religious beliefs, since the government has a fundamental, overriding

interest in eradicating racial discrimination and education that is compelling, and which substantially outweighs whatever burden the denial of tax benefits placed on the schools' exercise of their religious beliefs.

4. The IRS policy was founded on a neutral, secular basis, and did not violate the establishment clause of the First Amendment.[8]

Justice Powell concurred in part and concurred in the judgment to deny tax exemption, but he did not agree that the critical question in determining tax-exempt status was whether an individual organization provided a clear public benefit as defined by the court or that the IRS should be invested with such broad power so as to determine themselves which public policies are so strictly fundamental as to require denial of tax exemption when violated. Powell went on to list organizations that enjoyed tax exemption and asked pointedly if each served a "purpose that comports with 'the common community conscience.'" He wrote that the other jurists' opinions "suggest that the primary function of a tax-exempt organization is to act on behalf of the Government in carrying out governmentally approved policies. Such a view ignores . . . the diversity of association, viewpoint and enterprise essential to a vigorous, pluralistic society."[9]

Justice Rehnquist dissented on the grounds that (1) "nowhere [in §501(c)(3)] is there to be found some additional, undefined public policy requirement" for tax exemption. (2) The language and the legislative history of §501(c)(3) showed clearly that "Congress has decided what organizations are serving a public purpose . . . and has clearly set forth the characteristics of such organizations." (3) The IRS is requiring organizations "to meet a higher standard of public interest, not stated by Congress, but to be determined and defined by the IRS and the courts." (4) The history of §501(c)(3) shows that the interpretation of the section after 1970 "is at odds" with the position of the IRS for many years prior 1970, and that "the interpretation is unsupported by statutory language . . . and legislative history . . . and gives the IRS a broad power which until now Congress had kept for itself." If Congress intends for private, religious schools to be denied tax-exempt status because of racial policy, Congress knows how to act. However, "this Court should not legislate for Congress."[10]

To the disbelief of conservative commentators, the Court failed to judge the case on the First Amendment ramifications of the IRS action.[11] When the court found that a compelling public interest could "substantially" outweigh the exercise of religious belief, these thinkers pointedly asked, "Where were the civil libertarians who protected the First Amendment rights of the Black Muslims to discriminate against whites?"[12] They also pondered the question that because all students are treated equally at BJU and are not compelled to attend this private institution, against whom is the University discriminating?[13] Who determines overriding public policy and "whose religious obedience will the government deem 'anti-social' tomorrow?"[14] The case, as

Dr. Jones III had said repeatedly, was about religion, not race. The court had missed the point.

Immediately after the decision was announced, Bob Jones III was flooded with calls from across the country requesting statements or interviews. The two most commonly asked questions were "Do you pay the taxes or change your beliefs?" and "How much does the school owe the government?"

In answer to the first question, Dr. Jones answered, "We will never change beliefs that we base on the Word of God. We will pay our taxes if we have to pay them."[15] "The world moves by the mainspring of compromise," the President said, "but those who love the Lord are moved and motivated by allegiance to Him."[16]

The second question was a more long-lasting problem. When the suit was originally filed, the IRS asked for payment of nearly $490,000 plus interest and penalties for unemployment taxes for the years 1971-75. One source published in 1983 estimated the tax and penalties at $2.5 million.[17] It had not yet been determined whether the school owed back taxes on other federal levies, but it certainly had to pay federal income and unemployment taxes. The IRS would not speculate about the amount of the taxes owed, but a spokesman did say that "the bill could end up being substantial," and that "the interest charges on the . . . bill could exceed the amount" of the actual tax because of the number of years the case had been in court.[18]

After the decision was announced, Roy Barton, director of Financial Affairs for the University, expected to receive a tax bill from the IRS, and "I waited and waited," he said, "and I heard nothing." Finally, he called the appropriate IRS officer and inquired about the bill. The agent responded, "Your bill? You *are* going to change your policy aren't you? We'll give you your tax status back, just change your policy." Barton answered, "Sir, from 1971, we told you that this was a matter of conviction. It is still a matter of conviction. The issue is not whether we live or die without the tax exemption. The issue is a conviction. We are not going to change our policy."[19] The IRS apparently expected the school to capitulate after the decision was rendered, and they were unprepared to make a determination on the amount owed. The IRS therefore required the University to submit tax returns retroactive to 1971. The school was forced to go back and recalculate all of its financial records for 1971 through 1983—thirteen tax years in all—and file them as a profit-making corporation.

The director of Financial Affairs and its accountants put together the thirteen years' tax returns, making full use of corporate tax laws, and submitted them to the IRS for settlement. After nearly one full year of IRS study, for which the school had to pay additional interest, the IRS approved the returns and arrived at a figure approaching $1 million for taxes, penalties, and interest.[20] The University requested and received a statement from the IRS that the tax years in question were "closed forever" and were not open to review or reinterpretation following the payment of the income taxes, penalties, and interest.[21]

In the year following the Supreme Court's decision, Dr. Jones III announced that contributions had decreased by 13 percent because the school's supporters no longer enjoyed a deduction for their donations. Since the school did "not use contributions to operate," not much would change, except that the President "did not know how the school would compensate for the money it will pay in taxes."[22] School officials, though, reflected no panic. "We know the Lord has complete understanding," Roy Barton stated. "If He can create the world, He can meet our needs. I don't care about those taxes, they are irrelevant. God can feed us; He can pay our tax bill; He can do anything that needs to be done as long as this institution is faithful to the Word of God. . . . I've seen the Lord provide every one of our needs through every one of those tax problems."[23] Donations of cash gifts did initially drop off, but by the late 1980s they had stabilized, and in the early 1990s they actually began to rise.[24]

The most hard-hit aspect of the University's income was in the area of large estates and bequests totaling over $600,000.[25] The institution lost income from some large estates because of the estate tax liability which would be incurred by the estate's heirs. However, some large estates have come to the school because those making the bequests felt "led of the Lord" to do so or because federal estate tax liability was of little concern in the estate.[26] Unlike tax-exempt organizations, however, the University may now pay income tax on bequests depending on other factors found within the estate and tax law.

As a result of the tax case, Bob Jones University is now unique among American educational institutions as the only educational institution that is operated "for profit" and is therefore taxed. It is also the only "pervasively religious" organization in America that is taxed.[27] As such, the institution's various income-generating areas are constantly being studied to increase productivity and effectiveness.

Following the decision, the University's organizational structure underwent significant changes. The essential purpose of the organization was still education and all the areas of the school existed for the educational benefit derived by the student. The school therefore divided its activities along several different lines—education, ancillary services, and maintenance—operating for the benefit of the University's educational mission.

The educational arm, under the direction of Philip D. Smith, provost, and the academic deans, remains tightly organized around its four divisions: elementary school, junior high and Academy, University, and trade school. A media group, as a division of BJU, was organized around the Bob Jones University Press (est. 1973) to write, publish, and distribute Christian school textbooks and religious trade books. An ancillary division, under the direction of Fred Davis, was created to manage the institution's various support operations, such as the University farm with its meat and dairy production, the Cleaners, recording studio, costume room, Campus Store and Snack Shop, vending, campus hospital, and Dining Common. Maintenance was charged with the responsibility of tending to the many University buildings and University-owned faculty homes, beautifying the grounds, and keeping the vehicles and campus equipment in good condition.

These divisions have been able to expand the work and ministry of Bob Jones University in a way not possible before the court decision. The change in tax status made necessary a change in the faculty retirement plan, and the tax decision also paved the way for a change in thinking about such necessities as remodeling and renovating buildings and the acquisition of equipment.

The Founder's ideal was that each member of the faculty was hired for life, and he promised that the school would care for each member of the faculty, providing him or her with housing, food, medical care, and a small retirement salary until death. The school thus enjoyed a stable group of faithful, long-tenured faculty. With the change in tax structure and projecting costs into the future for the "growing and graying faculty," it was no longer feasible for the school to guarantee this promise, since all of these benefits would have to be funded with "after-tax dollars." In May of 1989 the school gained approval for a profit-sharing plan whereby the financial fruits derived from the University Press and other corporate investments were shared among all the faculty and were funded from "before-tax dollars." This move, in the first two years of the plan, saved the school from nearly $1 million in tax liability and provided a much-needed faculty retirement plan.[28]

Prior to 1983, the school's philosophy was to use every piece of equipment until it could no longer be repaired. For example, in 1983 the maintenance staff was still using panel trucks from 1941! These had been repainted and overhauled numerous times. After the case, corporate tax law provided the school with a tax benefit to purchase and depreciate an up-to-date fleet of vehicles that far surpassed the pains and gains of keeping forty-year-old vehicles running. The school has therefore taken great strides in updating and modernizing equipment with the dual effect of improving educational experiences for the students while providing a tax benefit to the institution.

As the University plant ages and needs regular face-lifts, corporate tax law has given impetus to an accelerated schedule of remodeling, modernizing, and renovation that otherwise may not have been possible. The long-term institutional effect of *Bob Jones University v. United States,* therefore, has not been the death blow to the school that many of the school's detractors hoped it would be.[29]

The national effect of the Bob Jones case was also nearly immediate. Within weeks of the BJU decision, the Gay Rights Coalition of the Georgetown University Law Center, a homosexual group in Washington, D.C., sued

Georgetown University (a Catholic institution) for official recognition and financial support. The group argued that official public policy opposed discrimination based on lifestyle, asked the Justice Department to move to revoke Georgetown's tax-exempt status, and cited the Bob Jones case as precedent.[30]

The United States Department of Education also moved against Grove City College, a small Presbyterian school, and claimed jurisdiction over it because it refused, on religious grounds, to offer coeducational physical education classes. The college was thus cited for sex discrimination. About four hundred Grove City students had received guaranteed student loans, but the school itself took no federal funds. The government argued that indirect payments through student loans brought the entire institution under "far-reaching anti-discrimination rules" which included sex discrimination in athletics.[31] The college countered that because the loans were to individual students, the school was not required to meet government regulations. Grove City College lost the case and the Bob Jones case was used as precedent.[32]

Indeed, a virtual Pandora's box has been opened wherein any tax-exempt organization can be denied the §501(c)(3) privilege based on a court's view of what constitutes pervasive public policy. Because of the Bob Jones decision, "it will be much simpler in the future for the courts and the politicians to decide that other religious practices are not in the general public's best interest." According to one observer, this may even involve the content of sermons "speaking out against homosexuality, abortion, euthanasia, and a host of uncovered social issues."[33] This, of course, is a two-way street. For example, if *Roe v. Wade* were reversed, and the "national public policy" on abortion changed to a pro-life position, organizations such as Planned Parenthood could be denied tax-exempt status because they were not in step with "public policy."

Detractors of Bob Jones University hoped that the negative effects from the Supreme Court decision of 1983 would fatally injure the University, limit its outreach, and create divisive internal change destructive to the institution. This has not been the case. The fact is that most, if not all, of the students and faculty greeted the open admission of minorities eagerly and anticipated a time when a large percentage of students would be minorities preparing their lives for Christian service. Within the Bob Jones University environment, each student is viewed as a unique person rather than a government-recorded statistic of color or national origin.

CHAPTER 22

◆

Just Keep in the Middle
of the Middle of the Road

Between 1965 and 1990, "good people" occasionally tried to use the school "to promote some pet cause" or turn it "aside from the task for which this institution was called into being by Almighty God."[1] Occasional controversies and their resolutions influenced the University's history and reinforced the Joneses' belief that "good men are reasonable"[2] and that the best policy was to "keep in the middle of the middle of the road."[3] The controversies, though short-lived, that created the greatest problems on the campus were Calvinism, the Charismatic gifts, "King-James-Only" ideas, and the Christian's responsibility in politics.

The Founder's philosophy stressed the essential elements of the Christian faith on which all conservative Christians could agree. Dr. Jones Sr., however, argued for charity and understanding toward those who disagreed about nonessentials. Saying that "we just don't agree about some things," the Founder told the student body in 1935 that "sometimes Christian people differ. Some people in the world want me to do just as they do about everything." Some Christians like ritual; some don't. Some "of us like to sing 'Amen' at the close of a hymn, some don't," he said. "Some Christians make their conscience the guide for everybody else in the world. The Bible is against that sort of thing. God preserves the integrity of the individual conscience," and he warned the students not to "discredit your brother because he doesn't believe as you believe about the nonessentials."[4]

From its earliest days the school was "nondenominational and interdenominational" and attempted, as much as possible, to stay out of sectarian debates about election, baptism, and so on. The University attempted to keep the student body from accentuating sectarian differences.[5] The school's leadership was largely successful in limiting schismatic debate that gave concerned parents of all Protestant backgrounds cause for relief.

Because BJC was originally located so far outside Panama City, students were required to attend Sunday worship on campus. A formal worship service was developed at which Dr. Jones Sr. or a member of the faculty would preach, gowned in formal robes. A formal choral anthem was sung by the choir, and a soloist from among the students or faculty would present a formal sacred solo. Women were required to cover their heads by wearing hats.

The required worship service continued in Cleveland and became more formal, with the addition of the reciting of the Lord's Prayer and singing the Gloria Patri. Following Vespers, most students attended Baptist Youth, Christian

Endeavor, or some other denominational function sponsored by the College and then attended church in the community. Sectarian debate was minimal.

As the College grew into a University in 1947, student Sunday school classes were organized by denomination. Classes for men and women for groups such as Southern Baptist, Regular Baptist, Conservative Baptist, Evangelical Lutheran, Bible Presbyterian, Southern Methodist, and others met every Sunday morning. Sectarian debate, again, was nearly nonexistent.

During the 1980s the number of denominations represented among the student body dwindled. By the 1990s most were either Baptists or from Bible or other independent churches, with only a smattering of other groups represented.[6] The University changed the student Sunday schools from meeting by denominations to meeting by literary society in the early 1980s.

In Greenville, the formal worship service continued until about 1990. When the administration realized that churches sending students to the University no longer had formal worship services, the school lessened the formality of the campus services. The Gloria Patri was replaced with the doxology, the Lord's Prayer was eliminated; the formal solo was changed to a gospel song; the choirs continued to sing anthems but were also allowed to sing arrangements of hymns and gospel songs; and the women students no longer were required to wear hats to Sunday services.

In the 1980s and 1990s students typically attended Sunday school classes, campus worship, and Vespers, and then were strongly encouraged to attend church on Sunday evening in one of the many Fundamentalist churches in the Greenville area. The school had always stressed involvement in the local church through extension ministries, many of which were run by local churches. Weekly, a large percentage of the student body left the campus on "extension"—participating in ministry opportunities in hundreds of churches throughout the region. Throughout the University's history, then, denominational battles were infrequent. But there were exceptions.

Calvinism

In the late 1960s and early 1970s, a furor developed over Calvinistic beliefs among some students and faculty and created aggressively polarized camps, especially among the students. That Calvinism should be the source of controversy at this time might seem surprising. BJU had long enrolled Calvinistic students and employed Calvinistic professors—usually Presbyterians—along with Arminians and every shade of belief between these two poles, as long as they unhesitatingly affirmed the creed. After World War II a new movement emerged in Great Britain that promoted the "rediscovery" of Calvinistic Puritan authors among British evangelicals. Termed "Neo-Puritanism" by historian D. W. Bebbington, the movement developed a small but loyal following.[7] Although British writer A. W. Pink (1886-1952)[8] is sometimes regarded as a precursor of Neo-Puritanism, its greatest popularizer was probably British minister D. Martyn Lloyd-Jones (1899-1981).

Lloyd-Jones drew on the Puritan theological heritage in his own popular preaching ministry, and the Puritan Conferences sponsored by him and others—notably evangelical J. I. Packer—influenced scores of ministers, students, and laymen. Publishing houses, notably the Banner of Truth Trust, specialized in reprinting classic Puritan works and publishing new works sympathetic to the Puritan perspective.[9] The movement spread to the United States, where it not only won support among traditional Calvinists but also sparked the growth of newer, consciously Calvinistic bodies such as the Reformed Baptists.[10] The spread of Neo-Puritanism, however, sometimes resulted in a conflict between often zealous promoters of Calvinism and those American evangelicals who did not wish to dogmatically embrace Calvinistic tenets. Some Fundamentalists unsympathetic to the movement sternly warned against "crusading Calvinism."[11] Even those who would have preferred not to take sides found themselves often forced to do so by the confrontational style taken by some of the newer converts to Calvinism.

BJU eventually felt the impact of this revival. When this movement created a stir among the students and staff, Dr. Jones Jr. said simply, "we do not have controversy" here about things that are not clear in God's Word, and on the point of election and predestination, good men disagree. He said, "the position of Bob Jones University, beyond our creed, is this: Whatever the Bible says is so. We do not permit some fellow to come here and knock us down with his Calvinism and rub our noses in it. We are not going to have it." He warned the students not to "argue in the dormitories and be making trouble and doing harm" to the point of causing "division among yourselves.[12]

Chapel messages stressed unity rather than division. The administration dealt with the issue directly in private conferences with the most outspoken of the students and one faculty member who was actively promoting Calvinist doctrine in his classes. Eventually, it became necessary to fire the faculty member and to expel a few students for continually pressing the discussion in classes, forcing debate about five-point Calvinism on others, and thereby creating division among the student body.[13] Interestingly, the students and faculty involved were not from backgrounds that had historically held to Calvinistic doctrine but were those who had newly discovered the doctrine.

The point stressed by Dr. Jones Jr. was one of common sense: "On the great fundamental doctrines you cannot be too extreme. The virgin birth, inspiration of the Bible, the atoning work of Christ on the cross, the resurrection of His body from the grave, the new birth—on these great doctrines you cannot be too extreme. But in matters of interpretation where good men differ . . . you had better not be too dogmatic about your interpretation."[14]

"I am firmly convinced," Dr. Jones Jr. wrote, "that when good saints of God like Wesley and Whitefield differ on the interpretation of the Scripture, the truth lies somewhere between."[15]

The Charismatic Movement

The national phenomenon of tongues and the Charismatic movement created some problems within the student body as well; several students in the late 1960s were expelled after speaking in tongues.[16] Because of the growth of the tongues movement and teachings about Charismatic gifts, the issue was dealt with firmly by Dr. Jones Jr. and Dr. Jones III in chapel.

To the Joneses, the Charismatic movement was "characterized by all types of uncleanness and excess," including materialism and widespread moral impurity; and the signs of true Christian faith were not evident among its proponents. For biblical separatists, the fact that the Charismatic movement was "the thread that ties the religions of the world together" in ecumenical alliance was also disturbing. The modern-day Charismatic movement was not producing better Christians, Dr. Jones III preached; "it is producing people who deny the Word of God."[17] The growth within the Charismatic movement of the "prosperity gospel"—the idea that if you plant a seed of faith (a donation of money) in a particular ministry, God will give you what you want—ushered in a spiritualized materialism that had heretofore been foreign to Christian thinking, was in opposition to the clear teaching of Scripture, and had to be openly refuted.[18]

There was an openness, however, toward those who genuinely held to Pentecostal belief and whose lives paralleled the scriptural commands to holiness, true piety, and humility.[19] In fact, Dr. Jones Jr. said in chapel that "this institution does not have an opposition to tongues. We believe in your freedom to interpret the Word of God for yourself." He continued by saying that when praying publicly and aloud, pray in a "language that people understand. . . . Anything that would disrupt us on this campus is not of God, it is of the Devil," and the appearance of tongues "is accompanied by the lust of the flesh."[20] The gifts of the apostolic age—tongues, healing, prophecy and so on—ended when the canon of Scripture was completed, Dr. Jones said.[21] "God is not the author of confusion," and we are commanded to "try the spirits to see whether they be of God," Dr. Jones III preached. "You do not need ecstatic utterances. You do not need any kind of special baptism of the Holy Spirit. Do not seek signs. Do not seek utterances—just seek Christ."[22]

The "King-James-Only" Controversy

The controversy surrounding the role of the King James Version was one of the most divisive issues to face the conservative church in general and Fundamentalism in particular.[23] Bob Jones University, to the irritation of those holding most belligerently to the belief, has consistently refused to be forced into the position popularly known as "King James Version Only."

The arguments for "KJV Only" seem to fall into two categories: arguments relating to textual criticism and arguments about the nature and meaning of biblical inspiration. Proponents of the KJV Only seem to fall into three subgroups within these categories: the English Version groups, the Received Text group, and the Majority Text group.[24]

The modern movement favoring the KJV Only appears to have been born after 1947 with the publication of several works by Harvard-trained divinity student Edward F. Hills, who advocated the superiority of the KJV based on textual arguments about the Textus Receptus.[25] The movement was also fueled by a plethora of new translations that hit the market in the late 1950s, 1960s, and 1970s, promulgated by groups espousing liberal theology and whose translations reflected their prejudices against the virgin birth of Christ, miracles, the inspiration of Scripture, and other fundamental doctrines.

After the publication of Hills's work, several Dallas Theological Seminary faculty members and students wrote articles and dissertations opposing use of the 1881 Greek testament of Westcott and Hort. This edition of the Greek New Testament was based on recently discovered manuscript evidence known as the Alexandrian Text. Some of the earliest fragments of this text were copied within one generation of the New Testament writers.[26] This was also the text on which many of the modern English translations were based.[27] The Dallas group strongly favored the Majority Text; this view holds that the most accurate and true reading of the Greek text is that found in the majority of the extant Greek manuscripts. Perhaps more significantly, they resurrected and modernized the textual arguments of John W. Burgon and a handful of other scholars who were contemporary with the 1881 Westcott and Hort work and antagonistic to it. One debate, therefore, has revolved around the question "Which Greek text is superior—the Received Text, the Alexandrian Text of Westcott and Hort, or the Majority Text?"[28]

The second and more serious debate focuses on the very nature and meaning of inspiration. Among the KJV Only adherents, opinion varies widely. Some hold that the KJV is inspired in the same sense that the original autographs were inspired, that is, that the KJV is "God breathed, and is thus infallible and inerrant, as were the original autographs." Thus, some argue for a "double inspiration: "God breathing His Word once to the original writers and once again to the King James translators.[29] A few state that all translations before and after the KJV are of satanic origin.[30] Some claim that the errors in the KJV are actually "advanced revelation" given its translators by God and that when disagreements in meaning occur, the Greek texts of the New Testament manuscripts should be corrected by the King James Bible.[31] Because "double inspiration" is a troubling term, other adherents of the KJV say that "the very words of God in English are found in the King James Bible and that other versions contain the very words of God in more or less quantity"; and that the authority of the Word of God is at stake if the authority of the KJV as an inspired version is impugned.[32]

To counter attacks made on the orthodoxy of Bob Jones University by several vitriolic polemicists, the most rabid of which was Peter Ruckman, both the Chancellor and the President issued statements to clarify the school's position, and the Bible Department crafted a statement as well. (See Appendix D.) The Founder had a great love for the Authorized Version.[33] Although he spoke with approbation of the American Standard Version of 1901, he studied, memorized, and read from the Authorized. He fought against the Revised Standard Version because of its clearly Modernist leanings, as represented by the work's omissions and word changes in clearly doctrinal passages. However, in the 1930s, Bob Jones Sr. did serve on the editorial board for the Amplified Bible, a study aid which provided all the possible meanings of the Greek words in the New Testament text. Dr. Jones III remembered that in chapel his grandfather "would often read his text from the KJV and then read it from the Amplified Bible to give the hearer a fuller and deeper understanding of exactly what that text is saying."[34]

The position of the old-time Fundamentalists who fought the battle against Modernism was presented in *The Fundamentals*: "The record for whose inspiration we contend is the original record—the autographs or parchments of Moses, David, Daniel, Matthew, Peter, or Paul as the case may be and not any particular translation or translations of them whatever."[35] R. A. Torrey, the great Bible teacher and Fundamentalist scholar, reinforced this: "No one, as far as I know, holds that the Authorized Version, or any English translation of the Bible, is absolutely infallible and inerrant. The doctrine held by me and by many others who have given years to careful and thorough study of the Bible is, that the Scriptures as *originally given* [emphasis in original] were absolutely infallible and Inerrant, and that our English translation is a substantially accurate rendering of the Scriptures as originally given."[36]

The University's position on the inspiration of Scripture continued to be the same as that held by the Founder and the same as that of the old-time Fundamentalists: "We believe in the verbal inspiration and absolute inerrancy of the Bible. We believe, as Fundamentalists have always believed, that this inspiration refers to the original manuscripts."[37] In addition, Dr. Jones III wrote, "We also believe that God has preserved His Word. We do not believe in the verbal inspiration of any translation, but of the original manuscripts." He stated that at BJU, the KJV exclusively is used for preaching and classroom teaching and that the AV is held "in the highest regard."

BJU, however, refused "to be drawn into the illogical and untenable position that [the KJV] is the only translation."[38] Dr. Jones Jr. wrote, "There are other good translations in the midst of all the bad ones. Unfortunately, there are no perfect ones, including the Authorized Version, as evidenced by the many corrections and amendments that have been made through the years."[39]

The Bible Department position was especially important. The statement authored by Stewart Custer and Marshall Neal was approved by the entire Bible faculty[40] and affirmed the belief in the verbal inspiration and absolute inerrancy of the Bible and "that this inspiration refers to the original manuscripts." It advocated use of the Greek Testament to provide fuller meaning to the student of Scripture and declared, "we have no sympathy with any version of the Bible that is not faithful to the Greek text." Casting their lot with most other conservative scholars, the department believed "that the text based upon the Alexandrian manuscripts is, as a whole, superior to the text based upon manuscripts of the Middle Ages." They considered "this not an issue of modernism versus conservatism but a matter of individual judgment on the part of Fundamental Christians." They concluded, "Christians should be free to choose and use either of these texts and still work together in harmony to teach and preach the Word of God to those who are without it."[41]

In keeping with the University's commitment to balance, among the University graduate school Bible faculty, some hold to the superiority of the Majority Text and others to the Westcott and Hort Alexandrian Text. None accepts the Textus Receptus of Erasmus as superior to either the Majority or Alexandrian texts. Men on each side, however, accept their colleagues on the other side as Christian brothers and without disputation choose to be united around God's eternal truth rather than to separate over textual preferences.

The Christian's Political Responsibilities

Early Fundamentalists, including Bob Jones Sr., had a history of political involvement that can be traced back to the progressive ideals of the early years of the twentieth century. They defended Prohibition and mourned its repeal; campaigned vigorously against Catholic and "wet" presidential candidate Al Smith in 1928; were involved in greater or lesser degrees in all political parties, including the Democratic, Republican, and Populist parties; and were a powerful electoral body.[42] As Fundamentalism lost its ascendancy in American culture and later divided into orthodoxy, Evangelicalism, and Fundamentalism, conservative Protestantism became an increasingly impotent political force and lost many of its elected representatives.[43]

Fundamentalism had never been a consciously political force except in a few instances (such as Prohibition and Al Smith's and John F. Kennedy's candidacies).[44] There was strong Fundamentalist backing for American participation in World War II, the Korean War, and the Vietnam War and against Communism. The judicial radicalism of the Warren Supreme Court and continued liberalism of the Burger Court was seen as a threat to conservative religious causes. Alarming decisions such as *Roe v. Wade* (1973) and the rise of aggressive liberal causes in the form of Gay Liberation and the Equal Rights Amendment gave the "Christian Right" further impetus. The national paroxysm over ethical scandals in the political and business communities, and "worry about the immorality of sex, pornography, and drugs . . . in a generation raised to think about nothing else but rock music and television," convinced many Fundamentalists that without their influence in politics, America was doomed.[45]

The alarms were also heard at BJU. Bob Jones Sr. and Bob Jones Jr. had played political hardball when dealing with the cities of Panama City, Cleveland, and Greenville.[46] Throughout his career, Dr. Jones Sr. had been deeply involved in politics and enjoyed the political spectacle. A parade of political figures (such as Bibb Graves of Alabama, Percy Priest of Tennessee, Strom Thurmond of South Carolina, George Wallace of Alabama, and Barry Goldwater of Arizona) had sought the support of students and faculty.[47] Until the early 1960s the faculty and students represented the spectrum of political beliefs but were moderate to conservative. Campuswide mock political conventions showed an even split in party loyalty among the students.

When Strom Thurmond switched to the Republican party, he spawned a movement in the state toward Republicanism that took hold on the campus. Events within the Democratic party also accelerated the campus shift toward Republicanism. Former dean Gilbert Stenholm put his considerable influence behind the reborn Republican party, and by the late 1970s several faculty, including Stenholm, communications professors Joyce Parks and Elmer Rumminger, mathematics professor Bob Taylor, and education professor George Youstra, were active in the local political process. With the help of alumni, they registered hundreds of voters; helped organize local precincts; elected delegates to the county, state, and national political conventions; and by 1980 had gained a foothold and a voice within the state Republican party.[48] BJU alumni were also elected to the Greenville City and County Councils, as well as to posts within South Carolina state government.

What differentiated the ideals of campus politicos and the Joneses from those of other religious conservatives was not the political issues—there was nearly universal agreement among conservatives, both believers and unbelievers alike, over abortion, homosexuality, feminism, children's rights, pornography, drugs, and other contemporary issues. The issue was "ecumenical politics" and alliances.[49] The Moral Majority, founded by Jerry Falwell, the well-known Baptist preacher and founder of Liberty University, was the focal point of the Joneses' larger concerns about the New Christian Right and ecumenical cooperation between Fundamentalists and Modernists "for the sake of saving America."[50]

The Moral Majority burst on the scene in June 1979 when "secular new rightists joined forces with evangelical conservatives" as one of "three organizations that would be the most visible part of the New Christian Right."[51] The tenets of the Moral Majority's political philosophy, simply stated, were "organize, register, and inform."[52] Its moral ideology was initially framed in Jerry Falwell's book *Listen, America!*[53] but underwent significant evolution as time wore on; questioning became more intense, and the goals became more diffuse and less immediately attainable.[54]

The Moral Majority published a helpful legislative action guide in which practical advice was given on how "to clean up America and make our great nation a symbol, rather than a cesspool."[55] The group, while denying any religious ties, also funded and published a thirteen-week Sunday school curriculum that dealt with the political and moral issues facing the nation.[56]

As helpful as these materials may have been, a basic scriptural issue was at stake: the "basic principles of scriptural separation." Dr. Jones Jr. wrote that "for something to be moral in God's eyes, it has to be scripturally right. As Christians, our morals are predicated upon God's Word. If the Moral Majority violates the Word of God, then it isn't moral." The primary goal of the Moral Majority, Dr. Jones wrote, "is to join together Catholics, Jews, Protestants of every stripe, Mormons, etc., in a common religious cause. Christians can fight on a battle field alongside these people, can vote with them for a common candidate, but they cannot be unequally yoked with them in a religious army or organization."[57]

Contrary to the statements by Falwell, the Moral Majority made broad religious appeals and included a more diverse group than Billy Graham's ecumenical evangelism.[58] Proclaiming that the Moral Majority was "Catholics, Jews, Protestants, Mormons, Fundamentalist Blacks, White farmers, housewives, businessmen, and businesswomen,"[59] the leadership of the New Right evangelicals, including Falwell, had the "real intention . . . to form a new ecumenical movement around those personal issues, family issues."[60]

When the University and the Joneses took a position against this new ecumenism, torrents of criticism assaulted BJU as an institution anachronistic and tragically distanced from the needs of American society. Falwell reportedly commented that "everybody is for the Moral Majority except Bob Jones, and they don't like me anyway."[61] Caught up in patriotic fervor as they were, many separated and conservative Christians "compromised the integrity of the gospel and the identity of the church," chose to seek religious ties in the name of political activism, and thereby moved the church from its "true mission of maintaining and proclaiming the pure gospel of Christ" toward that of a political agenda.[62] "While returning America to the precepts of her founding fathers is a noble goal, it is not worth the violation of the Word of God," Bob Jones III wrote.[63]

Even as this battle was being fought, presidential candidate Ronald Reagan visited the University for a campaign appearance in 1980. In 1992 Republican candidates, presidential hopeful Patrick Buchanan, and then–Vice President Dan Quayle made campaign stops at Bob Jones University, attempting to woo the vote of Fundamentalist Christians.[64] In the presidential primary season of 1995-96, presidential candidates Bob Dole, Patrick Buchanan, Phil Gramm, and Alan Keyes visited the campus as did Senator Strom Thurmond, who visited with former Vice President Dan Quayle. Additionally, numerous candidates for state and local office "pressed the flesh" at the Dining Common and sought meetings with and the endorsement of the University President prior to every election since 1980.[65]

The issue at BJU was not noninvolvement in the political arena; the issue was scriptural separation, even in the political arena. Contrary to the isolationist picture that Falwell and some Moral Majority supporters tried to paint of the University and its graduates, the resurgence of conservative Republicans to national prominence carried several BJU alumni to office. By 1992 seven alumni had made successful bids for the U.S. House of Representatives or to state houses in South Carolina, Michigan, Ohio, and Georgia.[66]

The attention political candidates gave to BJU was significant in that prior to Ronald Reagan's appearance in 1980, the school had only occasionally hosted political candidates for national office. The increased attention from candidates and Bob Jones III's willingness to invite them to campus signaled a growing interest on his part to involve the school in state and local issues and a growing desire on their part to court Fundamentalists' votes. Yet in these visits there were no calls for religious/political bridge building. The campaign stops were purely political and the reactions to them were purely political as well. As the presidential campaign of 2000 approached, campus leaders expected politics as usual but got hardball politics instead.

With a tight national Republican primary race shaping up, campaign organizers of various candidates approached BJU about appearances. Interest in BJU was multifaceted. The candidates saw campus appearances as an opportunity to get their message to six or seven thousand people representing nearly every state. Second, students and faculty were politically astute and a potent force at the ballot box. Third, candidates also could claim momentum for their campaign for having appeared before such a large and friendly assembly. As one state organizer put it, "In South Carolina there certainly are places that you hit when you're seeking office, and [Bob Jones] is one of them. You go to Bob Jones like you go to the Darlington Motor Speedway."[67]

By late January, all four Republican presidential hopefuls had contacted BJU about appearances: Texas governor and front-runner George W. Bush, publisher Steve Forbes, former ambassador Alan Keyes, and Arizona senator John McCain.[68] On February 2, 2000, an exhausted Bush, locked in battle with McCain and coming off a bitter defeat by him in New Hampshire, was the first to visit. He delivered an unremarkable speech of purely political stump talk to the audience of six thousand.[69]

Bush's visit to BJU was soon followed by national news headlines that screamed "bigotry" and "racism," and articles chastising Bush for his appearance referred to the speech as "Bush's Big Mistake."[70] The primary issue was BJU's historic Protestant view of Catholicism and secondarily its rule on interracial dating and marriage.[71] The rhetoric in the national media was vicious, publishing scurrilous and fabricated descriptions of campus life. Sensing a political opportunity, McCain took up the attack and in short order had his phone banks in Michigan, Ohio, and the Northeast states calling millions of voters informing them of BJU's anti-Catholicism.[72]

In the first two weeks following Bush's visit, BJU appeared in every major American news magazine and every national newspaper (including

USA Today, The New York Times, Washington Post, Chicago Tribune, and *Los Angeles Times*). Every weekly or daily news show and the political commentators all pompously joined in the castigation of BJU, its students, and its faculty. The only exception was conservative talk radio, where the hosts seemed to be more open-minded and interested in the real BJU, and in Reform party candidate Pat Buchanan's presidential campaign.[73]

National commentators eviscerated BJU with such comments as "a hothouse of bigotry" and "Holy Neanderthal!"[74] One writer accurately declared that BJU was the latest Democratic club to be used against Republican candidates, pressing their rivals to denounce the school and hoping to establish the GOP's guilt by association.[75] Democratic politicians pompously called for public repudiation of BJU, even offering resolutions of censure against the school in the U.S. Senate. "I think it's important for the Congress of the United States to have the last word," said Sen. Robert Torricelli (D-N.J.), who ironically was then under investigation by the Justice Department for serious financial and ethics violations.[76] A conservative Protestant writer summarized the entire mess this way: "What it really underscores is how allegedly well-informed people have completely lost touch with our religious and cultural past. You mean, Protestants are anti-Catholic? Tell me it isn't so!"[77]

Because of the furor, some alumni faced incidents of personal animosity, but the alumni rallied behind the school and had numerous opportunities to refute the charges and give testimony to God's saving grace. One U.S. congressman, a BJU graduate, related that he was stopped in the aisles of Congress by his peers and asked numerous questions about BJU. All in all, the rhetoric became so heated that the *Greenville News,* a paper often critical of BJU's conservative religious and social stance, twice rose in defense of the school. Beth Padgett, editorial page editor, wrote,

> The school, especially through its students and alumni, does a lot of good in the community. It helps to feed the hungry, care for the homeless, comfort the sick and take care of the elderly. So it is difficult to categorically condemn an institution that follows through, so faithfully, on its Matthew 25 responsibility to care for "the least of these."

> And finally, many of us in this community, even those who've crossed swords on occasion with BJU, realize how fundamentally unfair this blitzkrieg is. BJU is under such intense attack because this is politically expedient.[78]

The *News* later called the media's attacks "outrageous," the criticisms "shallow and unfair" and the national controversy "manufactured."[79] The American media and a political candidate had succeeded both in demonizing BJU and in introducing a new type of political correctness to the electoral process—that of demanding that Republican candidates examine and comment on the beliefs of every group to whom they speak![80] Seemingly, the American public accepted it uncritically.

After three weeks of trying to answer the attacks, the flood of requests for interviews and media visits, the President's patience wore thin. He closed the campus to the media and sought a forum in which to present the truth about the school. On March 3, 2000, BJU purchased a full-page advertisement in *USA Today* and other prominent newspapers to answer the charges leveled at the school. In "A Letter to the Nation from Bob Jones University," Dr. Jones III stressed that BJU was neither racially bigoted nor hateful of Catholics.[81] He pointed out that BJU's dominant presence on the political landscape of 2000 was purely for the political gain of John McCain and that the core issue was religious freedom—the same issue that had taken BJU to the Supreme Court.

On March 3, Dr. Jones appeared on *The Larry King Show*, a live television interview show, to answer critics. Following some general questioning about the school's history, King turned the conversation to Catholicism and interracial dating. Dr. Jones briefly explained BJU's biblically grounded and historically Protestant positions on Catholicism. When the conversation turned to dating, he told King that after much reflection and prayer, he had come to believe that the dating rule should neither represent the national reputation nor be the defining issue for the school.[82] Interestingly, twice in that previous year Dr. Jones had requested the Board of Trustees to discuss the policy and the wisdom of dropping it. Their near-unanimous concurrence followed, but agreement on the timing of the move was yet to come.

To everyone's surprise, Dr. Jones III announced that the rule against interracial dating, around which most of the national acrimony had centered, had been dropped: "Our concern for the cause of Christ, our concern for our graduates, our concern for our testimony, our concern for the school's broader usefulness is greater to us than a rule that we never talk about and that is meaningless to us."[83]

National reaction to the telecast was swift. The media was stunned.[84] Pundits rethought their earlier paroxysms of mock horror and some reported that "I completely revised my opinion of his institution. . . . I assumed it was provincial and benighted, not serious intellectually. . . . But that is not the way it is at all. [It] is a serious Baptist-Protestant institution with a deep Reformation coloring."[85] Letters arrived from religious leaders and colleges stated their support and praised the President for his clear presentation of the gospel, which closed the program.[86] Alumni reaction by the hundreds was swift: "Let me state how proud I was to be a BJU grad as I watched the Larry King show Friday night." One fourteen-year-old put it to the President, "You nailed it."[87]

Several thousand students, gathered in the Founders Memorial Amphitorium to watch the broadcast, greeted the news with silence, then applause, then a sigh of relief. Opposition to the one-world system of ecumenical religion, politics, economics, and education continued to be preached in chapel. The race aspect was now moot. Of greater concern was the cause of Christ and whether the middle course could again be established.

CHAPTER 23

◆

Progressing . . . Possessing

When Bob Jones III assumed the presidency in 1971, the University's foundation for the future had been solidly laid by the Founder and the Chancellor. As noted earlier, this foundation stressed fidelity to the school's Fundamentalist creed, emphasized biblical evangelism, embraced a high quality of culture and personal discipline, and underscored academic achievement among the faculty and the student body. When Dr. Jones III was inaugurated President, a faculty of 199 greeted him. By the end of his first decade as President, the faculty had increased by 70 members; by 1990 it had grown to 312. With staff and other support employees included, Bob Jones University was the twelfth largest employer in Greenville County by 1995, with 1,525 on the payroll. Only 20 percent—306—were teaching faculty.[1]

During these same years (1971-95) the academic complexion of the faculty changed. In 1970-71 the faculty's level of education was appropriate for the type of teaching demanded in most departments and the type of education offered: a thorough but more general liberal arts education. Following the Mercer situation, a number of faculty vacancies had occurred, and Dr. Bob Jr. had encouraged the newly hired young teachers to pursue graduate or advanced degrees.[2] As a result, by 1971 nearly 100 percent of the faculty held master's degrees and twenty-three teachers held doctorates. As Table 5 below indicates, the passing decades brought about a higher level of faculty preparation. Beginning about 1981, the deans urged many young and promising faculty members to go away for graduate school, earn advanced degrees, and then return to teach. As incentive, the University increased the financial assistance available and offered other incentives, such as extended leave schedules and diminished teaching loads, to encourage these faculty to complete dissertations.[3]

The response of the new generation of Bob Jones teachers is evident. They entered their teaching with enthusiasm and dedication, and they aggressively sought further education to strengthen their teaching. This enthusiasm was mirrored by the growth in the number of majors available, in the expansion of Bob Jones University's graduate school, and in the increase of those holding doctoral degrees. In 1971, for example, the University offered about 55 undergraduate majors in its five schools. By 1995 the number of available undergraduate majors was 105. By that year, some University departments were staffed almost entirely by teachers holding doctorates, many of whom had graduated from BJU in the 1970s. These teachers had a positive impact on student preparation, as well as within their respective fields.[4]

Table 5

Bob Jones University Faculty Degrees[5]

Year	Faculty	Grad Asst.	Drs.	% Dr.
1970-71	199	30	23	11.6
1974-75	202	43	36	17.8
1980-81	269	53	36	13.4
1984-85	294	53	54	18.4
1990-91	312	38	67	21.5
1994-95	306	39	78	25.5

In addition to the four-year majors offered in 1971, a three-year Bible college certificate program was available through the Institute of Christian Service. In school year 1981-82, the Institute was elevated to the sixth school of the University, was renamed the School of Applied Studies (SAS), and offered the associate of arts and the associate of science degrees in twelve fields.[6]

When Bob Jones III took office, the nation was at the midpoint of a two-decades' long increase in the number of college-age students. This period was followed by one decade of rather sharp decline in the college-age population. Bob Jones University continued to grow through the first decade and stabilized somewhat in the second. Explanations for the neutral trend in growth may be found in (1) the smaller size of the prospective student pool; (2) the University's tax case and fallout from the final decision; (3) the fact that competition among Christian schools became more intense about this time, with two very aggressive schools entering the "marketplace."[7] To attract students, many schools multiplied the number of scholarships they offered—often offering questionable "scholarships" to entice impressionable young students to attend.[8] BJU stayed its course, and, as Table 6 below shows, the enrollment managed to expand and then remain steady during these two decades.

Growth in the graduate program of the University was dramatic, with the number of graduate students doubling during the decade of the 1970s. This may be explained by the fact that the School of Education under Walter Fremont offered its first graduate degree in 1973, a master of science degree in school administration. It was specifically designed to "prepare administrators for a dynamic ministry in the Christian Schools," which by this time were expanding rapidly.[9] In the 1980s the size of the University's graduate program stabilized to between 250 and 300 students, with the program size to some extent related to the number of graduate and staff assistant positions available. The graduate school also expanded its summer offerings to encourage Christian school teachers to pursue master's degrees.

Table 6

First Semester Enrollment Bob Jones University & Academy, 1970-91[10]					
Year	Univ.	Academy	Grad./Spec.[11]	SAS[12]	Total
1970-71	3300	487	163	171	4121
1971-72	3415	505	155	200	4275
1972-73	3445	491	164	245	4345
1973-74	3562	509	172	268	4511
1974-75	3676	386	158	224	4444
1975-76	3778	394	183	232	4587
1976-77	4108	391	212	213	4924
1977-78	4158	379	277	226	5040
1978-79	4184	376	297	228	5085
1979-80	4286	336	311	273	5206
1980-81	4426	379	331	263	5399
1981-82	4322	421	331	281	5355
1982-83	4471	403	324	NA	5198
1983-84	4306	412	313	NA	5021
1984-85	4006	393	281	NA	4680
1985-86	3825	447	254	NA	4526
1986-87	3742	440	297	NA	4479
1987-88	3901	449	294	NA	4644
1988-89	4132	434	258	NA	4824
1989-90	4096	396	271	NA	4763
1990-91	4281	408	NA	NA	4689

In 1971 Bob Jones University offered twenty-five graduate degree programs, fifteen of which were in the School of Fine Arts, with the remainder in the School of Religion, including that school's five doctoral programs. By 1995 this number had grown to seventy-seven graduate programs, including ten doctoral degrees. Graduate study was available in such diverse fields as music performance and conducting, counseling, special education, cinema, and theology. The largest number of graduate degrees—thirty—was offered through the School of Education.[13] The School of Fine Arts offered twenty-eight graduate programs in music, speech, and cinema.[14] The School of Religion offered nineteen programs, including seven doctoral programs.[15]

The growth in the number of undergraduate and graduate majors was handled smoothly. Several of the new undergraduate majors attracted much attention and became quite popular with the students in the late 1980s. One example was the Department of Professional Writing and Publication, which was created in 1982 and included five majors.[16] By 1988, fifty-five students were enrolled as writing majors.[17] To give the students practical experience, Dr. Jones III announced that the University would begin publishing the *Collegian,* a campus newspaper, initially under the sponsorship of BJU Publishing coordinator Bob Whitmore, and later under Betty Solomon of the Professional Writing faculty. The student paper grew to be a popular and informative biweekly publication.[18]

Another program, noteworthy in its development, was the Division of Nursing. The University had offered a B.S. degree in nursing as far back as 1958 for those who had earned an R.N. elsewhere. It was designed as a two-year liberal arts program to "complement [the nurse's] specialized professional preparation."[19] While retaining the B.S. program, the University added the bachelor of science degree in medical missions in 1966, and the certificate in medical missions in 1968, both under the School of Religion.[20] In March 1979, a four-year bachelor of science in nursing (B.S.N.) degree was approved by the South Carolina State Board of Nursing and was greeted with great enthusiasm by the University students.[21] Because the approval was imminent, the University opened the program in the fall of 1978, and 62 students enrolled. The next year the enrollment nearly doubled to 113 students and then grew steadily through 1995 when 191 students were enrolled.[22]

A third program, nearly unique to Christian education, was the aviation program. This began in 1947 as the School of Aeronautics, one of the original schools of Bob Jones University.[23] That first year, over one hundred men, mostly former GIs, signed up for flying courses.[24] Within a few years, however, enrollment dropped to a handful, and flight training was eventually discontinued.[25]

In the 1960s and 1970s, commercial air travel out of Greenville was somewhat difficult. To accommodate the increasingly busy schedules of the Chancellor and the President, a friend of the University donated a Helio-courier to the school in the early 1970s. It was later sold, and an Aztec was purchased in 1974. BJU alumnus Larry Carver, a Greenville-based corporate pilot, was hired that year to be chief pilot, to revitalize the flight program, and to instruct the first group of seventeen primary flight students.[26] Even though Carver's availability to teach was unpredictable because of the exigencies of the Joneses' travel schedules, the program grew in equipment, faculty, and enrollment. The program took off in 1977, when more than thirty students were enrolled, requiring the full-time attention of both Carver and former navy pilot Cecil Tune, who joined the program as an instructor that same year. By 1995 sixty-four students were majoring in a flight-related program, with perhaps as many as thirty other nonmajors in various stages of flight training.[27]

At the outset, the curriculum was designed to take students through basic flight school, which qualified them for a private pilot's license. After Tune arrived, followed shortly by two other flight instructors and four aircraft mechanics, the school was able to expand the training to include commercial and instrument ground school, advanced flight instruction, and a maintenance program to meet the needs of the growing number of advanced students.[28]

In the fall of 1979, the University created Cornerstone Aviation at the Greenville Downtown Airport and leased a hangar, eventually building four more. Within two years, Cornerstone, a public aviation service company, was invited by the Greenville Airport Commission to become the fixed base operator at the airport because of the excellent reputation of the University's aircraft maintenance staff. The school operated Cornerstone until 1985, when it was sold to a Greenville businessman.[29]

Missionary aviation was added to the School of Religion as a major in 1980 and focused on developing the unique and demanding flying skills needed by missionary pilots. The next year the FAA approved a two-year airframe and power plant program under the School of Applied Studies. This program introduced students to all aspects of aircraft mechanics.[30] Six years later, 1987, a major in business and commercial aviation was offered in the School of Business to prepare pilots for careers in commercial and corporate aviation, flying multiengine planes. A second new major, designed as a five-year program, was added that same year in the School of Religion by combining the missionary aviation degree with the airframe and power plant program. Missionary pilots who completed this degree had thorough flight training as well as the knowledge and ability to repair their own aircraft engines and systems.[31]

BJU's flight program began in 1974 with only one airplane for student use: a 1967 Cessna found in Atlanta by board member Bob Wood. By 1995, through the business acumen of Wood, by then the executive vice president of BJU, the fleet had grown to fourteen aircraft, and included twelve training aircraft and two corporate planes (a Sabre twin-engine business jet and a turboprop Beechcraft KingAir). These planes added greatly to the flexibility of Dr. Jones III's speaking schedule and to the availability of faculty to speak at workshops, symposiums, and clinics.

These are but three of many examples of growth within the programs of the University. Others that underwent significant development include the English Department, which expanded its graduate offerings in concert with the School of Education; the Science Department, which added significantly to its programs in premed, pre-vet, and pre-physical therapy, as well as in its engineering fields; and the Speech Department, which moved into an integrated communications curriculum.

As dramatic as expansion was in the academic program of the University, the expansion of the physical campus was equally dramatic. The gigantic Founder's Memorial Amphitorium, dedicated at Thanksgiving 1973, was only "the tip of the iceberg" of campus development and construction. During the early 1970s, as inflation spiraled into double digits and sent the costs of room and board soaring, the executives expressed concern about containing the costs of a BJU education and maintaining the Founder's vision for a reasonably priced education. Hoping at the least to control some of the food costs in the Dining Common, the University purchased 609 acres of farmland in 1974 on which to breed and raise cattle.[32] There were some early problems with the herd, but by 1980 Pleasant Pastures supplied 50 to 75 percent of the University's beef requirements. The farm personnel next developed a dairy that eventually became the top-producing dairy in the state.[33] In spite of excellent product quality, the farm was unable to operate at a "break even" point and the goal of bringing savings to the University's food budget was never fully realized. After more than twenty-five years of University-subsidized operation, Dr. Jones III made the difficult decision to pull the school out of farming.

In the years since the purchase of the farm in 1974, Greenville's suburban growth moved steadily east, finally surrounding the Pleasant Pastures farm with housing developments. An offer to buy the land by a Greenville businessman was accepted by BJU's executives in June 2000, and Pleasant Pastures became a pleasant memory for all but the campus businessmen who had been responsible for making the operation pay for itself.

On the campus itself, building and renovation projects multiplied. With the growing student body of the 1970s came the need for expanded dormitory space "to alleviate the crowded conditions in the present dormitories" and

Bob Jones University's Pleasant Pastures Farm, Fountain Inn, South Carolina

to provide space for future growth.[34] Two new three-story dorms were dedicated in 1977—Mary Gaston Hall for women and R. K. Johnson Hall for men.[35] While Gaston and Johnson were being finished, the University air conditioned two men's and two women's dormitories and completed air conditioning the remaining four dormitories the next year.

Following the dorm construction, the crowded and overtaxed facilities of Mack Library were renovated. A 68,000-square-foot addition, which nearly tripled the size of the library, was opened after sixteen months of inconvenience to library patrons. The beautifully redone facility was dedicated on September 6, 1980, and was designed to meet student needs into the twenty-first century.[36] Besides books and other traditional library materials, Mack Library also boasted a new archives display area, presenting the history of BJU; a collection of rare Bibles housed in a reproduction of the Jerusalem Chamber of Westminster Abbey in which the King James Version translators worked;[37] and the beautifully appointed Earle W. Sargent Memorial Board-room, which featured two 1900-era Tiffany windows, one depicting Dorcas and the other the apostle Paul.[38] The room had rich, hand-carved walnut pilasters with their capitals, originally carved for the George Blumenthal mansion in New York,[39] and two crystal chandeliers that once hung in the Astor Hotel on Times Square in New York.[40] A third Astor Hotel chandelier was hung in the newly decorated main library lobby. The Mack Library also became the home of the University's first computer lab.

One facet of Mack Library that is only now becoming widely known is the Fundamentalism File, a collection currently containing more than eighty thousand documents pertaining to American Fundamentalism and religious issues. Described as "a library within a library," the file is used with increasing regularity by researchers, pastors, and teachers who seek current information on religious topics. Each of the more than forty-five hundred items added yearly to the collection is cataloged and computerized, abstracted, and cross-referenced to facilitate topic or author searches.[41]

As enrollment reached more than five thousand, the Student Center facilities could no longer contain the crush of students. An expansive addition to the Edwards-Riley Memorial Student Center named in memory of Dr. James D. Edwards, former dean of administration, and Miss Hazel Claire Riley, former dean of women, was dedicated on September 11, 1982.[42] The new addition, connected to the original structure by a glass-covered mall area, more than doubled the building's size. Anchored on the east by Stratton Hall (formerly called the Concert Center) and on the west by the War Memorial Chapel, the center held two social parlors, a game room, conference room, the campus post office, and the Snack Shop and Campus Store, as well as offices to serve the student body and campus guests.[43] In addition, the Student Center featured the one-hundred-seat Grace Levinson Chapel, in which the school's promotional multi-image presentation was shown.[44] The Edwards-Riley Student Center was renovated in 1995, following a late December fire that caused extensive damage to the Riley parlor.[45]

The late 1980s brought only "minor" construction—a pedestrian bridge across North Pleasantburg Drive,[46] an electricity generating plant,[47] and a new wrought iron fence with ornate entrance gates to the campus.[48] This minor construction, however, signaled to Greenville that BJU now saw itself as part of the community. The new decorative fence was a tangible sign of opening the campus to the city. The bridge showed local merchants that BJU intended to support them while protecting the safety of the student body. The cogeneration plant, in addition to saving money, also showed a campus-wide awareness for environmental concerns.

Because of the changing interests and needs of the student body, in 1988 Dr. Jones III announced plans to build an addition to expand the Howell Memorial Science Building.[49] The addition was designed to house two electrical labs, a home economics lab, two lecture rooms, and an advanced computing lab. Construction began on May 15, 1989, and the building was ready by September 1990.[50] Five years later the original Science Building was renovated to modernize this 1960s "relic."[51] Its lecture theaters were updated, as were all the laboratories, offices, and furnishings.

The Fremont Fitness Center, named for long-time dean of the School of Education, Walter Fremont, was begun in March of 1992. It was opened on January 22, 1993. The complex featured four racquetball courts, a fully equipped weight room, an aerobics exercise room, saunas, whirlpools, and locker rooms. The building also had an outdoor concession area for the Alumni Stadium.[52]

Numerous small projects and developments also took place. In 1986, the school acquired University Place, formerly known as the Wildwood Apartments, to house faculty and staff as well as to develop a Christian retirement community.[53] Between 1980 and 1995, ten faculty houses were constructed on the back campus area; an automotive and aircraft mechanic shop was built for the School of Applied Studies, along with a warehouse for the University Press. University Maintenance was moved to the former Wade Hampton Mall, which was purchased by the University in 1987. Mall space was subsequently converted for use by the Bob Jones Elementary School, the University Press, and other campus departments.

Remodeling and renovation projects also touched every part of the campus. Every summer following the departure of the student body, the University Maintenance Department busied itself with an average of 150 major projects, including such things as new roofs for buildings, new surfaces on the tennis courts, building redecoration, and new landscaping. For instance, over two years' time all the dormitories were updated, with new furniture, carpeting, paint, plumbing, and new electrical and computer connections. The Alumni Building received some new furnishings and was recarpeted and painted. And a new organ (donated by Dr. Jean Saito, a campus physician, in memory of her mother) and sound system were installed in the Amphitorium in 1994.

Dr. Jones III sought ways of opening the campus and bringing more young people in touch with the University. To do so, the school initiated a high school basketball tournament in 1973[54] and a high school fine arts festival in 1974.[55] With the cooperation of the physical education, science, and fine arts faculties, the school sponsored weeklong summer camps in soccer, basketball, volleyball, computers, nursing, criminal justice, art, band, orchestra, chorus, piano, and handbells. These attracted large numbers of prospective students to the campus.

The American Association of Christian Schools (AACS), headquartered in Kansas City, Missouri, and representing several thousand Fundamentalist Christian schools, was first invited to the campus for its national academic and fine arts tournament in 1977. The AACS Nationals annually brought to the campus over two thousand high school contestants from across the country for competition and judging in many academic areas. Though campus facilities were strained, the relationship between the AACS and BJU was cordial, and the group has returned to the campus annually for its national competition.[56]

During the 1970s and 1980s, activities for the students were developed to communicate a sense of the school's uniqueness and to show the students the personal interest that the faculty, staff, and administration took in them. Gold Rush Daze was one such example. Started in 1976, the first Gold Rush Daze was "designed to be really special in every college student's career." It provided a day of activity and fun. Scheduled for the first Tuesday after Bible Conference every fourth year, students had the morning free to rest and in the afternoon met on the athletic fields for "wacky and zany" events and games.[57] The goal was to get the entire University family involved in the games. These were followed by a fried chicken picnic and Faculty Body, a program in which the faculty, staff, and even administrators poked good-natured fun at BJU and at themselves.[58]

A second way of showing interest in the students' needs began in 1991. Since the beginning of the school, one day each semester was informally set aside as a special day of prayer. Students would go to the Social Parlor during free times to pray for the administrators, faculty, and requests from other students. However, in 1991, Dr. Jones III decided to suspend classes for one day a semester to put special emphasis on prayer. Beginning with a special chapel service, the day was filled with three forty-five-minute prayer sessions during which faculty and students shared prayer requests and prayed together. The day culminated with a service at which students and faculty shared testimonies about answered prayer.[59]

The Bob Jones University Alumni Association has played an important role in campus life by raising funds for needed projects, recommending students to the school, and supporting the institution in prayer. The association began as an alumni dinner that followed the Bob Jones College Commencement, apparently after the graduation of the first four-year class, and continued annually. On June 3, 1941, the Alumni Association discussed and approved an "organ of communication," which was named *Little Moby's Post,* taking its name from the campus store. During the formative years of the College, the association did not sponsor fund drives independent of the school but used the *Post* as a means of keeping in touch with alumni. In 1955 the Alumni Association Constitution and By-Laws were rewritten and *Little Moby's Post* was renamed *Voice of the Alumni.*[60] That same year the association began to take a more aggressive role in campus affairs, sponsoring its first project—air conditioning Rodeheaver Auditorium—and thereafter raising money for the student loan fund. The association officers and Dr. Jones III recognized the need for a permanent director in 1971, and on January 1, 1972, Bud Bierman began to serve as the director of Alumni Affairs.[61] Through his leadership, the association grew in size and importance in undertaking campus projects.[62]

For students who attended Bob Jones College in Tennessee or Bob Jones University in its early days in Greenville, it would have been difficult to imagine a day when the "old-timers" were no longer active. As time marched inexorably on, however, transitions were inescapable.

Dr. James D. Edwards, the dean of administration who had been bedrock in the operation of the school, died in 1981. At his death, his duties were divided between Dr. Philip D. Smith, who was named provost of the University,[63] and Jim Berg, who became dean of students.[64]

R. K. Johnson, business manager since 1936, member of the Executive Committee, and the administrative officer responsible for maintaining the financial vitality of the institution, passed away in 1971. He was followed after a three-year interim by Roy Barton, a successful Maine banker and community leader.[65]

Dr. Gilbert Stenholm retired as director of Ministerial Training in 1977 after having served in a variety of capacities at Bob Jones College and Bob Jones University.[66] For the next ten years, he served as staff evangelist, preaching for many of his Preacher Boys in their churches, an activity that gave him great personal satisfaction. Dr. Stenholm went home to be with the Lord in 1989. Richard Rupp was appointed director of Ministerial Training in 1977 and retired from the position in 1991.[67] Bruce McAllister succeeded Rupp that same year.

Dr. Walter Fremont, dean of the School of Education since 1953 and salesman extraordinaire for Christian education, was stricken with amyotrophic lateral sclerosis (ALS, or Lou Gehrig's disease) in 1986 and retired in 1990. He was succeeded by Dr. James Deuink.[68]

Hazel Claire Riley became dean of women in 1941 and held this position until her retirement in 1977. She passed away in 1982. Luena Barker, who assisted Miss Riley from 1961 through 1976, was named dean following

Riley's retirement and remained in the office through 1994, when Lynette Baker assumed the responsibility.

William Liverman, "the law and order" of BJU, was dean of men on the campus from 1953 through his retirement in 1981. He was a figure much feared by wrongdoers among the young men. Following his retirement, Tony Miller became dean of men.

Two other transitions of major importance to the institution's vitality and direction occurred in 1997 and 2000. The first was the death of the Chancellor, Bob Jones Jr. in 1997. The second came on May 5, 2000, when Stephen Jones (b. 1969), son of Bob Jones III, was appointed Vice President of Administration by the Board of Trustees. This move by the Board marked the official recognition of the next generation of executive leadership of Bob Jones University.[69]

Bob Jones Jr. remained a powerful influence in American Fundamentalism throughout the 1990s, traveling thousands of miles preaching and encouraging missionaries and pastors in their work. In 1996, his ministry was twice interrupted by illness. Following what was thought to be successful surgery for prostate cancer that summer, he resumed his preaching and traveling. By the summer of 1997 it became obvious to the University family that the Chancellor was not well. When school convened that fall, observers noted that his preaching had taken an interesting turn and that many of his comments focused on the glories of heaven, the wonder of salvation, and the prospect of seeing Christ. In January 1997, he asked the students in chapel:

> Did you ever stop to think how many paupers there are going to be in heaven? They got there by grace and will live in a mansion somewhere, but it is by grace. God expects you to earn the treasures of heaven. He gives the entrance by grace but in heaven you will be enjoying what you have earned and laid up—laying up treasure in heaven, souls won to Christ, testimony faithful in the midst of opposition and ridicule, dedication, love for the Lord, a life well-invested. That is the way you lay hold on eternal life. You have the gift, but oh, the poverty of a man or woman who stands in the presence of God and who has nothing except what He has given. . . . What a tragedy to live on a side street in a small house wearing a robe that He has given you but no crown on your brow, no treasure to lay at His feet.[70]

On September 29, 1997, upon his return from a preaching engagement at First Baptist Church of Troy, Michigan, Dr. Jones and his family learned the results of some previously administered medical tests—the diagnosis was abdominal cancer. Although he very much wanted to speak again in chapel, his health would not allow it. He recorded one final message, played to the students on October 29, in which he summarized his thoughts: "The wonderful thing about serving the Lord is that whatever He does for you is best and whatever He sends is the very best thing He can send. . . . Whatever the Lord sends is all right with me—His will is being done. . . . There is no satisfaction like knowing you serve Him, that you're His person in His will doing His task for His purpose to His glory.[71]

Two weeks later, on November 12, Dr. Jones III came to Founder's Memorial Amphitorium at the end of chapel to share the news with the student body. "Just before chapel today the Chancellor, my father, joined his Father in glory. . . . Dad sowed all he could sow, he produced all he could produce, and now he is at rest."

The reports of his death brought such comment as "To some, he was . . . the preacher who stood in the church doorway, looked across the changing social landscape and declared that he simply would not move."[72] Dr. Ian Paisley, Irish preacher, member of British Parliament, and the Chancellor's close friend called him "the *Mr. Valiant for the Truth* of this century" and reviewed the words of John Bunyan's *Mr. Valiant for the Truth* as Dr. Bob's final testimony:

> Then said he, I am going to my Father's, and though with great difficulty I have got hither, yet now I do not repent me of all the troubles I have been at to arrive where I am. My sword I give to him that shall succeed me in my pilgrimage, and my courage and skill to him that can get it. My marks and scars I carry with me, to be a witness for me that I have fought His battles who now will be my rewarder. As he went he said, "Death, where is thy sting?" And as he went down deeper, he said, "Grave, where is thy victory?"[73]

"So he passed over, and all the trumpets sounded for him on the other side."

The funeral on November 17, a "Celebration of His Homegoing," brought many thousands of alumni and former students to the campus. It was a triumphant occasion of tribute not only to a victorious and courageous Christian warrior at rest from the battle, but also to the God whom he had served. At the end of the service, the Chancellor's recorded voice, in trumpetlike tones, rose in eloquent prose. "You talk about the thunder of the tempest, the roaring of the sea in the hour of storm, the great throb of song as orchestra and choir lift their voices, the mightiest of pipe organs opens all the stops. My friend, the greatest music in the world is going to be the universal acclaim 'King of kings! Lord of Lords!'" Echoing the audience's response the University Chorale sang Handel's great chorus, "Hallelujah! For the Lord God Omnipotent reigneth. King of kings, and Lord of lords, Hallelujah!"

To the strains of hymns played by the University Wind Band, Bob Jones Jr. was laid to rest next to his mother and his father on the little island in the middle of the fountains in front of Rodeheaver Auditorium. Inscribed on his tombstone are these words by his son:

A prophet's eye,
A poet's voice,
A servant's heart,
A ransomed soul.[74]

CHAPTER 24

◆

Into All the World

One major interest of Bob Jones III as University President was to get the school out of the "cocoon" in which it found itself in 1971. Part of the reason for this cocoon was local and was formed when the University moved to Greenville and consciously isolated itself from the Greenville community because, as Bob Jones Jr. put it, "We didn't want to run the town [politically]."[1]

Part of the reason for the cocoon was national in scope and was spun by Fundamentalists' withdrawal from New Evangelicalism.[2] By the 1960s, the voices of Bob Jones Sr. and Jr. had been muted within evangelicalism by the eagerness with which the majority of the evangelical media and pastors uncritically accepted New Evangelicalism. The broader Christian lay public also discounted their voices because they perceived New Evangelicals as well intentioned, and not disobedient, brothers.

Bob Jones III began to take positive steps to minimize discord and to unify Fundamentalists around the essential doctrines of the Christian faith. He recognized the importance of fighting the good fight of faith but also realized the necessity for Fundamentalists to communicate in a positive manner. To this emphasis he dedicated the resources and influence of the University in the use of the electronic and print media and in educational and ministry outreaches.

Television

For years graduates had urged Dr. Jones III to consider having the school produce a national weekly television program. The time and money involved seemed prohibitive, but finally, Dr. Jones recalls, "I got liberty from the Lord to do it." By the mid-1970s the market for religious programming was booming, and in 1976 Bob Jones III directed that a pilot for a weekly television program be developed. Although the pilot was never aired, it was enough to persuade the administration to move into production.

Starting in October 1976, *Show My People*[3] was taped by an outside crew one week each month. By late summer 1978 the half-hour program was being taped, edited, and duplicated in-house.[4]

At its inception in 1977, the program was carried in nine major cities.[5] The number of outlets continued to grow until 1986, when the program was carried weekly by nineteen stations and twelve cable television systems.[6]

A typical *Show My People* program consisted of three or four musical numbers by an ensemble or choir, a solo, and a short message by Dr. Jones III. The President wanted the program to be a window to the campus through which viewers could see biblical Christianity at work. The primary motivation was both to inspire and to instruct Christians while retaining an evangelistic appeal to the unsaved.[7]

Finances were a major problem, but Dr. Jones III refused to ask the audience for money. Dr. Jones believed that, unlike other Christian television programs with their often specious claims of impending financial doom, the school's program should be one that the "unsaved person could view without the feeling that somehow the Gospel and dollar bill were inextricably joined."[8] To raise money, the University's Media Management department developed a three-pronged approach: banquets, rallies, and direct mail. *Show My People* Rallies and banquets were held in major cities throughout the country at which the Television Choir, faculty soloists, or student ensembles would sing and Bob Jones III would speak. At the rallies people were asked to pledge money toward purchasing airtime, while the University continued to underwrite the production and distribution costs.[9] Even though the rallies and banquets helped, the program was never able to meet expenses. By 1985 costs had risen to nearly $1 million a year, and the drain on University funds became critical.

On January 7, 1986, to a genuinely surprised faculty and student body, Dr. Jones III announced in chapel that *Show My People* was being discontinued. Not only was the expense of production debilitating to the University, but also the strain on the students and faculty in the School of Fine Arts, who did all of the music arranging, performing, recording, traveling, and writing for the program, had become excessive. Dr. Jones III later commented, "When the time came to end it, I was just as certain the time for ending was of the Lord as I was about the beginning."[10]

Publishing and the BJU Press

In 1973, seeing the need for a biblically based periodical written from a Fundamentalist perspective, the Chancellor founded *Faith for the Family.*[11] In the first issue of *Faith,* Bob Jones III wrote that he wanted to reach beyond the limits of the University family to touch the hundreds of Christian families who had limited contact with the school, as well as to address current and important religious issues.[12] Bob Jones Jr. wrote that the purpose of the magazine was to take a stand on current issues; inform the readers of these issues; and be comprehensive, Fundamentalist, Christian, and family-oriented.[13]

Faith, however, could not support itself from advertising and subscription sales, and Bob Jones III became concerned when the bulk of the University's advertising budget was being expended to keep the magazine afloat. Previously, the University had advertised in a variety of Christian and secular publications, giving the school widespread exposure. The readership of *Faith,* however, was primarily in churches with which the school already had an abundance of contact. The school therefore discontinued publication in April 1986. In its place Dr. Jones III asked Jerry Thacker, a media consultant and BJU alumnus, to develop a multifaceted public relations outreach that would diversify the school's advertising dollars as the University had done before *Faith.* The University maintained a magazine outreach, though, with *BJU Review,* a promotional quarterly.

Bob Jones University first entered trade book publishing full-scale in late 1973 with George Dollar's *History of Fundamentalism.*[14] It was not in trade books, however, that BJU Press would enjoy its greatest success. In the late 1960s and early 1970s, with the Christian school movement in America still in its infancy, two members of the University board surveyed the textbooks from their children's Christian schools and came to the conclusion that Christian schools needed Christian texts. They commissioned two members of the Bob Jones University science department to write a science text from a Christian perspective. The authors, physicist and astronomer George Mulfinger and physicist Emmet Williams, were interested in the potential of a Christian science text.[15] When the first draft of the book was completed, the board members presented it to Bob Jones III with a proposal that the University fund the printing of the book.[16]

The result was *PHYSICAL SCIENCE for Christian Schools,* a textbook that was designed exclusively for Christian schools and that was scholarly, academically sound, challenging for the student, and written by Christian scientists from a Christian perspective.[17] Because of its depth of content, design, illustration, and thoroughly Christian worldview, *Physical Science* became the benchmark by which other Christian texts were measured.[18] A second and more far-reaching result, however, was that Bob Jones University had opened the door to full-scale educational publishing. Thus, in two years' time, the University had launched a press and was printing a bimonthly magazine, trade books, and textbooks.

In 1974 Bob Jones University Press began work on an elementary Bible series and an elementary science series. Following in rapid succession were elementary math, high school biology, and elementary Heritage Studies (the Press name for social studies). Unlike other publishers in the Christian market who took out-of-print secular texts and marketed them as Christian, the BJU Press developed each book from scratch, using as its basis a Christian worldview and Christian philosophy of education.[19]

Initially, the Press had planned to publish only a few texts in areas where secular books were either philosophically flawed or academically deficient.[20] The success of the early books and the enthusiasm of the University faculty convinced Dr. Jones III that publishing a full spectrum of texts for Christian schools was wise, necessary, and possible.

In 1986 the Press branched out into biography and fiction for children and young adults as a way "of taking young readers from texts to literature." The Press worked to provide stories with a strong Christian message (the Light Line series) as well as books that were simply wholesome and appealing (the Pennant Book line).[21] In the first decade after the fiction line was inaugurated, the Press published more than seventy books by twenty-five different authors. Of these books, many have been awarded honors in national book competitions, such as that of the Boys Clubs of America and the C. S. Lewis Medal Contest.[22]

When the home school movement began to grow in the early 1980s, Dr. Jones III and the University administration expressed a supportive attitude toward home schoolers. As a result, the Press instituted home school fairs in major cities, sponsored home instruction workshops, and generally tried to be responsive to the needs of home schooling families. The Press created an academic testing division to provide home school families with the required state intelligence, aptitude, and achievement tests. The Press also developed the Academy of Home Education as a quality support system for home educators who were "teaching their teenage children upper-level courses" and preparing them for college.[23] Because of its supportive attitude, by 1988 the Bob Jones University Press was the largest textbook supplier to home school families in the nation.[24]

In 1990 the Press developed an annual weeklong Home Education Leadership Program (HELP) to "help home educators do the best job possible" in educating their children. More than 110 workshops and sessions were presented by University faculty in all curriculum areas. In its first year, over 850 families attended HELP. In its second year, the conference grew to nearly three thousand people.[25]

The outreach of the University and the Press was significantly expanded by BJ LINC—Bob Jones Live Interactive Network Classroom. Inaugurated on August 23, 1995, LINC transmitted nine different high school courses, ranging from advanced math to Spanish 2. They were taught live in Greenville, beamed to a geostationary satellite and back down to earth to receivers at subscribing schools. The students viewed the lessons and responded in "real time" through a special response keypad at each desk. The keypads also contained a voice microphone for verbal responses, questions, or conversations. Thus, students from across the country were linked together, with a live teacher, in one giant classroom through interactive technology.[26] The hope was that LINC would be a "huge boost to Christian schools who had difficulty finding qualified teachers" for advanced courses and would allow schools to expand their courses with minimal expense.[27] For the benefit of home schoolers, the Press initiated HomeSat (Home School Access Terminal), utilizing many of the same elements as LINC.

The LINC outreach led naturally to other avenues of broadcast education in addition to HomeSat, and the leadership of BJU Press in Christian education among home schools attracted another such opportunity. The Dominion DBS (Direct Broadcast Satellite) Television System approached the University in 1996 about providing educational programming for their system. The result was the scheduling of a series of expanding offerings: a single channel devoted to the enrichment of home education launched in late

1996, a full curriculum from kindergarten through twelfth grade to be broadcast beginning in September 1997, and finally multiple channels of instruction to become available in 1998. The publishing outreach of BJU Press had become a technological outreach that stretched around the world.

Educational Outreaches

Bob Jones Academy

In 1927 Bob Jones Academy opened with forty-seven students, grades seven through twelve, and class sizes were small—only four to six students per course. The first graduating class had five students, including Bob Jones Jr.[28] Because of its small size, the Academy shared facilities and teachers with Bob Jones College and was not considered a separate school until after it moved to Greenville in 1947.[29] The College dean administered the school in Tennessee, and after the move to Greenville, the academic deans made the operational decisions for the school. In 1970 the Academy became more independent, with the principal having a more dominant role. Finally, in 1978, the Academy's status as a separate school was completed when it published its own yearbook, the *Academian.*

Academy enrollment peaked at 357 students in 1952, then stabilized at this level through the 1960s.[30] The bulk of the student body, 91 percent, were dormitory students or faculty children, but a small number of children from Greenville also enrolled. As Greenville Christians became more aware of the problems in public education, and as the Academy's academic, artistic, social, and spiritual reputation became established, Academy day student enrollment began to grow dramatically. When the boom in Christian schooling hit in the early 1970s, however, dormitory enrollment declined just as dramatically. With 441 students by 1992, the Academy student body was composed of nearly 90 percent day students and only 10 percent dormitory students.[31] The Academy faculty also grew from eight teachers (who also taught in the College) in 1928 to fifty-three teachers assigned exclusively to the Academy in 1992.[32]

When the Academy moved to Greenville, the high school classes were held in the west end of the Alumni Building. In 1951 the first Academy building (one of six barracks moved from Cleveland, Tennessee) was dedicated. The school did what it could to decorate and update the buildings, but even so construction flaws and age took their toll. One teacher recalled that one day while he was teaching, the floor gave way beneath him, much to the delight of the students.[33]

Beginning in 1970 the University approved a series of modernization and beautification projects at the Academy that resulted in a new gymnasium and industrial arts building, air conditioning in all the buildings, redecoration, landscaping, and other improvements. In the mid-1980s, Academy Main underwent a face-lift, and the Brown Building was torn down and rebuilt. By 1995 all four Quadrangle buildings had either been dramatically improved, totally reconstructed, or razed and replaced, and the Academy occupied a total of seven classroom buildings. Besides regular classrooms, the Quadrangle also contained a four-hundred-seat auditorium; gymnasium; band room; orchestra room; and computer, biology, chemistry, physics, language, and home economics labs.

The Academy offered general and advanced courses in all subject areas, including English, speech, Bible, history, computers, mathematics and the sciences, and three foreign languages. An outstanding music program also developed and included band, orchestra, and choir, all of which were recognized in South Carolina as among the finest in the state. The school also had a nationally acclaimed forensics and debate program and a program of intramural sports to encourage participation and physical development.

More important than its academic success and reputation, however, was the spiritual emphasis at the Academy, which included more than just the required Bible classes and a daily chapel service. Academy students had opportunities to work in extension ministries at local nursing homes, children's homes, youth clubs, and area churches. Beginning in 1982, the Academy sponsored a weeklong mission team to New York City to do street evangelism, hold evangelistic services, and in other ways help local pastors.[34]

Bob Jones Junior High

When the junior high became a separate school in 1952, the thirty-three students shared building space, teachers, societies, and sports competitions with the Academy students. In 1964 the fifty-five seventh and eighth graders were separated from the high schoolers, and they formed their own societies and sports teams. One complete building of the Academy Quadrangle was assigned for their classes. By 1973 the student body had doubled, crowding the facility beyond its limits. In a move to ease the overcrowding and because of administrative concerns, in 1974 the junior high no longer accepted dormitory students. That same year, the junior high became completely independent from the Academy, with its own teachers and administration. Continued overcrowding made expansion necessary, and plans were laid for a new junior high building, which was dedicated in 1976.[35] School opened that fall in the new building with about 130 students.[36]

The junior high remained in its new quarters for only three years before moving back to the Academy Quadrangle to make room for the expanding School of Applied Studies. Shortly after the return to the Quadrangle, junior high enrollment rose until overcrowding again became critical and made yet another junior high building necessary. The design chosen had two stories, upper for the Academy, lower for the junior high. The new Hutto Building was dedicated in August 1990 for the 244 students who filled the nine classrooms. The building also included a library, teacher and administrative offices, and a cafeteria.[37]

Bob Jones Elementary School

When it opened its doors in 1970, BJES offered grades one through three, had four teachers and one secretary, and enjoyed a brand new building on the east side of the University campus. The next year the school added grades four through six and was using all twelve classrooms of the new building.

Even in its earliest years, the school carved out a reputation for academic excellence based on the students' performances on standardized tests. But as important as the intellectual preparation was, the school's promotional brochure stated that the major goal of the BJES teachers was "that all the children come to know the Lord Jesus Christ as Saviour." The teachers emphasized growth in Christian character in every aspect of school life, and they sought to develop depth and understanding in the children. Principal Melva Heintz warned the teachers "to guard against a shallow approach to academic skills and progress." She said, "I'd rather be thorough and move at a moderate pace, than be shallow and move rapidly."[38]

BJES rapidly grew to the point that 410 students were enrolled by 1976, three sections of some grades had been formed, part of one dormitory was allocated for class and music space, and the sixth grades were shifted to the junior high building. Sixteen classroom teachers, five music teachers, an art teacher, and a tutor oversaw the students' progress. But a physically divided school created problems that could be solved only by building a new elementary school building. Therefore, in 1981 a new building was erected for the 599 students. The school had thirty-five classrooms, a large cafetorium, a piano lab, an instrumental music room, an art room, tutors' offices, administrative offices, and a library.[39]

When the University acquired a nearby insurance office in 1985, the school remodeled it and developed a Beginnings Center with rooms for five sections of kindergarten.[40] Needing to expand again in 1988, the school renovated 21,000 square feet located in the Wade Hampton Mall into a Primary Center with thirteen classrooms (K4 and grades 1-3), a "gymnateria," offices, and space for tutors and speech therapists. Thus, in seventeen years, the school had grown from one building, 99 students, and four teachers, into a school of three buildings; 890 students; thirty-five full-time faculty; a music staff of thirteen instrumental, piano, and choral music teachers; an art teacher; two physical education instructors; two tutors; a librarian; a nurse; four secretaries; and an assistant principal.[41] By 1996, enrollment stood at 975 children.[42]

Community Outreaches

One community outreach initiated by Bob Jones III in 1984 was a Christian Business Luncheon to reach the Greenville business community. The luncheons gave local Christian businessmen and women the opportunity to bring coworkers and business associates under the message of the gospel. The luncheons were held twice monthly and averaged about 150 in attendance for a meal and a devotional challenge by a University faculty member.[43]

A second community outreach took form in 1986 when Dr. Jones III created the Community Relations Council to undertake special projects in the Greenville area. After the first project was completed, Greenville's mayor Bill Workman presented two national awards to the University for its role in the 1986 "Take Pride in America" campaign and to recognize the six hundred student volunteers who cleaned up and removed over five hundred cubic yards of trash from a Greenville park.[44] He stated that the city appreciated the school's efforts to be "not just a spiritual presence, but also a physical presence in the community."[45] Since the first cleanup day in 1986, the CRC has sponsored a wide range of activities, including organizing blood drives, fixing up dilapidated homes, cleaning camps and public areas, working at Special Olympics, and developing a long-term relationship with Camp Spearhead, a camp for the mentally and physically disabled.[46]

Church Planting

In his first year as President, Bob Jones III took action to reverse a trend in Fundamentalist Christianity that he had seen during his travels for the school. It was evident that an increasing number of churches were succumbing to New Evangelicalism and that large areas of the country had no Fundamentalist voice among the local churches. After some reflection, he became convinced that Bob Jones University could and should take up the challenge and provide leadership to plant new churches around the country.[47]

Prospective church planters selected an area of the country where few Fundamentalist churches existed and began surveying its potential. After trips to the area and much prayer for guidance, each person selected by the University received a salary and family insurance from the school for one year, thus enabling him to work full-time in organizing his church.[48] In return, the young pastor was required to submit reports of his services, attendance, contacts, and so on.[49] The University also provided a support framework of scheduled phone consultations, visits by school officials, and church planters' retreats to help the young pastors find solutions to the problems they faced.[50]

By 1994 Bob Jones University had sponsored nearly one hundred pastors in planting independent Fundamentalist churches in thirty-five states, at a cost of nearly $900,000. By 1996, some of these BJU-planted churches had grown dramatically and had themselves sponsored young pastors in church planting activities.[51]

In the mid-1980s Dr. Jones III also began to encourage new graduates to set aside their career goals for a time—two or three years—and select one of these small struggling churches, then go to that area, find work, and help that church and pastor as lay leadership. The need for trained leadership was great, Dr. Jones III thought, and a Bob Jones couple could be a great help.

Mission Teams

The impulse for missionary activity had always been strong among Bob Jones College and Bob Jones University students, and all of the Joneses actively encouraged the students to consider missionary work for their life's calling. It was not until the 1960s, however, that organized mission teams went out from the school. Until 1966 these were unofficial teams, organized through mission boards or by individual faculty members in connection with missionaries in various foreign lands.[52]

The first officially recognized mission team from BJU, however, was Project Compassion, a summer medical team formed in 1966. With the enthusiastic approval of President Bob Jones Jr., the team was directed by orthopedic surgeon and BJU faculty member Dr. John Dreisbach and his wife Betty, a registered nurse.[53] Though the University officially recognized the team, each member of the Project Compassion staff had to raise support for living expenses and transportation to the Windward Island of St. Lucia, the team's destination.

Project Compassion later took its medical missions project to such countries as the Philippines, Haiti, Mexico, Kenya, and Rumania. It also prepared the way for other official mission teams to go out under the auspices of Bob Jones University.

In 1974 Nelson McGeoch and Earl Nutz of the School of Religion organized teams to Canada to work with missionaries and pastors in Nova Scotia and Manitoba. The teams were a huge success, leaving "permanent results on the field" and giving "an effective training experience for each student."[54] Within three years, two more official teams had been added, one to Hawaii and one to Germany, and by 1991, thirteen official summer missionary teams were recognized by the University, with over 150 students and faculty participating.

Interestingly, the teams were not made up exclusively of Bible or missions majors as one would expect; a large percentage of each team majored in fields outside the School of Religion.[55] Each member was responsible for raising his own expenses, as had the Project Compassion teams. Teams focused on such missionary "support" projects as digging wells, constructing small buildings, and repairing machinery, as well as on more "spiritual" ministries such as child evangelism classes, Bible studies, camp counseling, street preaching, and regular church services.[56]

Perhaps the most intriguing of the summer teams was organized by Drs. Bill and Janie McCauley shortly after the Iron Curtain lifted in 1991. The Musical Mission Team spent fifty days in Poland, Czechoslovakia, the former East Germany, and Russia, holding concerts in connection with Fundamentalist churches. The students preached, sang, handed out gospel literature, and gave concerts in parks, on street corners, and in community halls. They also did street evangelism and found the Eastern Europeans open to the gospel, especially those in countries that had been most isolated by Communism. That summer over five hundred people, most of them in Russia, were converted. The national pastors were jubilant, and many of these converts were discipled and joined the churches.[57]

Timothy Program and WORLD Fund

In the 1970s the outlook for overseas American missionary activity was growing bleak. Fewer young people, it seemed, were interested in living a life of potential privation in a foreign land. In addition, many countries had expelled missionaries or threatened no longer to grant visas for Christian preaching or teaching activities. Furthermore, Mormonism, Buddhism, and Islam had expanded rapidly in foreign lands, making time of the essence. Gospel preaching from national pastors, Bob Jones III believed, would meet this challenge because "nationals can reach the people of their own country with the Gospel more effectively" than can American foreigners. Thus, the Timothy Program was born in 1977.[58]

BJU Timothy student Seth Mohenu, Bob Jones III, and Bob Jones Jr. (Commencement 1991)

The University limited the Timothy Program to men who wished to prepare for the ministry, who were actively preaching or teaching in their own countries, who displayed qualities of leadership, and who were recommended by missionaries or other Christian workers.[59] These students received their tuition and room and board partly in return for work performed on the campus. To start the program, the school received a gift from a board member, but to help with the students' costs, the University faculty and staff also collected monthly offerings. In addition, offerings collected from Dr. Jones III's Sunday speaking engagements and donations from interested friends went for this cause.

By 1996 thirty-four men had completed their ministerial studies and had returned to their countries to preach, found churches, and disciple converts.[60] The program has included men from Haiti, Brazil, Antigua, Singapore, Korea, Mexico, Bolivia, South Africa, Cypress, Cameroon, and the Philippines, among others.[61]

By 1985 many countries were completely closed to American missionaries of all kinds. Yet nationals educated in American universities who returned to their homelands with skills in computers, languages, the sciences, education, and the fine arts were welcomed. As this trend accelerated, Dr. Jones III believed that future world evangelization might well depend on the ability of foreign nationals, highly trained in secular fields, to carry on gospel ministries. He established the WORLD Fund (Workers of Righteousness Lending Dollars) in 1985 to provide financial assistance to foreign students who desired an education at a Christian university and who agreed to return to their home countries to work.

Unlike the Timothy Program, however, the WORLD Fund students included both men and women who were to be academically prepared in secular fields. To be eligible, a WORLD Fund student must have been actively involved in Christian ministry, have the recommendation of a missionary or pastor, meet BJU's academic requirements, meet the entry and language requirements set by the U.S. Immigration Service, provide his or her own transportation to and from the United States, and complete his or her academic programs within four years. All WORLD Fund students were also required to work on the campus to cover part of their expenses, while a portion was underwritten by the fund. Money for the fund came from special offerings at Bob Jones University, such as the Thanksgiving offering of 1989 and gifts from interested supporters.

Within five years of the fund's beginning, sixty-four students had attended Bob Jones University and seventy-one more had been accepted but were awaiting funding from the school.[62] By 1996, 109 WORLD Fund students had completed their education and had returned to their homelands. Because of the WORLD Fund, students from such diverse places as the Bahamas, South Africa, Mexico, Korea, Hong Kong, Brazil, Rumania, Poland, Bosnia, and Russia have received support. After the collapse of Communism, Dr. Jones III hoped to bring a larger number of students from former Soviet Bloc countries so that a Fundamentalist gospel witness could gain a foothold before cultists and Charismatics moved in.[63]

Bob Jones Jr. Memorial Seminary and Evangelism Center

One dream that had eluded the Chancellor during his life was erecting a seminary building on the campus. Since 1943, the University had an outstanding program of graduate studies in religion but the program had not a place to call its home. With other pressing construction needs through the years and though never far from the Chancellor's mind, the timing for a seminary building never seemed quite right.

Following the news of Dr. Jones Jr.'s illness in 1997, pastors, evangelists, and missionaries from around the world contacted the president and asked what the university could do to memorialize the Chancellor's vast contributions to the school. Recalling numerous conversations he and his father had had about a seminary building, the President moved forward with the idea. Just days before Dr. Bob Jr.'s homegoing, his son told him of the graduates' desire to build the Bob Jones Jr. Memorial Seminary.[64]

Ground was broken in January 1999.[65] A national fundraising campaign among churches pastored by BJU graduates began almost immediately and was chaired by Dr. David Innes, pastor of Hamilton Road Baptist Church in San Francisco. With a goal of 1.5 million dollars, he commented that raising money "is not very exciting. But this has been one of the most pleasant experiences of my life. I was taken aback by the marvelous response from the graduates of this institution."[66]

With a final cost of 2.1 million dollars, the Bob Jones Jr. Memorial Seminary and Evangelism Center was dedicated to the service of God on March 24, 2000. In a moving dedication, Dr. Ian Paisley and others who had fought shoulder to shoulder with Dr. Jones for Christ reviewed the Chancellor's ministry. He was a "preacher's friend from top to bottom and the proclamation of the gospel around the world was the deepest seated thing in his heart," Dr. Innes said. Bob Jones III commented that the building was dedicated "to the testimony, teaching, and preaching of the eternal, forever-settled Word of God." His desire for the seminary was that it "would train preachers who are discerning, evangelistic, balanced and willing to die for the testimony of Jesus Christ."[67]

Located to the west of the Alumni Building, next to Mack Library, the new construction added a dramatic architectural touch to the campus. The two-story building of nearly eighteen thousand square feet holds five lecture rooms, six offices, study areas, a teleconferencing room, and a video research facility. The building features a rotunda containing multimedia kiosks that present the history of American revivalism, the history of BJU's School of Religion, and a personal look at Bob Jones Jr. Dominating the rotunda's second floor is a massive mural of great American evangelists by artist Jim Brooks. In the downstairs lobby is a sampling of sermon notes, awards, honors, and memorabilia of the Chancellor.

With perhaps the most technologically advanced classrooms on the campus, every seminary student has computer access at his carrel for downloading lecture notes and other materials. The greatest feature of the seminary, however, is not the technological wizardry available to student and teacher. Nor is it the unique design of the building and informative but emotionally moving display area. The greatest feature of the Bob Jones Memorial Seminary is the quality of the godly men gathered to serve there. Seminary dean, Dr. Steve Hankins, put it this way: "We rejoice in the wonderful team that God gathered here to serve the Lord. God has been good to us to give us these men to help us pass the torch of ministry to the next generation."[68]

CHAPTER 25

♦

Chandeliers and Back Hall Lights

Bob Jones University has been the home of many memorable characters. Some are remembered for their eccentricities, some for their scholarship and teaching, and some for their faithfulness. It would be impossible to list all of those who have made a contribution to the institution and who, sometimes at personal sacrifice, have graced the offices, classrooms, studios, and hallways. Some of those included in this set of biographical sketches have been mentioned previously in the text but were not treated in detail even though they were an integral part of the institution for many years. Others are here because they and their classes embodied "the Bob Jones experience." Still others are representative of many who gave their lives to the benefit of the University.

Great men and women have walked here and continue to do so. They are great not because of human intellect, influence, wealth, or power, however. They are great because of their strength of character, their spiritual sight, and their dedication to the cause of Christ. As the Founder often reminded the student body, "The most important light in the house is not the chandelier in the parlor. It's that little back hall light that keeps you from breaking your neck when you go into the bathroom in the middle of the night." Within the next pages are both chandeliers and back hall lights.

Roy Aubrey Barton, 1931-

Roy Barton was born in Presque Isle, Maine, on December 1, 1931, the fifth of six children. His father was a district manager of the Maine Public Service Company. Barton's parents were devout and active Christian leaders in the United Baptist Church in Presque Isle. Roy came to know Christ as a boy of nine when his father led him to a saving knowledge of the Lord. Barton attended the public schools in Maine through high school and graduated from Caribou High School in 1949. That same fall he entered Bob Jones University, as all the other Barton children had done, and pursued a major in accounting. Because the Barton children were enrolled at BJU over twenty-four consecutive years, the older children helped the younger ones with school expenses, and all the children carried work-loan jobs on the campus as well. Roy delivered newspapers and was an usher. He eventually became head usher, a position of great responsibility, answerable directly to R. K. Johnson.

After graduation from BJU in 1953, he returned home, married his Maine sweetheart, Joyce McDaniel, and was offered the position of business and bookstore manager at a large New York City church. To preempt the draft during the Korean War, he joined the U.S. Navy and was accepted into Navy Officer Candidate School. He was commissioned as an ensign, rose to the rank of lieutenant, and was eventually assigned to service as a damage control officer on the U.S.S. *Des Moines,* a heavy cruiser.

After four years of military duty, Roy returned to Maine where he distinguished himself for seventeen years in banking. By 1974 he was vice president, treasurer, and a member of the executive committee of the Aroostook Trust Company; he was president of the chamber of commerce and a member of the board of development in Caribou, Maine; and he also taught in the American Institute of Banking. Barton was also active in his local church as chairman of the deacons, a teacher, lay preacher, and youth director. Because of the ungodly environment in their local public high school, the Bartons brought their oldest daughter to Greenville to enter Bob Jones Academy as a dorm student in 1970.

In February 1974 Dr. Jones III contacted Barton and asked him to consider coming to BJU to serve as business manager. His initial response was one of astonishment and doubt: a boy from rural Maine, working in a small bank, had little "to offer a sophisticated educational institution in the South."[1] Out of respect for the President and the Chancellor, he agreed to come to Greenville to discuss the matter.

On the one hand, he was overwhelmed by the thought of serving the Lord with men such as Dr. James D. Edwards and others for whom he had the utmost respect. On the other, he had been told that the "Dr. Bobs ran the school" and he "had a problem with that." Barton had been used to decision-making and "calling the shots" in his banking position. However, God began working in his heart through Scripture. He recalled reading Numbers 12, "where Miriam spoke against Moses and the Lord had to deal with her. She had asked, 'Hath the Lord indeed spoken only by Moses? Hath He not also spoken by us?' The Lord said He would speak to whom He would speak, and Miriam was smitten with leprosy. God spoke to me that day about my pride."[2]

He then came to realize that his decision would be a turning point in his family's life, just like the one that Israel faced when spying out the Promised Land. He asked himself, "Was I going to obey God and go, or was I going to disobey God and stay?" Shortly after this, the words of a song which expressed his personal desire were impressed on his mind—"I'm going to live the way He wants me to live. I'm going to give and give until there is no more to give." He recalled preaching about the fact that "God has a man for every job He needs doing," and Philippians 2:13 came to mind: "For it is God which worketh in you both to will and to do of his good pleasure." It was settled. The family would move to Greenville. They put their home up for sale in March, and the first person who came to see the house (in the middle of an ice storm at ten o'clock at night) bought it for the listed price.

Tucked away since 1974 in a second-floor office of the Administration Building, Roy Barton, with his BJU usher's grace, military discipline, and banker's insights, marshaled the school's financial assets during the University's court case. His business acumen helped the school to pay the fine and the fees. He reorganized the operation and was responsible for developing and funding the faculty retirement program, as well as overseeing all aspects of financial activity at the University, including its subsidiary divisions. "In hindsight," he said, "I marvel at how my background, my military, church, business, and civic experiences had prepared me for the work that had to be done at Bob Jones University. I still marvel at it."[3]

Charles Digory Brokenshire, 1885-1954

Imagine going to a concert and sitting next to a red-faced, white-haired professor who was reading a book on Ethiopic verb tenses, and who at intermission joked with you as he explained the syntax of this language. Such a man was linguist and scholar Charles D. Brokenshire.

He was born in Cincinnati, Ohio, on January 24, 1885, and lived in Rockford, Illinois, and Marietta, Ohio. He graduated from Marietta College Academy in 1903 and immediately entered Marietta College where he distinguished himself with an impressive record of scholarship. He excelled in Greek and German, and soon his great gift for languages was evident to all his teachers. He graduated in 1907, receiving both his B.A. (summa cum laude) and his M.A. degree in Greek. Brokenshire was described by the Marietta dean as the finest scholar "to go through Marietta in twenty-two years or longer."[4]

That fall, Brokenshire entered Princeton Seminary and studied with such luminaries of biblical scholarship and ancient languages as B. B. Warfield, Charles R. Erdman, J. Gresham Machen, and Robert Dick Wilson; he spent two years, after completing his bachelor of divinity degree, as a teaching assistant in Hebrew. Five years later, under Wilson, Brokenshire entered the Ph.D. program in Semitic philology at Princeton University. His declared dissertation topic was "A Study of Text of the Prophecy of Habakkuk in the Light of the Ancient Primary Versions." He reached his final examinations and inexplicably failed to finish. During his Princeton days, Brokenshire also spent three terms at the University of Heidelberg in Germany as a proctor traveling fellow, studying ancient languages and ancient history. He later attempted to finish a Ph.D. in the mid-1920s when he enrolled in the University of Chicago, completed his course work, announced the same dissertation topic, and passed his comprehensive examinations without ever finishing the dissertation. As late as 1941, Brokenshire was still investigating the possibility of earning a Ph.D. but was never able to do so. He did, however, study Japanese and Chinese at the University of Michigan.

As much as he loved language study, Brokenshire's first love was teaching, and in 1915 he took a teaching position in Biblical Literature and Religious Education at Alma College in Michigan. His faculty record from 1930 stated that he had "a reading knowledge or better" of French, Portuguese, German, Dutch, Spanish, Italian, Swedish, Norse, Latin, Greek (both classical and Koine), Hebrew, "Chaldee" (biblical Aramaic), modern Greek, Yiddish, Arabic, Syriac, Samaritan, Ethiopic, Babylonian, Coptic, Egyptian Hieroglyph, and Esperanto. By the end of his teaching career, he had added Chinese, Japanese, and Russian to the list.[5] In 1937 Alma honored him with the doctor of divinity degree, but his relationship with the school soured after that time. Brokenshire clashed with a new president of Alma, whom Brokenshire thought was misusing pension funds, and the president dismissed the linguist. In 1942 a new president reinstated him, but Brokenshire decided to pursue his teaching ministry elsewhere.

He came to Bob Jones College in 1943 and was appointed dean of the Graduate School of Religion. Brokenshire developed the College's graduate program by expanding the number of master's programs available, launched the Ph.D. program in 1943-44, and established the College's first seminary degree, the bachelor of divinity, in 1949. When BJC became BJU, he was the first dean of the School of Religion until 1950 when failing health made it necessary for him to step down.

When he arrived at Bob Jones College in 1943, Brokenshire was already a seasoned world traveler. He had studied in Europe and had traveled throughout the Middle East, visiting Algiers, Sicily, Greece, Turkey, Egypt, Syria, and the areas today encompassed by Israel, Jordan, and Lebanon.

Much of Brokenshire's lingering reputation comes from anecdotes about his idiosyncrasies. Around the Bob Jones campus he always traveled by bicycle, he collected keys for a hobby, and he loved to eat. It was widely reported that when students questioned him about a biblical topic, he would say, "Now, Mr. Smith, if you will go to the library and look under *R* for Rutherford, John H., and select his volume entitled, *Old Testament Interpretation Based on an Original Translation of the Book of Malachi,* and turn to chapter 5, page 173, and read until the second paragraph, I believe you will find your answer." Dr. Jones Sr. often introduced him to the student body by repeating such claims. It was also not uncommon before the chapel service for Dr. Jones Sr. to seek out Brokenshire and ask him for the precise meaning of a word or phrase from that day's Scripture text in the original Greek, Hebrew, or Aramaic.

Dr. Charles Brokenshire died on May 28, 1954, the day he turned in his second semester's final grades. Charles Brokenshire's knowledge of the sacred text gave him, not a sense of familiarity with, but an "awe for the character and person of God" that he communicated to his students. His expertise in language and his high standards of scholarship, honed at Princeton and Heidelberg as they were, had a deep and continuing impact at

Bob Jones College and Bob Jones University and on the students he trained.[6] A men's dormitory and the pulpit in the War Memorial Chapel were named in his honor.

John Floyd Collins, 1853-1932

J. Floyd Collins was born October 22, 1853, in Baldwin County, Alabama. When he was four, the family moved to Shubuta, Mississippi, where his father was an agent for the M & O Railroad. He attended school at the Academy for Boys at Pierce's Springs, Mississippi, where he received the foundation of a classical education. At sixteen, after the family moved to Jackson, Tennessee, he took up farming, learned some hard lessons of self-reliance, and, most importantly, was converted to Christianity. He became a member of the Methodist Church and began a lifelong pursuit of the "glorious adventure in spiritual discovery" and the "Victorious Life."[7] As a teen, Collins entered West Tennessee College, where he completed a classical education and came under the influence of a scholarly master teacher, Dr. Edmund L. Patton, from whom he studied Greek and Latin.

After completing college, Collins began teaching. While teaching in Thomasville, Alabama, he met and married his wife, Ruby Purcell, and they had four sons. During his fifty-year career, he taught or was school principal in twelve towns in Mississippi, Tennessee, and Alabama, including Fort Deposit, where he was principal of the high school which Fannie May Holmes attended.[8] J. Floyd Collins closed out his distinguished teaching career at Bob Jones College in Florida, which also conferred on him the honorary degree of doctor of literature.

Throughout his career, Collins taught Latin, Greek, and literature and was noted as an expert in southern literary history and literature; he was especially fond of the works of Sidney Lanier. Collins was a staunch defender of the "Lost Cause," a man of moral courage who was unyielding in the face of opposition, and was "frankly Southern in every fibre of his being, believing that the people of [the] Southland were God's last, best chance to build a worthy civilization in this Western World." He was a passionate speaker, a "radiant conversationalist" who "elevated conversation to an art," and he possessed "the very soul of chivalry and gallantry."[9] He wrote voluminously—as a news reporter he covered the revivals of Sam Jones—and wrote many articles on religious subjects, especially opposing Modernism, for the *Bob Jones Magazine* and Methodist religious publications. Collins had also made it a practice to memorize large portions of Scripture and was described as having "crystal sincerity," "unimpeachable character," and a "transparent soul."[10]

When he came to Bob Jones College at seventy-four years of age, he was named principal of the Academy and taught Latin and English in the "Preparatory Department," as well as handling the discipline of the boys in the military school. He helped establish the Bob Jones College Library and donated his extensive personal library to the College. Many of the students considered him to be the "perfect old southern colonel type."[11] Bob Jones Jr. described him as a "great cultural blessing by his example and by his life and by the broadness of his own culture to the students."[12] After J. Floyd Collins completed the 1931 school year in June, he fell ill and moved to Montgomery, Alabama, where he died on September 15, 1932.[13] A building at Bob Jones Academy is now named in honor of his service as the school's first principal.

James D. Edwards, 1914-81

Dr. Jones Sr. called him "Unc" because James Edwards had a nephew one year older than himself who attended Bob Jones College at the same time as Edwards did. His wife and friends called him "Jimmie D." Thousands of students who faced him at Discipline Committee, however, simply called him "Sir."

James D. Edwards was born in Eclectic, Alabama, on November 5, 1914, into a godly Methodist family. About 1920, James D., as his family called him, attended an evangelistic campaign at which Bob Jones Sr. preached, and the boy was converted. At daily family devotions his father would pray for Bob Jones, and when Bob Jones College began in 1927 he would pray simply for "the College." His father also purchased Bob Jones College Development Bonds which were later cashed in to pay for James's education.

There was no question as to which college he would attend—Bob Jones College was it. After finishing high school in 1932, he entered BJC at College Point, Florida, as a Bible major with a history minor. As a student, he held many offices, including president of the student body, and he was a monitor in the boys' dormitory. After James graduated at the age of twenty-one, Dr. Jones Sr. asked him to stay on at the school to become dean of men and teach U.S. history, a subject he taught for twenty-five years. Edwards received his M.A. degree in history from the University of Michigan, and the honorary doctor of laws was conferred on him in 1952 by Northwestern Schools in Minneapolis, Minnesota.

While a student at Bob Jones College, he met Elizabeth Reynolds, who was a speech major and a gifted actress. After a two-year courtship, they were married in 1939. The couple later had two children, James D. Jr. and Carolyn. A campus personality in her own right, Mrs. Edwards also earned an M.A. degree in speech from the University of Michigan and was a featured performer with the Classic Players and in the films *Wine of Morning, Flame in the Wind,* and *Sheffey.*

Dean Edwards had a dry sense of humor, which he often put to use in his classes. He would tell his classes that if "I put you to sleep, then I have the privilege of waking you up."[14] After telling his classes that "the only notes you take in this class will be history notes," he noticed a girl writing a post card. When she finished, he asked for the card and read part of it to the class. "How is your big toe?" it read. Several years later at graduation, as the girl passed Dean Edwards on the stage after receiving her diploma, he whispered to her, "How is your mother's big toe?"[15]

After announcing the Bible Conference attendance policy to the faculty, he once related the story of a faculty member from earlier days who decided to slip away from campus, miss the services, and go fishing. With a twinkle in his eye, the dean always closed the story by saying, "and he is still fishing." Bob Jones III related that Dr. Edwards's favorite story about himself had to do with a late-night call he once received from the inebriated father of a student.

"Hello, is this the do?"

"No, this is the dean."

"Dean who?"

"Dean Edwards."

"I want the do."

"I don't know the do, but this is the dean."

"Well, get me the do."

"How do I get the do when I don't know the do? I am the dean, and I'll be glad to help you."

"I don't want the dean, I want the do. Only the do can help me."

"Well, you'll have to try another number if you want the do."

"Thank you very much. I will. Goodbye."

Minutes after he returned to bed, the man called again and the conversation was repeated.

A trusted, loyal friend of Dr. Jones Jr., he held many administrative positions: dean of men, dean of the College, and dean of students. In 1953 he was appointed dean of administration. In addition, he was chairman of the Discipline Committee for forty years, head of the Scholarship Committee, and chairman of the Administrative Conference. He was also responsible for all required government reports on foreign students and veterans.

Dr. Edwards carried his responsibilities with patience and devotion, even though he suffered intense pain from rheumatoid arthritis, which also affected his mobility in his later years. He was universally respected by the faculty for his fairness, a quality he "prayed for the most," and he dealt with students and faculty alike with an even and reasonable hand. His burden of ministry was "to help the student" by not allowing him "to live a lie." His gaze and stoic manner caused many students to "come clean." To James D. Edwards, loyalty and dependability were a hallmark of godliness.

Following the dismissal of administrator Ted Mercer in 1953, Dr. Jones Sr. commissioned the new dean of administration by saying, "Dean Edwards, I charge you before God in the presence of these witnesses, to do your duty.

Rules in this school are made to be kept. Send home the students who won't obey. You owe that to this institution. You owe it to these young people. You owe it to God Almighty on Heaven's High Throne. You owe it to the cause of the Lord Jesus Christ."[16] Dean Edwards did his duty, with grace, dignity, and vigor, until his death on August 20, 1981.

Walter G. Fremont, 1924-

Walter Gilbert Fremont was born in Terre Haute, Indiana, to Christian parents on July 20, 1924. He was the second of five children. Walt's father was a highly principled, goal-oriented man, and although not even a high school graduate, he was nonetheless a well-educated man, achieving the position of educational director of the Standard Register Company. Walt's dad eventually became a professor at the University of Dayton, teaching there twenty years before retiring at age seventy-five, only to teach five more years in the Dayton, Ohio, public schools.

In his early years, Walt was sensitive to God and thought about spiritual things, but he did not know how to find God. Though he had been active in church all his life, he characterized himself as "religious and a church-going hypocrite."[17] He was born again as a sixteen year old, through the witness of his high school Boy Scout buddy, Bob Brown, and after this became active in a Dayton Bible study through which he made significant spiritual growth and became a fervent soulwinner. After graduating in 1942, he attended a Christian camp and dedicated his life to the Lord.

Walter never intended to go to college, planning rather to enter industry to become a tool designer and make money in real estate. After he had worked one year as a toolmaker at the National Cash Register Company, war intervened, and he was drafted into the army in 1943. The army assigned him to the Carnegie Technical Institute in Pittsburgh, Pennsylvania, for engineering training. After his training, he became an instructor, first with the Airborne Engineers and later with the Combat Engineers. He spent fourteen months in the Pipeline Engineers in charge of a mobile machine shop, following Patton across Europe. By the time of his discharge in 1946, he knew the Lord had called him to be a teacher and applied to Wheaton College for admission. Wheaton had chosen not to increase its enrollment to accommodate the large number of GIs seeking admission, so Fremont was turned away. He was accepted in the teacher training program at the University of Dayton, where his father taught psychology and time and motion study. At a Bible study he was introduced to Trudy Reed, a nursing student, and he arranged a date with her every day for one year. Walt proposed marriage during a New Year's Eve watch night service. During prayer, he asked her to marry him; she responded, "Yes!"; they kissed; and then they continued praying. Walt and Trudy were married in 1947. When they graduated in 1949, they were the first married couple to graduate together from the University of Dayton. That same fall he entered the University of Wisconsin and completed a master of science degree in curriculum development in 1950. Trudy earned her M.S. degree in nursing at the University of North Carolina nineteen years and three children later. Because Walt still had one year of GI benefits remaining, he decided to go to Bob Jones University because of its reputation for "instilling soul-winning fervor" into its students.[18]

Walt intended to enroll in BJU for only one year to study Bible. When the Fremonts arrived in Greenville, however, Walt was asked to teach educational psychology for the first semester. He agreed and took thirty hours of Bible training while teaching both semesters. Between 1950 and 1953, the Fremonts involved themselves in several extension ministries, including street preaching and work in a local children's home. Every Monday he sponsored a Young Life Club in a local high school, and every Thursday the Fremonts held a Bible study for teenagers in their home. He also taught Sunday school at a local church.

In 1951 he became a full-time member of the education faculty and was named dean of the School of Education in the summer of 1953. During his first year as dean, Fremont recognized his need for further education and enrolled for doctoral study at Pennsylvania State University. He completed his degree in 1961 and wrote his dissertation on the new field of Christian day schools.[19] His interest in Christian education had been stimulated some fourteen years earlier by Dr. Mark Fakkema in a correspondence course on the philosophy of Christian education. As a result of this course, Fremont became convinced of the need for Christian schools. As a doctoral student he had the opportunity to study the field in detail, and as dean of education he had the perfect platform from which to promote the Christian school movement, then in its germinal stages.

Under Dr. Fremont's leadership the School of Education's "meager offerings" became full-fledged professional programs in elementary and secondary education. He pioneered the development of BJU's graduate school in education; initiated the programs in individual subject areas, special education, and counseling; and developed the annual Principals' Recruitment Conference on the BJU campus in 1970.[20] Dr. Fremont was best known for teaching principles instead of just facts and for weaving Bible principles into the fabric of his teaching. He was an enthusiastic supporter of the Bob Jones University Press, and in 1976 he developed the Education Team to present in-service sessions for Christian school teachers.

In addition to his teaching, Walter Fremont was instrumental, with Ken Hay, in founding the Wilds Christian Camp and Conference Center in North Carolina, and he served on the board of directors of that organization for twenty-eight years. In addition, he served for twenty-six years on the executive committee of a Greenville-based mission board and helped start the Children's Gospel Club, serving on that board for thirty-three years. He and his wife have authored three books on family living, one on youth methods, and one in 1996 on Christian counseling. For twenty-six years the Fremonts traveled widely, giving weekend seminars on Christian family living.[21]

In 1986, members of the School of Education were saddened to learn that Dr. Fremont was suffering from amyotrophic lateral sclerosis (ALS, or Lou Gehrig's disease). He retired as dean in 1990 but continued to teach through 1991, although he was confined to a wheelchair. With his voice failing him, no longer could the students hear him shout at full voice, as he was prone to do, "How beautiful are the feet of them that preach the gospel of peace!" as he climbed atop the lecturer's desk, removed his shoes and socks, and displayed his wiggling toes. Nor could they hear him exult to a student, "Praise the Lord!" upon hearing of answers to prayer. Instead of anger or bitterness at his illness, the students saw his "positive faith attitude," that "I can do ALL THINGS through Christ who strengthens me."

Dwight L. Gustafson, 1930-

Inside Len's Fair Price Meats, tucked away on Seattle's Market Street, was a skinny little kid standing on a crate and grinding meat or sweeping or spreading new sawdust for his dad's meat market floor. No one who frequented the market would have then imagined that Dwight Gustafson would someday stand on a conductor's podium, in total command of a three-hundred-voice chorus and an eighty-piece orchestra.

Dwight Leonard Gustafson was born on April 20, 1930, in Seattle, Washington, the oldest of four children born to second-generation Swedish immigrant parents, Lennart and Rachel Gustafson. His father was a dynamic Christian who was totally committed to serving God. The family home was in Seattle, but the Gustafsons regularly went to the grounds of the Sammamish Bible Camp for special camp weeks. Finally, in 1947 the family sold their Seattle house and built one on the grounds of the camp. Len was extremely active in Christian work. He was chairman of their local church and of the Sammamish Bible Camp for many years; he helped organize the Seattle Christian Businessmen's Committee and often spent his weekends doing lay preaching at rescue missions, jails, and small area churches. The family would often accompany him to these meetings, and Dwight's mother would provide special music. Dwight would lead singing and sometimes sing solos before his father preached.

Dwight's mother was a pianist and a harpist and promoted music and art study among the four children. As a boy, Dwight took art lessons and studied violin with Rudy Peterson, the brother of gospel song writer John Peterson, at a local funeral parlor where Peterson worked. Those early lessons were often held in the parlor's "family room" behind the privacy lattice. Sometimes an occupied casket would even be in the room during his lessons. After several years of steady progress, he began taking lessons from the head of the string department at the University of Washington, who seemed to think the boy had talent.

As a lanky high schooler, "Gus" was deeply involved in music and art at Seattle's Queen Anne High School, where he took every art and music course that was offered. He sang in the choir and played violin in the school orchestra until he broke his collarbone twice within a year: once playing football with no shoulder pads and once when he fell in a locker room trying to escape from a towel fight. These injuries interrupted his violin study and redirected his interests toward art and design, which he developed to such a point that he became the cartoonist for the high school paper.

Dwight entered BJU as a freshman art major in 1948.[22] He auditioned and was selected to sing in the church choir and became immersed in the University's music program, singing with ensembles, in Vespers and in the operas, and traveling for the University on a summer music ensemble. He also worked on the stage crew painting scenery. In his sophomore year Dr. Jones Jr. asked him to make some sketches for *Cyrano de Bergerac,* and Dwight ended up designing the sets for the production. He also changed his major to voice and made rapid progress. In the church choir he met Gwen Adams, a beautiful soprano voice major. After a little more than a one-year courtship, they were married on their graduation day, May 28, 1952, in the lobby near Dr. Jones Sr.'s office. Dwight and Gwen remained at BJU for graduate school, and he earned the master of arts degree in sacred music in 1954. Sometime that spring, Dwight received a "call slip" to see Dr. Jones Jr. "The whole way to his office, I was trying to figure out what I had done wrong," he recalled. "I was flabbergasted when he asked me to become dean."[23]

After completing the master's degree, he assumed the position of acting dean of the School of Fine Arts in June 1954. At some point, about a year and a half later, the office manager announced to him that he was no longer "acting" dean and ordered new office stationery, which read, "Dwight Gustafson, Dean."

The new dean was responsible for a growing School of Fine Arts only a year after the Mercer affair, of supervising the work of his former teachers, and of learning the ropes of administration. The young Gustafson brought a much-needed stabilizing influence to the Fine Arts Department. "Gus," as Dr. Jones Jr. always called him, exuded confidence and poise, appreciating and building on the strengths of his faculty, even while knowing but not focusing on their quirks or weaknesses. He also brought to the office a familiarity with art, a knowledge of music, and a sense of stagecraft that allowed him to lead in all four divisions of the school from the beginning.

As a conductor his first big assignment was the opera *Aida* in 1955. In 1960 he was selected as one of ten young conductors to study conducting at the Aspen School of Music, and he was also selected as a participant in the

American Opera and Composers Forum, sponsored by the New York City Opera. After one summer's study at Florida State University in 1965, he was awarded a graduate fellowship for 1966 to study composition. He declared a minor in Renaissance art, studied voice, sang with the FSU opera, and was soloist with the FSU Choral Guild. He was selected as a participant in the FSU Conductors' Symposium in 1966, and he completed his doctor of music degree in composition in 1967. Dr. Gustafson is perhaps most widely known outside of Fundamentalist circles for his musical compositions.[24] He has written and arranged more than 160 works, including five film scores; two operas; and works for symphony orchestra, brass quintet, string quartet, soloists, and choir. His personal favorite work is *Three Psalms for Chorus and Orchestra* (1989), which contains settings of Psalm 100, Psalm 23, and Psalm 150.

As an administrator, "Dr. Gus" was greatly admired and highly respected. His talents as a symphonic conductor, opera conductor, composer, and teacher could easily have led him to try to develop a "group of dedicated disciples" to himself. He has, however, always deflected praise and focused credit for his talents on God, the Giver of all good things. After "getting his heart right with the Lord" as a sophomore in the University, he simply tried to step where God led him and tried to benefit the University, his place of calling. He said simply that "if lives have not been touched, then my work is a failure."

On August 24, 1993, Dwight Gustafson was honored by the faculty of the Divisions of Music, Speech, Art, and Cinema at a surprise banquet and celebration held on the stage of Rodeheaver Auditorium, where he had spent countless hours in rehearsals and performances. The event celebrated Gustafson's fortieth year as dean of the School of Fine Arts at Bob Jones University.[25]

Grace Haight, 1863-1955

"Miss H. is not much to look at but she is a fine character," Dr. J. Floyd Collins wrote Bob Jones Sr. "And she is a fighting fundamentalist. . . . She is all right "[26] "Fighting fundamentalist" is an apt description of this eccentric former missionary, author, poet, and prayer warrior. She was a "tiny little woman" who was noted for wearing her dresses to her ankles, high-button shoes, and a hat.

Grace Woodman Haight was born in Springfield, Massachusetts, on September 22, 1863, and lived in and attended school in Louisville, Kentucky. She graduated from the Louisville Female High School. Raised strictly in the Methodist Episcopal Church, South, Haight went to China in 1917 as a "missionary-helper" and was assigned to teach at Soochow Middle School No. 2, a Methodist school system that culminated in university-level training.[27] She was determined to serve God with her "WHOLE heart" and pledged herself "never [to] teach a lie" of Modernism."[28]

At Soochow, Haight became aware of division between the missionary-teachers over two doctrines: Creation and the virgin birth of Christ. When the school principal took an orthodox stand and the denominational hierarchy replaced him because of it, Haight realized how pernicious Modernism was. When the new school principal preached a sermon in which he explained the "divinity of Christ without believing in His Virgin Birth," she resigned, leaving the school after only two years. She then joined missionary friends at an independent mission work on the Nile River.

After several months in Egypt, she returned to the United States to work with Dr. R. A. Meek and edit the *Southern Methodist,* a Fundamentalist newsletter. When it ceased publication, Dr. J. Floyd Collins recommended her to Bob Jones Sr. who, in 1930, asked her to come to College Point to edit the *Fellowship News* and teach missions and hymnology courses. When Haight arrived at the College, she was sixty-six years of age but still full of fire. Once while she was leading her class in opening prayer, a knock came on the classroom door. She interrupted her prayer by saying, "Excuse me Lord; the Devil is at the door." To the amusement of everyone, she opened the door to Dr. Jones Sr., who had come to ask her a question. During one class, after a student asked her opinion of Cecil Rhodes, diamond magnate and imperialist, Haight turned her head, spat in the corner of the room, and said, "That's what I think of him. He ruined Africa for missionary activity."

As a writer, she took aim at Modernism, wrote doctrinal and devotional poetry, and researched the background of the great hymns. Eccentric in many ways, she would arise daily at 4 or 5 A.M., spread a map of the world on the floor, and pray specifically for missionaries she knew around the world. After her death in 1955, when preparing her body for burial, the undertakers discovered thick calluses on her knees, caused by years of praying.

The 1935 *Vintage* was dedicated to Grace Haight "for her staunch and uncompromising orthodoxy," calling her "that diminutive bundle of English Aristocracy and American Courage."[29] According to Dr. Jones Jr. she was "the most unusual woman I ever knew and one of the most godly."[30]

Eunice Hutto, 1904-47

Born in Ariton, Alabama, on December 18, 1904, Eunice Hutto possessed a brilliant, analytical mind. She entered the Women's College of Montgomery (later called Huntingdon College) at age sixteen and graduated at eighteen. She taught mathematics for five years in the public schools of Alabama and completed a master's degree in mathematics from the University of Alabama in 1929.

Hutto came to Bob Jones College in Florida in September 1928 and was appointed head of the Math Department in 1929. Two years later, she was appointed principal of the Academy and served in this capacity until 1936. Hutto was known as a strong, stubborn woman who would not compromise academic standards. Accordingly, she was appointed dean of the College in 1932, and at that time was the only female dean of a coeducational college in the country.

Hutto was assigned the responsibility of shaping up the somewhat disorganized academic programs of the College, and she worked at this aggressively. As dean, her traits of stubbornness, efficiency, precision, and strength enabled her to standardize the academic programs of the school, institute new programs, and gain acceptance of BJC course work by the University of Tennessee. Bob Jones Jr. recalled that because of her stubborn drive, the "work of the school really began to take shape."[31] In addition to the University of Alabama, she attended the University of California at Berkeley, the University of Michigan, and the University of Tennessee for further education in mathematics and in educational administration. She earned the doctor of pedagogy degree from Westminster College in 1939 and remained dean until her marriage to Jefferson Davis Morelock in September 1941. Following her marriage, she left the employment of the College for two years but was appointed to the Board of Trustees, serving on it from 1941 through 1947. After her return to teaching, she taught mathematics and supervised student teachers until her retirement in 1947. She died of leukemia on August 22, 1947, only eight months after the birth of her first son.[32]

Robert Kirthwood Johnson, 1910-71

R. K. Johnson was born in Lynchburg, Virginia, in 1910. His father died when R. K. was eight years old, and his mother placed him and his brother in the Odd Fellows Home, an orphanage in Lynchburg. His father had requested that the two boys be reared in the home because he knew their mother could not care for the family. The Odd Fellows Home provided schooling for the children, and "Lefty," as he was called, finished high school while living there. At the home, he worked in the automotive shop and was given charge of all the automotive equipment. Eventually, he did the purchasing of supplies for the home. He remained there until he was nineteen years of age.

In 1931 twenty-one-year-old Lefty arrived at Bob Jones College from Lynchburg, Virginia. The tall, handsome, auburn-haired young man soon became widely known on the campus and was a campus leader—an officer in his society, a member of the J Club, treasurer of student council, and president of the senior class. Even though he had majored in religion, he was made bookkeeper of the College in 1934, while still a student, and graduated from BJC in 1935. That fall he assumed the position of business manager. The next year he married Guye Ellenburg, a former Bob Jones College student from north Georgia, who had completed the one-year business course.[33] Lefty was appointed a member of the Executive Committee for

Expansion in 1946 and became the treasurer of the Board of Trustees, serving in this capacity until his death in 1971.[34]

Shortly after Johnson was appointed business manager, J. S. Mack, president of the G. C. Murphy Company and member of the BJC board, brought him to Pittsburgh, Pennsylvania, to receive training from Murphy accountants and to review the College's bookkeeping system. Mack also gave Johnson practical advice about buildings, grounds, and other institutional matters.

When the Greenville plant was being built in 1946-47, R. K. Johnson lived on the site in a trailer and supervised every aspect of construction. He was a hard-driving man, seemingly tireless, who was totally committed to the task at hand. It was not uncommon for him to travel all night by bus or car, transact business that day, travel again all night to Cleveland to complete the business, and return to Greenville by that same evening to check on progress at the campus. One report of a business trip to Texas, filed in 1962, demonstrated the dedication to the cause of the University which was characteristic of Johnson. He wrote that "it is hard to believe that so much can be accomplished in such a short time. I traveled all night to get to my office by 8:00 this morning, Tuesday, after being out of the office for only one day. . . . Even though I feel tired through and through, I feel so grateful for the opportunity that has been mine; and I feel so rewarded for the efforts put forth. I am thankful to God for letting me be a part of the greatest and most wonderful school in the world."[35]

Johnson was awarded the honorary degree doctor of laws from the Bible Institute of Los Angeles in 1957. He was president of the Alumni Association from 1954 to 1956, was active in numerous local, state, and national organizations, and was listed in *Who's Who in Commerce and Industry* and *Who's Who in the South and Southeast*.

His business sense was legendary among the Greenville business community. Lefty Johnson knew how to drive a hard deal. When negotiating for items for the campus, he would often say to the men involved something like, "That is a reasonable price. But this is God's school, can you do a little better?" and often they would. Sometimes they would even make a cash donation in addition. He never lost his enthusiasm for what God was doing on the campus and rejoiced daily in the miracles of provision, a subject about which he often spoke.

Virtually every business policy and system that the school had was devised by R. K. Johnson. He had a sense of duty and calling to the school which perhaps few other men have had. He was frugal, shrewd, and decisive. Because of his insistence on a "pay-as-you-go" policy, the school avoided many of the pitfalls that come with uncontrolled debt. His vision for Bob Jones University enabled the school to have the resources to survive the IRS tax settlement and still remain financially stable. Lefty Johnson never saw the final disposition of the case. He died of a heart attack on November 4, 1971, while vacationing in Acapulco, Mexico, with his wife.[36]

Beneth Peters Jones, 1937-

Beneth Peters was born in Albany, Oregon, and lived in Washington State until her early teens. When she was thirteen years of age, the family moved to Phoenix, Arizona, where she attended a public high school for two years. Beneth's father became very concerned about the influences within the high school and placed her in the Phoenix Christian High School for her remaining high school years. This school was one of only a handful of Christian schools in the country at the time, and though it was small, it offered courses in which she had an interest and in which she excelled. Beneth was a good student, and she did especially well in speech and music, although she today says she probably "took speech and choir to get out of phys. ed." Both of the high school teachers in these classes encouraged her to attend college—specifically, BJU—to refine her talents.

Beneth had never heard of BJU, but based on their recommendations she applied, was accepted, and found herself in the freshman class of 1955 with a major in interpretative speech. She was active on campus from the beginning and became a well-known campus personality, appearing often in Vespers and in other campus programs. Since her home was so far from the campus, the only way home at vacations was in a carload of other BJU students. Her freshman year she ended up driving home in a group which included Bob Jones III's best friend, Fletcher Anderson. After vacation ended and the students returned to campus, Fletcher went to Bob III and told him about a girl from out West, whom he ought to date. Beneth recalled that she knew there was a Bob III but "could not have cared less"—she was interested in someone else at the time. Fletcher's mention of Beneth piqued Bob's interest, and he started to watch for her on the campus.

In 1956 Beneth auditioned for a role in *Cyrano de Bergerac*. Both Katherine Stenholm, the play's director, and Bob III, playing the romantic role of Christian, agreed that she would be a perfect Roxane. Dr. Jones Jr. had the title role, and when he observed Bob and Beneth in rehearsals, he realized that "sparks were flying" and began to encourage the romance. In fact, when Beneth was considering sitting out a year of school to work, he saw her that summer at a West Coast BJU banquet and told her that she had better come back because Bob was getting interested in some other girls.

She returned, and Bob and Beneth were married in December 1959. Both graduated that next spring and immediately began graduate work together. In 1961 she completed her master of arts degree in speech and began teaching freshman speech and other classes, as well as directing Vespers and plays. In addition to directing, she has also played leading roles such as Katherine in *The Taming of the Shrew,* Ophelia and Gertrude in

Hamlet, Juliet in *Romeo and Juliet,* and Lady Macbeth, to list a few. She has also had major roles in Unusual Films productions, the largest of which was as the wife of Robert Sheffey.

Bob and Beneth Jones have three living children, Roxane, Bob IV, and Stephen. Their first child died shortly after birth, an event that has given Mrs. Jones the opportunity to counsel and encourage others who have gone through similar problems. She is a published author, currently with seven books to her credit,[37] and she records a syndicated radio commentary for Christian women, *Sunshine on the Soapsuds.* A woman of many talents and a woman of strong Christian character and conviction, she is a popular, visible, and active member of the BJU family. She travels extensively with her husband and is in great demand as a conference and seminar speaker.

Fannie May Holmes Jones, 1911-2000

The Holmes family lived in Fort Deposit, Alabama, a little town of about 1,200 people some thirty-five miles south of Montgomery. Born to Christian parents on February 5, 1911, Fannie May was one of ten children—five boys and five girls. Mr. Holmes, a godly man, made most of his living from harvesting pecans from his groves. He ruled his household with "an iron hand" but saw to it that all ten of his children received a thorough education. He was active in politics, and when Fannie May was about five, William Jennings Bryan visited their home and stayed the night.

The family's introduction to Bob Jones Sr. came a few years before, probably about 1908, when he held a revival in Fort Deposit. Mr. Holmes was active in the meetings, and as a result of Dr. Jones's ministry, the county called for a referendum and voted to go dry.[38]

Fannie May's education was in the public schools of Fort Deposit, where she was a good student. Because the name of Evangelist Bob Jones was so well known, and because the former principal of the Fort Deposit high school, J. Floyd Collins, was teaching at BJC, Mr. Holmes decided that all of his children who had not yet completed college would attend there. Fannie May entered BJC in September 1927 and met her future husband when she arrived on campus. As he told it, their first meeting was not pleasant. Fannie's sister had brought her to school, and fifteen-year-old Bob Jones Jr. was carrying luggage for the girls. When he came out to unload their car, Fannie's sister had just placed the boy in her memory. "I know that boy," she said. "He is a mean little kid. He used to ride the streetcar in his Starke uniform . . . and he was one of the boys who tried to flirt with all of the college girls from the women's college who rode the same streetcar. He used to stand on the back platform of the car and pull the trolley off the wire when it went around the curve." After this introduction, it took several years before Fannie May would pay much attention to Bob Jones Jr.[39]

Fannie May entered BJC and became a home economics major when that program was offered. When one of the faculty left the college in Fannie's senior year, she was asked to teach some of the lower-level home economics courses. After graduating in 1931, Dr. Jones Sr. asked her to remain on the faculty but told her she would need to earn a graduate degree. That summer, she attended Colorado State Teacher's College in Greeley, Colorado, and finished her M.S. degree in two summers and one quarter of study.[40] Shortly after finishing, Dr. Jones telegraphed and asked her to return to be dietician and to teach home economics courses. It was an offer she felt she could not refuse, and although shy, Miss Holmes was an effective, though reserved, teacher. In spite of her shyness, she accepted several roles in Shakespearean plays and sang solos in church, on Vespers, and at Bible Conference.

After several years of interest in her, and one year of dating, Bob Jones Jr. finally persuaded Fannie May to be his bride, and on June 1, 1938, they were married in the Margaret Mack Auditorium on the campus of Bob Jones College in Cleveland. After a short honeymoon in New York City, the new Mrs. Jones hit the road with her husband and helped him present the summer's itinerary of Curtain Calls. After Bob III was born, the family traveled for one summer with a BJC ensemble. When Jon was born, Mrs. Jones Jr. decided that traveling was too difficult and thereafter did not travel much.

In Greenville, Fannie May Holmes Jones was head of the Home Economics Department from 1947 to 1986. Never one to seek the spotlight, she tried to minister unseen from "behind the curtain" instead of "on the stage." Her daughter wrote that she "naturally prefers others and puts them before herself." To those on the campus she was always an example of selflessness, consistency, patience, and concern for others. This was especially evident to those who watched her care for Mrs. Jones Sr. in her declining years.[41]

Following Mrs. Jones Sr.'s death in 1989, Fannie May traveled occasionally with her husband but much preferred to remain in the background on the BJU campus. She remained strong and active in campus events through 1999. After a period of steady decline and the complications that accompany age, the last living graduate of the first four-year class of Bob Jones College died on October 31, 2000, and was laid to rest alongside her husband with whom she had shared the miracle of Bob Jones University.

Mary Gaston Stollenwerck Jones, 1888-1989

Mary Gaston Stollenwerck was born on a plantation near Uniontown, Alabama, on September 6, 1988, and a short time later moved with her parents to Mobile, where they lived until her father died shortly before her sixth birthday. Her mother's parents, the Siddonses, insisted that the family move back to Uniontown; and it was there that she grew up. The Siddonses were an "old-South" family of culture, education, and distinction; and Estelle Siddons Stollenwerck was no exception. Mary Gaston's mother radiated her cultured upbringing, and even though small in stature, she was full of grace, charm, and an indomitable character.

When Mary Gaston was a child, her mother attempted to teach her gentility and refinement. But Mary Gaston seemed to revel more in the activity of her brothers and was quick to defend them in neighborhood scraps. She was, in fact, known as "the little hellcat" of the community because of her antics.[42] She was often scolded for "unladylike" behavior, and her grandparents feared she "would never become a lady."[43] As a child, Mary Gaston was led to Christ by her grandmother. She desired to follow the Lord and do His will, but she also wished to enjoy life and attend the numerous parties to which she was invited.

As a young lady, living a good life, she began teaching a Sunday school class and studying her Bible; but she knew something was lacking. One summer as the community prepared for a revival with "young Bob Jones, the fiery evangelist," a boyfriend teased her about her life, saying, "Wait till Bob Jones gets here. He'll get you straightened out." She replied, "He won't affect me. You will see."[44] When the Bob Jones Revival Meeting arrived in Uniontown in 1907, she sang in the choir nightly and one night came under conviction, answered the altar call, and renewed her dedication to Christ. The evangelist had noticed her immediately during the first choir practice, and Dr. Bob Jones Sr. often said that "even to this day I can see Mary Gaston sitting there on the arm of the pulpit chair. She had all the culture and refinement that I lacked."[45]

She recalled that "the first time he ever saw me in his life, he told a friend, 'I'm going to marry that young lady if she'll have me.' The friend, who had come down to Alabama to work with him in the meeting, said, 'What are you talking about? You don't even know the young lady.' Robert said, 'No, but I'm going to know her.' He wrote me a letter that day in which he asked me if I would marry him. 'Don't open it now,' he said. 'Wait until after I'm gone.' All this happened in one day."[46]

Following a year's courtship, the refined and gracious Mary Gaston Stollenwerck and the rough-and-tumble twenty-four-year-old Bob Jones were married on June 17, 1908.

As the wife of an evangelist of growing reputation, Mary Gaston faced many situations for which her training and education had not prepared her. She possessed a quiet but determined spirit, however. An interest in people and an abiding love for her husband and his ministry enabled her to withstand the pressures, scrutiny, and attacks that eventually came her way. She traveled with her husband through much of his career; and when he began his years of union campaigns, Mary Gaston spoke to women's groups, taught them Bible lessons, led their prayer sessions, and in many other ways was an active participant in each campaign. She also was Bob Jones Sr.'s confidante and adviser.

When he began talking about founding a school, she took up the challenge and supported him as he did the impossible. When the Florida plant was being built, Mary Gaston became the on-site supervisor in the absence of her husband, making construction decisions and relaying her husband's instructions to the foremen. When the school moved to Tennessee, she and Bob Jones Jr. supervised the cleanup of the dilapidated Centenary College. In Greenville, Mary Gaston planned and directed much of the campus landscaping. She planted trees, bushes, and flower beds. She worked alongside of the faculty and staff to prepare the new plant for habitation and was an inspiration to them.

Mary Gaston was wise, disciplined, spiritually insightful, generous, "a canny businesswoman," and a keen judge of character. She also spoke her mind when necessary.[47] Her son wrote that "she and my father had what seemed to have been an ideal marriage for more than fifty-five years. She cheered him up, tried vainly to 'hold him down,' rarely complained; and, when he said God was leading him to do something, she always, whatever she felt about it, encouraged him."[48]

When Mary Gaston Stollenwerck Jones died at age one hundred on May 12, 1989, the era of the old-time evangelists died with her. Her legacy, however, lived on through the Chancellor, the President, and the hundreds of students to whom she had ministered.

John Ludwig, 1917-

John Ludwig, the supervisor of buildings and grounds from 1953 to 1977, was born in Michigan on December 26, 1917, of German immigrant parents. He was the youngest of nine children. John grew up on his parents' fruit farm where he learned how to work hard and how to fix almost anything. He trusted Christ as his Savior when he was a child and became active in his Michigan church as a musician—he led singing for services, played his horn, and sang in a men's quartet. He also took part in the radio ministry of his church. Ludwig went on to become the president of the local chapter of the Young People's Fellowship Club (YPFC), the youth organization founded by Bob Jones Sr.

In 1936 John Ludwig was selected to represent his local chapter of the YPFC at the national annual meeting, held during the Bible Conference at Bob Jones College in Cleveland, Tennessee. Up to then, he had given little thought to college. The conference stirred him greatly, but when he personally met Dr. Jones Sr. at the YPFC annual meeting, all doubt was dispelled—he would come to Bob Jones College. He returned to Michigan, tended an acre and a half of strawberries for two seasons, and saved his money to go to Cleveland. In 1938 John enrolled with a major in religion and a minor in English. He recalled that he "didn't have any money, but the Lord provided."[49] To pay his way through school, he worked on the yard crew and the maintenance crew and as the lighting technician on the stage crew. John also roomed with his future brother-in-law, who introduced him to his sister, Bea Comfort. After he graduated in 1943, Bea and John were married by Dr. Jones Sr. A few weeks after the wedding Dr. Jones simply asked, "John, how about helping us?"[50] The couple stayed, and in 1944 John became the head of maintenance and also worked on the Margaret Mack stage. When the school left Cleveland, Ludwig was responsible for loading the moving vans of furniture and equipment and getting them to Greenville, as well as moving the trailers and barracks units that followed.

In Greenville, Ludwig became Rodeheaver Auditorium stage manager for a time and also began work on a master's degree in church history. In 1953 he was appointed the physical plant manager (the title was eventually changed to superintendent of buildings and grounds). Bea became his secretary, and both served in this capacity until 1977, when John was appointed the supervisor of special projects. He retired in May of 1996.

Somewhere along the line he began arranging flowers for the sheer joy of it, and for more than forty years, John Ludwig weekly supplied fresh-cut flowers for the front of Rodeheaver Auditorium or the Founder's Memorial Amphitorium for church and Vespers, and for special occasions and weddings in the War Memorial Chapel.

His office in the maintenance complex contained a collection of choice items, all of which spoke to John Ludwig's character. One was a picture of Bob Jones Sr. as a twenty-one-year-old preacher, with the saying, "The door to the room of success swings on the hinges of opposition." There was a photo of Robert E. Lee, two blue pitchers from Cleveland's Dining Hall, a painting by one of his two daughters, and a German saying to remind him of his heritage, among other things. Truly a back hall light that glowed brightly for many years, John Ludwig remarked that his greatest satisfaction came from "seeing the students go out to preach the gospel. I know," he said, "that my work touches every life here."[51]

Marshall Neal, 1919-

Marshall Neal was born September 27, 1919, in Jackson, Mississippi, and was reared there as well. He was saved as a child and developed a fervent interest in serving the Lord as a result of contacts with several godly businessmen in Jackson. As a senior in high school, he dedicated himself to the gospel ministry and began planning for college. He took a job in a printing company in 1937 and worked there for three years before attending Bob Jones College as a religion major. When he arrived in 1940 as an older student, his maturity allowed him to appreciate the course work and gave him a desire to excel. Without doubt, his favorite courses were in Greek.

As a result of being delayed in attending college, Neal also was late in finding his life's partner. Anna Lloyd Pace, however, had also been somewhat delayed in finishing college. She had completed BJC's one-year business course and then had gone home to Chattanooga for three years to work. When she returned to Cleveland to complete her bachelor's degree, Marshall took note of her and decided that "she was worth pursuing."[52] They were married in 1945 and had a family of three boys. In 1945 he began teaching beginning Greek while taking courses leading to his master's degree. He earned a Ph.D. in religion in 1947, taking much of his course work from Dr. Charles Brokenshire.

In 1955 Neal was appointed registrar, a position he held until 1964, when he became the dean of the School of Religion. In the 1960s he led instructional tours to the Middle East, tracing the apostle Paul's journeys, and for several summers he also taught theology and Bible courses at pastors' schools in Poland and South Africa. Dr. Neal also pursued a ministry of writing. He spent many years as an editor of and contributor to *Biblical Viewpoint,* the journal of the School of Religion, and had his book *Seven Churches: God's Revelation to the Church Today* published by BJU Press in 1977.[53] He served as dean until his retirement from administration in 1978. He continued teaching graduate courses in New Testament Greek and theology, passing on Brokenshire's Princeton heritage of scholarship to new generations of Bible students until his retirement in 1994.

Edward Miran Panosian, 1930-

"And this has been our home, and calling, and ministry, and joy, and privilege, and mission, and delight, and burden"—thus, the historian, actor, author, and lecturer described his more than forty years' tenure at Bob Jones University.[54]

Edward Panosian was born in Elmira, New York, on August 19, 1930, to Armenian immigrant parents. Trying to escape the atrocities of Muslim Turks, his mother, of the Armenian Evangelical Church, had arrived in America shortly after World War I. His father, also a converted man of the Armenian Evangelical Church, had come over before the war, served in the American army, and after discharge from the service took a room at a boarding house managed by his future mother-in-law. The Panosians were married in 1920 and Ed's father established a shoe repair business in Elmira, that eventually grew into a small retail shoe chain.

Edward was educated in the public schools of Elmira and in the Sunday school of the Christian and Missionary Alliance Church in town. As a boy, he had been reared to be obedient, respectful, and honest; he recalled that he was not a gross sinner or a rebel. He was a leader among the church youth group, but he was not yet a believer—he "had never been convicted of heart" of his need of a personal Savior.[55]

On August 15, 1945, at a youth camp in southern New York State, Ed finally came to "know that I did not know" Christ, and he came to the Savior.

Describing his early life, Ed said that "growing up meant living in a godly family, assisting in the family business, having a minimum of social opportunities. . . . We were not affluent," he recalled. "We lived very simply. Dad had worked all his life and didn't know how to do anything else but work, and we learned integrity, and thrift, and obedience, and a godly example."[56]

Following high school, he chose to attend Bob Jones University because of the change and growth he observed in one of the church girls who attended the school. When Ed was a homesick freshman in 1948, Dr. Jones Sr. preached on the text "No man, having put his hand to the plow, and looking back, is fit for the kingdom of God" (Luke 9:62). All Ed could hear that night was "the problem with you is you're not fit. . . . not fit. . . . not fit." He felt as if the evangelist were speaking directly to him, but he determined at that time to be fit. He said, "Lord, I'm Yours. Do with me what You want."

He majored in religion and also took a large number of hours in history, but had no clear sense of calling. Ed was a brilliant student and a respected campus leader. As a senior he was accepted into the graduate program for a master's degree in church history, which he completed in 1954. During commencement week that year, Charles Brokenshire, his mentor, major professor, and the man he called "a legend" and "a noble scholar and a godly and good man" was found dead in his apartment. Suddenly the school was without a church history teacher, and since Ed Panosian had more training in the area than anyone else, he was asked to assume the position as well as to teach Reformation History the next fall.

That summer, Ed Panosian and Betty Jean Snyder, a young Pennsylvanian and speech major whom he had met in Educational Psychology class when he was a sophomore, were married. Their family soon consisted of three children—two boys and one girl.

In 1954 he began a doctoral program in church history by studying in the summers at Tulane University, the University of Chicago, Union Theological Seminary, and Columbia University, as well as taking work at BJU during the school years. In this way Panosian was able to study with the renowned American church historians of the era, including such scholars as Kenneth Scott Latourette and Sidney Mead. In 1959 he completed the Ph.D. in church history at Bob Jones University, with a dissertation on Luther's doctrine of scriptural authority.

As a graduate assistant, Panosian was suddenly thrown into a situation for which he had no direct preparation—he had to lecture to three classes of History of Civilization, three days a week. (GAs lectured to the freshman-level courses in those days.) When the system was later redesigned, he became *the* history lecturer for all History of Civilization students—an enlightening but sometimes fearsome experience for the freshmen who sat under his gaze and within sound of his commanding, regal voice—a voice so powerful that it was often used as the voice of God or one of the prophets in Vespers productions.

On the campus, Edward Panosian cut a tall and dignified figure, even on his bicycle, and he was revered by the students as much for his stage and film appearances as for his scholarship. His stage career came almost accidentally—the young man who was to have a major role in a play was expelled only a few weeks before the production. Since the young man's costume had already been made, the director decided to simply fill the role with whomever the costume fit. Since that time, Panosian has joked that "by an act of God, He had to expel a student whose costume fit me. So it was not my talent but my physique that got me my first real part."[57] Since that 1954 appearance, he has played numerous Shakespearean roles, including the tragic Moor in *Othello,* Prospero and the misshapen Caliban in *The Tempest,* Hotspur in *Henry IV,* and Petruchio to his wife's Kate in *The Taming of the Shrew,* among others. On film he began as a walk-on in *Wine of Morning,* progressed to an Italian waiter in *Miracle,* and eventually ended up with major roles in *Flame in the Wind, Beyond the Night,* and *The Printing.* In 1984 he developed seven dramatic historical monologues on different reformers and figures from church history, which he has presented in Russia and at churches in the United States and in Northern Ireland. He is a man of knowledge and understanding, but of humility also. His life, he said, was not all mapped out in his youth's mind years ago. He gave his life "to the Lord and didn't know what that meant or what that would mean." However, after more than forty years of teaching, Dr. Panosian said, "[the] lines [have] fallen unto me in pleasant places, and I am grateful, and I am rich in blessings."[58]

Monroe (Monk) Parker, 1909-94

Monroe Parker was born June 23, 1909, in Thomasville, Georgia, lived in Texas during his childhood, and moved to Alabama as a teenager. He was a strong, determined athlete who spent much of his time playing football or baseball—and fighting or recovering from fights. In 1926 he attended Birmingham Southern College on a football scholarship. Though potentially a brilliant student, he spent little of his time studying or working, choosing rather to party, carouse, and try to become a "big man on campus."

Like many other students at this time, Parker had grown up as a member of the Methodist Church and had taught Sunday school, but had never been converted by faith in Christ. When he got to college, he dropped the pretense of religion and became a skeptic. After hearing Bob Shuler preach during the summer of 1928, he came under the burden of his sin and trusted Christ as his Savior.

He transferred to Bob Jones College that fall, played football and baseball for the Swamp Angels, and graduated in 1931 as a classmate of Bob Jones Jr. with a B.A. degree in Bible. That summer Dr. Jones Sr. asked him to become a summer evangelist, preach daily on a new radio station in

Anniston, Alabama, and to hold other meetings for the College. This was the beginning of a long association with the school. In 1937, after Parker had spent several years as an evangelist and director of Bob Jones Gospel Centers in several communities, Dr. Jones Sr. invited him to become director of Religious Activities and join the faculty of the Bible Department. Parker became widely sought for evangelistic campaigns during his years at the College, and he traveled widely in evangelism between school terms. Parker received both his M.A. and Ph.D. degrees at Bob Jones College after studying under Charles Brokenshire.

Dr. Parker's first wife, Harriette, was a gifted organist and composer who was also head of the Music Department of the College. Shortly before her death in a tragic auto accident in 1946, she composed the music for the Bob Jones University Hymn.

When the school moved to Greenville, Dr. Parker took the position of assistant to the President but resigned in 1949, feeling compelled to enter full-time evangelism. After eight years in evangelism, Dr. Parker was appointed president of Pillsbury Baptist Bible College, a position he held until 1965. In 1969 he became general director of Baptist World Mission, located in Decatur, Alabama.

From 1933 until his death in 1994, Dr. Monroe Parker served on the BJU Board of Trustees; he was a member of the Executive Committee from 1957 until 1994; and he was a loyal and trusted friend of Dr. Jones Jr.[59]

Hazel Claire Riley, 1912-82

"Give her of the fruit of her hands; and let her own works praise her in the gates," said the wise man in Proverbs. Those who knew her well would agree that this verse exemplified the life of Hazel Claire Riley.

Born March 15, 1912, in Castleberry, Alabama, to a merchant and his wife, Hazel, as a child, helped her mother run a small tearoom and helped on the family's small farm. Through these experiences she learned to work hard, and she also developed a gracious spirit. Hazel made a good record in school, and her high school teachers encouraged her to go on to college. She was accepted to attend Florida State University and shipped off her personal belongings to Tallahassee during the summer of 1929. Two years earlier, Dr. Jones Sr. had held a revival campaign in a town close to her home, and he had told about his new school. The Rileys listened attentively but said little. In 1929, at breakfast the morning Hazel was to leave for FSU, her mother remarked that she had been restless all night "thinking about that college Dr. Jones is starting." She wondered aloud "if there [were] any more openings." Mrs. Riley persuaded her husband to telephone the school and inquire, and within minutes, Dr. Jones Sr. had sold them on sending Hazel to school at College Point.

At Bob Jones College, Hazel majored in speech, participated often in Vespers, and was a leader in her society, Sigma Kappa Rho. She also served in the Baptist Young People's Union and as a class officer. After her graduation in 1933, she signed a contract to work at an Alabama orphanage, but shortly after she signed the contract, the orphanage merged with another, and she was told that her services would not be needed.

Meanwhile, Bob Jones College had moved to Cleveland, Tennessee, and had grown in size. Hazel contacted the school, and soon she was at work as the checkout desk hostess; she also assisted in the dormitories. The next year she worked as a Dining Common hostess, and in 1935 she became an assistant to the dean of women. She was appointed dean of women in 1941, the position she held until her retirement in 1977. As dean of women, Miss Riley devised the system of prayer captains and assistant prayer captains in the dormitories and helped in designing the hall monitors' duties.[60]

For many years, Hazel Riley was pursued by a suitor, an Anglican Orthodox minister, who tried to persuade her to marry him. Because of her deep sense of calling to the ministry as dean of women, she refused marriage, however. She was a mainstay of Bob Jones University, both feared and respected. She projected an image of gentility and deep inner strength, but her sense of humor could shine, as when she appeared for "white glove inspection" in the women's dormitories wearing white dress gloves.[61]

She relinquished her duties as dean of women to Luena Barker in June of 1977. After several years of failing health, Hazel Claire Riley died on April 15, 1982.

Guenter Edward Salter, 1928-

Guenter Salter was born on November 22, 1928, in Bochum, Westphalia, Germany. The third of five children, he was born into the strictly disciplined home of a Baptist pastor and educated in a Lutheran elementary school. When he was ten years of age, Guenter returned home from school with an application form for Hitler Youth membership. His father refused to sign it, tore it up, and forbade his son to associate with "that band of godless creatures."[62] The elder Salter had already suffered at the hands of the Gestapo, who had subjected him to all-night interrogations to explain his beliefs, his preaching, and his views on the government. They also required him to obtain a license to preach.

In spite of not having submitted an application, Guenter was inducted into the Hitler Youth with his entire elementary school class, and he was required to attend party rallies, many of which were purposely held on Sundays to keep the children from attending church. Pastor Salter tried to keep his son from the rallies, often without success.

When war broke out, Guenter was only ten years old. By the time he was fourteen, his hometown and neighboring cities, the industrial heart of

Germany, were being bombed continually by the Allied air forces. The government removed all the children from Bochum and placed them in foster homes in rural eastern Germany. At age fifteen, he and all other boys his age were drafted into the German army and trained to man antiaircraft guns. Shortly after the Allied troops entered Germany, Guenter found himself in ground combat and, for the first time, came under intense strafing attacks and saw his first war casualty—a father of four who had not been able to dive into his foxhole.

On April 12, 1945, Guenter was ordered to stand guard duty at a crossroads. When his shift ended shortly after dusk, he left the post to return to the barracks but realized that he had forgotten something. Handing his rifle to his sergeant, he ran back to the crossroads only to face six American Sherman tanks that had rumbled into position. He dove to the ground, lay paralyzed with fear as the tanks opened fire, and was taken prisoner. The next day he learned that his entire unit had been annihilated in the attack on the barracks.

After more than ten months in French and American POW camps, Salter was released and simply walked through the wintry days until he reached his home, which had been totally destroyed. Following the war, Guenter completed Gymnasium studies and then studied international commerce and banking as a banking apprentice. At age eighteen, after realizing the folly of his long-held belief that he could "ride to heaven on the coattails" of his father, he accepted Christ as Savior.

In 1951 Guenter emigrated to the United States, settled in Detroit with members of the Salter family who had emigrated before the war, and began working in a tool and die shop. In Detroit he met his future wife, Johanna Kilgus, at the local German-English church, and they were engaged to be married in September 1952. Just weeks before the wedding day, however, he received a form letter from President Truman and a draft notice from the army, telling him to report for active duty in the Korean War. "That's great!" he said. "Hitler never wrote me, and here I've been in the States for only a year and the President of the United States writes to me!"[63] In order to qualify for citizenship, he decided not to claim alien status and thereby gain an exemption, but instead went to basic training. On December 20, 1952, he and Johanna were married, and in February 1953 he set sail for Korea. While on a stopover in Japan, he was one of twenty men selected from the four thousand on board to serve as a military policeman at a base in Yokohama. He said, "Because I went [to Japan] under the edict of the United States Army, I decided I was going to have a miserable time, and most of the time, I did."[64]

After the Korean War ended, he returned to Detroit, joined the international division of Chrysler Corporation, and rose in the ranks until he was assigned to be manager of the Rotterdam, Holland, office. Finding the work unfulfilling, he returned to Detroit, took a position with a cotton exporter, and again began to climb that corporate ladder. As a Christian, however, he began to question the rewards of materialism—which he characterized as the quest for having "better stereo equipment in the basement"—and began to ponder doing something that would count for eternity. He began thinking about a career in college teaching and discussed this new avenue of service with his wife.

Salter entered Wayne State University for his B.A. degree and graduated in 1964, after two and one-half years of study. Shortly after graduation, he visited Bob Jones University and "fell in love with the place."[65] At that time, Dr. Edwards asked him to teach German, but health problems stood in the way. In 1962 he had been diagnosed with bladder cancer and had undergone treatment. Within seven months of his diagnosis, he had three operations and one life-threatening infection. His daughter remembered that on the day of the third cancer operation, he was sitting in his hospital bed, an intravenous tube in his left arm, writing a paper for school with his right hand.[66] After five more cancer operations, the disease was conquered and he was clear of problems after 1972.

In 1967 Salter earned an M.A. degree in German literature, and in January 1967, the Salter family finally found themselves headed for South Carolina. In September of 1967 he was asked to chair the Modern Language Department, and in 1969 he left for Vanderbilt University to complete the residency requirements for the Ph.D. in literature and philosophy. While completing his Ph.D. degree, he also earned a second master's degree in comparative literature.

Dr. Salter taught undergraduate German literature courses and graduate philosophy courses, as well as Freshman Orientation. As a teacher, he is widely respected and has a fearsome reputation. He is no-nonsense, allows few exceptions, and does not tolerate excuse-making. Yet, under the stern German manner is a heart to minister to students and motivate them to strive to overcome obstacles and be excellent for their Savior.

In 1971 he became the dean of the College of Arts and Science, administrating the eleven majors then offered. Under his extraordinary leadership, the college grew to include a total of thirty-one majors, and the number of faculty was greatly expanded.[67]

Philip Daniel Smith, 1933-

Philip Smith was born into a Christian family in Dayton, Ohio, on December 25, 1933. Both of his parents were active in the local church, serving as Sunday school teachers and choir members, and his father served as a deacon. It seemed to him that every time the church doors were open, he was there. He did not resent the religious training he received as a child, but he did not understand it. When he was twelve years of age, however, he and his brother attended a youth meeting at which a missionary spoke.

During the meeting both boys were convicted of their sin, and that night both accepted Christ as Savior. Phil became active in the church, teaching Sunday school, leading singing, and working with the youth group. At a Youth For Christ meeting on New Year's Day 1949, he dedicated his life to full-time Christian service.

As a high school student, he worked in the school library and in the office of the assistant principal and decided to become a social studies teacher. Although he wanted to attend a local college in 1951, his parents persuaded him to attend Bob Jones University for at least one year. Philip stayed two years. He enjoyed campus life and his Epsilon Zeta Chi brothers and was blessed by the chapel messages preached by Dr. Jones Sr., but he convinced himself that BJU really did not offer the program of study that he wanted. Accordingly, he transferred to the University of Dayton in 1953. He also began dating Marilyn Brown, a girl from his church whom he had known all his life. They married on November 25 that same year.

During that junior year at Dayton, he began to realize the impact that BJU and the Founder had had on his life, and he missed the fellowship and Christian camaraderie that the school offered. He decided to return to Greenville and complete his degree as a married student. He graduated with a bachelor of science in secondary education (cum laude) and hoped to stay at the school and teach. Three things stood in his way, however: no teaching positions were open, he did not have a graduate degree, and BJU had no graduate programs in education. In 1956 he attended Miami (Ohio) University on a graduate assistantship and completed his master's degree in educational administration. While at Miami, he visited with Dr. Jones Jr. after a revival service and asked about returning to BJU to teach. Dr. Jones told him that if he was hired, he would have to be willing to do whatever the school asked, whether teaching in the Education or Social Studies Department or working in a staff position. Smith recalls that "if I was willing to come on that basis, he thought they might have a place for me."

Philip Smith returned and was the first Bob Jones University School of Education graduate to return to the institution to teach in the School of Education. Three years later, Walter Fremont, dean of the School of Education, encouraged Smith to consider doctoral work. That summer, 1959, he began doctoral study at the University of Colorado, and following a research offer from Pennsylvania State University, he transferred there to complete his degree. In 1961 Smith, on a leave of absence, visited BJU; during this visit, the dean of administration, Dr. Edwards, asked him to return to the school and become the dean of the College of Arts and Sciences. The twenty-seven-year-old was stunned by the offer, but felt that God had prepared him to assume the responsibility.

He was dean from 1961 through 1965, during which time he implemented the lecture/tutorial class organization for freshman history and English courses. In 1965 he was appointed registrar, the position he held until 1981, when he was appointed provost of the University. As provost, he superintended all areas of academic life at the institution, including the faculty, the curriculum, and all educationally related departments. He oversaw the educational work of Bob Jones Elementary School, Junior High, and Academy; the BJU Press; and the Center for Educational Technology. In addition, he was chairman of the Administrative Conference and the University Scholarship Committee and sat on numerous other University committees.

Philip's father, a factory worker with an eighth-grade education, stressed one thing in life: faithfulness to one's place of service. Philip Smith demonstrated that faithfulness and was willing to be a "back hall light." He realized that "God demands one's soul, one's life, and one's very all."[68]

Gilbert Ralph Stenholm, 1915-89

Evanston, Illinois, on the shores of Lake Michigan, was the home of Gilbert Stenholm. Born into a family of Swedish immigrants on February 15, 1915, Gilbert was saved as a child in the Swedish Covenant Church his family attended in Evanston. He began his career at Bob Jones College in Cleveland, Tennessee, as a freshman in 1934, majoring in religion. During his undergraduate years, he was a well-known and popular campus leader, class and society officer, and an outstanding athlete. He received his B.A. degree in 1938, after which he joined the dean of men's staff while working on his M.A. in Bible. In 1941 he married Katherine Corne and furthered his education with postgraduate studies at Northwestern University in Evanston, Illinois, and North Park Theological Seminary in North Park, Illinois, where some of his courses were taught in Swedish. Gilbert Stenholm received his Ph.D. from Bob Jones College in 1947.

At BJC, Stenholm assisted Dr. Jones Sr. with the Ministerial ("Preacher Boys") Class, teaching it when the Founder was away. During the war years, he taught everything from beginning Greek to typing and physical education classes. During the late 1940s and early 1950s, Stenholm, along with Bob Jones Jr. and Monroe Parker, was widely sought as a Youth For Christ speaker and as an evangelist. He maintained his ministry in evangelism for many years, holding his final meeting only weeks before his death. If in a Swedish church, he would sometimes preach in Swedish, and often sang as a solo "Tryggare Kan Ingen Vara" ("Children of the Heavenly Father") for special music.

In 1951 he was appointed dean of the School of Religion and director of Religious Activities, the positions he held until 1965, when he became director of Extension and Ministerial Training. In 1980 Stenholm retired from administration and traveled as a staff evangelist for the school until shortly before his death on December 12, 1989.

Gilbert Stenholm was a keen observer of the times and, as a hobby, kept a detailed diary of events, people, and ideas. His diaries stretch back to his first day on the Bob Jones College campus. They record everything from the names of chapel speakers and their sermon texts to the Big Ten football scores; they include everything from his personal teaching assignments and salary to Bob Jones Sr.'s travel schedule. Dr. Stenholm was noted for his precise recall of preachers, churches, organizations, and personalities and was instrumental in connecting hundreds of pastors and churches. He was also highly influential in establishing the South Carolina Republican Party, worked diligently in its organization, was chairman of the Greenville County Republican Party, and at times was a lone voice for conservatism among the party leadership.

Gilbert Stenholm loved to converse over a cup of "Swedish oil" (coffee) about his gifted wife and successful son, Gil Jr., but especially he loved to talk about his Preacher Boys and the Lord. In class, he enjoyed hearing them sing "We never will give in while souls are lost in sin. Souls for Jesus is our battle cry." One former student described him by saying, "He knew more about preaching and preachers and Fundamentalism" than any man except Bob Jones Sr. He poured his life into preachers' lives. He was an example of a soulwinner, and he was faithful.

Katherine Corne Stenholm, 1917-

Katherine Corne was born in Hendersonville, North Carolina, on June 19, 1917. "Kitty" was not a strong child—she was often sick, and because of illness she "never finished a single grade of grammar school." Each year the school superintendent would give her a test and allow her to pass to the next grade.[69] She attended Hendersonville High School and worked for the local newspaper as a movie reviewer to earn money for the family. She also directed local pageants and taught a ladies' Bible class at her church. In 1935, when Kitty was a senior in high school, she won a four-year scholarship to Wellesley College and fully intended to attend there until a Norman Greenway revival meeting changed her mind. While preaching, Greenway, a Canadian evangelist, made one statement that hit home with both Mrs. Corne and Kitty—that a Christian young person should attend a Christian college. At an after-service social, Kitty cornered the evangelist, asked him if he meant what he had said, and asked what school he would recommend. Though Greenway had never been to Bob Jones College and knew of it only through observing BJC students and graduates, he recommended the school to her.

The next day, while working at the Hendersonville Chamber of Commerce, she jotted a post card to the College and asked for information. Four days later, Mr. Loren Jones, Bob Jones Sr.'s song leader, arrived in Hendersonville to talk to her about coming to the College. She was familiar with only two Christian schools—Wheaton and Moody Bible Institute—but was put off by what she saw as the intellectual snobbishness of the Wheaton students and by the personal dowdiness of the Moody students. She had never heard of Bob Jones College before, but as she talked with Loren Jones and paged through the yearbook, the cultured view of the Christian life that she saw attracted her, as did the section devoted to the Classic Players and Shakespeare.

Because of the depression, the Corne family struggled financially. Katherine's father had been a real estate developer but during the depression was often without the means to care for the family. In fact, Katherine's earnings from the newspaper and the chamber sometimes supported the entire family. Even with the scholarship from Wellesley, she had no money for college. It appeared that even if she wished to go to BJC, it would be impossible. Jones was able to extract a pledge from Katherine's aunt Charlotte to pay $29.50 a month toward her expenses if Kitty would work off the remaining $10. Days later, in spite of tremendous pressure from well-meaning townspeople and church people who tried to persuade her to use her scholarship to Wellesley, Katherine Corne, her mother, and her Aunt Charlotte were on the train from Hendersonville to Cleveland, Tennessee. They agreed to look the place over and if "it is not all right, we'll know it when we get there. We'll just bring her back home on the train," they said.[70] They arrived at the College and attended chapel. After chapel, Aunt Charlotte looked at Mrs. Corne and said, "Well, Lulu, if we are going to make that two o'clock train, we better get us together and get down there." Katherine stayed. She met her future husband, Gilbert Stenholm, the very next morning at breakfast, and they were married six years later on June 4, 1941.

Katherine majored in speech and was an outstanding student, enjoying every aspect of life at Bob Jones. She assisted Bob Jones Jr. in directing *As You Like It* during her sophomore year and developed an interest in directing. She played in *King Lear* the next year, and in her senior year she was the private student of Bob Jones Jr. and directed Vespers. After she graduated in 1939, she went to Northwestern University for graduate work, where she studied with the renowned speech teachers Ralph Dennis, Alvina Krouse, and C. C. Cunningham. Katherine attended Northwestern for eleven straight summers, completing her M.A. in speech and all the requirements for a Ph.D. in interpretative speech with the exception of the foreign language require- ments. She even wrote a dissertation on the quantitative and qualitative aspects of rhythm in Stephen Vincent Benét's poetry. During the intervening years at BJC, she taught speech courses, gave private speech lessons, directed numerous plays and Vespers, and took major roles in many campus Shakespearean productions. Her favorite role was Ophelia in *Hamlet.* Yet when Dr. Jones Jr. approached her in 1950 about starting the University's film studio, she dropped her doctoral work and went to the University of Southern California to enter the film school. Thus she became one of only a handful of women in the United States to direct feature films and perhaps the first Christian woman ever to do so.

Her film career was indeed notable. She was keynote speaker at the Cannes Film Festival in Cannes, France, and addressed the Society of Motion Picture and Television Engineers and the International Congress of Motion Picture and Television Schools in Paris. She also published many articles in film trade and professional periodicals. Under her direction, Unusual Films produced and released seventy-two cinema efforts, including sermon films, religious documentaries, promotional films, multi-image presentations, client films, and the celebrated feature-length films *Wine of Morning, Red Runs the River, Flame in the Wind, Sheffey,* and *Beyond the Night.* The last film on which she worked was *The Printing.* While in the Soviet Union taking still photos and scenic footage, she suffered a mild stroke from which she eventually recovered. In 1986 she retired as director of Unusual Films and turned the studio over to one of her former students, Tim Rogers. After her recovery, she resumed doing what she believed she "did best of all—teaching" film directing.

Melvin Stratton, 1927-94

His nickname among the men who worked for him was "Chief," which to them meant "the leader" rather than "the boss." Lead is what Mel Stratton did; he led by his example as the Rodeheaver Auditorium stage manager.

Mel was born in Muskegan Heights, Michigan, on November 13, 1927, into a family of one brother and one sister. During the early 1930s, Mel's parents became Christians and began attending a local church. A few years later, when he was about ten years of age, Mel also accepted Christ as Savior during revival services at the Lake Harbor Baptist Church. He attended the public schools of Muskegan Heights, worked each afternoon and Saturdays at a printing business, and tore down auto engines as a hobby. He also worked with his father, who was a cabinetmaker. The church the Strattons attended was active in the Muskegan area Youth For Christ, and at these meetings Mel heard men from Bob Jones College preach. He was personally introduced to the College, however, when one of his high school buddies, George Jensen, left for Tennessee in early 1946 to attend Bob Jones Academy.

That fall, Mel joined Jensen at Bob Jones College in Cleveland, Tennessee, and began working on the stage crew to help with his expenses. He graduated from BJU in 1951 with a bachelor of arts degree and married his sweetheart, Gere, whom he met at Thanksgiving in 1950. After their wedding in Worcester, Massachusetts, Mel took a job at Continental Motors in Muskegan as a mechanic but struggled with some health problems caused by complications from an earlier operation. In April 1953 R. K. Johnson called and asked Mel to return to BJU. When he arrived on May 1, he was put in charge of the stage and managed the preparations for *Othello,* which was produced only three weeks later.

For forty-one years after that performance Mel Stratton was the leader backstage. Only rarely did he appear "out front" and then only momentarily. Dwight Gustafson recalled a production of *Tosca* by saying, "the opera doesn't have an overture. Three big chords start the opera and the curtain goes up. Mel was usually backstage checking things out at the last minute, and I always worried about him, but he seemed to have a sixth sense about when to move out of the way before the curtain went up. Well, we struck those three chords, the curtain went up and a flash of green went dashing offstage. It was Mel Stratton in his green overalls. I always kidded him after that and said it was the only opera appearance he'd ever made."[71]

Although he felt that he was "not equipped to do a lot of things like preaching or performing,"[72] Mel Stratton was equipped, with his mechanical genius, to design or customize stage equipment, scenery, props, and lights. In 1954 the University acquired the stage machinery, lifts, and turntables from the Center Theater in New York City, which was scheduled for demolition. Stratton flew to New York, observed the crew dismantle the three lifts, three turntables, and machinery over one week's time, then returned to Greenville and reconstructed the entire assembly, fitting it to the Rodeheaver stage. He also oversaw the installation of the third lift for the forestage orchestra pit, a process which required breaking out the concrete floor of the pit and digging out the area by hand before repouring the floor and installing the lift. All of this forestage work was done while the building was still being used daily for chapel, church, and Vespers.

Mel Stratton was unflappable, unhurried, diligent, and efficient; his life was characterized by "faithfulness, steady faithfulness."[73] He could build anything a stage designer could conceive and repair anything a stagehand could break. He died of a heart attack on December 29, 1994, while playing basketball, one of his favorite pastimes. Though he did not preach or perform, he did just what the Lord wanted him to do—backstage, for forty-one years.[74]

Robert Morris Wood, 1938-

Bob Wood was born in Lawrenceville, Georgia, on March 29, 1938. Bob's father was in the trucking business, and both of his parents were Christians. After living for a time in Atlanta, the Wood family settled in Tucker, Georgia, on the north edge of Atlanta, and the family began attending a large Southern Baptist church. When Bob was twelve years of age, he attended a revival service with his folks, went forward, was baptized, and joined the church. He also held a regular job at a local auto shop from the time he was in the eighth grade until he graduated from high school. When he was sixteen, as a baptized but unsaved young man, Bob became a Sunday school teacher at the church and taught until he was eighteen. As a high school senior, he took a job with a medical supply company, preparing to enter some area of medicine.

After he graduated from high school in 1956, he registered as a premed student at the University of Georgia, but he ended up attending a special school on advanced medical technology arranged and taught at Washington University in St. Louis, Missouri, on a full scholarship from the medical supply company. In St. Louis he fell in with a profligate group of students but successfully completed the training program. When he returned home, he exerted his will, rebelled against his parents and God, and ultimately left home. For the next two years, he was highly successful in medical sales, but he entered a business venture with a partner who turned out to be a thief. The business failed, leaving Wood broke, deeply in debt, and rapidly losing the desire to live. After six months without work, without money or friends, and without hope, he began to contemplate taking his own life.

During a particularly low period when he had basically given up, he saw the old Bible that his parents had given him. The Bible stimulated his thinking, and he prayed that God would give him something to live for. He decided to take an unused bowling bag back to Sears for a refund so that he could buy something to eat. As he waited for the store to open, the personnel manager, a man with whom Bob had played golf some years before, recognized him, questioned him about his life, and offered him a job if he would clean up and come back later that day. Bob returned to his apartment, cleaned himself up, and fell on his knees, telling God that if He would reveal Himself, he would serve Him for the rest of his life. That night he began reading the Bible and prayed for God to forgive him and love him. Three weeks later, at a small Baptist church in Lilburn, Georgia, Bob Wood responded to an invitation and made public the fact that he had accepted Christ as his Savior. He told his own parents about his conversion, but he was too proud to return to their home until God worked in his heart and brought a reconciliation with them.

At that little church he also met his future wife, Mary Cotter. Her parents would not let them date for a period of time because of Bob's reputation. Eventually, as they saw spiritual growth in him, they consented, and Bob and Mary Cotter were married on June 1, 1963.

He began studying the Bible and after a period of time began teaching a Sunday school class again. This time, however, he was teaching as a converted Christian, not as a lost church member. In 1964, after Bob had worked for four years on the staff of Brown Transport Corporation of Atlanta as a sales representative, the Woods started a Saturday evening Bible study in their home. That Bible study group eventually grew to about ninety people. From that group came Killian Hills Baptist Church in Lilburn, Georgia, which Bob began pastoring in 1972. That same year he was named vice president of the Brown Transport Corporation and served in that capacity while pastoring full-time. During this time, he joined the board of the Wilds Christian Camp and became well acquainted with Bob Jones III, who also served on this board.

At its annual meeting in 1976, the Board of Trustees of the University felt impressed to appoint Bob M. Wood to the office of executive vice president to help share some of the executive load of Dr. Jones III and provide executive leadership on the campus in the absences of both the Chancellor and the President. He assumed his duties of vice president on January 12, 1977. Wood is sought as a speaker for Christian business and school organizations around the country, and he serves on the boards of several Christian ministries. Bob Wood received the honorary degree of doctor of divinity from Maranatha Baptist Bible College in Watertown, Wisconsin, in 1979.

As a former vice president of a national transportation company, Bob Wood brought to the school a business acumen that complemented the financial skills of Roy Barton, a pastor's heart for the students, and a spirit of humility to serve the Lord and assist the President of the University.[75]

APPENDICES
◆

Appendix A:
The Fundamentalist-Modernist Controversy:
Basic Tenets

Three men appear to be largely responsible for the introduction of rationalistic German higher criticism into theological thought in America: William Rainey Harper, founder of the University of Chicago and later mentor of Shailer Mathews;[1] William Newton Clarke, professor of theology at Hamilton Institute (now Colgate-Rochester Divinity School) and mentor of Harry Emerson Fosdick;[2] and William Adams Brown of Union Seminary in New York.[3]

From 1870 to 1930 orthodoxy was formalized into Fundamentalism as a reaction to Modernism. In 1909, Lyman Stewart, chairman of the board of Union Oil Company of California, funded the writing, publication, and distribution of twelve paperback books containing ninety articles written by sixty-four conservative scholars and Bible teachers.[4] *The Fundamentals* were written to oppose modern currents in theology and to educate both the layman and the orthodox minister for the defense of conservative Christianity. The books were sent to "every pastor, evangelist, missionary, theology professor and student, Sunday school superintendent, YMCA, YWCA secretary in the English speaking world for which addresses could be obtained."[5] Each of the volumes contained articles dealing with the great doctrines basic to Christian belief, and they answered the specific attacks of modern theologians. Several articles dealt with the inerrancy, infallibility, and inspiration of Scripture. Some dealt with Christology; some with eschatology; others with the doctrines of God, salvation, and judgment; and still others with topics such as missions, evangelism, and everyday living.[6] The term *Fundamentalist* was coined by Curtis Lee Laws in 1920, somewhat after the publication of *The Fundamentals,* to identify those who "still cling to the great fundamentals and who mean to do battle royal for the fundamentals."[7] Fundamentalism was not primarily a rural, southern phenomenon, but was initially centered in the North and West,[8] with southern scholars and revivalists joining the fray at a later date as heresy established itself in southern pulpits and professorial chairs.[9]

The Fundamentalist movement was not primarily a reaction to social forces, urban-rural cultural tensions,[10] Darwinism,[11] or a type of political radicalism that "represents a misguided social revolution."[12] Fundamentalist and conservative reactions to liberalism were just what they claimed to be: reactions against modifications of traditional Christianity.[13] The hue and cry was, "The old time religion must be restored!"[14] Fundamentalists maintained that the issue was not sociological or cultural but hinged on the acceptance or rejection of unchanging truth. J. Gresham Machen of Princeton, one of the most respected of the Fundamentalist apologists, wrote, "Nothing in the world can take the place of truth."[15] To Machen and all Fundamentalists, "the God whom the Christian worships is a God of truth";[16] therefore, as the nature of God, truth was unchanging, inerrant, infallible, inspired, and authoritative.[17] Truth was the Bible: the Bible did not simply contain truth; the Bible *was* truth.[18] Doctrine was the application of truth; thus, doctrine was unchanging as well.

As an alternative to true doctrine, Modernist theologians found the spirit of Christ in the culture around them, in what is good and honest and brave, and in every person, in every work of art, in inventions, in education, and in social reform.[19] In the words of Shailer Mathews, dean of the University of Chicago Divinity School and a champion of the Modernist cause, the liberal, or "Modernist," was one who "regarded doctrines as relative to the needs begotten by new social and cultural conditions."[20] About doctrine, Harry Emerson Fosdick wrote, "[By the second decade of the twentieth century,] Christian doctrine had exceeded its Biblical support."[21] In Modernist thought, Christianity was based on a progressive revelation of truth that through the ages would change with perspective, historicity, and the intended use of that truth by the searcher.[22] Truth became evolutionary, and Scripture became largely allegorical, interpreted according to the situation, for the greater social good of man. One editorial in a New York paper hit the matter squarely when it said that in the present controversy the Fundamentalists lacked charity and the liberals lacked clarity.[23]

The *New Republic* and the *Nation,* however, both acknowledged that Fundamentalism had the force of logic on its side. Writers in the *Christian Century* reported, "Fundamentalists have succeeded in giving the liberal and intelligent leaders of the church the appearances of renegades who are sniping the church from the ramparts."[24] Invective flowed freely from both sides of the dispute.

Most liberals contended that Fundamentalists were those who for sociological reasons held on to the past in resistance to inevitable change. Liberal theologian Kirsop Lake wrote in 1925, "It is a mistake, often made by educated persons who happen to have but little knowledge of historical theology, to suppose that Fundamentalism is a new and strange form of thought. It is nothing of the kind: it is the . . . survival of a theology which was once universally held by all Christians. . . . The Fundamentalist may be wrong; I think that he is. But it is we who have departed from the tradition, not he, and I am sorry for the fate of anyone who tries to argue with a Fundamentalist on the basis of authority. The Bible and the corpus theologicum of the Church is on the Fundamentalist side."[25]

Liberal theologian Shailer Mathews viewed the conflict between Modernism and Fundamentalism as one not merely of theology; rather, he saw it as "a struggle between two types of mind, two attitudes toward culture."[26] Machen seems to agree when he writes, "The difficulty is perhaps not so much that we are brought face to face with new doubts as to the truth of Christianity. Rather it is the conflict of method, of spirit that troubles us. The scientific spirit seems to be incompatible with the old spirit of simple faith. In short . . . we are brought face to face with the problem of the relationship between knowledge and piety, or, otherwise expressed, between culture and Christianity."[27]

Yet Machen clearly thought that the basic issue was deeper than contradictions between knowledge and faith. Truth was the issue and the Scripture was the focus of controversy. Bob Jones Sr. wrote, "The greatest battle of the ages is being fought now. It is the battle between orthodoxy and modernism. Orthodoxy says the Bible is the Word of God. Modernism says the Bible contains the Word of God. Both of these positions cannot be true. . . . A person may take one of three positions in this battle between modernism and orthodoxy. The best position is to be orthodox. The next best is to be a modernist. The third best, to be neutral. . . . There are only two religions in the world—man's religion and God's religion. Man's religion is the fruit of his hands. God's religion is the shedding of blood. . . . This religion of man is no good."[28]

The following table summarizes the tenets of Fundamentalism and Modernism and is drawn from the works of those preachers, evangelists, educators, and scholars who were participants in the controversy.[29]

Fundamentalist and Modernist Doctrine

Fundamentalist Positions:

I. Scripture:

1. "To sum up, Our Lord Jesus says that the Bible is the Inerrant Word of God, the history of eighteen centuries has proclaimed the Bible to be the Inerrant Word of God, all the men and women who live nearest God and know God best declare that the Bible is the Inerrant Word of God, the Holy Spirit declares to the individual soul that puts himself in such an attitude that the Holy Spirit can speak to him, that the Bible is the Inerrant Word of God. Is the Bible the inerrant Word of God or is it not? Beyond the shadow of a doubt, it is."[30]

2. "If the Christian make full use of his Christian privileges, he finds the seat of authority in the whole Bible, which he regards as no mere word of man but as the very Word of God."[33] "The Bible is the Word of God and the whole Bible is the Word of God."[34]

Modernist Positions:

I. Scripture:

1. "We used to think of inspiration as a procedure which produced a book guaranteed in all its parts against error, and containing from beginning to end a unanimous system of truth. No well instructed mind, I think, can hold that now."[31] "The Bible must be allowed to say in terms of the generation when its books were written what its words in their historic sense actually meant."[32]

2. "[I believe] 'The Scriptures of the Old and New Testaments' contain the word of God but not that they are the word of God, and certainly I could not have applied the word 'infallible' to the whole Bible."[35]

3. "The Bible not only is an account of important things, but that account itself is true. . . . The resulting Book is the 'infallible rule of faith and practice.' "[36]

4. "The Bible is not only true, but inspired as well. By inspiration we mean that operation of the Holy Ghost on the minds of the writers, by which they were enabled to compose its books."[39]

3. "The Bible sprang from our religion, not our religion from the Bible."[37] "[We] approach the Bible as a treasury of inspiration and moral guidance. . . . We honor it as the germplasm of a developing religion."[38]

4. "Modernists believe in inspiration rather than inerrancy. But in the inspiration of men, not of words. Men were inspired because they inspire."[40]

II. Christ:

1. "The virgin birth of Christ is a fact and is an essential Christian Doctrine."[41]

2. "Begotten by the Holy Ghost and born of man, He was God and man."[43]

3. "The Jesus spoken of in the New Testament was no mere teacher of righteousness, no mere pioneer in a new type of religious life, but one who was regarded, and regarded Himself, as the Saviour whom men could trust. Jesus . . . is the object of faith."[45]

4. "In His suffering on the cross, Christ, as our vicarious atonement, took the place of sinful men. . . . Jesus Christ tasted death for every man."[47] "The Christian doctrine of the atonement is . . . rooted in the . . . doctrine of the deity of Christ."[48]

5. "The evidence (external historical, internal historical, circumstantial) proves to a certainty that the body of Jesus was raised from the dead."[52]

6. "The Lord will come again, and it will be no 'spiritual coming' in the modern sense. . . . He shall come again."[55]

II. Christ:

1. "God is not spoken of as the father of Jesus. . . . Joseph is the father of Jesus."[42]

2. "Arguments from the lower animals . . . [make] a virgin birth difficult to believe."[44]

3. "A man is vitally and inwardly a Christian only to the degree in which he himself possesses the kind of religion which Jesus Christ possessed."[46]

4. "Jesus made the concept [of divine forgiveness] thoroughly moral; he made God's pardon dependent on man's relationship with man."[49] "Jesus was a marvelously good man."[50] "Have done with your theological Christ and give us back Jesus the ethical teacher."[51]

5. "I do not believe in the resurrection of the flesh."[53] "He is still living personally in whatever may be the conditions in which the dead now are."[54]

6. "I do not believe in the physical return of Jesus."[56] "This is the Modernist's eschatology—an uplifting hope for the social order in which economic, political and all other institutions will embody the cosmic good will . . . of Jesus."[57]

III. Miracles:

1. "A miracle is the supernatural manifesting itself in the external world . . . an event that takes place by the immediate power of God."[58]

2. "Miracles are found not to be an excrescence in the New Testament account of Jesus, but belong to the very warp and woof. They are intimately connected with Jesus' lofty claims; they stand or fall with the undoubted purity of His character; they reveal the very nature of His mission in the world."[60]

IV. Creation:

1. "There are but two theories concerning the origin of the earth and of man—one is creation by a living God; the other is evolution by dead force. . . . We accept the fact of God as the Creator in [the] beginning."[63]

2. "To the question of how man came, I remark merely that over against the evolutionary hypothesis is the plain statement of the Bible that 'God created man in His own image.' "[65]

3. "The Darwinian hypothesis is still essentially unverified."[67]

4. "There is no 'natural selection'; [there is] supernatural selection."[69]

III. Miracles:

1. "In the Bible a story which seems to involve a ruptured law of nature . . . that story is antecedently improbable."[59]

2. "Stories of miracles are historically unreliable. . . . Miracles are practically undesirable. . . . If miracles had happened in the Bible and had not happened since, then God had changed his way of running the world."[61] "Miracles, instead of being the grounds for faith, become its stumbling block, for the Bible abounds in miracles."[62]

IV. Creation:

1. "Let us not mince matters in this connection: plants, animals, and man are either fixed and immutable products of special creation or else they have undergone changes and are undergoing changes today. . . . All lines of evidence point strongly to organic evolution. . . . [They] are utterly incompatible with . . . special creation."[64]

2. "The high degree of diversity within [*Homo sapiens*] is evidence of rapid evolution."[66]

3. "Never before in the history of science has there been so nearly a unanimous acceptance of the Principle of Evolution and so little consensus of opinion as to its causes."[68]

4. "Opinions as to the adequacy of this theory to explain in causal terms the phenomena it purports to explain are almost as numerous as are scientists who claim a right to such opinions."[70]

5. "The tendency of Darwinism, when taken seriously, is to undermine faith, first, in the Bible as an inspired book, and then in the miracles . . . ; next, repudiation of the virgin birth and the resurrection of Christ . . . and the rejection of Christ as Son and Savior. Lastly, Darwinism leads to the denial of the existence of a personal God."[71]

5. "We were ready to go with the evolutionist as far as reasonable interpretation of facts warranted. . . . Theological doctrines like the atonement, the deity of Christ, the personality of God and the worth of prayer were either outgrown or restated. . . . The substitution of the teaching of Jesus for authoritative doctrines, the conception of Christianity as a movement which undertakes to reproduce his attitudes and consequent behavior in our own day, the softening of God's sovereignty into a divine paternity, the development of the social gospel and the substitution of Christian nurture for supernatural conversion of children suffering from a corrupt human nature inherited from Adam, the modification of doctrines of the atonement were the direct result of the substitution of scientific attitude for that of implicit reliance on the Bible."[72]

Appendix B:
Rules of Bob Jones College, 1933

150 Demerits a semester automatically expels a student.

1. "Griping" will not be tolerated.

2. Hazing is positively prohibited. Penalty: Minimum 50 demerits.

3. The use of tobacco in any form by dormitory students is positively prohibited. Penalty: Expulsion. Day students who bring tobacco in any form on the campus will be expelled.

4. Dormitory students must take all meals at the college unless in company of an official chaperone. Penalty: Minimum 50 demerits. Exceptions may be made by the administration in the case of students who conduct religious services away from the local community.

5. Senior dormitory boys may leave campus at their pleasure provided this liberty does not conflict with any other school regulations. Junior boys have same privilege but must check out and in at night. Sophomore boys may leave campus at night by permission of the administration and check out and in. Freshman boys may leave campus three times a week but must have permission and must check out and in. If necessary for a freshman boy to leave campus more than three times a week, special permission must be given by acting head of the institution or by

some person to whom the administration designates authority. High school boys may leave campus twice a week provided they have permission and check out and in.

Dormitory girls may leave campus only in company of their parents or an authorized chaperone. Certain exceptions may be made in the case of upper class girls. Penalty: Minimum 100 demerits.

6. Students must protect and preserve all college property and any willful damage to college property will be punished with a minimum of 50 demerits. Any willful or unwillful damage to college property must be paid.

7. Dormitory students will not be permitted to have automobiles except for business and then only by written permission of administration.

8. The Bob Jones College endorses high class music. Students who persist in inflicting any other type music on the institution will be dealt with by the faculty committee.

9. No dormitory student will be permitted to go home unless a written or wired request from parent or guardian is sent direct to president or acting head of the college. This does not apply to students who are not subject to parent or guardian; however, such students must notify the administration when they are leaving. Penalty: suspension.

10. Gambling, drinking of alcoholic beverages, profanity, obscenity, dancing, card playing, dice throwing will not be tolerated.

11. Attendance at Chapel each week day and at morning Church service and Vesper service is compulsory. Penalty: 25 demerits. Students who work on Saturday may secure permission from the administration to miss Chapel on Saturday. Students who conduct religious services outside the local community may secure permission from the administration to miss Vespers; however, this permission will be granted only to students who are too far away to attend without great difficulty.

12. No day student may enter dormitory without permission of administration and no general permission will be given, but permission must be secured for each visit. Penalty: 10 demerits.

13. No dormitory student may visit any local home without permission of the administration. Penalty: minimum 25 demerits.

14. Students must avoid all communications through windows of dormitories or attempting to attract attention, such as waving, talking, passing notes, etc. Penalty: 10 demerits.

15. Any dormitory student leaving college premises without permission after 10:00 P.M. or entering a building after 10:00 P.M. without being accompanied by night watchman or an authorized chaperone will be expelled.

16. No dormitory student will be allowed to carry a charge account in Cleveland.[1]

Appendix C:
A Tribute and a Pledge—
Bob Jones Jr.

This should not be a day for weeping. This is a time for rejoicing. This should not be a moment of sorrow. This is an hour for gladness. A fight has been fought, a race has been won, a crown is laid up. Nevertheless, such is our human weakness that a son cannot today trust himself to speak and must therefore ask another to read the words which come from his heart.

It should not be thought strange that a son has written a father's eulogy. Aside from my mother, I am sure I knew my father better than anyone else. Others have seen him in the vigor of his great evangelistic campaigns; but I have known him in the quiet of the home as well. Others have listened to the sound advice of his chapel talks; but I have known, too, his chastening love and fatherly counsel in the private and quiet hours of my youth.

Faithful associates have borne with him the burden of the ministry of Bob Jones University and shared with him the fulfillment of his vision; but I saw the birth of the vision and knew not only the reality of his achievement, but also the burden upon my father's heart to which the University owes its existence.

Yet the language shall be limping, the picture unfinished, the story badly outlined. Only the pages of God's Heaven can reveal the measure of his life; only a recording angel report it fully.

Some say that it is only human to be inconsistent; but my father, who was of all men most human in his sympathies and understanding of man's weakness, was the most consistent man I ever knew. In private as in public he never turned for a moment aside from the principles by which his actions were shaped or departed in his own living from the convictions which fired his public statements and molded the lives of other thousands who sat under his ministry.

He was sure that he was right because he drew his convictions from the well of God's Word and rested his principles upon the sure foundation of the infallible Truth that is forever settled in Heaven. Because he would not sacrifice what he knew to be Truth for the pleasing of men, because he would not yield to the pressures of changing opinions or soften to accommodate to the softness of compromise with apostasy and sin, his enemies—and he had many, as all God's true servants have since the days of the Old Testament prophets—called him "bitter" and "unloving" and "stubborn."

Stubborn he was on matters of principle—thank God—but never on lesser things like method and means. Bitter and unloving he never was; and such was his nature that he could not be.

"Disloyalty," he often said, was "an unpardonable sin" where he was concerned. Loyalty to the cause he demanded in those who associated themselves with Bob Jones University; but I have seen my father when betrayed by one he trusted—one who in fact owed him more than could ever be repaid—moved not by bitterness but deep grief, try to understand a heart which many men would despise; and try to account for the action which deserved to be condemned. I have seen him, exhausted by lack of sleep and racked with physical pain, spend hours in loving effort to help a man who he knew was no friend.

He was not a patient man—either with himself or others—but he was a long-suffering man. How often have I heard him say, in deliberate disregard for grammar, "You can't do nothing for a fool"; and yet how often have I seen him try. His greatest weakness was his trustfulness. My mother and I have often said to him, "You take people at their face value too readily." Because he was so open and honest in his own heart and his own actions, he could not bring himself to believe—until he was faced with the proof—that others might not be all they pretended to be. He preferred to believe the good rather than the bad. He preferred to suffer the disappointment of being betrayed by one unworthy of his trust rather than to risk thinking a good man bad.

At every point Bob Jones had amazing gifts of perception. From the pulpit and in private conversations he might irritate his hearers with the truth about themselves; but so keen was his mind and so dynamic his personality he could never bore them. How often have I heard a student say, "I'd rather hear Dr. Bob preach the same sermon half a dozen times than listen to most men preach a new one." And no man who sat for a while under his ministry was ever able to escape completely thereafter from the impact of his words and the impression of his personality. Even those former students who have, for denominational approval or selfish gain or for lack of character, "sold God out" and betrayed the Lord that bought them—even they are still, years after, quoting his sayings (without acknowledging their source, of course) and preaching his sermons (mangled and emasculated and without the force of their author's conviction and that anointing of God which rested upon the man from whom they took them).

He had a way with words. He could paint pictures with language which were more moving than those a fine artist brought to canvas with his brush—yet never did his language soar higher than the thought. He delighted the ear to touch the heart. His homely philosophy is preserved bit by bit—like flies in amber—in the hearts of his "boys and girls" in the pithy sayings that have given direction to many a life.

"Good men are always reasonable men," he was wont to say; and I have found that he was right in that as in so many other things. And my father was himself the finest proof of it. He never expected perfection of others, but sought it in his own undertakings and was always himself most conscious of his own shortcomings. He had a gift for recognizing hidden talents and unrealized possibilities in the lives of young people; and many of you present today are spending yourselves in the Lord's service because of that sure sense of my father's that saw and awakened in you gifts you never dreamed you had.

What an unusual combination he was: at once deeply spiritual and intensely practical. Possessed of the gift of "the discerning of spirits," he could also discern a good business deal; and the financial stability of Bob Jones University gives the lie to the old adage that "good preachers are always poor businessmen."

Appendix C

Character and integrity were the qualities he most admired. "You can borrow brain," he used to tell us, "but you cannot borrow character." He said to me, "A man of bad character is better than a man with no character at all. Get him converted and he'll be a strong Christian; but a spineless man is no good to God or the devil."

Quick to recognize greatness in others, he never, I am sure, recognized the greatness in himself. As deep as was his faith, he used to rebuke himself for lack of it and declare, "I never had the measure of faith God gives to some men." Then he would add, "But I have found if you act as if you had faith you'll find things come out as well as if you had it; and that develops faith." He worked as if everything depended upon him and trusted as if all depended upon God. His faith was like a child's; his efforts those of an army.

He understood weakness and could sympathize with it; but he never could be for very long patient with it—especially in a Christian. And yet he found it difficult to be stern with a penitent student who had repented the same failure a dozen times before. Looking back, I can see now what an effort it cost him to punish me when I was a child; but his strong character demanded the effort and he made himself make it.

How he loved children! How, indeed, he loved people. So great was his interest in them that he took on their burdens and shared the secrets his sympathetic understanding led them to pour out to him when they would not open their hearts to anyone else.

My father responded intensely to beauty; but he preferred the colors of God's sunset to the colors in a painting of a sunset. He loved the old hymns. It was, I am sure however, the words to which his heart answered and not the notes, for he could never carry a tune; but "When the Lord comes," he would tell us, "I'll dip my tongue in the melody of the sky."

A man of deep sentiment, he loved to dwell on the memories of his boyhood and of his godly parents; and no man ever had deeper affection for his family than he had for us.

He loved the souls of men and spent his life striving to bring the lost to Christ. Even in these last months, old and forgetful in other things, he never forgot to inquire about the salvation of a visitor he did not remember or recognize. Nor did the ravages of time touch or mar his power in prayer.

But above all, he loved Jesus! "If there were one drop of blood in my veins that did not flow in love for Christ, I'd ask a surgeon to open that vein and let it out." This was the testimony of the evangelist who had met his Saviour at the age of eleven under the dim lamps of a country church in southeast Alabama and who grew up to take the light of the Gospel around the globe and to build the world's largest Christian education institution.

Almost every boy looks at his father and sees in him a great man. How few men at fifty-six can look upon the venerable face of a dead parent and realize their boyhood opinion confirmed a hundredfold. What a heritage he has left his son! His was a life of many talents, well invested, yielding for his Lord a return abundant. I would I might stand before God with his record or receive the reward for his faithfulness.

His is a fight well fought, a course well run, a faith well kept, a crown well won!

Having spoken as my father's son, it is time now for me to speak as his successor. The tired warrior rests, but the battle rages. The strife-scarred hero takes his repose, but the war continues. The great man is gone, but the work remains. The founder is departed, but the institution stands.

We will not betray the dead. We cannot avoid the challenge. We shall not flee the task. We would not escape the opportunity he has bequeathed to us. Here in the sight of his God and ours—standing beside this casket—we dedicate ourselves, our lives and talents afresh to the continuation of the ministry of the Gospel and the purpose for which he founded the institution which is at once his greatest achievement and his finest monument.

If it is the Lord's will, Bob Jones University shall continue to grow in its physical equipment and its scope, its outreach and its influence. But it shall stand unchanged and unchanging in its purpose and its philosophy. As long as it please God and the Board of Trustees that we shall be entrusted with the administrative responsibility of this university, Bob III and I shall continue unyielding in our warfare against Anti-Christ and shall undertake to assure that Bob Jones University shall remain a lighthouse of God's Truth amid the lengthening shadows of a great apostasy. We shall, in the words of our charter:

> conduct an institution of learning for the general education of youth in the essentials of culture and in the arts and sciences; giving special emphasis to the Christian religion and the ethics revealed in the Holy Scriptures; combatting all atheistic, agnostic, pagan, and so-called scientific adultera-tions of the gospel; unqualifiedly affirming and teaching the inspiration of the Bible (both the Old and the New Testaments); the creation of man by the direct act of God; the incarnation and virgin birth of our Lord and Saviour, Jesus Christ; His identification as the Son of God; His vicarious atonement for the sins of mankind by the shedding of His blood on the cross; the resurrection of his body from the tomb; His power to save men from sin; the new birth through the regeneration by the Holy Spirit; and the gift of eternal life by the grace of God.

Our students shall be continually reminded of their obligation to reach all men with the Gospel and of their privilege of being soul winners. The banner our founder raised here for the Lord Jesus Christ shall never be lowered. These colors we will never dip. The trumpet shall not cease to sound from these battlements nor shall that trumpet sound be muted or uncertain. God's holy, infallible, and living Word shall continue to be the Sword of our warfare and the Light of our path. We shall not depart from its precepts, cease from its procla-mation, or grow weary in its defence.

This is, I say, not a moment for weeping. This is a day of challenge. This is not a time for sorrow. This is an hour of dedication! I call upon all the members of the University family—trustees, faculty, students—young and old—upon the far-scattered alumni, upon the former students who are faithful to the institution that gave them their training and touched their eyes to see the vision of a needy world—upon you all I call—surrender your hearts afresh to the Christ whom our founder loved and served for more than seventy years.

Nothing is worthwhile that is not done for eternity. The brick of these buildings may go back to clay; but the living stones laid in the Temple of God through the founder's preaching are there forever. Let us build upon the foundation of God that standeth sure. Our founder was surely sent of God to meet a great need in his day. But the God of Elijah is the God of Elisha as well. The mantle has been dropped. We take it up in humility of heart and with reverent hands.

We thank God for the faithful friends who support this institution and who pray for this ministry. To them I say we need now, more than ever, the weight of your intercession behind us, the upholding hands of your petitions before the throne of God. Cease not day and night to pray for us. The weapons of our warfare are not carnal but spiritual.

To any present on this occasion or who hear this service broadcast or read the words in print and who have never put their trust in Christ, I say this: the same One who could take over the heart of a little country boy and make his life one of blessing to untold thousands can save you and bring you from death to life eternal. Nothing ever rejoiced my father's heart so much as seeing a man or woman come into the saving knowledge of Jesus Christ. May this be the moment when you shall receive Him as your Saviour.

To those of you saved under my father's preaching or living in the service of Jesus Christ because of his influence, and to all of you who rejoice with them in the blessed hope of Christ's glorious appearing, I would leave this final reminder and this assurance: God knows the future. Our times are in His hands and we are His. To Christ be the glory! His Kingdom is forever.[1]

Appendix D:
Position of the BJU Bible Department
on the Scripture

The dominating concern for all Bible-related courses, from English Bible to Theology and Ethics, in Bob Jones University is what the Bible teaches. This is of paramount importance to us because we believe in the verbal inspiration and absolute inerrancy of the Bible. We believe, as Fundamentalists have always believed, that this inspiration refers to the original manuscripts. "The record for whose inspiration we contend is the original record—the autographs or parchments of Moses, David, Daniel, Matthew, Peter, or Paul as the case may be and not any particular translation or translations of them whatever" (*The Fundamentals,* "Inspiration of the Bible," p. 127).

When we teach the content of the Bible, we naturally study a passage in the Greek Testament. To aid the students in understanding that passage, we will take to class the King James Bible, which often gives an exact rendering of the Greek.

Sometimes we will consult some other conservative translation, such as the American Standard Version of 1901 or the New American Standard Bible (not the liberal R[evised] S[tandard] V[ersion]), which at times gives the most accurate rendering of the Greek. We are always trying to help the students grasp the exact meaning of the original Greek text. There are a few passages in which the delicate shades of meaning in the Greek are missed by all English translations, in which cases we must explain from the Greek text itself those fine shades of meaning. We would not use a liberal paraphrase in class except as an illustration of a mistranslation, which we would at once correct by a true translation. We have no sympathy with any version of the Bible that is not faithful to the Greek text.

Because we believe in the inspiration of the original manuscripts of the Old and New Testaments, it is important that we have a Greek Testament that will be as close to the readings of the original as possible. Through the carelessness of scribes who copied manuscripts, many varying readings have crept into them. But God in His providence has preserved for us the original reading through the large number of manuscripts in existence that witness to the text of the New Testament. Today there are two Greek texts available. One is the Received Text, edited by Roman Catholic scholar, Erasmus, in the sixteenth century and based on manuscripts of the late Middle Ages. It is often called the "Byzantine" or the "majority text." The other is the Greek Testament, edited by Westcott and Hort in the nineteenth century and based upon the manuscripts of the fourth century, usually called the "Alexandrian text." The King James Version was based upon the "Received Text"; the American Standard Version was based upon the text of Westcott and Hort. We do not believe that either of these texts is "liberal" or "conservative." Not only Erasmus but also Westcott and Hort were seeking to present a close copy of the original text. We are interested in which one is closer to the original text of the New Testament.

Because (1) the Alexandrian manuscripts are much older and closer to the time the originals were written, (2) a careful comparison of these manuscripts with those of the Middle Ages has convinced us that a more accurate and careful job of copying was done by the Alexandrian scribes, and (3) Erasmus had to work in haste and with limited resources, it is our conviction that these Alexandrian manuscripts, which were not known to Erasmus, are, as a rule, the more accurate manuscripts to follow. Therefore, along with the great majority of conservative scholars, we believe that the text based upon the Alexandrian manuscripts is, as a whole, superior to the text based upon manuscripts of the Middle Ages.

The portion of the New Testament that has any substantial variation between the various manuscripts is only about one word in a thousand. These variations in no way change the teaching of the New Testament on any doctrine. Therefore, we consider this not an issue of modernism versus conservatism but a matter of individual judgment on the part of Fundamental Christians. Christians should be free to choose and use either of these texts and still work together in harmony to teach and preach the Word of God to those who are without it.[1]

NOTES
◆

Chapter 1: Bob Jones: The Man

[1]For a treatment of the life and ministry of BJsr, see R. K. Johnson, *Builder of Bridges: The Biography of Bob Jones, Sr.* (Greenville, S.C.: BJU Press, 1982).

[2]During the Battle of Chickamauga, both armies suffered 28 percent casualties, but the Alabama regiment with which Alex Jones fought suffered more than 50 percent casualties, the highest toll of the battle. See Johnson, *Builder,* p. 7.

[3]Johnson, *Builder,* pp. 7-9.

[4]MS, "Biographical Sketch of Bob Jones, Sr.," 14 November 1961 (GF: Memorabilia file); and Johnson, *Builder,* pp. 11-16.

[5]Johnson, *Builder,* p. 5.

[6]BJsr, *Things I Have Learned* (Greenville, S.C.: BJU Press, n.d.), p. 14.

[7]*Report on Economic Conditions of the South,* prepared for the president by the National Emergency Council (Washington, D.C., 1938), p. 45. Quoted in Thomas D. Clark, *Three Paths to the Modern South: Education, Agriculture, and Conservation* (Athens, Ga.: University of Georgia Press, 1965), pp. 29-30.

[8]John Samuel Ezell, *The South Since 1865* (New York: Macmillan Co., 1963), p. 158. See also C. Vann Woodward, *Origins of the New South: 1877-1913* (Baton Rouge: Louisiana State University Press, 1951), pp. 185-86.

[9]Quoted in Johnson, *Builder,* p. 15.

[10]BJsr, *Things,* p. 97. See also Melton Wright, *Fortress of Faith,* 3rd ed. (Greenville, S.C.: BJU Press, 1984), p. 2.

[11]Populism as a social and political movement is complex, springing from different roots in different parts of the nation. Generally, the populist movements were made up of common working folks, often rural farmers, somewhat uneducated, who fought a losing battle for agricultural interests to gain control of American government and to beat back the forces of urban industrialism. They stressed the "role of government in defending small voices against the powerful and the wealthy." Politically unfocused, populism grew out of farmers' protest movements of the 1890s. In social issues, populists generally supported the right, while in economic issues, populists tended to lean to the left (Jay M. Shafritz, *Dictionary of American Government and Politics* [Chicago: Dorsey Press, 1988], p. 424). For more information about American populism and the Farmers' Alliance, see Woodward, *Origins,* pp. 235-63; and Gene Clanton, *Populism: The Humane Preference in America, 1890-1900* (Boston: Twayne Publishers, 1991).

[12]Woodward, *Origins,* pp. 175-234.

[13]Wright, *Fortress,* p. 218.

[14]*Peru (Ind.) Republican,* 23 January 1914. See also Johnson, *Builder,* p. 18.

[15]MS, BJsr, chapel talk, 1 October 1935 (ABV: 1935).

[16]Ibid.

[17]MS, BJsr, chapel talk, n.d., 1936 (ABV: 1936). BJsr often alluded to soil and planting from his farm experiences. "Gifts planted in the soil of poor character will be a detriment to you. . . . It's not the gift, but the quality of the soil in which that gift is planted [that makes a difference]"(MS, BJsr, chapel talk, 14 December 1940 [ABV: 1940]). BJsr speaks of tariff laws when "[he] was a boy" and also breaking and driving yearlings in his book *Things I Have Learned,* p. 99.

[18]BJsr, *Things,* p. 98. See also MS, BJsr, chapel talk, 28 January 1947 (ABV: 1947). BJsr talks about losing a quarter in a sandbank on the road home from selling produce in Dothan. Also, MS, BJsr, chapel talk, 1 October 1935 (ABV: 1935).

[19]MS, "Biographical Sketch," 14 November 1961 (GF: Memorabilia file). See also Johnson, *Builder,* p. 20. See also BJjr, *Cornbread and Caviar: Reminiscences and Reflections* (Greenville, S.C.: BJU Press, 1985), p. 15.

[20]"Biographical Sketch." See also Wright, *Fortress,* p. 7; and Johnson, *Builder,* p. 20.

[21]Johnson, *Builder,* p. 15.

[22]Wright, *Fortress,* p. 5.

[23]BJsr, *Things,* pp. 10-11.

[24]MS, Oscar L. Newton, "A One Hundred Year History of the Beulah Church," 1949, p. 13. See also Johnson, *Builder,* p. 18.

[25]Johnson, *Builder,* p. 22.

[26]Quoted in Johnson, *Builder,* p. 23.

[27]Johnson, *Builder,* p. 26.

[28]Quoted in Johnson, *Builder,* p. 25.

[29]MS, Bob Jones University Department of Public Relations, "Dr. Jones, Sr., Biographical Sketch," 21 September 1962 (MLA: Box 13). Johnson records that at one time there were only two students in the entire school—Bobby and a smaller girl. All the other students were needed in the fields (Johnson, *Builder,* p. 29).

[30]Johnson, *Builder,* p. 18.

[31]MS, "Biographical Sketch," 14 November 1961.

[32]BJsr indicated in a chapel message in 1945 that he first heard this poem quoted by Dr. Sullins, a Methodist preacher and president of Centenary College in Cleveland, Tennessee. Centenary closed in 1929 and BJC took over the property in 1933 (BJsr, chapel talk, 16 October 1945 [ABV: 1945]).

[33]Charles Jefferson Hammitt, D.D. (1858-1935), was principal of the seminary from 1886 through 1899. Dr. Hammitt was a well-educated Philadelphian, having earned his doctorate from Yale. He was sent by the Methodist Church as a missionary to southern Alabama, where he pastored several circuits of churches, acted as seminary principal for three years, and made Kinsey, Alabama, his home. In the seminary Dr. Hammitt taught elocution (Nancy Michel, "Grandchildren Fondly Recall What the Hammitts Were Like," *Dothan (Ala.) Progress,* 22 October 1986, p. 1-C).

[34]Nancy Michel, "Landmark Eyes Another Piece of Heritage," *Dothan (Ala.) Progress,* 22 October 1986.

[35]Nancy Michel, "Mallalieu Seminary Had Major Role in Area Development," *Dothan (Ala.) Progress,* 22 October 1986. For a school of this type and in this location, the course offerings were diverse. Other courses taught during this time included plane geometry, botany, French, bookkeeping, and elocution.

[36]Michel, "Grandchildren."

[37]Fred S. Watson, *Hub of the Wiregrass: A History of Houston County, 1903-1972* (Anniston, Ala.: Higgenbotham, Inc., 1972), pp. 92-93.

[38]Michel, "Mallalieu Seminary."

[39]Interview, Carl O. Hammitt with Nancy Michel, 3 October 1986.

[40]MS, BJsr, chapel talk, 28 January 1947 (ABV: 1947).

[41]Interview, Nancy Michel with Evelyn Jarvis Smith, 8 October 1986.

[42]Johnson, *Builder,* pp. 32-35.

[43]Ibid., pp. 31-33.

[44]Ibid., pp. 32-35.

[45]Southern University became Birmingham Southern University in the 1920s.

[46]"Home Town Pays Tribute to Bob Jones U Founder," *Palm,* vol. 83, no. 4, December 1963, p. 23.

[47]Johnson, *Builder,* p. 39.

[48]MS, BJsr, Sunday sermon, 2 January 1945 (ABV: 1945).

[49]Johnson, *Builder,* p. 36.

[50]As a sixteen-year-old, BJsr was pastoring five churches in the Headland Circuit of the Marianna District of the Alabama Conference of the Methodist Church, for which he received a salary of twenty-five dollars a month. In summers, his residence was at Kinsey with the Hammitts (Interview, Nancy Michel with George Pabody, 26 September 1986).

[51]Johnson, *Builder,* pp. 36-37.

[52]Interview, Mrs. BJsr with Margaret Beall Tice, September/October 1973.

[53]"Jones-Sheffield," wedding report, unknown paper, n.d. (MLA: Box 38).

[54]Bernice Sheffield was born 18 September 1885 at Pine Hill in Wilcox County, Alabama. She "made a profession of religion" when she was eleven and joined the Baptist Church. She was educated at Judson College in Marion, Alabama, and graduated with honors in 1904. The next year she took a "post graduate course." How Sheffield and BJsr met is not known. After they married in October, she changed her membership to the Methodist Episcopal Church. Her final intelligible words reportedly were, "I know and can trust my Savior" (James A. Patton, "Mrs. Bernice Jones," *New Orleans Christian Advocate,* 25 October 1906). See also Wright, *Fortress,* pp. 11-12.

[55]Interview, BJjr, 28 May 1987.

[56]The *Gloversville (N.Y.) Morning Herald,* April through May 1916, published attendance records for the six-week campaign held there. By the end of the campaign, attendance topped 175,700 people, with total offerings in excess of ten thousand dollars. There were 1,780 converts to Christ during the meeting. It was not unusual for individual meetings to run 2,000 to 6,000 in attendance, depending on the size of the available structure.

[57]Interview, Mrs. BJsr with Margaret Beall Tice.

[58]BJsr, *Things,* p. 143. Examples of this type of palavering can be seen in the Sinclair Lewis novel *Elmer Gantry* and in the real-life scandal that surrounded popular female evangelist Aimee Semple McPherson (1890-1944).

[59]The Stollenwerck plantation house appears in a work by Hammond, entitled *Ante-Bellum Mansions of Alabama,* pp. 144-45. Prior to the Civil War, Mary Gaston's grandfather died, leaving several plantations, with about 450 slaves, to be run by his wife. Following the war, the family moved into the town of Uniontown, Alabama, and had the land sharecropped.

[60]BJjr recalls that Mrs. Stollenwerck was converted at fourteen in a campaign held by an evangelist named Bounds, "a preacher whose ministry had a tremendous effect everywhere he went at that time. She often mentioned this to me, and she was certainly soundly converted. . . . Mother once said that the week after her conversion, her older sister said, 'Telly, who are you going to the dance with on Saturday night?' Grandmother replied, 'I am converted and joined the church. I am not going to any more dances' " (BJjr to Dan Turner, personal correspondence, 14 March 1996).

[61]Interview, Mrs. BJsr with Margaret Beall Tice. As a girl she had heard Dwight Moody preach, and she had also heard Sam Jones. Yet she thought BJsr the greatest preacher who ever lived. According to Mary Gaston, her mother had read "everything that was good and worthwhile." In addition, she had memorized the books of Job and Revelation, as well as a large number of hymns (Interview, Mrs. BJsr, 28 August 1986). Estelle Siddons Stollenwerck had a profound effect on BJjr. She was instrumental in introducing him to literature and languages.

[62]Johnson, *Builder,* p. 25.

[63]BJsr to Rev. W. E. Middlebrooks, 3 August 1932 (BJsr, clipping book 9, no. 21). Though dating from the 1930s, this letter shows the extent of control the bishops felt they needed to exert over the pastors and church members of the era. The subject of this letter was the trial of BJC ministerial student Fred Brown for holding a tent meeting in Marianna, Florida, without the consent of the Marianna Circuit's presiding pastor.

[64]Johnson, *Builder,* p. 43.

[65]*Zanesville (Ohio) Times-Recorder,* 2 April 1917.

[66]See *Bob Jones Magazine,* vol. 2, no. 4, January 1930, p. 1, for a summary of the charges laid at the feet of both men and women. The issues included abortion, divorce, immodesty, prostitution, gambling, and drinking.

[67]In his fascinating essay, "The Meaning of the Progressive Movement," Richard Hofstadter lists the aims and accomplishments of the American Progressive movement, most of which revolved around the amelioration of social ills brought on by industrialism and urbanization. The issues about which BJsr preached and which are listed in the text are often found in Progressivist literature of the period, along with others such as community health, child welfare, public taxation, unionism, and labor strife. Progressives believed in a doctrine of progress and the improvability of man, and they believed science to have the answers to social problems. Closely allied with the political goals of the Progressives was the social gospel of Walter Rauschenbusch, a theological movement which stressed the amelioration of social ills, the need for social reform, and the salvation of man by remaking society. BJsr spoke out against the social gospel even though he supported many of the Progressive political and social aims of William Jennings Bryan and Bibb Graves. BJsr, like other Fundamentalists, preached that human conditions were the result of man's fallen nature and that only a heart changed by the gospel could truly make a difference in society. See Richard Hofstadter, ed., *The Progressive Movement 1900-1915* (Englewood Cliffs, N.J.: Prentice Hall, 1963), pp. 1-15. See also Robert Crunden, *Ministers of Reform: The Progressives' Achievement in American Civilization 1889-1920* (New York: Basic Books, 1982); and George Brown Tindall, *The Emergence of the New South, 1913-1945* (Baton Rouge: Louisiana State University Press, 1967), pp. 219-84.

[68]" 'Movies,' Saloons, and Prize Fights Rapped by Jones," *Joplin (Mo.) Globe,* 2 November 1915.

[69]"Square Politics Urgee [*sic*] by Jones in Sermon Today," *Montgomery (Ala.) Advertiser,* 1 June 1921.

[70]Charles A. Casad, "How Evangelist Bob Jones Lost His Dignity but Became Famous Preacher in One Night," *Gloversville (N.Y.) Morning Herald,* 14 April 1916. Casad reports that BJsr especially admired Bryan's unhesitating defense of the Bible and his stand on "principle." BJsr did not support all of Bryan's political beliefs, however. See also *New York American,* n.d., photo showing Bryan conferring with BJsr (MLA: Bob Jones clipping book 6); MS, BJsr, Bible Conference sermon, 3 April 1944 (ABV: 1944); and Johnson, *Builder,* p. 106.

[71]BJsr made one hundred speeches throughout the South against Al Smith and for Herbert Hoover between mid-August and November 5 (BJsr to Don Cochran, 9 August 1928 [GF: Cochran file]; BJsr, "Editorial," *Bob Jones Magazine,* vol. 1, no. 11, July 1929, p. 1; and BJsr, "Editorial," *Bob Jones Magazine,* vol. 1, no. 2, October 1928, p. 1). Fifty thousand copies of the Al Smith issue (November 1928) of the *Bob Jones Magazine* were distributed (BJsr to Don Cochran, 9 August 1928). BJsr alienated several members of his wife's family because of his support for Bibb Graves for governor of Alabama and Herbert Hoover for president of the United States. BJjr wrote, "A Republican was

something between a traitor and a demon to rabid Alabama Democrats in those days. . . . [The cousins] spent the whole meal being thoroughly disagreeable and making insulting remarks to my father. I was amazed at how gracious my father was" (BJjr, *Cornbread,* p. 18).

[72]MS, BJsr, chapel talk, 2 October 1945 (ABV: 1945); MS, chapel talk, 4 March 1935 (ABV: 1935); MS, chapel talk, 17 November 1945 (ABV: 1945).

[73]Interview, Mrs. BJsr, 30 August 1986. For information on the political reforms of Bibb Graves, see William E. Gilbert, "Bibb Graves as a Progressive, 1927-1930," *Alabama Review,* vol. 10, no. 1, January 1957.

[74]"Liquor, Dance and Cards Are Scored by Jones," *Peru (Ind.) Evening Journal,* 6 February 1914.

[75]Johnson, *Builder,* p. 142.

[76]MS, BJsr, chapel talk, 2 October 1945 (ABV: 1945). See also Johnson, *Builder,* pp. 88-90.

[77]MS, BJsr, chapel talk, 2 October 1945 (ABV: 1945).

[78]"Bob Jones, Evangelist, Takes Place of Sam," *Jacksonville (Fla.) Metropolis,* 12 May 1911.

[79]MS, BJsr, chapel talk, 2 October 1945 (ABV: 1945).

[80]Sam W. Small, "The Dream of Bob Jones," unknown paper, n.d. (MLA: Bob Jones clipping book 9, p. 43).

[81]"Evangelist Bob Jones Dies at 84," *Washington (D.C.) Post,* 17 January 1968.

[82]"Muskingum College to Honor Bob Jones," *Montgomery (Ala.) Journal,* 17 June 1921.

[83]"Ku Klux Klan Sends Money to Bob Jones," and "Ku Klux Klan Appears Here Tonight," *St. Petersburg (Fla.) Independent,* 10 November 1922; "Local Ku Klux Klan No. 29 Gives Bob Jones $1568," *Andalusia (Ala.) Daily Star,* 31 August 1925. It is reasonable to expect BJsr to have had the support of the Klan, since it was a self-professed Protestant organization made up of many leading citizens in the cities of the South, Midwest, and Southwest.

[84]Robert Moats Miller, "A Note on the Relationship Between the Protestant Church and Ku Klux Klan," *Journal of Southern History,* vol. 22, no. 3, August 1956, p. 356.

[85]"Revival Has a Dramatic Close Sunday Night," *Andalusia (Ala.) Daily Star,* 31 August 1925.

[86]MS, BJsr, chapel talk, 2 December 1949 (ABV: 1949). See also Miller, "Note," pp. 356-68. Miller points out that many Protestants, from Modernists like Harry Emerson Fosdick to Fundamentalists like John Roach Straton and the leaders of the Moody Bible Institute in Chicago, found the courage to oppose the Klan. It is impossible to say, as some Klan scholars and observers have, that any real connection existed between the Ku Klux Klan and Fundamentalism. It is reasonable to conclude that the Fundamentalist crusade and the Klan were parallel but independent currents in American history. The extent to which they intersected was only at the point of the involvement of individuals who happened to be both Fundamentalists and Klan members. The extant evidence suggests that the Klan was neither a direct instrument of Fundamentalism or Protestantism, nor that the church was a direct instrument of the Klan.

[87]BJsr recorded for broadcast a series of fifty-two radio messages in the 1920s entitled "The Fundamentals of the Faith," an exposition of Fundamentalist belief (ASTA).

[88]" 'The Unbeatable Game' Is Booked for Run at Philadelphia Theater," *Philadelphia Courier,* 9 May 1925.

[89]"Evangelist-Actor Denounces State Censorship for Slashing of Film," *Philadelphia Daily News,* 12 May 1925. A copy of the film has not survived. Film, as a medium for spreading the gospel, continued to fascinate BJsr, however.

[90]" 'The Perils of America,' Dr. Bob Jones's New Lecture Heard Here Wednesday Night," *Andalusia (Ala.) Star,* 25 February 1927. See also BJsr, "The Perils of America, or Where Are We Headed," sermon booklet (Cleveland, Tenn.: Bob Jones College, 1934).

[91]W. J. Hall, "Introduction," *Bob Jones Magazine,* vol. 1, no. 1, June 1928.

[92]W. E. Patterson, "Intelligence and Orthodoxy," *Bob Jones Magazine,* October 1928, cover.

[93]BJjr, "Pontius Pilate: A Religious Drama," *Bob Jones Magazine,* April 1929, p. 19.

[94]J. Floyd Collins, "The Atonement," *Bob Jones Magazine,* May 1930, pp. 2-3, 16.

[95]Howard Morse Skinner, "Music at the Bob Jones College," *Bob Jones Magazine,* April 1929, p. 6.

[96]Francis E. West, "Why I Am Not an Evolutionist," *Bob Jones Magazine,* October 1930, cover.

[97]Small, "Dream of Bob Jones."

Chapter 2: Why Start a College?

[1]Ezell, *The South,* p. 258. Ezell reports that 260 colleges were located in the South prior to the outbreak of hostilities. With only few exceptions, the colleges were private or denominationally affiliated and therefore reflected varying world views and curricular emphases.

[2]Ibid., p. 193. In 1865, with only one student remaining, the University of Alabama was forced to close. Louisiana State University continued to offer classes with only four students enrolled. Closed during the war, the University of South Carolina and the University of Virginia reopened in 1866, with Virginia matriculating some five hundred students.

[3]Charles Forster Smith, "Southern Colleges and Schools," *Atlantic Monthly,* 54 (1884), pp. 542-57. Quoted in Ezell, *The South,* p. 262.

[4]Charles W. Ramsdell, "The Southern Heritage," in W. T. Couch, ed., *Culture in the South* (Chapel Hill, N.C.: University of North Carolina Press, 1934), p. 17.

[5]Ezell, *The South,* pp. 265-67.

[6]The shift in educational emphasis may be clearly seen in American colleges. Perhaps the most influential leader in this movement was Charles W. Eliot, president of Harvard University from 1869 to 1909. Eliot, who chaired the national education study known as the Committee of Ten, also championed the elective system in colleges, pioneered the concept of graduate school, argued for the elimination of classical language studies, and took Harvard from a classically oriented institution to the forefront of progressive higher education. See Charles W. Eliot, *Educational Reform: Essays and Addresses* (New York: Centure, 1898); and *Harvard Memories* (Cambridge: Harvard University Press, 1923); see also Edward A. Krug, *Charles W. Eliot and Popular Education* (New York: Teachers College Press, 1961).

[7]Ferenc Morton Szasz, *The Divided Mind of Protestant America, 1880-1930* (University, Ala.: University of Alabama Press, 1982), pp. 15-41.

[8]James H. Leuba, *The Belief in God and Immortality: A Psychological, Anthropological and Statistical Study* (Boston: Sherman, French and Co., 1916). Leuba surveyed by questionnaire 927 students from nine colleges and one normal school (p. 186). He

surveyed 5,700 of the most prominent biological scientists, physical scientists, psychologists, philosophers, sociologists, and educators (pp. 248-51).

[9]William Jennings Bryan with Mary Baird Bryan, *The Memoirs of William Jennings Bryan* (Chicago: John C. Winston Co., 1925), p. 479.

[10]Leuba, *Belief*. The percentages as reported by Leuba are actually higher than 50 percent. Scientists who reported themselves as believing in God made up only 41.8 percent of the sample (p. 250). Those who reported themselves as believing in immortality made up 50.6 percent of the sample (p. 252).

[11]William Jennings Bryan, *The Menace of Darwinism* (New York: Fleming H. Revell Co., 1921), pp. 45-47.

[12]Leuba, *Belief*, pp. 280-81.

[13]Ronald L. Numbers, *The Creationists* (New York: Alfred A. Knopf, 1992), p. 40.

[14]For numerous stories of the ill effects of modern education, see Dan Gilbert, *Crucifying Christ in Our Colleges* (Washington, D.C.: Danielle Publishers, 1944), originally published in 1933. See also Bryan, *Menace,* pp. 47-51; and *Memoirs,* p. 479. For an early record, see Warren Candler, *Great Revivals and the Great Republic* (Nashville: Christian Literature Company, 1904), p. 320; John Roach Straton, *Fighting the Devil in Modern Babylon* (New York: George H. Doran Company, 1929), pp. 260-65; and BJsr, "Editor's Page," *Bob Jones Magazine,* vol. 1, no. 1 (June 1928), pp. 2-3.

[15]See Shailer Mathews, *New Faith for Old: An Autobiography* (New York: Macmillan Co., 1936). One such incident was recounted by the liberal theologian and former dean of the University of Chicago Divinity School, Shailer Mathews, who recalled going to his biology professor "and asking him for a book which showed that evolution was untrue." The professor remarked, "If science shows a fact which is contrary to Christianity, Christianity must be changed." Mathews wrote, "Such a reply shocked me but stirred me to undirected reading in the field of evolution. . . . I began to think critically. It was very poor thinking but it at least amounted to the organization of a tolerant attitude toward that which was not in current evangelicalism. Such an experience was typical of many college students of the time. They came under the influence of Darwin, Tyndall, Huxley, and Spencer. They were forced to make some sort of decision as to their religious life. In some cases . . . this decision led to an abandonment of evangelical affiliations" (p. 18). See also Harry Emerson Fosdick, *The Living of These Days: An Autobiography* (New York: Harper and Brothers, 1956). Fosdick writes of his change to belief in evolution (p. 49) and concludes that when he was assigned his first pastorate, "I could not have told clearly what I believed about any major Christian doctrine" (p. 57).

[16]James Lane Allen, *The Reign of Law: A Story of the Kentucky Hemp Fields* (New York: Macmillan Co., 1908), p. 295.

[17]See George Marsden, *Fundamentalism and American Culture: The Shaping of Twentieth-Century Evangelicalism: 1870-1925* (New York: Oxford University Press, 1980), pp. 141-64.

[18]Szasz, *Divided Mind,* pp. 15-41. See also John Roach Straton, *The Famous New York Fundamentalist-Modernist Debates: The Orthodox Side* (New York: George H. Doran Company, 1925); and *Fighting the Devil.*

[19]Walter Rauschenbusch is credited with the concept of the "social gospel." Rauschenbusch taught at Rochester Seminary in New York and argued that the aim of the Old Testament prophets and of Jesus Himself was to establish the kingdom of God on earth by social justice, the amelioration of social ills, and the humanitarian improvement of the world. The social gospel taught that the death of Jesus was the highest example of selfless giving for the poor and that Jesus was God's Son as all men are. The real power of Jesus' life, then, was the example to do good for others. For more, see

Walter Rauschenbusch, *The Theology of the Social Gospel* (New York: Macmillan Co., 1917). See also Szasz, *Divided Mind,* pp. 42-67.

[20]Willard B. Gatewood, *Controversy in the Twenties: Fundamentalism, Modernism, and Evolution* (Nashville: Vanderbilt University Press, 1969), p. 3.

[21]By the war's end, a major shift had occurred even in southern Protestantism. The changes that occurred in the South were pioneered in the denominational seminaries of the North in the 1870s and 1880s and came south as northern- and German-trained scholars took positions in southern colleges and denominational seminaries. To the religious liberal, the resulting changes were called progress. To the religious conservative, the changes were called heresy. As one writer put it, "Political and religious heresy in other sections of the country may be regarded as enlightenment or liberalism. In the South, heresy is still heresy with the vast majority of people" (Edwin McNeill Poteat Jr., "Religion in the South," in Couch, ed., *Culture,* pp. 250-51).

[22]See H. K. Carroll, *The Religious Forces of the United States* (New York: Christian Literature Co., 1893, rev. 1896), pp. viii-xv. The American Protestant Church by the 1920s had become essentially divided into conservative and liberal factions. Part of the conservative wing grew into Fundamentalism and that of two types: nonconformist and separatist. The liberal wing grew into Modernism and radicalism. The South was no exception to this. (David O. Beale, *In Pursuit of Purity: American Fundamentalism Since 1850* [Greenville, S.C.: Unusual Publications, 1986], pp. 3-12. Beale identifies the two important elements in American Fundamentalism as nonconformism and separatism. The term *nonconformism* may have been drawn from Fosdick, *The Modern Use of the Bible,* in which he describes those who oppose liberal thought as nonconformists.)

[23]Though enjoying sectarian debate and denominational competition, submitting to demagogy from the pulpit, and reveling in pulpiteering, the Protestants of the South freely supported many causes. Though from Los Angeles, R. A. Torrey expressed this attitude clearly when he wrote, "The old distinction between Presbyterians and Methodists, between Baptists and Congregationalists, between Lutherans and Episcopalians, have largely lost their significance for most of us. They have lost all of their significance for me. . . . I would not go across the road to make any other man a Presbyterian, but I would go a long ways and work hard to convince any that [the Bible] is the absolutely dependable Word of God" (R. A. Torrey, *Is the Bible the Inerrant Word of God?* [New York: George H. Doran Co., 1922], p. 14); see also Marsden, *Fundamentalism,* p. 70; and George W. Dollar, *A History of Fundamentalism in America* [Greenville, S.C.: BJU Press, 1973], pp.173-83).

[24]Poteat, "Religion," in Couch, *Culture,* p. 251.

[25]Szasz, *Divided Mind,* pp. 46-47. See also Shailer Mathews, *The Individual and the Social Gospel* (New York: Layman's Missionary Movement, 1914), for a brief apologetic on the meaning, application, and theology of the social gospel.

[26]Presbyterian J. Gresham Machen expressed clearly the contrast between the social gospel and orthodoxy when he wrote, "The older evangelism, says the modern liberal preacher, sought to rescue individuals, while the newer evangelism seeks to transform the whole organism of society: the older evangelism was individual; the newer evangelism is social" (*Christianity and Liberalism* [Grand Rapids, Mich.: Wm. B. Eerdmans Publishing Co., 1923], p. 152). Many Fundamentalists actively pursued social work and were, by most reports, tremendously effective in reaching men with the gospel even when social reform was unpopular. These workers were primarily interested in saving souls and spawning personal piety because they viewed the world as a "wrecked vessel" incapable of reclamation. Fundamentalist involvement in social reform seemed to end in

the 1920s when the social gospel gained popular acceptance and redefined the intent and need for reform.

[27]Straton, *Fighting the Devil,* p. 218.

[28]Marsden, *Fundamentalism,* pp. 91-93.

[29]See Edmund deS. Brunner, *Church Life in the Rural South: A Study of the Opportunity of Protestantism Based upon Data from Seventy Counties* (New York: George H. Doran Co., 1923), p. 45.

[30]Hunter Dickinson Farish, *The Circuit Rider Dismounts: A Social History of Southern Methodism 1865-1900* (Richmond: Dietz Press, 1938). This extensive work discusses Vanderbilt and documents its shift from evangelical faith into liberalism, the heresy charges, and the ultimate result (pp. 270-304). Virginius Dabney's *Liberalism in the South* (1932; reprint ed., New York: AMS Press, 1970) documents the struggles in academia about liberal theology (pp. 190-200, 287-308, 333-58, and 414-28). Howard K. Beale's *A History of Freedom of Teaching in American Schools* (New York: Charles Scribner's Sons, 1941) documents the degree of academic freedom in various sections of the country (pp. 251-64) and presents the charges brought against faculty at these and other schools as well as the outcome of the charges. See also Mathews, *New Faith,* pp. 52-89.

[31]In Nashville, at Vanderbilt University in 1878, geology professor Alexander Winchell was dismissed for teaching his belief that man existed on earth before the creation of Adam and Eve (Beale, *Pursuit,* p. 310; see also Ezell, *The South,* p. 349).

[32]In 1879 at Louisville's Southern Baptist Seminary, Crawford H. Toy was forced to resign because of his acceptance of the evolutionary hypothesis and his interpretation of the Old Testament based on the views of Wellhausen (David O. Beale, *S.B.C.: House on the Sand?* [Greenville, S.C.: Unusual Publications, 1985, pp. 24-26]. Toy later went to Harvard Divinity School to teach and became one of the more radical American theologians. He stressed the prevalence of myth in the Bible, saying, "The march from Egypt through the wilderness, and the exploits of Moses and Joshua must be regarded as a mass of legend" (Szasz, *Divided Mind,* p. 34). Liberal Harry Emerson Fosdick quotes Toy in *Modern Use,* p. 12, as support for his argument of the progressive nature of revelation of the Scripture. In 1917 two professors were removed from the faculty of Baylor University in Texas, and in 1926 religion and science professor Andrew L. Pickens was dismissed from Furman University in Greenville, South Carolina (Numbers, *Creationists,* pp. 47-48). In 1925 a widely publicized trial was held at Wake Forest College between President William L. Poteat and the Fundamentalists; it centered on the teaching of evolution as fact (Frederick A. Bode, *Protestantism and the New South: North Carolina Baptists and Methodists in Political Crisis, 1884-1903* [Charlottesville, Va.: University Press of Virginia, 1975], p. 9). Shailer Mathews, in *New Faith,* p. 80, called Poteat "a veritable Atlas of liberalism." See also Tindall, *Emergence,* p. 200.

[33]In 1884 at the Presbyterian Theological Seminary in Columbia, S.C., German-educated James Woodrow was dismissed for his position on evolution and the scientific accuracy of the Bible (Szasz, *Divided Mind,* pp. 5-7).

[34]Ibid., p. 273. University of North Carolina president Harry W. Chase was pursued by Fundamentalists to the point of resigning because of his support of academic freedom in the teaching of science and religion.

[35]Machen, *Christianity,* pp. 1-16.

[36]One instance of such Fundamentalist opposition to the teaching of evolution is contained in a joint resolution of the legislature of the state of Florida, 1924. Written by William Jennings Bryan, the resolution reads in part: "Whereas, the public schools and colleges of this State, supported in whole or in part by public funds, should be kept free

from any teaching designed to set up and promulgate sectarian views, and should also be equally free from teachings designed to attack the religious beliefs of the public. . . . Therefore, it is the sense of the Legislature of the State of Florida that it is improper and subversive to the best interest of the people of this State for any professor, teacher or instructor in the public schools and colleges of the State, supported in whole or in part by public taxation, to teach or permit to be taught atheism or agnosticism or to teach as true, Darwinism or any other hypothesis that links man in blood relationship to any other form of life" (Bryan, *Memoirs,* p. 459).

[37]For an example of this reaction, see E. H. Crowson, *The Betrayal of Southern College: A Study in the Technique of Modern Infidelity* (unpublished manuscript [ML]). Southern College was a small Methodist school in Lakeland, Florida, that was rocked by Modernism in the late 1920s and early 1930s. Crowson, a Methodist Fundamentalist, documents the proceedings and shows the insidious nature of Modernism.

[38]Quoted by H. L. Mencken in the *American Mercury,* vol. 3, no. 12, 1924, p. 416.

[39]Machen, *Christianity,* pp. 10-14.

[40]MS, BJsr, Bible Conference sermon, 3 April 1944 (ABV: 1944).

[41]"Bob Jones Says We Need the Rock of Ages—Not the Age of Rocks," *Bellingham (Wash.) American,* 16 November 1927.

[42]BJsr, "The Perils of America" (Chicago: Chicago Gospel Tabernacle, 1934), pp. 32-39.

[43]BJsr said in the course of a sermon, "We say we believe in the creation of man by the direct act of God. But we want our students to know what Darwin taught; we want them to know what Huxley taught; we want them to know what Spencer taught. We tell them that these men were just guessing" (MS, BJsr, Bible Conference sermon, 3 April 1944 [ABV: 1944]; see also MS, BJjr, "Speech at the DuBose Bible Conference," February 1939 [ABV: Odds & Ends]).

[44]Interview, Mrs. BJsr with Margaret Beall Tice.

[45]Ibid.

[46]BJsr, "Three College Shipwrecks," undated pamphlet (Greenville, S.C.: BJU [BJC], ca. 1930). "Shipwrecks" was reprinted in "Editorial," *Advent Review and Sabbath Herald,* vol. 108, no. 42, 15 October 1931. See also *Bob Jones Magazine,* vol. 1, no. 9; and vol. 2, no. 2.

[47]"Bob Jones Labors to Give Christian Education to Youth of the Future," *Birmingham (Ala.) News,* 20 June 1928. See also MS, BJsr, chapel talk, "Why I Founded Bob Jones University," 6 September 1950. This talk includes three such incidents from his evangelistic career.

[48]Wright, *Fortress,* pp. 25-26.

[49]BJsr, "Editorial," *Bob Jones Magazine,* vol. 1, no. 9 (June 1929), p. 1.

[50]BJjr, Interview, 28 May 1987. Moral looseness was a major sermon topic in the evangelistic career of BJsr. See also "Pleasure Loving Women Scored," *Galveston (Tex.) Morning Tribune,* 29 January 1911; "Liquor, Dance and Cards Scored by Jones," *Peru (Ind.) Evening Journal,* 6 February 1914; " 'Movies,' Saloons and Prize Fights Rapped by Jones," *Joplin (Mo.) Globe,* 2 November 1915; "Sins of America Subject of Sermon by Jones Tonight," *St. Petersburg (Fla.) Times,* n.d., 1922.

[51]As indicated by a sermon on 3 April 1944 (ABV: 1944) and 17 November 1945 (ABV: 1945), BJsr recalled talks with William Jennings Bryan on the subject of Darwinism and agreed fully with Bryan's opposition to it. BJsr assigned a faculty member, Francis E. West, on 22 October 1929, to write a position paper on "Why I Am Not an Evolutionist" (ABV: FMM, 22 October 1929). This paper was published in

October 1930 in the *Bob Jones Magazine*. Evolution was discussed in seven issues of the *Bob Jones Magazine* from June 1928 through its last issue in January 1931.

[52]Warner Ogden, "Evangelist Bob Jones Operates a Non-Profit College Where Fundamentalism Is Insisted On," *Knoxville (Tenn.) News-Sentinel*, 11 February 1934. It is interesting to note that among the sermon transcripts contained in the ABV, this researcher found four pages of hand-written notes (ca. 1933) identified by Iris Jackson, long-time office supervisor, as being written by BJsr, entitled "*Behaviorism* by Watson" (ABV: 1933). BJsr preached against behaviorism on several occasions, including a chapel talk on Genesis 3 (ABV: 1933) and a chapel talk on 2 April 1945 (ABV: 1945). In addition, *Bob Jones Magazine* asked the question on its cover "I wonder if the average every-day person knows what 'behaviorism' really means?" BJsr then wrote on the topic in a short editorial (*Bob Jones Magazine*, vol. 3, no. 1 [January 1931], cover).

[53]BJjr, Interview, 28 May 1987. Corroborative statements are found throughout the extant sermon transcripts of BJsr.

[54]BJsr, "Editorial," *Bob Jones Magazine*, vol. 1, no. 1 (June 1928), cover. See also Dolly Dalrymple, "Bob Jones Labors to Give Christian Education to Youth of the Future," *Birmingham (Ala.) News*, 20 June 1928.

[55]" 'Flapper Mothers' and Evolution Draw Fire from Evangelist Jones," *Birmingham (Ala.) News*, 9 May 1928.

[56]A. H. Perpetuo, "The Uniqueness of Bob Jones College," *Bob Jones Magazine*, vol 3, no. 1 (January 1931), pp. 14-15.

[57]BJsr, "Editorial," *Bob Jones Magazine*, vol. 1, no. 1 (June 1928), cover.

Chapter 3: The Founding of Bob Jones College

[1]Interview, Mrs. BJsr with Margaret Beall Tice. See also " 'Perils of America,' Dr. Bob Jones' New Lecture Heard Here Wednesday Night," *Andalusia (Ala.) Star*, 25 February 1927.

[2]MS, BJsr, chapel talk, 28 February 1950 (ABV: 1950).

[3]Interview, BJjr, 28 May 1987. Figures quoted in news clippings found in the Bob Jones clipping books, vols. 1-10 (MLA), corroborate BJjr's recollections.

[4]Interview, Mrs. BJsr with Margaret Beall Tice, "Founding of the School," tape 1, September-October 1973. At this time, though promoting and participating in union campaigns, BJsr was still a staunch member of the Methodist Episcopal Church, South. His thoughts about finding a college for his son may be reflective of the condition of Methodist schools like Southern University, which he attended, or Vanderbilt University in Nashville, Tennessee, in which widely publicized heresy charges had been leveled at professors. Had BJsr been reared in the Presbyterian or Baptist church, one wonders where BJjr would have been sent for college.

[5]Interview, Mrs. BJsr, "Founding," tape 1. From references in a promotion letter by BJsr, dated 7 December 1926, it seems probable that this event occurred in 1925. The exact date is unknown. See also Johnson, *Builder*, pp. 171-73. BJsr described the event by saying, "I am more sure that God called me to found this school than I am that He called me to preach. I thought He called me to preach—I just went to preaching. I didn't have any great compulsion to preach, I just sort of wanted to preach, I don't know why. I was converted at eleven years old. But I could take you to the spot today in Kissimmee, Florida, where God laid it on my heart so definitely, that I just had it to do. I remember it just as if it was yesterday—no 'ands,' 'ifs,' or 'maybe so's' about it. I just had to do it. . . . I told my wife about it. She said, 'You are in the evangelistic field all over the

country—you're getting along wonderfully.' I said, 'I know, but I see some signs—I see some conditions we're going to face, and there ought to be a school that would just take a stand and hold that stand regardless. . . . It should be in line with the Word of God. . . . Now, I know the public—I have access to the public, and I'm going to found that kind of school' " (MS, BJsr, radio talk [ASTA: 3 December 1959]).

[6]Warner Ogden, "Evangelist Bob Jones Operates a Non-profit College Where Fundamentalism Is Insisted Upon," *Knoxville (Tenn.) News-Sentinel,* 11 February 1934. See also "Bob Jones Makes Application for College Charter," unknown, n.d., BJsr clipping book 9, p. 10 (MLA). The date, though uncorroborated, comes from interview, Tommy Smith, 17 May 1988.

[7]It is interesting to note that two members of the BJC board were also members of the Bay County School Board. R. L. McKenzie and J. M. Sapp both sat as trustees on the three-member board in the county (Anne Williams Warwick, *Tides: Growing Up on St. Andrews Bay* [Panama City, Fla.: Boyd Brothers Printing, 1984], pp. 93-94).

[8]Johnson, *Builder,* p. 178.

[9]Ibid. Corroborated by Interview, Tommy Smith, 17 May 1988.

[10]"Flapper Mothers," *Birmingham (Ala.) News,* 9 May 1928.

[11]Gloria Jahoda, *Florida: A Bicentennial History* (New York: W. W. Norton and Company, 1976), p. 117.

[12]Frank Parker Stockbridge and John Holliday Perry, *Florida in the Making* (New York: de Bower Publishing Company, 1926), pp. 286-99. This period work asks the question, "Can the boom last?" and proceeds to answer it in the affirmative, stating, "The settlers are still coming."

[13]"Florida As It Is Today," *Florida State News,* 3 March 1927, quoted in Mark Dalhouse, "Bob Jones University and the Shaping of Twentieth Century Separatism, 1926-1991" (Ph.D. dissertation, Miami [Ohio] University, 1991), p. 83. Marlene Womack, "Bob Jones Made Dream a Reality," *Panama City (Fla.) News Herald,* 26 July 1987, reports that in late 1925 in north Florida, "two thousand lots were sold in one day for $3.00 each, then changed hands the next day for $5.00 each. Real estate men were known to have incomes of $10,000 a day," and records indicate that in one week, it was not uncommon for $5,000,000 worth of land to change hands.

[14]It is unclear how Dr. Jones was introduced to the Keith Corporation. The initial contact may have been arranged by real estate magnate and member of the Board of Trustees of the college, R. L. McKenzie. Interviewee Tommy Smith (17 May 1988) indicated that McKenzie was a founder of the Panama City community and was doing business with the Keith interests and their local representative, Berry Collins, at this time. McKenzie interested BJsr in locating the college in the Bay County area of Florida and showed him several tracts of land before BJsr decided on the Long Point area in Lynn Haven.

[15]There has been some disagreement as to whether Keith actually donated the land for the campus or whether he simply discounted the price. The earliest source (*Lynn Haven [Fla.] Free Press,* 4 December 1926) indicates that the company did indeed donate the land (Johnson, *Builder,* p. 175). See also Womack, "Bob Jones Made Dream."

[16]Interview, Mrs. BJsr, "Founding," tape 1. A beautiful structure, the original Jones home was built for $18,000 and is still standing. (The exact figure is in dispute: Mrs. BJsr recalled $18,000, while BJjr recalled $4,000.)

[17]Womack, "Bob Jones Made Dream." See also Dalhouse, "Shaping," p. 85.

[18]Johnson, *Builder,* pp. 175-76.

[19]Womack, "Bob Jones Made Dream."

[20]Interview, Mrs. BJsr, "Founding," tape 1.

[21]One letter reads,

I have asked my brother Tom and also Caleb Martin to see you in person, and outline to you some of the details of our college project. We are trying to do a big piece of work here and what we are trying to do will profit not only this country, but also south east [*sic*] Alabama. The usual method of building a College is to go out and solicit gifts, but we are not going to do this. We have made an arrangement by which a man can make a safe and undoubtedly profitable investment and at the same time do our College as much good as if they gave the money outright.

I am writing a few southeast Alabama friends and requesting them to purchase at least one lot in our subdivision and help us build this great College and at the same time help themselves by making a profitable investment. I am enclosing a little booklet which tells the whole story. Thanking you for your co-operation and with best wishes, I am

Yours very truly, Bob Jones (BJsr to "Friend," 26 February 1926 [MLA: Box 26])

[22]Interview, Mrs. BJsr with Margaret Beall Tice, "Evangelistic Days," September/October 1973. Also BJsr to "Friend," 29 June 1926 (MLA: Box 26). See also BJsr to Caleb Martin, 4 August 1926 (MLA: Box 26); and BJsr to "Sir," 5 August 1926 (MLA: Box 26), in which BJsr says, "Mr. Alex May, who you know, has asked you to represent the Bob Jones College in your locality and he wants you to come to Panama City NEXT THURSDAY if its [*sic*] the last trip you ever make. Bring someone who is able to buy a College Point lot and it will mean money in your pocket."

[23]The Bob Jones Tabernacle was apparently erected in the early 1920s and was used annually by the evangelist for several weeks of meetings. One report indicates that in January 1926, Bob Jones or an associate preached nightly through August at the Tabernacle. The Tabernacle meetings helped underscore the uniquely religious character of the school. For many years thereafter, the Bob Jones Tabernacle remained standing and served as a cultural and religious center to the people of Panama City (Warwick, *Tides,* pp. 119-20).

[24]Womack, "Bob Jones Made Dream." See also Dalhouse, "Shaping," p. 85.

[25]Sam W. Small, "The Dream of Bob Jones," unknown paper, n.d. (MLA: Bob Jones clipping book 9, p. 43). Small was assigned to cover the revival campaigns of Sam Jones, the popular Southern Methodist evangelist, for the *Constitution*. Small had been converted in a Sam Jones meeting at Collegeville, Georgia, and was delivered from alcoholism shortly after his conversion.

[26]Interview, Tommy Smith, 17 May 1988.

[27]The bonds were ten-year, 6 percent, first mortgage gold bonds issued 1 December 1926, with interest payable semiannually. The bonds were issued in $25, $100, $500, and $1,000 denominations. A. A. Payne, president of the First National Bank, and J. D. Sellars, president of the Commercial Bank, acted as bond trustees ("Up-to-the-Minute Facts About College Point and the Bob Jones College," 16 March 1927 [MLA: Box 26]).

[28]MS, BJsr, chapel talk, 28 February 1950 (ABV: 1950). See also BJsr to Howard Bailey, 20 March 1933. By 7 December 1926, $100,000 worth of bonds had been placed. One announcement reads, "The Minor C. Keith Florida Properties, Inc., . . . has purchased $80,000 worth of these bonds. Mrs. Jennie Brandenberg of Lynn Haven, Florida, has purchased $15,000 worth of these bonds. . . . They are six percent, ten year bonds with a provision that they can be taken up after three years" (BJsr, promotion letter, 7 December 1926 [MLA: Box 26]). *Bob Jones Magazine* also advertised in February 1929, $25,000 worth of bonds' being available for placement (*Bob Jones Magazine,* vol. 1, no. 6, February 1929).

[29]BJsr, promotion letter, 7 December 1926. The size of BJsr's constituency is unknown. It is known that he had preached in nearly every state of the Union and in every major city and had preached widely in Alabama, Georgia, and Florida for twenty-nine

years by the time the board was formed. Undoubtedly, the size of his supporting base was large. Eventually, the bonded indebtedness of the college "represented about 20 percent of the investment of the college" (BJsr to J. Paul Ray, 28 January 1952 [GF: Asbury Alumni Association]).

[30]*Lynn Haven (Fla.) Free Press,* 4 December 1926.

[31]Womack, "Bob Jones Made Dream."

[32]R. H. Hunt Company Architects, "The Bob Jones College, College Point—Bay County, Fla.," 16 March 1927 (MLA: Bob Jones clipping book 9, p. 10). Tommy Smith indicated that this building concept was arrived at jointly, the model being derived from the concept of building communities surrounding golf courses, as was the case with the Keith project at the Panama City–St. Andrews Bay Country Club (Interview, Tommy Smith, 17 May 1988).

[33]*College Point Development: Site of Bob Jones College,* printer's paste-up, p. 5, ca. 1926 (MLA: Box 26). Extant letters, sermon manuscripts of BJsr, and newspaper clippings, when dealing with this era of the school's history, do not mention a planned city or any urban development. The text quoted above may have been for the sole purpose of exciting sales rather than stating the development concepts of BJsr.

[34]Dolly Dalrymple, "Bob Jones Labors to Give Christian Education to Youth of the Future," *Birmingham (Ala.) News,* 20 June 1928.

[35]"The Creed of BJU" (ABV: Odds & Ends, 1950).

[36]"The Charter of Bob Jones College [University]," Office of the Provost, BJU, Greenville, S.C.

[37]BJsr often preached on points of the creed. Extant MSS include a chapel talk on the creed in 1945 (ABV: n.d. 1945); "The Creed of BJU," a chapel message preached in March 1950 (ABV: Odds & Ends); and daily mention of or allusion to the creed in a series of morning radio talks on the history, founding, and ethics of BJU, from 28 March through 21 April 1958 (ASTA).

[38]A. H. Perpetuo, "The Uniqueness of Bob Jones College," *Bob Jones Magazine,* vol. 3, no. 1, January 1931, pp. 14-15. Perpetuo categorized the institution's uniqueness in three areas: (1) BJC does not "tolerate any worldly amusements . . . [and] believes wholly in God's Word, without over-emphasizing any doctrine." (2) BJC is the only school "where the godliness of each faculty member is placed above scholarship, although the latter is not overlooked." (3) BJC is the "only school . . . where every class is opened with prayer. . . . Every session opens with a revival [meeting]."

[39]*American Mercury,* vol. 3, no. 9, 1924, p. 40. See also Small, "Dream of Bob Jones." For an excellent overview of the cynicism of Mencken and others, see Tindall, *Emergence,* pp. 285-317.

[40]MS, BJsr, chapel talk, 25 April 1946 (ABV: 1946).

[41]Specific reasons for Buswell's disapprobation have not been uncovered. Undoubtedly, the fact that Buswell became president of Wheaton on 1 April 1926 and immediately set about to enlarge the Wheaton student body had some bearing on his feelings. By 1927 Buswell had brought Wheaton into the North Central Association, gained official recognition from the University of Illinois, added $1 million to student endowment funds, raised faculty salaries, and begun a push to add more Ph.D.'s to the faculty. Proud of these early accomplishments, Buswell obviously believed that "one is enough." See Paul M. Bechtel, *Wheaton College: A Heritage Remembered 1860-1984* (Wheaton, Ill.: Harold Shaw Publishers, 1984), pp. 113-19.

[42]BJjr to Mark Dalhouse, 16 November 1989, quoted in Dalhouse, p. 90.

[43]BJsr to JRR, 12 May 1949 (GF: Buswell file). See also JRR, "Dr. J. Oliver Buswell's Charges Against Bob Jones University Answered," *Sword of the Lord,* June 1948.

[44]BJsr to "Brother," 6 April 1927 (MLA: Box 26).

[45]Interviewees Elizabeth Edwards, Karl Keefer, Monroe Parker, and Katherine Stenholm each reported that a pastor or area denominational leader tried to dissuade him or her from attending Bob Jones College. The arguments used were that the College was not "Methodist" (Edwards) or was "too strict" (Stenholm) or was "unaccredited and the college work would have to be validated" by the denominational leadership (Keefer).

[46]Alex M. Damon, "Lt. Commissioner and Mrs. Damon Visit Bob Jones College, College Point, Fla.," *War Cry,* 2 January 1932. See also "Editorial," *Advent Review and Sabbath Herald,* 15 October 1931. Monroe Parker wrote, "The Bible Conferences were held between semesters. My first year we had eight speakers each day; and though we got weary and some students had to take sofa pillows to the chapel to sit on, we loved every minute of it" (Monroe Parker, *Through Sunshine and Shadows: My First 77 Years* [Murfreesboro, Tenn.: Sword of the Lord Press, 1987]).

[47]A Holiness preacher and president of Asbury College in Wilmore, Kentucky, Henry Clay Morrison is credited by BJsr as being very helpful in the founding and development of the school. He spoke at chapel on a yearly basis (BJjr, *Cornbread,* p. 54). Morrison was a speaker at the first annual BJC Bible Conference, which ran from 27 January to 4 February 1929 (*Bob Jones Magazine,* vol. 1, no. 5, January 1929). BJC conferred on him the honorary degree of doctor of oratory in 1935 (GF: "Honorary Degrees Conferred by Bob Jones College").

[48]Noted American evangelist and friend of BJsr, Billy Sunday spoke at BJC yearly until his death. The school conferred on him the honorary degree of doctor of laws in 1935 (GF: "Honorary Degrees"). Mrs. Billy "Ma" Sunday was a member of the board from 1936 until her death in February 1957.

[49]Harry Ironside was of the Plymouth Brethren denomination and pastor of Moody Memorial Church, Chicago, Illinois, in the 1930s and 1940s. BJC offered Ironside an honorary doctorate in the 1930s, but he refused the degree, not wanting to offend any of his Plymouth Brethren friends who did not believe in divinity degrees (BJjr, *Cornbread,* pp. 56-58). Later he changed his mind, and in 1942 BJC conferred on him the honorary degree of doctor of divinity (GF: "Honorary Degrees").

[50]William Bell Riley was a Northern Baptist pastor from 1885-1947 and president of the Northwestern Bible College of Minneapolis, Minnesota, from 1902-44. Mrs. BJjr recalled Riley and his wife visiting BJC and their home on several occasions (Interview, Mrs. BJjr, 4 June 1987). Riley was offered an honorary degree but refused, saying he already had too many. He asked that the school confer the degree doctor of laws on his wife, which was done in 1941 (GF: "Honorary Degrees").

[51]Leander Whitcomb Munhall was an organizer of the World's Christian Fundamentals Association in 1918 and a Methodist. Munhall told BJsr, "Robert, remember this: God's Word says, 'If any man serve me, him will the Father honor.' " BJsr promised to exalt the Lord Jesus Christ in everything. BJC conferred on Munhall the honorary degree of doctor of divinity in 1931 (GF: "Honorary Degrees").

[52]William E. Biederwolf was a Presbyterian, the director of the Winona Lake, Indiana, Bible Conference, and a friend of BJsr. He spoke at BJC at Bible Conference sometime prior to 1931 (BJjr, *Cornbread,* p. 99). The school conferred on him the honorary degree of doctor of divinity in 1931 (GF: "Honorary Degrees").

[53]Pastor of Moody Memorial Church, Chicago, Illinois, from 1915-33, Paul Radar was a regular Bible Conference and chapel visitor (BJjr, *Cornbread,* p. 53). Radar

preached the Commencement Address on 28 May 1933 (Commencement Program of Bob Jones College, 1933 [MLA: Box 26]), and BJC conferred on him the honorary degree of doctor of divinity in 1933 (GF: "Honorary Degrees").

[54]John Roach Straton was a Baptist and pastor of Calvary Baptist Church, New York City. BJsr preached a summer series of revival messages yearly for Straton under a huge tent at West 124th Street and Morningside Drive in New York City.

[55]MS, BJsr, chapel talk, "The Creed of BJU," March 1950 (ABV: Odds & Ends).

[56]Marlene Womack, "Bob Jones Rode Crest of Area Boom," *Panama City (Fla.) News Herald,* 2 August 1987.

[57]BJsr, *Bob Jones Magazine,* "Editorial," June 1928.

[58]Interview, Mrs. BJsr, "Founding," tape 1.

Chapter 4: Bob Jones College: College Point, Florida

[1]Among those present were Alabama superintendent of education Dr. John C. Abercrombie; Florida superintendent of education Dr. W. S. Cawthorn; Dr. O. C. Carmichael, president of the Alabama College for Women at Montevallo; Dr. David Spence Hill, president of the University of Alabama; Director B. C. Riley of the University of Florida; and Dr. J. V. Brown of the Alabama Polytechnic Institute at Auburn. See "An Epoch in Education," reprint from the *Montgomery (Ala.) Advertiser,* 14 September 1927 (MLA: Box 26). See also Wright, *Fortress,* pp. 37-39.

[2]Interview, Mrs. BJsr, "Founding," tape 1. A banquet of fried chicken, mashed potatoes, asparagus, tomato aspic, iced tea, and dessert had been planned. Had it not been for Hattie, Jennie Brandenberg's cook, who helped in the kitchen, and Mrs. R. L. McKenzie, who decorated the dining room, the opening would have been a fiasco. Mrs. BJsr indicated that this was the last time Dr. Bob hired anybody for a service position without discussing it with her.

[3]Jennie Brandenberg Hall was named for a wealthy board member who made her home in Pittsburgh and wintered in Lynn Haven. She had supported BJsr in his evangelistic campaigns in Pennsylvania and had donated five thousand dollars for construction. She also purchased ten thousand dollars in College Development Bonds. When financial troubles threatened the school, she joined in the lawsuit that eventually forced the school to move to Tennessee. The name for Bama Hall was taken from Alabama, BJsr's home state.

[4]*An Epoch in Education: Facts About the Bob Jones College,* first college catalog (BJC: College Point, Fla., 1927), p. 8. BJsr described the first plant by saying it was "quite modern. We had a lovely girls' dormitory, a nice boys' dormitory, a wonderful dining room with equipment. . . . The other buildings were fair. Some of those were not built for permanent use; we intended to build some more [permanent ones] later" (MS, BJsr, chapel talk, 28 February 1950). Mary Lizzie Dixon and Mrs. R. L. McKenzie were sisters and planned and executed the landscaping for the new campus. In addition to donating time and money, they planted flower beds, shrubs, and trees, and in return the 1932 yearbook was dedicated to them for their efforts (*San Andros,* BJC yearbook, 1932).

[5]Wright, *Fortress,* p. 32. BJsr often mentioned the fact that he "borrowed the brains" to found and operate the College. Those from whom he borrowed brains included close friends such as Bibb Graves, governor of Alabama; Henry Clay Morrison, president of Asbury College; James M. Gray, president of Moody Bible Institute; Harry Ironside of the Bible Institute of Los Angeles and later pastor of Moody Church; as well as educational authorities in the state colleges and universities of Florida and Alabama. See

also MS, BJsr, Bible Conference message, 3 April 1944 (ABV: 1944); and MS, BJsr, radio talk (ASTA: 26 December 1959). See also Johnson, *Builder,* pp. 181-82. Interview data obtained from BJjr corroborates that H. C. Morrison was very helpful in providing advice to BJsr in the early days of the school and that leads for faculty members were occasionally obtained from Morrison. Morrison also advised BJsr to find faculty who were not "hirelings" but were called of God to the ministry (Interview, BJjr, 28 May 1987).

[6]MS, BJsr, radio talk (ASTA: 31 March 1958).

[7]MS, BJsr, chapel talk, 2 March 1933 (ABV: 1933).

[8]Interview, BJjr, 28 May 1987.

[9]Records indicate that by 1927 in church-supported schools such as the Methodists' Alabama College for Women at Montevallo, the "chapel" service often consisted of the reading of a verse of Scripture, an inspirational poem, and perhaps a song or solo. Preaching was unheard of. See Prince Leon Dorough, "A History of the Music Department of the University of Montevallo, Montevallo, Alabama" (Ed.D. dissertation, University of Illinois, 1986). BJsr's old school, Southern University, had daily chapel in which a portion of Scripture was read and a prayer said. By 1930 both of these schools had canceled or shortened the chapel programs or made attendance voluntary.

[10]Interview, Mrs. BJsr, "Founding," tape 1. Mrs. Jones continued the story by saying her mother went home and memorized all the verses to the song. She came down to breakfast devotions the next morning and said to BJsr, "Can I sing my hymn for you now or must I wait until chapel?"

[11]Interview, Mrs. BJjr, 4 June 1987.

[12]MS, BJsr, chapel talk, 19 December 1934 (ABV: 1934). The record of BJsr's dealing with cultural issues occurs in the earliest extant sermon MSS, including the following: 29 January 1933; 9, 11, and 12 February 1933; 2 March 1933; 19 December 1934; 3 January 1935; and 17 April 1935 (ABV: 1933-35).

[13]BJsr to "Friend," 6 April 1927. He wrote, "We propose to have as strong a Faculty as you can find anywhere in any Junior College."

[14]For more on Bob Jones Academy, see Chapter 24.

[15]MS, BJsr, radio talk (ASTA: 26 December 1959).

[16]"Epoch" (MLA: Box 26). During the 1928-29 school year, the College offered an associate degree in prelaw as well.

[17]*Bob Jones College Annual Bulletin,* volume 3, no. 1, April 1929 (MLA: *Bob Jones University Catalogue,* vols. 1-12, 1927-39). This bulletin states that "we advise students who desire to pursue courses leading to technical and professional degrees such as engineering, law, medicine, etc., to go elsewhere upon completion of the first two years, as we are maintaining the junior and senior years especially for those students who desire to enter some definite line of Christian work, or who want a thorough four-year course in arts and sciences" (p. 3). The *Bob Jones College Catalogue 1931-1932 and Announcements 1932-1933,* volume 5, no. 1, p. 37 (MLA: *Bob Jones University Catalogue,* vols. 1-12, 1927-39), states that "beyond the Sophomore year we retain only students who wish to major in music, speech, or religion. We give the A.B. degree only to students who major in one of these three subjects" (p. 8).

[18]*Catalogue 1931-1932,* vol. 5, no. 1, p. 37 (MLA: *Bob Jones University Catalogue,* vols. 1-12, 1927-39).

[19]In the spring of 1929 a five-member inspection team from the University of Florida sent a report to the state superintendent of education, W. S. Cawthorn, approving the school's academic program. By 1932, the University of Florida, Florida State University, and the Florida State College for Women had recognized the school's credits as well (FMM: 29

February 1932 [ABV]). See also Dalhouse, "Shaping," p. 91; and BJsr, *Bob Jones Magazine,* vol. 1, no. 9 (June 1928), p. 1.

[20]Extant FMM indicate that the standardization of the College's work was problematic, possibly because the College never received input from any outside source. Curriculum models were based on other institutions: it was announced by the dean on 16 September 1930 that "the University of Florida is to be our standard educationally thru [*sic*] the sophomore year." The college dean reminded faculty on a regular basis that the "most serious objection to our work . . . has been with reference to our abnormal number of A's and B's" (12 October 1931). Other mentions include 11 and 19 February, 25 March, and 16 September 1930; 28 February, 18 March, and 14 September 1931; 18 and 22 January, 29 February, and 14 October 1932 (ABV: FMM).

[21]FMM, 25 November 1929 (ABV). The informality of this arrangement was later corrected when the dean announced that an examination schedule would be posted.

[22]MS, BJsr, chapel talk, 1945 (ABV: 1945).

[23]These early graduates attended such institutions as the University of Chicago, the University of Pittsburgh, Princeton University, Union Theological Seminary, Columbia University, and Colorado State University. Interviewees from this era include three of the four graduates of the first four-year class: BJjr, Fannie May Holmes Jones, and Monroe Parker.

[24]W. E. Patterson, "Intelligence and Orthodoxy," *Bob Jones Magazine,* vol. 1, no. 2, October 1928.

[25]MS, BJsr, chapel talk, 30 March 1935 (ABV: 1935).

[26]BJsr, "Editorial," *Bob Jones Magazine,* vol. 1, no. 1 (June 1928), cover.

[27]"Epoch" (MLA: Box 26).

[28]MS, BJsr, Sunday sermon, "Prayer," 29 January 1933 (ABV: 1933).

[29]R. K. Johnson, *Miracle from the Beginning* (Greenville, S.C.: BJU, 1971), p.1.

[30]*Catalogue,* 1933-34, vol. 6, no. 1, p. 2. This motto may have been drawn from A. H. Perpetuo, "The Uniqueness of Bob Jones College," *Bob Jones Magazine,* vol. 3, no. 1 (January 1931), pp. 14-15. One sentence reads, "Bob Jones College is equal to any college its size and class educationally, and excels any school in its devotion to God's Word and in its Christian spirit."

[31]BJsr, "Editorial," *Bob Jones Magazine,* vol. 1, no. 1 (June 1928), cover.

[32]"Lt. Commissioner and Mrs. Damon Visit Bob Jones College, College Point, Fla.," *War Cry,* 2 January 1932.

[33]MS, BJsr, chapel talk, 1 October 1935.

[34]*Epoch,* p. 30.

[35]*Catalogue 1931-1932,* vol. 5, no. 1, p. 9 (MLA: *Bob Jones University Catalogue,* vols. 1-12, 1927-39).

[36]The first year's enrollment figures are open to question. Various sources quote differing figures, although it seems likely that the most accurate figures are those reported by the RO. The statistics quoted here are taken from official enrollment figures provided by the RO, which show that the College enrolled 85 and the Academy enrolled 47, for a total of 132 students ("Enrollment Statistics: First Semester," n.d.). In a chapel talk of the Founder, however, it was reported that the school opened with 88 students and matriculated 135 by the end of the second semester (MS, BJsr, chapel talk, 28 February 1950 [ABV: 1950]). See also Wright, *Fortress,* p. 40. Wright reports the total of matriculated students as 125.

[37]MS, BJsr, chapel talk, 28 February 1950 (ABV: 1950). Also mentioned in MS, BJsr, chapel talk, 2 January 1945 (ABV: 1945); and MS, BJsr, chapel talk, 24 January 1949 (ABV: 1949).

[38]BJsr, "A Frank Word About Our Boys and Girls," *Bob Jones Magazine,* vol. 1, no. 8 (April 1929), pp. 1, 23. See also Johnson, *Builder,* p. 184; and MS, BJsr, chapel talk, 28 February 1950 (ABV: 1950).

[39]Johnson, *Builder,* p. 184.

[40]MS, BJsr, chapel talk, 28 February 1950 (ABV: 1950). Although official enrollment statistics for these years do not show the size of the College enrollment, it seems somewhat unlikely that enrollment would have grown to over 200 by the second year. Official enrollment statistics show that the College and Academy together did not total more than 200 until 1934-35, at which time they totaled 210 students (RO: "Enrollment Statistics, First Semester," n.d.). Also, conflicting numbers of expulsions for 1928-29—thirty-five, forty, and fifty-two students—have appeared. BJsr mentions thirty-five expulsions in 1928. The number fifty-two is found in a sermon preached on 24 January 1949 (ABV: 1949). It was in the second year of the school that BJsr realized that admissions policies had to be changed in order to keep the student body from filling up with "bad boys" and to keep the school from turning into a "Reformatory."

[41]"Resolution," 23 January 1928 (MLA: Display).

[42]Interview, Elizabeth Edwards, 28 May 1987; Interview, Mrs. BJjr, 4 June 1987.

[43]For more on BJjr, see Chapter 11 and his autobiography, *Cornbread and Caviar.* For more information on Monroe Parker, James Edwards, and R. K. Johnson, see Chapter 25. Also see Wright, *Fortress,* pp. 355-59. For information on Parker, see his autobiography, *Through Sunshine and Shadows: My First 77 Years.*

[44]Interview, Mrs. BJjr, 4 June 1987. Extant FMM contain numerous records of discussions of student rules and policies—viz. 15 October 1929: "The faculty voted to close school at 3:00 Friday afternoon for the football game, but voted that no games be allowed in the future except on Saturdays"; 22 October 1929: "No student meetings [may] be called between Chapel and 9:00 classes, or at any time to interfere with any classes"; 29 October 1929: "Girls can go walking to the Bluff, to the Bay, to Lynn Haven with a student teacher"; 13 March 1930: "The faculty voted unanimously to expel Guyman from school. Other boys who were smoking were discussed" (ABV: FMM). See also Warwick, *Tides,* p. 121.

[45]*Bob Jones Magazine,* January 1929.

[46]Wright, *Fortress,* p. 49.

[47]MS, BJsr, chapel talk, 21 January 1941 (ABV: 1941).

[48]Interview, BJjr, 28 May 1987. Extant FMM record the faculty decisions relative to discipline on these dates: 29 October 1929, 19 and 25 November 1929, 3 December 1929, and at almost every meeting of the faculty for which minutes exist through 1933 (ABV).

[49]FMM, 8 March 1931 (ABV).

[50]Ibid., 15 April 1930.

[51]Ibid., 22 April 1930.

[52]Ibid. The following telegram was sent to his father: "I regret very much that the faculty have found it necessary to expel your son Wayne. He has committed offense after offense and broken many of the college regulations and the faculty feel they can do nothing more for him. Wire at once if you want him to come home. He is slightly indebted to the college and I do not think he has money. F. E. West."

[53]Unknown author, "An Unique Institution," n.d. (MLA: Box 16). In 1928 and 1929 transportation to College Point was rather difficult, and BJC did not own transportation. It was therefore necessary for teams to travel to the College. In later years, the College teams went into Panama City and other nearby towns to play games.

[54]*San Andros* (college yearbook), 1930, 1931. To be fair, it must be mentioned that the BJC teams played mainly high schools and vocational schools.

[55]Parker, *Sunshine,* p. 66.

[56]FMM, 3 December 1929 (ABV).

[57]Ibid., 7 October 1930.

[58]Ibid., 5 November 1930. This request was denied because "the rule passed last year was found to be that all players must pass their work."

[59]Ibid., 4 September 1931.

[60]Ibid., 15 October 1929. The faculty decided at this meeting to allow football games to be played only on Saturdays.

[61]BJjr to Lyle E. Eckly, 18 May 1964 (GF: Olivet Nazarene College file).

[62]Interview, Mrs. BJsr, "Founding," tape 1.

[63]FMM, 8 December 1933 (ABV). When this decision was reached, the school had been relocated to Cleveland, Tennessee. There were twenty-six faculty members at this time (*Bob Jones College Catalogue, 1933-34,* vol. 6, no. 1, p. 6).

[64]BJsr to J. Oliver Buswell, 12 May 1949 (GF: Buswell files).

[65]During this time literary societies were a national phenomenon in colleges and universities and were generally organized for students to read and discuss great literature. Societies would sponsor debates, story and poetry readings, and other literary events. See Bechtel, *Wheaton College,* pp. 136-38, for information on Wheaton's literary societies of this same era. See also William C. Ringerberg, *Taylor University: The First 125 Years* (Grand Rapids, Mich.: Wm. B. Eerdmans Publishing Co., 1973), pp. 52-53, 126-28.

[66]FMM record numerous instances of debate being a point of discussion. The first is found in minutes for 3 December 1929: "Too much time is taken up with debates and the Annual. Faculty agreed that no student can hold any office . . . [including] debate without a B average." College credit for debate was discussed on 10 December 1929 (ABV).

[67]*San Andros* (college yearbook), 1930.

[68]Parker, *Sunshine,* p. 83.

[69]MS, BJsr, chapel talk, 21 January 1941 (ABV: 1941). Corroborated by Mrs. BJjr, who added, "That really shook us all up. . . . He thought it was just awful to have it, much less play it" (Interview, Mrs. BJjr, 4 June 1987).

[70]FMM, 16, 23 November 1931 (ABV).

[71]MS, BJsr, chapel talk, 2 April 1945.

[72]Interview, Mrs. BJsr, "Founding," tape 2.

[73]Johnson, *Builder,* p. 180. The number of honorary doctorates among these is unclear. BJsr, President; Dr. W. E. Patterson, dean, psychology, education; Dr. W. J. Hall, history, religious education; W. F. Monk, mathematics; Ellen Laudenslager, Romance languages; Katie Nell Holmes, English; Dr. R. S. Gentry, science; P. W. Lott, Bible; Dr. J. Floyd Collins, English, Latin, preparatory division; Eunice Hutto, mathematics. There are no extant records to corroborate the first faculty. Several music teaching positions had not been filled by the time the school opened, but some teachers, such as Susie Kelly Dean, known to have been employed during the first year, are not found listed.

[74]Interview, BJjr, 28 May 1987.

[75]Interview, Mrs. BJjr, 4 June 1987.

[76]Marlene Womack, "Bob Jones Rode Crest of Area Boom," *Panama City (Fla.) News Herald,* 2 August 1987.

[77]Interview, BJjr, 28 May 1987.

[78]Ibid.

[79]MS, BJsr, chapel talk, 28 February 1950 (ABV: 1950).

[80]FMM, 25 November 1929 (ABV).

[81]For more on J. Floyd Collins and Eunice Hutto, see Chapter 25.

[82]*Bob Jones College Catalogue, 1932-33,* vol. 5, no. 1, p. 6.

[83]*Bob Jones College Catalogue, 1933-34,* vol. 6, no. 1, p. 6. Hutto was actually listed as "Registrar" of the College in 1933 and did not receive the title "Dean" until 1934 when the school had moved to Tennessee (*Bob Jones College Catalogue, 1934-35,* vol. 5, no. 1, p. 8).

[84]MS, BJsr, radio talk (ASTA: 26 December 1959). Collins was associated with the College through its Florida years but died shortly before the school moved to Tennessee (Interview, BJjr, 28 May 1987). See also "Prof. J. Floyd Collins, Litt.D.," *Alabama Christian Advocate,* 19 October 1933. Eunice Hutto was a native of Alabama with an academic background in education and mathematics (Johnson, *Builder,* p. 180).

[85]FMM, 19 November 1929 (ABV).

[86]Martha Grace Green, "Pockets for Our Aprons," *Piedmont Bible College Alumni Newsletter,* May 1986.

[87]Warwick, *Tides,* p. 121.

[88]MS, BJsr, chapel talk, 19 December 1934.

[89]Ibid., 17 May 1949 (ABV: 1949).

[90]Warwick, *Tides,* p. 128; Interview, Mrs. BJjr, 4 June 1987. Mrs. BJsr recalled one outing in Florida when the students "went out into the woods and gathered moss and gathered the greens to go with it. They made invitations, and fountains, and put them in the new auditorium, which was just a rough building. They took out all the pews and moved all the benches and set up tables. They made it like a Japanese garden—that was what their motif was. They made little bridges going all over through rocks, and had water [trickling] through. I don't know how they did it. It was one of the prettiest parties we ever had. And with soft lights, at night, it was almost ethereal it was so pretty. They had things hanging from the ceiling too, festooned garlands and all" (Interview, Mrs. BJsr, "Founding," tape 1).

[91]Interview, Mrs. BJsr, "Founding," tape 1. According to Anne Williams Warwick, the Chi Delta outings were the benchmark for BJC outings during these years. See Warwick, *Tides,* p. 128.

[92]Warwick, *Tides,* p. 122.

[93]*Epoch,* p. 10.

[94]"Twilight Musicales, Susie Kelly Dean, Director," handwritten program, dated 9 October 1927 (MLA: Box 26).

[95]Parker, *Sunshine,* p. 68.

[96]*Epoch,* p. 24. An announcement mailed to incoming students in 1927 reads, "It is the plan of the College to organize an orchestra, so each student who is interested in this kind of music is asked to bring such musical instruments as he or she may have" (W. E. Patterson to "Student," 20 August 1927 [MLA: Box 20]).

[97]FMM, 22 February 1932 (ABV).

[98]"Bob Jones College Glee Club Finishes Tour, Giving Concerts for 50 Schools," photo with caption, *Birmingham (Ala.) News-Age-Herald,* 27 May 1928 (MLA: Photo files, box 32).

[99]"Bob Jones College Conservatory of Music," recital program, 17 December 1930 (MLA: Box 26).

[100]Johnson, *Builder,* p. 49. BJsr said, "The sorrow of my life is I can't sing. My vocal chords [*sic*] and my ear—I don't understand it—just don't work together. I want to sing. You know, I'd rather be a singer than anything I know."

[101]FMM, 4 September 1931 (ABV). There is no evidence that he followed through on this request.

[102]Interview, Tommy Smith, 17 May 1988. Smith attended many of the school's performances and stated that one of the outstanding features of the College was its Shakespearean plays as well as its music.

[103]Three interviewees indicated that this policy was attractive to them when considering a college—Edwards in speech, Stenholm in speech, and Keefer in music. Even a casual observer would agree that music, speech, and art training would draw a different type of student from championship athletics.

[104]Figures for 1928-29 from *Epoch,* pp. 12-13. Figures for 1929-30 from photograph, *Bob Jones Magazine,* April 1929, p. 3.

[105]Bob Jones College, *Announcements,* vol. 5, no. 1, 1932-33, pp. 6-7.

[106]Although primary sources do not exist in Hall's personnel records that indicate the source and extent of his Modernistic thought and teaching, it is evident from numerous records that Hall was indeed the center of the controversy that broke on the College in the spring of 1929. By tracing BJsr's statements over the years, this researcher was able to identify Hall as the "Modernist." At various times, BJsr mentioned events surrounding the firing, providing scraps of description and evidence with each mention. Though never by name, BJsr spoke publicly of the man on the following dates: MSS, 20 December 1945, chapel talk; 28 February 1950, chapel talk; 21 April 1958, radio talk; and 13 May 1958, radio talk. Extant letters pertaining to the Hall situation were discovered in the GF in two letter files, "W. J. Hall" and "R. S. Gentry." Also, prior to January 1930, W. J. Hall was listed as associate editor of the *Bob Jones Magazine.* Beginning January 1930, A. H. Perpetuo was listed in Hall's place as associate editor with no announcement of a change, a highly unusual occurrence. Confirmatory data was found in a letter from BJsr to R. S. Gentry, dated 2 August 1933. The most complete account of the difficulty with Hall is the radio talk of 13 May 1958 (ABV).

[107]BJsr to R. S. Gentry, 2 August 1933 (GF: Gentry files).

[108]MS, BJsr, radio talk, 13 May 1958. The crux of the issue was the fact that Fosdick had by this time gone on record that the virgin birth of Christ was "piffle," acceptance of the virgin birth being a doctrinal tenet on which the College was founded. To allow any teacher to promote such thought in the classroom was, for BJsr, unthinkable and "a repudiation of the doctrine of Bob Jones College."

[109]W. J. Hall to BJsr, 18 September 1929 (GF: W. J. Hall files). BJsr then apparently wrote Dr. Hall a reprimand, to which Hall responded: "As to the matter about which you wrote me and I replied, I can only say that I shall keep the agreement to the last line. . . . Some day I shall be glad to go into any such matter with you and make a full explanation. Just now, others might become involved in any discussion, and I do think it much better, especially for the present, that that matter be a closed incident. Silence may mean, for me, misunderstanding; but I feel quite sure that it is in every way the wiser course. . . . The church unitedly and the town as far as my influence goes, will be with you and your work."

[110]MS, BJsr, chapel talk, 28 February 1950 (ABV: 1950). See also *Bob Jones Magazine,* vol. 1, no. 1 (June 1928).

Chapter 5: Bob Jones College: Depression and Collapse

[1]Johnson, *Miracle,* pp. 10-11.

[2]The College Development Bonds were secured by a note on the campus land, buildings, and furnishings. The agreement was apparently verbal, since several years later Dr. Jones could not find any written record of it.

[3]Dalhouse, "Shaping," pp. 96-97.

[4]BJC Board of Trustees Minutes, 9 January 1933 (MLA: Box 26).

[5]Interview, BJjr, 28 May 1987.

[6]Parker, *Sunshine,* pp. 89-90. He wrote,

When I stepped on the campus in September 1930, I had seventeen cents in my pocket. All of the money I received for my meetings that summer I used to pay debts I had incurred the year before. One Saturday afternoon just after lunch, I sat on the edge of my bed . . . reading the Bible. I turned to the fourth chapter of Philippians and read the nineteenth verse, "But my God shall supply all your need according to his riches in glory by Christ Jesus." I pondered that verse and my plight. It was Saturday. I would have to have forty dollars by Monday or leave school. As I sat there, I laid the Bible down on the bed by my side and crossed my foot on my knee. There was a hole worn almost through the sole of my left shoe. I began to fool with it and punched a hole through. I could not hold back the tears. There I sat, a big college man, weeping like a child. Then I picked up my Bible and looked again at that precious promise. . . . "But my God shall supply all your need according to his riches in glory by Christ Jesus." I said, "Forgive me, God. I don't have anything, but I am Thy child."

Parker went into Lynn Haven to the bank to ask about borrowing some money to pay his school bill, but the bank had closed, flat broke. He stopped to see a local pastor, who invited him to preach the next day. Following the service, the pastor felt moved to take an offering for young Monroe, and he received enough to pay his bill to the College and get a pair of shoes.

[7]Marlene Womack, "Depression Years Threw Bob Jones College into Ruin," *Panama City (Fla.) News Herald,* 9 August 1987.

[8]BJsr to "Bondholders," 15 November 1929. The bonded indebtedness represented about 20 percent of the total investment at BJC (BJsr to J. Paul Ray, 28 January 1952 [GF: Asbury Alumni Association]).

[9]Don Cochran to BJsr, 20 March 1931 (GF: Cochran file).

[10]FMM, 21 March 1932 (ABV).

[11]Ibid., 25 April 1932.

[12]Ibid., 28 May 1932.

[13]Johnson, *Builder,* p. 186.

[14]Ibid., p. 187.

[15]FMM, 28 May 1932 (ABV).

[16]Interview, BJjr, 28 May 1987.

[17]BJsr to Mr. Howard Bailey, 20 March 1933 (MLA: Box 26). Bailey served as counsel for the disgruntled bondholders. BJsr wrote, "You control a majority of the indebtedness of the college. You do not control a majority of the bondholders." W. J. Hall's name is listed among those who filed suit.

[18]MS, BJsr, chapel talk, 28 February 1950 (ABV: 1950).

[19]BJC Board of Trustees Minutes, 9 January 1933 (MLA: Box 26).

[20]Methodist school Taylor University, for example, was forced into receivership twice between 1929 and 1935. As its financial woes increased, Taylor eventually depleted its limited endowment to cover expenses. See Ringerberg, *Taylor University,* pp. 102-8.

[21]BJC Board of Trustees Minutes, 9 January 1933 (MLA: Box 26). The bankruptcy was reported in the *Pensacola (Fla.) Journal,* "Bob Jones College Is in Receivership," 12 January 1933.

[22]*Dothan (Ala.) Eagle,* 4 January 1932.

[23]BJsr to Howard Bailey, 20 March 1933.

[24]MS, BJsr, Sunday sermon, 29 January 1933 (ABV: 1933).

[25]MS, BJsr, chapel talk, 16 October 1945 (ABV: 1945).

[26]Johnson, *Builder,* p. 187.

[27]Quoted in Womack, "Depression Years."

[28]Invitations came from the state of Georgia; the state of Alabama; Anniston, Alabama; Newton, Alabama; and Cleveland, Tennessee, among others.

[29]BJsr to "Friend," 20 April 1933 (MLA: Box 26). This letter announced the move to Cleveland, Tennessee, and was sent to bondholders. See also "Bob Jones Is Given Hearty Welcome Here," *Cleveland (Tenn.) Daily Banner,* 3 May 1933; and "Bob Jones College, Located in Florida, Will Be Moved Here," *Lawrenceburg (Tenn.) Democrat-Union,* 5 May 1933.

[30]BJsr to Howard Bailey, 20 March 1933 (MLA: Box 26).

[31]BJsr to R. S. Gentry, 2 August 1933 (GF: Gentry file).

[32]Interview, Tommy Smith.

[33]Interview, Mrs. BJsr, "Founding," tape no. 2.

[34]MS, BJsr, chapel talk, 28 February 1950 (ABV: 1950).

[35]*Bob Jones College Catalogue 1931-1932 and Announcements 1932-1933,* vol. 5, no. 1, p. 4 (MLA: *Bob Jones University Catalogue,* vols. 1-12, 1927-39).

[36]Interview, Mrs. BJsr, "Founding," tape no. 2.

[37]Johnson, *Builder,* p. 190.

[38]Interview, BJjr, 28 May 1987.

Chapter 6: Bob Jones College: Cleveland, Tennessee

[1]"Bob Jones College, Located in Florida, Will Be Moved Here," *Lawrenceburg (Tenn.) Democrat-Union,* 5 May 1933.

[2]"Bob Jones Is Given Hearty Welcome Here," *Cleveland (Tenn.) Daily Banner,* 3 May 1933.

[3]Centenary College was founded in 1884 by Dr. George Stuart, a Methodist minister. Centenary became one of Tennessee's most esteemed women's colleges. For most of its fifty-year history, Centenary was under the auspices of the Holston Methodist Conference and was closed many times for lack of students. In 1928 it became a private women's college, offering a two-year program with courses in home economics, expression, physical education, playground supervision, commercial courses, and art. In 1929 Centenary College closed its doors for the final time and sat unused until June of 1933 when renovations for BJC began ("Old Centenary Had Record As Girls' School," *Cleveland (Tenn.) Daily Banner,* 6 September 1933; see also Wright, *Fortress,* pp. 50-51; and Johnson, *Miracle,* pp. 11-13).

[4]Wright, *Fortress,* p. 53.

[5]Travis K. Hedrick, "Bob Jones—His College," *Chattanooga Times,* 20 August 1933.

[6]Warner Ogden, "Evangelist Bob Jones Operates a Non-Profit College Where Fundamentalism Is Insisted On," *Knoxville (Tenn.) News Sentinel,* 11 February 1934.

[7]"Old Centenary Had Record," *Cleveland (Tenn.) Daily Banner.*

[8]MS, BJsr, chapel talk, 29 October 1944 (ABV: 1944).

[9]"Hearty Welcome," *Cleveland (Tenn.) Daily Banner; Bob Jones College Catalogue and Announcements 1933-1934,* vol. 6, no. 1, p. 4 (MLA: *Bob Jones University Catalogue,* vols. 1-12, 1927-39); and "The Bob Jones College Opens in Cleveland the 6th of September," *Kingsport (Tenn.) Times,* 6 August 1933.

[10]"Bob Jones to Speak Tuesday," *Cleveland (Tenn.) Daily Banner,* 1 May 1933.

[11]Johnson, *Builder,* pp. 190-91.

[12]"Bob Jones College Opens First Session Here Today," *Cleveland (Tenn.) Daily Banner,* 6 September 1933.

[13]Ibid.

[14]"Many Attend Opening of New College," *Cleveland (Tenn.) Daily Banner,* 8 September 1933.

[15]"Welcome Bob Jones Students, Teachers to Cleveland," *Cleveland (Tenn.) Daily Banner,* 6 September 1933.

[16]Interview, Charles Smith, 10 October 1985. Quoted in Michael S. Heiser, "The Move of Bob Jones College from Cleveland, Tennessee, to Greenville, South Carolina, in 1947," unpublished paper, p. 2.

[17]Ibid.

[18]Interview, Marshall Neal, 15 October 1985, quoted in Heiser, "Move of BJC."

[19]*Bob Jones College Catalogue, 1932-1933,* vol. 5, no. 1, p. 6.

[20]*Bob Jones College Catalogue, 1933-1934,* vol. 6, no. 1, p. 6.

[21]Johnson, *Builder,* pp. 194-95.

[22]*Bob Jones College Catalogue, 1934-35,* vol. 7, no. 1. Johnson is listed as bookkeeper. In *Catalogue, 1935-36,* vol. 8, no. 1, he is listed as business manager and treasurer of the Board of Trustees. BJsr was noted as a skilled financial manager, even during his early evangelistic career. For him to turn over to a new college graduate such responsibility is an indication of the financial ability that Johnson possessed. For more on R. K. Johnson, see Chapter 25.

[23]MS, BJsr, chapel talk, 10 March 1947 (ABV: 1947). See also MS, BJsr, chapel talk, 14 September 1948 (ABV: 1948).

[24]Interview, Katherine Stenholm, 8 June 1987.

[25]BJsr to J. S. Mack. Quoted in Johnson, *Builder,* p. 199.

[26]Robert P. Shuler, "California Pastor Declares Jones School 'Sensational,'" *Greenville (S.C.) News,* n.d. 1947 (MLA: Box 11).

[27]MS, BJsr, chapel talk, 28 February 1950 (ABV: 1950).

[28]Wright, *Fortress,* p. 69.

[29]The Gospel Fellowship Association was formed to establish a core of pastors, evangelists, and Christians who would stand for the fundamentals of the faith as found in the College creed. BJsr's goal was to develop an organization for Christian fellowship among like-minded believers and to raise funds for evangelistic and missions outreaches around the world. See Wright, *Fortress,* pp. 69-70; and Parker, *Sunshine,* pp. 122-33.

[30]Wright, *Fortress,* pp. 68-71. See also Parker, *Sunshine,* pp. 122-33. Monroe Parker, Henry Grube, Clifford Lewis, Jimmie Johnson, and others opened Bob Jones Gospel Centers in such cities as Pensacola, Florida; Mobile, Alabama; Spartanburg, South Carolina; and Birmingham, Alabama, to reach the cities for Christ. It is interesting to note that one Young People's Fellowship Club, started by Clifford Lewis in Greenville, South Carolina, would be influential in the future of the College.

[31]For more on Grace Haight, see Chapter 25. A dormitory in Greenville, now used for the Nursing Department, was named for her.

[32]J. S. Mack, who started his career as a store clerk, bought a single store, which he eventually parlayed into a controlling interest in a small chain of "five and dime" stores in 1911. He supervised its growth into a regional chain of more than two hundred stores in the Northeast and Midwest. G. C. Murphy Stores was second in size only to S. S. Kresge and Co. and was a leading and respected retailer of this era.

[33]Mack was a leading Christian philanthropist who donated the Ralph Gibson McGill Library to Westminster College and donated generously to the Piney Woods Negro Mission School in Kentucky. He donated $200,000 to the Indiana Hospital for

construction of a maternity wing and established a $300,000 trust for maintenance of the wing. He contributed more than $150,000 to his local hospital in McKeesport, Pennsylvania, among other acts of charity ("Death Takes Business Man Back to Childhood Scenes," *Pittsburgh Press,* 20 September 1940).

[34]This letter is reprinted in Johnson, *Builder,* pp. 197-200. The original has not been found.

[35]The role that John S. Mack and his wife played in the development of BJC cannot be overstated. Besides underwriting large portions of the major construction projects—often as much as 50 percent or more of the costs—they made regular, monthly contributions to the school, made several large gifts of G. C. Murphy stock, served on the Board of Trustees, paid for and provided special training for the business manager by Murphy Company CPAs, and in numerous other ways supported the College. The Board of Trustees, in appreciation to the Macks for their generosity, awarded him with an honorary degree of doctor of philanthropy, named the library in his honor, and named the Cleveland campus's auditorium in honor of Mrs. Mack. It was a blow to the school when J. S. Mack died on 27 September 1940. Records indicate that College donations increased more than $200,000 during 1940-41, perhaps reflecting the size of Mack's bequest to the College (BJC Financial Statement, ca. 1945-46 [Stone Realty: Bob Jones file]). For more detailed information about the role of the Macks, see Johnson, *Builder,* pp. 194-210.

[36]Heiser, "Move of BJC," p. 3. See also "BJC Purchases More Property," *Cleveland (Tenn.) Daily Banner,* 11 June 1942.

[37]Map of BJC, ca. 1943 (MLA).

[38]Johnson, *Builder,* p. 205. Each of the construction projects was a miracle of God's timing and provision. *Builder of Bridges* sets down the complete record of each building as a testimony to God's miraculous provision for the College. Everything from lumber to transportation came as a direct result of prayer.

[39]MS, BJsr, chapel talk, 16 October 1945 (ABV: 1945).

[40]Mrs. E. H. Peavy to BJsr, ca. 1932. One letter reads, "We are so sorry to have to take Cullie out of school. She hated to leave and says she intends going back next year if we are able to send her. We haven't any money and have borrowed on every thing we have to live. We lost every thing last June after signing up for her to go to your college. I am glad she got to go one semester for that has helped her."

[41]Ogden, "Bob Jones Operates a Non-Profit College." Files indicate that students were placed in at least eighteen businesses as part-time workers during 1934. Businesses that took student workers included Hardwick Stove Company, J. C. Penney, Hill Grocery, Hardwick Woolen Mills, and A & P Tea Company.

[42]BJsr to "Dean," Berea College, 10 May 1934. See Joseph C. Lewis to BJsr, 20 April 1934 (GF: Part-work scholarships).

[43]According to *Little Moby's Post, The Bob Jones College Alumni News,* the first student loan fund was announced in May of 1939 ("Alumni Loan Fund," *Little Moby's Post, The Bob Jones College Alumni News,* vol. 6, no. 4, May 1947).

[44]*Catalogue, 1933-34,* vol. 6, no. 1, p. 10.

[45]*Catalogue, 1936-37,* vol. 9, no. 1, p. 18.

[46]*Catalogue, 1946-47,* vol. 19, no. 1, pp. 26-27.

[47]Johnson, *Builder,* pp. 199-200.

[48]Ibid., p. 204.

[49]Ibid., p. 205.

[50]The number three hundred is found in both Wright and Johnson. The *Cleveland (Tenn.) Daily Banner,* 6 September 1933, reports the College's enrolling two hundred

students but states that all students had not yet reported. The official figures for this year are not listed in "Enrollment Statistics: First Semester," n.d. (RO), nor is there a figure for 1932-33. According to the official record, however, College enrollment did not top three hundred until 1936-37, making the number in Wright and Johnson inaccurate.

[51]MS, BJsr, chapel talk, 16 October 1945 (ABV: 1945).

[52]Wright, *Fortress,* p. 78. See also "Enrollment Statistics: First Semester," n.d. (RO).

[53]Enrollment Statistics: First Semester, n.d. (RO).

[54]"Building Plans," *Little Moby's Post,* vol. 4, no. 4, February 1946, p. 1 (MLA).

[55]Enrollment Statistics: First Semester, n.d. (RO). See also "The Opening of School," *Little Moby's Post,* vol. 5, no. 1, January 1947, p. 1.

[56]Data taken from the *Bob Jones College Catalogue, 1933-34,* vol. 6, no. 1, p. 6; *Catalogue, 1934-35,* vol. 7, no. 1, pp. 7-8; *Catalogue, 1935-36,* vol. 8, no. 1, pp. 8-9; *Catalogue, 1936-37,* vol. 9, no. 1, pp. 8-9; *Catalogue, 1937-38,* vol. 10, no. 1, pp. 8-9; *Catalogue, 1938-39,* vol. 11, no. 1, pp. 8-10; *Catalogue, 1939-40,* vol. 12, no. 1, pp. 8-10; and *Catalogue, 1946-47,* vol. 19, no. 1, pp. 11-15.

[57]For more on Charles Brokenshire, see Chapter 25. Also, Monroe Parker, a student of Brokenshire's at BJC, recorded personal recollections of his teaching in *Sunshine,* pp. 158-61. And for a biography of Brokenshire, see Mark Sidwell, "Charles Digory Brokenshire (1885-1954)," in *Biblical Viewpoint,* vol. 25, no. 1, April 1991, pp. 69-83.

[58]J. S. Mack to BJsr, n.d., quoted in Johnson, *Fortress,* p. 201.

[59]MS, BJsr, chapel talk, 4 March 1941 (ABV: 1941).

[60]During the early 1930s the final approval for the hiring of faculty resided principally with the President and the Acting President. Four interviewees from this era indicated that BJsr approached them with the opportunity to stay on: Monroe Parker, Elizabeth Edwards, Fannie May Holmes Jones, and Karl Keefer. See also Parker, *Sunshine,* pp. 97-109, 155-64.

[61]BJjr, *Cornbread,* p. 76.

[62]Interview, Karl Keefer, 27 July 1987. Monroe Parker also remembered,

> I arrived at Bob Jones College in time for the first faculty meeting for the academic year 1937-38. I was to teach General Survey of the Bible . . . and Bible Prophecy. . . . Then I was to have charge of Dr. Jones' class, Practical Instruction for Preachers, and would teach it in the absence of Dr. Jones. . . . I also had charge of the men's athletic department for the first four years I was on the staff. I organized the intramural system and used student assistants to lead the physical education classes. . . . I met with the administrative council . . . preached often at chapel and on Sunday mornings, organized the [campus] Sunday schools, Mission Prayer Band, Child Evangelism, and the various young people's societies, and approved the prayer leaders for the dormitory prayer groups. I was also responsible for all extension services, sending out faculty members and ministerial students to preach, as well as groups for various kinds of services. (Parker, *Sunshine,* p. 158)

[63]Although no interviewee from this era could recall specifically that the College paid his expenses, none could remember paying the expense himself. Some mentioned that BJsr arranged church meetings, radio broadcasts, or other types of Christian ministries for them in the area near their graduate school. The impression is that some type of support was forthcoming from the College. The type and extent of this support is unknown, although it may be that one reason for faculty salary bonuses at the end of each academic year was to help toward summer school expenses. See FMM, 12 April 1943 (ABV). (Confirmatory evidence is found in interviews with Elizabeth Edwards, Karl Keefer, Katherine Stenholm, and Monroe Parker.)

[64]FMM from 1940 record that "every teacher should go to school this summer or do some type of studying in case of those who have advanced degrees" (FMM, 19 February

1940 [ABV]). See also "Our Faculty in Summer School," *Little Moby's Post* (October 1944), p. 1. This report lists the faculty and their summer work.

> H. W. Berg, University of Kansas; Mrs. Helen Carruth and Mr. J. Hall, Columbia University; Miss Hazel Chalk, University of Southern California; Miss Louise Cherry, University of Wisconsin; Dr. Alfred Cierpke, Mr. Carruth, Mr. Robert Schaper, Union Theological Seminary; Mrs. Monroe Parker, American Conservatory in Chicago; Mr. Karl Keefer and Miss Sara Gayle H [unreadable], Cincinnati Conservatory; Miss D. Graves, University of Minnesota; Miss Julie Rose, Eastman Conservatory in Rochester; Miss Geraldine Williams, Northwestern; Mr. Herbert Hoover, Winona Lake School of Theology; Mr. Theodore Mercer, University of Chicago; Miss Harrison received her Bachelor's degree in Library Science at Peabody; Gilbert Stenholm, Northwestern; Ellen Herrmann and Miss Meta, Northwestern in Chicago; Mrs. Gilbert Stenholm received her M.A. degree from Northwestern; Mrs. Robert Schaper studied with Paul Althouse in New York.

[65]FMM, 17 May 1940 (ABV). See also FMM, 8 March 1943. Schools attended by the graduates of BJC from this era included Northwestern University, the University of Michigan, Colorado State College, Louisiana State University, Cincinnati Conservatory of Music, Columbia University, the University of Chicago, Ohio State University, the University of Southern California, the University of Tennessee, and Princeton University. Each of the interviewees from this period recalled being approached by BJsr or BJjr about attending a particular graduate school and doing work in a particular area of study. In each instance it was the sense of the interviewee that the graduate school had been selected by one of the Drs. Jones, most likely BJjr, for the express purpose of adding credibility to the College. For example, LSU was chosen for its history department, Northwestern for its speech department, Michigan for its speech and play production departments, Cincinnati for piano and the Zoo Opera, Chicago and Princeton for religion and philosophy, and Columbia for its education department.

[66]Giovanni Sperandeo to BJjr, 25 May 1936 and 2 June 1936 (GF: Sperandeo file). See also Zella Rose Emert, "How Can This Man Laugh?" *Chattanooga (Tenn.) Sunday Times,* 26 April 1936 (MLA: Box 29, Rachel Ayres scrapbook).

[67]BJjr to B. G. Osipoff, 17 April 1940, and Mrs. B. G. Osipoff to BJjr, 7 June 1940 (GF: Osipoff file).

[68]MS, BJsr, chapel talk, 30 January 1945 (ABV: 1945). "She walked around and said, 'You know, I'm so concerned. They have drama at Bob Jones College, and I think we should have a prayer meeting.' . . . She had a right to have it in for old William if she wanted to; that's her privilege. You don't have to love Shakespeare. . . . She didn't have to fall in love with old Bill. But she knew Bob Jones College loved Bill Shakespeare."

[69]Mrs. B. G. Osipoff to BJsr, 7 June 1940 (GF: Osipoff file).

[70]BJsr to Dorothy Seay, 16 December 1936; and BJsr to Dorothy Seay, 26 May 1938 (GF: Seay file).

[71]BJjr to Mrs. B. G. Osipoff, 2 July 1940 (GF: Osipoff file). BJjr says, in part, "We sincerely desire to do the will of the Lord in this institution. . . . We cannot use in our organization any one who is suspicious of decisions made by the administration or who is critical or unhappy in the organization. . . . We are trying to avoid the friction that the devil causes in most institutions that stand for the Gospel and the authority of the Bible. . . . The loyalty of every member of our organization must be above suspicion. . . . We are not suspicious people. We are slow to believe that anybody would come into a Christian organization . . . and not be loyal."

[72]BJsr, *Things,* pp. 76-79.

[73]MS, BJsr, chapel talk, 4 March 1935 (ABV: 1935).

[74]Anonymous [Dorothy Seay], "Accent on Sin," *American Mercury,* September 1940, vol. 51, no. 201, pp. 16-23.

[75]BJsr to Ruth Flood, 6 August 1937 (GF: Flood file).

[76]FMM, 26 September 1933 (ABV).

[77]Ibid., 27 September 1934 and 17 September 1945.

[78]BJsr to B. G. Osipoff, 3 June 1938 (GF: Osipoff file). The "bonus" concept appeared for the first time in a letter to Don Cochran from BJsr in 1935. Speaking of College income and bonuses, Dr. Jones wrote, "Whatever we make here, if there is any left over, the entire organization is welcome to it" (BJsr to Don Cochran, 19 August 1935 [GF: Cochran file]). Bonuses were one tangible way in which each member could share in the success of the institution and feel some reward for the year's efforts.

[79]Stenholm diary, 28 September 1940 and 5 September 1941.

[80]Dorothy Seay to BJsr, 16 December 1936 (GF: Seay file).

[81]Ruth Flood to BJsr, 4 August 1937; and BJsr to Ruth Flood, 6 August 1937 (GF: Flood file).

[82]BJsr to Giovanni Sperandeo, 26 May 1934 (GF: Sperandeo file). BJsr, perhaps noting the sizable salary agreement, did not promise Sperandeo a bonus, saying, "At the end of the year I will do more if I can, but I don't think I can do any better than that. This year we were able to give some of our faculty members a bonus but I would not want anybody to count on anything above the agreement which we make with each teacher."

[83]Gilbert Stenholm records on 12 April 1943, "Faculty received their bonus today. We received $475.00." This was a sizeable sum, equivalent to three months' salary (Stenholm diary).

[84]Joseph Free to BJsr, 25 May 1938.

[85]FMM, 19 May 1947 (ABV).

[86]"Odds and Ends," *Little Moby's Post,* October 1943, p. 4 (MLA).

[87]FMM, 29 January 1940.

[88]Ibid., 25 January 1943.

[89]"Business College in Connection with Bob Jones College," *Kingsport (Tenn.) Times,* 6 August 1933.

[90]*Catalogue, 1941-42,* vol. 14, no. 1, pp. 23-26; and *Catalogue, 1942-43,* vol. 15, no. 1, p. 24.

[91]*Catalogue, 1942-43,* vol. 15, no. 1, p. 69.

[92]*Catalogue, 1943-44,* vol. 16, no. 1, pp. 84-86.

[93]B. O. Duggan to Eunice Hutto, 5 September 1933 (GF: University of Tennessee file). Duggan's letter reads in part, "The outline of your teacher courses for Freshman and Sophomore years would meet the certification requirements of the State. . . . I am confident there will be no trouble about it."

[94]Although the Board of Education's approval is not reflected in the catalogs, a letter dated 9 July 1934 from BJsr to "Friend" indicates that Dr. Doak Campbell, secretary of the American Association of Junior Colleges, inspected the school and had recommended to the Tennessee State Board of Education that the students of the College be certified to teach in the state of Tennessee. A letter from Commissioner Walter D. Cocking of the Tennessee State Board of Education states that Dr. Campbell's recommendation was accepted and graduates of BJC could now be certified to teach in Tennessee (BJsr to "Friend," 9 July 1934 [MLA: Box 29, Rachel Ayres scrapbook]).

[95]In 1934 the University of Tennessee refused to accept BJC graduates into its graduate schools (R. F. Thomason to Marjorie Parker, 2 March 1934 [GF: University of Tennessee file]). Following lengthy correspondence between Thomason and BJsr, Tennessee agreed to accept BJC course credits on a provisional basis (R. F. Thomason to

BJsr, 10 May 1934 [GF: University of Tennessee file]). By 1 September 1939, UT had agreed to accept BJC graduates to the Graduate College on the same provisional basis as other nonaccredited schools (R. F. Thomason to BJsr, 1 September 1939 [GF: University of Tennessee file]). In response to a query from J. Oliver Buswell of Wheaton, the registrar of UT wrote,

> We grant only three years of credit for work taken in Bob Jones College. It is true that the University does not offer many of the subjects which Bob Jones does offer as special work, such as Music, Bible, and the like. However, that is not the only reason why we do not give more than three full years credit for the work. We have not yet thought that we should recognize them with a full four years of work though we may do so in the near future. Some schools in the state, as for example Peabody College, will recognize them with four years of work. P.S. The state Department of Education also recognizes them for four years of work. (R. F. Thomason to James O. Buswell, 25 February 1939 [GF: Buswell file])

[96]The correspondence files in each of the four cases investigated contain an unbroken string of dated correspondence on this issue. From 1929 through 1955, J. Oliver Buswell was one of the College's leading antagonists. In one instance in 1939, Buswell wrote to the country's three leading religious periodicals, including the *Sunday School Times* and *Moody Monthly,* in which BJC ran paid advertising, and demanded that the BJC ads be removed because of statements he claimed were misleading and false. These statements, he charged, left the impression that the College was accredited. The magazine editors wrote BJsr and informed him of the charges and that the BJC ads for the next month were going to be removed from the magazines until the situation could be clarified. At a face-to-face confrontation on 3 March 1939 BJsr produced documents from the University of Tennessee, Peabody College, and the Tennessee State Board of Education stating that the College was approved by them and that they accepted BJC credits and graduates and reporting the findings and recommendations of their evaluation teams. Buswell was forced to write a letter of apology to each of the editors involved and recant his charges against the College (BJsr to JRR, 12 May 1949 [GF: Buswell file]). The date March 3 is taken from a visit to Cleveland by Buswell, recorded by Gilbert Stenholm in his personal diary for 1936. This was Buswell's only visit to the school, at which time Bjsr also had Buswell preach in chapel.

[97]MS, BJsr, chapel talk, "The Creed of Bob Jones College," 2 April 1945 (ABV: 1945). Letters from John Walvoord of Dallas Seminary indicate that BJC graduates who had been enrolled and who were then currently enrolled had done work to the standard of all other Dallas Seminary students. Correspondence from Registrar R. F. Thomason of the University of Tennessee indicates that "we are always glad to have students from Bob Jones College and I should like to further add that you have sent us some very superior students" (R. F. Thomason to BJjr, 12 September 1935 [GF: University of Tennessee file).

[98]Johnson, *Builder,* p. 187.

[99]This association of religious schools became the National Association of Seminaries and ultimately included schools covering the spectrum of belief—from Catholic and Jewish seminaries to seminaries of Modernistic Protestant denominations.

[100]MS, BJsr, chapel talk, 17 September 1948 (ABV: 1948). Also BJsr to John Walvoord, 8 May 1944 (GF: Dallas Theological Seminary file). Dr. Jones on one occasion wrote,

> Let me make it clear: we have no objection to educational work highly standardized. . . .
> We, however, cannot conscientiously let some group of educational experts or some committee of experts who may have a behavioristic or atheistic slant on education control or even influence the administrative policies of our college. . . . Bob Jones College set

up its own educational standard in its own way [without the dictates of a Board of Regents]. When the standards were set up, the President of the college asked the Department of Education of the State of Tennessee to investigate the type work the institution was doing. . . . The Department . . . sent a special committee over to inspect our work and accredited the work we are doing. The Department of Education does not dictate any of the administrative policies of Bob Jones College. We decide on what condition we accept students and the type degrees we confer upon them.

It is interesting that following a New York State Board of Regents examination, Dr. Walvoord of Dallas Seminary informed BJsr that BJC degrees could no longer be recognized. BJC students, therefore, could not be accepted in master's degree programs at Dallas on an equal basis with other students without first completing a Dallas B.D. program or meeting other requirements. The Board of Regents had ruled that accepting students from nonaccredited schools was a violation of board policy and could result in the possible loss of accreditation for Dallas. After this, a special degree program, with somewhat different requirements from the recognized master's degree, was created at Dallas to accommodate students from nonaccredited schools. BJsr viewed this degree as discrimination against a Christian brother and vigorously registered his opinion. He also viewed as a violation of scriptural ethics unsaved men on a Board of Regents having control over policies at a Christian school (BJsr to John F. Walvoord, 8 May 1944 [GF: Dallas Theological Seminary file]; see also BJjr to John F. Walvoord, 26 April 1944 [GF: Dallas Theological Seminary file]). The issue of accepting credits from BJC was eventually put to rest as graduates entered the colleges and seminaries in question with equal standing as other transfer students.

[101] BJsr to James O. Buswell, 30 March 1942 (GF: Buswell file). Letters pertaining to accreditation may be found in the following files in the GF: "Buswell," "Dallas Theological Seminary," "Wheaton College," "Accreditation," and "University of Tennessee."

[102] BJsr to James O. Buswell, 12 May 1949 (GF: Buswell file).

[103] The College had 915 students, the Academy had 311, and the Graduate School enrolled another 38 students, totaling 1,264 ("Enrollment Statistics").

[104] BJC, "Rules of Bob Jones College" (MLA: Box 29, mimeograph, Rachel Ayres scrapbook). The thirty-five rules encompass areas from behavior in class to permission for leaving campus. Upper level students enjoyed fewer restrictions in certain areas than did freshmen or sophomores. Women students appear to have lived under generally tighter restrictions than did men students as evidenced by a third page of rules entitled "Dormitory Regulations for Women."

[105] "Resolved, that all boys who room above the auditorium be permitted to have light privileges since they are all upper classmen or special students and since many of them are writing theses" (FMM, 12 October 1933 [ABV]); this request was denied. "Resolved that the boys be allowed to enter the front door of the dining hall for all meals on Sundays. Prof. Martin made a motion, seconded by Miss Lee, that this request be granted. The motion passed without opposition. It was amended, however, to include a stipulation that the boys must clean their feet before entering" (FMM, 4 October 1934 [ABV]).

[106] Stenholm diary, 22 November 1938.

[107] BJsr, *My Friends* (Greenville, S.C.: BJU Press, 1983), pp. 53-54.

[108] "Rules of Bob Jones College," ca. 1933 (MLA: Box 29, Rachel Ayres scrapbook).

[109] BJsr to E. H. Peavy, 21 January 1937.

[110] MS, BJsr, chapel talk, n.d., 1945 (ABV: 1945).

[111]Interview, Katherine Stenholm, 8 June 1987. See also "Bob Jones Answers Anonymous Writer in American Mercury," *Cleveland (Tenn.) Daily Banner,* 5 March 1941.

[112]Faculty were charged with the responsibilities of maintaining student discipline within the classroom and chaperoning social events and dates. Not all faculty readily accepted the social rigor advocated by the school and some were eventually discharged. See also Anonymous [Dorothy Seay], "Accent," pp. 16-23.

[113]MS, BJsr, chapel talk, n.d. (ABV: "Odds & Ends," 1945).

[114]FMM, 4 September 1943 (ABV).

[115]BJsr, *Things,* p. 79.

[116]Interview, Elizabeth Edwards, 25 May 1993.

[117]"Giovanni Sperandeo, Lyric Tenor, Press Comments," n.d. (GF: Sperandeo file). Prior to joining the faculty, the Sperandeos had concertized extensively in the United States, playing in small communities such as Owensboro, Kentucky; Muscatine, Iowa; Platteville, Wisconsin; Tell City, Indiana; Sandusky, Ohio; Keokuk, Iowa; Ottawa, Illinois; and Gary, Indiana.

[118]BJsr to Giovanni Sperandeo, 26 May 1934 (GF: Sperandeo file).

[119]Giovanni Sperandeo to BJsr, 2 June 1936 (GF: Sperandeo file). Loren Jones and Mrs. Jones had traveled with BJsr for many years. Loren Jones had been BJsr's song leader and soloist, and Mrs. Jones had been the pianist and accompanist.

[120]"Bob Jones Spreads Gospel in Poland," *Chattanooga Times,* 25 November 1934.

[121]Giovanni Sperandeo to BJjr, 25 January 1936 (GF: Sperandeo file). This "incompetent" was Sarah Linton, a BJC graduate who was then a graduate student in piano performance at the Cincinnati Conservatory.

[122]BJjr to Giovanni Sperandeo, 24 January 1936 (GF: Sperandeo file).

[123]Giovanni Sperandeo to BJsr, 2 June 1936 (GF: Sperandeo file).

[124]BJsr to Giovanni Sperandeo, 28 May 1936 (GF: Sperandeo file).

[125]BJsr to E. A. Ralston, 24 January 1939 (GF: Flood file).

[126]"Student's Report on Miss Flood" (GF: Flood file).

[127]BJjr to Ruth Flood, 16 December 1936 (GF: Flood file).

[128]Stenholm diary, 1937. The entry reads, "Miss Ruth Flood came back after an absence of one semester."

[129]Dorothy Seay to BJsr, 21 August 1936 (GF: Seay file).

[130]Anonymous [Dorothy Seay], "Accent," p. 16.

[131]BJsr to Dorothy Seay, 16 December 1936 (GF: Seay file).

[132]Cena Mann to BJsr, 17 June 1938 (GF: Flood file). Ruth Flood's sister wrote, "I am actually surprised that you would tolerate a person, and even let them stay . . . in your employ, like Miss Seay. . . . Well, you can imagine my surprise, when I heard she was back on the faculty last year. I warned Ruth before she went back . . . to stay away from her. I found out afterward that it was impossible, because she spent so many hours in Ruth's room that [Ruth] did not have time to read, write, or rest, a lot of times when she wanted to do so." BJsr did not release Seay possibly because of the shortage of well qualified teachers, and Seay did have the credentials. He simply may have wished to give her the benefit of the doubt and time to adjust in the hope that she would come to hold the standards of the school. More likely, however, he was misled by others. He responded to Ruth's sister, "You raise the question about Miss Seay being returned this past year. Let me explain that. I had so much confidence in Ruth when she told me . . . that Miss Seay was absolutely loyal and had never said one word about which there could be a question, I took it for granted that my opinion must be wrong, so Miss Seay stayed on" (BJsr to Cena Mann, 20 June 1938 [GF: Flood file]).

[133]Anonymous [Dorothy Seay], "Accent," p. 16. Although published in the *American Mercury* in 1940, the use of the present tense throughout the article indicates that it may have been written while Dorothy Seay was still a member of the faculty. BJjr, remembering the article, called it "mean and dishonest."

[134]Stenholm diary, 23 May 1938.

[135]BJsr to Dorothy Seay, 26 May 1938. Corroborated by Stenholm diary, which records the student body meeting at which this took place, 23 May 1938.

[136]Joseph Free to BJsr, 25 May 1938 (GF: Free file).

[137]Ibid.

[138]Marjorie Foster to BJsr, 17 June 1938 (GF: Foster file). See also Free to BJsr, 25 May 1938.

[139]Free to BJsr, 25 May 1938 (GF: Free file).

[140]Interview, Katherine Stenholm, 25 May 1993; and Foster to BJsr, 17 June 1938 (GF: Foster file).

[141]BJsr to Cena Mann, 20 June 1938 (GF: Flood file).

[142]Ruth Flood to BJsr, 25 May 1938 (GF: Flood file).

[143]Interview, Gail Gingery, when discussing Robert Shaper and Ted Mercer.

[144]MS, BJsr, chapel talk, 2 April 1945 (ABV: 1945). BJsr would thunder, "A man that isn't loyal isn't anything. . . . Loyalty is necessary to success. An army can't win battles without loyalty. If you have traitors in the army, you lose the battle. You can't win any battles in life without loyalty. The moment you are disloyal in an institution like this . . . you will lose that wonderful substance that has set this school apart."

[145]BJsr, *Things,* p. 175.

Chapter 7: Combing Out the Cultural Kinks

[1]BJU, "Charter" (Office of the Provost, BJU).

[2]The dean of administration reminded the faculty as late as 1959 that the school had been founded on these three principles: the Bible, discipline, and culture (FMM: 22 April 1959).

[3]MS, BJsr, chapel talk, 29, 30 October and 1, 2 November 1944 (ABV: 1944).

[4]William D. Upshaw, "Bob Jones Stirs and Blesses Atlanta, Georgia," unknown paper, 1911 (MLA: 1911 clipping book).

[5]BJsr, chapel talk, 3 April 1944 (ABV: 1944). He said, "I am the founder of this college, but I am not a scholar. I am not a literary genius. I am not an authority on books. I borrow the educational and technical brains to run this college."

[6]" 'The Perils of America' Dr. Bob Jones' New Lecture Heard Here Wednesday Night," *Andalusia (Ala.) Star,* 25 February 1927. See also, BJsr, "The Perils of America, or Where Are We Headed," sermon booklet (Cleveland, Tenn.: BJC, 1934).

[7]See BJsr, *Bob Jones' Revival Sermons* (Wheaton, Ill.: Sword of the Lord Press, 1948); "The Unbeatable Game: A Sermon to Men," sermon booklet (Cleveland, Tenn.: BJC, n.d.). Also, "Square Politics Urgee [*sic*] by Jones in Sermon Tuesday," *Montgomery (Ala.) Advertiser,* 1 June 1921; "Tabernacle Constructed Here in 1917 for Revival Meetings," *Zanesville (Ohio) Times Recorder,* 13 March 1960; "Bob Jones Delivers Blunt, Forceful Sermon to Churchmen at Tabernacle: Evangelist Rebukes Sham, Humbuggery and Dishonesty in the Church and Demands More Honesty in Business, Cleaner Politics and More Prayer in the Homes," *Gloversville (N.Y.) Morning Herald,* 15 April 1916.

[8]In chapel talks and sermons, there are 125 occurrences of BJsr's dealing with the cultural issue of personal refinement or standards of behavior. The first occurrence is

chapel talk, 11 February 1933 (ABV: 1933); the final occurrence is in the last year of chapel talks and messages surveyed (14 December 1954 [ABV: 1954]).

[9]Wright, *Fortress,* p. 280.

[10]Alan Peshkin, *God's Choice: The Total World of the Fundamentalist Christian School* (Chicago: University of Chicago Press, 1986). Although a recent volume, Peshkin's accurately portrays the world view to which Fundamentalist Protestants have historically subscribed. BJC, in its early days, was perhaps the first to define the "total world" and is the only college in which theological and disciplinary emphases have remained relatively unaffected by the passage of time and changes of administration.

[11]MS, BJsr, chapel talk, 28 December 1944 (ABV: 1944). BJsr clearly enunciated his position on cultural development and the "total world" when he said, "Everything you do and say and think is our business if you are a Bob Jones College student." He then enumerated some areas of personal refinement that he felt clearly established the cultural norm of the College: courtesy, thankfulness, punctuality, cleanliness, proper deportment, and so on.

[12]MS, BJsr, chapel talk, March 1950 (ABV: 1950). For early statements of his position, see BJsr, *Bob Jones' Sermons* (Montgomery, Ala.: State Press, 1908).

[13]See BJsr, *Revival Sermons.*

[14]MS, BJsr, chapel talk, 19 January 1950 (ABV: 1950); MS, BJsr, chapel talk, 30 October 1944 (ABV: 1944).

[15]The presupposition here is that "the actions of man, though willed by him, are always under the superintendence and sovereign control of God and therefore that the facts of history are actions either directed or permitted by God. As such they are God's doings, while man's" (BJU, *The Christian Teaching of History* [Greenville, S.C.: BJU Press, 1981], p. 2). Man, as a fallen creature with moral agency, to know God as He intended, must come to God through accepting the atoning sacrifice of God's Son, Jesus Christ, for sin. Only in this way may fallen man be restored to fellowship with his Creator.

[16]"Dr. Jones Goes After Modern Church Crowd," *Cleveland (Tenn.) Daily Banner,* December 1935 (MLA: Rachel Ayres scrapbook). MS, BJsr, chapel talk, 3 April 1944 (ABV: 1944). In this sermon BJsr places the blame for the social ills of America—juvenile delinquency, immorality, civil unrest, social upheaval—on Darwinian evolution and behaviorism in education and on permissivism in American homes. See also Straton, *Debates;* and Isaac Massey Haldeman, *Dr. Harry Emerson Fosdick's Book: "The Modern Use of the Bible"* (Philadelphia: Sunday School Times Company, 1925).

[17]"Let America Shun Entanglement of Coming War, Urges Bob Jones," *Cleveland (Tenn.) Daily Banner,* n.d., 1936 (MLA: Rachel Ayres scrapbook). See also Ruth Taunton, "Christianity, Not Warships, Can Save Civilization, Says Fighting Educator," *San Diego Union,* 21 March 1939. Also, MS, BJsr, chapel talk, 4 January 1945 (ABV: 1945).

[18]"Famous Evangelist Says Communism Creates Real Danger for Uncle Sam," *Mobile (Ala.) Press Register,* 7 December 1941. See also MS, BJsr, chapel talk, 30 October 1944 (ABV: 1944).

[19]"Sir Prophet, Here Is a Job for You—To Save New York," unknown paper, 1916 (MLA: Bob Jones clipping book 3, p. 42); and "New York Women on Road to Ruin Lure Men to Tread It with Them, Says Rev. Bob Jones," unknown paper, 1916 (MLA: Bob Jones clipping book 3, p. 41). See also "Sins of Men Are Discussed," *Hartford City (Ind.) Times-Gazette,* n.d., 1915 (MLA: Bob Jones clipping book 3, p. 26). Also, BJsr, *Revival Sermons.* See also John Roach Straton, *The Menace of Immorality in Church and State: Messages of Wrath* (New York: George H. Doran Co., 1925).

[20]Machen, *Christianity,* p. 8.

[21]MS, BJsr, radio message, 18 March 1965 (ASTA).

[22]MS, BJsr, chapel talk, 13 May 1945 (ABV: 1945).

[23]Ibid., 16 May 1945 (ABV: 1945).

[24]For a concise treatment of Fundamentalist thought toward Catholicism, see Robert E. Wenger, "Social Thought in American Fundamentalism, 1918-1933" (Ph.D. dissertation, University of Nebraska, 1973), pp. 152-212.

[25]Wenger, "Social Thought," pp. 169-70. Though an oversimplification, this is basically accurate. Modernists felt that immigration would add to the social burden of the cities, and Fundamentalists feared the political influence of the papacy and religious persecution from Catholics in power.

[26]*Bob Jones Magazine,* vol. 1, no. 9, June 1928, cover.

[27]See *Bob Jones Magazine,* vol. 1, no. 3, November 1928. This volume contains articles critical of Al Smith, the Democratic party, and Roman Catholicism. Articles included are "Al and His Church," by E. C. Glover; "Roman Catholicism vs. Protestantism," by W. J. Hall; "Why Not Al?" by J. Floyd Collins; and "An Open Letter to Mr. Kohn," by BJsr. *Bob Jones Magazine* in October 1928 carried an editorial by BJsr attacking Al Smith and pledging BJsr's support to Herbert Hoover. Al Smith was opposed for the following reasons: "First, Al Smith is a Catholic. . . . America stands for public schools. The Catholic church does not. . . . America stands for freedom of thought. The Roman . . . church stands for ignorance and superstition ànd the slavery of the human soul. Second, I am against Al Smith because he is wet. . . . Third, Al Smith represents Tammany Hall. . . . Tammany stands for everything that is corrupt. Fourth, Al Smith stands for the foreign domination of America. . . . He stands for the opening of our doors to millions more of [uneducated] foreigners. Fifth, Al Smith represents the city idea of American government. Sixth, Al Smith . . . is not fit to be president" (BJsr, "Editorial," *Bob Jones Magazine,* vol. 1, no. 2, October 1928, p. 1). Interestingly, though opposing Catholic polity and theology, BJsr felt a closer commonality of belief with Catholics than with Modernists. Catholics believe in the virgin birth of Christ, the bodily resurrection, miracles, and the inspiration of Scripture, whereas Modernists deny the possibility of these (MS, BJsr, "Religious Liberty," radio talk, 17 September 1960).

[28]"Perils," *Andalusia (Ala.) Star.* The eight perils were (1) "the peril of the city," showing concern for changes in American demographics and the morality of the masses; (2) "the peril of thoughtlessness," presenting the lack of reflective thought; (3) "the peril of extreme wealth and extreme poverty," presenting his understanding of prevailing social conditions in the cities; (4) "the spirit of [social] unrest," presenting one result of Modernism's faith in science, Darwinism, and behaviorism; (5) "the peril of the future," presenting man's finite existence and God's eternal providence; (6) "the peril of lawlessness," giving a call to law and order; (7) "the peril of a Nation without a Sabbath," dealing with the emerging issue of Sunday commercialism; and, (8) "the peril of sensuality," presenting his view of the final link in the moral chains that bind nations.

For studies of the social thought presented in "Perils," see Daniel L. Turner, "Fundamentalism, the Arts, and Personal Refinement: A Study of the Ideals of Bob Jones, Sr., and Bob Jones, Jr." (Ed.D. dissertation, University of Illinois–Urbana-Champaign, 1988); and Dalhouse, "Shaping."

[29]"Perils," *Andalusia (Ala.) Star.*

[30]Taunton, "Christianity, Not Warships."

[31]BJsr, "Perils."

[32]"Kicking Bob Jones," *Scranton (Pa.) Times,* n.d., 1913.

[33]BJsr, "Perils," 1934. For a thorough presentation of the dominant social thought of early twentieth-century Fundamentalists, see Wenger, "Social Thought." Wenger makes the point that there was nearly universal agreement among Fundamentalists of

this time about these issues. There was, however, no consensus as to solutions. On the whole, Fundamentalists of the period, BJsr included, were content with the American economic system; took a moderate nationalistic stance; condemned greed, avarice, and lust in every setting in which they were found, including the economic and social; and supported the cause of conservative education (pp. 290-93).

[34]Taunton, "Christianity, not Warships."

[35]MS, BJsr, chapel talk, 5 December 1948 (ABV: 1948).

[36]Ibid., n.d., 1945 (ABV: Odds & Ends).

[37]Ibid., 30 March 1935.

[38]Wright, *Fortress,* p. 281.

[39]"We live by rule. . . . If [the students] do not live up to the game, we have prayer with them and give them a chance. Then if they do not live up to the rules, we send them home" (BJsr, *Bob Jones Magazine,* back cover, January 1929). See also William T. Bruner Jr., "Is a Really Christian College Possible?" *Western Recorder,* 22 February 1940, p. 12; and " 'Flapper Mothers' and Evolution Draw Fire from Evangelist Jones," *Birmingham (Ala.) News,* 9 May 1926.

[40]MS, BJsr, chapel talk, 10 November 1949 (ABV: 1949). "Anybody around here that doesn't like what this administration does, you can come to the administration and ask about it and express your feelings. But you can't go around here and gripe about it to anybody else."

[41]MS, BJsr, radio talk, "The Ethics of the Bible," 26 December 1959 (ASTA). With every message preached on the creed, time was spent defining the "ethics" of the Scripture.

[42]MS, BJsr, chapel talk, 17 May 1949 (ABV: 1949).

[43]Interview, Karl Keefer, 27 July 1987; corroborated by Interview, DG, 19 June 1987.

[44]Interview, Karl Keefer.

[45]MS, BJsr, chapel talk, 2 March 1933 (ABV: 1933).

[46]Ibid., 10 November 1949 (ABV: 1949).

[47]Ibid., December 19, 1934.

[48]Martha Grace Green, "Pockets for Our Aprons," *Piedmont Bible College Alumni Letter,* May 1968 (MLA: Box 16), contains an eyewitness account of one of these lectures on etiquette. Interviewee Robert Pratt has vivid memories of Mrs. BJsr's etiquette lectures when he was a student in 1942 (Interview, Robert Pratt, 8 June 1987); and Leonard Holliday commented, "They taught you not to eat until the hostess gave the signal. . . . They would announce that. You were taught where to put your utensils when you were done. The very fact that you were being served by waiters and waitresses gives you the atmosphere . . . where you are to use manners. And then [they tell] you to seat the ladies" (Interview, Leonard Holliday, 22 June 1987). Also, BJjr's "Design for Culture at the World's Most Unusual University," magazine article draft, n.d., reads, "At mealtime, rules of etiquette are frequently dropped as 'apples of gold on leaves of silver.' "

[49]See FMM, 25 November 1929; and 23 September 1930 (ABV).

[50]Ibid., 29 October 1929.

[51]"School Calendar," *Little Moby's Post,* vol. 1, no. 1, March 1942; and vol. 1, no. 2, June 1942. All students except those working the meals as waiters or waitresses were required to attend. Such banquets were held every year. As the school grew larger, however, the formal banquets grew fewer in number until, by 1971, there were only three.

[52]MS, BJsr, chapel talk, n.d., 1945 (ABV: Odds & Ends).

[53]Ibid., 17 April 1935 (ABV: 1935).

[54]Ibid., n.d., 1945 (ABV: Odds & Ends).

[55]Ibid., 13 April 1935 (ABV: 1935).

[56]Ibid., 27 November 1945 (ABV: 1945).

[57]Ibid., 3 January 1935 (ABV: 1935).

[58]"A man who is not loyal is not anything" (Ibid., 8 December 1948 [ABV: 1948]).

[59]"You've got to learn discipline; that is one of the essentials of culture" (Ibid., n.d., 1945; also 24 November 1949 [ABV: Odds & Ends]).

[60]Ibid., 19 December 1934 (ABV: 1934).

[61]Ibid., 5 December 1948 (ABV: 1948).

[62]Ibid., 31 January 1949 (ABV: 1949). FMM from 1933 to 1947 record much concern for the students' personal table etiquette. As has been previously noted, the College in the early days provided lectures in etiquette for the students and monitored opportunities to apply these lessons. This type of instruction continued through the history of the school in Freshman Orientation classes with lectures pertaining to basic courtesy, table manners, concert etiquette, and so on.

[63]MS, BJsr, chapel talk, 15 February 1945 (ABV: 1945).

[64]Interview, BJjr, 28 May 1987.

[65]MS, BJsr, chapel talk, 7 May 1947 (ABV: 1947).

[66]Ibid., n.d., 1945 (ABV: Odds & Ends).

[67]Ibid., 9 May 1947 (ABV: 1947).

[68]Ibid., 25 January 1946 (ABV: 1946).

[69]Ibid., n.d. 1945 (ABV: 1945).

[70]Ibid., 9 May 1941 (ABV: 1941).

[71]FMM, 4 October 1943 (ABV).

[72]MS, BJsr, chapel talk, 15 March 1941 (ABV: 1941). In the sermons of BJsr from 1927 through 1954, at least sixty-two mentions of the fine arts were made. Although he often recited poetry, spoke poetically in the pulpit, occasionally visited art galleries and museums, attended opera, saw great performers such as Paderewski and Heifetz, and was widely traveled, his ideas of music, drama, and the other fine arts did not surface until later in his life.

[73]Ibid., 11 February 1933 (ABV: 1933). "You don't inherit culture." This is not to say that he was not interested in the arts prior to 1934; however, aside from one article in the *Bob Jones Magazine* of April 1929, there are no printed sources extant which refer to culture until a chapel talk in 1933.

[74]Based on James 1:17—"Every good gift and every perfect gift is from above, and cometh down from the Father of lights." The sense in which BJsr uses "good" is entirely moral. His meaning is that as art carries a morally uplifting message or invokes emotion that is edifying, it is good. BJsr did not develop an aesthetic by which to judge inherent musical, dramatic, or artistic worth outside the realm of the moral.

[75]The term "original state" presupposes a culture existing after the creation of man to that time of the Fall of man in the Garden of Eden. Thus, the creative activity of man during this time would be activity reflecting only the eternal nature and purity of man's expressive soul as an unfallen creation.

[76]MS, BJsr, chapel talk, 13 December 1949.

[77]MS, BJsr, chapel talk, 1 April 1945 (ABV: 1945).

[78]Howard Morse Skinner, "Music at Bob Jones College," *Bob Jones Magazine,* vol. 1, no. 8, April 1929, p. 6.

[79]MS, BJsr, chapel talk, 13 December 1949.

[80]The use of the apostle Paul to justify cultural endeavor occurred in extant chapel talks of 9 March 1941; 30 November 1946; and 18 November 1948.

[81]MS, BJsr, chapel talk, 18 November 1948 (ABV: 1948). This is the most detailed statement of BJsr relating to the importance of culture in the life.

[82]Ibid., n.d. 1945 (ABV: Odds & Ends).
[83]Ibid., 10 March 1947 (ABV: 1947).
[84]Ibid., 12 January 1945 (ABV: 1945).

Chapter 8: Culture Comes to Cleveland

[1]Howard Morse Skinner, "Music at the Bob Jones College," *Bob Jones Magazine,* vol. 1, no. 8, April 1929, p. 6.

[2]Interview, Mrs. BJjr, 4 June 1987. According to Mrs. BJsr, this occurred only once, although references are made to similar events in Gilbert Stenholm's diaries from 1934 and 1935.

[3]Interview, BJjr, 28 May 1987. Most interviewees of the era, including Mrs. BJjr, credit the beginning of the Musicales to BJjr. He takes no credit for these programs, however, attributing them to Mrs. Dean. Extant Vespers programs indicate that Susie Kelly Dean directed every Musicale that first year. Also, Interview, Tommy Smith, 17 May 1988.

[4]Twilight Musicale program, 9 October 1927 (MLA: Box 26). See also *An Epoch in Education: Facts About the Bob Jones College,* vol. 1, no. 1, 1928, p. 10.

[5]Susie Kelly Dean, "Large Crowd Present at College Twilight Musicale," handwritten press release, n.d. (MLA: Box 26). The program was produced "under the direction of the Music and Dramatic Arts Departments, Mrs. Susie Kelly Dean—Director and Accompanist."

[6]Interview, BJjr, 28 May 1987; corroborated by Interview, Mr. Tommy Smith, 17 May 1988. One student from this era recalls that "Vespers . . . were professional and gave the students wonderful opportunities for developing their talents. They were well planned cultural and inspirational programs of the best of music, drama, literature and art. Faculty and students took part, and occasionally visiting artists entertained. These productions were open to the public, and people came from all over the area and filled that large auditorium. Those in charge were perfectionists, and if we were invited to be on a Vespers program we knew it meant hard work and doing our best" (Warwick, *Tides,* p. 127).

[7]The program consisted of four vocal solos of the religious art song genre, one vocal duet, a mixed vocal quartet, a male quartet, two piano solos, and one address ("Twilight Musicale, Bob Jones College," 9 October 1927, typewritten program [MLA: Box 26]). See also Susie Kelly Dean, "Large Crowd Present" (MLA: Box 26).

[8]The program included the "Morton March" performed by the orchestra; "The Bells" and "Tinkle-oo," by the Glee Club; a "Musical Reading"of Luke 2:8-20, by BJjr; Randolph Sparkes and BJjr singing "Silent Night," accompanied by a violinist; a male quartet; several readings; and a variety of other vocal and instrumental solos ("Twilight Musicale, Bob Jones College," 11 December 1927, mimeographed program [MLA: Box 26]). Programs from the year 1927-28 record several instrumental selections chosen for performance. For example, the first piano solo presented on a Twilight Musicale was "The Last Hope" by Gottschalk on 9 October 1927 ("Twilight Musicale," 9 October 1927 [MLA: Box 26]). On 1 April 1928, a student performed the "Riggoletto [*sic*] Fantasy" by Liszt ("Twilight Musicale, Bob Jones College," 1 April 1928, handwritten program [MLA: Box 26]).

[9]Selections such as "Bloom Brightly, Sweet Roses" by Fowler ("Twilight Musicale," 1 April 1928 [MLA: Box 26]); "Would That We Were Maying" by Nevin ("Twilight Musicale, Bob Jones College," 18 March 1928, handwritten program [MLA: Box 26]);

"The Palms" by Fauré ("Twilight Musicale," 1 April 1928 [MLA: Box 26]); and "Honey Chile" by White brought the first year's students a taste of "culture."

[10]Charles W. Mountain was a graduate of the Moody Bible Institute and held a bachelor of music degree from Northwestern University in Evanston, Illinois. He was the head of the music conservatory, taught voice, and directed the choir.

[11]FMM, 4 September 1931, indicate that BJjr was "placed in charge of the first Vesper program of the year. It was also determined that the speech and music departments should furnish a certain number of selections for each Vesper program and that credit for this be given with the details to be worked out between the heads of the various departments" (ABV).

[12]Rehearsal was scheduled from 6:30 to 8:00 P.M. See FMM, 15 December 1932 (ABV).

[13]These dramas, staged and costumed as well as possible, were written by speech majors, as in the case of *Pontius Pilate: A Religious Drama,* by BJjr, performed in April 1929 (reported in *Bob Jones Magazine,* vol. 1, no. 8, April 1929, p. 19) or were prepared from outside scripts ("Twilight Musicale—Bob Jones College," 22 February 1928, handwritten program [MLA: Box 26]). The play *Easter Morning* was presented as part of the "Musicale" on 1 April 1928 ("Twilight Musicale—Bob Jones College," 1 April 1928, handwritten program [MLA: Box 26]).

[14]For more on Ruth Flood, see Chapter 6.

[15]Interview, BJjr, 28 May 1987.

[16]Ibid.

[17]Interview, Mrs. BJjr, 4 June 1987. Interview, BJjr, 28 May 1987. See also Hugh Fellows, "The College Chronicle," *Cleveland (Tenn.) Daily Banner,* 24 October 1933; and Monroe Parker, *Sunshine,* p. 83.

[18]Interview, Tommy Smith, 17 May 1988.

[19]Interview, BJjr, 28 May 1987. BJjr described his role in the early days by saying, "I was pushing all the time for the drama."

[20]Ibid.

[21]Ibid. This included buying costumes, fabric, equipment, stage curtains, lights, and so forth, for the early productions.

[22]"Bob Jones University Classic Players," repertory list 1930-56 inclusive (MLA: uncataloged document).

[23]Interview, Elizabeth Edwards, 28 May 1987. See also "BJU Classic Players."

[24]"BJU Classic Players."

[25]*Hamlet* played in the city auditorium to a standing-room-only audience, "hundreds being turned away from the door." The performance was extremely well received, perhaps not so much out of love for the Bard as for the admission price.

> The Bob Jones College players presented Shakespeare's 'Hamlet' at the Municipal Auditorium in Dothan last Saturday evening before an audience of something over 2,000. The huge building, which will accommodate comfortable [*sic*] seven hundred people, was overflowing long before the performance started, so that instead of the curtain rising at seven as scheduled the play began at six, one hour ahead of schedule. All available seating space was taken early in the evening and it was estimated that besides the two thousand who were admitted to see the production, between three and five thousand were turned away for lack of space in the auditorium. Hamlet was put on out of appreciation to the young people of that section for their co-operation in the recent revival campaign put on there by Dr. Jones, and no admission was charged. (Tom Ham, "College Pointers," unknown paper, n.d., 1932 [MLA: Box 29, BJC publicity scrapbook, 1929-39])

See also "Bob Jones College to Present Hamlet." This article says, "Hamlet will be presented January 19, 1932" (unknown paper, n.d. [MLA: Box 29, BJC publicity scrapbook]). "Bob Jones University Classic Players" records *Hamlet* as playing 11 February 1932 at the College. Since the article "Hamlet Coming to Dothan Again" records the return engagement as being 11 February 1932 and states that the play packed the auditorium "three weeks earlier," it is probable that the "Classic Players" document is in error on the date of this performance. *Hamlet* was also performed in Montgomery, Alabama ("Pupils Present Hamlet at Lanier," unknown paper, n.d., 1932 [MLA: Box 29, BJC publicity scrapbook, 1929-39]).

[26]"Commencement Program: Bob Jones College," 27 May–1 June 1932 (MLA: Box 26). According to this program, *The Taming of the Shrew* was presented at 2:00 P.M. and *Hamlet* was presented at 8:00 P.M., Tuesday, 31 May 1932. BJjr played Petruchio in *Shrew* and Hamlet.

[27]Interview, Karl Keefer, 27 July 1987.

[28]Interview, Elizabeth Edwards, 28 May 1987. Mrs. Edwards cites a stronger theme orientation as the primary development in Vespers performances during the Cleveland era.

[29]One program was on the theme of "Hills" and was based on Psalm 121:1: "I will lift up mine eyes unto the hills, from whence cometh my help." It contained songs and readings that dealt with hills or used the words "Lift up mine eyes," and it ended with an original play entitled *Hills* ("Play to Feature Vesper Services," [*sic*] *Cleveland [Tenn.] Daily Banner,* n.d.).

[30]Another program from 1940 on the theme "God in Nature" included a reading, "A.B.C. in Green," and a vocal solo, "Trees." On the same program a male quartet sang "The Spacious Firmament" and a violinist played the second movement of a Beethoven violin concerto; there was also Scripture from Psalm 19 and a vocal solo ("The Blind Plowman"), among other selections (Elizabeth Adams, "God in Nature," Vespers production notes, 21 April 1940 [Vespers songs files]).

[31]"Play at College Draws Overflow Audience," unknown paper, n.d. (MLA: Box 29, Rachel Ayres scrapbook).

[32]"The Star in the East Pageant to Be Given at Vesper Services," unknown paper, n.d. (MLA: Rachel Ayres scrapbook).

[33]Helen Loose, "Israel," Vespers production notes, 4 February 1940 (Vespers songs files).

[34]Fellows, "College Chronicle."

[35]"Dedicate New Auditorium on Easter Sunday," *Cleveland (Tenn.) Daily Banner,* 10 April 1936.

[36]Thomas Brahan, "Gossip of Screen and Stage: Birthday Greetings," *Chattanooga Times,* 28 May 1939. The director of one visiting troupe, following their performance at the College, remarked, "Bob Jones College has the best stage and equipment of any college that we have seen in America, and we have played in hundreds of schools from coast to coast" ("Director of White Hussars Praises BJC Stage and Equipment," unknown paper, n.d. [MLA: Box 8, Artist Series]).

[37]*Vintage,* 1940, pp. 67-69. BJjr established a resident costume department in Florida that grew along with the school and its costuming demands.

[38]Interview, Elizabeth Edwards, 28 May 1987.

[39]MS, BJsr, chapel talk, 23 January 1941 (ABV: 1941).

[40]Interview, BJjr, 28 May 1987. In Florida the performances were given at the Dixon-McKenzie Auditorium. In Tennessee the performances were given at Arnold School, a local elementary school, until the Margaret Mack Auditorium was completed.

[41]"Bob Jones College Classic Players Tenth Anniversary," booklet, 30 May 1939 (MLA: Box 29, BJC publicity scrapbook). The Classic Players on at least one occasion presented a matinee performance for the students of local Cleveland schools. The play

was introduced by BJjr, who gave a synopsis of the plot prior to performance. The aim of this performance was to give the school children a "better appreciation and understanding" of Shakespeare, with the hope of generating interest in his works ("Dr. Jones Says Vivid Imaginations Required to Read Drama with Profit," *Cleveland [Tenn.] Daily Banner,* 9 February 1939).

[42]"Hamlet at Lanier." See also "Students Present Shakespearian Play," unknown paper, n.d. 1932 (MLA: Box 29, BJC publicity scrapbook, 1929-39). See also Thomas Brahan, "Gossip of Screen and Stage: Notes on 'King Lear,' " *Chattanooga Times,* 27 March 1938.

[43]Apparently a performance of *Othello,* given 13 October 1939, fell short of previous productions. One Chattanooga critic wrote, "Mr. Jones was hampered by the fact that the group had only three weeks to spend in rehearsal. That 'Othello' seems less successful than others of the Classic Players' performances is due not to Friday the 13th being an unlucky date, but a premature one" (Thomas Brahan, "Classic Players Present 'Othello,' " *Chattanooga Times,* 15 October 1939). Also, "Classic Players Give 'Merchant of Venice' Here," *Cleveland (Tenn.) Daily Banner,* 26 November 1938; and Thomas Brahan, "Gossip of Screen and Stage: Birthday Greetings," *Chattanooga Times,* 28 May 1939.

[44]Warner Ogden, "Evangelist Bob Jones Operates a Non-profit College Where Fundamentalism Is Insisted On," *Knoxville (Tenn.) News-Sentinel,* 11 February 1934. See also "Bob Jones Players Now in Ninth Year," *Chattanooga Free Press,* 20 February 1938.

[45]Samuel A. Tannenbaum, "The Classic Players and *King Lear,*" *Shakespeare Association Bulletin,* vol. 14, no. 2, April 1939, p. 128.

[46]Interview, Elizabeth Edwards, 28 May 1987. Also, BJjr to Mr. Paul Soper, 15 May 1944 (GF: Southern Association of Teachers of Speech file). This convention unfortunately was canceled at the request of the Department of Transportation, Office of War Preparedness.

[47]Wenger, "Social Thought," p. 222. See also W. B. Riley, *The Crisis of the Church* (New York: Charles C. Cook, 1914), p. 171; and Straton, *Menace,* p. 62.

[48]*Theater* appears to have been used by many Fundamentalists as a generic term covering any type of presentation on a stage, ranging from burlesque and vaudeville to monodrama and Shakespeare. Rarely does one find a definition of theater, especially among its Fundamentalist opponents.

[49]Straton, *Fighting the Devil,* pp. 110-11.

[50]Straton, *Menace,* p. 58. See also Riley, *Crisis,* p. 170; and William B. Biederwolf, *The Christian and Amusements* (Grand Rapids, Mich.: Wm. B. Eerdmans Publishing Co., n.d.), pp. 15-31.

[51]Interview, Mrs. BJsr, 28 August 1986.

[52]BJjr, *Cornbread,* p. 48. See also Brahan, "Birthday Greetings," *Chattanooga Times;* and "Bob Jones Players," *Chattanooga Free Press.*

[53]BJjr, *Cornbread,* p. 48.

[54]Dale Savidge and BJjr, "Shakespeare and Shylock: An Interview with Bob Jones," videotape interview (BJU Division of Speech, Department of Dramatic Productions), 1987. See also BJjr, *Cornbread,* pp. 46-48.

[55]BJjr, *Cornbread,* p. 46.

[56]There are no letters or articles from religious papers extant from the early days of the school to corroborate this point. There are notable examples, however, remaining from the 1940s and 1950s. There is no indication that criticism aimed at the school as late as 1955 would differ substantially from that reportedly given the school in the 1930s. Mrs. BJsr, Mrs. BJjr, BJjr, and Monroe Parker all corroborated the existence of a critical element of supporters in the early days of the school.

[57]BJjr, *Cornbread,* p. 48.

[58]Interview, Mrs. BJsr, 28 August 1986. The fear of subverting the direction of the school was occasionally expressed in chapel talks and letters. BJsr preached, "It is possible to hide God behind the eloquence of a preacher. It's possible to hide God behind the spectacular of a great program. . . . It is so easy to get fascinated with something we like . . . that we bow the knee [to it] in worship" (MS, BJsr, chapel talk, 20 December 1945).

[59]"Bob Jones College Stresses Dramatics," unknown paper, n.d. 1934 (MLA: Box 29, Rachel Ayres scrapbook). See also MS, BJjr, chapel talk, 11 September 1950 (ABV: 1950). Many ministerial students did participate in the Shakespearean productions, and in one production of *Julius Caesar* on 4-5 November 1949, all four major men's roles were played by ministerial students (Wanda Walden, "Julius Caesar," *Little Moby's Post,* vol. 9, no. 3, November-December 1949, p. 1; also, Interviews, Monroe Parker and Karl Keefer, 27 July 1987). DG asserted that some of the school's most successful graduates now pastoring large churches credit some of their preaching success to their Shakespearean experience (Interview, DG, 19 June 1987).

[60]BJjr, *Cornbread,* pp. 47-48. See also Interview, Mrs. BJsr, 28 August 1986; and Interview, BJjr, 28 May 1987.

[61]"G-Man Heard by Students Here Monday," *Cleveland (Tenn.) Daily Banner,* 9 November 1937.

[62]"Ruth Bryan Owen to Speak Here 23rd," *Cleveland (Tenn.) Daily Banner,* 16 October 1937.

[63]" 'New Germany' Is Lecture Text: Von Wormer Walsh, World-Famed Traveler, to Appear Here Saturday," *Cleveland (Tenn.) Daily Banner,* 28 February 1939.

[64]"Publisher to Lecture," *Cleveland (Tenn.) Daily Banner,* 11 December 1939.

[65]"Richard Halliburton Coming Here Oct. 29: Bob Jones College to Present World-Famed Traveler" *Cleveland (Tenn.) Daily Banner,* n.d.

[66]"*The Messiah,* presented by the Bob Jones College Chorus," concert program, 26 January 1934 (MLA: Box 29, Rachel Ayres scrapbook).

[67]"Bob Jones College Commencement Concert," program, 25-29 May 1934 (MLA: Box 29, Rachel Ayres scrapbook).

[68]The Artist Series offered a variety of attractions at the College: dramatic monologuists, pianists, operatic singers, choral ensembles, instrumental ensembles, and American folk musicians. On rare occasions a performer who performed some folk dance was also included on the schedule. Such was the case with Ish-Ti-Opi, American Indian baritone.

[69]BJjr to Mr. James Heaton, 19 May 1937 (GF: Winona Lake files). The first student ticket fees were five dollars per semester and were adopted for school year 1936-37 (*Bob Jones College Catalogue,* vol. 9, no. 1, 1936-37, p. 18).

[70]"A Costume Recital by V. L. Granville," recital program, dated 6 February 1934 (MLA: Box 29, Rachel Ayres scrapbook). Granville apparently made a return appearance at the College. The 1934-35 *Vintage* displays a photo montage of programs, recitalists, music groups, and guest artists. One of these programs, that of Granville, is included and is dated 15 October 1934. No corroborative data has been uncovered.

[71]*Vintage,* 1933-34.

[72]"Singer Delights College Audience," *Cleveland (Tenn.) Daily Banner,* 27 March 1937. Doria's program was described as "the eighth number of the Artist Series sponsored by the college." College clipping files, scrapbooks, and the yearbook give no indication as to the nature of the other performances. Interestingly enough, Gilbert Stenholm's diary records that Miss Doria was accompanied by Ruth Newlin, a student at BJC at the time (Stenholm diary, 25 March 1937).

[73]BJjr to Mr. James Heaton, 14 May 1937 (GF: Winona Lake files).

[74]James Heaton to BJjr, 17 May 1937 (GF: Winona Lake files).

[75]Cornelia Otis Skinner was involved in one-woman shows, presenting her own original material. She and Ruth Draper were the pioneers in the field of original monologue, a field overwhelmingly rejected by authorities in the drama field for a number of years. BJjr had a great interest in monologue and solo shows, as evidenced by his own Curtain Calls.

[76]A similar program at Wheaton College was not initiated until 1954. See Bechtel, *Wheaton College,* p. 241.

[77]See *Cleveland (Tenn.) Daily Banner,* 2, 4, 11, and 12 November 1938; *Chattanooga News,* 5 November 1938; and *Chattanooga Times,* 10 November 1938. The program was replaced with the Wagnerian Festival Singers, a choral ensemble of young Metropolitan Opera hopefuls. The singers drew lavish praise from the Cleveland and Chattanooga press, who said that they were "decidedly the most outstanding group ever heard here" ("Wagnerian Festival Singers Delight Cleveland Audience," *Cleveland [Tenn.] Daily Banner,* 6 December 1938).

[78]Interview, BJjr, 28 May 1987.

[79]BJjr, *Cornbread,* p. 19. See also Interview, Gail Gingery, 5 June 1987.

[80]Interview, BJjr, 28 May 1987.

[81]Memo, "Bob Jones University Opera Productions," FAO. See also *Opera News,* 17 January 1944, vol. 8, no. 12, p. 15.

[82]BJjr to Dan Turner, personal correspondence, 14 March 1996.

[83]Interview, Mrs. Oliver Steiner, 18 June 1987.

[84]Ibid.; and Interview, Karl Keefer, 27 July 1987.

[85]Interview, Karl Keefer, 27 July 1987.

[86]Four large photographs with captions from the *Cleveland (Tenn.) Daily Banner* are extant in the BJU Archives. Judging from the photograph size (4" x 6"), one would assume that the paper believed this to be a major event in the community (MLA: Box 8, Artist Series).

[87]Interview, Mrs. Oliver Steiner, 18 June 1987. See also *Little Moby's Post,* June 1942, p. 4; and *Little Moby's Post,* February 1943.

[88]Ralph McGilvra, " 'Aida' Termed Great Success," unknown paper, n.d. (MLA: Box 29).

[89]"Bob Jones' Aida," *Opera News,* vol. 8, no. 12, 17 January 1944, p. 15.

[90]Interview, Karl Keefer, 27 July 1987. See also "Campus Highlights," *Little Moby's Post,* December 1944, p. 4.

[91]For example, *Il Trovatore* was staged on 16 December 1942, and the *St. Matthew's Passion* (with the same soloists) was performed on 17 December 1942. In 1943 *Aida* and the *Messiah* were performed by the guests with one day of rest between.

[92]Some of the eminent singers of the 1940s appeared in the BJC Opera Association productions. Among them are Doris Doe, Robert Weede, Marjorie Lawrence, George London, Eugene Connally, Ramon Vinay, Ebe Stignani, Frederick Jagel, and Nicola Moscona (names taken from opera program files, FAO).

[93]Interview, Karl Keefer.

[94]*Ernani* was staged on 19 and 20 December 1945 ("Pre-Christmas Festival," *Little Moby's Post,* February 1946, vol. 4, no. 4, p. 1).

[95]Interview, BJjr, 28 May 1987.

[96]There is no record of another performance of an oratorio until December 1937, when the *Messiah* was performed in Cleveland.

[97]Verdi, performed 31 March 1945; Bach, performed 17 December 1942; Rossini, performed 29 and 30 March 1946; and Brahms, performed 7 April 1956.

[98]MS, BJsr, chapel talk, 13 December 1949 (ABV: 1949).

Chapter 9: Closing the Book on Cleveland

[1]Stenholm diary, 15 December 1941.

[2]Ibid., 22 February 1943. ("Today I have to take over two typing classes. Narramore is in the army now.")

[3]"Odds and Ends," *Little Moby's Post,* October 1943, p. 4; and "Odds and Ends," *Little Moby's Post,* April 1944, p. 4.

[4]Stenholm diary, 21 March 1942.

[5]Ibid., 7 February 1943.

[6]Ibid., 11 February 1944; 19 October 1944; and 23 March 1945.

[7]Ibid., 6 August 1945.

[8]*Little Moby's Post* ran a feature called "In Memoriam" in which the College published the names of those killed in action. Between 1941 and 1946 this column contained the names of only nine former students. There were probably others about whom the College remained uninformed.

[9]Between 1941 and 1946 *Little Moby's Post* printed letters from BJC servicemen in a feature called "In the Military." Many were in frontline duty; others became chaplains or chaplain's assistants and had numerous opportunities to deal with men about their spiritual condition. Many times the letter writers would report the conversions of shipmates, buddies, and others.

[10]Johnson, *Builder*, pp. 211-18.

[11]Ibid., pp. 213-14.

[12]Ibid., p. 217.

[13]Ibid., p. 214.

[14]MS, BJsr, chapel talk, 2 November 1944 (ABV: 1944).

[15]Campus Map, Cleveland, Tennessee (GF).

[16]*Lighted Pathway,* vol. 17, no. 8, August 1946. See also Wright, *Fortress,* p. 59.

[17]Stenholm diary, 13 January 1944; 30 January 1946.

[18]Ibid., 23 December 1942.

[19]All figures derived from "Enrollment Statistics: First Semester," n.d. (RO). All enrollment figures are for the first semester. BJU does not keep enrollment figures for the second semester of each year. Rather, the school reports matriculated students for second semester of each school year. Grad./Spec. indicates students on the graduate level and those admitted under some type of special status. Apparently Bob Jones Seminary existed in 1935-37, and the Graduate School started in 1942.

[20]See Davis R. B. Ross, *Preparing for Ulysses: Politics and Veterans During World War II* (New York: Columbia University Press, 1969), for an excellent study of the legislative history of the bill. See also Keith W. Olson, *The G.I. Bill, the Veterans, and the Colleges* (Lexington: University Press of Kentucky, 1974). This is a useful study of the implementation of the bill in American colleges.

[21]Dianne Ravitch, *The Troubled Crusade: American Education, 1945-1980* (New York: Basic Books, 1983), pp.12-15. The Veterans' Administration determined the applicant's eligibility for assistance, the veteran selected the college, and the college determined admission. This insured the veteran's freedom to select his school and gave schools the freedom to control their admissions and curricula without federal intervention.

[22]Lawrence Cremin, *American Education: The Metropolitan Experience 1876-1980* (New York: Harper & Row Publishers, 1988), p. 250.

[23]During the seven years of the first GI Bill, 7.8 million veterans used benefits to get education. Of this number, more than 2.2 million attended college (Ravitch, *Crusade,* p. 14). One of the most important rule changes was allowing married students to remain in school. Prior to the war, marriage "provided grounds for expulsion in many colleges because tradition held that marriage and college did not mix" (see Olson, *G.I. Bill,* p. 33).

[24]Tindall, *Emergence,* pp. 711-31. Also see Ravitch, *Crusade,* pp. 19-26.

[25]Tindall, *Emergence,* pp. 634-35.

[26]BJsr, as described by George Marsden, "related fundamentalism to Southern political conservatism, including racial segregation" (Marsden, *Fundamentalism,* p. 279). Marsden's assertion is without citation and therefore undocumented. In the period of study of his work, the conservatism to which BJsr subscribed was the populism espoused by William Jennings Bryan and the progressivism practiced by his friend and supporter Bibb Graves. In studying all of BJsr's printed messages, clippings of revival campaigns, and chapel messages from the earliest extant in 1933 through 1959, this researcher found few references to race until the late 1950s, when the Civil Rights movement began and the practice of civil disobedience was adapted from the Indian politics of Ghandi to the American movement. In the late 1950s, BJsr denounced the movement for several reasons: (1) God separated the races and intended them to be distinct from each other. Integration would ultimately lead to a commingling that was not ordained by God. (2) The leaders of the movement were radical and Modernistic Protestants and Catholics. To officially join them in support of worthy social change would be unscriptural. (3) Civil disobedience as a course of action is unscriptural. "It is never right to do wrong, to get a chance to do right," BJsr often said. And the political powers that be are ordained of God. (4) The government had no right to coerce any organization that was private and that did not have its hand in the public till. BJsr would say often, "If you want to have a school for bowlegged people, you ought to be able to have one" without interference. While it is true that BJC practiced segregation during the Cleveland years, it must be remembered that segregation was de jure in the South until 1964 and that desegregation did not generally occur until 1966-68.

[27]See Chapter 20, note 9.

[28]Johnson, *Miracle,* p. 14. Also Stenholm diary, 19 October 1945.

[29]FMM for 3 December 1945 read: "If anyone knows of a room for rent for the second semester, please inform Mr. Johnson of this as soon as possible, as it is necessary for him to find accommodations for twenty-eight GI couples the second semester."

[30]The government office was probably the National Housing Administration, which administered a program made possible through the Lanham Act of 1940. The Lanham Act authorized the government to give barracks and other buildings to colleges for student housing if the colleges were willing to move the structures to their campuses. Later amendments to the act in 1944, specifically the Reuse Program, directed the armed services to turn over unused barracks, huts, and empty apartment buildings on government bases to colleges and universities who could demonstrate the need to house students. Nationwide, at its peak, the program provided housing for some 300,000 GIs. These housing units were supplied with no government strings, the act stating that each college should administer the housing according to its standards of discipline and academics. Other reuse programs existed which, for example, provided classroom buildings and instructional space at no charge to the colleges. This particular program, however, required that the government oversee and approve the use of the buildings. Some colleges, such as Wheaton and BJC, found this requirement to be intrusive and therefore

did not avail themselves of the opportunity to gain classroom space at essentially no cost to themselves. For further information, see Olson, *G.I. Bill,* pp. 59-78.

[31]Johnson, *Builder,* pp. 217-18. See also Johnson, *Miracle.*

[32]"Building Plans," *Little Moby's Post,* vol. 4, no. 4, February 1946, p. 1 (MLA).

[33]Stenholm diary, 2 February 1946. According to his diaries, work at the trailer camp continued at least until 5 February 1946.

[34]These barracks were probably obtained because of the amendments to the Lanham Act. See note 30.

[35]Johnson, *Builder,* p. 218.

[36]BJsr to K. B. Miles, 24 May 1946 (GF: Chamber of Commerce file). FMM for 18 February 1946 indicate that BJsr had already received an official offer to purchase the campus. It is possible that the delegation from the Church of God called for a response and not to tender an offer (ABV).

[37]Gilbert Stenholm records that Bill Bright of Campus Crusade regularly came to BJU to recruit summer staff members and full-time staff members. By August 1957 there were "twenty-six from BJU on the Campus Crusade staff, one from Wheaton and one from Westmont" (Stenholm diary, 1 August 1957).

[38]Gilbert Stenholm records that beginning in 1945, BJsr and BJjr were speaking regularly at Youth For Christ meetings all over the country—22 September 1945, BJjr speaking in Birmingham, Alabama; 6 October 1945, BJsr speaking in Birmingham; and 17 November 1945, BJjr speaking in San Antonio, Texas, and BJsr speaking in Miami, Florida. These speaking engagements at YFC continued through the 1950s. According to his diary, Gilbert Stenholm's first Youth For Christ appearance was 16 February 1946 in Winston-Salem, North Carolina, and Monroe Parker's first appearance was on 22 November 1946 in Kansas City (Stenholm diary, 1945 and 1946).

[39]William Martin, *A Prophet with Honor: The Billy Graham Story* (New York: William Morrow and Company, Inc., 1991), p. 103.

[40]FMM, 15 April 1946 (ABV). The College received hundreds of letters similar to this one:

> Is there any opportunity to enroll in your college as a student for the coming Fall term? I definitely desire going to a Christian College because the Lord has been leading me into the Ministry of the Gospel. . . . It was while in the service that I first felt the Call, until then I had never recognized the plan of God's will for my life.
>
> Having served almost four years I am eligible under the G.I. Bill of Rights to Government aid in my schooling.
>
> I am married with one child, 25 years old and willing to do whatever necessary to fall into line with your schedule. (Evan Shaffer to "Sir" [BJC Admissions Dept.] 5 July 1946 [GF: Shaffer file])

[41]All colleges faced the same decision. Wheaton, for example, chose to maintain itself basically at its prewar enrollment levels. In 1941 Wheaton opened with 1,193 students, and by 1946 the student body numbered 1,524 (Bechtel, *Wheaton College,* pp. 165, 184). BJC, on the other hand, had 455 students in 1941 and 1,585 in 1946.

[42]FMM, 17 December 1946 (ABV).

[43]BJsr to K. B. Miles, 24 May 1946.

[44]MS, BJsr, chapel talk, 29 October 1944 (ABV: 1944).

[45]One business owner complained that the students did not patronize his establishment, to which BJsr responded, "our students don't go to beer joints [and] eat in dirty places." (MS, BJsr, chapel talk, 22 February 1946 [ABV: 1946]). See "Banner Endorses Plan to Help Keep Bob Jones College Here," *Cleveland (Tenn.) Daily Banner,* n.d., 1946.

The exemption enjoyed by the College applied to all tax-exempt organizations: schools, churches, hospitals, and so on.

[46]His speech outline read:

> Bob Jones College does not belong to me. I do not own B.J.C.
>
> Reconstructed. College not more problems.
>
> Turning Ocoee Street into business street.
>
> I did not locate a college on Ocoee Street.
>
> Bob Jones College has a right to expand.
>
> Ocoee has no reason to complain.
>
> Ocoee no more to me than Parker, Nineteenth, or some other street.
>
> Bob Jones College is buying property and doesn't have to pay taxes. I didn't pass an act of the legislature in Tennessee making churches, Christian institutions, and schools which are corporations not for profit tax exempt. If you don't like it, take it up with the legislature and change the law.
>
> Does not cooperate with the ——— [indistinguishable word]
>
> Calls the school a prison.
>
> Says students that come here are too poor to be worth anything to town. (BJsr, speech outline, n.d. [MLA: Box 8])

[47]"Banner Endorses Plan."

[48]Johnson, *Builder,* p. 219.

[49]Ibid., pp. 218-25. There is no evidence to suggest that the owners of the properties in question had organized in opposition to the College. Extant evidence indicates that the owners were simply holding out independently for a better price, not believing that the College would actually consider leaving Cleveland (MS, BJsr, Special Meeting #2, "School Moving to South Carolina," 25 April 1946 [ABV: 1946]). See also *Chattanooga Times,* 2 March 1946; and *Chattanooga Free Press*, 26 April 1946.

[50]"Banner Endorses Plan."

[51]"Cleveland Has 3 Days to Save Jones College," *Cleveland (Tenn.) Daily Banner,* 1 April 1946.

[52]Interview, BJjr, 16 October 1985. Quoted in Heiser, "Move of BJC," p. 5.

[53]"The Need for Expansion," *Cleveland (Tenn.) Daily Banner,* n.d., 1946.

[54]*Chattanooga (Tenn.) Times,* 2 March 1946. Reprinted in "Plans to Move Campus," *Little Moby's Post,* vol. 4, no. 5, March 1946, p. 1 (MLA).

[55]Interview, Charles Smith, 10 October 1985. Quoted in Heiser, "Move of BJC," p. 7.

[56]Stenholm diary, 26 March 1946.

[57]"Cleveland Has 3 Days."

[58]Ibid.

[59]Robert S. Shuler, "California Pastor Declares Jones School 'Sensational,' " *Greenville (S.C.) News,* n.d. 1947 (MLA: Box 11).

[60]MS, BJsr, chapel talk, 25 April 1946 (ABV: 1946). See also *Chattanooga Times,* 2 March 1946; and *Chattanooga Free Press,* 26 April 1946.

[61]MS, BJsr, chapel talk, 25 April 1946 (ABV: 1946).

[62]BJsr, BJjr, and R. K. Johnson were appointed to this special committee. "Resolutions adopted at a special call session of the Board of Trustees of Bob Jones College on 4 Apr. 1946," quoted in *Little Moby's Post,* vol. 4, no. 6, May, 1946, p. 4 (MLA).

[63]FMM for 15 April 1946 indicate that the faculty was apprised of developments as they occurred, and their reaction to each site was requested by the Expansion Committee (ABV).

[64]Telegram, Walter T. Wilson, 23 May 1946 (GF: Greenville Chamber of Commerce file).

[65]Interview, BJjr, 16 October 1985. From Heiser, "Move of BJC," p. 8.

[66]"College Sold to Church of God," *Cleveland (Tenn.) Daily Banner,* n.d. 1946.

[67]Ibid.

[68]MS, BJsr, chapel talk, 28 February 1950 (ABV: 1950).

[69]Interview, Charles Smith, in Heiser, "Move of BJC."

[70]Wright, *Fortress,* pp. 90-92.

[71]"College Moving to Greenville," *Cleveland (Tenn.) Daily Banner,* n.d. 1946.

[72]Stenholm diary, 23 April 1946.

[73]Telegram, Willard J. Parks to K. B. Miles, 24 May 1946 (GF: Greenville Chamber of Commerce file).

Chapter 10: Miracles, Pressed Together

[1]Johnson, *Builder,* p. 220.

[2]Interview, Martha Stone, 4 June 1993.

[3]Ibid. See also Interview, E. Roy Stone Jr., 4 June 1993.

[4]E. Roy Stone Sr. to James D. Edwards, 6 October 1944 (GF: Stone file).

[5]Interview, Martha Stone, 4 June 1993.

[6]E. Roy Stone Sr. to BJsr, 8 April 1946 (GF: Stone file).

[7]Interview, E. Roy Stone Jr. See also Johnson, *Builder,* pp. 220-21; and "New Location Chosen," *Little Moby's Post,* vol. 4, no. 6, May 1946, p. 1.

[8]Ken Miles to BJsr, 16 April 1946 (GF: Miles file).

[9]Telegram, Ken Miles to BJsr, 17 April 1946 (GF: Miles file).

[10]Interview, E. Roy Stone Jr. See also Johnson, *Builder,* p. 220.

[11]Stenholm diary, 22 April 1946; and Interview, E. Roy Stone Jr.

[12]Quoted in Johnson, *Builder,* p. 222.

[13]Johnson, *Builder,* p. 222.

[14]Ibid.

[15]Telegram, K. B. Miles to BJsr, 24 April 1946 (GF: Chamber of commerce file).

[16]Johnson, *Builder,* p. 223.

[17]The four sent from Greenville were Ken Miles, R. C. McCall, E. Roy Stone, and Walter Goldsmith.

[18]MS, BJsr, chapel talk, 25 April 1946 (ABV: 1946). In a chapel talk on 28 February 1950, BJsr said, "We didn't owe anybody a cent of money. We had all that property paid for and $300,000 cash in the bank. There wasn't any place to build. We couldn't buy a foot of land. There we were—a little patch here, a little patch there" (ABV: 1950). See also *Chattanooga Times,* 2 March 1946; and *Chattanooga Free Press,* 26 April 1946.

[19]BJsr to K. B. Miles, 25 April 1946 (GF: Chamber of commerce file).

[20]MS, BJsr, chapel talk, 25 April 1946 (ABV: 1946).

[21]The Greenville papers indicate that the presidents of these institutions met with BJjr (*Greenville [S.C.] Piedmont,* 30 April and 3 October 1946). See also Telegram, K. B. Miles to BJjr, 30 April 1946 (GF: Chamber of commerce file). Also, Interview, E. Roy Stone Jr.

[22]Johnson, *Builder,* p. 226.

[23]Telegram, BJsr to K. B. Miles, 30 May 1946.

[24]K. B. Miles, "Bob Jones College," information bulletin of the Greenville Chamber of Commerce, n.d. (GF: Chamber of commerce file). Six teams had five members, with a seventh team of four. Each team member was asked to raise $3,500 for the Bob Jones College Fund, for a total of $119,000.

[25]K. B. Miles to Guyla Pearson, 15 May 1946. Also, "Options Are Set on Land for College," unknown paper, n.d. (GF: Chamber of commerce file). Also, "Bob Jones College As We See It," *Greenville (S.C.) Piedmont,* 31 May 1946.

[26]*Greenville (S.C.) News,* 22 May 1946. Problems developed with the land promised. Before the monies could be raised for purchase, one section was subdivided and sold. The owner of the land was a soldier stationed in Europe, so it appeared that one very important parcel was gone. After some quick maneuvering by the chamber, however, the land was repossessed and brought back into the promised tract (Johnson, *Builder,* p. 321).

[27]K. B. Miles to "Gentlemen," 28 June 1946 (GF: Chamber of commerce file). Miles's memo gave the following information:

> Present Status: (1) Official College headquarters are established in Greenville. (2) Options on all land needed have been acquired. (3) Approximately $90,000 of land has been purchased and paid for. (4) Page ads in several nationally known periodicals stating Greenville, South Carolina, as location beginning with academic year 1947-48 are prepared and contracted for. (5) C.P.A. construction authority for 19 buildings—$2,930,000 has been granted. (6) Daniel Construction Company has begun work. Office, warehouse, sawmill and other needed utilities now being constructed. (7) Construction program will accommodate 3,000 students and 125 faculty members. (8) Officials estimate that with college and student expenditures there will be more than $4,000,000 spent annually in Greenville. (9) Past experience proves students have three visitors annually, or 9,000 visitors staying average of 4 days at $10 per day—$360,000 annually.

[28]K. B. Miles, "Bob Jones College" (GF: Chamber of commerce file).

[29]Stone Realty Office: Bob Jones file.

[30]BJsr to "Friend," 5 January 1948 (GF: Chamber of commerce file).

[31]Earl Johnston to E. Roy Stone Sr., 24 May 1946 (Stone Realty Office: Bob Jones file). Interview, E. Roy Stone Jr.

[32]Interview, E. Roy Stone Jr. Prior to the move to Greenville, BJsr contacted Dr. Plyler, and Plyler indicated unqualified support for the new institution. As time passed, however, Plyler changed his position to one of opposition to the Fundamentalist position of the school and the school itself. Dr. Jones often stated that if Furman had shown any hesitation about the school's coming to Greenville, BJU would have gone elsewhere (BJsr to Dr. Louie Newton, 2 October 1951 [GF: Newton file]).

[33]Interview, Martha Stone, 4 June 1993. Corroborated by Interview, E. Roy Stone Jr.; Interview, BJjr, 16 October 1985; and Interview, Charles Smith, 17 October 1985. This fear on the part of Greenville's religious elite was well founded. According to one report, the first year the school was in Greenville, BJU "preacher boys conducted more than fifteen thousand services and dealt with more than forty thousand persons about their spiritual condition, all in the Greenville area" (Margaret Beall Tice, "Bob Jones Campus: The Older We Get, the More Beautiful She Becomes," *Voice of the Alumni,* vol. 45, no. 4, December 1971, p. 9).

[34]BJsr to John McSween, 27 October 1948 (MLA: File 1).

[35]BJjr to Preston S. Marchant, 9 June 1962.

[36]Interview, E. Roy Stone Jr.

[37]FMM, 17 September 1945 (ABV).

[38]"Bob Jones College As We See It," *Greenville (S.C.) Piedmont.*

[39]W. W. Pate to "Friend," 2 October 1946 (GF: Chamber of commerce file).

[40]BJsr to "Friend," 5 January 1948 (GF: Chamber of commerce file).

[41]Sometime during late May or early June of 1946, Richard Arrington was hospitalized for thirty days with a major illness. He died shortly after the school's groundbreaking in September. The loss of Arrington's influence was a major blow to those who supported BJU because he was highly visible as president of one of the area's largest and

most successful textile firms, and he wielded great power within the Greenville financial community. He aggressively supported BJC and was the glue that held together the BJC supporters within the chamber board. If Arrington had remained on the scene, it is highly likely that the chamber would have met its obligation.

[42]The University received an area bordered by U.S. Highway 29, S.C. Highway 291, part of Springdale Drive, Old Spartanburg Highway, and White Oak Road. The school was not able to purchase the Gifford property, White property, Wilson property, or several other smaller parcels, which made the edges of the BJU tract something of a checkerboard.

[43]Johnson to BJsr, 7 December 1961 (GF: Chamber of commerce file).

[44]Johnson, *Builder,* p. 240.

[45]BJsr to James H. Price Sr., 14 February 1951 (GF: Chamber of commerce file). Price, the school's lawyer at this time, had to threaten the chamber with a lawsuit before they would assume the upkeep of these lines as they had originally promised to do.

[46]Dictated by BJsr, signed by R. K. Johnson, to Tally Fox, 7 March 1953 (GF: Chamber of commerce file).

[47]Johnson to BJsr, 14 March 1953. See also Thurman Wisdom to "Secretary, Greenville Chamber of Commerce," 10 April 1959 (GF: Chamber of commerce file). Letters to BJU administrators, the Founder, and the President from chamber officials, after K. B. Miles's tenure ended, seem to be curt and reflect a combative and generally uncooperative spirit.

[48]BJiii to Carrol D. Gray, 20 May 1984 (GF: Chamber of commerce file).

[49]Wright, *Fortress,* p. 82. See also, Johnson, *Miracle,* p. 18. On the day BJU received its permits, the WPB denied a state university permission to construct a $2 million project.

[50]*Chattanooga Times,* 2 March 1946. Reprinted in "Plans to Move Campus," *Little Moby's Post,* vol. 4, no. 5, March 1946, p. 1.

[51]Johnson, *Builder,* pp. 232-34. The story of the loan is unique in itself. The president of Jefferson Standard had agreed to a loan of $1.25 million with BJsr. However, before the papers could be signed, the man died in an accident. The Jefferson board later reviewed the loan application, had second thoughts, and backed out of the deal. BJsr flew to North Carolina, met with the board, explained the school and its needs, and was amazingly granted a loan for $650,000 more than was originally sought. The loan for $1.9 million was approved on 18 April 1947 (Stenholm diary).

[52]MS, BJsr, chapel talk, 25 April 1946 (ABV: 1946).

[53]Johnson tells of two incidents when tensions between himself and employees involved in construction created problems—one when a building supervisor questioned Johnson's authority to review building decisions, and one when tension between Johnson and the architects caused them to resign from the project. The latter case was eventually patched up fourteen days later by Charles Daniel, the construction company owner, who agreed to build two construction site offices next to his project manager's: one for the architects and one for Johnson. See Johnson, *Builder,* pp. 229-31.

[54]Johnson, *Miracle,* p. 18.

[55]BJjr to Dan Turner, 14 March 1996.

[56]Johnson, *Builder,* p. 229.

[57]John G. Garth, "A Modern Miracle in Christian Education," unknown periodical, 1 July 1947, p. 7 (MLA: Box 10).

[58]MS, BJsr, chapel talk, 25 April 1946 (ABV: 1946).

[59]"Bob Jones University Dedicated to God on Thanksgiving Night," *Little Moby's Post,* vol. 7, no. 1, December-January 1947-48, p. 1.

[60]BJjr to Dan Turner, 22 July 1986.

[61]The stage itself measures "one hundred fifty feet from wall to wall and sixty-five feet from stage to grid and is equipped with a central revolving stage twenty-seven feet in diameter." It contains three folds on each side, an orchestra pit with a lift, two screw-type lifts measuring forty-four feet by nine feet, three inches, with an elevation range of twelve feet in both directions. There are also three turntables of various sizes. Thirty to thirty-five curtains may be hung at any one time, and the curtains include a contour curtain and a cyclorama. The lighting system at the time of construction was considered state of the art, with solo spots, three battans, and second and third border lights, as well as all types of stand spots and floods. By 1960 the stage had over two hundred scenic drops available for use, as well as stage pieces, armor, and weapons of nearly every imaginable size and shape (see "Rodeheaver Auditorium Seats 3,000; Has Screw Lift Stages," *Greenville [S.C.] News,* D2, n.d. October 1967; and Interview, Mr. Melvin Stratton, 26 June 1988).

[62]Johnson, *Miracle,* p. 20.

[63]Ibid., pp. 18-19.

[64]Anonymous, "A Look at Mr. John Ludwig," unpublished paper, n.d., p. 3.

[65]Johnson, *Miracle,* p. 22.

[66]Ibid., pp. 18-21.

[67]Ibid.

[68]Stenholm diary, 5 December 1946.

[69]This account taken from two sources—Johnson, *Builder,* pp. 235-38; and *Miracle,* pp. 22-24.

[70]Stenholm diary, 7 December 1946.

[71]For details on negotiations, construction, and relocation, see Johnson, *Builder,* pp. 218-43. See also Wright, *Fortress,* pp. 81-88.

[72]Johnson, *Builder,* p. 235.

[73]Parker, *Sunshine,* pp. 162-67.

[74]Stenholm diary, 28 May 1947 ("Dr. Bob announced that Bob Jr. was now President of Bob Jones University").

Chapter 11: Bob Jones Jr.

[1]BJjr, *Cornbread,* p. 27. BJjr speaks lovingly of Emma and writes that she was "cook, nursemaid, laundry woman—a kind of general factotum in the household."

[2]Katherine Stenholm reported this incident as told to her by Mrs. Stollenwerck, BJjr's grandmother (Interview, Katherine Stenholm, 8 June 1987). Several interviewees repeated the same story, including Edwards, Gingery, and DG, but did not credit it directly to Mrs. Stollenwerck.

[3]Interview, Mrs. BJsr, 28 August 1986.

[4]BJjr, *Cornbread,* pp. 41-42. Mrs. BJsr recalled many nights listening to her mother read stories and recite poetry to BJjr (Interview, Mrs. BJsr, 28 August 1986).

[5]BJjr, *Cornbread,* p. 35. BJjr occasionally makes mention of memorizing the entire hymnal and in the course of sermons quotes verses to some rather obscure hymns.

[6]Ibid., p. 37.

[7]Ibid., pp. 27-40. One chapter of *Cornbread and Caviar* is titled "Teachers I Have Persecuted." BJjr writes, "I loved literature and history and hated just about everything else in the curriculum, and I am afraid I was in a state of continual warfare with those who tried to ram some of these subjects down my throat. . . . I hope, in truth, I was not half as bad as I remember being" (p. 37).

[8]Ibid., p. 28. Miss Woodruff must have made an influence on BJjr. He referred to her no less than twenty times in the sample of chapel talks studied.

[9]MS, BJjr, chapel talk, 14 November 1946 (ABV: 1945).

[10]Starke was a cultured Virginia gentleman who operated one of the two private boys' military schools in Montgomery. Starke had been converted to Christianity as a Methodist layman during a week-long Bible Conference which BJsr had organized in Montgomery years earlier. Starke's Academy was chosen because of its fine reputation for discipline and academics. BJsr said, "I had just one boy. . . . He was artistic and loved the beautiful and the artistic. [He] didn't like mathematics and Latin, didn't like military drilling. I put him in a little military school where they taught him mental arithmetic. [They] made him drill, made him mix with people" (MS, BJsr, chapel talk, 14 February 1945 [ABV: 1945]).

[11]BJjr, *Cornbread*, p. 46.

[12]Ibid., p. 83.

[13]Ibid., p. 37.

[14]Ibid., p. 32.

[15]Interview, Mrs. BJjr, 4 June 1987.

[16]"Starke's University School Commencement Exercises," program, Montgomery, Alabama, 1926-27 (MLA: Box 29).

[17]BJjr, *Cornbread*, p. 31. See also MS, BJjr, chapel talk, 14 November 1946 (ABV: 1946). Shortly after this event, the minister of the Court Street church was replaced with a Bible-believing pastor.

[18]BJjr went on to say, "I never again saw anything as disgraceful as their performance until I watched the 1972 Democratic Convention on television. Then some of the candidates were as contemptible in their behavior and ideas as the Tammany crowd of the galleries were in Bryan's day" (BJjr, *Cornbread*, p. 38). See also BJsr, *My Friends*, p. 46; and *Andalusia (Ala.) Star*, 25 February 1927.

[19]By 1927 it was reported that the Jones family had visited England, Spain, Italy, Egypt, and the Holy Land (*Andalusia [Ala.] Star*, 25 February 1927).

[20]BJjr, *Cornbread*, pp. 39-40. Graves made the appointment on the condition that BJjr never ask him to issue a pardon to a prisoner. About this experience, BJjr wrote that he "learned a lot that has proved useful in my ministry. I learned what human nature is like and what unregenerate human nature can do" (p. 40). In a chapel message, BJjr said jokingly, "After dealing with prisoners, I can cope with students. It is good training for a man who is going to be president of an institution to have to be a prison chaplain for a while" (chapel talk, 5 April 1960 [ABV: BJjr, 1960]).

[21]Savidge and BJjr, "Shakespeare and Shylock," videotape interview.

[22]Wright, *Fortress*, p. 97.

[23]He wrote of his experiences at the opera, "Auntie loved music and all of the arts and always made a pilgrimage to Atlanta at the time of the Metropolitan Opera's annual spring visit, attending every performance. When I was sixteen and a senior in high school, she paid my way to come and attend the performance there with her. . . . I used to go down to the auditorium every morning and watch them set the stage and lay out the costumes for the next performance. Why they tolerated a sixteen-year-old kid wandering around backstage, I still do not know, but I never got thrown out. Among the performers whom I heard were Rosa Ponselle, Giacomo Lauri-Volpi, and Lucrezia Bori and among operas, *Rigoletto, Aida,* and *La Gioconda*" (BJjr, *Cornbread*, p. 19).

[24]Interview, Mrs. BJjr, 4 June 1987.

[25]He read all the works of Sir Walter Scott and many by Washington Irving. He completed John Ruskin's *Essays on Art, The Golden Bough, Pilgrim's Progress, The*

Yellow Peril, Machiavelli's *The Prince,* and, though he does not recommend them, *The Satyricon* and Boccaccio's *Tales.* He also read the works of the ancient historians Josephus and Herodotus, as well as the complete works of Shakespeare and modern drama by Scandinavian and Russian dramatists (BJjr, *Cornbread,* pp. 43-44).

[26]MS, "Acting Career," Office of Public Liaison: Bob Jones file, BJU 1987.

[27]Interviewees from each era of the school's history recalled that criticism was directed at the school by some Fundamentalists because of the Shakespearean plays.

[28]Leiber took note of BJjr's acting career and corresponded on occasion with him. One telegram received by BJjr on 29 May 1934 reads, "Good Luck and success in your performance of King Lear tonight—Fritz Leiber" (MLA: Box 29).

[29]Agnes Mathis Cherry to BJjr, 15 April 1937 (GF: Program Magazine file). Reported in Wright, *Fortress,* pp. 95-96.

[30]His thesis was "American Evangelism: A Study of the Vocational Evangelist Following the Civil War" (M.A. thesis, University of Pittsburgh, 1933).

[31]"Bob Jones Jr. Attending Northwestern This Summer," unknown paper, 1936 (MLA: Box 29, Rachel Ayres scrapbook).

[32]*Bob Jones College Catalogue, 1932-1933,* vol. 5, no. 1, p. 6.

[33]*Bob Jones College Catalogue, 1933-1934,* vol. 6, no. 1, p. 6.

[34]BJjr, *Cornbread,* p. 54. BJjr was awarded honorary degrees from Chung-ang University, Seoul, Korea; John Brown University, Siloam Springs, Arkansas; Houghton College, Houghton, New York; Northwestern Schools, Minneapolis, Minnesota; and Midwestern Bible College, Pontiac, Michigan.

[35]Program, "The Life of King Henry the Fifth" (MLA: Box 29, BJC Publicity). Interview, BJjr, 27 May 1986.

[36]BJjr, *Cornbread,* p. 68.

[37]Otis Skinner had been introduced to BJjr by his niece, Cornelia Otis Skinner, who operated the hostel. Otis Skinner advised BJjr to "go on the stage. But be sure not to take a job unless the star of the company is a skilled actor. Most young actors will unconsciously pick up the mannerisms and peculiarities of the stars with whom they work, especially during the first season. You do not want to pick up bad habits" (Ibid., pp. 68-69).

[38]"Bob Jones, Jr., and Two Aids Go On Dixie Tour," *Cleveland (Tenn.) Daily Banner,* 20 October 1933. See also BJjr to James Heaton, 18 February 1935 (GF: Winona Lake). BJjr's Curtain Calls was a yearly attraction at the annual Pre-Christmas Festival. The earliest documented booking of Curtain Calls at the College came on 3 December 1937 (BJC publicity scrapbook, 1929-39 [MLA: Box 29]). It is almost certain, however, that BJjr's recital was presented at the College prior to 1937, based on the letters to Heaton in 1935 and one news report dating from 1933.

[39]BJjr to James Heaton, 30 April 1935. He was carried by the Alkahurst Agency of Atlanta and the Dixie Bureau in Dallas. He was also carried by the Doris Roe Agency of New York for one year, 1937-38 (Samuel A. Tannenbaum to Doris Roe, 30 September 1937 [Office of the Chancellor: Shakespeare Association of America file]).

[40]"Bob Jones, Jr., and Two Aids Go On Dixie Tour." See also BJC annual, *The Vintage,* 1945. Undoubtedly, the pressures of designing and building the Greenville campus brought to an end his one-man show.

[41]"Bob Jones, Jr., Presents 'Curtain Calls,'" handbill, n.d. (Office of the Chancellor). Samples of the music used in the performances were found in boxes labeled "Curtain Calls—Music to Accompany" (MLA: Box 29). Two basic programs were available from which concert managers could select. Although there was no set order for the characterizations, the first program consisted of presentations of Shylock in "a court of justice" from *The Merchant of Venice;* Othello in "the bedchamber in the castle at Cypress";

Richard II "at Westminister Hall in London" and "the Landing Scene"; Falstaff at "the Boarshead Tavern" from *The Merry Wives of Windsor;* Richard, Duke of Gloucester, in "a room in the Tower of London" from *Henry IV, Part III;* King Lear, mad on the "open heath"; and Hamlet at the "Royal Castle at Elsinore in Denmark." The second program was made up of Jaques in "the Forest of Arden" from *As You Like It;* Macbeth in his castle at Forres; Antony in "the Roman Forum" from *Julius Caesar;* Launce on "a street in Verona" from *Two Gentlemen of Verona;* Cardinal Wolsey in "the royal palace in London" from *Henry VIII;* and Mercutio on "a street in Verona" and Romeo in "Friar Lawrence's Cell" and at "the Tomb of the Capulets" from *Romeo and Juliet.* BJjr also presented material from Browning and Marlowe ("Bob Jones, Jr., Presents 'Curtain Calls,' " two programs: "Great Characters from Shakespeare and the Classics, December 15," and "From the Plays of William Shakespeare, December 17," n.d. [MLA: Box 29]).

[42]Samuel Tannenbaum to BJjr, 31 October 1935. Tannenbaum, secretary of the Shakespeare Association and editor of the *Shakespeare Association Bulletin,* invited BJjr to perform at the national convention held on 19 November 1935. The performance was favorably received: "Bob Jones Jr. . . . entertained the audience with brilliant interpretations (in costume!) of Richard III . . . and Hamlet. He charmed all with his person" (Samuel A. Tannenbaum, "The Annual Celebration," *Shakespeare Association Bulletin,* vol. 11, no. 1 [January], 1936, p. 57). BJjr was also invited to perform for a second time at the national convention on 21 December 1936 (Samuel Tannenbaum to BJjr, 31 October 1936 [Office of the Chancellor: Shakespeare Association of America file]). In 1937 Tannenbaum wrote one booking agent about BJjr, "He is good to look at, speaks clearly, distinctly, and beautifully, reads his lines intelligently and understandingly, and has a sensitive appreciation of Shakespeare's poetry. He's a fine artist and will undoubtedly delight his audiences" (Samuel A. Tannenbaum to Doris Roe, 30 September 1937 [Office of the Chancellor: Shakespeare Association of America file]).

[43]Hugh Fellows to BJjr, n.d. (Office of the Chancellor: Curtain Calls). The International Lyceum Association convention in Indianapolis, held in November 1939, voted Curtain Calls "the best on the program." According to the *Cleveland (Tenn.) Daily Banner,* Curtain Calls was reported to be one of the nation's most popular lyceum attractions (*Cleveland [Tenn.] Daily Banner,* 22 November 1939). See also "Has Role of 'Petruchio' in 'Taming of the Shrew,' " *Cleveland (Tenn.) Daily Banner,* 28 April 1936.

[44]"Has Role of 'Petruchio.' "

[45]*Reading (Penn.) Times,* n.d. (Office of the Chancellor: Curtain Calls).

[46]*Huntsville (Tex.) Houstonian,* n.d. (Office of the Chancellor: Curtain Calls).

[47]Quoted from "Bob Jones, Jr., Presents 'Curtain Calls,' " handbill, n.d. (Office of the Chancellor: Curtain Calls).

[48]Quoted in MS, Jack Tillman, "To Him the Mantle Is Passed," 6 June 1969 (Office of Public Liaison: Bob Jones file). About this performance, BJjr wrote, "I really was ashamed of the program at Hunter College. Having only a little over one hour to get set up and ready, the light's failure to operate, I do not feel that the performance was very creditable" (BJjr to Samuel A. Tannenbaum, 27 November 1937 [Office of the Chancellor: Shakespeare Association of America file]).

[49]Savidge and BJjr, "Shakespeare and Shylock," videotape.

[50]BJjr, *Cornbread,* p. 46.

[51]Included were men such as Leander Whitcomb Munhall, R. A. Torrey, Harry Ironside, Billy Sunday, James M. Gray, John Roach Straton, I. M. Haldeman, Henry C. Morrison, William E. Biederwolf, Governor Bibb Graves, Congressman William Upshaw, and William Jennings Bryan. By virtue of his position as BJsr's son and his office of Acting

President of the College and later as President of the University, BJjr has known nearly every major leader in conservative Christianity and politics since 1930.

[52]BJjr, *Cornbread,* pp. 3, 8-9, 72.

[53]Ibid., pp. 73-74.

[54]BJjr was ordained to the gospel ministry after transferring his membership from the Methodist Church to the Christian and Missionary Alliance Church. As he tells it, a short time after joining the CMA Church, "they sent me a certificate of ordination. I presume now that they were taking for granted because I had been preaching that I was ordained in the Methodist Church, which I was not." BJjr chose the CMA Church because he knew a number of fine men who were pastors in that group, and he had always thought of them as a fellowship rather than a denomination. Denominationalism, he believed, always led to ecclesiastical control and tyranny over groups of local believers (BJjr, *Cornbread,* p. 74).

[55]Only those ordained to the gospel ministry can rightfully carry the title of evangelist, pastor, or minister. BJjr was not at this time ordained even though he was preaching; he never sat under the examination of an ordination council.

[56]Wright, *Builder,* p. 102.

[57]MS, BJjr, chapel talk, 6 May 1945 (ABV: BJjr, 1945). See also MS, BJjr, chapel talk, 2 February 1946 (ABV: BJjr, 1946) in which BJjr stated categorically his beliefs, all of which parallel those of his father and other Fundamentalists. R. K. Johnson compared the two when he wrote, "Bob's advantages, his background in Hebrew History . . . his foundation in Bible, his speech training and acting ability, and his sound spiritual slant, destined him in some ways to excel his father. Both men have been leaders in the religious and educational world, and both have been fighters, differing only in their approach. Dr. Bob had the rough-and-tumble, bulldog tenacity, saw-dust aisle approach; Bob has the polished, well-educated approach, with a voice that flows like ripples of water in a clear running mountain stream" (Johnson, *Builder,* p. 259).

[58]By 1953 BJjr estimated that he had been to Europe eighteen to twenty times (MS, BJjr, chapel talk, 15 May 1953).

[59]For a personal view of BJjr's art collecting, see his autobiography, *Cornbread and Caviar,* pp. 48-51.

[60]Stenholm diary, 28 May 1947.

[61]Interview, BJiii, 3 June 1987. BJiii indicated that his father was keenly interested in the financial affairs of the school so that the various cultural programs of the school could be funded. BJsr always felt that he had to keep the financial reins tight on his son or he would "go wild on the cultural expenditures." Corroborated by Mrs. BJsr, Interview, 28 August 1986.

[62]Interview, BJjr, 28 May 1987. Corroborated by Interview, BJiii, 3 June 1987.

[63]His preaching took him to such disparate places as the Pentagon in Washington, D.C.; mission outposts in India, Australia, Japan, Korea, and South America; military chapels at bases in Europe and the United States; and churches throughout Europe, Asia, North and South America, and Africa. He was received by and held conferences with foreign heads of state, ambassadors, prime ministers, and politicians as a representative of American conservative Christianity.

[64]Alan Ehrenhalt, *The United States of Ambition: Politicians, Power, and the Pursuit of Office* (New York: Random House, 1991), pp. 96-97.

Chapter 12: "The Most Wonderful Place in the World"

[1]Stenholm diary, 22, 25, 26, 29 September 1947.

[2]BJsr to Evan L. Shaffer, 5 July 1946 (GF: Shaffer file).

[3]Stenholm diary, 21 September 1947.

[4]Mark Edward Sidwell, " 'It's Right to Do Right': William E. Liverman and the Dean of Men's Office at Bob Jones University," unpublished paper (MLA), p. 4.

[5]Interview, Gail Gingery, 5 June 1987.

[6]One story that was widely carried, which to the skeptics showed just how unusual the University was, read, "Not long ago the University placed its second order for freshman Greek texts with a new publisher, ordering 375 copies. The publisher wired back anxiously: 'Wire stated 375 copies. 75 copies largest order ever shipped any school. Sending 75 copies.' But Bob Jones wired back, and got its 375 new copies. This University believes in classic learning" (Burke Davis, "Teachers and Students Live by Strict Creed at Bob Jones U.," *Charlotte (N.C.) News,* 3 October 1947 [MLA: Box 11]).

[7]John G. Garth, "A Modern Miracle in Christian Education," unknown periodical, 1 July 1947, p. 8 (MLA: Box 10).

[8]Davis, "Teachers and Students."

[9]Enrollment Statistics: First Semester, n.d. (RO).

[10]*Greenville (S.C.) Piedmont,* 27 September 1947.

[11]Those who lived in the trailer parks spoke with some fondness and a sense of pioneer spirit when discussing the community bathhouse, the limited toilet facilities, the mud, and general living conditions. Life was exciting for them, even in one-room trailers.

[12]Interview, Iris Jackson, 29 July 1993.

[13]At this time, the gymnasium was located on the east end of the Student Center, where Stratton Hall (formerly the Concert Center) is now located.

[14]Stenholm diary, 1 October 1947.

[15]FMM, 6 January 1947 (GF).

[16]"Outline of the Educational Program of Bob Jones University 1947-1948," *Little Moby's Post,* vol. 6, No. 3, April 1947, p. 1. The full announcement reads:

THE COLLEGE OF ARTS AND SCIENCES

The Bachelor of Arts degree in the humanities without a field of concentration. The Bachelor of Arts degree with concentration in English, French, Italian, Latin, German, Russian, Spanish, history, mathematics, or science. The Bachelor of Science degree in home economics.

THE SCHOOL OF FINE ARTS

The Bachelor of Arts degree in art. The Bachelor of Science degree in music pedagogy. The Bachelor of Arts and Master of Arts degrees in piano, violin, voice, organ, or sacred music. The Bachelor of Science degree in speech pedagogy. The Bachelor of Arts and Master of Arts degrees in interpretive speech, public speaking, dramatic production, or radio production. The Master of Fine Arts degree in the combined fields of speech and music.

THE SCHOOL OF EDUCATION

The Bachelor of Science degree in elementary education, secondary education, or educational administration.

THE SCHOOL OF AERONAUTICS

Training in accordance with the requirements of the Civil Aeronautics Administration will be offered as follows: Basic and advanced ground school training. Primary, commercial, and instrumental flying instruction. Aircraft and engine maintenance.

THE SCHOOL OF RELIGION

The Bachelor of Arts degree in English Bible, Christian Education, or Christian Missions. The Master of Arts degree in religion. The Doctor of Philosophy degree in religion.

THE SCHOOL OF COMMERCE

The Bachelor of Science degree in accounting, office administration, or business administration.

[17]*Bob Jones University Catalogue,* 1947-48, vol. 20, no. 1.

[18]MS, BJjr, chapel talk, 7 November 1949 (ABV: 1949). The first group of administrative officers were Karl Keefer, dean of the School of Fine Arts; Hal Carruth, dean of the College of Arts and Sciences; Charles D. Brokenshire, dean of the School of Religion; Laird Lewis, dean of the School of Education; Gilbert Stenholm, director of Ministerial Training and Extension; James D. Edwards, dean of students; Ted Mercer, assistant to the President; Hazel Claire Riley, dean of women; and Robert Shaper, dean of men.

[19]Interview, John Ludwig, 7 July 1993.

[20]Comments during the service were offered by BJsr and BJjr. Mayor J. Kenneth Cass welcomed the University to Greenville, and Rev. M. C. Patterson of the Greenville Ministerial Association and Mr. P. D. Meadows, President of the Greenville Chamber of Commerce, offered greetings to the students and faculty. Dr. John Plyler, president of Furman University, extended his school's greetings, Dr. Thomas Mosely of the Missionary Training Institute of Nyack, New York, offered thanks to God for the spirit of evangelism that he sensed on the campus, and Mrs. Billy Sunday, among others, spoke briefly to the crowd. Greenville's school districts were represented, as were every college in South Carolina and the state departments of education of Tennessee and South Carolina (Ruth Walker, "Thousands Attend Jones Dedication," unknown paper, n.d. [MLA: Box 11]; see also "Bob Jones University Dedicated to God on Thanksgiving Night," *Little Moby's Post,* vol. 7, no. 1, December-January 1947-48, p. 1).

[21]Walker, "Thousands Attend."

[22]Ibid.

[23]Stenholm diary, 16 December 1947.

[24]Interview, Gail Gingery, 4 October 1985. Reported in Heiser, "Move of BJC," p. 19.

[25]Garth, "Modern Miracle," p. 8.

[26]Interview, Eva Carrier, 14 July 1993.

[27]Interview, Iris Jackson, 1 July 1993.

[28]BJjr, quoted by Margaret Beall Tice, "Bob Jones Campus: The Older We Get, the More Beautiful She Becomes," *Voice of the Alumni,* vol. 45, no. 4, December 1971, p. 8.

[29]Ibid., p. 9.

[30]The first unit was the Rodeheaver Auditorium; Alumni Building; Administration Building; Mack Library; first Dixon-McKenzie Dining Common; Student Center; Bibb Graves and J. Y. Smith Halls for men students; Margaret Mack, Nell Sunday, and Grace Haight Halls for women students; the Academy building; music practice studios; Faculty Court apartments; six prefabricated buildings used as classrooms; the Maintenance Shop; and the tennis courts and athletic field. Construction that followed after the first unit included radio station WMUU, 1949; Unusual Films Studio, 1950; Museum and Art Gallery, 1951; another men's dormitory, later named Brokenshire Hall, 1951; a hospital wing with operating room, 1951; Academy classroom building, 1952; fifteen prefab housing units, 1953; four administrators' homes, 1954; Georgia Creel Hall and two administrators' homes, 1955; and Fine Arts Building, 1956. Other major projects were undertaken during this time also and included such things as air-conditioning Rodeheaver Auditorium in 1953. All of this progress was extremely costly, as were the fledgling cinema program and the new art collection and gallery.

[31]"New Studio," *Little Moby's Post,* vol. 9, no. 6, May-June 1950, p. 1. Radio station WMUU continued operation until it was sold by the University following the court case in 1983. It is currently operated by a Greenville mission board.

[32]Andrea Neely, "A History of Bob Jones Academy," unpublished paper (MLA).

[33]"Significant Change in Loan Fund Plan," *Little Moby's Post,* vol. 25, no. 6, March 1952, p. 1.

[34]One unusual event, which drew national attention to the University, was the Mid-Century World Outlook Conference, sponsored by BJU in December 1950. The conference brought speakers from all over the world to present political and economic issues. It included such well-known figures as J. Strom Thurmond, governor of South Carolina; the Honorable Moshe Keren from Israel; the first secretary of the French Embassy, Henri Ruffin; and the son of Bethlehem's mayor and delegate to the United Nations from Trans-Jordan, Yusif el Bandek. Others who spoke included members of the international diplomatic community such as representatives from Sweden, Egypt, Czechoslovakia, Yugoslavia, Armenia, the Philippines, Iraq, Norway, England, Belgium, the Netherlands, Pakistan, Finland, Greece, Estonia, and China. For more on the conference, see Wright, *Fortress,* pp. 146-52. Transcripts of all conference speeches are located in the MLA.

[35]Karl Keefer to "Friends and colleagues," 10 July 1953 (Stone Realty: BJU file).

Chapter 13: Clouds on the Horizon

[1]For a scholarly treatment of the NAE and BG, see Dalhouse, "Shaping." Also, readers should consult Martin, *Prophet.* This definitive biography clearly shows the conflict between BJU and other Fundamentalists and BG and accurately records the impact of BG on conservative Christianity.

[2]Readers should take note that the issue of "loyalty in all particulars" is not one unique to BJC or BJU. Loyalty to administrative or executive decision is fundamental to most military, business, educational, or religious organizations' success. No successful enterprise long survives that allows unbridled criticism and complaint by its employees toward the policies or conditions of the enterprise. For two of numerous examples, one from a religious organization and one from secular higher education, the reader may consult Mark Edward Sidwell, "The History of the Winona Lake Bible Conference" (Ph.D. dissertation, BJU, 1988), pp. 221-32, for the issue of loyalty to administrative decision; and Albert Harrison, "A History of the School of Music of the University of Illinois, 1940-1970" (Ed.D. dissertation, University of Illinois), which documents numerous uproars created by internal unrest, criticism, and disagreement over policy.

[3]Interview, Millie Butts, 15 July 1993.

[4]Ibid.

[5]DG to Dan Turner, 4 April 1988.

[6]Many of those hired between 1947 and 1950 carried academic credentials from colleges and universities in the United States, Europe, and the Far East. Among the institutions represented among the faculty's advanced degrees were Harvard University, Yale University, Central University (China), Nihon University (Tokyo), Cambridge University, Royal Conservatory of Toronto, Paris Conservatoire, and the Collège Moderne (Le Havre, France).

[7]Interview, BJjr, 28 May 1987; corroborated by Gail Gingery, 5 June 1987; and DG, 1 April 1988.

[8]DG to Dan Turner, 4 April 1988.

[9]Ibid.

[10]All data taken from the *Bob Jones University Catalogue, 1947-48,* vol. 20, no. 1, through the *Catalogue, 1991-92. Catalogue* issue 1948-49, vol. 21, is not extant. This reckoning does not include graduate teaching assistants (GAs) because the majority of these held degrees from the University prior to their tenure in limited teaching roles.

[11]The decline in faculty may be explained by the fact that enrollment in the University was declining because of a limited pool of students. Through attrition, the faculty size was gradually reduced to be more in line with the student population. Also, these figures do not represent the fact that the graduate teaching faculties were no longer listed in the undergraduate course bulletins. All of these data are drawn from the BJU catalogs for the years listed.

[12]Stenholm diary, 30 September 1947.

[13]Interview, Bob and Doris Harris, 9 July 1993. Bob Harris indicated that the second semester bonus was usually larger and made it possible for many of the faculty wives not to work during the summer.

[14]One faculty member recalled that if a family had an emergency or a child-related discipline matter that occurred before a meal, causing them to be late, they could not eat. Money was so tight that missing a meal at the Dining Common was a great hardship (Interview, Gail Gingery, 5 June 1987).

[15]DG to Dan Turner, 4 April 1988.

[16]This percentage was derived from data taken from the *Bob Jones University Catalogues* for the years 1947-48 through 1954-55. The reader will note that data for the years 1948-49 are missing as no catalogs from this school year are extant. The reader will also note that data for the years 1951-53 are combined. The *Catalogue* for these two years was published as a combined volume, making it impossible to separate each year's figures. The data are as follows:

Table 7

Percentage of Faculty Turnover, 1947-55

Year	Total Faculty	# Leaving	% Turnover
1947-48	79	26	33
1949-50	80	26	33
1950-51	93	14	15
1951-53	96	24	25
1954-55	96	53	55

One letter of 1953 reports that "23 full-time teachers" were not returning and "we have 25 new full-time teachers coming" (BJsr to Matthew Welde, 15 August 1953 [GF: Welde file]).

[17]DG to Dan Turner, 4 April 1988.

[18]Interview, Iris Jackson, 29 July 1993.

[19]During these years, the Red Scare and Cold War were on, and the national perception of imminent Communist attack was woven into American thinking. These feelings of national threat may account for the high incidence of preaching on loyalty to authority and government. Of course personal loyalty, as noted, was a common topic.

[20]MS, BJjr, chapel talk, 24 September 1948 (ABV: 1948).

[21]MS, BJsr, 10 March 1947 (ABV: 1947).

[22]Interview, Mrs. Oliver Steiner, 18 June 1987. Bill Kintigh of the College math faculty remembers that in 1946-47 his family shared a large, two-story house with

Dr. Brokenshire of the Bible faculty and two other families. The house was partitioned in such a way that each had its own entrance and private living space, although it was necessary to share a bathroom between two families.

[23]DG to Dan Turner, 4 April 1988. See also Olson, *G.I. Bill,* pp. 65-66.

[24]Interview, Gail Gingery, 5 June 1987. One student from the early Greenville days recalls being told by a faculty member from Cleveland that the administration, before moving to Greenville, made the promise that every faculty member would have his own house provided by the school.

[25]According to Gilbert Stenholm's personal diary, housing arrangements in Greenville were discussed by BJjr in a faculty meeting on 12 May 1947. Though details of this discussion are not extant among FMM, the perception of the faculty was that each would have his own place. E. Roy Stone Jr. indicates that his father's firm helped faculty families find homes suitable for purchase or rent during the early years in Greenville (Interview, E. Roy Stone Jr., 4 June 1993).

[26]Fairly or not, many people blamed Johnson for their situations, since he was charged with the financial and staff affairs. He was in the precarious and unpopular position of meeting people's true needs while trying to assuage their perceived needs.

[27]Interview, Gail Gingery, 25 January 1988.

[28]Wright, *Fortress,* pp. 425-27.

[29]Interview, Iris Jackson, 29 July 1993.

[30]Interview, Karl Keefer, 27 July 1987. Corroborated by Gail Gingery, DG, and Iris Jackson.

[31]Interview, Karl Keefer, 27 July 1987.

[32]Interview, DG, 29 July 1993. He recalls that after coming onto the faculty as a newly married man, he and his wife were having difficulty meeting their monthly expenses, including the repayment of school loans. Within a day or two of a discussion about this with Johnson, they received a letter from BJsr outlining a strategy to use in repaying the loans over the span of several years.

[33]Karl Keefer, who left the school in 1953, recounted that after taking concerns about his wife's workload and her health to Johnson and receiving the most unkind treatment and comments, he brought the situation to BJjr's attention. Shortly thereafter, the President talked with Johnson, who then issued an apology. The wife's workload was also immediately improved (Interview, Karl Keefer, 27 July 1987).

[34]Pauline Rupp to Ernest Qvarnstrom, 9 October 1951 (GF: Qvarnstrom file). One piece of correspondence, written by BJjr's secretary, reads, "I just talked to Dr. Bob on the phone, and he said that he was behind Mr. Johnson in whatever he did to run the school right. . . . This is Mr. Johnson's responsibility, and he is going to stand by him in whatever decisions he makes." See also BJjr to Ernest Qvarnstrom, 18 October 1951 (GF: Qvarnstrom file).

[35]Interview, DG, 29 July 1993. Corroborated by Interview, Iris Jackson, 29 July 1993. She indicated that at this time if a person did not fit in or did not do his job, BJsr would call him in and "take care of the problem."

[36]R. K. Johnson to Ernest Qvarnstrom, 7 October 1951 (GF: Qvarnstrom file).

[37]Ibid., 10 October 1951.

[38]Interview, DG, 29 July 1993.

[39]Interview, Gail Gingery, 3 August 1993.

[40]"Some Denominations Represented at B.J.U.," February 1948, p. 1.

Chapter 14: The Storm of '53

[1]BJsr to Karl Keefer, 18 June 1953 (GF: Keefer file).

[2]BJsr and R. K. Johnson to BJjr, 15 June 1953 (GF: Mercer file).

[3]BJjr to Keefer, 18 June 1953 (GF: Keefer file).

[4]Minutes of the Board of Trustees, BJU, Executive Committee, 15 June 1953 (ABV). The official record reads, "There was a full discussion of the situation that had developed, different members stating how they had talked with Dr. Mercer and had tried to help him. But the further we went into the discussion, the more every member saw that it was impossible to keep him in the employ of the institution any longer. Mr. James H. Price made a motion which was unanimously carried that the Executive Committee write Dr. Bob Jones, Jr., president, instructing him to dismiss Mr. Mercer."

[5]Minutes of the Board of Trustees, 8 July 1953.

[6]Stenholm diary, 15 June 1953.

[7]BJsr to Martha Caddell, 8 May 1953 (GF: Mercer file).

[8]BJjr to Ted Mercer, 1 June 1953 (GF: Mercer file).

[9]Stenholm diary, 6 June 1953.

[10]Theodore C. Mercer, "A Statement Concerning My Dismissal from Bob Jones University," 28 July 1953, pp. 5-6.

[11]Josephine Cox to BJsr, 27 June 1953 (GF: Welde file). The Coxes' letters did not reveal their specific concerns. Millie Cox was an officer in the Future Teachers of America, whose faculty sponsor was Mercer, and her boyfriend, Matt Welde, was an officer in the student body. They worked closely with Ted Mercer in their leadership capacities.

[12]Interview, BJjr, 30 July 1993.

[13]Interview, DG, 29 July 1993.

[14]Theodore C. Mercer, "A Third Statement," 10 August 1953 (GF: Mercer file).

[15]Charles Blankenship to R. K. Johnson, 3 November 1952 (GF: Blankenship file). This is an official report filed by the night watchman on the incident. Mercer subsequently claimed that this student, who was later expelled for similar rules violations, was shipped because "he made the fatal mistake of saying I understood him and his problems" (Mercer, "A Statement," p. 8).

[16]Interview, Joyce Parks, 29 July 1993. Corroborated by Matthew Welde to BJsr, 16 July 1953 (GF: Welde file).

[17]Matthew Welde to BJsr, 16 July 1953 (GF: Welde file). Corroborated by Stan Dyer to Ted Mercer, 29 May 1951 (GF: Dyer file).

[18]Matthew Welde to BJsr, 16 July 1953 (GF: Welde file).

[19]Ibid.

[20]Interview, DG, 29 July 1993.

[21]Mercer, "A Statement," p. 8.

[22]Hazel Claire Riley to Mrs. Homer Cox, 10 June 1953 (GF: Welde file).

[23]Interview, Iris Jackson, 29 July 1993.

[24]BJsr and R. K. Johnson to BJjr, 15 June 1953 (GF: Mercer file). The letter read,

Dear President Jones:

We are addressing you formally because this letter is official. Members of the Executive Committee, after having checked certain facts, have unanimously authorized the chairman and the secretary of the Board to write you and call your attention to the following:

First: Under the charter and by-laws of Bob Jones University, it is mandatory that every employee of the institution be discharged if at any time he breaches his contract by hobnobbing with students or by being a party to or even encouraging any kind of clique in the faculty or employees of the institution or being disloyal in any particular.

Second: On the basis of the evidence we have, we are convinced that Dr. Theodore Mercer should be immediately discharged as an employee of the institution. We, therefore, recommend that you discharge him at once but give him a check through the current month. . . .

The secretary of the Board has informed members of the Executive Committee that he and the Dean of Students, Dr. Edwards, and the Dean of the School of Religion, Dr. Stenholm, called Dr. Mercer into the office several weeks ago and told him that his conduct was not in line with what was expected of a member of this organization and especially not in line with what is expected of the assistant to the president. Dean Riley informs us that weeks before the executives had this conference with Dr. Mercer, she, herself, warned Dr. Mercer about his relationship with certain students.

I think we should say that we did not give the members of the Executive Committee certain detailed information which we had about Dr. Mercer's relationship to the institution. Nevertheless, the information we gave was enough to warrant the members of the Committee to instruct us to write this letter.

[25]BJsr to Mrs. Alice Mercer, 16 June 1953 (GF: Mercer file). The check was intended as severance pay to help with the family's expenses, as well as a gesture of good will toward Alice Mercer and the couple's children. Though it was not widely known, when an employee was fired, BJsr frequently initiated such payments to help with moving expenses, and so on. (GF: Qvarnstrom file).

[26]Laird Lewis to BJsr, 7 July 1953 (GF: Lewis file). As the evidence came in, no immoral conduct was ever shown, although he was shown to be dispossessed of the good judgment and decorum befitting his office.

[27]MS, BJsr, chapel talk, 9 September 1953 (ABV: 1953). BJsr said, "I've been sorry for myself two or three times this summer" and talked about being depressed. This message also indicates the Founder's wishes if the school were to close. He says, "We'd sell the property. Take all the money here and divide it up" among the employees for their retirement and take the balance and distribute it to spread the gospel around the world.

[28]BJsr to Mrs. Homer Cox, 20 June 1953 (GF: Welde file); and BJsr to James H. Price, 19 April 1954 (GF: Price file).

[29]Mercer, "A Statement," p. 5.

[30]Theodore C. Mercer, "An Additional Statement to the Alumni and Board of Trustees of Bob Jones University," 4 August 1953. This second tract also deals with accreditation by a regional educational agency and covers many issues that would be examined in accreditation reviews. This booklet may indicate more of Mercer's motivations than the other two—it shows a rationalism born of a desire for acceptance by academics. BJsr felt that a conspiracy existed, but it may have been that Mercer's dissatisfaction with BJU developed as he researched accreditation and attended registrars' conferences at which accreditation issues were major topics of discussion.

In fact, following his dismissal, Mercer went to Muskingum College in Ohio and later to Bryan College in Dayton, Tennessee, where he led that college through its accreditation process. For most areas of campus life, curriculum development, and funding, accreditation was education's panacea in the 1950s. Mercer undoubtedly realized that as long as BJsr and BJjr led the institution, accreditation—the national solution to faculty salaries, housing, education, and the good life in academia—could remain only a whispered topic of discussion. Mercer's ultimate motivation may have been to bring the institution into an accreditation association for what he considered its ultimate good. To do so, however, would require a philosophical restructuring away from a spiritual perspective, toward an "enlightened," "rational" one, and the ultimate denial of the founding precepts of the institution.

What Mercer did not see in terms of accreditation, however, was that the good an association may have brought to the school in the short term in salaries, faculty degrees, library size,and so forth, would have been undone by the social and religious demands brought to bear on the school. For example, some associations have demanded racial and gender "equity" (i.e., quotas) in hiring; they have required homosexual and lesbian representation in the student body and faculty; they have demanded that Creation not be taught in science courses, that chapel attendance be optional, that rules be suspended on weekends; and they have made other demands that would have altered the fabric that makes BJU unique.

[31]Mercer, "A Third Statement."

[32]These stratagems were all revealed within weeks of the firing. Students from across the country called and wrote the school asking about the situation, saying they had received material about it in the mail. BJjr recalled a textbook representative who came to him and asked, "What kind of guy is this? He's sending me all this stuff, and as a Christian, I can't see what he is going to accomplish by this." BJsr received calls from the National Education Association and Future Teachers of America asking for clarification of certain charges Mercer made to them. The breadth of the attack was incredible (Interview, BJjr, 30 July 1993).

[33]"Registrar Is Fired; BJU Deans Resign," *Greenville (S.C.) News,* 27 June 1953.

[34]Laird Lewis to BJsr, 7 July 1953 (GF: Lewis file).

[35]BJsr, quoted in *Greenville (S.C.) News,* 28 June 1953. An Asheville, N.C., newspaper carried an anonymous letter to the editor in which the writer stated that "reliable reports indicate that petty jealousy on the part of the veteran head was the prime factor" in the firing. The letter went on to compare BJsr with the Pharisees, assigning "unsavory qualities" to him and stating that the whole incident "smells to high heaven. Many a man since King Uzziah has grown too big for his britches," and the writer apparently thought BJsr had (unknown Asheville, N.C., newspaper, n.d. [GF: Mercer file]).

[36]The attitude of the Board of Trustees toward Mercer and the three deans was that the board was "out of sympathy with your newspaper interviews." In a joint letter, two board members wrote that Mercer showed a "real animosity underlying" his remarks, an animosity that obviously had "built up only after a period of time." They continued that "since this is your attitude, then the administration is wise in your dismissal for you can only harm the school and yourself" (Rosa M. Bailey and Mrs. P. B. Mayfield to Ted Mercer, dated 4 July 1953, recorded in Minutes of the Board of Trustees, BJU, 8 July 1953). The exceptions to this were Loren Jones, BJsr's song leader, and his wife. They had become very close to the Mercers and wrote letters to BJjr supportive of Mercer. As a result, they were asked to resign from the board, and the dormitory that had been named for Jones was renamed Charles D. Brokenshire Hall (GF: Loren Jones file).

[37]*Greenville (S.C.) News,* 28 June 1953. This report quotes Mercer as saying that forty faculty members resigned in protest following his dismissal. On another occasion he was quoted as saying that the faculty turnover rate for 1953 was 30-40 percent—approximately fifty to seventy professors. It has been found, by comparing the names of faculty and staff published in the *BJU Catalogue, 1953-54,* with those appearing in the *BJU Catalogue, 1954-55,* that forty-eight faculty and graduate assistants did not return for the 1954-55 school year. After accounting for those graduate assistants whose degrees and contracts were completed, marriages of single faculty, and calls to Christian service (i.e., church pastorates, youth ministries, and mission fields), one concludes that only about 16 percent of the faculty left with Mercer—a number significantly below those he quoted. Faculty

loyalty to Mercer may be understood because he often presided at faculty meetings, did some of the prospective faculty interviewing and some hiring, mediated some minor faculty disputes, socialized among the faculty a great deal, and was a very popular and present figure among the students.

[38]Some of the disgruntled faculty completed their contracts for school year 1953-54 and then resigned in order to remove the Mercer stigma from themselves (Interview, Iris Jackson). Some students and alumni, not knowing which side to trust, allowed their loyalty to waver and simply remained friendly while distancing themselves from the school.

[39]Stenholm diary, 28 August 1953. One meeting was attended by Gilbert Stenholm, who recorded in his diary, "I took Tonnetti, Lopusti with me . . . to attend meeting called by Dilks and Keefer at the 4th Presby. Church. Picked up Otis Holmes . . . called for Ken Ouelette at the Rescue Mission. We sure did surprise them by our visit. It turned out to a complete flop and farce. We 'poured' it on to them. There were 26 present and the numbers must have been about 20 to 6, in favor of Dr. Bob."

[40]Robert Dilks to BJsr, 12 August 1953 (GF: Mercer file). Dilks refers to BJsr as a "rabble rousing demagogue" who should "have the decency to resign." This letter also describes the school as run by a "Gestapo" controlled by a "diabolical system." See also MS, BJsr, chapel talk, 19 September 1953.

[41]Some who sided with Mercer went so far as to call themselves "Mer-people" as a way of showing their allegiance (Ted Mercer to "Mer-people," undated post card [GF: Mercer file]). Interestingly, a group of Mer-people met in Hendersonville, N.C., as recently as the summer of 1992 for a celebration of their freedom from BJU.

[42]Interview, BJjr, 30 July 1993.

[43]MS, chapel talk, 14 September 1953. In chapel talks on 9, 10, 12, and 18 September 1953, BJsr dealt with issues apparently raised by Mercer.

[44]W. Robert Holmes to JRR, copy, n.d.; and JRR to W. Robert Holmes, 22 July 1953 (GF: Rice file).

[45]Enrollment Statistics: First Semester. Graduate School enrollment was 91 in 1953-54 and following two years of increases dropped to 86 in 1957-58. Academy enrollment increased steadily each year from 289 to 345 by 1957-58.

[46]Interview, Alice Christman Gingery, 25 January 1988.

[47]Interview, Gail Gingery. Corroborated by DG, 4 April 1988.

[48]It is interesting to note that a number of faculty members such as DG, Edward Panosian, Gail Gingery, and others who received undergraduate degrees in 1952 and 1953, who then became teaching assistants as graduate students, remained on the faculty through the 1990s (Interview, BJjr, 30 July 1993).

[49]DG to Dan Turner, 4 April 1988.

[50]BJsr, chapel talk, 9 September 1953 (ABV).

Chapter 15: "What Difference Does It Make?"

[1]Bruce L. Shelley, *Evangelicalism in America* (Grand Rapids, Mich.: Wm. B. Eerdmans Publishing Co., 1967), p. 7.

[2]MS, BJsr, chapel talk, 17 November 1945 (ABV: 1945).

[3]Shelley's definition of terms is helpful. "Evangelical" is used in an inclusive way to categorize all Christians who are concerned with a "personal experience with Christ." "Orthodox Christians" is used to describe those who accept the cardinal doctrines of historic Protestantism. "Conservative" is sometimes used as a synonym for evangelical

to connote a shade of meaning more doctrinal than operational. "Fundamentalist" is used for those who most vigorously fight for the "defense of the faith" (Shelley, *Evangelicalism,* pp. 7-9).

[4]Much of the material for this chapter is drawn from Bob Jones IV, "Middle Ground: Bob Jones University and the Evolution of Separation," unpublished paper, BJU, 1995 (MLA); and from Dalhouse, "Shaping."

[5]The list of signatories of this call to action reads like a veritable Who's Who of American conservative Protestantism, and besides BJsr, includes William Ward Ayer, William Culbertson, Charles E. Fuller, Frank Gaebelein, Harry Ironside, Harold Ockenga, Harry Rimmer, and Charles Woodbridge (James Murch, *Cooperation Without Compromise* [Grand Rapids, Mich.: Wm. B. Eerdmans Publishing Co., 1956], p. 54).

[6]Murch, *Cooperation,* pp. 54-55.

[7]Shelley, *Evangelicalism,* pp. 69-71.

[8]Ibid., p. 70.

[9]The statement affirmed that

1. We believe the Bible to be inspired, the only infallible, authoritative Word of God.

2. We believe that there is only one God, eternally existent in three persons, Father, Son, and Holy Ghost.

3. We believe in the deity of our Lord Jesus Christ, in His virgin birth, in His sinless life, in His miracles, in His vicarious atoning through His shed blood, in His bodily resurrection, in His ascension to the right hand of the Father, and in His personal return in power and glory.

4. We believe that for the salvation of lost and sinful man regeneration by the Holy Spirit is absolutely essential.

5. We believe in the present ministry of the Holy Spirit by whose indwelling the Christian is enabled to live a godly life.

6. We believe in the resurrection of both the saved and the lost; they that are saved unto the resurrection of life and they that are lost unto the resurrection of damnation.

7. We believe in the spiritual unity of believers in our Lord Jesus Christ. (Ibid., pp. 71-72; see also Murch, *Cooperation,* pp. 65-66)

[10]Shelley, *Evangelicalism,* p. 70.

[11]BG to BJsr, 3 April 1951 (GF: Graham file). BJsr became an original member of the NAE's Committee on Evangelism and was offered the commission chairmanship in 1949 (Dalhouse, "Shaping," p. 127). BJsr was also one of the original members of the board of directors for the NAE's National Religious Broadcasters organization (Murch, *Cooperation,* p. 77).

[12]BJsr, "Dr. Bob Jones Reports on the Recent National Convention of Evangelicals," *Churchill Tabernacle Evangelist,* June 1944 (MLA).

[13]Murch, *Cooperation,* p. 77. BJsr served with M. R. DeHaan, Theodore Epp, and Walter Maier, among others.

[14]Ibid., p. 181. Serving on this committee were BG, JRR, and Oswald Smith, among others.

[15]Dalhouse, "Shaping," p. 127. This board of seventeen men served under the six-member Executive Committee and the six elected officers (Murch, *Cooperation,* p. 67).

[16]Dalhouse, "Shaping," p. 128. BJjr recalled that he had already left the NAE Convention when his name was put up for the office. He wrote, "I had left the convention quietly but with the firm intention of writing a letter of resignation, handling it this way so as not to be 'divisive.' I was elected vice president by that convention after I had already left it; and I was not present, or I would never have permitted myself to be nominated or brought up as a possibility" (BJjr to Dan Turner, 26 February 1996).

[17]Shelley, *Evangelicalism,* p. 81.

[18]Murch, *Cooperation,* p. 53.

[19]Ibid., p. 185.

[20]Carl McIntire, *Twentieth Century Reformation* (Collingswood, N.J.: Christian Beacon Press, 1945), p. 13. Quoted in Jones IV, "Middle Ground," p. 10. George Marsden, in *Reforming Fundamentalism: Fuller Seminary and the New Evangelicalism* (Grand Rapids, Mich.: Wm. B. Eerdmans Publishing Co., 1987), writes, "McIntire was constitutionally unable to play any other role than chief." Some in the NAE board felt that McIntire intended for the NAE to subsume itself under the ACCC and McIntire's leadership, rather than the tiny ACCC melding itself into the much larger NAE.

[21]Jones IV, "Middle Ground," p. 10.

[22]BJsr to R. L. Decker, 9 September 1949 (GF: Decker file).

[23]Ibid., 11 October 1949 (GF: Decker file).

[24]BJjr "Comments Regarding the Dissertation Entitled 'Bob Jones University and the Shaping of Twentieth Century Separatism, 1926-1991' " (MLA: unpublished manuscript, n.d.).

[25]Jones IV, "Middle Ground," pp. 12-14.

[26]One of the earliest issues concerned the Committee on Evangelism, which had been one of BJsr's original reasons for supporting the organization. Because of his many years of experience in evangelism, BJsr logically thought that he should be made chairman; instead he was made a junior member of the committee and was asked to rubber-stamp a report that approved ineffective methods. He wrote, "I tried to work to save all I could from the rubbish of the mistakes that the Committee on Evangelism was making" (BJsr to R. L. Decker, 9 September 1949 [GF: Decker file]). And he found that at any time he made a complaint, he "was misunderstood." He wrote, "I do not have the physical, mental, and nervous strength to work with an organization when I am under suspicion" (BJsr to Frederick Fowler, 13 November 1950 [GF: Fowler file]).

[27]See Jones IV, "Middle Ground," p. 15.

[28]See Murch, *Cooperation,* pp. 82-96.

[29]Jones IV, "Middle Ground," p. 16; see also Murch, *Cooperation,* p. 87. The committee convened in April 1946, with the membership selected by a committee from the NAE Commission on Education Institutions, of which BJU had been a member since 1943. Committee members were from the following institutions: Stony Brook School, Wheaton College, University of Minnesota, Fuller Theological Seminary, Asbury Theological Seminary, Greenville College, Houghton College, and Fort Wayne Bible College. In addition, a group of consultants was formed that consisted of representatives from Princeton Theological Seminary, Moody Bible Institute, Stony Brook School, Juniata College, Westmont College, Houghton College, Columbia Bible College, Nyack Missionary Training Institute, the Bible Institute of Los Angeles, and several public secondary schools (Frank Gaebelein, *Christian Education in a Democracy* [New York: Oxford University Press, 1951], pp. v-vi]). Considering the other colleges represented, BJU was indeed conspicuous by its absence.

[30]BJsr to Frederick Fowler, 23 September 1950 (GF: Fowler file).

[31]BJjr to Carl F. H. Henry, 21 January 1948 (GF: Henry file).

[32]Gaebelein, *Education,* pp. 88-90. The report is replete with admonitions for Christian schools to seek and maintain accreditation. The report summarizes the need for accreditation by saying that "accreditation represents an important beginning toward lifting these institutions to an approved level of educational practice" (p. 286). While arguing for schools' being independently controlled, the commission failed to recognize that accreditation brings controls much more pernicious than those exerted by religious

forces. While arguing against government intrusion into religious schools, the commission also failed to account for the government's role in establishing accreditation criteria.

[33]Ibid., p. 286.

[34]Ibid., pp. 148-49.

[35]Carl F. H. Henry to BJjr, 27 January 1948 (GF: Fuller Theological Seminary file).

[36]Gaebelein, *Education,* pp. 286-87.

[37]Carl F. H. Henry to BJsr, 6 January 1949 (GF: Fuller Theological Seminary file). For the story of Fuller's founding, see Marsden, *Reforming Fundamentalism,* pp. 50-60.

[38]BJsr to Carl F. H. Henry, 14 January 1948 (GF: Fuller Theological Seminary file).

[39]Carl F. H. Henry to BJsr, 26 January 1949 (GF: Fuller Theological Seminary file). Interestingly, six months before Carl F. H. Henry wrote BJsr asking for evidence of the acceptability of BJU graduates, Fuller Seminary had accepted only two students, and when Fuller opened, it had thirty-nine students, almost all from secular campuses and very few from Christian colleges (p. 54).

[40]The NAE requested BJsr to forward them a list naming the colleges he considered to be unbiblical, but he refused to substantiate his claim, saying that "definitely . . . was not our policy, that we did not put our finger on any individual school" (BJsr to Frederick Fowler, 13 November 1950 [GF: National Association of Evangelicals file]).

[41]BJsr to R. L. Decker, 9 September 1949 (GF: Decker file). In this letter BJsr writes, "I do not see how Bob Jones University can be of any further service to the organization. Bob can do whatever he pleases personally." See also BJsr to James Murch, 26 May 1951 (GF: NAE file). According to R. L. Decker to BJsr, 21 June 1953 (GF: Decker file), James Murch, editor of the NAE publication *United Evangelical Action,* "insisted on publishing the lists of non-member schools" and in Decker's mind, this was "a great mistake."

[42]BJjr to Frederick Fowler, 6 September 1950 (GF: NAE file).

[43]BJjr to Frederick Fowler (2), 6 September 1950 (GF: NAE file).

[44]R. L. Decker to BJsr, 21 June 1953 (GF: Decker file).

[45]BJjr recalled that one of his reasons for resigning was that the organization had "approved Billy Graham to be their official evangelist after he had already begun to show signs of compromise" (BJjr to Dan Turner, 26 February 1996). In *Cornbread and Caviar,* BJjr also notes the visible animosity held toward McIntire's group as a factor in his decision. See also BJjr to Frederick Fowler, 6 September 1950 (GF: Fowler file). The Dalhouse thesis is that BJjr had a separatist impulse as an integral part of his personality. The correspondence to Fowler and others, of which Dalhouse knew nothing, shows otherwise.

[46]BJsr to Frederick Fowler, 23 September 1950 (GF: NAE file).

[47]A thorough account of one division that resulted from the New York campaign is found in Marsden, *Reforming Fundamentalism,* pp. 153-71. The debate and division that developed at Fuller appear to be representative of the national debate in conservative theological circles. For a more generalized treatment of the topic, see Ernest D. Pickering, *The Tragedy of Compromise: The Origin and Impact of the New Evangelicalism* (Greenville: BJU Press, 1994).

[48]See Martin, *Prophet,* pp. 218-19. Of the many biographies of BG, Martin's is the most thorough and objective. The Marshall Frady biography, *Billy Graham: A Parable of American Righteousness* (Boston: Little, Brown and Company, 1979), is less objective and "overwrought but often insightful" (Martin, *Prophet,* p. 596). For comment on the scriptural issues, see Johnson, *Builder,* pp. 273-309; BJjr, *Cornbread,* pp. 153-61; Dollar, *History,* p. 252; and Beale, *Pursuit,* pp. 9, 257, 262-68, 283-84. Historian William G. McLoughlin Jr. in *Billy Graham: Revivalist in a Secular Age* (New York: Ronald Press, 1960) takes a very positive stance toward BG.

⁴⁹For an excellent discussion of JRR and BG, see Howard Edgar Moore, "The Emergence of Moderate Fundamentalism: John R. Rice and *The Sword of the Lord*" (Ph.D. dissertation, George Washington University, 1990).

⁵⁰Martin, *Prophet,* pp. 66-71. See also John Pollock, *Billy Graham: The Authorized Biography* (New York: McGraw-Hill Book Co., 1966), pp. 11-13. Pollock reports that BG found the BJC regulations on dating "galling." Letters from BG's parents indicate some type of medical concern, but BJjr recalls that it was generally supposed that "Billy wanted to go to Florida because his ambition was to be a ball player" and the professional teams wintered there (BJjr to Dan Turner, 26 February 1996).

⁵¹Martin, *Prophet,* p. 70. Interestingly, Phillips, who was much older and had already graduated from Moody Bible Institute, left BJC in January 1937 without completing his first semester examinations, thus losing a semester of credit. On 16 June 1942 Phillips wrote BJsr asking to be re-admitted to the College and said, "Last winter I told you of my earnest desire to complete my studies at Bob Jones College. I would rather be a graduate of Bob Jones College than any other college in America. Your practical help alone is worth the price of the course" (Wendell Phillips to BJsr, 16 June 1942 [GF: Phillips file]). Phillips also sent his daughter to BJU (Wendell Phillips to Gilbert Stenholm, 13 August 1956 [GF: Phillips file]).

⁵²Martin, *Prophet,* p. 70. Letters in the GF indicate that BJsr had at least three conversations with BG, and he wrote about these to BG's parents. Although Phillips withdrew from school immediately, BJsr advised BG to stay and finish at the least his first semester examinations in order to receive his credits from the semester of work. BJsr's final letter reads, "I have advised Billy to go down to Florida to the Bible Institute and take his work regularly and orderly. I have advised him that Wendell [Phillips] is not the type fellow he should have with him. . . . As one father to another and as a Christian brother to another, I advise you to write Billy to go to Florida . . . and that you do not want him to go with Wendell" (BJsr to W. F. Graham, 11 January 1937 [GF: Graham file]).

⁵³There was no apparent ill will toward BG for leaving BJC. On 27 July 1943 BJsr wrote to BG, "May God bless you, Billy, in your work. I hope you will stay close to God. There has never been such an opportunity for preaching as now. . . . Evangelists of the right kind are so badly needed now" (BJsr to BG, 27 July 1943 [GF: Graham file]).

⁵⁴Florida Bible Institute occupied a large old hotel on the outskirts of Tampa, part of which was also used as a Christian winter retreat and Bible conference center. In conjunction, there was an old eighteen-hole golf course, which was a strong attraction for BG. The school itself was run by Dr. W. T. Watson, a Christian and Missionary Alliance pastor who, with one other CMA pastor, composed the bulk of the full-time teaching faculty. The school "did not pretend to be a college . . . or attempt a general education; nor was it a seminary." Its aim was to give experience in practical Christian service. The curriculum included such offerings as prophecy, modern missions, Bible customs, hymnology, and one course in gospel magic. BG was not a serious student at FBI; he spent a great deal of time golfing, caddying, swimming, playing tennis, courting young ladies, and attending spring training games of professional baseball teams (Pollock, *Authorized,* pp. 8-15; and Frady, *Parable,* pp. 105-7; see also Martin, *Prophet,* pp. 71-79).

⁵⁵The YFC message was clearly Fundamentalist and evangelistic and had not yet adapted Christianity to a "popular" style of presentation. During these early years of YFC, BJsr, BJjr, Monroe Parker, Gilbert Stenholm, and others from BJC and BJU were featured speakers at Saturday rallies. According to Stenholm's 1946 diary, BJjr left BJC on 1 February 1946 to preach at YFC in Miami. Stenholm preached in Winston-Salem on 16 February 1946. BJjr preached in Indianapolis on the same day Monroe Parker was in Kansas City, 23 November 1946.

[56]T. W. Wilson first joined BG for a Los Angeles youth rally at which T. W. spoke to a crowd of over six thousand young people, the largest crowd he had ever seen. One Chicago rally, which capped off twenty-one consecutive Saturdays of filling Chicago's Orchestra Hall for YFC programs, was attended by seventy thousand young people. It featured a three-hundred-piece band, a five-thousand-voice choir, and a missionary pageant with hundreds participating, and was a masterpiece of organization and showmanship.

[57]See Frady, *Parable,* pp. 200-202; Martin, *Prophet,* pp. 94-100, 130; and BJjr, *Cornbread,* p. 154.

[58]Martin, *Prophet,* pp. 94-95. Martin writes that BG and the other YFC staffers recognized the importance of Hearst's publicity. For example, when departing for a series of rallies in Europe, the group booked the first transatlantic flight from Chicago, which in itself was newsworthy. The YFC staff organized a large sendoff rally, complete with a prayer meeting on the tarmac posed for newspaper photographers who had been sent to cover the historic flight. Frady writes that the photographers, after each "Amen," shouted, "Keep praying! Keep praying!" while they snapped pictures, the other passengers gaped, and the group obligingly knelt reverently on the tarmac beside the loading ramp (Frady, *Parable,* p. 164). The purpose of the publicity was to project an image of sincere and simple faith while utilizing the most effective Madison Avenue techniques. Graham's understanding and use of publicity has never failed him, as Martin clearly demonstrates in *Prophet.*

[59]BG wrote, "I have no clear indication from the Lord that I am to succeed Dr. Riley. God called me into evangelism. . . . However, if it would ease or be of any help, I would be glad to become *Interim* President in case of an emergency, until the Board could make some disposition of the office" (BG to BJsr, 11 December 1947 [GF: Graham file]).

[60]Martin, *Prophet,* p. 103.

[61]BG gave, at most, only one week a month of full attention to the affairs of the college. T. W. Wilson ran the day-to-day affairs of the school (BG to BJsr, 11 December 1947 [GF: Graham file]). Letters for advice include 11 December 1947, 29 December 1949, and 23 October 1950. BJsr's letter of December 1947 is especially interesting because he states this concept of finance and says, "Remember this: If you have got somebody in your organization that will leave you because he can get more money elsewhere, you don't want that fellow there, anyhow" (BJsr to BG, 11 December 1947 [GF: Graham file]).

[62]Quoted in Martin, *Prophet,* p. 111. Frady (*Parable,* pp. 178-82) and Pollock (*Authorized,* pp. 50-52) provide similar records of the conversation.

[63]Pollock, *Authorized,* p. 52.

[64]Stanley Rowland, "Billy Starts Tiring of Evangelism," *New York Times,* 9 February 1957.

[65]Frady, *Parable,* p. 201.

[66]BJjr, *Cornbread,* p. 153. See also BJsr to BG, 5 April 1951 (GF: Graham file).

[67]Gilbert Stenholm's diary records that he attended the BG meeting on March 7 and was introduced in the meeting by Cliff Barrows. Stenholm at this time was director of ministerial training at BJU (Stenholm diary, 7 March 1950). See *Little Moby's Post,* March/April 1950, p. 1. See also Martin, *Prophet,* p. 129.

[68]BG to BJjr, 24 May 1951 (GF: Graham file).

[69]"Heaven, Hell, and Judgement Day," *Time,* 20 March 1950, pp. 72-73. See also Martin, *Prophet,* pp. 129-30, and Pollock, *Authorized,* pp. 68-72.

[70]Martin, *Prophet,* p. 129.

[71]Graham's campaign manager initially refused the chapel service because of BJU's outspoken stand. After several letters between BJsr and BG, an apology was forthcoming from BG, the chapel service was arranged, and the campaign manager was replaced. Later, BJsr wrote, "I know what has been said to you by the [religious] bosses. I know what they said to you in South Carolina when they tried to keep you from coming here to our school and you wanted to get out and leave us dangling and would have done it if it had not been for [my] pressure" (BJsr to BG, 5 April 1951).

[72]Stenholm diary, 18 March 1950.

[73]Ibid., 20 March 1950.

[74]Willis Haymaker was campaign advance man for BJsr starting before 1920 and continuing through at least 1951. BJsr had taught Haymaker the techniques that became so well known with BG's crusades: publicity committees, finance committees, preachers' committees, music committees, extensive cottage prayer meetings, women's prayer meetings, men's prayer meetings, businessmen's campaign organizations, and the use of personal conferences to handle renegade local preachers. The Haymaker file is replete with letters from BJsr outlining organizational ideas, giving advice on everything from tabernacle sizes and locations to the necessary committees for successful campaigns. For BG, Haymaker replaced the term *campaign* with *crusade* in order to project an image of lasting or continuing action, and applied BJsr's advice from 1931: "The most important thing you are doing is to start prayer meetings. If you can do that in a community, you are successful" (BJsr to Willis Haymaker, 19 May 1931 [GF: Haymaker file]).

[75]Martin, *Prophet*, p. 244. Note also pp. 142-54, 244-50, 284-316, and 350-99, which chronicle BG's relationship with Presidents Kennedy, Johnson, Nixon, Ford, Carter, Reagan, and Bush.

[76]BG to BJsr, 23 October 1950 (GF: Graham file).

[77]"Thank you for the nice things you say, Billy. We love you and love all the rest of [your team]. I trust that God will bless and use you in Atlanta" (BJsr to BG, 25 October 1950 [GF: Graham file]).

[78]BJsr to BG, 5 April 1951 (GF: Graham file), and BJjr to BG, 10 May 1951 (GF: Graham file). BJjr writes, "I have been . . . hurt by the fact that no mention is made in any of the publicity that you release of the fact that you ever went to Bob Jones University. It rather puts me on the spot, and it has very definitely embarrassed my father. Years ago you told him to consider you one of his boys. This was long before you came into the limelight. He took you at your word and mentioned you [widely and often]. . . . Dad thinks you do not mention [BJU] because you feel that there are lots of folks who are enemies of Bob Jones University and you are trying to get along with everybody. . . . It is a case that looks to him like you don't want to stand with us."

[79]BJsr to BG, 5 April 1951 (GF: Graham file).

[80]BJsr to BG, 22 May 1952 (GF: Graham file). It is interesting to note that some of BG's most publicized activities have been related to politics and politicians. Not only has BG met with and consulted many world leaders, but he and his influence have been cited as a moral proof for many social schemes, including Lyndon Johnson's "War on Poverty." BG endorsed the "War" before members of Congress and made a film with Sargent Shriver, director of the Office of Economic Opportunity, highlighting several antipoverty initiatives. BG was called to the White House numerous times to offer prayers during the Vietnam War and Richard Nixon's presidency and during the Persian Gulf War under George Bush.

[81]BG to BJsr, 3 June 1952 (GF: Graham file).

[82]BJsr to BG, 30 December 1953 (GF: Graham file). In 1956 the liberals made a major attempt to do just that. The National Council of Churches employed Chuck

Templeton as a full-time evangelist, holding crusades under the auspices of the National Council. The former YFC personality, associate of BG, and now agnostic preacher, had no spiritual success in his campaigns.

[83]BG to BJsr, 23 October 1950 (GF: Graham file).

[84]Ibid., 3 April 1951 (GF: Graham file).

[85]BJsr to BG, 5 April 1951 (GF: Graham file).

[86]See Pollock, *Authorized*, p. 43; and Martin, *Prophet*, p. 102.

[87]Ockenga, who had been awarded an honorary doctorate by BJC in 1944, was pastor of Park Street Congregational Church in Boston and a professor at Fuller Seminary. He became the leading exponent of the New Evangelicalism.

The "New Evangelicalism," as Ockenga defined it, differed from Fundamentalism in three key areas: (1) a repudiation of the practice of separation; (2) a summons to greater social involvement; and (3) a determination to engage in theological dialogue with liberalism. He listed four major agencies to accomplish the spread of the New Evangelical movement: (1) the National Association of Evangelicals; (2) Fuller Theological Seminary in Pasadena; (3) the religious publication *Christianity Today;* and (4) the Billy Graham organization (Beale, *Pursuit*, p. 262). For a complete treatment of Fuller Theological Seminary, see Marsden, *Reforming Fundamentalism.*

The connection between these four agencies is not accidental. BG and his staff members were highly active in and the most visible members of the NAE. BG has been the featured speaker at NAE conventions since 1947. Fuller Seminary was founded in 1947 for the express purpose of becoming the educational vehicle for the movement. *Christianity Today,* edited by Carl Henry of Fuller Theological Seminary, was founded at the urging of BG and with monies raised by him. Carl Henry was selected by BG to be the editor, even though BG felt that Henry was too much identified as a Fundamentalist and would elicit a negative response among liberal or Neo-orthodox readers. In 1955 BG asked Henry to "soft-pedal" the differences between Fundamentalists and Modernists for a two-year period and instead stress the common features of belief between the two groups. BG's father-in-law, Nelson Bell, was appointed executive editor (Martin, *Prophet,* p. 215). *Christianity Today* was embraced by the New Evangelicals as a mouthpiece publication.

Up to 1955, BG retained the public support of BJsr, BJjr, JRR, and most other Fundamentalists.

[88]Martin, *Prophet,* p. 218.

[89]The 1948 Amsterdam meeting brought together the leaders of all forms of religious belief for the purpose of finding common ground on which to unite religiously. Most of the leaders attending denied some, if not all, of the fundamental doctrines of Christianity. At this meeting, survey results gathered from world religious leaders concluded that "the fundamentalists should subordinate their 'impregnable maxim' of verbal inspiration to the findings of historico-scientific methods so that the words may have meaning. . . . They are tied to the Bible which is only human words. The 'form' of the Apostles is a stumbling block, preventing modern man from listening" (Arthur Johnston, *World Evangelism and the Word of God* [Minneapolis: Bethany Fellowship, Inc., 1974], p. 223).

Because of its lack of a coherent biblical faith and its hodgepodge of religious and pseudo-Christian philosophies, the World Council of Churches was quickly denounced by Fundamentalists as part of the coming church of the Antichrist.

[90]Interestingly enough, there was no Fundamentalist outcry against BG's attending the early WCC meetings. His thoughts as to the value of those meetings were not immediately forthcoming, thus the Fundamentalists had to take him at his word. See Martin, *Prophet,* pp. 103-4.

[91]Martin, *Prophet,* p. 327. The WCC in Evanston heard position papers on evangelism that redefined conversion by replacing biblical definitions of the term with social definitions; replaced man's need for personal salvation with the saving of society; stressed universalism; and minimized or rejected the personality of Satan as "illusory," replacing him with "real" social, political, and religious dominations that must be addressed by an authoritative church working for social renewal. See Arthur Johnston, *The Battle for World Evangelism* (Wheaton, Ill.: Tyndale House Publishers Inc., 1978), pp. 98-119.

[92]The WCC and its American counterpart, the National Council of Churches, reject the verbal inspiration, inerrancy, and infallibility of Scripture, citing rather the "implicit errors and the human authors." They reject the authority of Scripture as rule for faith and practice because of its human authorship and see it as a "continuing source of disunity" among Christians. And they reject the Bible as the very Word of God but accept it as "becoming" the word as men find their truth in it in time of need (Johnston, *Evangelism and the Word,* pp. 255-57).

[93]Martin, *Prophet,* p. 180-81.

[94]Quoted in Ian R. K. Paisley, *Billy Graham and the Church of Rome* (Greenville, S.C.: BJU Press, 1972), p. 47.

[95]Much of this account is taken from James E. Bennet to Jack Wyrtzen, 29 October 1956 (BJU: Graham packet #1). This is the single clearest and most detailed account available. In 1955 BG flew Bonnell to Scotland to participate in a campaign; in 1956 Bonnell, as a member of the Protestant Council and on the record in opposition to Fundamentalist doctrine (Martin, *Prophet,* p. 222), was a sponsor of the New York crusade. The later "representation" issue clearly indicates the shift in BG's campaign organization practices in demanding that all churches be represented. Please note that "all churches," to the Graham organization, meant all liberal and Modernist churches, primarily those who maintained membership in the NCC ministerial association, but not all conservative, Fundamentalist, separatist, or Bible-believing churches.

[96]BJsr wrote in 1957, "BG could have gone to New York under the sponsorship of the conservatives that did all they could to get him. . . . The liberals did not invite BG to New York. The conservatives invited him; but BG's organization, by its pressure, brought the modernists into the picture" (BJsr, to "Friend," 6 March 1957 [BJU: Graham packet #1]).

[97]See G. Archer Weniger to Walter Smyth, 20 December 1957 (BJU: BG packet). Weniger addresses the major criticisms of the New York crusade by showing Smyth how he was being less than open and forthright about these questions. From the evidence now available, it is obvious that members of the BG team both on the national level and at the local level would falsify, misstate, and openly lie in response to serious questions in order to "be all things to all men" and thus win the support of the questioner. If the questioner persisted, he was dismissed as Fundamentalist troublemaking rabble. See also Martin, *Prophet,* pp. 225-31. One member of the committee was the well-known Neo-orthodox positive thinker Norman Vincent Peale.

[98]Martin, *Prophet,* p. 220.

[99]BG to unnamed, 8 May 1958 (GF: Graham file).

[100]Martin, *Prophet,* p. 222.

[101]"Billy Starts Tiring of Evangelism," *New York Times.*

[102]Wilfred Bockelman, "A Lutheran Looks at Billy Graham," *Lutheran Standard,* 10 October 1961.

[103]Martin, *Prophet,* p. 241, quoted from *Christian Beacon,* 9 January 1958.

[104]The term "cooperative evangelism" came from the book entitled *Cooperative Evangelism: Is Billy Graham Right or Wrong?* (Grand Rapids, Mich.: Zondervan

Publishing House, 1958), by BG Evangelistic Association researcher and author, Robert O. Ferm. In this work Ferm laid out ten arguments by which New Evangelicals rationalized and defended the embracing of Modernists and liberals in evangelistic outreaches, and BG's evangelistic outreaches specifically. Ferm asserts that all the early evangelists—Wesley, Whitefield, Finney, Moody, Sunday, and by implication, BJsr and JRR—willingly cooperated with a wide range of church leaders, not examining their sponsors' beliefs too carefully. *Cooperative Evangelism* showed a lack of historical understanding, since Modernist viewpoints were not greatly influential in American pulpits until the early 1900s. The earliest debates were those of Unitarianism and Universalism in the 1760s, which resulted in the emasculation and liberalization of Congregationalism by the 1830s. None of the early evangelists, with the possible exception of Finney at the end of his life, would have allowed in their meetings any representation by Unitarians among the sponsoring ministers. Modernism in the Protestant pulpit, in its full-blown form of denial of the basic Christian doctrines, was a twentieth-century development, and therefore, not applicable to Wesley, Whitefield, or Moody.

Modernism was, however, active in northern seminaries and Congregationalist churches prior to the 1870s. The inroads of "science as faith," following the 1859 publication of Darwin's *Origin of Species,* wrought some retrenchment among pastors as they tried to reconcile the seemingly insurmountable evidences for evolution with the Genesis record. Yet many of the men who acquiesced and thereafter held to theistic evolution—Creation days comprised of eons of time—clearly were stalwart in defense of the historic faith, including God's creation of man. Full-blown Modernism—the denial of the doctrine of Christ and the doctrine of the inspiration of Scripture—in the pulpits came in post–World War I America with the popularization of Harry Emerson Fosdick, the widespread acceptance of Modernist higher criticism in higher education, and the rise of faith in science as the new savior of the race. Thus, Wesley, Whitefield, Moody, and even BJsr, through the 1920s and early 1930s, did not worry about the orthodoxy of sponsors; almost all were still orthodox. By the mid-1930s BJsr had noticed a change in belief and attitude on the part of southern Methodists. Upon mentioning this to Willis Haymaker, Haymaker responded, "I have also noted this change too. It has come about in this way. . . . The ecclesiastical and denominational program that they have been trying to put over was a mistake and . . . the spiritual life of many of their churches is about dead. . . . The Lord has no use for any group of people who go into apostasy or who try to substitute man's program for God's program" (Willis Haymaker to BJsr, 22 March 1939 [GF: Haymaker file]).

[105]See Moore, "Emergence," pp. 182-366. Moore documents JRR's position on BG and places JRR to the left of BJsr in his views of separation, calling JRR "a centrist." He notes that long after BG had publicly declared his opposition to Fundamentalism, JRR was still actively defending him in the *Sword.* JRR hoped that citywide union campaigns of the past, such as those of Moody, Sunday, and BJsr, could be maintained, and in spite of the compromises would support BG out of this hope and JRR's own desire to "win souls." Moore points out that JRR finally adopted a critical stance toward BG only because of BJsr's urging.

[106]See John 14:15, 21.

[107]It is difficult to imagine how such issues as the deity of Christ, His virgin birth, the blood atonement, and the inspiration of Scripture could be considered nonessentials.

[108]Martin, *Prophet,* pp. 222-24.

[109]"What's the Next Step," interview with BG, *Christian Life,* June 1956, pp. 20-23. Quoted and paraphrased in Marsden, *Reforming Fundamentalism,* p. 163; and Martin, *Prophet,* p. 221.

Chapter 16: "Wounds of a Friend, Kisses of an Enemy"

[1]Proverbs 27:6: "Faithful are the wounds of a friend; but the kisses of an enemy are deceitful."

[2]Though not yet openly critical of BG, JRR was one of those about whom the "strict Calvinist" claims were made by virtue of his association with BJsr. Such claims were, of course, unfounded. JRR, an evangelist and editor of the *Sword of the Lord,* sponsored yearly soulwinning conferences. BJsr as an evangelist won thousands of souls to Christ and saw revival in many churches through his preaching and influence; and BJjr, University President and also an evangelist, though younger than JRR, was constantly in revival meetings and seeing many saved.

[3]T. W. Wilson's relationship to BJsr is interesting. Wilson had very little money as a BJC student and had difficulty paying his bill. On one occasion, BJsr personally paid Wilson's tuition so that he could stay in school. On another occasion Wilson got into some difficulty on his night watchman's job, and the dean of students wanted to send him home. BJsr intervened, and Wilson was allowed to stay in school (MS, chapel talk, BJjr, 18 January 1968 [ABV: 1968]).

[4]T. W. Wilson to BJsr, 21 May 1957 (GF: Wilson file).

[5]BJsr, as President of the Interdenominational Evangelists Association of Winona Lake, Indiana (1920-22), sponsored a resolution calling on the membership of the organization to refuse any campaigns or meetings in which the sponsorship included Modernists. The resolution passed unanimously ("125 Volunteers to Take Part in Tabernacle Day," *Owensboro [Ky.] Messenger,* 28 February 1926).

[6]Martin, *Prophet,* p. 224.

[7]Shelley, *Evangelicalism,* p. 120.

[8]BJsr to Willis Haymaker, 21 March 1951 (GF: Haymaker file).

[9]BG to BJjr, 19 May 1956 (GF: Graham file).

[10]Willis Haymaker, whom BJsr had trained to be an advance man for his campaigns and who joined the Billy Graham Evangelistic Association in 1950, was fully aware that BJsr would not allow a Modernist to serve on a committee. BJsr wrote Haymaker in 1941 saying, "I would not want to go in with any preacher who does not believe in the Virgin Birth and the Blood" (BJsr to Willis Haymaker, 2 December 1941 [GF: Haymaker file]). As a twenty-one-year-old evangelist, BJsr had been invited to hold a meeting for "the leading Methodist preacher of the South. This preacher did not believe that Moses wrote the Pentateuch, and I told him I could not come" (BJsr to Charles T. Cook, 25 April 1957 [GF: Cook file]). In 1947 Haymaker wrote a report on a proposed campaign in West Palm Beach, Florida, in which he said, "The First Presbyterian man is a modernist and does not believe in this sort of thing, so that lets him out" (Willis Haymaker to BJsr, 16 October 1947 [GF: Haymaker file]).

[11]BJsr to Charles T. Cook, 25 April 1957 (GF: Cook file).

[12]JRR, *Sword of the Lord,* 27 April 1957.

[13]Quoted in Martin, *Prophet,* p. 222.

[14]BG to unnamed, 8 May 1958 (GF: Graham file). The hole in logic here is readily apparent. Without an inerrant Word, one has no trustworthy record of Christ, His incarnation, life, words, death, resurrection, and ascension to the right hand of the Father. Therefore, there is nothing on which to base His deity besides human speculation.

[15]Ernest Pickering, *Biblical Separation: The Struggle for a Pure Church* (Schaumburg, Ill.: Regular Baptist Press, 1979), p. 82.

[16]See T. W. Wilson to BJsr, 6 March 1956 (GF: Graham file). Wilson at this time was writing as an official representative of the BG organization and may be considered

to be speaking for BG. For a time JRR also seemed to agree with this position. About the New York crusade, JRR wrote, "We rejoice to hear that there have been big crowds and many people coming forward. . . . The one thing dearest to my heart . . . has been the winning of souls." JRR also mentioned that Norman Vincent Peale's church received more decision cards from BG than any other congregation (JRR, "Souls Saved in Billy Graham's New York Crusade," *Sword of the Lord,* vol. 23, no. 24, 14 June 1957; quoted in Moore, "Emergence," p. 265).

[17]BJsr to T. W. Wilson, 18 February 1956 (GF: Wilson file).

[18]BJsr to BG, 17 January 1956 (GF: Graham file).

[19]BJjr to BG, 12 May 1956 (GF: Graham file).

[20]BJjr to Ralph W. Mitchell, 7 November 1956 (GF: Graham file).

[21]BJsr to "Friend," 6 March 1957 (BJU: Graham packet #1).

[22]See II Timothy 4:1-5 and Ephesians 4:11-16.

[23]L. Nelson Bell to BJsr, 19 March 1957 (GF: Graham file).

[24]BJsr to L. Nelson Bell, 26 March 1957 (GF: Graham file).

[25]Moore, "Emergence," pp. 266-67.

[26]Interestingly, BG organization requests for formal prayer meetings for the New York crusade were also denied by Lee Roberson and Chattanooga's Tennessee Temple Schools, a Fundamentalist Bible college. Neither Roberson nor Tennessee Temple were mentioned by Bell or any BG associate. About this, Moore writes, "Roberson had declined for reasons identical to BJU's, yet the Graham organization had remained silent. Obviously, someone had elected to make an example of BJU" (Moore, "Emergence," p. 267).

[27]L. Nelson Bell to BJsr, 7 May 1957 (GF: Graham file).

[28]*Sword of the Lord,* 11 October 1957.

[29]BJsr to L. Nelson Bell, 11 May 1957 (GF: Graham file).

[30]BJjr to Ralph W. Mitchell, 7 November 1956 (GF: Graham file).

[31]Johnson, *Builder,* pp. 297-99.

[32]MS, BJjr, chapel talk, 22 January 1965 (ABV: 1965).

[33] Ibid., 8 February 1965 (ABV: 1965).

[34]"Bob Jones Says Billy Graham Doing More Harm to the Cause of Christ than Any Living Man," *Greenville (S.C.) News,* 4 March 1966. That BG would be unsure as to the cause is absolutely amazing, given the large number of letters exchanged among the Founder, the President, and him.

[35]Ibid.

[36]See BG to unnamed, "Open Letter," 8 May 1958 (GF: Graham file). L. Nelson Bell wrote BJsr, applying Gamaliel's pragmatic advice from Acts 5:38-39—"if this . . . work be of men, it will come to nought: but if it be of God, ye cannot overthrow it"—to BG's crusades (L. Nelson Bell to BJsr, 7 May 1957 [GF: Graham file]). In a letter to JRR, BG noted the large crowds (BG to JRR, 10 January 1956), which prompted BJsr to say that crowds are not emblematic of God's blessing in revival.

[37]BJsr to L. Nelson Bell, 11 May 1957 (GF: Graham file).

[38]See Paisley, *Church of Rome,* for detailed information about the early days of BG's cooperation with Roman Catholics.

[39]Those who believed such included the great Reformers Jon Huss (1373-1415), John Knox (1505-72), Martin Luther (1483-1546), John Calvin (1509-64), and John Bradford (1510-75) and twentieth-century evangelists and Bible teachers R. A. Torrey, James Gray, Billy Sunday, W. B. Riley, Harry Ironside, and BJsr.

[40]William McElwain, title unknown, *Pittsburgh Sun-Telegraph,* 6 September 1952, quoted in "Significant Statements" (GF).

[41]*Protestant Church Life,* quoted in "Significant Statements."

[42]*Chicago Daily News,* 20 June 1957, quoted in "Significant Statements."

[43]G. Archer Weniger, "The Blu-Print," 10 June 1958. On 4 June 1958, convert cards from the San Francisco Crusade Office were sent to the following churches, among others: Lakeside Unity Temple, Grand Avenue Seventh-Day Adventist Church, Market Street Seventh-Day Adventist Church, Our Lady of Kazan (Russian Orthodox Catholic), Church of the Holy Trinity (Greek Orthodox), Fellowship of All Peoples, and Berkeley Seventh-Day Adventist.

[44]W. H. Martindale to unnamed, 29 February 1968 (BJU: Graham packet #3). See also Jerry Beavan to Evan L. Shaffer, 30 October 1952 (GF: Graham file).

[45]"Storm over Graham," *Sydney (Australia) Daily Mirror,* 6 April 1959 (BJU: Fundamentalism File document 0446757).

[46]Arlene Grimes, "Cardinal Has Praise for Graham Crusade," *Boston Herald,* 16 September 1964; and "Historic Encounter: Graham-Cushing," *United Evangelical Action,* November 1964, pp. 21-22. See also "Cardinal 100 Per Cent for Graham," *Greenville (S.C.) News,* 8 October 1964.

[47]Paul Smith, "Belmont Abbey Confers Honorary Degree," *Gastonia (N.C.) Gazette,* 22 November 1967.

[48]George Dugan, "Dr. Graham Envisions a New Era for Christianity," *New York Times,* 9 November 1963.

[49]Bill Rose, "Billy Graham Wins Praise of Catholic," *Oakland (Calif.) Tribune,* 29 July 1971.

[50]Martin, *Prophet,* pp. 328-34.

[51]"Bob Jones, Jr., Called 'Pharisee' in Graham Dispute," *Christian Beacon,*17 March 1966.

[52]BJsr to Charles T. Cook, 25 April 1957 (GF: Cook file).

[53]Robert Shaper, a former BJU dean, went to Fuller Theological Seminary as a faculty member. Following an intense but rather short battle over New Evangelicalism and BG, Fuller became one of the nation's academic centers for New Evangelical studies. Several other dissidents eventually landed at Bryan College in Tennessee, a Christian college that is in the New Evangelical camp.

[54]Enrollment Statistics: First Semester (RO).

[55]All figures derived from "Enrollment Statistics: First Semester," n.d. (RO). BJU does not keep enrollment figures for the second semester of each year; rather, the school reports matriculated students for second semester of each school year. "Grad./Spec." indicate students on the graduate level and those admitted under some type of special status.

[56]Other students are night school students (1950-54) and Institute of Christian Service students (1957-present).

[57]Loren Jones to BJsr (GF: Jones file).

[58]T. W. Wilson to BJsr, 17 May 1957 (GF: Wilson file).

[59]Cliff Barrows to BJsr, 22 May 1956; and BJsr to Cliff Barrows, 26 May 1956 (GF: Barrows file).

[60]William Piper to BJsr, 16 November 1957 (GF: Piper file).

Chapter 17: "Not Letting the Devil Grind His Ax"

[1]MS, BJsr, 10 September 1953 (ABV: 1953).

[2]See Turner, "Fundamentalism."

[3]Interview, BJjr, 28 May 1987. Corroborated by DG, 16 June 1987.

[4]MS, BJsr, chapel talk, 19 November 1944 (ABV: 1944). "Don't you get so in the habit of [saying] this Lord's Prayer on Sunday morning here, and so in the habit of saying the creed, that you actually begin to substitute things like that for God."

[5]"Great Contribution to Culture," *Easley (S.C.) Progress,* 22 January 1948. At the outset in 1937, the Artist Series programs were funded by a ten-dollar per year student fee. By 1971 ticket costs were included in the matriculation fee, which had been raised to one hundred dollars per year. Since the matriculation fee covers other small fees, it is difficult to determine the exact cost of the Artist Series. The University, however, has never underwritten these programs; they are funded through student fees and the sale of the remaining seats to the public (*Bulletin,* 1970-71, p. 30; Interview, BJiii, 3 June 1987).

[6]"Great Contribution," *Easley (S.C.)Progress.* Corroborated by Martha Stone.

[7]This is evident from the critiques published in the Greenville papers during the 1960s and 1970s. The local arts critic, Dale Perry, consistently made inane references to BJU's moral rectitude in his pieces. One interviewee described the press review of an opera performed at another area college—performed without orchestra, with "tacky" scenery, poor singing, wooden acting, and "awful" costuming—as not just highly complimentary, but as "raves." That year's BJU production, with full orchestra, beautiful sets and costumes, and outstanding singing by Metropolitan Opera stars, was panned for its tone (Interview, Gail Gingery, 16 June 1994).

[8]"Bob Jones Players Give Stirring Performance, Colorful Play," *Greenville (S.C.) News,* 15 January 1948.

[9]"Editorial," *Easley (S.C.) Progress,* 22 January 1948.

[10]JRR, "A Visit to Bob Jones College," *Sword of the Lord,* 8 June 1945. JRR wrote, "If it were worth my studying [as a student] and reading now, I see no reason why it is not worth acting also. I think that [simply] as education, the play was abundantly worth-while. But there were much greater values to those who took part." He continued that the actors

> learned what were the customs of the times, what kind of clothes people wore, how society was organized, how the kings, lords, bishops and common people of the time lived; how their wars were fought. And they got the finest practice in the world, being drilled and drilled in speaking clearly so that their words could be heard over the big auditorium, every line; in learning to put feeling and emotion and meaning into their voices. They developed voices, developed courage, developed personality, developed poise and ease before the crowd. . . . If lessons in expression are worth-while, if lessons in speech and voice culture or elocution are worth-while, then certainly the giving of "Richard III" was worth-while. . . . For too long we have tried to train preachers in the thinking of their messages but not in the delivery. Too often our schools turn out timid, self-conscious preachers whose voices cannot be heard in a good auditorium and who do not speak with authority and boldness, not with charm, nor pathos, nor conviction.

[11]JRR to BJjr, 8 June 1960 (GF: Rice Files). JRR writes,

> I did not get to tell you how greatly I enjoyed *The Merchant of Venice* on the Tuesday night of Commencement. I know the pressure you are under, and I know that you are constantly pressed with the thought that you will not long have time for the Shakespearean plays. However, I remind you that you give very great pleasure to many of us, and besides that, that you make classic literature and culture momentous and intriguing and fascinating to thousands who otherwise would be tempted to count it dead and dull. . . . [I] rejoice that all man's God-given talents may yet be recognized and sanctified to good uses at Bob Jones University. And that much of the culture of the ages is not lost to good Christians.

[12]As reported earlier, Buswell's animosity toward BJsr extended back to 1925, when Buswell unsuccessfully attempted to recruit BJsr to lead a national fight against educational standardization. In 1927 Buswell castigated BJsr for starting another Christian

college. This was followed in 1938 by Buswell and several associates' forming an accrediting organization that BJsr and the College would not join. In 1939 Buswell attempted to force three Christian publications to cancel BJC advertising on the grounds that the BJC ads were erroneous and misleading. Buswell was forced to write an apology and retraction of the charges. (See Chapter 6, note 96.)

As president of Wheaton, Buswell opposed dramatic studies and kept the performance of all plays out of the extracurricular offerings (Buswell to JRR, 2 July 1949). Student opinion at Wheaton apparently favored an expanded cultural program, but President Buswell remained intransigent, and drama was kept from the Wheaton campus until after his dismissal. An interview with Helen Torrey Remich by Robert Shuster, 17 May 1982 (Wheaton College Archives: Buswell papers) indicates that in the 1930s, when Torrey was a student, there were no drama, no acting, no Shakespeare, and no plays.

One student wrote the Wheaton campus newspaper that the cultural level of the campus needed to be raised by bringing to it high standards of faith and culture, thus helping the students develop "an appreciation of all that is fine and good" (*Wheaton Record,* 6 June 1928). Another student wrote in 1927 that if it is right to read Shakespeare in the classroom, is it not right to perform it on the stage (*Wheaton College Record,* 27 April 1927)? As late as 1939 a student wrote of the need for "good music, good interpretation and good lectures" to be offered on the campus (*Wheaton Record,* 4 April 1939).

[13]J. Oliver Buswell, *Bible of Today,* May 1949, pp. 215-16.

[14]JRR, "Dr. J. Oliver Buswell's Charges Against Bob Jones University Answered," *Sword of the Lord,* June 1949. Letters exchanged among BJsr, JRR, and Buswell brought no resolution to the issue (see BJsr to J. Oliver Buswell, 12 May 1949; BJsr to JRR, 12 May 1949; BJsr to JRR, 14 June 1949; JRR to Buswell, 28 June 1949; BJsr to JRR, 1 July 1949; Buswell to JRR, 2 July 1949; and BJsr to JRR, 1 August 1949 [GF: Buswell file]).

[15]In one instance, the Founder answered, "On Bob Jones University campus, life is not divided into the secular and the sacred. The Shakespearean programs open with prayer just like any other programs. We are not training people for the stage. We are training them for Christian work, and this is a part of the training. If your son stays here as a student, he is going to have to go along with the rest of the students and do the things that are officially approved. . . . If you want to take him home, you can do that; but if he stays here, he is going to have to go through the play" (BJsr to Mr. and Mrs. Henry P. Stover, 19 May 1955).

[16]Since 1960 the school has offered a greater variety of productions, including "one-man shows" by faculty and original dramas written by students and faculty.

[17]For example, four consecutive programs presented in 1953, all planned by different directors, took the themes of "Hands" (27 September 1953), "Love" (4 October 1953), "Prayer" (11 October 1953), and "Music" (18 October 1953). Each program used poetry; dramatic readings; Scripture; and vocal, instrumental, and choral music to set the mood and illustrate the theme (FAO: Vespers files: 1953-54). Two Vespers directors, Elizabeth Edwards and Gladys Besancon, also published a volume of twenty complete programs entitled *Sound His Glories Forth* (Grand Rapids, Mich.: Baker Book House, 1965).

[18]BJjr, "Memo to the Vesper Staff," n.d., duplicated (FAO: Vespers file—Vespers regulations). The music selections featured eventually included more gospel songs and hymns than in the Cleveland years and classical music was regularly included and used to open the programs or to set a mood. During one semester of programs, it would not be uncommon for the music of Gabrielli, Vivaldi, Bach, Handel, Haydn, Beethoven, Chopin, Liszt, Schubert, Vaughan Williams, and other classical composers to be performed on Vespers. One program from 1960 included four classical selections, by Nevin, Kuhlau, Beethoven, and Bach (Robert Pratt, "Grace and Works," Vespers Program, 4

December 1960 [FAO: Vespers files]. By 1990 the use of classical music had diminished somewhat, but the music was still "easily recognizable, pleasant to listen to, and not extreme" (BJjr to Marilyn Hertel, 8 April 1969 [FAO: Vespers file—Vespers regulations]).

[19]BJjr to DG, 3 May 1971. He chided the Vespers directors by writing, "The so-called reading on Sunday at Vespers was not a reading. It was an essay or a sermon, the very kind of thing we said we do not want on Vespers. All readings are supposed to be dramatic readings or incidents that carry a narrative and a story—not essays and not preaching. Vespers is not a preaching service."

[20]Interview, Robert Pratt, 8 June 1987. One sample letter from the College's executive offices reads, "Our music (speech) students have unusual advantages . . . for practical experience on our radio programs, Sunday afternoon Vesper Services, and recitals" ("Letters to Parents, Disciplinary Measures, and Regulations" [MLA: Box 8]).

[21]Interview, BJjr, 28 May 1987.

[22]Robert Pratt of the speech faculty, after returning from Northwestern University, introduced the technique in Vespers with huge success. This innovation allowed directors to present narrative materials, Scripture, or dramatic readings in a new way and with a heightened sense of drama (Interview, Robert Pratt, 8 June 1987).

[23]Other changes in the Vespers since 1948 include an increased reliance on drama; the gradual elimination of most poetry; a move to less formal staging; and the diminished use of classical music. By 1991 classical music was used almost exclusively for prelude or offertory music, and in 1994 classical music was eliminated from the programs unless the number had "a strong reason for existing in terms of its dramatic or thematic content relating to the body of the program." Including music simply for the sake of cultivating good taste in the students was seen as a less important aspect of the Vespers productions. The cultural background and tastes of the typical University student had declined, and it was thought that inculcating strong values in sacred music was a worthwhile goal in itself (DG to Vespers Speech and Music Supervisors, Vespers Directors, 25 March 1994 [FAO: Vespers file]; also Interviews, Lonnie Polson, 14 July 1994; and Robert Pratt).

[24]One dramatic example was a program performed in 1992 that centered on abortion. Powerfully presented and with a strong didactic and spiritual message, the program utilized lecture and sermon material and had an impact on the students.

[25]"The objective," the President wrote, "is changed lives and growth in godliness. . . . The programs, above all, must move the heart of hearers through the exaltation of Christ in an aesthetically pleasing way which does not call undue attention to the aesthetics" (BJiii to Lonnie Polson, 15 July 1993 [FAO: Vespers file]).

[26]"Aida Pleases Audience Here," *Greenville (S.C.) News,* 16 January 1948. The reviews said that the school did the opera "full justice." Amazingly, the production of *Aida* was one night after and in the same auditorium as a performance of *Richard III. Richard* was presented on January 14 and 16; *Aida* was presented on January 15 and 17.

[27]The 1954 production of *Rigoletto* was conducted by John Canfield, director of the University band (*Little Moby's Post,* vol. 27, no. 5, March 1954, p. 2). One opera was conducted by Frank Garlock during DG's doctoral leave of absence, and two performances of *The Elixir of Love* were conducted by Jay-Martin Pinner.

[28]John Ardoin, " 'La Juive' Southern Style," *Musical America*, May 1963, p. 14. Performances were considered well done from the standpoint of the student orchestra, sets, costuming, and staging. The problems that developed, however, were nearly always with the guest singers. Chief among those problems were singers who did not know their parts. In 1960, for example, an Italian bass, contracted to sing Scarpia in *Tosca,* arrived but did not know the music or the basic stage movement required for the part. After the piano rehearsal and the full dress stage rehearsals, it became apparent that some drastic

measure had to be taken. The bass was fired and put on an airplane; Cesare Bardelli, with whom the soprano had just sung the same opera, was contacted, and when he arrived the next day the cast walked though the stage movement. That night he sang the first performance without any musical rehearsal.

Both BJsr and BJjr made it a practice to drop in on rehearsals and, on occasion, made comments or mediated minor artistic disputes. At one dress rehearsal, the singers were having difficulty with a love duet when BJsr shouted from the back of the auditorium in jest, "Forget she's an old woman. Be more romantic!" (Interviewees Karl Keefer, DG, Gail Gingery, Katherine Stenholm, and Elizabeth Edwards all provided data to confirm this.)

After sitting in on a rehearsal, BJjr would sometimes demand that an inaccuracy of scenery, stage decoration, or costuming be corrected before the performance. BJjr's costuming and stage expertise and his critical eye are legendary on the campus. On one occasion in the 1952 production of *Tosca*, he attended the dress rehearsal and noticed that the staging for one scene was "just backwards." He gave directions for the scenery to be reversed, and it was as he directed for the opening performance the next day (Interview, Gail Gingery, 5 June 1987). In another instance, a pair of dyed tennis shoes worn by a cast member threw him into an impassioned discourse on costume accuracy (Interview, DG, 19 June 1987).

[29] Among them are Eleanor Steber, Ebe Stignani, Astrid Varnay, Lili Chookasian, Joann Grillo, Herva Nelli, Phyllis Curtin, Martial Singher, Jarmila Novotna, Norman Treigle, Jon Crain, Richard Cassilly, Brian Sullivan, Giuseppe Valdengo, Sherrill Milnes, Samuel Ramey, and the great bass Jerome Hines (FAO: Opera program files).

[30] Between 1942 and 1990 only two twentieth-century works were staged—*The Hunted* by DG, performed in May 1960 and 1977, and *Amahl and the Night Visitors* by Gian Carlo Menotti in December 1990. Menotti's operetta *Help! Help! The Globolinks!* was also presented for one Commencement Concert in the 1970s.

Among the operas performed most often on the campus between 1942 and 1990 was Gounod's *Faust,* performed eight times. *Faust* is considered by BJjr to be a very moral story even though it is the story of the "seduction of a woman and her death, and her having a baby which she kills in her insanity. In the long run, there is no greater lesson in the effects of sin and the grace of God in pardoning sinners than in *Faust*" (Interview, BJjr, 28 May 1987).

Rigoletto has been performed six times. BJjr considers *Rigoletto* to be a strong lesson against evil and wickedness. "Although Rigoletto is a wicked and evil man himself, he gets back exactly what he has been bringing to the other characters" (Interview, BJjr, 28 May 1987).

Aida has been performed six times. According to BJjr, *Aida* is a lesson in betrayal, tyranny, and treason. There is no sexual immorality presented in the opera. Some viewers have been troubled by the presentation of Egyptian gods, priests, and priestesses on the stage, however (Interview, BJjr, 28 May 1987).

Other operas performed include *Il Trovatore* (six times); *Lucia di Lammermoor* (five times); *Tosca* (five times); *The Barber of Seville* (four times); *Samson and Delilah* (four times); and *Romeo et Juliette, Madame Butterfly, The Magic Flute, Mefistofele, The Merry Wives of Windsor, Nabucco, Norma, Andrea Chenier,* and *Fidelio.* (All information taken from "Opera Productions" [FAO].)

[31] The last American performance of *La Juive* had been at the San Francisco Opera in 1936.

[32] John Ardoin, *Musical America,* May 1963, p. 14. Ardoin wrote, "The strength of the production was more visual than vocal. Conductor Gustafson designed the handsome

sets which took on a different function in each act. . . . Projections were used for the atmospheric backgrounds. . . . The costumes and stage direction were both by Eva Carrier, and both were of the highest order. The chorus groupings in particular were imaginative and resourceful. . . . The university's excellent chorus sang with vigor and authority. The school's orchestra was not as strong as it might be."

[33]The President continued, "We do not put on performances which are immoral or suggestive. . . . There is nothing about them any spiritual man or woman would find offensive in any way" (BJjr to Mrs. Melvin Renalds, 9 January 1964 [GF]).

[34]Interview, BJjr, 28 May 1987. The operas were usually sung in their original language, a practice which kept the story somewhat obscure. "I think it's better if you don't know what they're singing about," BJjr commented half seriously.

[35]This widely known radio orchestra performed 25 November 1947.

[36]Performers who have graced the University stage include guitarists Andrés Segovia, Christopher Parkening, and the Romeros; violinists Henryk Szeryng and Fritz Kreisler; pianists Byron Janis, Lili Kraus, Phillipe Entremont, and Gina Bachauer; opera stars Kirsten Flagstad, Norman Thomas, Jan Peerce, Eileen Farrell, Jerome Hines, Robert Merrill, James McCracken, and Sherrill Milnes; the Eastman Brass Quintet and the Empire Brass Quintet; the Curtis String Quartet; the Norman Luboff Choir; the Roger Wagner Chorale; the King's Singers; the Detroit Symphony; the French National Orchestra; the Japan Philharmonic Orchestra; actors Hal Holbrook, Claude Rains, and Raymond Massey; and mime Marcel Marceau; to list a few.

[37]Over the years the number of programs in the series has varied from as many as twelve in 1940-41 to as few as four in 1969-70, but the trend has been toward fewer programs largely because of the exorbitant fees demanded by topflight performers. Also, modern programs have to be more "popular" in the sense that they require a broader audience appeal to compete equally with other artist series that are now available in the Greenville community.

[38]Interview, BJjr, 28 May 1987.

[39]When one performer refused to have a printed program, BJjr wrote the agent.

> I am a little concerned that Mr. Massey is not having a printed program, since it does not give us any idea in advance of the material he will be handling.
>
> I know Mr. Massey is not only a fine actor but he is also a gentleman and a man of great discernment and good taste. However, quite often material that would be acceptable in the theater and cause no problem and give no offense to a member of the audience might be entirely out of place here in this Christian institution.
>
> Our standards in these matters are extremely high—so high in fact that sometimes we are accused of being old fogies. In preparing the Shakespearean prompt books for our own Classic Players, we expurgate expressions and cut out some scenes which would be included in the average performance. Even Shakespeare can't cuss here! We cannot have any type of profanity, even such mild profanity as "hell" and "dam" [sic]. Such expressions as "my God" or "for God's sake," or any use of the Lord's name profanely—or as an expletive—we do not permit. (BJjr to Mr. Mason Bliss, 11 September 1958 [GF: Artist Series]

Interviewees Monroe Parker, Karl Keefer, and DG, all familiar with the guest artists of their era, indicated that the artists were most accommodating in this regard.

[40]BJjr preached, "We want you students to learn something about everything possible. . . . You'll hear great minds . . . commune with your mind in the language of beauty. It will help your soul stretch and grow. It helps your character to develop some muscles and some stamina—a broadness of culture and an appreciation of beauty will make your whole life rich. You will begin to understand what great [artists] are trying to say. You'll begin to hear the voice of men—dead and gone to dust—as they speak through

their art to you. It will do something for you." More than this, "you will be able to use it in service for the Lord" (MS, BJjr, chapel talk, 16 October 1951).

[41]MS, BJjr, chapel talk, 9 October 1953. The student cut the performance of Metropolitan Opera star Claramae Turner.

[42]See MS, BJjr, chapel talks, 26 November 1949; 16 October 1951; 9 October 1953; and 28 October 1963.

[43]MS, BJjr, chapel talk, 9 October 1953.

[44]Gail Gingery recalled that "John Charles Thomas, the great American baritone, came for a concert and was just marvelous. I still remember him singing *Figaro,* the main aria from that opera in which he would do a great whistle. It was just fantastic. We also had Fritz Kreisler. He must have been in his eighties. He could hardly dodder out onto the stage. His accompanist appeared to be even older and they just barely got out on the stage, but once they got there, nobody doubted that they were there because the playing—the piano and the violin—was just marvelous" (Interview, Gail Gingery, 5 June 1987). Another student recalled the recitals of Norman Thomas and of Kirsten Flagstad and Astrid Varnay, and the concerts of the Detroit Symphony, the Buffalo Symphony, and the French National Orchestra as being "topnotch" (Interview, Karl Keefer, 27 July 1987).

[45]Amy J. Marshall, "Artist Series: The Beginning of a Tradition," *Collegian,* vol. 6, no. 2, 1 October 1992. See also "Press Release, Salzburg Mozarteum Orchestra," 23 March 1956 (GF: Public Relations).

[46]BJjr to W.O.H. Garman, 18 June 1959.

[47]BJjr to Norman Mayfield, 23 April 1963. Mayfield maintained that Farrell was a jazz singer who should not have been allowed to perform.

[48]Hamilton was known as a man of strong Christian character and conviction who had attended BJsr's early citywide evangelistic campaigns in the Northeast.

[49]Stephen D. Pepper, *Bob Jones University Collection of Religious Art: Italian Paintings* (Greenville, S.C.: BJU Press, 1984), p. iv. Hamilton at one time owned masterpieces like Bellini's *Feast of the Gods,* now in the National Gallery, and the Botticini altarpiece in the Metropolitan Museum.

[50]It was reported in "Old Masters Gather in Greenville" (*Southern Living Magazine,* March, 1988, p. 23) that collecting was begun in 1951 with an acquisition fund of thirty thousand dollars.

[51]Murray Havens, "Foreword," in BJU, *Selected Paintings from the Bob Jones University Collection of Sacred Art* (Greenville, S.C.: BJU, 1952). See also Pepper, *BJU Collection: Italian,* pp.vi-vii.

[52]Reasons for this disfavor may be explained by the compositional style; the common use of the heroic, mythological, or biblical for subject matter; or the sheer size of many of the canvases. Some baroque works in the BJU collection measure 75 x 96 inches, 86 x 118 inches, or larger (Interview, Joan Davis, 2 June 1987).

[53]David H. Steele Jr., *Baroque Paintings from the Bob Jones University Collection* (Raleigh, N.C.: North Carolina Museum of Art, 1984), p. 5.

[54]"Old Masters," *Southern Living,* p. 23.

[55]*St. Vincent, Martyr* by Goya, *Madonna and Child with Angel* by Sandro Botticelli, *Madonna and Child with Infant St. John and Angels* by Francesco di Giovanni Botticini, *The Nativity* by David Ghirlandaio, *The Cross Laid Upon Jesus* by Sebastiano del Piombo, *The Visit of the Queen of Sheba to Solomon* and *Christ in Gethsemane* by Jacopo Tintoretto, *Mary Magdalene* by Paolo Veronese, and *Christ Crowned With Thorns* by Jusepe de Ribera. The *Christ Crowned with Thorns,* or *Head of Christ,* was named one of the "best Spanish paintings in the world" by José Gudiol, Director of the Spanish

Library of Art at Barcelona. ("Spanish Art Authority Discovers Emphasis on Display in Galleries," unknown paper, dated 22 September 1961 [Art Gallery scrapbook]).

[56]Among the art historians on whom BJjr has relied are Max Friedlaender of Amsterdam; Herman Voss of Munich; Roberto Longhi of Florence; William Sueda and Stephen Pepper of the United States; Alfred Scharf (who wrote the "Introduction to the Italian Paintings," *The BJU Collection of Religious Paintings: Italian and French Paintings* [Greenville, S.C.: BJU, 1962], pp. 11-14); José Gudiol (who wrote the "Introduction to the Spanish Paintings," *Art of the BJU Collection, Vol. 2: Flemish, Dutch, German, and Spanish Paintings,* pp. 315-16); Georges Marlier (who wrote the "Introduction to the Flemish, Dutch and German Paintings," pp. 195-201); and Hans Tietze (who wrote the "Foreword," *Bob Jones University Collection of Religious Paintings* [Greenville, S.C.: BJU Press, 1954], pp. i-iii). For personal recollections of these and other art historians, art dealers, and art buffs, see BJjr, *Cornbread,* pp. 49-51.

[57]"Open House for Bowen Museum," *Little Moby's Post,* vol. 25, no. 5, January 1952, pp. 1, 4. See also Interview, Joan Davis, 2 June 1987; corroborated by *Little Moby's Post,* "Open House." See also Stenholm diary, 11 April 1944. The Bowen Collection was donated to BJC in 1943 and opened to the public on 11 April 1944.

[58]The number of paintings originally displayed in the gallery is in dispute. BJjr recalls twenty-five paintings in the first gallery (in Pepper, *BJU Collection: Italian,* p. v). A published report in *Little Moby's Post* ("Open House" pp. 1, 4), and the *Atlanta Journal-Constitution* (Wylly Folk St. John, "You Can Make An Easter Pilgrimage," March 1952), number the paintings at twenty-eight. See also Pepper, *BJU Collection: Italian,* p. iv; David H. Steele Jr., *Baroque Paintings.*

[59]*BJU Collection of Religious Paintings,* 1954.

[60]DG and Murray Havens, "The New Fine Arts Building," *Voice of the Alumni,* vol. 30, no. 2, September 1956, pp. 1-2. See also Joseph Aronson, *Furniture in the Bob Jones University Collection* (Greenville, S.C.: BJU Press, 1976). Aronson, in his "Foreword," says, "The Bob Jones University collection [of furniture] may be unique in America in developing one single theme: the earliest phases in form and decoration of furniture *as we know it,* the groundwork of an evolutionary idiom in furniture as an art form."

[61]Tondi are relatively small, circular paintings. Those in the BJU collection all depict the Madonna and are displayed on walls of black marble. The other rooms display only pictures from the locale and period after which each room is named.

[62]Elmer Rumminger, "The New Art Gallery," *Voice of the Alumni,* vol. 30, no. 3, October 1956, pp. 1, 3.

[63]Some of the newer works included *Christ on the Cross* and *The Dead Abel* by Rubens, *Madonna and Child* and *Mother of Sorrows* by Anthony Van Dyck, *The Hiding of Moses* by Sebastien Bourdon, *Song of Miriam* by Luca Giordano, and *Abner Stabbed by Joab* by Lucas Cranach the Elder.

[64]"Gallery Praised," *Voice of the Alumni,* vol. 34, no. 9, April 1961, p. 2 .

[65]"BJU Obtains Seven Paintings by England's Benjamin West," *Greenville (S.C.) Piedmont,* n.d., 1965 (Art Gallery scrapbook). West served as "Painter to the King" and was one of the founders of the Royal Academy of London. These works are all extremely large. *The Ascension of Our Lord,* for example, measures 17.5 feet in height.

[66]BJU, *Supplement to the Catalogue of the Art Collection: Paintings Acquired 1963-1968* (Greenville, S.C.: BJU Press, 1968), pp. 185-91. See also Wright, *Fortress,* p. 303. There were to have been more than thirty pictures in the series, only seven of which were completed. The paintings are *Esau and Jacob Presented to Isaac, Moses and Aaron Before Pharaoh, The Brazen Serpent, Isaiah's Lips Anointed with Fire, Christ*

Coming Up Out of the Jordan, The Ascension of Our Lord, and *Peter Preaching at Pentecost.*

[67]*Art Journal,* Winter 1965, vol. 25, no. 2, pp. 154-62. Participants in the symposium included Dr. David Carter, director, Montreal Museum of Fine Arts; Dr. Charles Parkhurst, director, Baltimore Museum of Art; Dr. John Coolidge, director, Fogg Art Museum, Harvard University; Dr. Theodore Rousseau, curator of paintings, Metropolitan Museum of Art, New York City; Dr. Anthony Clark, director, Minneapolis Institute of Arts; and Dr. John Walker, director, National Gallery of Art in Washington, D.C. See also, photo, *Greenville (S.C.) Piedmont,* 15 November 1965; and Wright, *Fortress,* p. 327.

[68]"A New Museum for BJU," *Voice of the Alumni,* vol. 39, no. 4, December 1965, pp. 8-10. The Cole Collection was a gift to the University and came from the Imperial Chapel in Vienna. Among the items are several gifts from Marie Antoinette to her mother, Empress Maria Theresa.

[69]See "The Bob Jones University Collection of Religious Art," *Art Journal,* vol. 25, no. 2 (Winter), 1965, pp. 154-62. New works displayed for the first time in 1965 included Guercino's *King David Penitent,* Dolci's *Madonna and Child,* and a sixteenth-century carved ceiling eighty feet in length, installed as part of a Renaissance corridor ("A New Museum," p. 9). Also added to the collection was Rembrandt's *Head of Christ.* The gallery contained "distinguished examples" of the Spanish, French, German, Dutch, and Flemish Schools, and the galleries were enriched by a number of fine paintings, "a few of which are of real art-historical importance" (*Art Journal,* p. 156).

[70]"A New Museum," p. 10. The exact number of the paintings used in all of the NBC film projects is unknown. "BJ Paintings on Telecast " (*Greenville [S.C.] Piedmont,* n.d.), reports that nine paintings were used in the production of "The Coming of Christ."

[71]Interview, Joan Davis, 2 June 1987. See BJU, *Supplement: 1963-1968.* See also "BJU Has New Director of Art Gallery," *Voice of the Alumni,* October 1970, p. 5.

[72]Tina Crawford, "BJU Art Gallery, Museum Evolve into Finest in Western Hemisphere," *Collegian,* vol. 4, no. 6, 21 November 1990.

[73]Many of the newspapers and magazines that have written about the gallery have brought out the Catholicity of the collection. For example, see Ruth Berenson, "Ars Sacra in the Peruna Belt," *National Review,* 20 July 1973; and Richard, "Baroque," *Washington Post.* BJjr usually answered the criticism that many of the paintings were executed by "Catholics" with a short history of the Protestant Church, pointing out that all of the arts in the fourteenth and fifteenth centuries, before the influence of the Reformation, were under the domination of the Roman Catholic Church and were, for the most part, religious in nature and reflected the theology of the Roman Catholic Church (BJjr to Firman Smith, 5 December 1957). The Catholic Church was the repository of painting, sculpture, music, literature, and nearly every other activity of cultural life. Thus, the paintings in the collection dating from the fourteenth through sixteenth centuries, or from countries which after the Reformation remained under the sway of Romanism, portray religious events in a "Romish" manner (BJjr to Walter L. Wilson, 12 December 1957; and BJjr to Jerry Counts, 1 November 1975).

[74]BJjr to Norman Mayfield, 23 April 1963.

[75]BJjr to Larry Carrier, 9 January 1979.

[76]BJjr to Mr. George A. Bowdler Sr., 18 December 1957.

[77]For more information on Unusual Films, see Wright, *Fortress.* Also significant is the fact that the cinema department and all of its productions until 1990 were directed by a woman. This fact was cited by a UPI story reprinted in the *Voice of the Alumni,* vol. 37, no. 10, May 1964, pp. 1-2. Katherine Stenholm indicated that of more than 3,700

feature films to date, only a handful have been made by women, and she was one of the first, in 1952 (Interview, Katherine Stenholm, 8 June 1987).

[78]" 'The Unbeatable Game' Is Booked for Run at Philadelphia Theater," *Philadelphia Courier,* 9 May 1925.

[79]Interview. Ralph McGilvra, February 1989. BJsr "pulled several moving picture cameras, film cans, and light banks out from a storage closet, handed them to me and in essence said, 'Learn how to use this stuff and try to make a film about the college.' " Though McGilvra remembers that he tried to learn how to use the equipment, it was too big an order, and he gave up after several weeks.

[80]See "Rank's Retreat," *Time,* 24 October 1949, pp. 96-97, for information on the Rank Studios, the largest film studio in Great Britain.

[81]Wright, *Fortress,* p. 167. See also MS, BJjr, chapel talk, 11 October 1950; and Lucille B. Green, "Widely Acclaimed Films Produced at University," *Greenville (S.C.) News,* 2 October 1967.

[82]The studio adjoined Rodeheaver Auditorium and included a sound stage, offices, costuming and make-up rooms, editing rooms, and sound recording rooms, as well as cinema classrooms ("New Studio," *Little Moby's Post,* vol. 9, no. 6, May-June 1950, p. 2). The cost of the total project was estimated at $150,000, including construction and equipment.

[83]Katherine Corne was reared in Hendersonville, North Carolina, and had a long acquaintance with Hollywood movies. Prior to attending BJC as a student in 1935, she was the movie critic for the Hendersonville newspaper and wrote reviews weekly. Every Hollywood film that played in Hendersonville between 1931 and 1935—the "Golden Age of Hollywood"—fell under her critical gaze. During this time she also directed community and school pageants and taught a weekly women's Bible study at her church. As a result of her school grades and community service, she was offered a full scholarship to Wellesley College but instead chose to attend BJC (Interview, Katherine Stenholm, 8 June 1987).

[84]Her first directorial experience came in 1939 for a production of *As You Like It.* Katherine was a sophomore in the College and was assigned by BJjr to direct the rehearsals for a four-week period while he was away giving Curtain Calls. Her first solo opportunity to direct came in 1940 for *Comedy of Errors,* for which she did her own prompt book and blocking. She assisted in the directing of the first *Faust* as well.

After graduating from BJC, she married Gilbert Stenholm and became a faculty member teaching speech and dramatic production courses. She completed a Master of Arts degree in Interpretative Speech from Northwestern University in Evanston, Illinois, and completed the course work for a Ph.D. in speech. She also had leading roles in several BJC Shakespearean productions and directed numerous Vespers, Shakespearean productions, and operas (Interview, Katherine Stenholm, 8 June 1987). (For more on Gilbert and Katherine Stenholm, see Chapter 25.)

[85]Green, "Acclaimed Films." She adapted one of Sternod's techniques, used in the Hollywood production of *Mutiny on the Bounty,* to give the impression of large, violent waves in a storm scene for *Wine of Morning.*

[86]Wright, *Fortress,* p. 163.

[87]"Unusual Films," *Little Moby's Post,* vol. 10, no. 3, February 1951, p. 5. The project was delayed when BJjr was hospitalized with pleurisy.

[88]"Light of the World," *Little Moby's Post,* vol. 10, no. 4, April 1951, p. 4.

[89]Interview, Fred Pachter, film historian, Unusual Films, 19 February 1988. *Macbeth* had a cast of more than sixty members drawn from University students and faculty, and the film's music was composed and conducted by Richard Girvin of the music faculty

and recorded by the University Orchestra ("BJU Begins Its Twenty-Fifth Year," *Little Moby's Post,* vol. 25-26, no. 3, September 1951, p. 1).

[90]Katherine Stenholm to George Wilson, 31 December 1951 (Unusual Films: BG television file). Unusual Films apparently produced three complete *Hour of Decision* programs and produced either sound or film footage for several more. The three complete programs, numbers 15, 16, and 17 of the *Hour of Decision,* cost a total of $2,021.83. In gratitude for the work that was done, the BG Evangelistic Association sent a $600 cash bonus to be split among the production staff and the musicians who worked on the project.

[91]Green, "Acclaimed Films." Also "Awards Won by Unusual Films," Unusual Films, internal memo, November 1985.

[92]George Gilbert, "Divinity School's Commercial Terms," *Variety,* 23 February 1955. See also "Biographical Sketch, Katherine Corne Stenholm" (Unusual Films: Stenholm personal files); also, *Voice,* May 1957, p. 2. *Frontiers* was broadcast in fifty-four television markets, covering most of the major American metropolitan areas, including Atlanta, Chicago, Detroit, Denver, Los Angeles, Cincinnati, Seattle, and Boston (NBC " 'Frontiers of Faith' with Dr. Bob Jones Jr.," promotion flyer, 22 September 1957 [GF: Public Relations file]).

[93]Katherine Stenholm wrote a technical report of the production's problems and their solutions entitled "*Wine of Morning*—A Film with a Purpose." This appeared in *American Cinematographer,* December 1950. The picture was called "a slightly romanticized story of the life of Barabbas . . . of decidedly religious inspiration," in a report of the Fifth International Congress of Motion Picture School Directors published in the Italian magazine *Bianco e Nero* (quoted in *Voice of the Alumni,* October 1958).

[94]The music was composed and conducted by Joseph Schmoll of the University music faculty ("Big-scale University Film Production," *American Cinematographer,* vol. 35, no. 12, December 1954, p. 625). See also "Sermons on Celluloid," *Philadelphia Enquirer,* 24 October 1954.

[95]Steven Knudsen to Katherine Stenholm, 12 March 1958. Stenholm was invited by the UFPA to be a keynote speaker at this congress on the subject of directing (Don Williams to Katherine Stenholm, 25 March 1958). See also "BJU Movie Chosen for Film Fest," *Greenville (S.C.) Piedmont,* n.d. Also, "Bob Jones University," *Journal of the Society of Motion Picture and Television Engineers,* vol. 69 (November 1960), p. 826. See also "Film Department Praised," *Voice of the Alumni,* vol. 32, no. 3, 1958.

[96]National Evangelical Film Foundation, "Christian Oscars," news release, n.d. See also Katherine Stenholm to Harry Bristow, 7 May 1957 (Unusual Films: Bristow file).

[97]In 1964 *Red Runs the River* won four medals from the National Evangelical Film Foundation, including best motion picture and best actor (Harry Bristow to Katherine Stenholm, 30 March 1964). *River* was also selected that year by the University Film Producers Association to represent the United States at the International Congress of Motion-Picture and Television Schools in Budapest, Hungary, and also represented the United States at the International Book Fair in Cracow, Poland (Blaine Watson to Katherine Stenholm, 22 July 1963 [Unusual Films: UFPA file]; see also "Awards Won by Unusual Films" [Unusual Films: Internal memo, November 1985]). For the premiere of this film, nearly twelve thousand attended the showings in Greenville ("Red Runs the River, A Feature-Length Civil War Epic," *Voice of the Alumni,* vol. 36, no. 9, April 1963, p. 1).

[98]During location filming in Russia, Dr. Stenholm was taken ill and production was delayed. Tim Rogers was subsequently named as Director of Unusual Films and head of the BJU Cinema Department.

[99]In 1989, for example, Dave Burkhardt's senior project (on a Georgia old-time steam railroad company) placed second nationally in the Motion Picture Arts and

Sciences 16th Annual Student Film Awards Competition ("Cinema Student Wins Academy Award," *Collegian,* July 1989).

[100]Reported in "BJU Among Big Three in Cinema," *Voice of the Alumni,* vol. 31, no. 4, October 1957.

[101]United States Office of Education, *Motion Picture Production Facilities of Selected Colleges and Universities,* bulletin, 1963, OE-51005, no. 15, p. 237.

[102]Interview, Katherine Stenholm, 8 June 1987.

[103]DG, sample letter, n.d. (FAO).

[104]Interview, BJiii, 3 June 1987. As one administrator wrote,

> If the Christian is to function as a member of society and communicate the gospel effectively, he needs to understand the world in which he lives; and he needs to be able to deport himself and to communicate fluently so that what he says is clear and cogent, even to the ears of a Godless society. The Bible does not forbid the Christian from seeking and enjoying that which is beautiful, but rather encourages him to take into his life that which is good and honest and beautiful and to use discrimination in his choices (Phil. 4:8). In the case of opera or any special forms of music, art, or literature, we will exercise discriminating choices to bring to our students the finest examples of great masterworks to aid their cultural education. As a Christian institution we will also protect our students from degrading, worldly influences and by example and word teach them principles of moral choice so that they will make the right choices in their own lives. (DG to unknown, n.d. [FAO: Sample letter file])

[105]BJsr to James Oliver Buswell, 12 May 1949 (GF: Buswell file).

Chapter 18: "Brains are No Substitute for God!"

[1]MS, BJsr, chapel talk, 21 November 1944 (ABV: 1944).

[2]Ibid.

[3]While not a member of any regional or national association, BJU was listed in *Accredited Higher Institutions: 1952* as having a teacher training program accredited by the South Carolina State Board of Education (Theresa Birch Wilkins, *Accredited Higher Institutions: 1952* [Washington, D.C.: United States Office of Education, Bulletin, 1952, no. 3], p. 52). The teacher training program has been accredited by the state yearly through this study's publication date. The University of South Carolina accepted BJU graduates unconditionally into graduate programs related to the undergraduate background of the student (p. 92).

[4]"Educational Department Wins National Honor," *Little Moby's Post,* May 1952, p. 1.

[5]The "A's" and "B's" referred to were the levels of teacher certification then available in South Carolina ("Excerpts from a Recent Release Concerning the Educational Progress of the University in 1950-1951," *Little Moby's Post,* vol. 24-25, no. 2, July 1951, p. 1). Students in the School of Education had to maintain a C+ average in order to take the NTE.

[6]"Education News Notes," *Voice of the Alumni,* May 1957, p. 1.

[7]"NTE Scores High," *Voice of the Alumni,* vol. 35, no. 9, April 1962, p. 2.

[8]"High Scores," *Voice of the Alumni,* vol. 36, no. 10, May 1963, p. 2.

[9]"BJU Seniors Score High Again," *Voice of the Alumni,* May 1970, p. 2.

[10]"Greenville Teachers" and "Christian Education," *Voice of the Alumni,* vol. 34, no. 8, March 1961, p. 3.

[11]"Seniors Score High Again."

[12]George H. Dooms, "An Alumnus Speaks," *Voice of the Alumni,* vol. 29, no. 2, 22 September 1955, p. 7. Dooms writes, "We have found that Bob Jones University trained

people are able to fit into any situation and are excellent at any task they are called on to perform. We are glad that being dependable is second nature to Bob Jones students. . . . Another attribute that BJU trained men acquire is punctuality."

[13]"Seniors Rank High on National Test: One Student Achieves 100 Percentile," *Voice of the Alumni,* vol. 35, no. 8, March 1962, p. 1; and "High Scores," p. 2.

[14]Wright, *Fortress,* p. 313. "BJU Accounting Seniors 42% Above National Average," *Voice of the Alumni,* vol. 37, no. 9, March-April 1964, p. 10.

[15]"Lautenbach to Retire," *Voice of the Alumni,* May 1969, pp. 2-3.

[16]"Bob Jones Ministerial Association," *Little Moby's Post,* October 1950, p. 1

[17]"Ministerial Class," *Vintage,* 1961, p. 74.

[18]BJjr, quoted by Margaret Beall Tice, "Bob Jones Campus: The Older We Get, the More Beautiful She Becomes," *Voice of the Alumni,* vol. 45, no. 4, December 1971, p. 10.

[19]Photograph: Pensacola Christian Grade School, *Voice of the Alumni,* vol. 29, no. 5, December 1955, p. 5. Although this is a photo from the 1950s and not of a Bible college, it does make the point that BJU's influence among Christian schools has been enormous. This Christian school had eight full-time teachers and all were BJU graduates, including its founder. From the Pensacola Christian School of 1955 came Pensacola Christian College, the initial faculty of which was almost entirely BJU-educated. See Buzz Baker, "To Win Boys and Girls to the Lord," *Voice of the Alumni,* vol. 41, no. 6, April 1968, pp. 5-6.

[20]From author's personal conversation with B. Myron Cederholm, former president of Pillsbury Baptist Bible College and founder and president of Maranatha Baptist Bible College. These schools include Tennessee Temple College, Pillsbury Baptist Bible College, Maranatha Baptist Bible College, Baptist University of America, Lynchburg Baptist College, Faithway Baptist Bible College, Pensacola Christian College, and most recently, Northland Baptist Bible College.

[21]*"Biblical Viewpoint:* BJU's New Religious Periodical," *Voice of the Alumni,* vol. 40, no. 5, January 1967, p. 1. The first volume focused on Paul's Epistle to the Romans and featured an article by Charles Woodbridge.

[22]"Miss Levinson Honored," *Voice of the Alumni,* vol. 35, no. 1, June 1961, p. 3. Also, "Art Exhibit" and "Alumna Authors Book," *Voice of the Alumni,* vol. 35, no. 8, March 1962, p. 3.

[23]"High Scores," *Voice of the Alumni,* vol. 35, no. 10, May 1962, p. 2.

[24]Albert Clary, "1972 Report to the American Association of Collegiate Registrars and Admissions Officers on *Credit Given by Educational Institutions"* (Washington, D.C.: American Association of Collegiate Registrars and Admissions Officers, 1972), p. 92.

[25]Schools represented included Middlebury College, Boston University, the University of Michigan, the Juilliard School of Music, the Eastman School of Music, Peabody Conservatory, Union Theological Seminary, the University of Chicago, the University of Minnesota, Florida State University, Harvard University, Yale University, Duke University, Pennsylvania State University, the University of Southern California, the University of North Carolina, the University of Virginia, the University of Wisconsin, Northwestern University, and the University of Illinois.

[26]"Project Compassion," *Voice of the Alumni,* vol. 40, no. 4, December 1966, p. 1.

[27]"New Course of Study Announced," *Voice of the Alumni,* vol. 30, no. 7, March 1957, p. 1.

[28]Ken Hay directed the Institute of Christian Service from 1957 through 1971 when he left BJU to become full-time director of the Wilds Christian Camp and Conference Center. Thurman Wisdom was appointed the director until 1978 (Willie Thompson,

"The School of Applied Studies: Past and Present," unpublished paper, BJU, 4 April 1988, p. 2).

[29] Wright, *Fortress,* pp. 287-88. Also, Thompson, "School of Applied Studies."

[30] Enrollment Statistics: First Semester (RO).

[31] R. K. Johnson to Yates B. Britt, 11 October 1961 (GF: Internal Revenue Service file).

[32] The owners of the land, W. Harrell Wilson and his family, filed an application with the Greenville Planning and Zoning Board to rezone the property from residential to commercial status so that they could construct a shopping center on the land bordered by Wade Hampton Boulevard, White Oak Drive, Karen Drive, and Buena Vista Drive, to the west of the campus ("Boundaries of Wilson Property Shown," photo, *Greenville [S.C.] News,* 22 July 1962 [MLA: BJU rezoning controversy notebook, metal file #1]).

[33] In fact, 174 complaints were filed by residents with the zoning board, of which the BJU complaint was one. See Ruth Walker, "Dismissal of BJU Suit Suggested," *Greenville (S.C.) News,* 4 January 1963 (MLA: BJU rezoning controversy notebook, metal file #1).

[34] Ted Shelton, "Council Again Okays Re-zoning Near BJU," *Greenville (S.C.) News,* 23 June 1962 (MLA: BJU rezoning controversy notebook, metal file #1).

[35] "BJU Studies New School Site," *Greenville (S.C.) Piedmont,* 29 May 1962 (MLA: BJU rezoning controversy notebook, metal file #1). Citing the economics of the situation, BJjr stated that the school had spent over $45 million in the Greenville area since moving and was entitled to consideration of its interests. The school went so far as to distribute surveys to the student body to determine the students' choice for relocation (survey form, MLA [BJU rezoning controversy notebook, metal file #1]). The form read, "If BJU moves, I would prefer it to locate in . . ." Pennsylvania, Texas, Missouri, Virginia, Florida, Indiana, Michigan, and California were listed as possible options. Also, at the annual Board of Trustees meeting, board member JRR made the motion for the school to investigate other sites to which to move if the situation in Greenville demanded.

[36] Ruth Walker, "Complaint Filed by Bob Jones University," 6 July 1962, *Greenville (S.C.) News* (MLA: BJU rezoning controversy notebook, metal file #1). See also Sam Ayers, "BJU Asks Court to Halt Zoning," *Greenville (S.C.) Piedmont,* 5 July 1962 (MLA: BJU rezoning controversy notebook, metal file #1).

[37] At a hearing, the presiding judge, the Master at Equity, found that the 174 complainants had failed to file their objections properly and within the time limits required by the law. The complaints were therefore to be ignored. He also found that creating a buffer zone of residential land between BJU and commercial interests was unnecessary for the welfare of the community at large (Walker, "Dismissal").

[38] Wilson sold the land to Bubba Cain of Cain Realty, who tried and failed to develop the whole of it. He built a strip shopping center bordering Wade Hampton Boulevard and owned the land for several years before selling it to Shaw, who offered it to BJU. The Wilson land had originally been promised to BJU by the chamber of commerce in 1946 but was one of the parcels for which money was not raised, and the owners were uncooperative.

[39] Enrollment Statistics: First Semester (RO).

[40] All figures derived from "Enrollment Statistics: First Semester," n.d. (RO). All enrollment figures are for the first semester. BJU does not keep enrollment figures for the second semester of each year. Rather, the school reports matriculated students for second semester of each school year. "Grad./Spec." indicate students on the graduate level and those admitted under some type of special status.

[41] *Catalogue, 1947-48,* p. 30.

[42] *Catalogue, 1970-71,* p. 27.

[43]"Significant Change in Loan Fund Plan," *Little Moby's Post*, vol. 25, no. 6, March 1952, p. 1. Contained in this article is the announcement that 50 percent of all funds received were to be used for missionary projects around the world.

[44]Only one of the buildings in the Quadrangle was for the Academy—the Main. The other three buildings contained the University Science Department and laboratories, the Home Economics Department, and the campus infirmary.

[45]The War Memorial Chapel was constructed as part of the original plant, on the west end of the University Student Center. The chapel was intended as a memorial for BJC and BJU students who had been killed as soldiers in the armed forces, a fact that is underscored by two brass howitzer shell casings that sit at the front of the room. The chapel is also intended as a memorial for BJC and BJU faculty and staff who have died "in spiritual battle" while teaching and working for the Lord, a fact that is underscored by bronze plaques in the foyer that bear their names and birth and death dates. The chapel originally had one painting, a primitive-style mural painted across the entire front wall. The picture depicted a millennial scene of swords being beaten into plowshares and spears into pruning hooks. The mural was painted by the father of Nate Saint, a missionary martyred by Auca Indians in South America in the 1950s. The seating originally was folding theater seats, which were replaced by regular wooden pews in 1965. When the school obtained the West canvases, the Saint mural was hidden by dark wood paneling so that *The Ascension* could be hung at the front. In 1988 the electronic organ in the room was replaced by an eighteen-rank pipe organ, which the school miraculously obtained from a Methodist church in Phoenix, Arizona (Yvette Goubeaud, "War Memorial Chapel Ages with Grace," *Collegian,* vol. 5, no. 13, 16 April 1992).

[46]For details about the Dixon-McKenzie Dining Common, see Fred Davis, "The Dixon-McKenzie Football Field," *Voice of the Alumni,* vol. 39, no. 6, January 1966, pp. 3-7. When constructed in 1966, the new Dining Common was state-of-the-art in food service. The main dining room, the Varsity Room, designed to seat 2,508 students at 114 tables for family-style meals, measured 298 feet by 85 feet, with a 30-foot ceiling (more than 750,000 cubic feet of space). The building also contained three other dining rooms: the Family Room for faculty with young children, the Faculty Room (or Red Room) for faculty with older children, and the Administrative Dining Room (or Blue Room). The Dining Common was designed so that all dining rooms could be operating at the same time and be promptly served. The kitchen area contained a bakery, a vegetable and meat preparation department, and a dairy department, plus huge ovens (large enough to cook five thousand pounds of meat at one time), convection ovens (large enough to cook sixty-six trays of food at a time), giant freezers, refrigerators, and mixers. There was also a large warehouse located under the Varsity Room.

[47]"The Little Angels of Korea," Artist Series, 7 December 1970 (Cultural and Activities Calendar of BJU, 1970 [GF: Public Relations]). Story recounted by Rob Loach.

[48]Author's recollection.

[49]"Wanted: 7,300 Seats," *Voice of the Alumni,* vol. 44, no. 3, October 1970, p. 3.

[50]Margaret Beall Tice, "The Construction," *Voice of the Alumni,* vol. 47, no. 4, December 1973, pp. 8-11. The total project cost more than $4 million.

[51]"Amphitorium Receives Award," *Voice of the Alumni,* vol. 48, no. 4, February 1975, p. 3.

[52]"Society Outings," *Little Moby's Post,* February 1948, p. 1.

[53]James D. Edwards to Merl F. Holderman, 2 December 1954 (GF: Bethel College file). Edwards states that one purpose of the societies is to encourage participation and that "an exceptionally high percentage of student participation is secured." Competition

offered at this time included soccer, speedball, basketball, softball, track, volleyball, tennis, badminton, table tennis, horseshoes, and archery.

[54]*Vintage,* 1981, p. 148.

[55]The University purchased the first set of soccer and basketball uniforms for the pioneer societies and took a more positive approach in general. The students' response to the pioneer effort was excellent, which was gratifying to the administration.

[56]"Campus Radicals Not Welcome: Bob Jones University Goes Own Quiet Way," *Wall Street Journal,* 27 March 1967.

[57]*McCall's,* March 1967.

[58]*Esquire,* 1967. See also Larry L. King, "Buckle in the Bible Belt," *Harper's,* June 1966, pp. 51-56; and Robert G. Sherrill, "Bob Jones University: New Curricula for Bigotry," *Nation,* 29 March 1965, pp. 326-33.

[59]Gil Rowland, "Fundamentalists Envied," quoted in *Voice of the Alumni,* vol. 43, no. 14, April 1970, p. 22.

[60]MS, chapel talk, BJjr, 4 February 1965 (ABV: 1965).

[61]BJjr, "Thirty-seventh Academic Year Begins," *Voice of the Alumni,* vol. 37, no. 3, 22 October 1963, p. 1.

[62]MS, BJjr, chapel talk, 29 January 1965 (ABV: 1965). This message dealt with the Air Force Academy cheating scandal of 1965 and stressed personal discipline and accountability. See also MS, BJjr, chapel talk, 9 February 1965 (ABV: 1965), in which BJjr preached on Samson and self-control. He said, "Samson wasn't blinded when the Philistines put out his eyes; he was already blind to truth and values when he stayed with Delilah and sold God out. . . . You can sacrifice God's blessing for the smile of some ecclesiastic. You can sacrifice truth for money. You can sell out the Word of God for the approval of men. . . . Make up your mind that there are some things worth dying for and there are some things more important than anything you may get in this life."

[63]MS, BJjr, chapel talk, 25 January 1965 (ABV: 1965).

[64]Ibid., 28 May 1965 (ABV: 1965).

[65]Wright, *Fortress,* pp. 290-91.

[66]Johnson, *Builder,* p. 351.

[67]Interview, Beneth Peters Jones, 9 May 1996.

[68]Sam W. Small, "The Dream of Bob Jones," unknown paper, n.d. (MLA 9-43).

[69]At the Founder's death, when most who knew him were turned to affectionate reminiscences and praise to God for His faithful old servant, T. W. Wilson of the BG team, the one who had accused BJsr of being influenced by the "green-eyed old Monster of Jealousy," announced his intention to attend the funeral. The Jones family denied him an invitation but said that any other member of the BG team would be welcome to attend. In a telegram to Wilson, BJjr wrote, "See from the papers that you are representing the Graham organization at the funeral. In view of the vicious letter you wrote my father some years ago, a man who had done everything for you, the family prefers that you not attend the funeral. . . . When my father's heart had been broken by your wicked and unkind letter, I wrote you without his knowledge and urged you for the sake of your own conscience to apologize while he was still living. We do not want you coming to stand with pious pretense over his casket now" (BJjr to T. W. Wilson, telegram, 16 January 1968 [GF: Wilson file]).

[70]"Rugged Fundamentalist," *Columbia (S.C.) State,* 18 January 1968.

[71]"Dr. Jones' Consistency," *Greenville (S.C.) Piedmont,* 19 January 1968.

[72]BJjr, "A Tribute and a Pledge," quoted in Johnson, *Builder,* pp. 356-60.

[73]Noel Smith, "Dr. Bob Jones, Sr.," *Voice of the Alumni,* memorial issue, 1968, p. 7.

[74]BJjr, "Tribute," quoted in Johnson, *Builder,* p. 356.

Chapter 19: Bob Jones III

[1]Lucille B. Green, "Bob Jones III Takes Over as President of University," *Greenville (S.C.) News,* 3 June 1971. See also "Bob Jones University Has New President and Chancellor," *Bob Jones University Newsletter,* vol 34, no. 17, June 1971. See also Wright, *Fortress,* p. 343.

[2]Wright, *Fortress,* p. 344. Also reported in Johnson, *Builder,* p. 265.

[3]Interview, Beneth Peters Jones, 9 May 1996.

[4]Ernest I. Reveal was a smallish man noted for his soulwinning zeal and holy life. Crippled as a child, Reveal wore a steel leg brace and walked with difficulty. He had been a "drunken bricklayer" but was converted as a result of reading the Bible, and he gave himself immediately to "the Lord's work." He was trained for rescue mission work by Pat Withrow in Charleston, West Virginia. Highly individualistic, "Pappy" Reveal visited the University campus many times, speaking in chapel and Bible Conference services. He served on the board, and a men's dormitory is named for him. For more on Reveal, see BJjr, *Cornbread,* pp. 113-18.

[5]Paul Vanaman pastored in Clarkston, Michigan, until his drowning on a church missions trip early in 1992. He was a man of great wit and humor, who, according to Beneth Jones, had a unique gift of ministry and "a huge heart" that caused him to "make countless phone calls and write numerous letters just to say, 'We love you. We are praying for you.'" He did special things to "encourage and brighten the days" of BJiii. His death was a great personal loss to BJiii, as well as a loss to the University (Interview, Beneth Peters Jones).

[6]Reveal's expression "hooked on at the Mercy Seat" connotes that Reveal prayed for BJiii regularly and often. Dr. Reveal was known as a "prayer warrior" because of his fervent prayer life and childlike faith in the power of God. See Johnson, *Builder,* pp. 265-68.

[7]Interview, Beneth Peters Jones.

[8]Quoted in Johnson, *Builder,* p. 266.

[9]Interview, Beneth Peters Jones.

[10]Ibid.

[11]In 1955-56, BJiii had completed most of his high school requirements and therefore took University classes part-time. He graduated from Bob Jones Academy in the spring of 1956 but had entered BJU in the fall of 1955.

[12]Interview, Beneth Peters Jones.

[13]Johnson, *Builder,* p. 268.

[14]*Bob Jones University Bulletin,* vol. 23, no. 6, February 1960, p. 198.

[15]*Bob Jones University Bulletin,* vol. 35, no. 6, February 1962, p. 212.

[16]*Bob Jones University Bulletin,* vol. 38, no. 5, February 1965, p. 215. See also Wright, *Fortress,* pp. 290-91.

[17]Interview, Beneth Peters Jones.

[18]Larry L. King, "Bob Jones University: The Buckle on the Bible Belt," *Harper's,* 232:51-58, June 1966.

[19]Quoted in James M. Wall, "Bob Jones Speaks, General Motors Listens," *Christian Century,* 30 March 1977, p. 291.

[20]Kenneth R. Clark, "Television's Holy War Rages On," *Greenville (S.C.) Piedmont,* 25 March 1981.

[21]Quoted in Perry C. Cotham, ed., *Christian Social Ethics* (Grand Rapids, Mich.: Baker Book House, 1979), p. 166.

[22]The broadcast was eventually sponsored by Proctor and Gamble, who picked it up only days before the scheduled broadcast.

[23]*Phil Donahue Show,* videotape, January 1982 (BJU: Media Center Tape Library).

[24]Quoted in Wright, *Fortress,* p. 349.

[25]James Johnson to BJiii, 24 January 1996 (GF: Johnson file).

[26]Interview, Beneth Peters Jones.

[27]Ibid.

[28]Ibid., corroborated by DG.

[29]Riddle, "Learning Is Fundamental," *Atlanta Journal-Constitution,* 31 December 1995.

[30]Interview, DG, 9 May 1996.

[31]Ibid.; corroborated by Beneth Peters Jones.

[32]BJjr's disdain for computers was well known on the campus and was a topic he often touched on with humor.

[33]Interviews, Beneth Peters Jones and DG. Personal correspondence, BJiii to Dan Turner, 16 October 1995.

[34]Interview, Beneth Peters Jones.

Chapter 20: "It's Religion, Not Race"

[1]Each section of the U.S. had laws aimed at minority groups. Native Americans faced discrimination in the Midwest and Far West but not in the East or South. Blacks faced discrimination in the South but not in the Far West. Other groups fared similarly. For example, a California legislative report of 1876 stated: "the Chinese are inferior to any race God ever made. . . . [They] have no souls to save, and if they have, they are not worth saving." In response to pressures from the West, Congress passed the "Chinese Exclusion Act" in 1882 to restrict the flow of Orientals into the U.S. (Taken from Steven Tozer, Paul Violas, and Guy Senese, *School and Society: Educational Practice as Social Expression* [New York: McGraw-Hill, 1993], pp. 120-21). For more, see Ronald E. Butchart, *Northern Schools, Southern Blacks, and Reconstruction Freedmens Education, 1862-1875,* (Westport, Conn.: Greenwood Press, 1980). Robert A. Margo, *Race and Schooling in the South, 1880-1950.* (Chicago: Univ. of Chicago Press, 1960). Leonard Dinnerstein, *Ethnic Americans: A History of Immigration and Assimilation.* (New York: Harper Row, 1987).

[2]Gary Orfield, *The Reconstruction of Southern Education* (New York: John Wiley & Sons, 1969), pp. 356-61. *Brown* set aside the principle established in *Plessy v. Ferguson* (1896)—that facilities may be "separate but equal." In *Brown,* the court ruled that "separate educational facilities are inherently unequal" and are therefore unconstitutional. The Court further directed that all school facilities be desegregated "with all deliberate haste" (*Brown-sequel* [1955]). For further information on the effects of *Brown,* see Raymond Wolter, *The Burden of Brown: Thirty Years of School Desegregation* (Knoxville: University of Tennessee Press, 1984).

[3]Orfield, *Reconstruction,* p. 357.

[4]MS, BJjr, chapel talk, 13 February 1970 (ABV: 1970).

[5]Bjsr, radio address, 17 April 1960. BJsr said, "There is no trouble between a born-again white man and a born-again colored man. . . . Born-again, Bible-believing Christians do not have trouble. . . . Let's use our heads. Let's be intelligent. Let's not try to kick the Bible off the center table. We are one in Christ. There is no trouble between a colored Christian and a white Christian. They operate as individuals and deal with each other as Christians who have their citizenship in heaven."

[6]MS, BJjr, chapel talk, 18 March 1965 (ABV: 1965). BJjr preached a five-message series on the law in chapel, in which he dealt with the Christian's responsibility to moral

law and social justice. BJjr said, "The legitimate thing to do is to get a law changed if it's wrong, but you haven't any right to break a law just because it pleases you to do so. That is unscriptural and it is wrong." BJjr was highly critical of Martin Luther King Jr. because of his Modernist theology. When King was murdered, however, BJjr commented, "I hope they bring [the murderer] to justice" (MS, BJjr, chapel talk, 8 April 1968 [ABV: 1968]).

[7]MS, BJjr, chapel talk, 12 February 1965 (ABV: 1965). See also MS, BJjr, chapel talk, 14 September 1970 (ABV: 1970). BJjr said, "We are American citizens and we have to obey the law whether we think the law is a criminal law or a good law."

[8]MS, BJjr, chapel talk, 18 March 1965 (ABV: 1965).

[9]BJsr, to Louis Gasper, 10 June 1952 (GF: Gasper file).

[10]BJsr, radio talk, 17 April 1960. See also MS, BJjr, chapel talk, 13 February 1970 (ABV: 1970). BJjr said, "My dad wanted to build a school for black people. He said, 'As soon as we get Bob Jones University on a self-supporting basis . . . I want to start a school for Negro people.' When we first came here twenty-three years ago, we looked around at property nearby where we could build a negro institution and get the same kind of training you get in Bob Jones University." Rumor at that time had it that the school had even purchased a tract of land about five miles east of the present for just such a purpose.

[11]BJsr, radio talk, 17 April 1960.

[12]MS, BJjr, chapel talk, 13 December, 1965 (ABV: 1965).

[13]MS, BJjr, chapel talk, 12 February 1965 (ABV: 1965). See also MS, BJjr, chapel talk, 13 May 1965 (ABV: 1965).

[14]MS, BJjr, chapel talk, 3 February 1967 (ABV: 1967). See also MS, BJjr, chapel talk, 18 March 1965 (ABV: 1965). One of BJjr's most powerful denouncements of Marxism and communism is found in MS, chapel talk, 4 October 1965 (ABV: 1965).

[15]See MS, BJjr, chapel talk, 5 January 1967 (ABV: 1967), in which BJjr stated that Martin Luther King Jr. "doesn't believe in the virgin birth—he does not believe anything." Nailing down King's theological views is a difficult task. Black evangelical evangelist Tom Skinner sympathized with King and his cause, but he nonetheless wrote, "I am not sure that Martin Luther King knew Jesus Christ in the evangelical Christian context. . . . King rejected the idea of original sin; that is, he rejected the concept that a person is born separated from God. Martin Luther King accepted the deity of Jesus Christ, and the fact that Jesus Christ was divine, only in the sense that He was one with God in purpose; he believed that Jesus Christ so submitted His will to God's will, that God revealed His divine plan through Jesus Christ; but he did not accept the fact that Jesus Christ was actually God or actually the Son of God, or God manifested in the flesh. Reflecting much of the liberal instruction he received in liberal institutions, he considered the virgin birth a mythological story which tried to explain that Jesus Christ had moral uniqueness, rather than the fact that His birth was a literal fact—that is His virgin birth." (Tom Skinner, *Black and Free* [Grand Rapids: Zondervan, 1970], p. 142).

[16]MS, BJjr, chapel talk, 22 March 1965 (ABV: 1965). Citing men from the French Revolution, he said, "They talk about revolutionaries as if they are great heroes. The great revolutionaries of history have been monsters in their own human lives . . . full of hatred and bitterness. They were against the status quo because their hearts were full of hate, and they wound up murderers."

[17]MS, BJjr, chapel talk, 24 April 1965 (ABV: 1965).

[18]MS, BJjr, chapel talk, 31 May 1965 (ABV: 1965).

[19]U.S.C. §2000(D)-Civil Rights Act of 1964, Title VI: Section 601: "No person in the United States shall, on the ground of race, color, or national origin, be excluded from participation in, be denied the benefits of, or be subjected to discrimination under any program or activity receiving Federal financial assistance." The documents in question

stated that the signers agreed to comply with all future regulations of HEW regarding civil rights and guaranteed agreement and compliance with all future civil rights legislation. Failure to sign the documents of compliance would cause the government immediately to withhold federal funding of student loans and other educational aid programs. BJU's difficulty with this was the issue of agreeing to comply with future regulations, sight unseen and many years in advance of their being conceived and written.

[20]MS, BJjr, chapel talk, 12 February 1965 (ABV: 1965). See also MS, BJjr, chapel talk, 13 May 1965 (ABV: 1965). After BJjr refused to sign the documents, an employee of HEW was quoted as saying that BJU could have "anything they wanted if they did not have such a stubborn old fool for a president" MS, BJjr, chapel talk, 13 February 1970 [ABV: 1970]).

[21]Readers should keep in mind that the BJU policy at this time was not unique. Many American colleges and universities, including those in the Northeast and Midwest, were segregated, and all Southern schools were segregated. Both the University of South Carolina and Clemson University were integrated in 1963 by court order and went through a period of student unrest, and Furman University integrated quietly in 1965 by accepting two married black students, who were also Greenville County school teachers, into their night school for graduate courses (Alfred Sandlin Reid, *Furman University: Toward a New Identity, 1925-1975* [Durham, N.C.: Duke University Press, 1976] p. 199).

[22]MS, BJjr, chapel talk, 5 January 1967 (ABV: 1967).

[23]"A Statement from the Chairman of the Board of Trustees and the President of Bob Jones University," 10 September 1971 (GF: IRS files).

[24]BJiii, interview, 12 June 2000.

[25]Some radical groups have used Scripture in an attempt to "prove" that cultural and genetic superiority exists among the Caucasian races and that non-Caucasian races are inferior. Some claim that the curse that God placed on Noah's son Ham was the "curse" of black skin. In their chapel talks, neither BJsr nor BJjr, when dealing with race, took a position that "blackness" was the Hamitic curse and that all blacks therefore suffered under the curse of God. BJjr said simply that people "accuse those of race prejudice who do not believe that integration is the answer to the problem and that integration is not scriptural." (MS, BJjr, chapel talk, 5 January 1967 [ABV: 1967]).

[26]MS, BJjr, chapel talk, 5 January 1967 (ABV: 1967). See also BJsr, radio talk, 17 April 1960.

[27]BJsr, radio talk, 17 April 1960, "Whenever you get a situation that rubs out the line that God has drawn between races, you are going to have trouble. . . . The established order cannot be overthrown without having trouble. That is what wrecked Paradise. It is man's rebellion against a holy God. . . . Let's approach this thing in a Christian way. Let's make the battle a Christian battle. Do not let people run over you by coming along and talking about the Universal Fatherhood of God and the Universal Brotherhood of man. There is no Universal Fatherhood of God and Universal Brotherhood of man. There is not a word about that in the Bible."

[28]BJsr, radio talk, 17 April 1960.

[29]MS, BJjr, chapel talk, 14 May 1970 (ABV: 1970). BJjr said, "God said to these people after the flood, 'I want you to scatter abroad.' He was going to send man out in the areas of the earth that He had never permitted man to occupy before. . . . God sends men out. He says to them, 'You go to your place. I have made a place for you.' They said, 'We are not going to be scattered abroad . . . God, you go and tend to your business and leave us alone. . . .' And God came down and confused their tongues. . . . He used the force of a confused tongue and a language barrier to make them move out."

[30]George S. Schuyler, "Negro Newspaperman Speaks Out: 'Civil Rights Leaders Should Blame Themselves' " (*Human Events,* 28 August 1965. Quoted in *Congressional Record,* 26 August 1965, pp. 22054-55).

[31]"IRS Announces Position on Private Schools," Internal Revenue Service News Release, 10 July 1970 (GF: IRS files).

[32]*Green v. Kennedy,* 309 F Supp 1127 (DC, 1970).

[33]This corresponds to the period in which the most rapid growth occurred in the Christian school movement. All Christian schools were brought under suspicion and grouped with the small number of private schools that were known as "segregation academies." These schools presumedly were found primarily in the South and were founded after 1964 when the Supreme Court struck down "freedom of choice" plans, which enabled school districts to remain substantially segregated by claiming that the students' choice of school was being honored (*Griffin v. Prince Edward County,* 377 U.S. 218 [1964]). David Nevin and Robert Bills in *The Schools That Fear Built: Segregationist Academies in the South* (Washington, D.C.: Acropolis Books, 1976) took the thesis that schools established after 1964 were founded to foil desegregation. Nevin and Bills identified several purely segregationist schools but grouped with these all church-related, Christian schools, claiming segregationist ideology as their raison d'être. V. D. Nordin and W. L. Turner, in "More Than Segregated Academies: The Growing Protestant Fundamentalist Schools" (*Phi Delta Kappan,* February 1976, pp. 391-94) disproved Nevin and Bills's thesis and took them to task for their shoddy research and inflammatory rhetoric.

[34]H. W. McLeod to BJU (IRS Doc. 400:EO) 30 November 1970 (GF: IRS files). The survey simply asked, "What are the present policies and practices of your school on admissions? ❑ Racially Nondiscriminatory ❑ Racially Discriminatory ❑ Other."

[35]"IRS Announces Position on Private Schools" (IRS document), 10 July 1970.

[36]H. W. McLeod to Bob Jones University (IRS Doc. 400:EO), 30 November 1970 (GF: IRS files). See also "Private School Survey," Internal Revenue Service Fact Sheet 71-2, 30 November 1970 (GF: IRS files).

[37]Richard J. Stakem to James T. Broyhill, 6 May 1971 (GF: IRS files).

[38]Sam J. Ervin to Mark C. Bullock, 9 February 1971 (GF: IRS files). Ervin, chairman of the Senate Judiciary Committee, wrote that the IRS had informed him that "an assertion of nondiscriminatory policy is sufficient to accord a school tax-exempt status." According to the IRS commissioner, one hundred schools in Mississippi alone chose not to adopt such a policy and faced the IRS in court (Jerome Kurtz, "News Release: Remarks Before the PLI Seventh Biennial Conference on Tax Planning for Foundations' Tax-Exempt Status and Charitable Contributions," IRS, 9 January, 1978 [GF: IRS files]).

[39]IRS commissioner Jerome Kurtz said, "We have no specific statutory guidance; our authority and obligations on racial issues derive from the constitutional doctrine announced in *Brown v. Board of Education* in 1954, and cases enforcing and interpreting it, and from the broad national policy announced in the 1964 Civil Rights Act" (Kurtz, "Remarks").

[40]BJjr put the suit in this light: "If the government can dictate our admissions policies, then they will presume [eventually] to . . . say who qualifies for church membership. . . . We are fighting for the religious freedom of every Christian in America. We are not spending a few thousand dollars to keep a few colored people out of Bob Jones University. We are fighting for the right, under our Bill of Rights and the Constitution of the United States, to exercise our religious freedom in America. A Christian institution has a right to religious convictions." (MS, BJjr, chapel talk, 31 May 1971 [ABV: 1971]).

[41]The first black student was Willie Thompson, a former Marine who wished to use his GI Bill benefits. Shortly after the IRS moved against BJU, the VA, with the Justice

Department, following another Supreme Court ruling, changed its GI Bill provisions to exclude benefits to any veteran enrolled in a discriminatory institution. The courts had ruled that veterans' benefits, originally intended for the support of the veteran and paid directly to him to be used at his discretion, were actually a government subsidy to the school. Therefore, schools to which veterans paid tuition must be in compliance with all civil rights legislation or the veteran would be dropped from receiving benefits. The irony of this is that BJU's first black student was denied GI benefits for attending school because BJU had been listed as a discriminatory institution. Thompson completed both his bachelor's and master's degrees at BJU, and is a member of the Bible faculty in the School of Applied Studies, a pastor, and announcer for a local religious radio station.

[42]"A Statement from the Chairman of the Board of Trustees and the President of Bob Jones University," 10 September 1971 (GF: IRS files).

[43]*United States Supreme Court Reports,* "Lawyers' Edition," 1985, *Bob Jones University, Petitioner, v. United States* (no. 81-3), p. 167.

[44]BJU, "Religious Freedom Imperiled: The IRS and BJU," pamphlet, 1982, p. 4.

[45]*Bob Jones University v. William E. Simon, Secretary of Treasury, et. al.,* 1974.

[46]*Runyon v. McCrary,* 427 U.S. 160 (1976).

[47]BJiii to O. Jack Taylor, 29 May 1975 (GF: IRS files). Obviously the school's change in admissions policy came before *Runyon v. McCrary* was announced by the Supreme Court. The change may have been effected after the decision was rendered at the circuit court level.

[48]General Information Letter, BJiii to [no name], March 2000 (President's Office). The letter continues, "I said until I was blue in the face that we were not defending our policy but our right to the policy. The policy was not understood by most people, even the staunchest Christians. It was based upon the broader principle of the Bible's teaching against the one-world government which is fast encroaching upon us."

[49]BJiii to O. Jack Taylor.

[50]H. E. Kenworthy to Bob Jones University, 19 January 1976 (GF: IRS files).

[51]CNN Transcript: *Larry King Live,* 3 March 2000 (wysuwtg://11/http://cnn.com/TRANSCRIPTS/0003/03/lkl.00.html).

[52]*United States Supreme Court Reports,* "Lawyers' Edition," p. 167.

[53]In this ruling, Judge Robert F. Chapman declared that the IRS had violated BJU's guarantee of freedom of religion and stated that "there is no clearly defined federal policy against prohibiting interracial social practices" or against discrimination by religious organizations. The IRS "has overstepped its authority and usurped that of Congress," Chapman wrote. Quoted from Rebecca V. Tabler, "Bob Jones University versus Internal Revenue Service," unpublished paper, 23 November 1992 (author's possession).

[54]The court cited *Green v. Connally,* 330 F Supp 1150 (DDC 1971) for its definition of *charitable.*

[55]The court read §501(c)(3) as meaning that an organization must be charitable *and* educational, charitable *and* religious, etc. This is in stark contrast to the careful wording of §501(c)(3): "religious, charitable, scientific testing for public safety, literary, *or* educational purposes, or for the prevention of cruelty to children or animals" (italics added). Each category is clearly discrete and independent of any other. (Quoted in Albright G. Zimmerman, "Epilogue: Speculations and Conclusions," in Ronald C. White, Jr., and Albright G. Zimmerman (eds.), *An Unsettled Arena: Religion and the Bill of Rights* (Grand Rapids, Mich.: Wm. B. Eerdmans, 1990), p. 69.

[56]*United States Supreme Court Reports,* "Lawyers' Edition," pp. 171-75.

[57]Goldsboro had been denied tax-exempt status by the IRS because of its admissions policy, which, though a religious conviction based on racial types as descended from

Noah's sons, was racist in that it argued against the cultural mixing of the races. (Supreme Court of the United States, Syllabus, *Goldsboro Christian Schools, Inc., v. United States of America* [no. 81-1], p. 7).

[58] Lynn Nabers Riddle, "Religious Groups Join Bob Jones University Tax Fight," *Greenville (S.C.) Piedmont,* 1 December 1981 (ML: Vertical file). Such diverse groups as the Mormon Church, the National Association of Evangelicals, the National Jewish Commission for Law and Public Affairs, the American Baptist Convention, the United Presbyterian Church, the General Conference Mennonite Church, the National Committee for Amish Religious Freedom, and the Christian Legal Society's Center for Law and Religious Freedom filed *amicus curiae* briefs.

[59] James J. Kilpatrick, *The Morning Call.* Quoted in Tabler, p. 5.

[60] "Faith, Hope and Charity," *Wall Street Journal,* 15 January 1982, p. 24. Because the case had become so laden with the social baggage of race, the Reagan administration's announcement was a political disaster that sent his aids scrambling to explain it.

[61] "President Has Few Alternatives in Tax Exemption Case," *Greenville (S.C.) Piedmont,* 10 February 1982. See also "Reagan Muddies Waters on Bob Jones Tax Status," *Greenville (S.C.) News,* 13 January 1982; and "Reagan Tax Exemption Stand Raked over Coals," *Greenville (S.C.) News,* 5 February 1982.

[62] BJU, "Religious Freedom Imperiled: The IRS and BJU," pamphlet, 1982, p. 5.

[63] Quoted in Tabler, "Bob Jones University," p. 5.

[64] "Civil Rights Groups to Battle Tax Decision," *Greenville (S.C.) News,* n.d. (ML: Vertical file).

[65] Patrick Buchanan, "Hooks Proudly Claims Tolerance, but Where Is It?" syndicated column in the *Birmingham (Ala.) News,* 15 January 1982. Quoted in "Religious Freedom Imperiled," p. 6.

[66] BJiii, "The Issue Is Religion, Not Race," *Washington Post,* 24 January 1982.

[67] Ibid.

[68] BJiii to "Friend," 7 June 1982.

[69] "Administration to Ask Justices to Consider Bob Jones Case," *Greenville (S.C.) Piedmont,* 25 February 1982 (ML: Vertical file).

Chapter 21: "The Power to Tax Is the Power to Destroy"

[1] Goldsboro denied black students admission and argued against the social and cultural mixing of the races. BJU accepted black students but argued, on religious grounds, against interracial dating and marriage. The University felt that this was a major difference in the merit of the cases.

[2] Marilyn Rauber, "Supreme Court Hears Bob Jones Tax Plea," *Greenville (S.C.) News,* 13 October 1982.

[3] Supreme Court of the United States, October term, 1981, "Brief for Petitioner," pp. 8-9 (ML: Vertical file).

[4] Phil Randall, "High Court Hears Bob Jones Case," *Greenville (S.C.) Piedmont,* 12 October 1982 (ML: Vertical file).

[5] Ibid.

[6] Rauber, "Supreme Court."

[7] BJiii, "The Initial Reaction of Bob Jones University to the Supreme Court Decision," *Faith for the Family,* July/August 1983, reprint.

[8] *Bob Jones University v. United States,* 461 US 574.

[9] Ibid, pp. 158, 184-85.

[10]*Bob Jones University v. United States,* J. Rehnquist, dissenting, 24 May 1983, pp. 1-12.

[11]The glee of the media reporting the decision was unabashed: "Tax-Exempt Hate, Undone," and "Bob Jones U. Trounced," they intoned. "As for Bob Jones University, stop discriminating, or pay the price," they said (BJU, "The Bomb and Its Fallout: *Bob Jones University v. United States,*" pamphlet, 1983, p. 22).

[12]Patrick J. Buchanan, "The Bob Jones Decision Reflects 'New Intolerance,'" *Tribune Company Syndicate,* June 1983.

[13]Ibid.

[14]"Rethinking Bob Jones," *Washington Times,* 3 June 1983.

[15]BJiii, "Initial Reaction."

[16]BJiii, "Ramifications of Court Ruling," *Faith for the Family,* July/August, 1983, reprint.

[17]BJU, "Bomb," p. 14.

[18]Lynn Nabers Riddle, "IRS Official Says Bob Jones Owes at Least \$489,000," *Greenville (S.C.) Piedmont,* 25 May 1983 (ML: Vertical file). Both the IRS and the University expected to have to litigate the actual amount owed in interest and penalties.

[19]Interview, Roy Barton, 27 July 1995 (tape in author's possession).

[20]The \$1 million figure is reported in Lynn Nabers Riddle, "Learning Is Fundamental," *Atlanta Journal-Constitution,* 31 December 1995. No confirmation from BJU is available.

[21]Interview, Roy Barton.

[22]Riddle, "IRS Official."

[23]Interview, Roy Barton.

[24]Ibid. The initial decrease in donations may be explained by the fact that since the Reagan tax program came into effect, some 85 percent of American taxpayers file short form returns in which there is no deductibility available for donations.

[25]According to Roy Barton, the law allows that bequests in any size (up to the total of the estate) can be made to BJU from any estate that totals \$600,000 or less without any federal estate tax consequences. Thus, an individual with an estate less than \$600,000 may designate any amount up to the total of the estate as a bequest to the school.

[26]Interview, Roy Barton.

[27]Ibid.

[28]Ibid. The school's plan was conceived in early 1989, approved and in place by May, and the first contribution to the plan was paid that same month. A second contribution for the next tax year was made again later in 1989. Each contribution saved the school 34 percent in taxes that would have been due on that money.

[29]Ibid.

[30]The federal courts, ruling to "protect minority rights," forced Georgetown University, against its religious values and beliefs, to recognize and support a campus organization for homosexuals. The court, in essence, freed the homosexuals from any jeopardy or discipline resulting from their practices, including proselytizing. The case never reached the Supreme Court because Georgetown finally capitulated to the pressure of the lower courts and the demands of homosexual and liberal media groups. Catholics were stunned that Georgetown would capitulate and that the lower courts would rule without regard to the First Amendment. See Albright G. Zimmerman, "Epilogue," in Ronald C. White Jr. and Albright G. Zimmerman, eds., *An Unsettled Arena: Religion and the Bill of Rights* (Grand Rapids, Mich.: Wm. B. Eerdmans Publishing Co., 1990), pp. 154-56. See also *Georgetown University, et al., v. Gay Rights Coalition of Georgetown University Law Center, et al.,* in *U.S. Supreme Court Report, Lawyers' Edition,* vol. 98, p. 641.

[31]Zimmerman, "Epilogue," p. 154.

[32]For a complete explanation of Grove City, see Thomas J. Flygare, "The Court's Title IX Decision: Who Won?" *Phi Delta Kappan,* 65 (May 1984), pp. 640-41. Interestingly, the court found in favor of the Department of Education but soundly criticized the department for its overzealous pursuit of Grove City.

[33]Larry Burkett, *What Ever Happened to the American Dream* (Chicago: Moody Press, 1993), p. 75. See also White and Zimmerman, eds., *Arena,* pp. 77-81, 154-56.

Chapter 22: Just Keep in the Middle of the Middle of the Road

[1]BJjr, *Cornbread,* p. 215.

[2]Quoted in Wright, *Fortress,* p. 282. If good men are reasonable, it follows that an unreasonable man is not good.

[3]Words to a Negro spiritual which says simply, "just keep in the middle of the middle of the middle of the road" ("Keep in the Middle of the Road," Negro spiritual, arranged by Marshall Bartholomew, G. Schirmer, 1930).

[4]MS, BJsr, chapel talk, 4 March 1935 (ABV: 1935).

[5]Sectarian debate was minimal because unity on fundamental truths was stressed. Students enjoyed denominational youth meetings every Sunday following Vespers in Florida and Cleveland. In Greenville, even without the denominational meetings, unity remained the same. BJjr preached, "This is not a Presbyterian school; this is not a Baptist school; this is not a Lutheran school; this is not a Holiness school. This is a Christian institution, nondenominational, whose testimony is, 'I believe in the inspiration of the Bible'; and right on through to 'the gift of eternal life by the grace of God.' That is all we are dogmatic about around here." MS, BJjr, chapel talk, 14 November 1967 (ABV: 1967).

[6]"Lifestyle Survey Results," Office of Dean of Students, 1993.

[7]D. W. Bebbington, *Evangelicalism in Modern Britain: A History from the 1730s to the 1980s* (Grand Rapids, Mich.: Baker, 1992), pp. 261-62.

[8]See Iain Murray, *Arthur W. Pink: His Life and Thought* (Edinburgh: Banner of Truth Trust, 1981).

[9]Most literature on Neo-Puritanism, aside from brief notices such as Bebbington's, has come from within the movement. Probably the best place to start is Iain Murray, *David Martyn Lloyd-Jones: The Fight of Faith, 1939-1981* (Edinburgh: Banner of Truth Trust, 1990). See also Iain Murray, "The Story of the Banner of Truth Trust," *Banner of Truth,* November 1993, pp. 15-23; and introduction to *The Puritans: Their Origins and Successors,* by D. Martyn Lloyd-Jones (Edinburgh: Banner of Truth Trust, 1987).

[10]H. Leon McBeth, *The Baptist Heritage: Four Centuries of Baptist Witness* (Nashville: Broadman, 1987), pp. 770-76, gives a good overview of the various Calvinistic Baptist bodies formed since World War II. McBeth indicates that British Neo-Puritanism is but one source of the Calvinistic revival, at least among Baptists.

[11]George Dollar, *The Fight of Fundamentalism: American Fundamentalism, 1973-1983* (Sarasota, Fla.: G. W. Dollar, 1983), pp. 99-104. For other Fundamentalist critiques of the Calvinistic revival, see Robert L. Sumner, *An Examination of Tulip: The Five Points of Calvinism* (Brownsburg, Ind.: Biblical Evangelism Press, 1972), and JRR, "Hyper-Calvinism—A False Doctrine," *Some Serious, Popular False Doctrines Answered from the Scriptures* (Murfreesboro, Tenn.: Sword of the Lord Publishers, 1970), pp. 273-89.

[12]MS, BJjr, chapel talk, 9 December 1969 (ABV: 1969).

[13]BJjr to Mike Mulvaney, 12 September 1969 (ABV: Subject file).

[14]MS, BJjr, chapel talk, 9 December 1969 (ABV: 1969). In *Cornbread* the Chancellor writes, "It has been my observation that where good, Bible-believing theologians hold to opposite and contradictory positions on the interpretations of Scripture . . . the truth usually lies somewhere between" (p. 186).

[15]BJjr to Stuart Latimer, 25 November 1967 (GF: Subject file).

[16]BJjr to Mike Mulvaney.

[17]MS, BJiii, chapel talk, 24 February 1977 (ABV: 1977). By the mid-1980s the whole of the Charismatic movement was under suspicion and investigation as national TV leaders/performers, who displayed insatiable appetites for adulation, wealth, fame, and power (such as Robert Tilton, Jim and Tammy Bakker, and Jimmy Swaggart) fell into gross immorality and had their libertine lifestyles exposed.

[18]Ibid.

[19]BJjr made it clear that he was not unfriendly to Pentecostals. In 1969 a Church of God pastor served on the board, and a small group of conservative Pentecostal people helped support the school (see BJjr to Mike Mulvaney, 12 September 1969). In 1977 BJiii said, "the real old-time Pentecostal people are deeply embarrassed to be identified with modern-day Charismatic efforts. I have good friends who are Pentecostal people. The Pentecostal people originally were just simply in their purest forms, trying to be a holy people. They had some excesses, and they had some beliefs and doctrinal positions that I personally do not subscribe to; but they were sincere, God-fearing, separated people, and they sought after a closer relationship to the Lord in holiness. Holiness characterized their entire movement and practice."

[20]MS, BJjr, chapel talk, 9 December 1969 (ABV: 1969).

[21]BJjr preached, "Bear this in mind—before the Bible was complete, God gave His revelation through men. In Old Testament times He gave His revelation through the prophets, dreams, through the casting of lots—the Urim and Thummim. They were the priestly means of casting lots to determine the will of God. Remember, they had no revelation of God in the written Word of God. . . . In the New Testament, God gave His revelation in the assembly—in the Christian church as they gathered together, through the mouth of the apostle whom He had sent there to preach . . . God also gave His revelation through what are called here prophets; that is somebody in the congregation . . . who is just preaching. It does not mean some strange message about what is going to come to pass. . . . 'When that which is perfect is come, . . . that which is in part shall be done away.' Prophecy shall cease, knowledge shall fail, and tongues shall be silenced when that which is perfect is come. This [Bible] is that which is perfect prophecy; this is perfect revelation; this is all God has for you to know, this whole Bible—not just the New Testament" (MS, BJjr, chapel talk, 14 December 1967).

[22]MS, BJiii, chapel talk, 24 February 1977 (ABV: 1977).

[23]BJiii to "Friend," 4 May 1988 (Office of the President).

[24]For a concise treatment of these groups and their beliefs, see Thurman Wisdom, "Light on the Bible Text Debate," BJU Press, pamphlet, 1984. James R. White, *The King James Only Controversy: Can You Trust the Modern Translations?* (Minneapolis: Bethany House, 1995), categorizes those within KJV Only into five groups: (1) "I Like KJV Best"; (2) "The Textual Argument"; (3) "Received Text Only"; (4) "The Inspired KJV Group"; (5) "The KJV as New Revelation." A thorough discussion of the issues is found in D. A. Carson, *The KJV Debate: A Plea for Realism* (Grand Rapids, Mich.: Baker, 1979), and White, *Controversy.* For good coverage of the KJV Only issue, see James B. Williams (ed.), *From the Mind of God to the Mind of Man: A Layman's Guide to How We Got Our Bible* (Greenville, S.C.: Ambassador-Emerald International, 1994).

[25]The term *Textus Receptus,* or "Received Text," was lifted from a promotional preface to an edition of the Greek New Testament published in 1633, twenty-two years after the publication of the KJV. Both the term and the text took hold, and this text of the Greek Testament dominated scholarly study for generations. It is textually very similar to the first published Greek Testament, edited by the great humanist and Augustinian Catholic priest Desiderius Erasmus in 1516. The manuscripts from which these Greek Testaments were produced came from the Byzantine, or Greek Orthodox, family. Naturally, this family represents the majority of existing Greek manuscripts, since Greek was this church's native tongue through its whole history. Thus, in spite of slight differences to which scholars are sensitive, the terms *Byzantine Text, Majority Text,* and *Received Text* have all come, in popular usage, to signify the same textual family and are often used synonymously. ("Families" of manuscripts developed within geographical regions, where manuscripts were copied from one another in genealogical relationship to one another.)

Virtually no one contends today for the superiority of Erasmus's first edition of the Greek New Testament. Though a gifted scholar, Erasmus had only a small number of manuscripts from which to work, and the earliest of those dated from the tenth and eleventh centuries. To complete the Greek text for which he had no manuscripts (as in the case of the Book of Revelation), he translated the Latin Vulgate back into Greek. He had a mere "handful" of manuscripts when compared to those available in 1880 or today (see Thurman Wisdom, "Textus Receptus: Is It Fundamental to our Faith?" *Faith for the Family,* October 1979, pp. 3-4). For a clear presentation of the development of KJV textual criticism, see Samuel Ellsworth Schnaiter, "The Relevancy of Textual Criticism to the Modern English Version Controversy for Fundamentalists" (Ph.D. dissertation, BJU, 1980).

[26]Wisdom, "Textus Receptus." As any historian will attest, evidence dated closer to the occurrence of an event is always considered more reliable than a document dated several hundred years later that relates similar information. This is also true of retranslation, wherein a secondary translation is considered more accurate than a tertiary translation or than a translation done in the primary source's language but from secondary sources.

[27]The logic of many of the critics of Westcott and Hort's text is this: modern translations are Modernistic in theology. The translators of the modern versions used Westcott and Hort's text. Therefore the text is modernistic. The reality is that regardless of which text was used these biased translators would have arrived at the same result.

[28]The textual debate has taken many twists and turns of logic, even going to the point of arguing that the KJV translators were more brilliant in their acumen than present-day linguistic scholars. There is no doubt that the KJV translators were unusually gifted men. There is also no doubt that today's conservative translators are also gifted men. See D. A. Waite, *Four Reasons for Defending the King James Bible* (Collingswood, N.J.: Bible for Today Publishers, n.d.), p. 17. Waite's four reasons are (1) superior texts, (2) superior translators, (3) superior technique, and (4) superior theology.

[29]Many KJV-Only adherents deny this aspect of the debate.

[30]Tom Corkish, "What Do Colleges Think of the King James Bible," *Flaming Torch,* extra edition, spring 1995. Corkish, in an attitude that appears to be common among this group, proposes that if poor renderings or KJV sections based on poor manuscript evidence (such as I John 5:7-8) are changed, then the authority of the whole is open to question and doctrine is at stake.

In the case of I John 5:7-8, Corkish states that the verses are a "great guard for the doctrine of the Trinity" in spite of the fact that conservative scholars agree that the passage is found in only "four or five" Greek manuscripts, none of which were done before the sixteenth century. See *Holy Bible, New King James Version* (Camden, N.J.: Thomas Nelson, Inc., 1990), p. 1499, note 5:7. See also *Holy Bible, New International Version*

(Grand Rapids, Mich.: Zondervan Publishing House, 1984), p. 907, notes c7, 8. The doctrine of the Trinity is guarded more fully by other Scriptures that have greater manuscript authority.

[31]See BJjr, "Editorial," *Faith for the Family,* July/August 1979, p. 2.

[32]White, *Controversy,* p. 6. In cases in which the English word selected by the KJV translators for the Textus Receptus Greek was clearly wrong, they made arguments similar to the following. One writer, in commenting on Acts 12:4, wrote that "the Greek phrase in verse 4 is plainly *meta* to *pascha*—which normally would be translated 'after the Passover.'" The KJV, however, reads "after Easter." This writer thus concluded that "the Holy Spirit has thrust himself into the AV committee of 1611 and said, 'WRITE . . . [Easter, not Passover].' " Quoted in Wendall Mullen, "A Word of Warning by Pastor Mullen," mimeograph, 1 July 1979 (MLFF: Gilbert Stenholm papers).

[33]BJjr, "Statement: Amplified N.T.," n.d. (Office of the Chancellor).

[34]BJiii "Para/KJV," n.d. (Office of the President).

[35]Quoted in BJU, "Position of the Bible Department."

[36]Torrey, *Inerrant,* pp. 76-77.

[37]BJU, "Position of the Bible Department."

[38]BJiii to "Friend," 4 May 1988 (Office of the President). For a concise statement of the University's position, see Edward M. Panosian, "What Is the Inspired Word of God?" *Faith for the Family,* February 1979. See also JRR, "Some Questions for King James Fans," *Sword of the Lord,* 30 March 1979.

[39]BJjr to "Friend," 11 October 1994 (Office of the Chancellor). According to some estimates, the corrections made to the 1611 Authorized Version since its appearance number as high as seventy thousand. The American Bible Society recently counted twenty-four thousand discrepancies between five KJV editions. The 1613 revision by the King James translation committee itself introduced over three hundred changes. Other revisions to the KJV were made in 1629 and 1638 and have continued to the present. Thus to argue for an inerrant and infallible 1611 version, or to argue that a 1611 translation is itself the work of men verbally inspired by God, is to agree that God made between twenty-four thousand and seventy thousand errors in everything from misspellings and word omissions to biblical numbers. Clearly, if the KJV record were inerrant, the seventy thousand corrections would have been unnecessary.

One writer asked, "Where in the Bible does God guarantee that any translator of the Bible, anyone who copies the Bible, anyone who preaches the Bible, or anyone who teaches the Bible, will be infallibly correct?" He then proceeded to answer, "There is no such Scripture. The doctrine of infallibility of the translation in the King James is not a Bible doctrine; it is a manmade scheme . . . partly influenced by bad judgement" (JRR, "Some Questions").

[40]Both Stewart Custer and Marshall Neal were maligned, vilified, and ridiculed in the most mean-spirited, hateful, and un-Christian manner this writer has ever observed. Their names appear frequently in print followed by epithets that are antithetical to the authors' claims of spiritual maturity, insight, and Christian scholarship. See White, *Controversy,* pp. 109-21.

[41]BJU, "Position of the Bible Department."

[42]For information on the political activities of BJsr, see Turner, "Fundamentalism," pp. 189-208.

[43]For a concise treatment of twentieth-century political activities of Evangelicals and Fundamentalists, see Richard V. Pierard, "The New Religious Right in American Politics," in George Marsden, ed., *Evangelicalism in Modern America* (Grand Rapids, Mich.: Wm. B. Eerdmans Publishing Co., 1984), pp. 161-67.

[44]Some scholars also believe that most Evangelicals refused to support Kennedy more on the grounds of his liberalism than his Catholicism. Fundamentalists still saw the Catholic Church as a mortal enemy and wished no papal representative elected president.

[45]Robert Wuthnow, "The Religious Right and Symbolic Politics," in James E. Wood Jr. and Derek Davis, eds., *The Role of Religion in the Making of Public Policy* (Waco, Tex.: J. M. Dawson Institute of Church-State Studies, Baylor University, 1991), p. 95.

[46]The Founder was not afraid to use the power of the ballot box. During the 1962 zoning controversy between BJU and Greenville, BJsr, when speaking to the city council, said he had "four hundred votes in his pocket and in any election he would have control over who would be elected" ("Minutes," Greenville City Council, 26 April 1962 [Greenville City Hall: Microfiche]).

[47]David Bibb Graves (1873-1942) was elected three-time governor of Alabama (1927-31, 1935-39) and died before taking office for his third term. J. Percy Priest (1900-1956) was a member of the editorial staff of the Nashville *Tennessean* (1926-40) and was elected eight times to Congress. J. Strom Thurmond (b. 1902) was a South Carolina teacher, school superintendent, lawyer, judge, and long-time U.S. senator (1954-present). George C. Wallace (1919-98), a short-time professional boxer, was also an Alabama circuit judge, four-time governor of Alabama, and Democratic candidate for the presidency in 1968 and 1972. Barry Goldwater (1909-98) was elected five times to the U.S. Senate from Arizona and made an unsuccessful run for the U.S. presidency in 1964.

[48]Attempts to gain a voice within the Democratic party met with failure because of the larger attendance at Democratic precinct meetings, the ideology of most of the Democrats, and the racial makeup of the Democratic party.

[49]Frank Bumpus, "Ecumenical Politics," *Faith for the Family,* March 1985, pp. 6-7.

[50]Ibid., p. 7.

[51]Richard V. Pierard, "Religious Right," p. 170. The three most visible organizations were Christian Voice (Gary Jarmin), the Moral Majority (Jerry Falwell and Robert Billings), and the (Religious) Roundtable (Ed McAteer).

[52]James M. Perry, "The Moral Majority Finds Its Own Units May Need Guidance," *Wall Street Journal,* 12 February 1981, p. 1.

[53]Jerry Falwell, *Listen, America!* (New York: Doubleday, 1980). The book is divided into three parts. Part I is a loosely organized political history of the United States, ending with a review of "The Miracle Called Israel." Part II contains Falwell's list of America's national problems (the family, children's rights, the feminist movement, the right to life, homosexuality, television, pornography, education, music, and drugs and alcohol). Part III consists of "A Biblical Plan for Action" and "The Imperative of Moral Involvement." Throughout the convincingly written book he calls for revival and a return to God and faith in American ideals but devotes only one paragraph out of 266 pages to a presentation of personal salvation (p. 264).

[54]Richard J. Mouw, "Assessing the Moral Majority," *Reformed Journal,* June 1981, pp. 13-15. Mouw writes, "I was impressed at how many times Rev. Falwell attempted to qualify, modify, or retract earlier statements . . . systematically softening earlier hard-line positions." See also R. Gustav Niebuhr, "Why 'Moral Majority,' A Force for a Decade, Ran Out of Steam," *Wall Street Journal,* 25 September 1989, p. 1.

[55]Jerry Falwell, ed., *How You Can Help Clean Up America* (Washington, D.C.: Moral Majority, Inc., 1981), p. 6.

[56]Jerry Falwell, Truman Dollar, A. V. Henderson, William W. Pennell, eds., *Issues for the Eighties: A Thirteen-Week Sunday School Curriculum Series* (Detroit: Fundamentalist Church Publications, 1982). Topics for study included abortion, feminism, divorce and remarriage, the death penalty, pornography, and homosexuality. Typically, each lesson

would give a short Scripture text, provide other Scripture references, give a Bible verse for memorization, and then lay out the conservative political interpretation for each issue, citing Scripture references where germane. Though published by Fundamentalist Church Publications, it is general enough to be used in nearly any church setting.

[57]BJjr, "The Moral Majority," *Faith for the Family,* September 1980, pp. 1, 27-28.

[58]Falwell, *Listen, America!,* pp. 255-57. Calling for a new inclusivism, Falwell wrote, "I am well aware of the crucial issues of personal and ecclesiastical separation that divide fundamentalists . . . from evangelicals and liberals. I do not believe it is right to compromise the truth in order to gain an opportunity to do right. In doctrinal and spiritual matters, there is no real harmony between light and darkness. . . . When the entire issue of Christian survival is at stake, we must be willing to band together on at least the moral issues of the day."

[59]Moral Majority advertisement quoted in Cline E. Hall and Jerry H. Combee, "What Really Was the Moral Majority?" *Liberty,* July-August, 1986, p. 20.

[60]Ibid.

[61]BJjr, "Moral Majority," p. 1.

[62]BJiii, "The Ultimate Ecumenism," *Faith for the Family,* September 1985, pp. 1, 9-10.

[63]Ibid., p. 10.

[64]Don Harrelson, "Quayle, Buchanan Come to BJU to Fight for Conservative Votes," *Collegian,* vol. 5, no. 11, 12 March 1992.

[65]All were Republicans and included Congressman Bob Inglis of Greenville, three Republican candidates for governor, two mayoral candidates, several state representatives, and local councilmen.

[66]Beth Hunter, "Election Roundup: BJU Grads Finish Strong in Local and National Races," *Collegian,* vol. 6, no. 5, 12 November 1992.

[67]Juliet Eilperin, Hanna Rosin, "Bob Jones: A Magnet School for Controversy" *Washington Post,* 20 February 2000.

[68]Bush and Keyes came to campus. Forbes, failing to garner support in the New Hampshire primary, withdrew from the race and canceled his already-scheduled appearance. Although denied by McCain later in the campaign, his staff had approached BJU about an appearance but the school declined to give him a platform. Angered by this, he apparently sought a way to harm Bush's campaign and pay back the institution as well.

[69]Governor Bush was accompanied by two former S.C. governors, several members of the House of Representatives, and scores of local politicians.

[70]Ben Macintyre, "Embracing Sexism, Racism, Homophobia? George W. Bush's Big Mistake." *London (U.K.) Times,* 30 March 2000. Bush's visit seems to have been first noted by Democratic senator and then presidential candidate Bill Bradley. Bradley "chided Mr. Bush for addressing more than 5,000 students at Bob Jones University, a bastion of Christian conservatism in South Carolina." Noting that the college had lost its tax-exempt status in the 1970s because it did not allow interracial dating, he said, "We had to fight to deny tax-exempt status to Bob Jones University unless it changed that policy. And yet the Republican candidate for president yesterday goes to Bob Jones University to make a speech about what conservatism is in this country. Well, ladies and gentlemen, that is what conservatism is, Bob Jones University, and it should be rejected" (James Dao, "Bradley Blasts Bush for Talk at Bob Jones U." *New York Times,* 4 February 2000).

[71]At issue were *Faith for the Family* articles from the 1970s and 1980s archived on the BJU website. Of the more than 315 articles, only three seemed to directly mention Catholicism. If BJU were pervasively bigoted against Catholic practitioners, far larger numbers of articles about Catholicism would be expected. Strong, biblically accurate Re-

formation language was used by BJjr in discussing Catholicism: "It is a satanic counterfeit, an ecclesiastic tyranny over the souls of men, not to bring them to salvation but to hold them bound in sin and to hurl them into eternal damnation. It is the old harlot of the book of the Revelation—"the Mother of Harlots." Catholics as individuals were never mentioned. All references to Catholicism dealt with the political and spiritual organization of the Church of Rome.

[72]Hoping to use BJU as a wedge issue, McCain attacked Bush and BJU, even though one of his leading S.C. supporters, Terry Haskins, the speaker pro tem of the S.C. Senate, and McCain's S.C. campaign manager were alumni. Within days of McCain's attacks, Haskins dropped his support.

[73]Buchanan, a Catholic, had appeared at BJU twice in previous campaigns and was eager to show his displeasure with the media for unfair treatment of BJU. After the furor erupted, Buchanan contacted BJU and asked to come for a campaign appearance.

[74]Rod Dreher, "Keeping Up with Catholic-Bashing Joneses," *New York Post*, 8 February 2000.

[75]Emil Guillermo, "No Bob Jones University?" *San Francisco (Cal.) Examiner,* 9 February 2000.

[76]"I think it's important for the Congress of the United States to have the last word," said Sen. Robert Torricelli, D-N.J., not realizing that censure of one religious belief was tantamount to censure of all, a violation of constitutionally protected religion, and a dangerous legislative precedent. Quoted in Janelle Carter, Associated Press report, "Democrats in Congress seek condemnation of Bob Jones U.," (www.star-telegram.com/new/doc/1047/1:RELIGION35/1:RELIGION350229100.html).

[77]Rob Schlapfer, "Will the Real Bob Jones Please Stand Up?" (www.antithesis.com/news/bju.html).

[78]Beth Padgett, "Bob Jones Finds Friends Among Critics," *Greenville (S.C.) News,* 6 March 2000.

[79]"BJU Becomes Lightning Rod," *Greenville (S.C.) News,* 4 March 2000.

[80]Democratic candidates remained uncriticized for appearances at an Orthodox Jewish synagogue at which all women and children were officially segregated and for speeches to a black racist's organization in New York City.

[81]BJiii, "A Letter to the Nation from Bob Jones University." *USA Today,* 3 March 2000.

[82]At one point, BJiii said simply, "Larry, we don't hate anybody." On the interracial dating matter, he explained the school's rule, stating that no Bible verse directly forbade interracial marriage. He emphasized that Scripture and BJU stood against all one-world views—one religion, one-world economy, one-world political system—and a fractional part of this was the breaking down of racial boundaries into one race.

[83]CNN transcript: *Larry King Live,* 3 March 2000 (wysuwtg://11/http://cnn.com/TRANSCRIPTS/0003/03/lkl.00.html)

[84]Ken Garfield, "Dating Ban Dropped." *Charlotte (N.C.) Observer,* 4 March 2000. Most of the media assumed that such a rule could be based only on racial hatred and that such feelings were part of the fabric of the institution and its teaching. To have the rule rescinded in the spirit in which it was, was a myth-shattering moment for them.

[85]Jeffrey Hart, "Revisiting Bob Jones." King Features Syndicate, 6 March 2000.

[86]Letters were received from such varied sources as Franklin Graham, Tim LaHaye, Paige Patterson of the Southern Baptist Convention, Pillsbury Baptist Bible College, evangelist Ron Comfort, and others.

[87]Electronic mail, Virginia A. Banks to BJiii, 7 March 2000.

Chapter 23: Progressing . . . Possessing

[1] "Greenville: A Reference Guide," *Greenville (S.C.) News,* 30 April 1995; and *Bob Jones University Bulletin, Catalogue and Announcements,* vol. 68, 1994-95.

[2] BJjr to "Friend," 12 February 1958. "Any full-time faculty member who does not have an M.A. degree should plan to do at least six hours work in the field in which he is teaching, even if he has an M.A. in some other field." The school agreed to lend the cost of tuition and fees at 4 percent interest and to cancel the principal after three years of service.

[3] Though the administration was supportive of teachers pursuing advanced education, as demonstrated by BJjr's letter quoted in note 2 above, the difficulty with pursuing advanced work in the 1950s and 1960s was that often these teachers were critical to the success of a major or were necessary in order to offer specific courses. Therefore, they were not able to take the necessary leave to complete residency requirements and still retain their positions at BJU. In the event that a teacher was to go on for doctoral residency and return to BJU, the teaching load upon return was such that virtually no time was available for research or writing of the dissertation during the school year, and the salary schedule was such that it was impossible to save enough to spend the summer writing. Thus, by the 1960s there were a large number of ABDs ("All But Dissertation") among the faculty, most married with children, who simply were unable to finish.

[4] Because BJU is a teaching, rather than a research, institution, the faculty are expected to teach. A large number also participate in scholarly research. Between 1971 and 1995, one member of the education department, Dr. George Youstra, was appointed to the U.S. Department of Education as an undersecretary of education. In the 1970s, A. Duane White, a member of the University piano department, contributed an article on composer Anton Eberl for inclusion in the *New Groves Dictionary of Music and Musicians.* More recently, the American Council of Learned Societies and the National Endowment for the Humanities awarded research grants to Drs. Carl Abrams and John Matzko of the history faculty (Amy Bollinger, "Political Science Prof. Wins Grant for Historical Research on Fundamentalism," and "BJU Professor Wins NEH Archaeology Grant," *Collegian,* vol. 2, no. 1, 15 September 1988). Dr. Kathleen Crispin, chairman of the Division of Nursing, was appointed to the S.C. State Board of Nursing in 1995 (LeAnne Blackburn, "Chairman of Nursing Division Appointed to State Board," *Collegian,* vol. 8, no. 11, 16 March 1995). Dr. Ron Horton, chairman of the English Department, was awarded the South Atlantic Modern Language Association Award in 1976 for his study on Edmund Spenser's *Faerie Queene* ("Alumnus Wins Book Award," *Voice of the Alumni,* vol. 50, no. 3, December 1976, p. 8). Horton also had a paper on Spenser selected for publication by the Renaissance Society of America in 1991 ("Dr. Horton's Paper Published," *Collegian,* vol. 5, no. 4, 31 October 1991). In addition, he has authored textbooks for BJU Press, including *British Literature for Christian Schools* (Greenville, S.C.: BJU Press, 1992). Dr. Janie McCauley of the English Department was invited to read a paper on Spenser at Princeton University ("Dr. Janie McCauley at Princeton," *Collegian,* vol. 4, no. 2, 27 September 1990). Dr. Sue Quindag of the Music Education Department was invited to present two papers, one at the Music Educators' National Conference convention in Kansas City in 1995, and another that same year in Amsterdam, Holland, at the World Conference of the International Society for Music Education. Numbers of faculty have authored textbooks, student study guides, teacher's guides, and so on for BJU Press.

[5] This accounting includes part-time as well as full-time faculty. Honorary degrees were not counted, nor were terminal degrees such as M.F.A. degrees tabulated. All figures gathered are from *Bob Jones University Bulletin, Catalogue and Announcements,* vols. 43, 47, 54, 58, 64, and 68.

[6]The Institute of Christian Service was started in 1957 as a three-year Bible college program, which, at that time, was representative of Fundamentalist higher educational approaches. It was enlarged in 1978 to include the newly developed Institute of Christian Tradesmen, which offered two-year certificate programs in such fields as aircraft maintenance, automotive service, carpentry, construction, and electricity. In 1982 the ICS became the School of Applied Studies and was organized in two divisions: the Division of Church Service and the Division of Trades and Technology, which offered the associate of applied arts degree in Christian lay leadership, daycare supervision, ministerial training, and missionary preparation; and the associate of applied science degree in aircraft maintenance, general office procedures, library technical assistance, and trade management (BJU, *Bulletin,* vol. 56, February 1982-83, p. 133). Within two years, the SAS program had grown to include the associate of applied science degree in automotive service, carpentry, cosmetology, diesel service, and farm management (BJU, *Bulletin,* vol. 58, February 1984-85, p. 137). Following Ken Hay as director was Thurman Wisdom, who remained until 1978, when he became dean of the School of Religion. Mr. Nelson McGeoch was appointed director of the SAS in 1978 and was director through the years of expansion. (See Willie Thompson, "The School of Applied Studies: Past and Present," unpublished paper [MLA]; also, "New and Improved," *Voice of the Alumni,* vol. 55, no. 4, February 1982, pp. 10- 11.)

[7]Liberty University attracted a few potential BJU students, and Pensacola Christian College attracted even more. Both LU and PCC developed their student bodies through widespread tuition discounts and "scholarships."

[8]Some schools, for the first time, initiated fees such as campus studio fees, locker fees, storage fees, lock fees, and so on; then as incentives to students, offered "fee waivers." Other schools offered "scholarships" that required the student to sign a contract guaranteeing that he would stay four years and would work for the school. If the student left school before four years were up, the "scholarship" money was to be repaid. These were not presented to the students as work loans, but as merit scholarships. See William Ihlanfeldt, *Achieving Optimal Enrollments and Tuition Revenues* (San Francisco: Jossey-Bass, 1980), and "The Current Marketing Environment in Higher Education," in *Marketing in College Admissions: A Broadening Perspective* (New York: College Entrance Examination Board, 1980), pp. 70-91. See also Edward B. Fiske's "Ethical Issues in Recruiting Students" (*New Directions for Higher Education,* no. 33, 1981), pp. 41-48; and "The Marketing of the College" (*Atlantic Monthly,* October 1979), pp. 93-98.

[9]BJU, *Bulletin: Catalogue, 1972-73,* vol. 45, February 1972, p. 130. The catalog description goes on to say that "certification or public school preparation is not a goal of this program."

[10]All figures derived from "Enrollment Statistics: First Semester," n.d. (RO). All enrollment figures are for the first semester. BJU does not keep enrollment figures for the second semester of each year. Rather, the school reports matriculated students for second semester of each school year. "Grad./Spec." indicates students on the graduate level and those admitted under some type of special status.

[11]NA indicates that the total number of graduate students is not available.

[12]NA indicates that the total number of students for the SAS program (the former ICS) is included in the University total.

[13]The School of Education offered the master of arts in teaching (M.A.T.) and the master of education (M.Ed.), both of which required specialized study in one of eight academic disciplines. The M.A.T. areas from which the student could choose were elementary education, special education, English, mathematics, art, history, music, and speech. The M.Ed. differed by not offering the degree with a concentration in speech, but offer-

ing a concentration in secondary education. The master of science (M.S.) degree was offered in counseling, educational administration and supervision, and personnel services. The specialist in education (Ed.S.) degree was offered in counseling, educational administration and supervision, personnel services, elementary education, special education, English, mathematics, history, and music. The doctor of education (Ed.D.) degree was offered in curriculum and instruction—secondary; curriculum and instruction—elementary; and educational supervision (BJU, *Graduate Bulletin: Catalogue and Announcements, 1995-96,* vol. 69, February 1995, pp. 57-58).

[14]Through the Division of Art, the School of Fine Arts offered the master of arts (M.A.) degree in art, graphic design, and illustration. The Division of Music offered the master of music (M.M.) degree in church music—conducting, or church music—voice, organ, piano, or orchestral instrument; and in organ, piano, voice, or orchestral instrument performance (including flute, oboe, clarinet, bassoon, saxophone, trumpet, horn, trombone, euphonium, tuba, violin, viola, or cello). The Division of Speech Communication offered the M.A. degree in interpretative speech, platform arts, rhetoric and public address, dramatic production, radio and television broadcasting, and broadcast management. The Division of Cinema offered the M.A. in cinema and video production. The M.A. in Fine Arts, an interdisciplinary degree, was also available (BJU, *Graduate Bulletin: Catalogue and Announcements, 1995-96,* vol. 69, February 1995, pp. 51-55).

[15]The School of Religion offered the following seminary programs: master of ministry, specialist of ministry, master of divinity, doctor of ministry, and doctor of pastoral theology. The Division of Graduate Studies offered the certificate of medical missions, the certificate of biblical studies, and six master of arts degrees in Bible, teaching Bible, theology, pastoral studies, church administration, and church history. The Doctor of Philosophy degree provided advanced study in Old and New Testament interpretation, theology, and church history (BJU, *Graduate Bulletin: Catalogue and Announcements, 1995-96,* vol. 69, February 1995, p. 34).

[16]BJU, *Bulletin: Catalogue, 1982-83,* vol. 56, February 1982, pp. 43-44.

[17]The majors included print journalism, public relations journalism, broadcast journalism, technical writing, and creative writing. For practical experience, students majoring in PWP also are assigned writing internships with business and publishing groups.

[18]See "Students Covering the News," *Voice of the Alumni,* vol. 61, no. 5, Summer 1988. The *Collegian* began in October 1987. It actually followed in the footsteps of the *Conqueror,* a monthly paper published by the student body of BJC, beginning in 1936. The *Conqueror* was published for only two or three years. It was described as a "literary publication" but contained stories about campus events (BJC, *Catalogue: Announcements for 1937-38,* vol. 10, no. 1, p. 19). Such articles as "Senior Personality," "Book Nook," and a weekly calendar of coming events were featured. Grace Haight was the faculty adviser (BJC, *Conqueror,* vol. 2, no. 1, 9 October 1939 [MLA: Box 27]).

[19]BJU, *Bulletin: Catalogue, 1958-59,* vol. 31, February 1958, p. 70. Students in the B.S. degree program in nursing were required to take seventy hours of course work, including Bible and a foreign language. From 1958 through 1962, only one nursing course, nursing education, was included in the curriculum. In 1962 a second required nursing course was added (BJU, *Bulletin: Catalogue, 1962-63,* vol. 35, February 1962, p. 60).

[20]BJU, *Bulletin: Catalogue, 1966-67,* vol. 35, February 1966, pp. 73-74.

[21]"Nursing Program Offered at BJU," *Voice of the Alumni,* vol. 53, no. 1, June 1979, p. 7. See also "School of Nursing: A Ministry of Caring," *Voice of the Alumni,* vol. 59, no. 2, fall 1985, pp. 12-13. The first director of the Nursing Division was Jewell Chambers, the administrative assistant at Presbyterian Medical Center School of Nursing in Denver, Colorado. The B.S.N. program, developed in partnership with the Greenville Hospital

System, enables the graduates to sit for the R.N. examinations as well as to complete the bachelor of science degree.

[22]The nursing program was designed as a rigorous academic program. Of the sixty-two students who entered in 1978, twenty completed all requirements and graduated in 1982. The next year, the largest class to date, fifty-one, graduated. All figures from RO.

[23]In its first year the School of Aeronautics offered eight courses in basic and advanced ground school, primary flying, advanced flying, missionary flying, and instrument flying. For more information, see BJU, *Bulletin, 1948-49*, pp. 151-52. Royal Grubb was hired as the first head of this school. In the summer of 1947, he left Cleveland,Tennessee, to visit his home before coming to Greenville. A member of the Air Force Reserve, he received orders to join his group and became chief officer on a K99 tanker plane, assigned to the newly born Strategic Air Command. When the aeronautics program started that fall, there was no director. Winfield Arn became the director of the program in 1948, but he was replaced the next year by Curt Wetzel. Wetzel was interested in evangelism, so he mounted loudspeakers under the wings of his plane to play gospel music as he flew. He also used the loudspeakers to announce evangelistic campaigns. He left the program to enter full-time evangelism in 1950. After Wetzel left, Raymond Baltz became director. He was followed in 1953 by Ken Platte, who remained director until the program was dropped (Interview, Shawn D. Williams with Ken Platte, 25 January 1992 [MLA]).

Only two other Christian schools have had aviation programs: Moody Bible Institute in Chicago and Piedmont Bible College in Winston-Salem, North Carolina. Of these, Piedmont closed its program within a few years.

[24]Surprised by the interest, the school was unprepared for such a large number of students and had to scour the area for aircraft and instructors. Two local men were hired as instructors and the school rented fifteen J3 Cubs from Southern Aviation (which became Piedmont Airlines and was eventually acquired by USAir).

[25]Interview, Williams with Ken Platte. By 1959 the course offerings had diminished to only five. By 1960 few students were enrolled, government regulations had changed, and the cost to meet the regulations was prohibitive. According to Platte, the FAA required controllable pitch propellers and retractable landing gear on training aircraft after 1960. In 1967 the Aeronautics Department was shifted to the School of Religion and was operated within the Missions Department until flight courses were discontinued two years later after the school's trainer plane was destroyed in a crash.

[26]Prior to the purchase of the Aztec, the University leased a plane and pilot, Tom Mull, from a local aviation company for several years. During one particularly bad flight, Mull was forced to land in North Carolina because of severe thunderstorms. After BJiii and Mull reached a motel, the President was able to lead Mull to saving faith in Christ. Shortly after this, Mull left the area, and the school decided to hire a full-time pilot. Carver was recommended for the position by Harry Ward, an administrative assistant to BJiii. On flights that summer, Carver suggested to the executives that the school revive the old flight program. They agreed, and by September, the flight program was in place and had been approved by the FAA. Dr. Phil Smith worked through the flight curriculum with the FAA and found a way to fit the requirements into a semester's organizational pattern. Interview, Shawn D. Williams with Larry Carver, 6 February 1992 (MLA).

[27]Figures provided by RO.

[28]Two pilots, Mel Wilhite and David Hill, and four mechanics, Dick Becker, Bruce Brown, Ron Campbell, and Eldon Anderson, soon joined the program.

[29]Cornerstone was sold to Larry Jackson, a BJU board member and partner in Jackson-Dawson Communications, a Detroit-based advertising corporation.

[30]The FAA required a minimum of 1,900 hours of training, "out of which at least 400 hours [were] required in airframe curriculum and 750 hours in the power plant curriculum" ("Aviation Expansion," *Voice of the Alumni,* vol. 56, no. 4, February 1983, pp. 4-7).

[31]"Aviation Expansion," p. 7.

[32]The farm was located eighteen miles from Greenville in Laurens County, about eight miles east of Fountain Inn, S.C., bordering the Enoree River. The Pleasant Pastures Dairy was constructed in 1988 and produced milk, cream, and buttermilk, as well as ice cream. See "Books and Barns: A New SAS Program," *Voice of the Alumni,* vol. 59, no. 1, Summer 1985, pp. 8-10; and Deanna Meadows, "Dairy Processing Plant to Cut Costs, Increase Efficiency," *Collegian,* vol. 2, no. 10, 1989. See also Stacy M. Cowles, "Improvements Breed Better Results at Farm," *Collegian,* vol. 3, no. 7, 1989.

[33]Pleasant Pastures received numerous awards for its soil and water conservation practices, production techniques, and land use, including being named the 1992 Outstanding Cooperator by the Greenville County Soil and Water Conservation District ("BJU Farm Receives Award," *Collegian,* vol. 6, no. 1, 1992) and the 1995 top commercial beef herd in South Carolina. The dairy was recognized for its production and high quality of its milk and was named the top producer of the Greenville Livestock Association in March 1996.

[34]Wright, *Fortress,* p. 418.

[35]Both buildings were designed so that additional floors could be added in the future. Each building had 253 air-conditioned rooms. post office, meeting room, study lounge, laundry and vending areas, prayer room, and music practice studios. All the furniture, 4,807 pieces in all, was custom designed, fabricated, and finished in the BJU cabinet shop. The accounting of all the materials is immense. The furniture project took 113,091 pieces of birch cabinet plywood; 12,065 handles; 3,036 hinges and an equal number of sliding door tracks; 1,012 formica tops; 3,289 pieces of trim; 759 mirrors; 759 closet bars; and 4,048 doors ("New Dormitories on Campus," *Voice of the Alumni,* vol. 5 1, no. 2, October 1977, pp. 15-16).

[36]The old building was essentially "enclosed" by the new structure, at a cost of $2.8 million. The new building had seating for over fifteen hundred students and included over six hundred individual study carrels. The building was also designed to hold approximately 340,000 bound volumes on open stacks, as well as microforms and periodicals.

[37]The Jerusalem Chamber at Westminster dates from the fourteenth century and probably took its name from the subject of the tapestries originally hung there. The room's fame in literature was enhanced by Shakespeare's use of it in *Henry IV.* The chamber was used by the translators of the KJV in 1611, as well as by the committees of the Revised Standard Version of 1885 and the New English Bible of 1961. BJU's reproduction was made possible through the cooperation of Peter Foster, Esq., Surveyor of the Fabric of Westminster Abbey (the resident architect), and was financed by Dixie Baptist Church of Clarkston, Michigan, pastored by Paul Vanaman (Wright, *Fortress,* p. 421).

[38]The windows were executed by Lewis Comfort Tiffany, of the famed Tiffany Glass and Decorating Company, around 1900. The Dorcas window titled "Full of Good Works" represents good works, Christian love, and charity; the Paul window is titled "I Have Kept the Faith"; it portrays the apostle as the essence of faithfulness in the proclamation of the gospel and an uncompromising stand for the Word of God and its truth (see Wright, *Fortress,* p. 422; and Kathy Bell, "Show Windows in Stained Glass," *Voice of the Alumni,* vol. 59, no. 1, Summer 1985).

[39]The carved walnut pilasters at one time formed part of the reception room of the Blumenthal mansion. When the building was dismantled, the woodwork was procured by the antique dealer French and Company, who presented these pieces to the Chancellor.

[40]The three chandeliers, two of which hang in the boardroom and one of which lights the main library lobby, were the gift of Mr. and Mrs. W. H. B. Simpson of Greenville.

[41]Interview, Hala M. Khoury with Joe Allen, 5 October 1990, quoted in Hala M. Khoury, "The Mack Library of Bob Jones University," unpublished paper (MLA).

[42]The original building contained 27,530 square feet; the new addition added about 34,500 square feet, for a total of just over 62,000 square feet, at a cost of $1.7 million in 1982.

[43]These include interview rooms, the Office of Student Services, Unusual Tours Travel Agency, Unusual Films Photo Studio, and the Office of the Director of Career Development and Placement.

[44]Grace Levinson was for many years chairman of the Department of Voice in the Division of Music.

[45]Kelley Deegan, "Fire Forces Unexpected Renovations to Riley Room," *Collegian,* vol. 9, no. 8, 1 February 1996. A campus security officer was in the room when a Christmas tree caught fire. He tried but could not contain the blaze, and within five minutes the Greenville Fire Department was on the scene and the blaze was extinguished. Because of the Riley Room's open design, it sustained approximately $250,000 of damage even though the fire was small—it took about twenty-five gallons of water to extinguish. Heat damaged the ceiling, several walls, and furniture, and smoke damaged the draperies, upholstery, and the walls. The wallpaper had to be removed, a job that took more than fifteen hundred yards of new wallpaper, and all the furniture had to be re-covered.

[46]"Bob Jones University Dedicates Bridge over North Pleasantburg," *Greenville (S.C.) Piedmont,* 19 June 1986.

[47]Cogeneration is the production of two or more kinds of energy from a single source. The University's plant, designed by BJU engineer Chuck Alderson, was to produce 4,650 kilowatts of power, plus steam and hot water to heat all the dormitories. Total savings provided by the plant were in excess of one thousand dollars a day, and the electrical power was also sold to Duke Power during times of peak usage. See Denise Hughes, "Co-gen Facility Cranks Up," *Collegian,* vol. 1, no. 10, 14 April 1988. Also, "Maintenance Department Prepares Campus for Fall," *Collegian,* July 1989.

[48]"BJU Plans to Install New Type of Fence," *Greenville (S.C.) Piedmont,* 3 March 1987. The new fence bordered the 1,800-foot frontage of the campus on Wade Hampton Boulevard.

[49]Denise Hughes, "Science Building Addition to Ease Crowding," *Collegian,* vol. 1, no. 9, 24 March 1988. The addition was 13,000 square feet.

[50]"Science Building Addition Underway," *Collegian,* July 1989. See also Don Harrelson, "New Science Building Labs Provide Technology, Practical Experience," *Collegian,* vol. 4, no. 5, 8 November 1990.

[51]Ryan Elliot and Rachel Menillo, "Bible Conference Offering Goal Set at Record Amount for Science Building Renovations," *Collegian,* vol. 8, no. 10, 2 March 1995.

[52]"Fremont Fitness Center Opens," *Voice of the Alumni,* vol. 66, no. 6, Summer 1993.

[53]"University Place," *Voice of the Alumni,* vol. 59, no. 4, Spring 1986, p. 17.

[54]"First Annual Christian High School Invitational Basketball Tournament," program, 23-26 January 1973 (MLA).

[55]DG to "Pastor," 4 September 1973 (MLA).

[56]Bobby Jones, "University Hosts AACS Tournament," *Collegian,* vol. 1, no. 10, 14 April 1988.

[57]"Craig Olsen: The Dean of Fun Arts," *Voice of the Alumni,* vol. 62, no. 5, Spring 1989, pp. 18-19.

[58]"Highly entertaining spoofs have included the dean of the School of Fine Arts lip-synching "My Old Flame" by Spike Jones; the dean of men acting out a dating scenario; a soft-shoe by a musicology professor; mountain clogging by the director of the School of Applied Studies; the chairman of the Division of Graduate Studies in Religion reading poetry using Victor Borge's "phonetic punctuation"; and BJiii and his wife spoofing themselves. See "Faculty Body and Gold Rush Daze, April 1981" *Voice of the Alumni,* vol, 55, no. 1, June 1981.

[59]Don Harrelson, "Classes to Be Cancelled for Special Day of Prayer," *Collegian,* vol. 5, no. 4, 31 October 1991.

[60]Changes announced in *Voice of the Alumni,* vol. 29, no. 1, July 1955. The bylaws were rewritten in 1962 to make the document current.

[61]BJiii, "Welcome," *Voice of the Alumni,* vol. 45, no. 5, January 1972, p. 14.

[62]The association raised the $100,000 to build Alumni Stadium in 1968; to light the stadium field, pave the track, and light the tennis courts, the association raised an equal amount between 1975 and 1977. They purchased a coach bus in 1986. The association also raised $95,000 to install an elevator in the Alumni Building in 1990. These projects filled definite needs and helped transform the campus. The association also created the Alumni Child Tuition Aid Grant to help current students who were children of alumni.

[63]*Voice of the Alumni,* vol. 63, no. 3, Spring 1989, pp. 10-11, 20.

[64]Ibid., vol. 64, no. 6, Summer 1990, p. 10.

[65]Ibid., vol. 62, no. 3, Fall 1988, pp. 20-22. Before Barton came to BJU, the responsibilities of business manager had been divided between Don Tice and Keith Mock.

[66]Ibid., vol. 63, no. 5, Spring 1990, p. 5. The date of Stenholm's leaving the position of director of Ministerial Training is incorrect in this article. University service records in the RO indicate that Stenholm held this office from 1951 through the end of school year 1977. Rupp assumed his responsibilities on 1 September 1977.

[67]Faculty Service Records (RO).

[68]*Voice of the Alumni,* vol. 63, no. 3, Spring 1989, pp. 20-21, 23.

[69]Many observers believed that Bob Jones IV would become active in the administration of the institution at some point in the future. This appears somewhat unlikely, however, because of Bjiv's decision to join a Christian news journal, *World Magazine,* as national editor. (See Bob Jones III, "A Open Letter to BJU Alumni," *Voice of the Alumni,* vol. 71, no. 4, Winter 1997, p. 14.)

[70]MS BJjr, chapel talk, 1 January 1997 (ABV). Other examples may be found in MS BJjr, chapel talk 4 April 1997; MS BJjr, chapel talk 16 April 1997; MS BJjr, chapel talk 7 July 1997; MS BJjr Sunday sermon, 17 August 1997. The next to last chapel message preached by the Chancellor is especially instructive. In it he talked of some of his own age-related problems while making three points with the student body from his text in Ecclesiastes 12: (1) The passing of time cannot be changed. (2) The coming of darkness (death) awaits all men. (3) The certainty of judgment follows everything done in life. MS BJjr chapel talk, 18 September 1997.

[71]BJjr. audio tape, 29 October 1997 (ASTA). See also "Bob Jones Jr." *BJU Review,* vol. 12, no. 4, Spring 1998, p. 10.

[72]Eric Frazier, "University Leader Bob Jones Jr. Dies," *Charleston (S.C.) Post and Courier,* 13 November 1997.

[73]Ian R. K. Paisley, "My Tribute to my Beloved Friend, Dr. Bob Jones," *Voice of the Alumni,* vol. 71, no. 4, Winter 1997, p. 7.

[74]For more on the funeral of BJjr., see *BJU Review,* vol. 12, no. 4, Spring 1998.

Chapter 24: Into All the World

[1] "Bob Jones University, 'Please Come to Greenville, We Need the Spiritual Impact of the School,' " unknown paper, n.d. (MLA). BJjr indicated that the administration decided at the time of the move to Greenville that it would not involve the institution in local political affairs. As a result, for many years the school failed in building common ground with many Greenvillians unless they took the initiative.

[2] As previously noted, the theological challenge of the 1950s and 1960s—New Evangelicalism—was vague and more difficult to define than the indisputably false teachings of Modernism propagated by a liberal and unbelieving clergy in the 1920s and 1930s.

[3] The title *Show My People* was taken from Isaiah 58:1: "Cry aloud, spare not, lift up thy voice like a trumpet, and shew my people their transgression, and . . . their sins."

[4] Interview, Dan Boone, June 1995.

[5] Wright, *Fortress*, p. 404.

[6] Ibid.

[7] BJIiii to Dan Turner, 29 July 1994 (author's personal file).

[8] Ibid.

[9] Wright, *Fortress*, p. 406.

[10] BJiii to Dan Turner.

[11] *Faith for the Family* replaced the *Fellowship News,* a four-page weekly newsletter that first appeared in 1934 with BJsr as editor and Grace W. Haight as associate editor. It was sent to all members of the Young People's Fellowship Clubs and those in the Gospel Fellowship Association. The paper carried articles about College events; "A Word from the President," by BJsr; "A Look at the Book," by BJjr; "The Story of a Great Hymn," by Grace Haight; and sermon excerpts. When Haight and BJsr were no longer able to continue the *News,* BJjr and Guye E. Johnson took the editorships.

[12] BJiii, "A Word from the President," *Faith for the Family,* vol. 1, no. 1, March/April 1973, p. 17.

[13] BJjr, "Editorial," *Faith for the Family,* vol. 1, no. 1, March/April 1973, p. 2.

[14] Dollar, *History.* Dollar's book was the first history of Fundamentalism by a Fundamentalist scholar.

[15] The date 1974 is commonly reported as the beginning of the BJU Press (George Mulfinger and Emmet Williams, *Physical Science for Christian Schools* [Greenville, S.C.: BJU Press, 1974]. Williams was chairman of the department of physics, with a B.S. and M.S. in metallurgical engineering from Virginia Polytechnic Institute and a Ph.D. in materials engineering from Clemson University. Mulfinger held a B.S. and M.S. from Syracuse University in physics. He had done doctoral study at Syracuse and Harvard.

[16] From an interview with Elmer Rumminger. Board members Bob Garrett and Walt Rumminger paid the salaries of Mulfinger and Williams during their summers of writing.

[17] For an explanation of the "Christian perspective," see "The Christian Teaching of Science," in *Christian Education: Its Mandate and Mission* (Greenville, S.C.: BJU Press, 1992).

[18] The book contained more than four hundred photographs, illustrations, and diagrams, many in full color. According to George Collins, who prepared the first edition of this book for publication, *Physical Science for Christian Schools* compared favorably to any secular science text in every area, and far surpassed anything available from any other Christian textbook publisher. The book was not without its problems, however. Collins wrote that in a chapter on the diffraction of light, a beautiful photograph of a western sunset had been selected. " 'Note the delicate pinks, yellows, and oranges' said the caption to a picture that was reproduced in black and white" (George Collins, "For Christian Schools," *Voice of the Alumni,* vol. 68, no. 6, Summer 1995, p. 5). Collins, former direc-

tor of production of BJU Press, also stated that the book was more than simply anti-evolution. It was written from a thoroughly Christian conceptual base, with a consistent Christian philosophy, attempting to teach students to think, not merely to memorize.

[19]Interestingly, the Christian publishers who reprinted secular texts from the 1940s and 1950s trumpeted their books as "traditional" and openly equated traditional education with Christian education. While labeling the books of BJU Press as "progressive education," these publishers apparently did not recognize the inherent philosophical problems with "traditionalism"—its essential humanism, reliance on faculty psychology and memoriter learning, and extreme authoritarianism. Oddly, though proclaiming their texts "traditional," they selected popular textbooks written during the progressivist era, all of which reflected the underlying progressivists' stance presented in the "Cardinal Principles of Education" and promoted by the Progressive Education Association.

[20]Wright, *Fortress,* p. 401.

[21]See Deb Richardson-Moore, "BJU Press Has Quietly Risen to Top in Homeschool Publications," *Greenville (S.C.) News,* 26 May 1996.

[22]Richardson-Moore stated that the C. S. Lewis Contest, a national competition for Christian literature, named twenty-four BJU Press titles to its list of the top five hundred books for the years 1990-94 (Richardson-Moore, "BJU Press"). The contest is sponsored by a Christian school organization and considers more than three hundred books each year from fifty to seventy publishers. *With Daring Faith,* the story of Amy Carmichael by Rebecca Henry Davis, was the 1987 National Gold Medal winner of the C. S. Lewis Contest (Gloria Repp, BJU Press children's trade editor, telephone interview, 27 May 1996).

[23]Gretchen Nebergall, "New Program Announced at H.E.L.P. Conference," *Collegian,* summer issue, 8 June 1992.

[24]Sean Sachon, "Home Schooling Takes Off," *Collegian,* vol. 2, no. 3, 13 October 1988. See also Richardson-Moore, "BJU Press."

[25]Heidi Nebergall, "Conference to Aid Home Educators," *Collegian,* 25 January 1990. See also Jennifer Horton, "Second Annual H.E.L.P. Conference Underway," *Collegian,* 3 June 1991. In the first year, about 1,400 adults, 125 teens, 1,600 children ages four through twelve, and 300 children below age three attended (Dave McQuaid, "University Hosts H.E.L.P. Conference," *Collegian,* June 1990).

[26]George Collins, "Distance Education and Christian Education," *Balance,* vol. 15, no. 8, April 1996.

[27]Collins, "Distance Education." At the time of this writing, the cost for LINC service was ten thousand dollars per year.

[28]The principals of Bob Jones Academy have been John Floyd Collins, 1927-28; Woodrow Patterson (dean of Bob Jones College), 1928-30; August Greisel (dean of Bob Jones College), 1930-32; Eunice Hutto (dean of Bob Jones College), 1932-36; Lillian Lee Brown, 1936-64; Gene Fisher, 1964-68; Cleo Aldrich, 1968-70; George D. Youstra, 1970-71, 1972-79; James Monro (acting principal), 1971-72; Ross Penix, 1979-85; C. Sidney Cates 1985-96; Steve Tompkins, 1996-99; and David Fisher, 1999-present. Dr. Fisher is the first Academy principal to also be an Academy graduate.

[29]Dennis M. McKinsey reported that the school was known by several names until the late 1970s. Some of the names included Bob Jones College High School, the University prep school, and Bob Jones University's Academy (Dennis M. McKinsey, "A History of Bob Jones Academy Compared to Selected Other Christian Schools" [Ed.D. dissertation, BJU, 1992, p. 183]).

[30]Enrollment Statistics: First Semester (RO).

[31]McKinsey, "History," p. 264. The exact percentages are 89.3 percent day students, 10.7 percent dormitory.

[32]Ibid., pp. 325-26.

[33]Andrea Neely, "A History of Bob Jones Academy," unpublished paper, p. 7 (MLA).

[34]McKinsey, "History," p. 218.

[35]Ibid., p. 182. The new junior high building featured eight classrooms, a large assembly room, teachers' offices, and a central lobby with a principal's office (Wright, *Fortress,* p. 417).

[36]McKinsey, "History," p. 262.

[37]Ibid.

[38]"BJES: Elementary Excellence," *Faith for the Family,* vol. 2, no. 6, January/February 1975.

[39]Incidentally this school was built on the property previously owned by the Wilson family. See Chapter 18.

[40]The insurance office sat on property on which the Wilson home and chicken coops had been sitting in the early 1960s, which had been part of the land originally promised to BJC before the move to Greenville; it finally came into the school's possession in 1985.

[41]"The Lord's Leading," *Voice of the Alumni,* vol. 64, no. 3, Fall 1990, p. 14.

[42]All figures from Stan Smith, assistant principal, Bob Jones Elementary School, electronic mail note, 29 May 1996.

[43]Abby Merkle, "Bible Study Luncheons Provide Fellowship and Attract Scores of Visitors from the Greenville Area," *Collegian,* vol. 5, no. 5, 14 November 1991.

[44]"BJU: The Opportunity Place," *Voice of the Alumni,* vol. 60, no. 1, Summer 1986, pp. 10-11.

[45]Bobby Jones, "Workman, Eastwood Praise BJU Efforts," *Collegian,* vol. 1, no. 1, 9 October 1987.

[46]Vanessa Hartman, "BJU Students Assist with the Special Olympics and Camp Spearhead," *Collegian,* 16 April 1992.

[47]Otis R. Holmes, "Church Planting in North America," *Voice of the Alumni,* vol. 68, no. 4, Winter 1994.

[48]Dan Olinger, "Show Windows Through Church Planting," *Voice of the Alumni,* vol. 58, no. 3, Winter 1985, pp. 5-6, 15. According to an article published the year after the program was established, the men selected had to possess a "pioneer spirit and a desire for a longterm ministry in one church" ("Go Ye," *Voice of the Alumni,* vol. 46, no. 2, September 1972).

[49]For several years BJU sponsored a church planting team of five or six young men who worked with selected new churches in evangelism. They would spend eleven days in a town, holding revival services and children's meetings and doing door-to-door evangelism on behalf of the newly established church (Stuart Smith, "Helping Lay Foundations," *Voice of the Alumni,* vol. 51, no. 1, June 1977; see also Holmes, "Church Planting").

[50]Bruce McAllister, "Church Planting: The Denver Model," *Voice of the Alumni,* vol. 68, no. 4, Winter 1994, pp. 18-19.

[51]The range of this activity has not been isolated to one region of the country. By 1994 church planters had built ministries in thirty-five states and several Canadian provinces. While many of the churches have remained relatively small, several of the urban churches have grown in attendance to over five hundred. See "Church Planters Complete New Buildings," *Voice of the Alumni,* vol. 64, no. 5, Spring 1991, p. 23.

[52]Mission boards that organized summer teams included Baptist Mid-Missions and Gospel Fellowship Association.

[53]"Project Compassion: 1966," *Voice of the Alumni,* vol. 40, no. 1, December 1966, pp. 1-3. The students received academic credit for their participation in the project.

[54]"Outreach: Summer Missions Teams," *Voice of the Alumni,* vol. 51, no. 3, December 1977, pp. 13-14.

[55]Majors on the 1990 missions teams included aviation, carpentry, nursing, modern languages, accounting, music, education, premed, prelaw, and radio and television production. See "Talk Back," *Collegian,* vol. 3, no. 13, 5 April 1990.

[56]Kathleen Frank, "This Class Meets 24 Hours a Day for Seven Weeks," *Voice of the Alumni,* vol. 49, no. 1, June 1975.

[57]Jennifer Horton, "Musical Mission Team Sees Hundreds Saved in USSR," *Collegian,* vol. 5, no. 1, 19 September 1991.

[58]*Vintage,* 1986, p. 142.

[59]Interview, Brenda Pritchard (Timothy/WORLD Fund secretary), 16 May 1996. One Timothy Fund graduate, Eduard Lassegue of Haiti, earned the B.S. degree in Bible education and the M.S. degree in educational administration and supervision from BJU. On his return to Haiti, he was employed by the Haitian Department of Education as the head of the Office of Assistance to Private Schools. His ministry was to teens in Haiti through Bible clubs ("Determination: A Christian Example," *Voice of the Alumni,* vol. 61, no. 5, Summer 1988, pp. 8-9).

[60]The first Timothy graduate was Eliseo Cuenca of Mexico, who graduated from BJU in 1981. He is currently serving as a missionary in Mexico.

[61]Interview, Brenda Pritchard.

[62]Bob Jones IV, "WORLD Fund Students: The Next Generation of Missionaries," *Voice of the Alumni,* vol. 63, no. 5, Spring 1990, p. 6.

[63]See Beth Hunter, "Eastern European Students Train for Future Service in Homeland," and Hunter's "Students Reveal Experiences with Religious Persecution in Europe," in *Collegian,* vol. 6, no. 10, 25 February 1993. This article chronicles the story of several students from Russia, Ukraine, and Rumania in the Timothy and WORLD Fund programs.

[64]Interview, BJiii, 12 June 2000.

[65]Photo, *Voice of the Alumni,* vol. 72, no. 5, Spring 1999, p. 16.

[66]Anita Feliciano, "Seminary Building Dedicated, *Collegian,* vol. 13, no. 12, 2000, p. 1, 6.

[67]Ibid.

[68]Ibid.

Chapter 25: Chandeliers and Back Hall Lights

[1]Roy Barton to Dan Turner, 26 July 1996.

[2]Ibid.

[3]Ibid.

[4]Quoted in Mark Sidwell, "Charles Digory Brokenshire (1885-1954)," *Biblical Viewpoint,* vol. 25, no. 1, April 1991, p. 71.

[5]Ibid., p. 75.

[6]For more on Brokenshire, see Sidwell, "Charles Digory Brokenshire," pp. 69-84. See also "Dr. Charles D. Brokenshire—Dean of the Graduate School," *Little Moby's Post,* vol. 2, no. 1, May 1943, p. 1; and Ken Casillas, "Dr. Brokenshire Known as a Man of Humor, Spiritual Zeal," *Collegian,* 28 September 1989.

[7]"J. Floyd Collins," *Alabama Christian Advocate,* 19 October 1933 (MLA: BJsr scrapbook 2-24).

[8]Interview, Mrs. BJjr, 4 June 1987.

[9]"Collins."

[10]Ibid.

[11]Interview, Mrs. BJjr, 4 June 1987.

[12]Interview, BJjr, 28 May 1987.

[13]"Collins."

[14]Mark Palmer, "The Life of James D. Edwards," unpublished paper, 1980, p. 6 (MLA).

[15]Ibid., p. 7.

[16]Ibid., p. 10.

[17]James L. Hays, "Walter G. Fremont: An Oral History," unpublished paper, 17 April 1985, p. 4 (MLA).

[18]James D. Deuink, ed., *Balance,* vol. 10, no. 9, May 1990.

[19]His dissertation was titled "Administrative Competencies in Christian Day Schools."

[20]This conference has yearly drawn more than 180 Christian high school principals to the campus to recruit teachers since 1970.

[21]These seminars have been videotaped and are available from the BJU Press.

[22]Interestingly, between September and May that school year, he grew five inches taller and gained two shoe sizes, reaching his commanding height that first year.

[23]Denise Hughes, "Dr. Gustafson," *Collegian,* vol. 1, no. 5, 21 January 1988.

[24]DG's music has won prizes in composition contests, including first prize in the Erskine College Contest in Musical Composition Based on Psalm Texts (*Voice of the Alumni,* vol. 38, no. 1, June 1964, p. 3), and he was the winner of the Twentieth Annual Charleston, S.C., Choral Society's Composers' Competition, for which he entered settings of Walt Whitman's "Three Songs of Parting: 'Joy, Shipmate, Joy'; 'The Dismantled Ship'; and 'Now Finale to the Shore.' "

[25]See "40th Anniversary Celebration August 24, 1993," *Voice of the Alumni,* vol. 67, no. 3, Fall 1993, p. 14.

[26]Quoted in Janiece K. Robinson, "Analysis of Grace Haight's Life as a Fighting Fundamentalist," unpublished paper, December 1988 (MLA: Haight file).

[27]Elmer T. Clark, ed., *Missionary Yearbook of the Methodist Episcopal Church, South, 1927* (Nashville: Board of Missions, 1927), p. 198.

[28]Robinson, "Analysis," pp. 18-19.

[29]*Vintage,* 1935.

[30]BJjr to H. Thomas Haight, 24 January 1975 (MLA: Haight file).

[31]BJjr to Dottie Harris, 15 February 1977 (GF: Hutto file).

[32]"Present with the Lord!" *Little Moby's Post,* December-January 1947-48, p. 3.

[33]For information on Guye Ellenburg Johnson, see Bea Hackstedde Ward, "Guye Ellenburg Johnson: Behavior That Becometh Holiness," *Voice of the Alumni,* vol. 58, no. 1, Summer 1984, pp. 6-8.

[34]Jean Martin, "Love Was the Essence of the Man," *Voice of the Alumni,* vol. 45, no. 4, December 1971, pp. 4-5.

[35]R. K. Johnson to BJsr and BJjr, "Report," 13 March 1962 (GF: Ragan file).

[36]BJU: "Long-time Business Manager of BJU Dies," news release, n.d. (MLA).

[37]*Sunshine on the Soapsuds, More Sunshine on the Soapsuds, Beauty and the Best, Ribbing Him Rightly!, Words Fitly Spoken, With Heart and Hand* (coauthored with Bobbie Yearick), and *Mount Up on Wounded Wings.*

[38]See BJjr, *Cornbread,* p. 9, for more on this story.

[39]Ibid., pp. 8-9.

[40]Her master's thesis was done on the newly discovered vitamin C and the amounts of the substance in potatoes prepared in different ways. When she completed her degree, she intended to go to Walter Reed Hospital in Washington, D.C., to continue her education.

[41]Dianne Carter, "In Honor Preferring One Another," *Voice of the Alumni,* vol. 65, no. 5, pp. 17-18.

[42]Johnson, *Builder,* p. 57.

[43]Guye Ellenburg Johnson, "Mary Gaston Jones," *Voice of the Alumni,* vol. 62, no. 3, Fall 1988, pp. 4, 5, 7.

[44]Ibid., p. 5.

[45]Johnson, *Builder,* p. 57.

[46]Interview, Dan Turner with Mrs. BJsr, 28 August 1986.

[47]BJjr, *Cornbread,* pp. 10-11. Her keen judgment was dismissed only once when she tried to persuade BJsr not to appoint Ted Mercer to a position of high responsibility.

[48]Ibid., p. 11.

[49]Quoted in Amy J. Marshall, "Faculty Member Wears Many Hats over 50-Year Career at University," *Collegian,* 15 April 1993.

[50]Doris Fisher Harris, "Patient Perseverance," *Voice of the Alumni,* vol. 45, no. 7, May 1972.

[51]Ibid.

[52]"An Interview with Marshall Neal," *Voice of the Alumni,* Fall 1995, pp. 8-9, 18-19.

[53]For a comprehensive list of Marshall Neal's writings, see Mark Sidwell, "In Honor of Dr. Marshall P. Neal," *Biblical Viewpoint,* vol. 25, no. 2, 1991, pp. 3-7.

[54]Interview, Edward Miran Panosian with Kathy Eveland, 16 February 1995.

[55]Ibid.

[56]Ibid.

[57]Ibid.

[58]Ibid.

[59]For more information on Monroe Parker's ministry, see his autobiography, *Through Sunshine and Shadows: My First 77 Years.*

[60]Johnna K. Hines, "She Shall Be Praised," unpublished paper, 14 December 1982, pp. 4-5 (MLA).

[61]Doris Fisher Harris, "Her Own Works Praise Her," *Voice of the Alumni,* vol. 46, no. 5, 1973, pp. 1ff.

[62]Lori Ann Boland, "Guenter Edward Salter," unpublished paper, n.d., p. 2 (MLA).

[63]Ibid., p. 10.

[64]Ibid., p. 11.

[65]Ibid., p. 14.

[66]Ibid., p. 15.

[67]*Bob Jones University Bulletin,* vol. 69, February 1995, p. 50.

[68]Much of the information for this sketch was drawn from Interview, Philip D. Smith with Dan Turner, 27 May 1987 (MLA); "The Lord's Leading," *Voice of the Alumni,* vol. 63, no. 3, Fall 1989, pp. 10-12; and "Faculty Service Records," RO.

[69]Interview, Katherine Corne Stenholm with Dan Turner, 8 June 1987 (MLA).

[70]Ibid.

[71]Quoted in Jason Mauk, "Rodeheaver Stage Manager Dies at 67," *Collegian,* vol. 8, no. 8, 2 February 1995.

[72]Mark Lauger, "Interviews with Melvin Stratton," 10 February and 17 February 1986 (MLA).

[73]Mauk, "Stage Manager."

[74]Lauger, "Stratton," p. 16.

[75]Information taken from BJU, "News Release," Office of Vice President, n.d. Information also taken from Bob Wood, "Personal Testimony" (ASTA: #771001).

Appendix A

[1]Shailer Mathews, *New Faith for Old: An Autobiography* (New York: Macmillan Co., 1936), pp. 60-65.

[2]For more on Clarke, see George W. Dollar, *A History of Fundamentalism in America* (Greenville, S.C.: BJU Press, 1973), pp. 15-20. See also Harry Emerson Fosdick, *The Living of These Days: An Autobiography* (New York: Harper and Brothers, 1956), pp. 65-66, 254-55.

[3]Dollar, *History,* p. 12. See also George M. Marsden, *Fundamentalism and American Culture: The Shaping of Twentieth Century Evangelicalism: 1870-1952* (New York: Oxford University Press, 1980), p. 105.

[4]For an index of *The Fundamentals,* see David Beale, *In Pursuit of Purity: American Fundamentalism Since 1850* (Greenville, S.C.: Unusual Publications, 1986), pp. 41-45.

[5]Foreword to *The Fundamentals,* quoted in Ferenc Morton Szasz, *The Divided Mind of Protestant America, 1880-1930* (University, Ala.: University of Alabama Press, 1982), p. 79.

[6]Ernest R. Sandeen, *The Roots of Fundamentalism* (Chicago: University of Chicago Press, 1970), pp. 188-207.

[7]Beale, *Pursuit,* p. 195.

[8]See Robert E. Wenger, "Social Thought in American Fundamentalism, 1918-1933" (Ph.D. dissertation, University of Nebraska, 1973). Wenger presents Fundamentalism's geographical scope after comparing the place of residence in 1920 of Fundamentalists and Modernists. He reports that approximately 78 percent of Fundamentalists were located in the East and far West corridors of the country. A majority lived in the metropolitan areas of New York, Philadelphia, Boston, Chicago, and Los Angeles (pp. 55-62).

[9]Marsden, *Culture,* p. 103. Most analyses of Fundamentalism list among its most important leaders W. B. Riley of Minneapolis, J. Gresham Machen of Princeton, John Roach Straton of New York City, James M. Gray of Chicago, Harry Ironside of Chicago, B. B. Warfield of Princeton, and R. A. Torrey of Los Angeles, to name a few. Even those works that claim the movement to be of southern origin are hard-pressed to list among the movement's leaders any southerners of note, except J. Frank Norris of Texas and evangelists Sam Jones and BJsr (p. 179).

[10]Among works holding this thesis are Stewart Cole, *The History of Fundamentalism* (1931; rpt. Hamden, Conn.: Archon Books, 1963); Reinhold Niebuhr, *The Social Sources of Denominationalism* (New York: Henry Holt and Company, 1924); and Willard Gatewood, *Preachers, Pedagogues, and Politicians* (Chapel Hill, N.C.: University of North Carolina Press, 1966).

[11]Works holding this thesis include Gatewood, *Preachers;* Furniss, *The Fundamentalist Controversy* (New Haven: Yale University Press, 1954); and Maynard Shipley, *The War on Modern Science: A Short History of the Fundamentalist Attacks on Evolution and Modernism* (New York: Alfred A. Knopf, 1927).

[12]George Brown Tindall, *The Emergence of the New South, 1913-1945* (Baton Rouge: Louisiana State University Press, 1967), p. 219.

[13]Marsden, *Culture,* p. 116.

[14]Gatewood, *Preachers,* p. 7.

[15]J. Gresham Machen, *Christianity and Liberalism* (Grand Rapids, Mich.: Wm. B. Eerdmans Publishing Co., 1923), p. 48.

[16]Ibid., p. 75.

[17]The best defense of Fundamentalist doctrine from this era is found in Machen's *Christianity and Liberalism*. See pp. 17-53 and 69-79.

[18]R. A. Torrey, *Is the Bible the Inerrant Word of God?* (New York: George H. Doran Co., 1922), pp. 51-53.

[19]Marsden, *Culture,* p. 126.

[20]Mathews, *New Faith,* p. 278.

[21]Fosdick, *Autobiography,* p. 64.

[22]See Harry Emerson Fosdick, *The Modern Use of the Bible* (New York: Macmillan Co., 1924). *Modern Use* is a major apologetic work for liberal Protestantism's view of Scripture. See Shailer Mathews, *The Faith of Modernism* (New York: Macmillan Co., 1925).

[23]Quoted in Fosdick, *Modern Use,* p. 182.

[24]Quoted in Marsden, *Culture,* p. 175.

[25]Kirsop Lake, *The Religion of Yesterday and To-morrow* (Boston: Houghton-Mifflin, 1925), pp. 61-62. Quoted in Beale, *Pursuit,* p. 4.

[26]Shailer Mathews, "Fundamentalism and Modernism: An Interpretation," *American Review,* 2 (1924): 1-9. Quoted in Gatewood, *Preachers,* p. 17.

[27]J. Gresham Machen, "Christianity and Culture," *Princeton Theological Review,* 9 (1913): 3.

[28]Melton Wright, *Fortress of Faith,* 3rd ed. (Greenville, S.C.: BJU Press, 1984), p. 270.

[29]The areas of comparison shown are based on the Five Famous Points of the 1910 Presbyterian General Assembly. Though not a definitive statement and not universally accepted by all who termed themselves Fundamentalist, these are considered the last rallying point of conservative Christians. The Five Points parallel other short creeds of orthodoxy and with the addition of "creation" represent the general topics on which the controversy centered. Interestingly, premillenialism, a position most often associated with Fundamentalism by its Modernist opponents, is not represented as one of the basics of the controversy. Nor was premillenialism included in any of the conservative creeds of the early twentieth century. The doctrine of the Second Coming is represented, however.

[30]Torrey, *Is the Bible,* p. 32.

[31]Fosdick, *Modern Use,* p. 30.

[32]Ibid., p. 273.

[33]Machen, *Christianity,* pp. 75-76.

[34]Torrey, *Is the Bible,* p. 53.

[35]Fosdick, *Autobiography,* p. 169.

[36]Machen, *Christianity,* p. 73.

[37]Mathews, *New Faith,* p. 50.

[38]Ibid., p. 53.

[39]James M. Gray, *The Bulwarks of the Faith* (Elgin, Ill.: Brethren Publishing House, 1899), p. 117.

[40]Mathews, *Modernism,* p. 52.

[41]John Roach Straton, *The Famous New York Fundamentalist-Modernist Debates: The Orthodox Side* (New York: George H. Doran Company, 1925), p. 171.

[42]Mathews, *Modernism,* pp. 141-42.

[43]William Bell Riley, *Christ the Incomparable* (New York: Fleming H. Revell Co., 1924), pp. 40-41. The classic orthodox treatment of the subject is found in J. Gresham Machen's *Virgin Birth of Christ.*

[44]Mathews, *Modernism,* p. 142.

[45]Machen, *Christianity,* p. 85,

[46]Fosdick, *Adventurous Religion* (New York: Harper and Brothers, 1926), p. 308.

[47]Straton, *Debates,* p. 243.

[48]Machen, *Christianity,* p. 126.

[49]Fosdick, *Modern Use,* p. 226.

[50]Ibid., p. 270. See also Harry Emerson Fosdick, *The Manhood of the Master* (New York: Association Press, 1917).

[51]Fosdick, *Modern Use,* p. 245.

[52]Torrey, *Is the Bible,* p. 165.

[53]Fosdick, *Modern Use,* p. 98.

[54]Mathews, *Faith of Modernism,* p. 154.

[55]Machen, *Christianity,* p. 49.

[56]Fosdick, *Modern Use,* p. 104.

[57]Mathews, *Faith of Modernism,* p. 167.

[58]Machen, *Christianity,* p. 99.

[59]Fosdick, *Modern Use,* p. 143.

[60]Machen, *Christianity,* p. 107.

[61]Fosdick, *Modern Use,* pp. 143, 151, 154.

[62]Mathews, *New Faith,* p. 233.

[63]Straton, *Debates,* pp. 56, 72.

[64]Shailer Mathews, *Contributions of Science to Religion* (New York: D. Appleton Co., and 1924), pp. 166, 209.

[65]Straton, *Debates,* p. 72.

[66]Mathews, *Contributions,* p. 187.

[67]Straton, *Debates,* p. 81.

[68]Mathews, *Contributions,* p. 165.

[69]Straton, *Debates,* p. 82.

[70]Mathews, *Contributions,* p. 165.

[71]William Jennings Bryan, *The Menace of Darwinism* (New York: Fleming H. Revell Co., 1921), p. 4.

[72]Mathews, *New Faith,* pp. 230-31.

Appendix B

[1]Bob Jones College, "Rules of Bob Jones College," ca. 1933, Rachel Ayres scrapbook (MLA: Box 29, mimeograph).

Appendix C

[1]BJjr, "A Tribute and a Pledge," quoted in R. K. Johnson, *Builder of Bridges: The Biography of Bob Jones Sr.* (Greenville, S.C.: BJU Press, 1982), pp. 356-60.

Appendix D

[1]BJU, "Position of the Bible Department of Bob Jones University on the Scripture," mimeograph, n.d. (Office of the President).

BIBLIOGRAPHY

◆

Correspondence

Correspondence to and from Bob Jones Sr., Bob Jones Jr., and Bob Jones III was invaluable in the preparation of this work. Their letters illuminate in a unique way the three men's differing personalities and approaches to problems and in many instances were the only extant evidence to document ideas, statements, or events. Over 170 individual pieces of correspondence have been cited from the thousands made available, and those cited have been given full bibliographic treatment in the footnotes.

Sources of the correspondence were the General Files (GF) of Bob Jones University; the University Archives located in the J. S. Mack Library (MLA); the Office of the President of Bob Jones University; the Office of the Chancellor of Bob Jones University; and the offices of various deans of the schools of Bob Jones University.

At the present time, correspondence in the General Files is periodically cleared, which has led to the destruction of many pieces of material.

Sermons and Addresses

The unpublished sermons, chapel talks, and radio talks by Bob Jones Sr., Bob Jones Jr., and Bob Jones III are a particularly valuable source of information on the theology, politics, cultural ideals, and events that affected Bob Jones College and Bob Jones University. Between the 1920s and the mid-1950s, American evangelists and pastors would often collect and publish volumes of sermons for the study and edification of other believers. On the campus of Bob Jones College and Bob Jones University, a secretary was assigned to stenographically record each chapel message preached by one of the Joneses and prepare a typescript, which was later read and corrected (if necessary) by the speaker. These were stored for future use or publication. The verbatim record of the Joneses is therefore nearly complete, beginning in January 1933 through the 1980s when the practice was discontinued in favor of audiotape recordings, which are left untranscribed.

Several thousand of these sermon documents are stored, by year preached, in the Administration Building of Bob Jones University and are a gold mine for scholarly study. These documents first came to my attention during doctoral research, when I perused hundreds of sermons for certain key words and phrases. As a source for future study for scholars of American Fundamentalism, they are invaluable.

Bibliography

Many chapel talks were also recorded by tape in addition to having a typescript made. All of these sermons, including those preached since 1980, are found in the archives of the Bob Jones University Audio Services, as are copies of more than one thousand short radio talks given by the Founder. These primary sources were available for use, and 118 of the more than 900 studied have been cited. Full bibliographic record for each citation appears in the footnotes.

The differences in rhetorical style among the three Joneses are striking, and a study of their styles would be valuable in itself.

Interviews

Forty-five interviews collected over an eight-year period were all helpful in clarifying events and adding detail and perspective to campus life. All the interviews were tape-recorded, with the exception of those by Nancy Michel, which were obtained from the Dothan, Alabama, Landmark Historical Society files.

Most interesting among the interviews were those with Mrs. Bob Jones Sr.; Bob Jones Jr.; Tommy Smith of Panama City, Florida; and Martha Stone and her brother, E. Roy Stone Jr., of Greenville, South Carolina. These are just some of the fascinating people who have walked the campus of Bob Jones College and Bob Jones University.

Primary Source Documents

Uncataloged and unpublished documents for this study appeared in numerous places: the Bob Jones University Vespers files, the University Archives of J. S. Mack Library, the General Files of Bob Jones University, and the files of E. Roy Stone Realty in Greenville, South Carolina. Of particular help and interest for the years 1927-35 were the Minutes of the Faculty, found in the storage vault located in the BJU Administration Building. Citations identify the location of each document. Those listed were among the most valuable in documenting this work.

Adams, Elizabeth. "God in Nature" (program). Vespers files, 21 April 1940.

"A Bill to Amend the Internal Revenue Tax Code of 1954 . . ." MLA: vertical file, n.d.

Bob Jones clipping books, vols. 1-9, MLA.

Bob Jones College Board of Trustees Minutes. MLA, box 26, 9 January 1933.

Bob Jones College Campus Map, Cleveland, Tennessee. GF, n.d.

"Bob Jones College Classic Players Tenth Anniversary" (booklet). MLA, box 29, BJC publicity scrapbook, 30 May 1939.

"Bob Jones College Commencement Concert" (program). MLA, box 29, Rachel Ayres scrapbook, 25-29 May 1934.

"Bob Jones College Conservatory of Music" (program). MLA, box 26, 17 December 1930.

Bob Jones College Financial Statement. E. Roy Stone Realty, Bob Jones file, ca. 1945-46.

Bob Jones College. *An Epoch in Education: Facts About the Bob Jones College.* Vol. 1, no. 1, 1928.

Bob Jones College. Minutes of the Faculty. 1929-35.

"Bob Jones University Opera Productions" (memo). BJU Fine Arts Office, n.d.

Bob Jones University. "Charter of Bob Jones College [University]." Office of the Provost, Greenville, South Carolina.

Bob Jones University. "Honorary Degrees Conferred by Bob Jones College" (office document).

Bob Jones University. "Minutes of the Board of Trustees, Executive Committee."

Bob Jones University. "Position of the Bible Department of Bob Jones University on the Scripture" (mimeograph). Office of the President, n.d.

"College Point Development: Site of Bob Jones College" (printer's paste-up). Ca. 1926.

"Commencement Program: Bob Jones College." MLA, box 26, May 27–June 1, 1932.

"A Costume Recital by V. L. Granville" (program). MLA, box 29, Rachel Ayres scrapbook, 6 February 1934.

Dean, Susie Kelly. "Large Crowd Present at College Twilight Musicale" (handwritten press release). MLA, box 26, n.d.

"Discipline Committee Resolution." 8 January 1937.

"First Annual Christian High School Invitational Basketball Tournament" (program). MLA, January 23-26, 1973.

Greenville City Council. "Minutes." Greenville City Hall: Microfiche, 26 April 1962.

"IRS Announces Position on Private Schools" (IRS document). 10 July 1970.

Jones, Bob, Jr. "Comments Regarding the Dissertation Entitled 'Bob Jones University and the Shaping of Twentieth Century Separatism, 1926-1991' " (unpublished manuscript). MLA, n.d.

———. "Statement: Amplified N.T." Office of the Chancellor, n.d.

Jones, Bob, Sr. Speech outline. MLA, box 8, n.d.

Jones, Bob, III. "para/KJV." Office of the President, n.d.

Kurtz, Jerome. "News Release: Remarks Before the PLI Seventh Biennial Conference on Tax Planning for Foundations' Tax-Exempt Status and Charitable Contributions." Internal Revenue Service, 9 January 1978.

"Lifestyle Survey Results." Office of the Dean of Students, 1993.

Loose, Helen. "Israel" (production notes). Vespers files, 4 February 1940.

Mercer, Theodore C. "An Additional Statement to the Alumni and Board of Trustees of Bob Jones University." 4 August 1953.

———. "A Statement Concerning My Dismissal from Bob Jones University." 28 July 1953.

———. "A Third Statement." 10 August 1953.

"The Messiah, Presented by the Bob Jones College Chorus" (program). MLA, box 29, Rachel Ayres scrapbook, 26 January 1934.

"Opera Productions" (document). FAO.

"Rules of Bob Jones College" (mimeograph).

Savidge, Dale, and Bob Jones Jr. "Shakespeare and Shylock: An Interview with Bob Jones" (videotape). Bob Jones University Division of Speech, Department of Dramatic Productions, 1987.

Stenholm, Gilbert. Personal diaries, 1935-70.

"Student's Comments on Prof. Sperandeo." GF, Sperandeo file, n.d.

"Student's Report on Miss Flood." GF, Flood file, n.d.

"Twilight Musicale." MLA, box 26, 9 October 1927.

"———, Bob Jones College" (handwritten program). MLA, box 26, 9 October 1927.

———. MLA, box 26, 11 December 1927.

———. MLA, box 26, 22 February 1928.

———. MLA, box 26, 18 March 1928.

———. MLA, box 26, 1 April 1928.

"Twilight Musicales, Susie Kelly Dean, Director" (handwritten program). MLA, box 26, 9 October 1927.

Wilson, Walter T. Telegram. GF, Greenville Chamber of Commerce file, 23 May 1946.

Books

Primary Sources

Bob Jones College Annual Bulletin. Vols. 3-19.

Bob Jones University. *Catalogue.* Vols. 20-63.

———. *The Vintage* (yearbook). 1934-95.

Brunner, Edmund deS. *Church Life in the Rural South: A Study of the Opportunity of Protestantism Based upon Data from Seventy Counties.* New York: George H. Doran Co., 1923.

Bryan, William Jennings. *The Menace of Darwinism.* New York: Fleming H. Revell Co., 1921.

———, with Mary Baird Bryan. *The Memoirs of William Jennings Bryan.* Chicago: John C. Winston Co., 1925.

Carroll, H. K. *The Religious Forces of the United States.* New York: Christian Literature Co., 1893, rev. 1896.

Clark, Elmer T., ed. *Missionary Yearbook of the Methodist Episcopal Church, South, 1927.* Nashville: Board of Missions, 1927.

Clary, Albert. "1972 Report to the American Association of Collegiate Registrars and Admissions Officers on *Credit Given by Educational Institutions.*" Washington, D.C.: American Association of Collegiate Registrars and Admissions Officers, 1972.

Fosdick, Harry Emerson. *Adventurous Religion.* New York: Harper and Brothers, 1926.

———. *The Living of These Days: An Autobiography.* New York: Harper and Brothers, 1956.

———. *The Manhood of the Master.* New York: Association Press, 1917.

———. *The Modern Use of the Bible.* New York: Macmillan Co., 1924.

Gaebelein, Frank. *Christian Education in a Democracy.* New York: Oxford University Press, 1951.

Gray, James M. *The Bulwarks of the Faith.* Elgin, Ill.: Brethren Publishing House, 1899.

Haldeman, Isaac Massey. *Dr. Harry Emerson Fosdick's Book: "The Modern Use of the Bible."* Philadelphia: Sunday School Times Co., 1925.

Jones, Bob, Jr. *Cornbread and Caviar: Reminiscences and Reflections.* Greenville, S.C.: Bob Jones University Press, 1985.

Jones, Bob, Sr. *Bob Jones' Revival Sermons.* Wheaton, Ill.: Sword of the Lord Press, 1948.

———. *Bob Jones' Sermons.* Montgomery, Ala.: State Press, 1908.

———. *My Friends.* Greenville, S.C.: Bob Jones University Press, 1983.

———. *The Perils of America.* Chicago: Chicago Gospel Tabernacle, 1934.

———. "The Perils of America, or Where Are We Headed" (sermon booklet). Cleveland, Tenn.: Bob Jones College, 1934.

———. *Things I Have Learned.* Greenville, S.C.: Bob Jones University Press, n.d.

———. "Three College Shipwrecks" (pamphlet). Greenville, S.C.: Bob Jones University (Bob Jones College), ca. 1930.

———. "The Unbeatable Game: A Sermon to Men" (sermon booklet). Cleveland, Tenn.: Bob Jones College, n.d.

Leuba, James H. *The Belief in God and Immortality: A Psychological, Anthropological and Statistical Study.* Boston: Sherman, French and Co., 1916.

Machen, J. Gresham. *Christianity and Liberalism.* Grand Rapids, Mich.: Wm. B. Eerdmans Publishing Co., 1923.

Mathews, Shailer. *Contributions of Science to Religion.* New York: D. Appleton and Co., 1924.

———. *The Faith of Modernism.* New York: Macmillan Co., 1925.

———. *The Individual and the Social Gospel.* New York: Layman's Missionary Movement, 1914.

———. *New Faith for Old: An Autobiography.* New York: Macmillan Co., 1936.

Murch, James. *Cooperation Without Compromise.* Grand Rapids, Mich.: Wm. B. Eerdmans Publishing Co., 1956.

Parker, Monroe. *Through Sunshine and Shadows: My First 77 Years.* Murfreesboro, Tenn.: Sword of the Lord Publishers, 1987.

Rauschenbusch, Walter. *The Theology of the Social Gospel.* New York: Macmillan Co., 1917.

Riley, William Bell. *Christ the Incomparable.* New York: Fleming H. Revell Co., 1924.

San Andros (BJC yearbook). 1930.

Straton, John Roach. *The Famous New York Fundamentalist-Modernist Debates: The Orthodox Side.* New York: George H. Doran Company, 1929.

———. *Fighting the Devil in Modern Babylon.* New York: George H. Doran Co., 1925.

———. *The Menace of Immorality in Church and State: Messages of Wrath.* New York: George H. Doran Co., 1925.

Torrey, R[euban] A. *Is the Bible the Inerrant Word of God?* New York: George H. Doran Co., 1922.

Wilkins, Theresa Birch. *Accredited Higher Institutions: 1952.* Washington, D.C.: United States Office of Education, Bulletin 1952, no. 3.

Books

Secondary Sources

Allen, James Lane. *The Reign of Law: A Story of the Kentucky Hemp Fields.* New York: Macmillan Co., 1908.

American Association of Collegiate Registrars and Admissions Officers. *Credit Given by Educational Institutions.* Washington, D.C.: American Association of Collegiate Registrars and Admissions Officers, 1972.

Aronson, Joseph. *Furniture in the Bob Jones University Collection.* Greenville, S.C.: Bob Jones University Press, 1976.

Beale, David O. *In Pursuit of Purity: American Fundamentalism Since 1850.* Greenville, S.C.: Unusual Publications, 1986.

———. *S.B.C.: House on the Sand?* Greenville, S.C.: Unusual Publications, 1985.

Beale, Howard K. *A History of Freedom of Teaching in American Schools.* New York: Charles Scribner's Sons, 1941.

Bebbington, D. W. *Evangelicalism in Modern Britain: A History from the 1730s to the 1980s.* Grand Rapids, Mich.: Baker, 1992.

Bechtel, Paul M. *Wheaton College: A Heritage Remembered 1860-1984.* Wheaton, Ill.: Harold Shaw Publishers, 1984.

Biederwolf, William B. *The Christian and Amusements.* Grand Rapids, Mich.: Wm. B. Eerdmans Publishing Co., n.d.

Bob Jones University. *Art of the BJU Collection, Vol. 2: Flemish, Dutch, German, and Spanish Paintings.* Greenville, S.C.: Bob Jones University, 1962.

———. *The BJU Collection of Religious Paintings: Italian and French Paintings.* Greenville, S.C.: Bob Jones University, 1962.

———. *The Bob Jones University Collection of Religious Paintings.* Greenville, S.C.: Bob Jones University Press, 1954.

———. "The Bomb and Its Fallout: *Bob Jones University v. United States*" (pamphlet), 1983.

———. *Christian Education: Its Mandate and Mission.* Greenville, S.C.: Bob Jones University Press, 1992.

———. *The Christian Philosophy of Education.* Greenville, S.C.: Bob Jones University Press, 1978.

———. *The Christian Teaching of History.* Greenville, S.C.: Bob Jones University Press, 1981.

———. *Selected Paintings from the Bob Jones University Collection of Sacred Art.* Greenville, S.C.: Bob Jones University, 1952.

———. *Supplement to the Catalogue of the Art Collection: Paintings Acquired 1963-1968.* Greenville, S.C.: Bob Jones University Press, 1968.

Bode, Frederick A. *Protestantism and the New South: North Carolina Baptists and Methodists in Political Crisis, 1894-1903.* Charlottesville, Va.: University Press of Virginia, 1975.

Bibliography

Brereton, Virginia Lieson. *Training God's Army: The American Bible School, 1880-1940.* Bloomington, Ind.: Indiana University Press, 1990.

Burkett, Larry. *What Ever Happened to the American Dream.* Chicago: Moody Press, 1993.

Burnham, George, and Lee Fisher. *Billy Graham and the New York Crusade.* Grand Rapids, Mich.: Zondervan Publishing House, 1957.

Candler, Warren. *Great Revivals and the Great Republic.* Nashville: Christian Literature Company, 1904.

Carson, D. A. *The KJV Debate: A Plea for Realism.* Grand Rapids, Mich.: Baker, 1979.

Church League of America. *Billy Graham: Performer? Politician? Preacher? Prophet? A Chronological Record Compiled from Public Sources.* Chicago: Church League of America, 1979.

Clanton, Gene. *Populism: The Humane Preference in America, 1890-1900.* Boston: Twayne Publishers, 1991.

Clark, Thomas D. *Three Paths to the Modern South: Education, Agriculture, and Conservation.* Athens, Ga.: University of Georgia Press, 1965.

Cohen, Gary. *Biblical Separation Defended: A Biblical Critique of Ten New Evangelical Arguments.* Philadelphia: Presbyterian and Reformed Publishing Co., 1966.

Cole, Stewart. *The History of Fundamentalism.* 1931; rpt. Hamden, Conn.: Archon Books, 1963.

Cothan, Perry C., ed. *Christian Social Ethics.* Grand Rapids, Mich.: Baker, 1979.

Couch, W. T., ed. *Culture in the South.* Chapel Hill, N.C.: University of North Carolina Press, 1934.

Cremin, Lawrence A. *American Education: The Metropolitan Experience 1876-1980.* New York: Harper Row, 1988.

Crowson, E. H. *The Betrayal of Southern College: A Study in the Technique of Modern Infidelity* (unpublished book manuscript). 1933.

Crunden, Robert M. *Ministers of Reform: The Progressives' Achievement in American Civilization 1889-1920.* New York: Basic Books, 1982.

Dabney, Virginius. *Liberalism in the South.* 1932; rpt., New York: AMS Press, 1970.

Dalhouse, Mark Taylor. "Bob Jones University and the Shaping of Twentieth Century Separatism, 1926-1991." Ph.D. dissertation. Miami (Ohio) University, 1991.

Dollar, George W. *The Fight of Fundamentalism: American Fundamentalism, 1973-1983.* Sarasota, Fla.: G. W. Dollar, 1983.

———. *A History of Fundamentalism in America.* Greenville, S.C.: Bob Jones University Press, 1973.

Dorough, Prince Leon. "A History of the Music Department of the University of Montevallo, Montevallo, Alabama." Ed.D. dissertation. University of Illinois, 1986.

Dunn, Charles W., ed. *American Political Theology.* New York: Praeger, 1984.

Ehrenhalt, Alan. *The United States of Ambition: Politicians, Power, and the Pursuit of Office.* New York: Random House, 1991.

Ekirch, Arthur A., Jr. *Progressivism in America: A Study of the Era from Theodore Roosevelt to Woodrow Wilson.* New York: New Viewpoints, 1974.

Eliot, Charles W. *Educational Reform: Essays and Addresses.* New York: Centure, 1898.

———. *Harvard Memories.* Cambridge: Harvard University Press, 1923.

Ezell, John Samuel. *The South Since 1865.* New York: Macmillan Co., 1963.

Falwell, Jerry. *Listen, America!* New York: Doubleday, 1980.

———, ed. *How You Can Help Clean Up America.* Washington, D.C.: Moral Majority, Inc., 1981.

———, Truman Dollar, A.V. Henderson, and William W. Pennell, eds. *Issues for the Eighties: A Thirteen-Week Sunday School Curriculum Series.* Detroit: Fundamentalist Church Publications, 1982.

Farish, Hunter Dickinson. *The Circuit Rider Dismounts: A Social History of Southern Methodism, 1865-1900.* Richmond, Va.: Dietz Press, 1938.

Ferm, Robert O. *Cooperative Evangelism: Is Billy Graham Right or Wrong?* Grand Rapids, Mich.: Zondervan Publishing House, 1958.

Frady, Marshall. *Billy Graham: A Parable of American Righteousness.* Boston: Little, Brown and Company, 1979.

Furniss, Norman F. *The Fundamentalist Controversy.* New Haven, Conn.: Yale University Press, 1954.

Gatewood, Willard B. *Controversy in the Twenties: Fundamentalism, Modernism, and Evolution.* Nashville: Vanderbilt University Press, 1969.

———. *Preachers, Pedagogues, and Politicians.* Chapel Hill, N.C.: University of North Carolina Press, 1966.

Harrison, Albert. "A History of the School of Music of the University of Illinois, 1940-1970." Ed.D. dissertation. University of Illinois, 1987.

Bibliography

Heiser, Michael S. "The Move of Bob Jones College from Cleveland, Tennessee, to Greenville, South Carolina, in 1947." Unpublished paper, n.d.

Hofstadter, Richard, ed. *The Progressive Movement 1900-1915.* Englewood Cliffs, N.J.: Prentice Hall, 1963.

Huff, Archie Vernon, Jr. *Greenville: The History of the City and County in the South Carolina Piedmont.* Columbia, S.C.: University of South Carolina Press, 1995.

Hulse, Erroll. *Billy Graham—The Pastor's Dilemma.* Honslow, Middlesex, England: Maurice Allan, Inc., 1966.

Jahoda, Gloria. *Florida: A Bicentennial History.* New York: W. W. Norton and Company, 1976.

Johnson, R. K. *Builder of Bridges: The Biography of Bob Jones, Sr.* Greenville, S.C.: Bob Jones University Press, 1982.

———. *Miracle from the Beginning.* Greenville, S.C.: Bob Jones University, 1971.

Johnston, Arthur P. *The Battle for World Evangelism.* Wheaton, Ill.: Tyndale House Publishers, Inc., 1978.

———. *World Evangelism and the Word of God.* Minneapolis, Minn.: 1974.

Jones, Bob, IV. "Middle Ground: Bob Jones University and the Evolution of Separation." Unpublished paper. MLA, 1995.

Jones, D. Martyn-Lloyd. *The Puritans: Their Origins and Successors.* Edinburgh: Banner of Truth Trust, 1987.

Kolko, Gabriel. *The Triumph of Conservatism: A Reinterpretation of American History, 1900-1916.* London: Collier-Macmillan, 1963.

Krug, Edward A. *Charles W. Eliot and Popular Education.* New York: Teachers College Press, 1961.

Marsden, George. *Fundamentalism and American Culture: The Shaping of Twentieth Century Evangelicalism: 1870-1952.* New York: Oxford University Press, 1980.

———. *Reforming Fundamentalism: Fuller Seminary and the New Evangelicalism.* Grand Rapids, Mich: Wm. B. Eerdmans Publishing Co., 1987.

———. *Understanding Fundamentalism and Evangelicalism.* Grand Rapids, Mich.: Wm. B. Eerdmans Publishing Co., 1991.

———, ed. *Evangelicalism in Modern America.* Grand Rapids, Mich.: Wm. B. Eerdmans Publishing Co., 1984.

Martin, William. *A Prophet with Honor: The Billy Graham Story.* New York: William Morrow and Co., Inc., 1991.

Marty, Martin E., and R. Scott Appleby, eds. *Accounting for Fundamentalisms: The Dynamic Character of Movements.* Chicago: University of Chicago Press, 1991.

―――. *Fundamentalisms and Society: Reclaiming the Sciences, the Family, and Education.* Chicago: University of Chicago Press, 1993.

―――. *Fundamentalisms and the State: Remaking Politics, Economics, and Militance.* Chicago: University of Chicago Press, 1993.

―――. *Fundamentalisms Observed.* Chicago: University of Chicago Press, 1991.

McBeth, H. Leon. *The Baptist Heritage: Four Centuries of Baptist Witness.* Nashville: Broadman, 1987.

McKinsey, Dennis M. "A History of Bob Jones Academy Compared to Selected Other Schools." Ph.D. dissertation. Bob Jones University, 1992.

McLoughlin, William G., Jr. *Billy Graham: Revivalist in a Secular Age.* New York: Ronald Press, 1960.

―――. *Modern Revivalism: Charles Grandison Finney to Billy Graham.* New York: Ronald Press, 1959.

Moore, Howard Edgar. "The Emergence of Moderate Fundamentalism: John R. Rice and *The Sword of the Lord.*" Ph.D. dissertation. George Washington University, 1990.

Murray, Iain. *Arthur W. Pink: His Life and Thought.* Edinburgh: Banner of Truth Trust, 1981.

―――. *David Martyn Lloyd-Jones: The Fight of Faith, 1939-1981.* Edinburgh: Banner of Truth Trust, 1990.

Neuhaus, Richard John, and Michael Cromartie, eds. *Piety and Politics: Evangelicals and Fundamentalists Confront the World.* Washington, D.C.: Ethics and Public Policy Center, 1987.

Nevin, David, and Robert Bills. *The Schools That Fear Built: Segregationist Academies in the South.* Washington, D.C.: Acropolis Books, 1976.

Newton, Oscar L. "A One Hundred Year History of the Beulah Church." Unpublished manuscript. 1949.

Niebuhr, Reinhold. *The Social Sources of Denominationalism.* New York: Henry Holt and Company, 1924.

Numbers, Ronald L. *The Creationists.* New York: Alfred A. Knopf, 1992.

Olson, Keith W. *The G.I. Bill, the Veterans, and the Colleges.* Lexington, Ky.: University Press of Kentucky, 1974.

Orfield, Gary. *The Reconstruction of Southern Education.* New York: John Wiley and Sons, 1969.

Paisley, Ian R. K. *Billy Graham and the Church of Rome.* Greenville, S.C.: Bob Jones University Press, 1972.

Bibliography

Palmer, Mark. "The Life of James D. Edwards." Unpublished paper. MLA, 1980.

Pepper, D. Stephen. *Bob Jones University Collection of Religious Art: Italian Paintings.* Greenville, S.C.: Bob Jones University Press, 1984.

Peshkin, Alan. *God's Choice: The Total World of the Fundamentalist Christian School.* Chicago: University of Chicago Press, 1986.

Pickering, Ernest D. *Biblical Separation: The Struggle for a Pure Church.* Schaumburg, Ill.: Regular Baptist Press, 1979.

————. *The Tragedy of Compromise: The Origin and Impact of the New Evangelicalism.* Greenville, S.C.: Bob Jones University Press, 1994.

Pollock, John. *Billy Graham: The Authorized Biography.* New York: McGraw-Hill Book Co., 1966.

Ravitch, Dianne. *The Troubled Crusade: American Education, 1945-1980.* New York: Basic Books, 1983.

Reid, Alfred Sandlin. *Furman University: Toward a New Identity, 1925-1975.* Durham, N.C.: Duke University Press, 1976.

Rice, John R. *Some Serious, Popular False Doctrines Answered from the Scriptures.* Murfreesboro, Tenn.: Sword of the Lord Publishers, 1970.

Riley, William Bell. *The Crisis of the Church.* New York: Charles C. Cook, 1914.

Ringerberg, William C. *Taylor University: The First 125 Years.* Grand Rapids, Mich.: Wm. B. Eerdmans Publishing Co., 1973.

Robinson, Janiece K. "Analysis of Grace Haight's Life as a Fighting Fundamentalist." Unpublished paper. MLA: Grace Haight file, December 1988.

Ross, Davis R. B. *Preparing for Ulysses: Politics and Veterans During World War II.* New York: Columbia University Press, 1969.

Sandeen, Ernest R. *The Roots of Fundamentalism.* Chicago: University of Chicago Press, 1970.

Schnaiter, Samuel Ellsworth. "The Relevancy of Textual Criticism to the Modern English Version Controversy for Fundamentalists." Ph.D. dissertation. Bob Jones University, 1980.

Shafritz, Jay M. *Dictionary of American Government and Politics.* Chicago: Dorsey Press, 1988.

Shelley, Bruce L. *Evangelicalism in America.* Grand Rapids, Mich.: Wm. B. Eerdmans Publishing Co., 1967.

Shipley, Maynard. *The War on Modern Science: A Short History of the Fundamentalist Attacks on Evolution and Modernism.* New York: Alfred A. Knopf, 1927.

Sidwell, Mark Edward. "The History of the Winona Lake Bible Conference." Ph.D. dissertation. Bob Jones University, 1988.

Skinner, Tom. *Black and Free.* Grand Rapids, Mich.: Zondervan, 1970.

Steele, David H., Jr. *Baroque Paintings from the Bob Jones University Collection.* Raleigh, N.C.: North Carolina Museum of Art, 1984.

Stockbridge, Frank Parker, and John Holliday Perry. *Florida in the Making.* New York: de Brower Publishing Co., 1926.

Suhr, Bryan M. "The First Amendment: The Dispute over Semantics and the Subsequent Treatment of Private Education by the United States Supreme Court." Unpublished paper, 1994.

Sumner, Robert L. *An Examination of Tulip: The Five Points of Calvinism.* Brownsburg, Ind.: Biblical Evangelism Press, 1972.

Szasz, Ferenc Morton. *The Divided Mind of Protestant America, 1880-1930.* University, Ala.: University of Alabama Press, 1982.

Tabler, Rebecca V. "Bob Jones University Versus Internal Revenue Service." Unpublished paper. 1992.

Thompson, Willie. "The School of Applied Studies: Past and Present." Unpublished paper. Bob Jones University, 4 April 1988.

Tindall, George Brown. *The Emergence of the New South, 1913-1945.* Baton Rouge, La.: Louisiana State University Press, 1967.

Turner, Daniel L. "Fundamentalism, the Arts, and Personal Refinement: A Study of the Ideals of Bob Jones, Sr., and Bob Jones, Jr." Ed.D. dissertation. University of Illinois at Urbana-Champaign, 1988.

Waite, D. A. *Four Reasons for Defending the King James Bible.* Collingswood, N.J.: Bible for Today Publishers, n.d.

Warwick, Anne Williams. *Tides: Growing Up on St. Andrews Bay.* Panama City, Fla.: Boyd Brothers Printing, 1984.

Watson, Fred S. *Hub of the Wiregrass: A History of Houston County, 1903-1972.* Anniston, Ala.: Higgenbotham, Inc., 1972.

Weisberger, Bernard A. *They Gathered at the River: The Story of the Great Revivalists and Their Impact upon Religion in America.* Boston: Little, Brown and Co., 1958.

Wenger, Robert E. "Social Thought in American Fundamentalism, 1918-1933." Ph.D. dissertation. University of Nebraska, 1973.

White, James R. *The King James Only Controversy: Can You Trust the Modern Translations?* Minneapolis, Minn.: Bethany House, 1995.

White, Ronald C., Jr., and Albright G. Zimmerman, eds. *An Unsettled Arena: Religion and the Bill of Rights.* Grand Rapids, Mich.: Wm. B. Eerdmans Publishing Co., 1990.

Wisdom, Thurman. "Light on the Bible Text Debate" (pamphlet). Bob Jones University Press, 1984.

Wood, James E., Jr., and Derek Davis, eds. *The Role of Religion in the Making of Public Policy.* Waco, Tex.: Baylor University J. M. Dawson Institute of Church-State Studies, 1991.

Bibliography

Woodward, C. Vann. *Origins of the New South: 1877-1913.* Baton Rouge, La.: Louisiana State University Press, 1951.

Wright, Melton. *Fortress of Faith.* 3rd ed. Greenville, S.C.: Bob Jones University Press, 1984.

INDEX

The letter *n.* following a page number refers to a note citation on that page. For example, "328 n. 66" refers to note 66 on page 328.

Index

Index

Index

Index

Flood, Ruth, 70-74, 88-89, 129, 356 nn. 128, 132

Florida Bible Institute, 167, 392 nn. 52, 54

Florida State University, 286, 299, 341 n. 19; 412 n. 25

Fogg Art Museum, 408 n. 67

Forbes, Steve, 248, 429 n. 68

Ford, Gerald R., 394 n. 75

Fort Wayne Bible College, 390 n. 29

Fosdick, Harry Emerson, 46, 311-12, 329 n. 86; 331 n. 15; 333 n. 32; 346 n. 108; 397 n. 104

Foster, Peter, 435 n. 37

Founder's Memorial Amphitorium, 196, 206-8, 217, 256, 295

Free, Joseph, 72-75, 159

Freeman Report, The, 218

Fremont, Trudy, 282-84

Fremont, Walter, 188, 201, 219, 252, 258, 260, 282-84, 303

Fremont Fitness Center, 258

Friedlaender, Max, 407 n. 56

Fuller, Charles E., 389 n. 5

Fuller Theological Seminary, 165-66, 390-91 nn. 29, 39; 395 n. 87; 400 n. 53

Fundamentalism/Fundamentalists, vii, 29, 118, 131, 161, 259, 286-87, 358 n. 10; 388-89 n. 3; 392 n. 55; 399 n. 26; 445 n. 29. *See also* Graham, Billy, and Fundamentalism; Jones, Bob, Jr./Sr./III, and Fundamentalism

and Bob Jones College/University, 36-37, 58, 64, 85, 109, 145, 148, 152, 158, 205, 208-9, 240, 251, 257, 270-71, 373 n. 32

and Calvinism, 240-41

and Catholicism. *See* and Roman Catholicism

and culture, 81

and ecumenicism, 395 n. 89

and evolution, 333 nn. 32, 34, 36

and Modernism, 16-19, 186, 311-316, 332 n. 22; 334 n. 37; 445 n. 29

and New Evangelicalism, 166, 181, 263, 270, 395 n. 87

and politics, 245-50

and Roman Catholicism, 79, 186, 359 nn. 24, 25; 428 n. 44

and sectarianism, 31

and social issues, 80, 328 n. 67; 332 n. 26; 359-60 n. 33

and the fine arts, 36, 92, 190, 365 n. 48

and the King-James-Only controversy, 242-45, 322-23

mischaracterizations of, 30, 36

Fundamentalism File. *See* Mack Library, Fundamentalism File of

"Fundamentalism, the Arts, and Personal Refinement," vii

Fundamentals, The, 244, 311, 322

Furman University, 114-18, 138, 333 n. 32; 373 n. 32; 381 n. 20; 419 n. 21

Future Teachers of America, 201, 387 n. 32

Gaebelein, Frank, 389 n. 5

Garlock, Frank, 403 n. 27

Garrett, Bob, 438 n. 16

Gay Atheists Society, 218

Gay Liberation, 246

Gay Rights Coalition, 237

Gentry, R. S., 344 n. 73

Georgetown University, 423 n. 30

Georgetown University Law Center, 237

Georgia Creel Hall (dormitory), 206, 381 n. 30. *See also* Jones, Georgia Creel

Ghandi, Mahatma, 369 n. 26

Ghirlandaio, David, 194, 406 n. 55

GI Bill of Rights, 101, 138, 369-70 nn. 23, 40; 421 n. 41. *See also* GIs

Gingery, Gail, 388 n. 48

Giordano, Luca, 195, 407 n. 63

Girvin, Richard, 409 n. 89

GIs, 145, 149, 254, 282-83, 369 n. 30. *See also* Bob Jones College, Cleveland, Tennessee, and GIs; GI Bill of Rights

Gold Rush Daze, 259

Goldsboro Christian School, 229, 231, 421-22 nn. 57, 1

Goldwater, Barry, 246, 428 n. 47

Index

Index

Index

Index

Index

Oratorio Society. *See* Bob Jones University, Oratorio Society

Origin of the Species, 397 n. 104

Owen, Ruth Bryan, 93

Packer, J. I., 241

Paisley, Ian, 262, 437 n. 73

Panosian, Betty, 297

Panosian, Edward, 188, 211, 296-98, 388 n. 48

Parkening, Christopher, 405 n. 36

Parker, Harriette, 63, 123, 299

Parker, Monroe, 39, 42, 47, 63, 104, 123-24, 151, 153, 298-99, 304, 339 nn. 45, 46; 347 n. 6; 349 n. 30; 392 n. 55

Parkhurst, Charles, 408 n. 67

Parks, Joyce, 246

Parks, Willard J., 110

Patterson, Woodrow E., 35-36, 43, 344 n. 73; 439 n. 28

Patton, Edmund L., 279

Patton, George S., Jr., 282

Payne, A. A., 337 n. 27

Peale, Norman Vincent, 396 n. 97; 399 n. 16

Peerce, Jan, 405 n. 36

Penix, Ross, 439 n. 28

Pennsylvania State University, 283, 303, 412 n. 25

Pensacola Christian College, 412 n. 20; 432 n. 7

Pentecostalism, 164, 242, 425 n. 19

Pepper, Stephen, 407 n. 56

"Perils of America, The," 12, 19, 79, 359 n. 28

Perry, Dale, 401 n. 7

Persian Gulf War, 394 n. 80

Peters, Beneth. *See Jones,* Beneth Peters

Peterson, John, 284

Peterson, Rudy, 284

Phil Donahue Show, The, 218, 230

Phillips, Wendell, 167, 392 nn. 51, 52

Physical Science for Christian Schools, 438-39 n. 18

Pickens, Andrew L., 333 n. 32

Pickering, Ernest, 166

Piedmont Bible College, 434 n. 23

Pillsbury Baptist Bible College, 216, 299, 412 n. 20

Pink, Arthur W., 240

Pinner, Jay-Martin, 403

Piombo, Sebastiano del, 406 n. 55

Planned Parenthood, 238

Platte, Ken, 434 n. 23

Pleasant Pastures (University farm), 237, 256, 435 nn. 32, 33

Plessy v. Ferguson, 417 n. 2

Plyler, John, 115, 373 n. 32; 381 n. 20

Populism, 3, 78, 245, 325 n. 11

"Position of the BJU Bible Department on the Scripture," 244-45, 322-23

Poteat, William L., 333 n. 32

Pound of Flesh (Unusual Films), 197

Powell, Lewis, 233-34

Pratt, Robert, 188, 360 n. 48; 403 n. 22

Preacher Boys, 59, 202, 260, 305, 366 n. 59; 373 n. 33

Presbyterian College, 114

Presbyterian Theological Seminary, 333 n. 33

Price, James H., 374 n. 45; 385 n. 4

Priest, Percy, 246

Princeton Theological Seminary, 67, 168, 277, 312, 390 n. 29

Princeton University, 342, 431 n. 4

Printing, The (Unusual Films), 198, 299, 307

Progressivism, 10, 245, 328 n. 67; 439 n. 19. *See also* Jones, Bob, Sr., and Progressivism

Prohibition, 10-12, 245

Protestantism/Protestants, vii, 11-12, 15, 17, 26, 29, 31, 66, 79, 163-64, 172, 174, 185-86, 239, 329 nn. 83, 86; 332 nn. 21, 22, 23; 354 n. 99; 358 n. 10; 369 n. 26; 388-89 nn. 3, 5; 397 n. 104; 408 n. 73; 445 n. 22

Puritanism, 131, 240

Index

Index